The Geology and Climatology of Yucca Mountain and Vicinity, Southern Nevada and California

edited by

John S. Stuckless
U.S. Geological Survey
MS 421, Box 25046, Denver Federal Center
Denver, Colorado 80225
USA

Robert A. Levich
U.S. Department of Energy
Las Vegas, Nevada 89134
USA

THE
GEOLOGICAL
SOCIETY
OF AMERICA®

Memoir 199

3300 Penrose Place, P.O. Box 9140 ▪ Boulder, Colorado 80301-9140, USA

2007

Published by The Geological Society of America, Inc.
3300 Penrose Place, P.O. Box 9140, Boulder, Colorado 80301-9140, USA
www.geosociety.org

Printed in U.S.A.

GSA Books Science Editor: Marion E. Bickford

Library of Congress Cataloging-in-Publication Data

The geology and climatology of Yucca mountain and vicinity, Southern Nevada and
    California / edited by John S. Stuckless, Robert A. Levich.
        p. cm. (Memoir ; 199)
    Includes bibliographical references.
    ISBN-13 9780813711997
        1. Geology--Nevada--Yucca Mountain Region. 2. Geology--California. 3. Radioactive
    waste sites--Nevada--Yucca Mountain Region--Evaluation. 4. Nevada--Climate. 5.
    California--Climate. I. Stuckless, John S. II. Levich, Robert A., 1941- . Memoir
    (Geological Society of America) ; 199.

QE138.Y83 G46 2007
557.93′34--dc22

                                        2007061015

Cover: Pseudoperspective elevated view of Yucca Mountain and surroundings depicted by high-resolution aeromagnetic image superimposed on color-processed Landsat image mosaic. View to the northwest. The aeromagnetic image extends from the western part of Little Skull Mountain west to the western edge of Crater Flat, and from the Amargosa Desert north to the northern edge of Yucca Mountain. Landsat image processing by John Dohrenwend. Illustrated features discussed by O'Leary, chapter 4.

10 9 8 7 6 5 4 3 2 1

Contents

Preface

In October 1996, scientists from the U.S. Department of Energy's (DOE) Yucca Mountain Project began development of the Yucca Mountain Site Description. The Yucca Mountain Site Description is a compilation of more than twenty years of scientific research and the resulting understanding of the geology and hydrogeology of the Yucca Mountain Site. This regulatory document was developed to support the license application for a deep geologic repository for the disposal of high-level nuclear waste, which the DOE intends to submit to the U.S. Nuclear Regulatory Commission, as required by federal regulations.

This memoir evolved from the Yucca Mountain Site Description and summarizes the current understanding of the geology and climatology (past, present, and future) of the Yucca Mountain area. Similarly, a second volume, currently in preparation, will summarize the understanding of the hydrology and geochemistry of the Yucca Mountain area. However, because of its differing emphasis and content, the Yucca Mountain Site Description had to be completely transformed and rewritten to develop these volumes.

Scientists from the DOE, the U.S. Geological Survey (USGS), and the DOE national laboratories have long advocated publishing the basic science supporting Yucca Mountain as a proposed repository, and this memoir is an outgrowth of these recommendations. Hundreds of scientists from the DOE, the USGS, the U.S. Bureau of Reclamation, Lawrence Berkeley National Laboratory, Lawrence Livermore National Laboratory, Los Alamos National Laboratory, Sandia National Laboratories, and universities, research organizations, and geotechnical consultants collected, compiled, and interpreted the data upon which these volumes are based. In addition, several dozen scientists contributed directly to the development of both the Yucca Mountain Site Description and the memoirs.

All the authors of this memoir have been supported by the DOE Office of Civilian Radioactive Waste Management, and all the research reported, except for most of the regional geology, also has been supported by the DOE. Richard Quittmeyer and Kathryn Mrotek (Bechtel SAIC) played important roles in the organization, compilation, and development of the Yucca Mountain Site Description. Both Ardyth Simmons (Los Alamos National Laboratory) and Claudia Newbury (DOE) were instrumental in creating this published work.

One further note: the engineering properties chapter of the Yucca Mountain Site Description was rewritten by Mala Ciancia as Chapter 3, "Geotechnical properties of the tuffs at Yucca Mountain, Nevada," in the Geological Society of America Special Paper 408, *Tuffs—Their Properties, Uses, Hydrology, and Resources*, edited by Grant Heiken.

The editors of this memoir are grateful to all who contributed to the scientific studies of the Yucca Mountain area, and the development of this volume.

Geological Society of America
Memoir 199
2007

Yucca Mountain, Nevada—A proposed geologic repository for high-level radioactive waste

Robert A. Levich

U.S. Department of Energy (Retired), Consulting Geologist, 405 Norwood Lane, Las Vegas, Nevada 89107, USA

John S. Stuckless

U.S. Geological Survey, MS 421, Box 25046, Federal Center, Denver, Colorado 80225

ABSTRACT

Yucca Mountain in Nevada represents the proposed solution to what has been a lengthy national effort to dispose of high-level radioactive waste, waste which must be isolated from the biosphere for tens of thousands of years. This chapter reviews the background of that national effort and includes some discussion of international work in order to provide a more complete framework for the problem of waste disposal. Other chapters provide the regional geologic setting, the geology of the Yucca Mountain site, the tectonics, and climate (past, present, and future). These last two chapters are integral to prediction of long-term waste isolation.

Keywords: nuclear waste, waste management, site selection, laws and regulations, geologic repository.

INTRODUCTION

Since the dawn of the Atomic Age more than 60 years ago, the operation of nuclear power plants, as well as the development and manufacture of nuclear weapons, has generated large amounts of radioactive waste. Some of the radioisotopes in this waste are in low concentrations or have short half-lives. Most of these "low-level" wastes can be disposed of in shallow trenches. Other radioactive waste contains radioisotopes in higher concentrations or isotopes with long half-lives, greater than 1000 years. These "high-level" wastes must be disposed of in a manner that will isolate them from the biosphere for tens of thousands of years.

Worldwide, there has been a long-standing scientific consensus that the best method for permanent disposal of high-level radioactive waste is in deep geologic repositories (e.g.,

see National Academy of Sciences, National Research Council report, 1957, and Nuclear Energy Agency report, 1995). There are many analogues that support this conclusion, e.g., ore deposits that have existed for millions of years, organic materials that have existed in caves for hundreds of thousands of years, and anthropogenic items that have been preserved underground for thousands to tens of thousands of years (Winograd, 1986; Brookins, 1986a; Alexander and Van Luik, 1991; Miller et al., 1994; Stuckless, 2000, 2002)

Nuclear waste destined for disposal comes from several sources. The largest quantity is commercial spent nuclear fuel, consisting of fuel assemblies from civilian nuclear power plants that contain enriched uranium fuel pellets that have been removed after completing their useful life in the production of electricity. Approximately 20% of our nation's electricity is produced at 74 sites in 33 states that host 118 commercial nuclear power

Levich, R.A., and Stuckless, J.S., 2007, Yucca Mountain, Nevada—A proposed geologic repository for high-level radioactive waste, *in* Stuckless, J.S., and Levich, R.A., eds., The Geology and Climatology of Yucca Mountain and Vicinity, Southern Nevada and California: Geological Society of America Memoir 199, p. 1–7, doi: 10.1130/2007.1199(01). For permission to copy, contact editing@geosociety.org. ©2007 Geological Society of America. All rights reserved.

reactors, more than 100 of which are still in operation. Currently (2006), more than 40,000 metric tons of heavy metal are stored in 33 states at 72 commercial reactor sites and a single storage site (Commonwealth Edison's consolidated storage facility at Morris, Illinois). It is estimated that if the existing nuclear power plants continue to operate for their license periods of 40 years, they would generate ~87,000 metric tons of heavy metal of spent nuclear fuel. If each reactor were granted an additional 10 years by license extension, they could produce a total of ~105,000 metric tons of heavy metal of spent nuclear fuel (cf. Dyer and Voegele, 2001; U.S. Department of Energy, 2001).

Other sources of waste include:

1. U.S. Department of Energy (DOE) spent nuclear fuel—spent nuclear fuel from reactors aboard naval vessels and irradiated fuel from weapons production and research reactors.
2. High-level radioactive waste—radioactive by-products resulting from the reprocessing of commercial or defense spent nuclear fuel, which fails to separate small amounts of plutonium and other transuranic elements.
3. Surplus weapons plutonium.
4. Transuranic wastes—by-products from fuel assembly and the manufacture of weapons.

HISTORY OF NUCLEAR WASTE MANAGEMENT

The Atomic Energy Act of 1954 assigned to the U.S. Atomic Energy Commission (AEC) the responsibility of managing spent nuclear fuel from civilian reactors. This act also permitted private industry to construct and operate nuclear reactors for generating electricity. In the following year, the National Academy of Sciences (NAS), at the request of the AEC, began a study of waste disposal and in 1957 reported "…that radioactive waste can be disposed of safely in a variety of ways and at a large number of sites in the United States." The NAS also indicated that "…the most promising method of disposal of high-level waste…is in salt deposits" (National Research Council, 1957). As a consequence, the AEC commissioned the U.S. Geological Survey (USGS) to review the nation's salt deposits. On the basis of investigations between 1962 and 1969, an abandoned salt mine near Lyons, Kansas, was selected for further study. However, owing to the technical problems such as the discovery of old abandoned wells, as well as intense local opposition to the development of a waste disposal site, the project was canceled. As a consequence, the search for alternative geologic repositories was broadened to investigate salt deposits in other states, as well as a variety of other rock types, as discussed below.

In addition to the search for geological repositories in the United States, there was a perceived need to investigate other geologic and nongeologic means for nuclear waste disposal, which included widely diverse alternatives as represented by the following.

1. Sub-seabed disposal—spent nuclear fuel and/or devitrified high-level waste sealed in specially designed canisters and buried within deep sea sediments of an abyssal plain in a tectonically stable area far from plate boundaries.
2. Island disposal—isolation of waste in a deep geologic repository beneath an uninhabited island that lies in a remote area and lacks natural resources.
3. Ice sheet disposal—storage of waste in containers to be placed on the surface of ice sheets (Greenland or Antarctica), with heat from radioactive decay causing the container to melt its way toward the bottom of the ice sheet.
4. Deep-hole disposal—placement of waste-filled canisters in drill holes as much as 10,000 m (6 mi) deep, below circulating groundwater and far below the accessible environment.
5. Rock-melt disposal—placement of waste in liquid or slurry form in a deep drill hole or underground rock opening, with the heat of radioactive decay eventually melting the surrounding rock to form a molten solution of waste and rock that would eventually solidify into a relatively insoluble mass resistant to leaching.
6. Deep well injection—injection of waste into a deep geologic formation capped by a layer of impermeable rock.
7. Space disposal—several alternative concepts were considered, including (1) transport to and injection of waste into the sun, (2) emplacement of waste on the moon, and (3) sending reprocessed waste into orbit midway between Earth and Venus.
8. Long-term surface storage—continued storage in (1) water pools that cool spent fuel rods and shield workers from radiation, or (2) dry storage casks; these are considered to be temporary measures requiring constant monitoring and security.

Treatment methods to mitigate the waste-disposal problem also were considered. Reprocessing of waste is a chemical process in which spent nuclear fuel is dissolved, fissile uranium and plutonium are recovered, and the remaining high-level waste is vitrified (Cowley, 1997). The process is expensive but produces a greatly reduced volume of waste. During President Carter's administration (1977–1980), the United States established the policy of not reprocessing commercial spent nuclear fuel. Partitioning and transmutation of radioactive waste as an adjunct to reprocessing also was considered (Cowley, 1997). In this method, the actinide waste is combined with uranium (or uranium + plutonium), fabricated into mixed oxide, and reinserted into a reactor. After numerous cycles the waste actinides would be converted to stable isotopes or ones with very long half-lives; however, additional waste streams are generated during each reprocessing cycle. Furthermore, transmutation does not reduce the quantities of long-lived fission products including ^{99}Tc and ^{129}I, and these must be disposed of in a geologic repository.

Inherent technical difficulties and other serious disadvantages limit consideration of most nongeological alternatives for waste disposal, and thus the effort to find an acceptable geologic solution was expanded. In 1972, The AEC contracted with the USGS to evaluate several different methods of geologic disposal, principally in geologic media other than salt. Five modes of disposal were to be considered: (1) very deep drill holes (9140–15,250 m), (2) geometric array of shallow to moderate depth drill holes (300–6100 m), (3) shallow mined chambers (300–3000 m), (4) cavities with man-made (engineered) barriers, and (5) explosion cavities (610–6100 m). The final report (Ekren et al., 1974) cited 30 previous reports on geologic disposal and concluded that hydrologic isolation was of paramount importance. One specific recommendation was "the Basin and Range Province of the western United States, particularly the Great Basin exclusive of seismic-risk zone 3[1], appears to have potential for mined chambers above deep water tables in tuff, shale, or argillite" (Ekren et al., 1974, p. 2). The body of the report provides several examples of favorable geologic features at the Nevada Test Site.

During the 1970s and 1980s, the DOE (and predecessor agencies) investigated several alternative sites and rock types:

1. Salt sites (other than Lyons, Kansas)—three salt domes (two in Mississippi and one in Louisiana) and four bedded salt units (Paradox Basin in Utah and Permian Basin of West Texas) were evaluated (U.S. Department of Energy, 1984a, 1984b; 1986a, 1986b, 1986c).

2. Basalt Waste Isolation Project, Hanford, Washington—investigation of layered basalts of Miocene age in the Cold Creek Syncline of the Columbia Plateau, on the Hanford Nuclear Reservation (U.S. Department of Energy, 1986d).

3. Crystalline rocks—following a survey of crystalline rocks largely in the regions of the Appalachian Mountains and the North American Shield, 12 areas in Georgia, North Carolina, Virginia, New Hampshire, Maine, Minnesota, and Wisconsin were recommended for further study (OCRD, 1983; U.S. Department of Energy, 1986e).

4. Sedimentary rocks—widely distributed claystones and shales were considered as appropriate media for geologic disposal of nuclear waste by the National Academy of Sciences (1957). The DOE supported several investigations in this medium (Merewether et al., 1973; Shurr, 1977; Dames and Moore, 1978; and Brookins, 1986b).

5. Tuffaceous rocks, Nevada Test Site—included tuffs in both the unsaturated and saturated zones that had been examined in considerable detail as part of other investigations on the Test Site (U.S. Department of Energy, 1986f, 1986g). This site received the endorsement of USGS Director Vincent McKelvey, who wrote to the DOE in 1976 pointing out the remoteness of the site, its varied geologic environments, and the existence of 900 man-years of data collection and interpretation.

Throughout the 1970s and 1980s, in addition to working with the DOE in specific areas, the USGS was tasked by Congress to study and comment on the problem of disposal of high-level radioactive waste. A report released in 1978 concluded that (1) salt was less than ideal as a disposal medium; (2) shales, tuffs,

and crystalline rocks should be considered; (3) major studies of flow and transport were needed, especially in fractured rock; (4) more tools were needed for dating water and materials older than ~40,000 years; and (5) the severe limitations of Earth science predictions needed to be recognized (Bredehoeft et al., 1978).

In 1980, the Office of Nuclear Waste Management of the DOE and the USGS of the Department of Interior released jointly a draft plan for disposal of radioactive waste in a mined repository (U.S. Department of Energy and USGS, 1980). The report was written by 17 scientists from five organizations and concluded that there was a need to redirect research from generic characterization to four or five specific sites, that detailed study plans should be prepared for each site, and that research and development at the current level should be sufficient to resolve major technical issues within the next 10 years. They also noted a need for research on thermo-mechanical effects on hydrology. The search for more specific sites was started in 1981, when the USGS, in cooperation with seven state agencies (Arizona, California, Idaho, Nevada, New Mexico, Texas, and Utah), began evaluating the Basin and Range Province for possible repository sites. The results were published in eight Professional Papers in the 1370 series; the region encompassing Yucca Mountain is described by Bedinger et al. (1989).

THE YUCCA MOUNTAIN SITE

The Yucca Mountain site is located in Nye County in southern Nevada, ~160 km (100 mi) northwest of Las Vegas (Fig. 1). The entire proposed repository is located on Federal lands, a principal consideration in facilitating further study. The eastern portion is located on the Nevada Test Site; the northwestern corner is located on the Nevada Test and Training range of the U.S. Air Force; and the southwestern corner is located on land managed by the Bureau of Land Management.

Scientific investigations began at Yucca Mountain at the end of the 1970s. The area had already been mapped at 1:24,000 (Lipman and McKay, 1965; Christiansen and Lipman, 1965), and the geology was known to be uncomplicated. The gently dipping volcanic strata of fairly uniform thickness over a large area could be characterized easily, and Yucca Mountain was well removed from the region of active nuclear weapons testing. Initial efforts focused on the saturated zone, but preliminary drilling showed that the water table was very deep (nearly 600 m), the temperature at the water table was moderately elevated (30–35 °C), and the rocks in the saturated zone were highly transmissive, making containment of any leaked waste difficult if not impossible.

The general benefits of an unsaturated zone had already been pointed out by Winograd (1974, 1981), including greater ease of (1) characterizing the site, (2) monitoring stored waste, and (3) retrieving waste should it become necessary. In February 1982, USGS geologists indicated in a letter to the DOE that the thick unsaturated zone at Yucca Mountain might offer considerable

---

[1]Seismic-risk zone 3 corresponds approximately to the east and west province margins, where extension is most active.

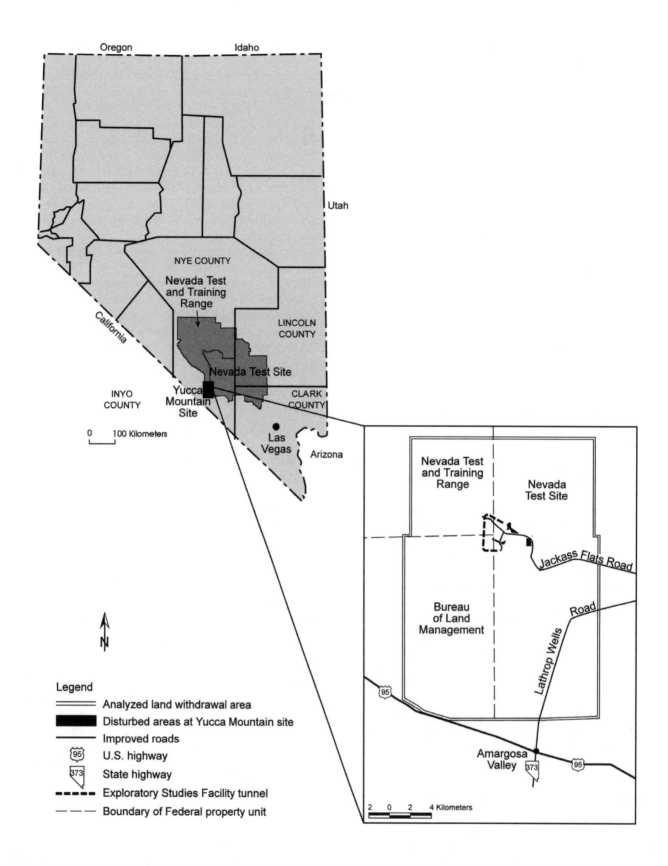

Figure 1. Map showing the location of the proposed repository at Yucca Mountain, Nevada.

advantages for disposing of radioactive waste. The rationale was that only a small amount of water would reach the underground repository, and the repository could be designed so as to permit this water to pass through into deeper permeable rocks and thus have only minimal contact with the stored waste containers. Furthermore, there was a thick zeolitic unit above the water table that would impede the movement of water to the saturated zone and sorb several of the radioactive elements should there be any leakage. A more complete discussion of the advantages on the unsaturated zone at Yucca Mountain is presented by Roseboom (1983). In July 1982, the DOE changed the target horizon for a possible repository to the unsaturated zone.

At the end of 1982, the focus of high-level radioactive waste disposal changed with the passage of the Nuclear Waste Policy Act (NWPA), which directed the DOE to develop specific criteria for recommending candidate sites and prohibited characterization work at any site until a site-characterization plan had been developed. Work at Yucca Mountain was allowed to continue because it was already in progress. The DOE developed siting criteria, which were published as 10 CFR 960 (U.S. Department of Energy, 1984c), and nine sites were selected for judging against these criteria. By 1986, three sites remained: a bedded salt at Deaf Smith, Texas; the basalt flows of Hanford, Washington; and the ash-flow tuffs of Yucca Mountain, Nevada. At the end of 1987, Congress amended the Nuclear Waste Policy Act, directing the DOE to characterize only Yucca Mountain.

The designation of Yucca Mountain as the only site for continued study was based on several important factors. It is located at the west edge of the Nevada Test Site, an area in which many years of geologic, geophysical, hydrologic, and related investigations had been conducted in support of the underground nuclear weapons testing program, as well as preliminary studies of various parts of the area as potential nuclear-waste disposal sites. The preliminary studies had illuminated several favorable conditions for siting a geological repository as noted previously, and no major adverse conditions had been found. However, the DOE was instructed to notify Congress immediately and to stop work if anything was discovered that made the site unsuitable.

Hydrologic conditions in both the saturated and unsaturated zones were of major importance in the designation of Yucca Mountain as the only site to be characterized. These will be discussed in a companion volume. A series of papers covering aspects of both zones can be found in Bodvarsson et al. (2003), and a description of the regional flow system can be found in D'Agnese et al. (2002).

The DOE, as directed by the NWPA, developed an extensive Site Characterization Plan (U.S. Department of Energy, 1988), and the details of how characterization was to proceed were written into more than 100 study plans. Studies included, but were not limited to, regional and site geology, volcanic stratigraphy, Quaternary deposits, climate and paleoclimate, erosion, unsaturated zone hydrology, saturated zone hydrology, mineralogy and petrology, rock and fluid geochemistry, fracture fillings characterization, rock mechanics, thermal testing, coupled processes testing, radionuclide transport, tectonics and tectonic models, seismic and volcanic hazards analysis, geophysics, and natural resources evaluation. Some of the results of these investigations are discussed in the following chapters of this volume. Combined, the results of the entire suite of investigations provide ample documentation that Yucca Mountain is one of the most thoroughly studied geologic features on Earth. Each of these subjects is discussed in detail in the Site Description (Bechtel SAIC Company, 2004). This publication will discuss the regional and site geology, tectonics, and climate (past, present, and future).

REGULATORY INFORMATION

The Yucca Mountain project has been one of the most heavily regulated and scrutinized projects in the history of geology. This section provides a brief overview of this aspect of the project. The NWPA of 1982 (1) established a comprehensive national policy for management and disposal of spent nuclear fuel and high-level radioactive waste, which still remains the framework for the nation's geologic disposal program; and (2) designated three agencies with the authority and responsibility related to waste disposal: (a) the DOE, for siting, licensing, constructing, operating, and closing a repository; (b) the U.S. Environmental Protection Agency, for developing and issuing standards for radiological release from a repository; and (c) the Nuclear Regulatory Commission (NRC), for establishing requirements and criteria for approving or disapproving a license for a repository. The NWPA also established a fund derived from a 1.0 mil per kilowatt-hour assessment on electricity generated by nuclear power plants. This fund would cover costs associated with site characterization, licensing, construction, and operation of a repository (with some additional funding from the Department of Defense for handling of their radioactive waste).

The NWPA also provided for use of the nuclear waste fund in the form of grants for monitoring and independent characterization activities by the state in which site characterization was active as well as monitoring by other affected governmental agencies and affected Native American tribes. In addition, funds have been made available to the NRC for the same purposes. The NWPA required DOE to provide Congress with annual reports on all site-characterization activities and findings.

The Nuclear Waste Policy Amendments Act added another layer of oversight by creating the U.S. Nuclear Waste Technical Review Board. The 11 members of this board are appointed by the president of the United States from a slate of nominees provided by the National Academy of Sciences. The board was also given investigatory powers by the act.

A rigorous quality assurance program provides an internal oversight of all project work. All scientific activities must conform to several standards. Among these are the following. Each activity must be fully described in a planning document before any data collection can take place. The rationale as to why the study is needed is given. The methods to be used are listed along with an explanation of how these methods will attain the desired answers or what should be done if unexpected results are found. All personnel performing quality-affecting work must have their qualifications documented and verified, and their training must be documented. Procurements supporting quality-affecting work must be reviewed for appropriate quality assurance requirements and be procured from approved sources that are audited. All instruments to be used must be calibrated; the tolerances for calibration must be given, and all calibrations must be within the tolerance limits or else the data are discarded back to the date of the last known acceptable calibration. All data are collected according to detailed written procedures, and all samples are controlled and tracked. Finally, all data and records are reviewed and entered into a project database. Any part of the quality assurance program is subject to internal audit and/or audit by the NRC.

The NRC, in 10 CFR 63, mandated that the license application for the Yucca Mountain site include a computer model that will assess how the engineered and natural systems, as a whole, will act to isolate radionuclides from the accessible environment. All data collected by the project have been synthesized into subsystem models and abstracted into a Total System Performance Assessment (TSPA). Much of the data in this volume are included in process models that form the basis for TSPA, either as frameworks within which a model must operate (e.g., the basic geologic data for the site) or as input to a model (e.g., future climate as an input to future unsaturated-zone flow and transport). For a more comprehensive discussion of this complicated model and its results, see Bechtel SAIC Company (2003).

ACKNOWLEDGMENTS

The authors of this chapter wish to thank Eugene Roseboom and Isaac Winograd (U.S. Geological Survey, retired), Michael Voegele (Science Applications International Corporation, retired), Claudia Newbury (Department of Energy) and Stephen Brocoum (Department of Energy, retired), who collectively have more than a century of work in high-level radioactive waste disposal, for very helpful reviews and numerous helpful discussions.

REFERENCES CITED

Alexander, D.H., and Van Luik, A.E., 1991, Natural analogue studies useful in validating regulatory compliance analyses, *in* Validation of geosphere flow and transport models (GEOVAL): Proceedings of a NEA/SKI Symposium, Stockholm, Sweden, May 14–17, 1990, Paris, France, Organization for Economic Cooperation and Development, p. 589–597.

Bechtel SAIC Company, 2003, Total system performance assessment–license application methods and approach: Las Vegas, Nevada, Bechtel SAIC Company, TDR-WIS-PA-000006 REV 00 ICN 01.

Bechtel SAIC Company, 2004, Yucca Mountain site description: Las Vegas, Nevada, Bechtel SAIC Company, TDR-CRW-GS-000001 REV 02 ICN 01, 2 volumes.

Bedinger, M.S., Sargent, K.A., and Langer, W.H., 1989, Studies of geology and hydrology in the Basin and Range Province, southwestern United States, for isolation of high-level radioactive waste—Evaluation of the regions: U.S. Geological Survey Professional Paper 1370-F, 8 plates, 49 p.

Bodvarsson, G.S., Ho, C.K., and Robinson, S.A., eds., 2003, Yucca Mountain Project: Journal of Contaminant Hydrology, v. 62-63, 750 p.

Bredehoeft, J.D., England, A.W., Stewart, D.B., Trask, N.J., and Winograd, I.J.,

1978, Geologic disposal of high-level radioactive wastes—Earth-science perspectives: U.S. Geological Survey Circular 779, 15 p.

Brookins, D.G., 1986a, Natural analogues for radwaste disposal—elemental migration in igneous contact zones: Chemical Geology, v. 55, p. 337–344, doi: 10.1016/0009-2541(86)90034-3.

Brookins, D.G., 1986b, Proceedings of the First Geochemical Workshop on Shale: Martin Marietta, Oak Ridge National Laboratory, ORNL/TM-9865.

Christiansen, R.L., and Lipman, P.W., 1965, Geologic map of the Topopah Spring NW quadrangle, Nye County, Nevada: U.S. Geological Survey Geologic Quadrangle Map GQ-444, scale 1:24,000.

Cowley, K.D., 1997, 1997, Nuclear waste disposal—the technical challenges: Physics Today, June 1997, p. 32–39.

D'Agnese, F.A., O'Brien, G.M., Faunt, C.C., Belcher, W.R., and San Juan, C., 2002, A three-dimensional numerical model of predevelopment conditions in the Death Valley regional ground-water flow system, Nevada and California: U.S. Geological Survey Water-Resources Investigations Report 2002-4102, 114 p.

Dames and Moore, 1978, Baseline rock properties—Shale: Office of Waste Isolation, Report Y/OWI/TM-36/6.

Dyer, J.R., and Voegele, M.D., 2001, The Yucca Mountain site characterization project for the United States, *in* Witherspoon, P.A, and Bodvarsson, G.S., eds., Geological challenges in radioactive waste isolation—Third worldwide review: Lawrence Berkeley National Laboratory Report LBNL-49767, Berkeley, California, p. 298–312.

Ekren, E.B., Dinwiddie, G.A., Mytton, J.W., Thordarson, W., Weir, J.E., Jr., Hinrichs, E.N., and Schroder, L.J., 1974, Geologic and hydrologic considerations for various concepts of high-level radioactive waste disposal in conterminous United States: U.S. Geological Survey Open-File Report 74-158, 219 p.

Lipman, P.W., and McKay, E.J., 1965, Geologic map of the Topopah Spring SW quadrangle, Nye County, Nevada: U.S. Geological Survey Geologic Quadrangle Map GQ-439, scale 1:24,000.

Merewether, E.A., Sharpe, J.A., Gill, J.R., and Cooley, M.E., 1973, Shale, mudstone and claystone as potential host rocks for underground emplacement of waste: U.S. Geological Survey Open-File Report 73-184, 44 p. plus maps.

Miller, W., Alexander, R., Chapman, N., McKinley, I., and Smellie, J., 1994, Natural analogue studies in the geological disposal of radioactive wastes: Amsterdam, Elsevier, 328 p.

National Research Council, 1957, The disposal of radioactive waste on land: Report of the Committee on Waste Disposal of the Division of Earth Sciences, National Research Council, National Academy of Sciences, Publication 519, 42 p.

Nuclear Energy Agency, 1995, The environmental and ethical basis of geological disposal, a collective opinion of the NEA Radioactive Waste Management Committee: Paris, Organization for Economic Co-Operation and Development, 30 p.

OCRD, 1983, A national survey of crystalline rocks and recommendations of regions to be explored for high-level radioactive waste repository sites: Columbus, Ohio, Battelle Memorial Institute, Office of Crystalline Repository Development (OCRD), OCRD-1, 110 p.

Roseboom, E.H., Jr., 1983, Disposal of high-level waste above the water table in arid regions: U.S. Geological Survey Circular 903, 21 p.

Shurr, G.W., 1977, The Pierre Shale, northern Great Plains—A potential isolation medium for radioactive waste: U.S. Geological Survey Open-File Report 77-776, 27 p.

Stuckless, J.S., 2000, Archaeological analogues for assessing the long-term performance of a mined geologic repository for high-level radioactive waste: U.S. Geological Survey Open-File Report 2000-181, 27 p.

Stuckless, J.S., 2002, Natural analogues—One way to help build public confidence in the predicted performance of a mined geologic repository for nuclear waste: Waste Management 2002 symposium, Tucson, Arizona, 15 p.

U.S. Department of Energy and U.S. Geological Survey, 1980, DOE Office of Nuclear Waste Management and U.S. Geological Survey, Earth science technical plan for disposal of radioactive waste in a mined repository (Draft): DOE/TIC-11033 (draft) and USGS (draft report), 211 p. (available from National Technical Information Service, Springfield, Virginia).

U.S. Department of Energy, 1984a, Environmental assessment overview Cypress Creek Dome, Mississippi: OCRWM, DOE/RW-0011, 26 p.

U.S. Department of Energy, 1984b, Environmental assessment overview Swisher County Site, Texas: OCRWM, DOE/RW-0015, 26 p.

U.S. Department of Energy, 1984c, General guidelines for the recommendation of sites for the nuclear waste repositories; final siting guidelines: 10

CFR 960.

U.S. Department of Energy, 1986a, Environmental assessment overview for Richton Dome, Mississippi: OCRWM, DOE/RW-0078, 37 p.

U.S. Department of Energy, 1986b, Environmental assessment overview for Deaf Smith County Site, Texas: OCRWM, DOE/RW-0075, 36 p.

U.S. Department of Energy, 1986c, Environmental assessment overview for Davis Canyon Site, Utah: OCRWM, DOE/RW-0077, 38 p.

U.S. Department of Energy, 1986d, Environmental assessment overview for reference repository location, Hanford Site, Washington: OCRWM, DOE/RW-0076, 34 p.

U.S. Department of Energy, 1986e, Area recommendation report for the Crystalline Repository Project: OCRWM, DOE/CH-15(1), v. 1.

U.S. Department of Energy, 1986f, Environmental assessment, Yucca Mountain Site, Nevada Research and Development Area, Nevada: OCRWM, DOE/RW-0073, 3 volumes.

U.S. Department of Energy, 1986g, Environmental assessment overview for Yucca Mountain Site, Nevada Research and Development Area, Nevada: OCRWM, DOE/RW-0079, 36 p.

U.S. Department of Energy, 1988, Site Characterization Plan—Yucca Mountain Site, Nevada Research and Development Area, Nevada: U.S. Department of Energy, Office of Civilian Radioactive Waste Management, DOE/RW-0199, 353 p. Accessed online January 9, 2007, at http://www.lsnnet.gov/. Search on Participant number HQO.19881201.0002.

U.S. Department of Energy, 2001, Yucca Mountain science and engineering report: OCRWM, DOE/RW-0539, section 1, 45 p.

Winograd, I.J., 1974, Radioactive waste storage in the arid zone: Eos (Transactions, American Geophysical Union), v. 55, p. 884–894.

Winograd, I.J., 1981, Radioactive waste disposal in thick unsaturated zones: Science, v. 212, p. 1457–1464, doi: 10.1126/science.212.4502.1457.

Winograd, I.J., 1986, Archaeology and public perception of a transscientific problem—Disposal of toxic wastes in the unsaturated zone: U.S. Geological Survey Circular 990, 9 p.

MANUSCRIPT ACCEPTED BY THE SOCIETY 18 OCTOBER 2006

Geological Society of America
Memoir 199
2007

Geology of the Yucca Mountain region

John S. Stuckless
Dennis W. O'Leary
U.S. Geological Survey, MS 421, Box 25046, Denver Federal Center, Denver, Colorado 80225, USA

ABSTRACT

Yucca Mountain has been proposed as the site for the nation's first geologic repository for high-level radioactive waste. This chapter provides the geologic framework for the Yucca Mountain region. The regional geologic units range in age from late Precambrian through Holocene, and these are described briefly. Yucca Mountain is composed dominantly of pyroclastic units that range in age from 11.4 to 15.2 Ma. The proposed repository would be constructed within the Topopah Spring Tuff, which is the lower of two major zoned and welded ash-flow tuffs within the Paintbrush Group. The two welded tuffs are separated by the partly to nonwelded Pah Canyon Tuff and Yucca Mountain Tuff, which together figure prominently in the hydrology of the unsaturated zone.

The Quaternary deposits are primarily alluvial sediments with minor basaltic cinder cones and flows. Both have been studied extensively because of their importance in predicting the long-term performance of the proposed repository. Basaltic volcanism began ca. 10 Ma and continued as recently as ca. 80 ka with the eruption of cones and flows at Lathrop Wells, ~10 km south-southwest of Yucca Mountain.

Geologic structure in the Yucca Mountain region is complex. During the latest Paleozoic and Mesozoic, strong compressional forces caused tight folding and thrust faulting. The present regional setting is one of extension, and normal faulting has been active from the Miocene through to the present. There are three major local tectonic domains: (1) Basin and Range, (2) Walker Lane, and (3) Inyo-Mono. Each domain has an effect on the stability of Yucca Mountain.

Keywords: general geology, structure, stratigraphy, repository.

INTRODUCTION

Yucca Mountain, located ~160 km northwest of Las Vegas, Nevada (Figs. 1A and 1B), is one of the prominent uplands characterizing the terrain of southwestern Nevada. It is a tilted block of mid-Tertiary volcanic rocks erupted from a series of volcanic centers that form the southwest Nevada volcanic field (see Fig. 9). The complex geology of this highly deformed and still tec-tonically active region has been studied by numerous investigators, leading to the publication of a wide variety of descriptive and interpretive maps and reports. The primary purpose of this chapter is to summarize the principal results of these studies as they contribute to a basic understanding of the regional geologic setting of the proposed repository site for the disposal of high-level radioactive wastes at Yucca Mountain. Emphasis will be on features that generally lie within 100 km of the site. Detailed

Stuckless, J.S., and O'Leary, D.W., 2007, Geology of the Yucca Mountain region, *in* Stuckless, J.S., and Levich, R.A., eds., The Geology and Climatology of Yucca Mountain and Vicinity, Southern Nevada and California: Geological Society of America Memoir 199, p. 9–52, doi: 10.1130/2007.1199(02). For permission to copy, contact editing@geosociety.org. ©2007 Geological Society of America. All rights reserved.

Figure 1. Maps showing (A) approximate location of the physiographic features of western North America.

discussions of the geology of the site area proper are given by Keefer et al. (this volume).

GEOGRAPHIC SETTING

The Yucca Mountain region lies in the north-central part of the Basin and Range Physiographic Province, within the northernmost subprovince (commonly referred to as the Great Basin) that encompasses nearly all of Nevada as well as adjacent parts of Utah, Idaho, Oregon, and California (Fig. 1A). The southern margin of the Great Basin subprovince is considered to be the Garlock fault and its northeast projection (Fig. 1B). South of this fault lies the northeastern part of the Mojave Desert (Figs. 1A and 1B), characterized by relatively small, irregularly shaped basins and ranges.

Landforms in the region are characterized by more or less regularly spaced, generally north-south trending mountain ranges and intervening alluvial basins. Accordingly, elevation changes

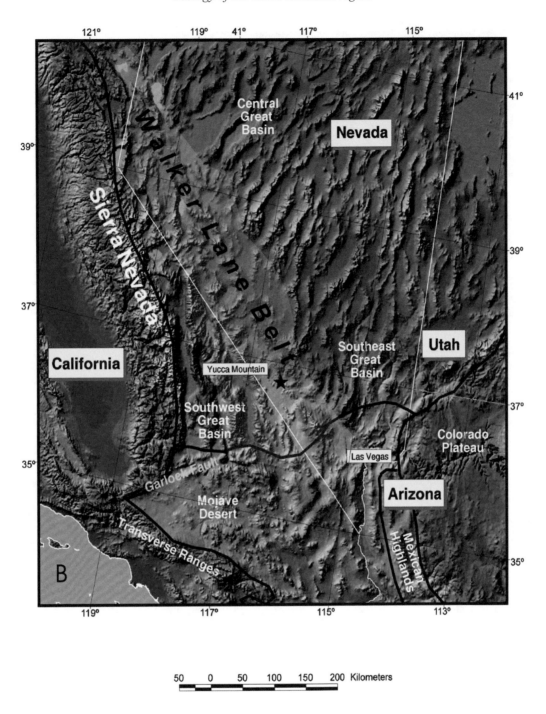

50 0 50 100 150 200 Kilometers

Figure 1. (B) approximate location of the Walker Lane belt and subdivisions of the southern Great Basin (modified from Stewart, 1988; O'Leary, 1996).

and topographic relief are considerable. Lowlands east and west of Yucca Mountain, for example, Jackass Flats and Crater Flat, respectively (Fig. 2), range in elevation from ~850–1000 m above sea level, whereas the crest of Yucca Mountain rises to as much as 1930 m. Death Valley (Fig. 3A), ~80 km west of Yucca Mountain, is the lowest point in the Western Hemisphere, with an elevation of 86 m below sea level at its lowest point.

Yucca Mountain lies near the center of the upper Amargosa drainage basin, which originates in the Pahute Mesa–Timber Moun-

tain area to the north (see Fig. 3A) and includes the main tributary systems of Beatty Wash and Fortymile Wash (Fig. 2). The basic drainage pattern of the area was established soon after caldera collapse and resurgent dome formation that followed the late Cenozoic eruptions in the southwest Nevada volcanic field, and the gross pattern has changed little since then (Huber, 1988).

Surface-water runoff is ephemeral in the region and at Yucca Mountain is mainly through Fortymile Canyon and south through Fortymile Wash (Fig. 2). Jackass Flats to the east is topographically

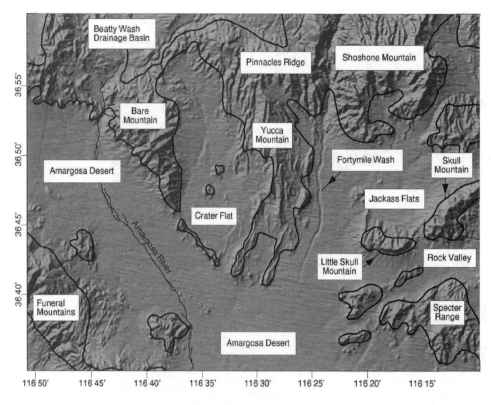

Figure 2. Physiographic features of the Yucca Mountain area.

open, with drainage also into and along Fortymile Wash. The Fortymile Wash drainage, in turn, intersects the Amargosa River in the Amargosa Desert ~15 km southwest of Yucca Mountain (Fig. 2). The Amargosa River enters Death Valley at its southern end, turns to the northwest, and terminates near the center of the valley (Fig. 4). The Great Basin is entirely internally drained (Fig. 1A).

PHYSIOGRAPHIC SETTING

The region surrounding Yucca Mountain can be subdivided further into several well-defined physiographic areas that reflect regional variations in their geologic characteristics. These areas include (Figs. 1A and 1B):

1. The large elongate north-northeast-trending basins and ranges of the central Great Basin;
2. The somewhat smaller, more arcuate, and more closely spaced basins and ranges of the southeast Great Basin;
3. The massive ranges and deep basins of the southwest Great Basin (Inyo-Mono subsection of Carr [1984, p. 9 and 26]); and
4. The highly variable terrane of the Walker Lane belt, which trends northwest between the southeast and southwest segments of the Great Basin to the south, and between the central Great Basin and the Sierra Nevada to the north (Fig. 1B). The Yucca Mountain area is located within this

physiographic area. The geologic relations suggest that many (perhaps most) of these landscape features in this subprovince took on their basic topographic form during the period 12.7–11.7 Ma (Fridrich, 1999).

The mountain ranges of the Great Basin, most of which are tilted, fault-bounded blocks, may extend for more than 80 km, are generally 8–24 km wide, rise 300–1500 m above the floors of the intervening basins, and occupy ~40–50% of the total land area. The deep structural depressions forming the basins contain sedimentary-fill deposits of late Tertiary and Quaternary ages, ranging in thickness from a few hundred meters to more than 3 km. The floors of closed basins are nearly level to gently sloping and are commonly covered, in part, by playas. Open basins generally are moderately to deeply dissected with axial drainage ways. Within this landscape, erosion and erosional processes are concentrated in the high, steep, and relatively wet uplands, whereas deposition and depositional processes generally are concentrated in the low, relatively arid lowlands.

Climatic conditions in the Yucca Mountain region, and over Nevada and much of the southwestern United States, are described in several publications that address this general subject (e.g., Spaulding, 1985; Houghton et al., 1975). In general, the climate of south-central Nevada can be characterized as arid to semiarid, with average annual precipitation ranging from 100 to 200 mm in most lowland areas, 200–400 mm over parts of the uplands, and more than 400 mm along some mountain crests.

This climate exists because the Sierra Nevada Mountains (Figs. 1A and 1B) are a major barrier to moist air moving in from the west. Precipitation from Pacific air masses that do reach the potential repository area accounts for ~50% of the total amount and occurs during November through April. Precipitation in the form of snow is infrequent.

Summer is generally the driest time of year; the sparse summer precipitation commonly occurs as localized thunderstorms rather than from large-scale frontal activity. These storms have a much greater flood potential than the frontal precipitation that occurs during the winter months because of their release of significant amounts of rainfall in relatively short periods of time. Thunderstorm activity produces a secondary precipitation peak during July and August. More details on the regional climatic conditions are given in a later chapter (Sharpe, this volume)

The area surrounding Yucca Mountain can be subdivided into eight clearly defined physiographic elements (Fig. 2) that combine to produce a variable and diverse terrane typical of the Walker Lane belt (Fig. 1B). Two of these elements (Yucca Mountain and Fortymile Wash) are described in the following chapter on site geology (Keefer et al., this volume). The remaining six are described as follows.

1. The Amargosa Desert occupies a broad northwest-trending basin ~80 km long and as much as 30 km wide. The basin is one of the largest in the southern Great Basin. Its floor slopes gently southeastward from elevations of ~975 m at the north end, near Beatty (Fig. 4), to ~600 m toward the south end. The channel of the Amargosa River, into which the streams that drain the Yucca Mountain area empty, extends southeastward along the basin axis, then turns westward and northwestward and terminates in the internal drainage system of Death Valley (Fig. 4).

2. Bare Mountain is an upfaulted block consisting of complexly deformed sedimentary and metasedimentary rocks of Paleozoic and Precambrian age that bounds the west side of Crater Flat (Fig. 2). The range, roughly triangular in plan view, is ~20 km long and from less than 2 km to ~10 km wide. Adjacent piedmont surfaces, sloping southwestward into the Amargosa Desert basin and eastward into Crater Flat, respectively, generally are steep and slightly to moderately dissected proximal to the range flanks, but flatten and are largely undissected toward the basin centers. The piedmont-range junction on the east side of Bare Mountain rises gradually from ~915 m at the south end to almost 1200 m at the north end. Elevations along the range crest vary between 1460 and 1925 m. The southwestern flank of the range is embayed by steep, flat-floored valleys. The eastern flank is sharply defined and only slightly embayed, being structurally controlled by the bounding high-angle, east-dipping Bare Mountain normal fault (see Fig. 10) that was active into Quaternary time.

3. Crater Flat (Fig. 2), flanked by Bare Mountain on the west and Yucca Mountain on the east, is a structural basin ~24 km long and 6–11 km wide. The basin has the overall form of a graben, its west side having been down-dropped several kilometers along the east-dipping Bare Mountain fault and its east side down-dropped a few hundred m along a series of west-dipping normal faults next to the western slope of Yucca Mountain (Carr, 1984, p. 64–66; Simonds et al., 1995; Fridrich, 1999, p. 170–171). The axial part of the basin floor, covered by alluvial deposits that overlie a thick (as much as 3 km) sequence of Late Cenozoic volcanic rocks, rises gradually from altitudes of ~840 m at the south end to as much as 1280 m at the foot of Yucca Mountain to the north. Four basaltic vents and their associated lava flows form prominent cones that attain heights ranging from 27 to 140 m above the alluviated surface of the central basin area.

4. Jackass Flats (Fig. 2) is an asymmetric alluviated basin, 8–10 km wide and nearly 20 km long, that lies east of Yucca Mountain and Fortymile Wash. It is formed principally by piedmonts that slope away from bounding highlands to the north, east, and south, merge in the central basin area, and descend gradually westward and southwestward toward Fortymile Wash. Toward the highlands, the piedmont areas are moderately dissected, with shallow (5–10 m deep) arroyos and rounded interfluves; elsewhere, the basin floor is largely undissected. Topopah Wash is the main axial drainage.

5. Pinnacles Ridge (Fig. 2) is a roughly triangular upland, ~11 km long and 6 km wide, and bounded by Beatty Wash drainage basin on the north, Fortymile Wash on the east, and Yucca Mountain on the southwest. The ridge is contiguous with and extends southeastward from the northeastern flank of Yucca Mountain. Its south flank is structurally and lithologically similar to Yucca Mountain, and its crest is the eroded southern margin of the Timber Mountain caldera (Fig. 3A; Carr, 1984, Fig. 29 therein), one of the main centers of eruption in the southwestern Nevada volcanic field. The ridge crest rises 250–670 m above the prominent washes that surround it, and tributaries to these washes have cut deep, linear valleys into its flanks.

6. Beatty Wash (in the center of Beatty Wash Drainage basin, Fig. 2), one of the larger tributaries of the upper Amargosa River, drains an irregularly shaped area of ~250 km^2 north of Yucca Mountain and Pinnacles Ridge. The basin topography generally is steep and irregular, with valley depths ranging from ~200 to 790 m. Total relief from the mouth of the basin to the crest of Timber Mountain (Fig. 3A) to the north exceeds 1200 m.

TECTONIC SETTING

The Yucca Mountain region lies in parts of three major tectonic domains—from northeast to southwest, the Basin and Range domain, the Walker Lane domain, and the Inyo-Mono domain (Fig. 5). Their principal characteristics are summarized below.

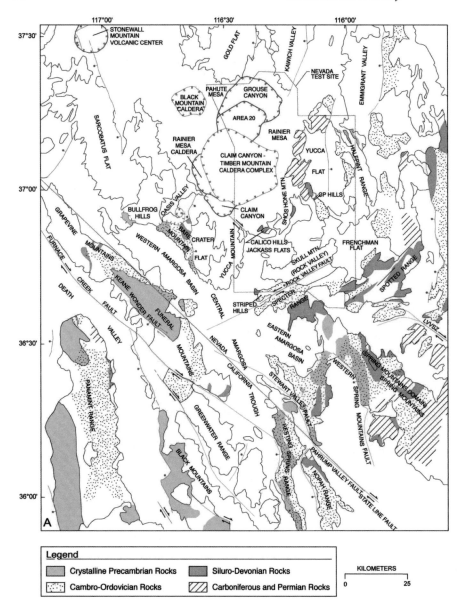

Figure 3. Generalized geologic maps of the Yucca Mountain region (compiled from Frizzell and Shulters, 1990; Stewart and Carlson, 1978; Tschanz and Pampeyan, 1970; Jennings, 1977; Burchfiel et al., 1983; and Carr and Monsen, 1988). Areas of exposed bedrock are indicated by outline. (A) Exposed Precambrian and Paleozoic rocks.

Legend

Crystalline Precambrian Rocks	Siluro-Devonian Rocks
Cambro-Ordovician Rocks	Carboniferous and Permian Rocks

KILOMETERS

0   25

Basin and Range Domain

The Basin and Range domain is dominated structurally by generally north-south–trending mountain ranges separated by basins filled with thick alluvial deposits (Figs. 1A and 1B). The ranges are separated by distances as much as 25–30 km, but many arc toward one another and merge along strike. The general small-scale spatial pattern was aptly likened by Gilbert (1875) to an "army of caterpillars marching north out of Mexico." This structural pattern is the result of a generally east-west–directed extension that began in Tertiary time and continues at the present time (e.g., see Stewart, 1980; Hamilton and Myers, 1966). Rocks of all geologic ages, from Precambrian to Pleistocene, are deformed within this extensional regime. Deformation typically is expressed as complex normal faulting that has facilitated

the rotation of blocks to various dips around nearly horizontal axes. Thus, each range is fundamentally an assemblage of tilted fault blocks and is bounded by a major range-front fault. Seismic reflection profiles show that this style of deformation extends beneath alluvium of the intervening basins (Catchings, 1992).

Walker Lane Domain

Yucca Mountain lies within the Walker Lane domain, an ~100-km-wide (locally much wider) structural belt along the west side of the Basin and Range domain (Fig. 5). The domain, also referred to as the Walker Lane belt (Stewart, 1988) or simply the Walker Lane, extends northwestward from the vicinity of Las Vegas, Nevada, subparallel to the Nevada-California border, into northern California. The domain is characterized by an

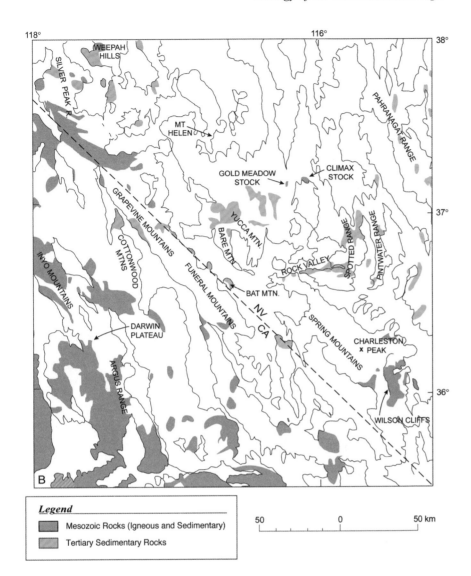

Figure 3. (B) exposed Mesozoic and Tertiary rocks. Tertiary faults and caldera margins shown on 3A in red. LVVSZ is the Las Vegas Valley shear zone and R is Range.

Legend
■ Mesozoic Rocks (Igneous and Sedimentary)
▨ Tertiary Sedimentary Rocks

50   0   50 km

assemblage of crustal blocks separated by discontinuous northwest-striking right-lateral faults and northeast-striking left-lateral faults (Stewart, 1988; Carr, 1990). Because of its structural heterogeneity, the Walker Lane is recognized as a tectonic terrane distinct from the Basin and Range only at a regional scale. The local northwest-striking faults give the domain its overall structural grain and deformation style, obscuring basin and range structure to varying degrees. Although there is no definitive eastern structural boundary to the Walker Lane domain as a whole, the Las Vegas Valley shear zone (Fig. 5) may be interpreted as an eastern bounding structure for the domain's southern segment.

The Walker Lane domain is subdivided into sections (Fig. 5), each of which is characterized by a distinct structural pattern (Stewart, 1988). With respect to the tectonic setting of Yucca Mountain, only three are of concern: (1) the Goldfield section, which includes the Yucca Mountain site area, is characterized by irregular (in places arcuate) ranges, lack of major northwest-striking strike-slip faults, and a scarcity of major "basin-range" faults (Stewart, 1988); (2) the Spotted Range-Mine Mountain

section, which abuts the Goldfield section to the south and is dominated by northeast-striking left-lateral faults; and (3) the Spring Mountains section, which is dominated by Paleozoic and Precambrian rocks that largely preserve pre-Basin and Range structural patterns.

Inyo-Mono Domain

The Inyo-Mono domain includes all of the extended terrane west of the Furnace Creek-Death Valley fault zone (FC on Fig. 5), east of the Sierra Nevada front, and north of the Garlock fault (G on Fig. 5). Its northern end is defined by the termination of the Fish Lake Valley fault (see Fig. 15) and a major right step in the population of active northwest-striking faults along a "northeast-striking structural zone" (Carr, 1984). However, on the basis of gross structure and landform pattern, the domain could be projected northward to the northern terminus of the White Mountains (WM on Fig. 5; Stewart, 1988, Fig. 3 therein). It includes modern basins and ranges with great structural and topographic

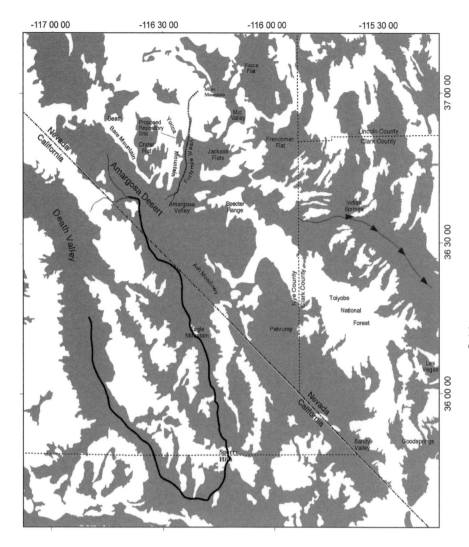

Figure 4. Pleistocene depositional basins and drainage features.

Legend

relief, including Death Valley as a low and the Panamint Range as a high (Fig. 3A). Because of its ongoing tectonic activity and exposure of originally deep-seated to mid-crustal rocks, the Inyo-Mono domain is an important part of the regional geologic setting; it contains some of the more tectonically active structures in the region that lies within 100 km of Yucca Mountain.

The Inyo-Mono domain was identified by Carr (1984) as a subsection of the southwest Great Basin, distinct from the Walker Lane domain. Carr (1984, p. 26) emphasized the pronounced northwest structural and physiographic trends, particularly the "long, linear valleys of north-northwest trend that are outlined by pronounced thoroughgoing structures with abundant evidence of Holocene and local historic faulting." He contrasted this tectonic pattern with the display of "adjacent transform-like offsets or large-scale oroflexing common to many elements of the Walker Lane belt." Stewart (1988), citing Carr (1984), also recognized the distinct tectonic character of the Inyo-Mono domain, but he included it as a section of the Walker Lane domain because of the major north-northwest–striking right-lateral faults.

The Inyo-Mono domain is dominated by dextral strike-slip and oblique transtension, resulting in elevated crustal blocks and intervening deep, high-relief basins (Blakely et al., 1999). Structural relief is large in places, because detachment faulting has unroofed some of the ranges, including the Funeral Mountains

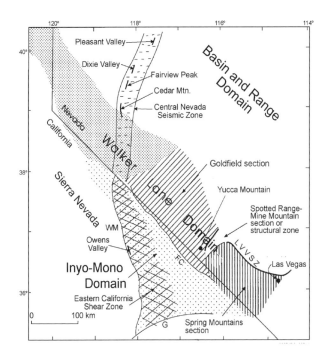

Figure 5. Regional tectonic domains for Yucca Mountain and surrounding environs, plus sections of the Walker Lane belt and five named zones of historical seismic activity shown schematically as short dark lines (modified from Stewart, 1988). LVVSZ—Las Vegas Valley shear zone; G—Garlock fault; FC—Furnace Creek fault; WM—White Mountains.

and Black Mountains (Figs. 3A and 3B). Distinctive as this domain is, it may be partly represented within the Walker Lane domain by less developed features, including Sarcobatus Flat and Amargosa Desert(Figs. 3A and 4), and perhaps even the Amargosa Desert rift zone of Wright (1989).

REGIONAL STRATIGRAPHY

Figure 3A shows the general distribution of exposed Precambrian and Paleozoic rocks in the Yucca Mountain region, and Figure 3B is an outcrop-location map for Mesozoic rocks and Tertiary sedimentary rocks. Two stratigraphic charts (Figs. 6 and 7) show the hierarchy of geologic names that has been established for Jurassic and older rocks in various parts of the region. A third chart (Fig. 8) contains a detailed listing of the units that compose the largely volcanic suites forming the bulk of the rocks exposed at Yucca Mountain and in the surrounding areas.

Pre-Cenozoic rocks in the Yucca Mountain region primarily are upper Precambrian (Proterozoic) siliciclastic strata and Paleozoic limestones and dolomites (Fig. 6). Carbonate rocks within the Paleozoic sequence are the main regional aquifers (Winograd and Thordarson, 1975). Mesozoic rocks are of relatively minor importance to Yucca Mountain, as they are preserved only in the western part of the Inyo-Mono domain (chiefly marine strata) and near the southern part of the Walker Lane domain (chiefly

nonmarine strata) (Fig. 3B). Small Mesozoic igneous intrusions are present near Yucca Mountain. Regionally, there is abundant evidence of large-scale pre-Cenozoic tectonism, but because of limited exposures in the area of the southwest Nevada volcanic field and within the Goldfield section of the Walker Lane belt, the pre-middle Miocene structural configuration of the pre-Cenozoic rocks near Yucca Mountain is uncertain.

At Yucca Mountain and in the surrounding area, Cenozoic rocks overlie complexly deformed Paleozoic and Precambrian rocks along a profound erosional unconformity (Scott, 1990). The distribution, geometry, and attitudes of these older rocks, and the extent to which these factors influenced the distribution and structure of the Cenozoic units, is indeterminable, given the present lack of subsurface data. The age of the regional unconformity also is unknown, but erosional downcutting, possibly associated with extension, most likely was under way in Late Cretaceous (post-Santonian) time. The age of the basal Cenozoic deposits is unknown. The oldest such deposits within a 100 km radius of Yucca Mountain are at least late Oligocene, but such deposits may include older basal colluvium or lag conglomerates. The total thickness of the pre-Tertiary section at the Nevada Test Site is estimated at ~11,500 m (Frizzell and Shulters, 1990).

Precambrian Rocks

Precambrian rocks comprise two major assemblages: an older, metamorphosed basement assemblage (no basal contact is exposed), and a younger, metasedimentary assemblage, the uppermost unit of which is time transgressive and partly Cambrian. The older assemblage primarily consists of quartzofeldspathic gneisses and quartz-feldspar-mica schists of metasedimentary or metaigneous origin. The gneisses and schists typically are intruded by migmatitic veins or larger, deformed bodies of granite or pegmatite.

The Upper Proterozoic formations are widely exposed in the Panamint Range of the Inyo-Mono domain (Labotka et al., 1985, p. 10,359); in the Spring Mountains section of the Walker Lane belt; in the Funeral Mountains; and at Bare Mountain, the Striped Hills, and the Specter Range (cf. Figs. 3A and 3B, 4, and 5 for locations). The Stirling Quartzite and the Wood Canyon Formation are exposed locally east and north of Yucca Mountain (Ekren et al., 1971, p. 7 and 9). The metamorphic facies of the Upper Proterozoic strata is lower greenschist over wide areas of exposure, but in some places, notably the northwestern corner of Bare Mountain, the section as high as the Wood Canyon Formation reaches garnet-amphibolite facies of metamorphism.

Regionally, the Upper Proterozoic units become increasingly calcareous from southeast to northwest (Stewart, 1970, p. 7; Diehl, 1976, p. 58). They form the basal units of a miogeoclinal section and represent a marine depositional environment characterized by passive margin conditions and simple lithologies, chiefly siliciclastic rocks that grade upward into Paleozoic

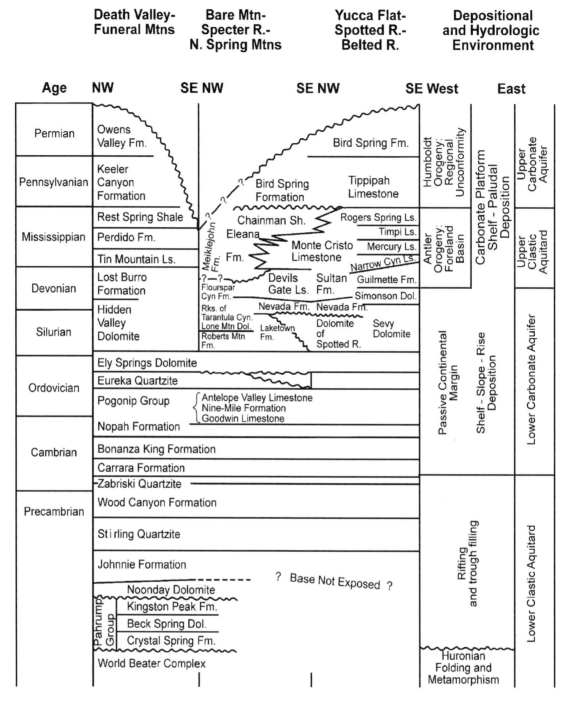

Figure 6. Precambrian and Paleozoic stratigraphic units of the Yucca Mountain region. Mtns—Mountains; R—Range; Fm—Formation; Sh—Shale; Ls—Limestone; and Dol—Dolomite.

carbonate rocks. The cumulative thickness of the exposed Pre-cambrian section in the Yucca Mountain region ranges from 100 m to more than 6 km and forms a sedimentary wedge that thickens to the northwest (Stewart, 1970, p. 7). The Proterozoic rocks, with their weakly to strongly metamorphosed fabrics, form a regional aquitard or barrier to groundwater flow (Winograd and Thordarson, 1975, p. C39).

Paleozoic Rocks

Paleozoic rocks in the Yucca Mountain region comprise three lithosomes: a lower (Cambrian through Devonian) dominantly carbonate lithosome; a middle (Mississippian) fine-grained siliciclastic lithosome; and an upper (Pennsylvanian to Middle-Permian) carbonate lithosome. The lower carbonate

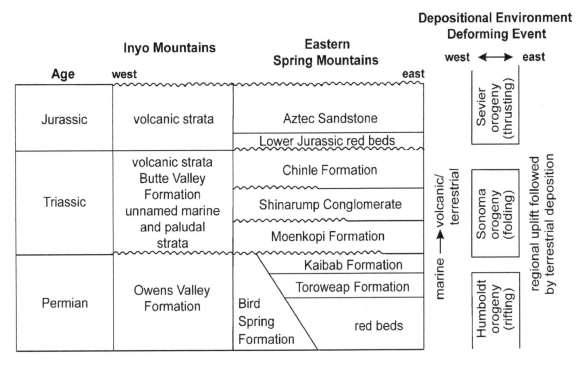

Figure 7. Permian and Mesozoic stratigraphic units of the Yucca Mountain region.

lithosome represents deposition in a deep to shallow marine passive continental margin (outer shelf to upper rise) setting (e.g., see Poole et al., 1992, p. 46). By Late Devonian time, these conditions were interrupted by the Antler Orogeny, the main result of which in the Yucca Mountain region was an influx of clay, silt, and sand into the depositional record (Trexler et al., 1996, p. 1739). A carbonate platform (continental shelf) depositional environment was reestablished in Pennsylvanian time across much of the region, except in the Inyo-Mono domain, where a deeper trough or slope environment was formed (Stewart, 1980, p. 46; Dunne, 1986, p. 5).

Although the Cambrian carbonates are strong and resistant to erosion, in many places they are characterized by stratally confined brecciation. At least two generations of breccia are present, the oldest of which may be of primary origin (submarine debris flows). One or more post-consolidation breccias, most likely of tectonic origin, are associated with interclastic voids in many parts of the calcareous section. This condition has enhanced cavernous dissolution, favoring the flow of groundwater. This feature, as well as the regional extent and uniformity, provides the conditions that make the lower carbonate lithosome a regional aquifer (the lower carbonate aquifer of Winograd and Thordarson [1975, p. C14]).

The character of the Cambro-Ordovician carbonate section differs markedly from that of the Upper Ordovician Eureka Quartzite. The upper part of the Eureka Quartzite is typically a dense, white, sucrose quartzite that forms a unit as much as 150 m thick that is closely fractured. The fractured sections are

locally an aquifer. The Eureka Quartzite is succeeded by the shallow-water Ely Springs Dolomite, which marks a recurrence of the carbonate depositional regime. Ordovician strata grade up through the Ely Springs Dolomite, interrupted by minor erosional gaps, into dolomites that form the Siluro-Devonian section (Stewart, 1980, p. 25, 28).

The Silurian system is thin and areally restricted relative to the rest of the Paleozoic section in southern Nevada (Stewart, 1980, p. 28); it is generally ~600 m thick in the Yucca Mountain region (Stewart, 1980, p. 28). At Yucca Mountain rocks of this age were penetrated below 1244 m, well UE-25p#1 (see M.D. Carr et al., 1986, Plate 1 therein).

The Devonian section is thick and extensive across southern Nevada, and in the Yucca Mountain region, it consists of a succession of limestone and dolomite that typically includes intervals of thick-bedded, gray, crystalline dolomite; fossiliferous, thin- or slabby-bedded or cherty limestone; and silty-sandy or quartzitic beds. The lithologic and stratigraphic variability, the fossil assemblage, and the presence of numerous erosional breaks indicate deposition in shallow (shelf to upper slope) water, dominated at times by reef-bank environments. Devonian strata tend to be siltier upsection and toward the northwest, a lithostratigraphic distinction that becomes more pronounced in the overlying Mississippian section (Stevens et al., 1991, p. 884).

Mississippian strata in the Yucca Mountain region are represented by sharply contrasting but locally intertonguing lithologies: a shale-siltstone section that thickens to more than 3000 m toward its westward source (Stewart, 1980, p. 41), and a comparatively thinner and more uniform carbonate section that

Yucca Mountain
Region

Funeral and Grapevine
Mountains
Death Valley Region

Age		AGE GROUPING UNIT	AGE (Ma)
Plio -	Pleistocene	**Pliocene and Quaternary Volcanics;** (Interbedded with alluvium)	
		Lathrop Wells cone	0.074-0.084
		Bishop Tuff ashfall	0.76
		Creater Flat cinder cones	0.77-1.17
		Older Crater Flat flows	3.7
Miocene	late	**Latest Miocene Units;**	
		Late Miocene basin fill (locally includes)	(10-7)
		Spearhead Tuff	7.5 ± 0.03
		Unnamed ashfall	8-8.5
		Thirsty Canyon Tuff	9.4
		Rocks of Rainbow Mountain	10.47
		Rock-avalanche breccia	10.5
		Twisted Canyon basalt and tuff	10.7
		Major Volcanic Period (11-14 Ma) Units;	
		Rock-avalanche breccia	(11.5)
		Timber Mountain Group:	
	middle	Ammonia Tanks Tuff	11.45±0.03
		Rainier Mesa Tuff	11.6±0.03
		Rhyolite of Fluorspar Canyon	11.6-7
		Rock-avalanche breccia	12.6-11.8
		Windy Wash lavas & tuffs	12.5
		Paintbrush Group:	
		Tiva Canyon Tuff	12.7.±0.03
		Yucca Mountain Tuff	-
		Pah Canyon Tuff	-
		Topopah Spring Tuff	12.8±0.03
		Calico Hills Frn.	12.9±0.04
		Wahmonia Salyer Fms.	
		Crater Flat Group:	13.1
		Prow Pass Tuff	13.25±0.04
		Bullfrog Tuff	13.35
		Rhyolite of Propector Pass	13.45
		Tram Tuff	13.9
		Lithic Ridge Tuff	15.2-14
	early	Older Tuff (Tuff of Yucca Flat)	15.1±0.06
		Pre-Southwest Nevada Volcanic Field Units:	
		Rocks of Pavitts Spring and rocks of Joshua Hollow	(14?-16)
		"Green conglomerate"	(16?-20)
		Winapi Wash/Titus Canyon Fm.	(25?-30)
		Slide Breccia	?
Oligocene		Monotony Tuff	27.3

Funeral and Grapevine Mountains Death Valley Region:

Funeral Formation	basalt	
	cgl.	
Furnace Crook Fm (2000 m)	fluvio-	
	lacustrine alluvium	
	local basalt	
Artist Drive Fm (~2500 m)	ss. cgl.	Esmeralda Formation
	volcanics and basal ls	
Bat Mtn. Frm	ss. fangl.	
Kelley's Wells Ls (100 m)	ls	
Amargosa Valley Fm (800 m)	ls tuff	Titus Canyon
	red ss	
	ls, tuff	
	cgl.	

Sources: Sawyer et al. (1994); Cemen et al. (1999, p 69); Wright et al. (1999); Slate et al. (1999, pp 23, 33); Fridrich (1999, p. 175); Turner (1990); Cemen et al. (1999, p.69); and Wright et al. (1990)

extends southeastward from the vicinity of Mercury (cf. Fig. 14) and the Spotted Range, where it is ~300 m thick (Barnes et al., 1982).

Barnes et al. (1982) mapped three Mississippian carbonate units at the Nevada Test Site (Fig. 3A), but along the west side of Yucca Flat, the Mississippian section is mostly the shaley, western facies, represented by the Eleana Formation (Fig. 6). The upper part of the Eleana Formation primarily is calcareous turbidites, which is represented farther east and south by the Chainman Shale (Fig. 6), a monotonous siltstone or mudstone several hundred meters thick, interbedded with sparse quartz sandstone. The Chainman Shale crops out in the CP Hills and the core of the Calico Hills (Maldonado et al., 1979, p. 1; Cole et al., 1994, p. 68, 71; Sawyer et al., 1995, p. 29; Potter et al., 2002a) (exposures too small to display in Fig. 3A). About 770 m of Chainman Shale were penetrated by borehole UE-25 a-3 in the Calico Hills. The hole bottomed in Silurian or Devonian dolomite (Maldonado et al., 1979, p. 1). The borehole revealed low-grade thermal metamorphism of the shale, which provides one possible explanation for a magnetic anomaly that encompasses the Calico Hills (Majer et al., 1996, Plate 2 therein). Alternatively, the anomaly could be explained by a depositionally thick section of Miocene tuff above the Paleozoic contact.

Rocks of Pennsylvanian to Permian age in the Yucca Mountain region are represented by the Tippipah Limestone (Fig. 6), a thick- to thin-bedded, gray limestone, but is locally silty and cherty (Frizzell and Shulters, 1990). The Tippipah is exposed only at the east side of the Nevada Test Site, along the western edge of Yucca Flat (Fig. 4), and at the southern end of the CP Hills (Fig. 3A), where it is disconformable with the Chainman Shale (Fig. 6; Cole et al., 1994, p. 75).

Mesozoic Rocks

Stratified Mesozoic rocks have not been found within the 100 km radius of Yucca Mountain; their closest occurrence to Yucca Mountain is at the periphery of this area, south and east of Charleston Peak in the Spring Mountains (Figs. 3A and 3B). There, a thick, well-exposed section of Mesozoic rock forms Wilson Cliffs at the latitude of Las Vegas (Longwell et al., 1965; Fig. 3B). Although Mesozoic strata are not a factor in the hydrologic or tectonic phenomena relevant to Yucca Mountain, a discussion is included here as an integral part of the geologic history of the Yucca Mountain region.

Carbonate deposition in the Yucca Mountain region continued into Late Permian time, but gradual uplift, accompanied by erosion, resulted in an unconformity. Deeper (and older) stratigraphic levels were exposed toward the west, whereas deposition

of younger strata encroached from the east, progressively covering much of the eroded carbonate rock. Consequently, Lower Triassic strata unconformably overlie Middle to Lower Permian parts of the Bird Spring Formation (Fig. 6) in the western Spring Mountains. In the southeastern Spring Mountains, the Permian section is more nearly complete and contains Permian red beds and the Toroweap and Kaibab Formations (Fig. 7). Farther east, in the Colorado Plateau, a virtually complete Permian through Triassic section is present. As the erosional hiatus across the unconformity diminishes toward the east, the younger Paleozoic strata below the unconformity reflect shallower, near-shore depositional environments, as do the Lower Triassic strata that lie above the unconformity.

The Lower Triassic strata are assigned to the Moenkopi Formation (Fig. 7; Stewart, 1980, Table 3.2-2 therein). This unit includes interbedded silty limestone, reddish-brown siltstone to fine-grained sandstone, gypsum, and local limestone pebble conglomerates, facies that indicate a shoaling marine to alluvial near-shore environment of deposition. Upper Triassic strata comprise the Chinle Formation and its basal member, the Shinarump Conglomerate (Fig. 7). The Shinarump consists of widespread chert-pebble conglomerate in sandstone matrix; the Chinle is chiefly weakly consolidated red shale, claystone, siltstone, and fine sandstone. Unconformably above the Chinle are Lower Jurassic red beds equivalent to the Moenave and Kayenta Formations of the Colorado Plateau. Conformably above these beds lies the Lower Jurassic Aztec Sandstone, the youngest Mesozoic unit in the region (Fig. 7). The Aztec consists of conspicuously cross-bedded, pink to red, fine- to medium-grained quartzose sandstone as much as 750 m thick in the Wilson Cliffs (Fig. 3B). The top of the Aztec Sandstone either is eroded away or sliced off by an overthrust Paleozoic section along the Keystone thrust (Longwell et al., 1965).

The Mesozoic section in the Spring Mountains (Fig. 3B) indicates that regional uplift continued and expanded eastward in Middle to Late Triassic time, exposing strata of the Moenkopi Formation (Fig. 7) to slight erosion and, during a later phase of uplift, also exposing the Chinle Formation (Fig. 7) to erosion (Marzolf, 1990). By Early Jurassic time the region evolved from an alluvial plain to a desert, and dune sands of the Aztec Sandstone were laid down (Marzolf, 1990).

In California, Mesozoic strata are present in a band that stretches along the Inyo Mountains, the Darwin Plateau, and into the Argus Range (Fig. 3B; Stone and Stevens, 1986). The section includes two Triassic lithosomes: a Lower Triassic marine to near-shore alluvial lithosome consisting of ~800–900 m of micritic limestone and mudstone (Lewis et al., 1983; Dunne, 1986), and an Upper Triassic (and possibly younger) continental volcanic and volcaniclastic lithosome as much as 3000 m thick (Dunne, 1986). In those areas, as in Nevada, the change in environment of deposition, from marine to continental, reflects regional uplift associated with tectonism. The Upper Triassic lithosome in California comprises an eastward prograding assemblage of fan deposits that were derived from the evolving

Figure 8. Tertiary and Quaternary stratigraphic units of the Yucca Mountain region. Mtns—Mountains; Fm—Formation; ls—limestone; ss—sandstone; cgl—conglomerate; and fangl—fanglomerate.

Sierra Nevada (Figs. 1A and 1B) plutonic/volcanic terrane to the west (now represented by the exposed Sierra Nevada batholith; Dunne, 1986; Dunne et al., 1978). Most of the California Triassic rocks are metamorphosed as a result of igneous intrusion and concomitant crustal thickening (Dunne, 1986). Igneous intrusion in that region occurred from ca. 186–147 Ma (Chen and Moore, 1982; Dunne et al., 1978; Miller, 1978) and from 80 to 70 Ma (Labotka et al., 1985).

Mesozoic rocks younger than Early Jurassic in the Yucca Mountain setting are intrusive, consisting of widely scattered granitic stocks and mafic dikes. Granitic stocks near Yucca Mountain (Fig. 3B) include the Climax and Gold Meadow stocks (101 Ma and 93.6 Ma, respectively; Naeser and Maldonado, 1981) and a buried intrusive body near Yucca Flat (102 Ma; Cole et al., 1993), as well as numerous lamprophyre dikes (ca. 101 Ma; Cole et al., 1994). In California, a widely distributed population of mafic dikes that are aligned about N25°W (the Independence dike swarm; Moore and Hopson, 1961; Chen and Moore, 1979) is Late Jurassic (ca. 148 Ma; Chen and Moore, 1979). The dikes represent an early phase of regional extension oriented N65°W (Chen and Moore, 1979). The intrusion of granitic stocks represents a period of crustal thickening and heating that culminated probably in Late Jurassic to Early Cretaceous time. Metamorphism of the Proterozoic rocks in the Funeral Mountains (Fig. 3A) has been attributed to regional metamorphism in Mesozoic time that likely continued into the Tertiary. Many of the intrusive rocks are exposed at structural levels that indicate removal by erosion of several kilometers of rock since the time of intrusion and crystallization.

Cenozoic Rocks

Cenozoic rocks of the Yucca Mountain geologic setting fall into three general groups: pre-Middle Miocene sedimentary (including volcaniclastic) rocks that predate creation of the southwestern Nevada volcanic field; the Middle to Late Miocene volcanic suite that constitutes the southwestern Nevada volcanic field; and the Plio-Pleistocene basalts and basin sediments. These lithostratigraphic groups are not well defined in terms of system boundaries (e.g., Tertiary or Quaternary), so systemic distinctions will not be emphasized in the following sections.

Tertiary Rocks

Pre-middle Miocene sedimentary rocks are widely distributed in Nevada (Stewart, 1980, p. 87). The distribution and heterogeneous continental character of the Tertiary deposits implies that they were laid down in restricted basins that may have been precursors to the present basins (cf. Stewart, 1980, p. 92). The deposits in the Yucca Mountain area typically comprise a basal conglomerate, lacustrine limestone, and tuffs. The conglomerate is composed of locally derived clasts (Precambrian or Paleozoic provenance), commonly of cobble to boulder size, and typically is poorly sorted and set in an oxidized matrix. Its textural characteristics range from those associated with colluvial deposits to those associated with

fanglomerates and stream-channel gravels. The conglomerate typically intertongues with and is overlain by a characteristically pinkish-cream to buff or tan crystalline or clayey-silty lacustrine limestone. In outcrop, the limestone commonly shows soft-sediment deformation features, local slump folding, and algal mat structures. Upsection, the limestone is interbedded with and ultimately overlain by tuffaceous sandstone and distal air-fall tuffs of uncertain provenance. Strata of this lithologic assemblage and pre-middle Miocene age (Fig. 8) are found in and near Rock Valley, east of Yucca Mountain (Figs. 2 and 3A).

The presence of air-fall tuffs high in the Oligocene section heralds a period of catastrophic explosive volcanism that culminated in the creation of the southwestern Nevada volcanic field 15–7.5 Ma (Stewart et al., 1977, p. 67; W.J. Carr et al., 1986, p. 3; Sawyer et al., 1994, p. 1304) (Fig. 9). The earliest of these great eruptions is represented by the Monotony Tuff (Fig. 8), a unit dated 27.3 Ma and exposed mainly north of Yucca Mountain in the Belted Range and the Rhyolite Hills, which are located just off the northeast corner of the Nevada Test Site (Sawyer et al., 1995, p. 28). The Monotony Tuff has a maximum exposed thickness of ~700 m; it originated from a caldera located in the area of the present Pancake Range and northern Reveille Range (Fig. 9; Ekren et al., 1971, p. 25; Sawyer et al., 1995, p. 28). (The Pancake Range is north of the Reveille Range.) The sequence of upper Oligocene through middle Miocene tuffs and associated sediments forms an important part of the Tertiary section in the setting north and east of Yucca Mountain; Ekren et al. (1971, p. 24) cited more than 6000 m of such strata ranging in age from 27 to 7 Ma.

Deposition of the tuffs and establishment of the great caldera complexes interrupted and locally obliterated the established Tertiary depositional regime in the Yucca Mountain geologic setting. This regime continued elsewhere, however, with modifications imposed by tectonism, until nearly the end of the Miocene, when fundamental changes in climate and regionally active extensional faulting put an end to it throughout the southern Great Basin.

In the vicinity of Yucca Mountain, in Rock Valley (Figs. 2 and 3B), the Oligocene rocks of Winapi Wash are succeeded by a complex assemblage of bouldery and poorly sorted stream gravel, volcanic arkose, shale and siltstone, freshwater limestone and marl, and a variety of tuffs. This assemblage is informally designated "rocks of Pavits Spring" (Hinrichs, 1968) (Fig. 8). The fluvial-lacustrine environment inherited from the Oligocene persisted in Rock Valley until the Ammonia Tanks Tuff (Fig. 8) was deposited at 11.4 Ma. Gravel (unit Tsd, M.D. Carr et al., 1986, Fig. 12 therein, p. 28, 30) possibly correlative with the rocks of Pavits Spring was penetrated by well UE-25 p#1 at Yucca Mountain, near the Paleozoic unconformity (cf. Keefer et al., this volume).

The explosive volcanism, during the evolution of the southwestern Nevada volcanic field, is the most significant depositional event of the Cenozoic era with respect to Yucca Mountain. It resulted in the formation of at least six major calderas from ca. 15–7.5 Ma (Sawyer et al., 1994, p. 1304), created

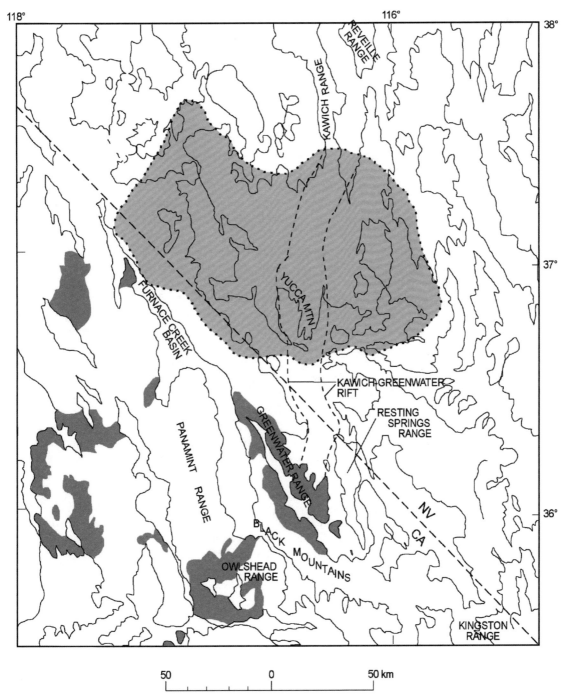

Figure 9. General extent of the southwest Nevada volcanic field (shown in gray) and Coeval Igneous Rocks (shown in yellow) of the Inyo-Mono Domain (modified from Carr, 1990, and Jennings, 1977).

Yucca Mountain, and brought to a close the regional deposition that spans domains of the Yucca Mountain geologic setting. The record of regional tuff deposition begins within the rocks of Pavits Spring. Tuff deposition also is documented in the eastern part of the Nevada Test Site, where Redrock Valley Tuff (15.3 Ma) (Sawyer et al., 1995, p. 26) and the tuff of Yucca Flat (15 Ma) (Sawyer et al., 1995, p. 26) are large components. The suc-

cession of tuff and lava units that form Yucca Mountain are listed on Figure 8 and described in detail in the site geology chapter (Keefer et al., this volume)

The lowest of the tuffs that form the foundation of Yucca Mountain is the Lithic Ridge Tuff (Fig. 8), which is 15.2–14 Ma (Sawyer et al., 1994, p. 1305). Although pre-Lithic Ridge tuffs are found in the rocks of Pavits Springs and beneath Yucca

Mountain, little is known about their extent, age, and stratigraphic relationships. Younger units that are widely distributed in the southwestern Nevada volcanic field (Fig. 8) include the Crater Flat Group (ca. 13.1 Ma), the Calico Hills Formation (12.9 Ma), the Paintbrush Group (12.8–12.7 Ma), and the Timber Mountain Group (11.6–11.4 Ma) (Sawyer et al., 1994, p. 1305). The caldera sources for all but the Tiva Canyon Tuff of the Paintbrush Group and the Timber Mountain Group tuffs are uncertain (Sawyer et al., 1994, p. 1304). Peak volcanism in the southwestern Nevada volcanic field occurred during eruption of the Paintbrush and Timber Mountain Groups when more than 4500 km^3 of magma were erupted in two episodes separated by a span of ~1.1 m.y. (Fig. 8; Sawyer et al., 1994, p. 1311; Keefer et al., this volume).

The Wahmonie Formation (Poole et al., 1965), a sequence of andesite and dacite lava flows erupted from a source north of Skull Mountain and south of Shoshone Mountain (Fig. 3A), forms a distinctive marker between the Crater Flat Group tuffs and the Calico Hills Formation (Fig. 8) east of Yucca Mountain. Rocks of the Wahmonie Formation characteristically are biotite-rich and, therefore, dark and Fe-rich. They are generally massive, thick-bedded lava flows, autoclastic breccias, and agglomerates. The lower part of the Wahmonie Formation includes interbedded volcaniclastic sediments—debris flows, lahars, and mudslides—that indicate initial deposition in a relatively high-relief setting. The basal volcanic and volcaniclastic interval was formerly called the Salyer Formation (Poole et al., 1965; Frizzell and Shulters, 1990), but is now reduced to member status (Sawyer et al., 1995, p. 19).

The Calico Hills Formation (Fig. 8) is named for exposures in the northwestern part of the Calico Hills (Sawyer et al., 1994, p. 1307). It consists of rhyolite lavas, bedded and locally zeolitized tuffs, and nonwelded ash-flow tuffs. In the Yucca Mountain area, it is 50–300 m thick (Sawyer et al., 1994, p. 1307; 1995, p. 18). In earlier maps and reports, the unit is referred to informally by various designations, such as Rhyolite of Calico Hills (Lipman and McKay, 1965), tuffs and lavas of Calico Hills (W.J. Carr et al., 1986, p. 4, Fig. 2 therein), or rhyolite lavas and tuffaceous beds of Calico Hills (Frizzell and Shulters, 1990).

The largest and most important contribution to the volume of volcanic rocks at Yucca Mountain is the Paintbrush Group (Fig. 8). It consists of a succession of well-stratified rhyolites and quartz latites totaling ~610 m thick at Yucca Mountain. The group includes four members, in ascending order, the Topopah Spring Tuff (12.8 Ma), the Pah Canyon Tuff, the Yucca Mountain Tuff, and the Tiva Canyon Tuff (12.7 Ma). The Topopah Spring Tuff is subdivided into 2 members and 9 informal units (Day et al., 1998) based on crystallinity, degree of welding, and development of lithophysae. The Topopah Spring Tuff is the host rock for the proposed radioactive waste repository and is described in more detail in the chapter on site geology (Keefer et al., this volume).

The Paintbrush Group was faulted and eroded following deposition of the 12.7 Ma Tiva Canyon Tuff, thus forming an unconformable contact with the overlying Timber Mountain Group (Fridrich, 1999, p. 184). Although the Timber Mountain Group (Fig. 8) forms a major eruptive volume of siliceous rhyolites and quartz latites, it is sparsely present at Yucca Mountain (primarily as a small outcrop on the west side of Yucca Mountain [Day et al., 1998]). In general, distribution of the two major units of the Timber Mountain Group, the Rainier Mesa and Ammonia Tanks Tuffs (Fig. 8), is extensive within the western half of Crater Flat basin and at the western end of the south-bounding cuesta. Outcrop thicknesses as great as 240 m are recorded (Fridrich, 1999, p. 187).

Other eruptive centers and calderas associated with the southwestern Nevada volcanic field are shown on Figure 3A including the Black Mountain caldera (9.4 Ma), and the Stonewall Mountain volcanic center (7.5 Ma) (Sawyer et al., 1994, p. 1305–1306). The various tuffs and lavas erupted in the post–11 Ma period form important volumes of rock in the Pahute Mesa-Sarcobatus Flat–Bullfrog Hills area northwest of Yucca Mountain (Fig. 3A). They are not, however, directly relevant to the history or makeup of Yucca Mountain. The youngest tuff at Yucca Mountain is the Rainier Mesa Tuff of the Timber Mountain Group (Fig. 8; Keefer et al., this volume).

Physical properties of the tuff and lava units of the southwestern Nevada volcanic field contrast greatly across formational contacts, but tend to be uniform laterally over wide areas. This characteristic results from:

1. The conditions of deposition—large batches of homogenized material laid down quickly over large areas;

2. Differences in initial composition of each eruptive batch; and

3. Post-depositional processes of welding, vapor-phase crystallization, autolytic and pneumatolytic alteration, and gas dispersion.

As a result, some of the tuff units are physically similar to ceramics or glass, whereas others are loose and porous, or vesicular and closely fractured or chemically altered. Understanding the spatial variation of these properties contributes to modeling the behavior of a proposed repository under thermal loading and to modeling of hydrologic processes.

Miocene rocks west and south of Yucca Mountain, in the Inyo-Mono domain (Fig. 5), that are chiefly of igneous origin are younger than ca. 16 Ma. These include the central Death Valley volcanic field (Wright et al., 1981, p. 7) and an irregular belt of volcanic rocks that extends from the Owlshead Range and southern Panamint Range eastward toward the Kingston Range, the Greenwater Range, the Black Mountains, and the Furnace Creek basin (Fig. 9). Tuffs of the Artists Drive Formation date from ca. 14–6 Ma (Wright et al., 1991). Above these lie the Furnace Creek and Funeral Formations, with a combined total thickness of ~3600 m of pyroclastic sediments, basalt flows, intertonguing conglomerates, sandstones, and mudstones. Basalts near the base of the Funeral Formation are dated at ca. 4 Ma (McAllister, 1973). Wright et al. (1991) note that this rock assemblage is most likely the direct result of Neogene local-basin subsidence and extension.

The central Death Valley volcanic field is underlain by the Willow Springs Pluton, a diorite dated between 11.6 and 10 Ma, exposed along the west side of the Black Mountains (Fig. 9) (Asmerom et al., 1990, p. 224–225). The diorite is intruded by small granite bodies. Basalt extrusion in the Resting Springs Range (Fig. 9) of about the same age (11.7 m.y.) was followed by extensive silicic to mafic volcanism during the 10.5–5 Ma period. Volcanism culminated in the 8.5–6.5 Ma period with eruption of the Shoshone volcanic suite, chiefly dacites and rhyodacite tuffs (with associated sediments) exposed in the eastern Black Mountains and southern part of the Greenwater Range (Fig. 9). Silicic volcanism ceased in this area ca. 5–6 Ma with deposition of rhyolites of the Greenwater volcanic suite (Noble 1941, p. 956; Drewes 1963, p. 42). Thereafter, diminishing basaltic volcanism continued into late Pleistocene time, as in the Goldfield section of the Walker Lane domain to the east (Fig. 5).

The advent of basaltic volcanism at ca. 11 Ma signaled the end of crustal magmatism in the construction of Yucca Mountain. It indicates generation of small, discrete batches of basaltic magma at upper mantle depths (60 km) capable of making their way quickly to the surface in Crater Flat basin (Crowe et al., 1995, p. 5-16–5-17). The history, evolution, and character of Plio-Pleistocene basaltic volcanism proximal to Yucca Mountain (within 25 km of the proposed repository) is discussed in Crowe et al. (1995) and Vaniman et al. (1982).

The oldest basalts in Crater Flat are dated at ca. 11.3 Ma, indicating that episodes of basaltic volcanism began very shortly after eruption of the Ammonia Tanks Tuff (11.45 Ma). However, no further basaltic volcanism occurred in Crater Flat until 3.7 Ma, when a large lava flow and a group of five northwest-aligned scoria cones were emplaced in southeastern Crater Flat (Fig. 10). This latter episode represents the largest volume basaltic emplacement in Crater Flat. The complex formed largely from Hawaiian-type fissure eruptions and aa flows. Lava-filled fissures and feeder dikes are oriented north-south. The deposit subsequently was cut by faulting that produced dip-slip offsets of more than 1 m, west side down (Crowe et al., 1995, p. 2-19–2-20).

Quaternary Rocks and Sediments

Quaternary deposits consist of alluvial sediments and infrequently erupted basalts. The basaltic eruptions represent a continuation of the activity during the Late Tertiary. Following the episode at 3.7 Ma, a subsequent basaltic eruption episode occurred from 1.7 to 0.7 Ma. This eruptive episode consists of four cinder cones (Little Cones, Red Cone, Black Cone, and Makani Cone) aligned north-northeast along the axis of Crater Flat (Fig. 10). Most of the volume from this episode is associated with Red and Black Cones. The area of this episode spatially overlaps the area of the earliest basaltic eruption (11.3 Ma).

The most recent episode of basaltic volcanism created the Lathrop Wells Cone (Fig. 10). The Lathrop Wells Cone complex comprises fissure eruptions; spatter, scoria, and cinder cones; and aa flows. Satellite spatter cones at the east base of the main cone have a northwest alignment. The Lathrop Wells Cone complex is probably ca. 80 ka (Heizler et al., 1999, p. 767–768). The complex emplacement history of this volcanic center is discussed by Crowe et al. (1995) and Heizler et al. (1999).

Other basaltic centers in the Yucca Mountain vicinity include the 380 ka Sleeping Butte centers, located 45 km northwest of Yucca Mountain, and the Amargosa Valley basalt, located ~3 km south of crossroads at Amargosa Valley (Fig. 4; Crowe et al., 1995, p. 2–19). The basalt is buried, but was sampled by drilling; basalt samples gave $^{40}Ar/^{39}Ar$ isochron ages of 3.8 and 4.4 m.y. (Crowe et al., 1995, p. 2–19).

Apart from sporadic and volumetrically minor basaltic volcanism, Quaternary deposition in the Yucca Mountain geologic setting primarily is restricted to alluvial basin deposition. In many basins, alluvial deposition is a continuation of sediment infilling that was well under way in late Miocene time. For example, in Mid Valley (Fig. 4), a continuous alluvial section 300–400 m thick includes a several-meter-thick interval of 7.5 Ma ash-fall Spearhead Tuff (McArthur and Burkhard, 1986, p. 26–27, 41). The tuff, penetrated by two boreholes, is overlain by ~360 m of fine to coarse sand and sandy gravel derived from the basin flanks.

Closed basins in the area received alluvial sediment hundreds of meters thick throughout the Plio-Pleistocene, in response to continuing faulting, subsidence, and range flank erosion. Frenchman Flat and Yucca Flat basin, Mid Valley, Crater Flat basin, and especially the basins of the Inyo-Mono terrane (Fig. 5) contain sediment that includes coarse alluvial clastic facies (e.g., debris-flow deposits, colluvium, fan-sheet gravel) and lakebed-playa deposits (e.g., siliceous clays, marls, evaporites). In some basins, such as Crater Flat basin, aggradation has reached levels sufficient to have formed spillways, so that alluvial deposition is graded to an adjacent valley (here Amargosa Desert) (Fig. 4) or basin.

Within the Yucca Mountain region, broad valley or trough-like areas of subsidence are linked by graded fan assemblages and washes to form two separate drainage systems: the Las Vegas Valley watershed (cf. Las Vegas Valley shear zone, Fig. 12) and the Amargosa Desert watershed (Fig. 4). Colluvium and scree commonly litter the range flanks. This sediment typically is brought to the basins as debris flows or mud flows during the infrequent torrential rains that are characteristic of the present interpluvial climate.

Swadley and Carr (1987) identified fine-grained marl and silt deposits in the Amargosa Desert (Fig. 4) as lake and marsh deposits. The southward decrease in elevation of these deposits was interpreted as evidence for an overall regional tilt to the south, established during the past 8 m.y. (Carr, 1984, p. 82). The proposed regional tilting seemed consistent with the southward regional drainage and a general ponding at the southern ends of major basins and associated spillways. However, these fine-grained deposits in the Amargosa Desert, Las Vegas Valley, and Pahrump Valley are now recognized as paludal ground-water discharge sites that preferentially trapped silt (Forester and Smith, 1994; Quade et al., 1998; Paces et al., 1997; Lundstrom et al., 1999; Paces and Whelan, 2001; Quade et al., 2003).

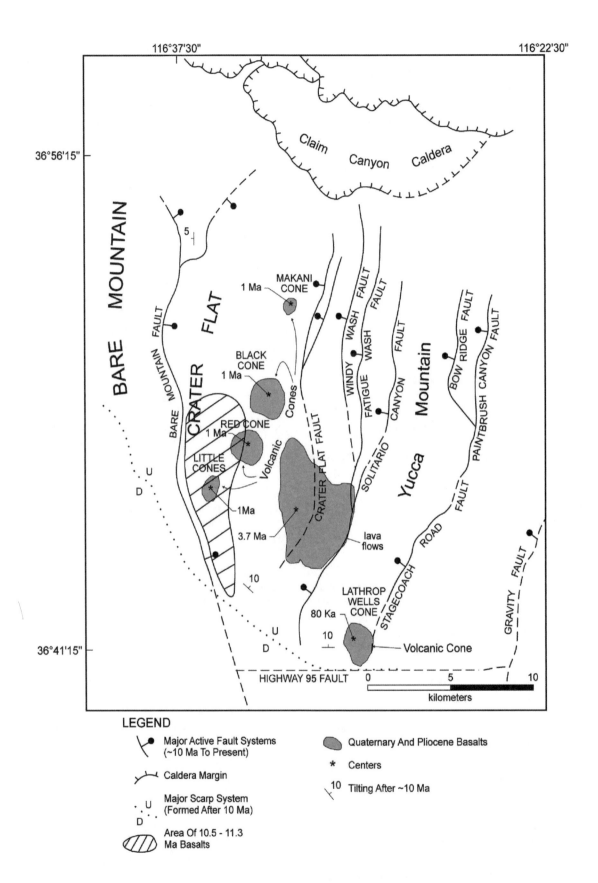

Figure 10. Pliocene and Quaternary features at and near Yucca Mountain (modified from Fridrich, 1999).

The largest of the fine-grained sedimentary deposits is in Tecopa Valley (the depositional basin south of Eagle Mountain and north of the Sperry Hills, Fig. 4) where the thickness attains 100 m (Morrison, 1999). Morrison (1999) attributes the sediments to Lake Tecopa, which persisted for more than 5 m.y. until 1 Ma, fluctuated between a playa and shallow lake, but during the middle Pleistocene, the lake deepened to more than 100 m until at 186 ka it breached its containment to the south and filled Lake Manly. Hillhouse et al. (2005) examined ostracodes from the Tecopa deposits and found no evidence for a deep lake, but rather the evidence supports ground-water discharge deposits and seasonal surface water. The Lake Tecopa beds currently are being incised as drainage flows through the Sperry Hills, then west into Death Valley (Fig. 4).

Although present deposition and erosion generally occur at very low rates and sporadically because of the arid climate, the middle to late Pleistocene depositional record (locally dated by distal ash layers like the 760 ka Bishop ash) indicates a highly variable and localized succession of sedimentary deposits, perhaps analogous to the Miocene rocks of Pavits Spring (Fig. 8), but without the tuffaceous volcanic component. Sediment input is dominated by highly local sources that control the lithologies of the coarse clastic components; lake or pond deposits are virtually the only datable records because they contain fine sediment and rare but radiometrically datable volcanic ash beds. In some places, large accumulations of eolian silts and sands are banked up against range flanks or as dune accumulations, notably Big Dune, south of Bare Mountain (Fig. 4). Details of Pleistocene stratigraphy and depositional and erosional processes are given by Keefer et al. (this volume).

REGIONAL STRUCTURE AND TECTONIC DEFORMATION

The geologic setting of Yucca Mountain is characterized structurally by two distinctly different tectonic deformation styles: an earlier compressional "mountain building" style of regional folding and thrusting, and a later extensional "basin-forming" style of regional normal and strike-slip faulting. The following sections discuss the structures resulting from these two styles of deformation.

Compressional Tectonics of the Yucca Mountain Region

The compressional style records orogenic events that occurred during the Paleozoic, followed by a peak event that occurred in the Mesozoic and terminated marine deposition. Compressional deformation of Precambrian age also is recorded in Proterozoic and older rocks, but no orogenic pattern has been determined from the sparsely exposed rocks.

The earliest mountain building event that affected Paleozoic rocks in the Yucca Mountain geologic setting is the Antler Orogeny (Fig. 6; Stewart, 1980, p. 36, Fig. 22 therein). Antler orogenic deformation is expressed chiefly by the Roberts Mountains overthrust belt, which is located well north of Yucca Mountain. The thrusting created a mountain range and a marine foredeep basin along its eastern margin into which the coarse sediment that eroded from the thrust belt was deposited. An alternative interpretation (Ketner, 1998) characterizes the Antler Orogeny as involving primarily vertical tectonics, without a strong compressional component.

The coarse, clastic sediment derived from the Antler highlands beginning in Middle Devonian time and continuing into the Mississippian period constitutes the Eleana Formation (Fig. 6), exposed at the Nevada Test Site (Trexler et al., 1996, p. 1740). Farther east, a correlative section of Chainman Shale (Fig. 6) was deposited in an environment that has aspects of an inner shelf as well as a subsiding basin (Trexler et al., 1996, p. 1750); east of that was a carbonate platform environment unaffected by the Antler Orogeny. Similar depositional effects of the Antler Orogeny are found in the Inyo-Mono domain, where the Upper Mississippian Rest Spring Shale (Fig. 6) and the shaley lower part of the Lower Mississippian Tin Mountain Limestone (Fig. 6) represent erosion of the Antler highlands (Dunne, 1986, p. 5) and, therefore, are part of the Eleana-Chainman lithosome.

The Antler Orogeny is significant in the Yucca Mountain region for two reasons:

1. The fine-grained, terrigenous lithology of the Eleana (and especially the Chainman Shale) lithosome forms a major Paleozoic aquitard north and east of Yucca Mountain, as well as a potential source rock for hydrocarbons; and
2. The juxtaposition of three distinct but coeval facies (i.e., Antler-derived clastic debris, black Chainman Shale, and Mississippian and older carbonates) aids in recognizing the structural configurations that formed during the subsequent Sevier (Cordilleran) Orogeny.

Mountain building in the near vicinity of Yucca Mountain began with eastward-encroaching uplift in latest Permian to Triassic time and culminated during the Mesozoic with the Sevier Orogeny (Stewart, 1980, p. 77; Fleck, 1970a; Armstrong, 1968, p. 429f). The Sevier Orogeny resulted in a broadly north- to northeast-trending fold-thrust system (Fig. 11). The thrust sheets typically are complicated by overturned or dismembered folds and local reverse or overthrust faults. The major thrusts are continuous along strike for distances of more than 100 km and exhibit stratigraphic juxtapositions that indicate translations of tens of kilometers. Nevertheless, the history of thrust faulting in the Yucca Mountain region and the identity of each fault from place to place is uncertain because of erosion, subsequent extension, and burial beneath Tertiary and Quaternary rocks and surficial deposits over wide areas. Therefore, only a general treatment, with an emphasis on geometric relations relevant to issues concerning Yucca Mountain, is presented below.

Two major thrusts are recognized in the vicinity of Yucca Mountain (Fig. 11): the Belted Range thrust (Caskey and Schweickert, 1992, p. 1318; Cole and Cashman, 1999, p. 8) and the CP thrust (Caskey and Schweickert, 1992, p. 1316; Barnes and Poole, 1968, p. 233; Carr, 1984, p. 52). The Belted Range thrust

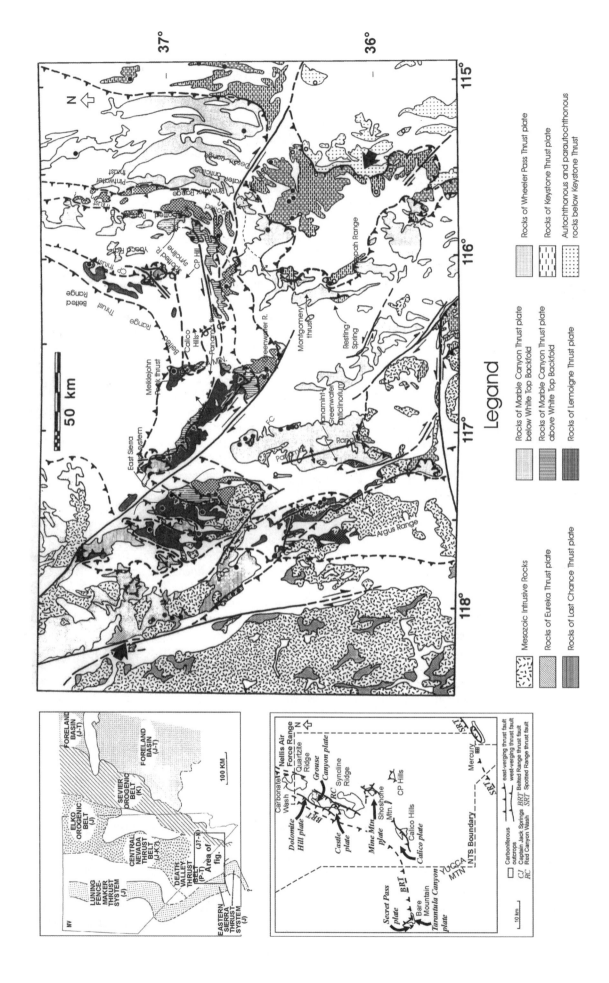

Figure 11. Generalized compressional features of the Yucca Mountain region (modified from Snow, 1992; Taylor et al., 1993; and Trexler et al., 1996). Dots are points of stratigraphic control used by Snow (1992); FC is the Furnace Creek Fault; and Tertiary rocks are not shown.

(Fig. 11) is the structurally lower and older thrust. It is represented in outcrop at Bare Mountain (there referred to as the Meiklejohn Peak thrust), perhaps in the core of the Calico Hills (see discussion of Calico Hills below), and by exposures at the southern end of the Belted Range west of Yucca Flat (Fig. 11; Caskey and Schweickert, 1992, p. 1318, 1321; Cole and Cashman, 1999, p. 7). Displacement across the Belted Range thrust is estimated from at least 7 km (Cole and Cashman, 1999, p. 8) to more than 25 km (Caskey and Schweickert, 1992, p. 1320). Below the Belted Range thrust, a stack of imbricate slices or "plates" place Middle Devonian strata and the Mississippian Eleana Formation over the Mississippian Chainman Shale along a subhorizontal thrust exposed in the Eleana Range (Trexler et al., 1996, p. 1756). Thrusts that form the base of this duplex zone cut upsection into Mississippian strata, then form a décollement within the weak Chainman Shale (Trexler et al., 1996, p. 1757). The duplex stack extends ~7 km east of the main Belted Range thrust; it includes structures at Calico Hills (Calico Hills plate), Mine Mountain (Mine Mountain plate), the Eleana Range (Castle plate, Dolomite Hill plate, and Grouse Canyon plate), and Quartzite Ridge at the northern border of the Nevada Test Site (Fig. 11) (Trexler et al., 1996, p. 1739; Cole and Cashman, 1999, p. 10, 11). A component of the duplex stack in this northern area was identified as the Tippipah thrust by Robinson (1985, p. 7).

The CP thrust is a west-vergent back-thrust that lies to the east of, and is structurally above and possibly younger than, the Belted Range thrust (Fig. 11) (Caskey and Schweickert, 1992, p. 1326). It generally emplaces Precambrian through Cambro-Ordovician strata over Mississippian and Pennsylvanian strata. The CP thrust, originally defined from a small patch of outcrop in the CP Hills, which form the west flank of Yucca Flat (Fig. 11) (Barnes and Poole, 1968, p. 233), is a large, complex structure that extends for more than 180 km on strike and has ~8.5 km of stratigraphic throw (Caskey and Schweickert, 1992, p. 1318, 1327). Rocks of the upper plate are imbricately faulted, highly folded, and locally overturned to the west, and large-scale, west-vergent, nearly recumbent folds occupy both the lower and upper plates (Caskey and Schweickert, 1992, p. 1316). Early work at the Nevada Test Site assigned all thrust structures in the area to the CP thrust (Barnes and Poole, 1968, p. 233; Carr, 1984, p. 52), but Caskey and Schweickert (1992, p. 1314) distinguished the CP thrust from the Belted Range thrust on the basis of lower plate folds that indicate westward thrusting of the CP thrust in opposition to eastward thrusting of the Belted Range thrust.

The complex structural relations between the Belted Range and CP thrust systems are reflected in the conflicting interpretations that have been presented in various geologic reports. For example, exposures north and west of the CP Hills have been variously interpreted. East-vergent thrusting at Mine Mountain (Fig. 4) is cited by Burchfiel et al. (1970, p. 213) and Ekren et al. (1971, p. 69) and assigned to the CP thrust; Barnes and Poole (1968, p. 238) and Caskey and Schweickert (1992, p. 1318) recognized west-vergent thrusting at Mine Mountain and linked the Mine Mountain and CP thrusts. Carr (1984, p. 52) and Robinson

(1985, p. 16) tentatively proposed that the older over younger block assemblage at Mine Mountain could be a dismembered gravity slide. This was substantially documented by Cole et al. (1989, p. 444). Cole et al. (1989) considered that the structure at Mine Mountain, the CP Hills, and the Calico Hills could best be interpreted as low-angle gravity sliding of middle Miocene age; only the faults at Bare Mountain could be considered indisputable thrusts. More recently, structure at Mine Mountain is interpreted to be a complex overprinting of west-vergent thrusting of the CP thrust over the lower plate of the older east-vergent Belted Range thrust, as well as later extensional faulting (Cole and Cashman, 1999, p. 16).

Caskey and Schweickert (1992, p. 1324) carried the CP thrust west through the Calico Hills and correlated it to the Panama thrust in the southern part of Bare Mountain (Fig. 11). This interpretation suggests that the CP thrust extends through the Paleozoic substrate beneath Yucca Mountain (Potter et al., 2002b), possibly placing Silurian rocks above buried Eleana Formation rocks or forming a north-vergent thrust south of and subparallel to the inferred Belted Range thrust duplex mentioned above. In other words, beneath Yucca Mountain there may exist two opposing thrusts, one correlating with the Meiklejohn Peak thrust and the other with the Panama thrust at Bare Mountain (Fig. 11). Potter et al. (2002b) show two opposing thrusts beneath southern Calico Hills (Belted Range thrust) and Jackass Flats (CP thrust). However the Belted Range thrust is not shown at depth beneath Yucca Mountain because it is projected to the north of the north-south cross-section line.

The structure exposed in the core of the Calico Hills could be assigned to gravity sliding or to the Belted Range thrust (Trexler et al., 1996, p. 1756; Cole and Cashman, 1999, p. 18), the CP thrust (Caskey and Schweickert, 1992, p. 1324), or both (Cole and Cashman, 1999, p. 25). Uncertainty exists because of the difficulty in recognizing indisputable thrust-related deformation that expresses vergence, and because either or both thrust systems reasonably could be projected through the Calico Hills. Simonds and Scott (1996, p. 34) could not resolve the uncertainty, but tentatively advocated a thrust structure rather than a gravity-slide structure.

The contact between the Paleozoic and Miocene rocks was not recovered during the drilling of UE-25p#1 (M.D. Carr et al., 1986; cf. Keefer et al., this volume, Fig. 8 therein), but the permeability of that contact is small enough to preserve a 20 m greater hydraulic head in the Paleozoic carbonate rocks. In the Calico Hills, the contact between Paleozoic and Miocene rocks is formed by a dense layer of secondary carbonate, which Simonds and Scott (1996) attribute to faulting, but it could be a more widespread feature that formed at the base of the volcanic rocks.

Apart from the Calico Hills exposure, the east- and west-vergent thrust systems are separated by a span of rock that probably was never overthrust. Conodont alteration-indices data indicate that the Chainman Shale at Syncline Ridge, located between the thrust systems (Fig. 11), was never tectonically buried, hence neither thrust ever extended much beyond its present position

(Trexler et al., 1996, p. 1757). Conodont alteration indices from the Silurian rocks penetrated by well UE-25 p#1 at Yucca Mountain indicate the rocks reached maximum temperatures of 140° to 180 °C. M.D. Carr et al. (1986, p. 49) concluded that these temperatures could have been achieved by normal burial depths for Silurian rocks in the Great Basin. This observation supports an interpretation that the Silurian rocks in UE-25 p#1 were not overthrust. The gap between the thrust fronts probably extends to Bare Mountain, where the Meiklejohn Peak thrust (Belted Range thrust system) and the Panama thrust (CP thrust system) presently are separated by ~6.5 km. Small klippen of the Panama thrust near the center of the mountain (Monsen et al., 1992) indicate the gap, if it existed, originally was smaller, or perhaps the Panama thrust originally overrode the Meiklejohn Peak thrust (Cole and Cashman, 1999, p. 27).

Farther east, the Spotted Range thrust, named for its exposure in the Spotted Range (Fig. 11) (Barnes et al. 1982), placed Middle Cambrian strata over Upper Devonian and Mississippian strata, with more than 25 km of offset (Caskey and Schweickert, 1992, p. 1318, 1320; Tschanz and Pampeyan, 1970, p. 108). Lower plate strata have tight to isoclinal folds overturned to the southeast. Accordingly, the Spotted Range thrust cannot be correlated with the CP thrust (as proposed by Barnes and Poole, 1968, p. 235). Caskey and Schweickert (1992, p. 1320) observed that the lower plate of the Spotted Range thrust is structurally equivalent to the upper plate of the west-vergent CP thrust . Therefore, the Spotted Range thrust is possibly an eroded, eastern outlier (klippe) of the Belted Range thrust.

The Spotted Range thrust has been extended westward by correlation with the Specter Range thrust (Wernicke et al., 1988a, p. 257). The Specter Range thrust is exposed for a strike distance of ~4 km in the Specter Range (Sargent and Stewart, 1971), where it is expressed as a N60°E to N50°E and 60° dipping fault that places the Cambrian Bonanza King Formation (Fig. 6) over Lower and Middle Ordovician strata (Sargent and Stewart, 1971; Burchfiel, 1965, p. 179), a stratigraphic displacement of more than 1700 m (Burchfiel, 1965, p. 179). The correlation with the Spotted Range thrust was argued by Snow (1992, p. 96) on the basis of structural position, stratigraphic throw, association with a footwall syncline, and distance from other distinctive structures. However, Cole and Cashman (1999, p. 30) pointed out that the Specter Range thrust and the Spotted Range thrust represent different stratigraphic levels (cf. Burchfiel, 1965, p. 185; Caskey and Schweickert, 1992, p. 1326), and that stratigraphic displacement decreases to the east such that the Specter Range thrust dies out beneath Mercury Valley. Burchfiel (1965, p. 186, Plate 3 therein) inferred that the Specter Range thrust continues east and south of Mercury Valley (cf. Fig. 14) as a strike-slip fault, forming the northern end of the Las Vegas Valley shear zone (discussed below).

East of Yucca Mountain, The Gass Peak thrust (Fig. 12) is a large, east-vergent thrust that places upper Precambrian and Cambrian rocks over highly folded and locally overturned Pennsylvanian and Permian carbonate strata (Longwell et al.,

1965, p. 76; Guth, 1981, p. 767) for at least 140 km along the east side of the northern part of the Sheep Range and through the Las Vegas Range (Longwell et al., 1965, p. 75). It has been correlated southward across the Las Vegas Valley Shear Zone into the Spring Mountains (as the Wheeler Pass thrust) because of its consistent structural level (Fig. 12) (Guth, 1990, p. 240). Net horizontal displacement may exceed 30 km (Guth, 1981, p. 764). Because no major thrusts occur between the Gass Peak thrust and klippen of the Spotted Range thrust (Fig. 12), the lower plate of the Spotted Range thrust also is equivalent to the upper plate of the Gass Peak thrust (Caskey and Schweickert, 1992, p. 1322). Therefore, the Gass Peak thrust and the CP thrust define the eastern and western structural boundaries of the same allochthon.

Late Paleozoic and Mesozoic thrust systems in the Inyo-Mono domain (Fig. 5) are more extensive and complex than any exposed east of the Funeral Mountains (Fig. 3A), but their structural relations are more clearly defined. The most extensive thrust system, the Last Chance thrust system (Fig. 12), includes (from oldest to youngest) the Last Chance, the Talc City, the Race Track, the Marble Canyon, and the Lemoigne thrusts (Dunne, 1986, p. 9; Corbett et al., 1988). The system comprises imbricate, northeast-trending, generally east-vergent thrusts having at least 7–35 km of total displacement and placing rocks as old as Precambrian on rocks as young as Permian. Deformation typically involves locally recumbent and isoclinal folds in the overridden plates, but most folds are upright and open. The system probably was most extensively active from Middle Triassic to Early Jurassic time (Dunne, 1986, p. 11), but thrusting could have begun as early as Permian time (Snow, 1992, p. 102). The Last Chance thrust system predates the 167–185 Ma Hunter Mountain batholith (Dunne et al., 1978, p. 197). It may predate intrusion of the pre-Late Triassic White Top stock in the Cottonwood Mountains (Fig. 3B; Snow, 1992, p. 91; Caskey and Schweickert, 1992, p. 1327). The Last Chance thrust system essentially comprises the Death Valley thrust belt (Snow, 1992, p. 81).

Numerous attempts have been made to correlate thrusts of the Death Valley thrust belt across the Furnace Creek–Death Valley fault into the Walker Lane belt and the Nevada Test Site area. Caskey and Schweickert (1992, p. 1326) argued that only three thrust plates exist at the Nevada Test Site, not five as in the Death Valley thrust belt (Snow, 1992, p. 81; Wernicke et al., 1993, p. 453):

1.   Strata above the Belted Range thrust;
2.   Strata below the Belted Range thrust and the CP thrust; and
3.   Strata above the CP thrust and the Gass Peak thrust.

Accordingly, Caskey and Schweickert (1992, p. 1325) tentatively correlated only two thrusts, the Belted Range thrust with the Last Chance thrust. Caskey and Schweickert (1992, p. 1317, Fig. 3) and Snow (1992, p. 94) continued the Belted Range thrust west, connected it with the Grapevine thrust, and thereby correlated it with the Last Chance thrust system (Fig. 12). Snow (1992, p. 97) correlated the Meiklejohn Peak duplex zone (Calico Hills plate of Trexler et al. [1996, p. 1739]) with the Racetrack duplex

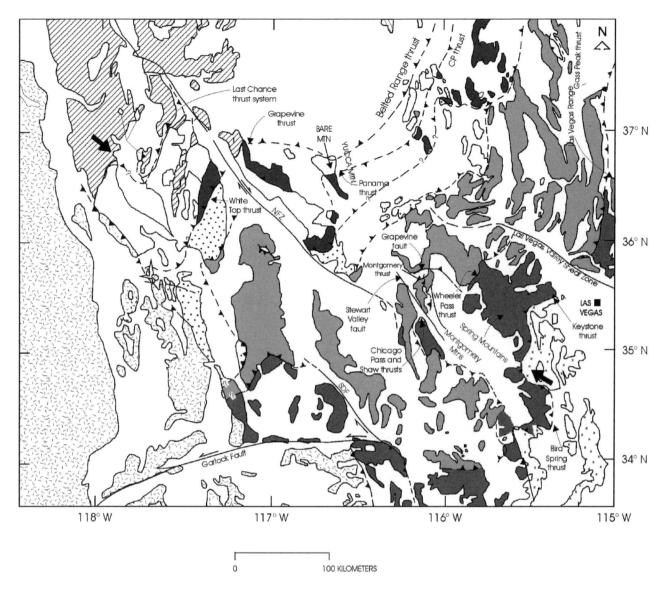

Figure 12. Correlative thrusts of the Yucca Mountain region (modified from Wernicke et al., 1988a; Burchfiel et al., 1983).

Legend

Bar stipple (along left side of figure) is Sierra Nevada block; diagonal rule is rock above the Last Chance thrust; no pattern is rock below the Last Chance and White Top thrusts; dark gray is rock above the White Top thrust; dot stipple is rock below the White Top thrust; light gray is rock above the Wheeler Pass, Gass Peak, Chicago Pass, and Shaw thrusts; medium gray is rock between the Wheeler Pass and Keystone thrusts; and x-pattern (lower right part of figure) is rock below the Keystone thrust.
SDF = Southern Death Valley fault; NFZ = Northern Death Valley-Furnace Creek fault zone.

zone beneath the Last Chance thrust. Snow (1992, p. 84, Table 1 therein) also correlated the White Top thrust (or backfold) with the Panama thrust-CP thrust (Fig. 12), but this correlation is disputed by Cole and Cashman (1999, p. 33). The Marble Canyon thrust is correlated with the Specter Range thrust via the Schwaub Peak thrust in the Funeral Mountains (Wernicke et al., 1988a, p. 257; Snow, 1992, p. 94, 96; Cole and Cashman, 1999, p. 33).

Attempts to trace thrusts across the Spring Mountains section of the Walker Lane domain into the Inyo-Mono domain are hampered because of dextral offset along the Stewart Valley fault and as much as 3.5 km of normal offset along the Grapevine fault (Fig. 12) (Burchfiel et al., 1983, p. 1371). The structurally lowest thrust in the Spring Mountains section, and in the entire Yucca Mountain geologic setting, is the Bird Spring thrust (Fig. 12), which places the Bonanza King Formation on the Lower Jurassic Aztec Sandstone (Fig. 7); however, at its northern end, the thrust loses throw and merely duplicates Permian red beds (Burchfiel and Davis, 1988, p. 89). The Bird Spring thrust is the base of a duplex sheet of imbricate faults and folds, all cut out by the overlying Keystone thrust (Fig. 12), which puts the Bonanza King Formation over younger Cambrian and overturned Triassic strata.

In tracing thrusts west out of the Spring Mountains and into the Montgomery Mountains, Burchfiel et al. (1983, p. 1375) tentatively concluded that the Wheeler Pass thrust is correlative with the Chicago Pass and Shaw thrusts in the northern part of the Nopah Range (Figs. 11 and 12). The Chicago Pass thrust and the closely related Shaw thrust have a net stratigraphic throw of ~5 km to the south. The thrust overrides a footwall syncline that infolds lowest Devonian to highest Carboniferous strata with a 300 m wavelength (Burchfiel et al., 1983, p. 1367 and 1369). The Montgomery thrust places Stirling Quartzite over Ordovician rocks and Devonian Devils Gate Limestone (Fig. 6) in a tight overturned syncline having a wavelength of ~1 km across a dip of ~30° to the northwest (Burchfiel et al., 1983, p. 1366–1367). Wernicke et al., (1988b, p. 1743), Wernicke et al., (1988a, p. 257), and Snow (1992, p. 82) correlated thrusts as far west as the Panamint Range (Fig. 9) or the Slate Range in eastern California with the Wheeler Pass–Gass Peak thrust system (Fig. 12).

At present, the only aspects of the Mesozoic orogeny that are well known in the Yucca Mountain geologic setting are the geometry and the stratigraphic relations among the various thrust sheets. Questions regarding where the faults are rooted, how they climb sections, and to what levels of the crust thrusting is involved remain unresolved.

Many thrust systems in the Yucca Mountain region are associated with regional folds. One example of a large fold is the Panamint-Greenwater anticlinorium (Fig. 11; Wright et al., 1981, p. 10), described by Dunne (1986, p. 15) as a "northwest-pointing tongue of Precambrian rock exposed in the Panamint, Black, and Greenwater Ranges." The fold is bounded by west-dipping strata of the East Sierra thrust system in the Argus Range, and by east-dipping strata in the Resting Spring and Nopah ranges (Fig. 11). Structural relief is probably ~7 km. The fold may be a large ramp anticline resulting from the generally eastward movement of a thrust stack of Proterozoic crystalline basement up and over a west-facing ramp (Dunne, 1986, p. 15). Robinson (1985, p. 5) inferred that the major Mesozoic structure encompassing Yucca Mountain is a synclinorial basin spanning the area between Bare Mountain and the Halfpint Range (along the eastern boundary of the Nevada Test Site; Fig. 3A), a distance of more than 80 km. In his interpretation, the basin is asymmetric, having steep to overturned limbs on the Bare Mountain side and along Rock Valley. The basin is bounded to the south at the position of the modern Rock Valley fault zone and to the northeast by a "major northeast-trending thrust system," the Tippipah thrust zone (Robinson, 1985, p. 5) (the Belted Range thrust of Caskey and Schweickert [1992] and Trexler et al. [1996]). The principal deformation

within the basin consists of broad, concentric folds 8–24 km apart that trend about N30°E and plunge northward (Fig. 13). Robinson (1985, p. 5, 19) based his interpretations of fold structure on exposed dips, data from well UE-25 p#1, and aeromagnetic data. As a corollary to this tectonic interpretation, Robinson (1985, p. 16) inferred that the Mine Mountain and CP thrusts are minor structures; he suggested they were local slides that occurred in response to regional folding. Whether Robinson's (1985) assessment of fold geometry, and the relative magnitudes of folding and thrusting, is correct, there is little doubt that large-amplitude, regional folds have accompanied thrust faulting in the region.

East of Yucca Mountain, the Gass Peak thrust plate (Fig. 12) is folded into large, north-trending open folds (Guth, 1990, p. 238) and, more broadly, arched to form the Pintwater anticline (Longwell, 1945, p. 111f) and the Spotted Range syncline (Barnes et al., 1982), a regional fold pair traceable for ~100 km and having a combined width that spans four mountain ranges (i.e., the Sheep, Desert, Pintwater, and Spotted Ranges) (Fig. 11). Structural relief is probably as much as 7 km (Caskey and Schweickert, 1992, p. 1322). The west limb of the Pintwater anticline probably controls the ramp-like Pintwater thrust (Longwell et al., 1965, p. 72), a steeply west-dipping thrust fault that extends ~25 km along the west side of the Pintwater Range (Fig. 11) and has ~1 km of stratigraphic separation (Guth, 1990, p. 241).

Burchfiel et al. (1983, p. 1366, 1375) argued that a large, recumbent east-trending anticline-syncline pair in the northwestern Spring Mountains (Montgomery thrust) correlates with the east-trending Pintwater anticline at the southern end of the Spotted Range. The Pintwater anticline and the Spotted Range syncline represent a broad regional fold pair having a pre-extensional structural relief of as much as 7 km (Caskey and Schweickert, 1992, p. 1322). The Montgomery thrust is inferred to pass through the northwestern part of the Spring Mountains, degenerating into a fold pair ultimately correlating with the Pintwater Range anticline (see Figure 11 for location).

It is unclear when overthrusting and regional folding generally ceased in the Yucca Mountain region. The presence of undeformed Late Cretaceous intrusives indicates that deformation did not continue through Cretaceous time. The Belted Range thrust, as correlative to the Last Chance thrust, probably originated prior to latest Middle Triassic and ceased activity by ca. 93 Ma, the age of the Climax stock (Naeser and Maldonado, 1981, p. 46), a granodiorite intruded in complexly folded Ordovician strata north of Yucca Flat (Houser and Poole, 1960). The age of the CP and the Gass Peak thrusts, which cut the Belted Range thrust, would be younger. The Keystone thrust (Fig. 12) probably was moving by Early Jurassic time (Burchfiel et al., 1974, p. 1021). By Late Jurassic time, deformation was well under way in the Great Basin (Armstrong, 1968, p. 449). Thus, the Sevier orogeny (Armstrong, 1968, p. 451; Fleck, 1970a, p. 1718) was a short-lived compressional event in the Yucca Mountain region. Compressional tectonism in the Inyo-Mono terrane appears to have ceased completely in Paleogene time (Dunne, 1986, p. 16).

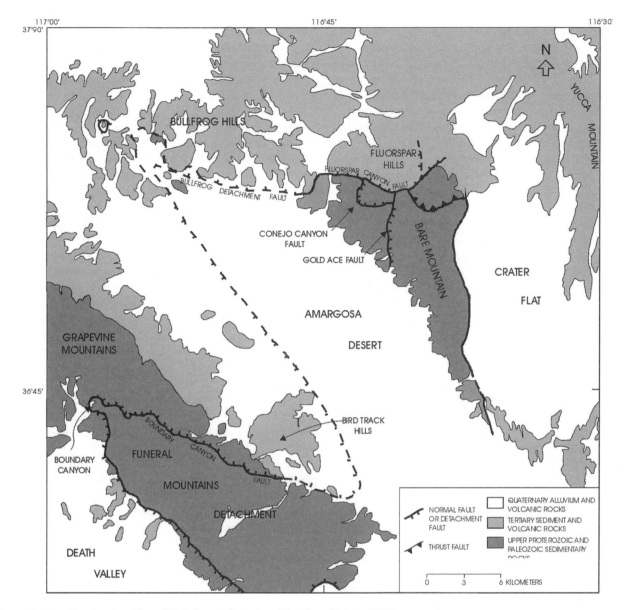

Figure 13. Map Showing Location of Detachment faults (modified from Hoisch, 2000).

Extensional Tectonics of the Yucca Mountain Region

Extension in the Yucca Mountain region was active by late Oligocene time (Axen et al., 1993, p. 64; Sawyer et al., 1994, p. 1314; Hardyman and Oldow, 1991, p. 285; Ekren and Byers, 1984, p. 214; Dilles et al. 1993, p. 425) and probably earlier (Eaton, 1982, p. 412; Hodges and Walker, 1992, p. 563; Axen et al., 1993, p. 64; Applegate et al., 1992, p. 519; Smith, 1991, p. 189). This early phase of extension, sometimes referred to as "pre–basin and range faulting" (Zoback et al., 1981, p. 420), continued into middle Miocene time. It is thought to have evolved by gravitational collapse of thrust-thickened crust following diminution of subduction-generated compression from the west (Stewart, 1978, p. 25; Wernicke et al., 1987, p. 203; Cole et al.,

1993; Hodges and Walker, 1992, p. 566–567; Scholz et al., 1971, p. 2987). The result was a thinner, closely faulted crust and lithosphere heated and elevated by upper mantle convection (Stewart, 1978, p. 26; Hamilton, 1989, p. 770; Eaton, 1982, p. 411, 422; Scholz et al., 1971, p. 2981, Fig. 3). Extension during this early phase is thought to have migrated from east-northeast to west-southwest and to have been unaffected by oblique shear (Seedorff, 1991, Figures 5–8). Although this phase of regional extension progressed under the influence of a generally uniform west- to southwest-directed least principal stress (Zoback et al., 1981, p. 204), northwest-directed oblique shear also influenced extension toward the west side of the widening province at an early date (Stewart, 1992, p. 7, 9). By early Miocene time (and likely by middle-late Oligocene), the characteristic features of the

Walker Lane belt had been established, namely discontinuous north-northwest–striking dextral faults and east-northeast–striking sinistral faults (Ekren and Byers, 1984, p. 203; Hardyman and Oldow, 1991, p. 289; Stewart, 1988, p. 686). Deep-seated detachment also may have been a significant mechanism of Paleogene extension in this region. Geobarometry and fission-track age dates indicate that subhorizontal mylonites, presumably indicative of predetachment shear (Hamilton, 1987, p. 157, 165; Hamilton, 1988, p. 80), were generated at depths of at least 15 km beneath the Funeral-Bare Mountains area during this phase of deformation (Hoisch and Simpson, 1993, p. 6823–6824; Hoisch et al., 1997, p. 2830). More recent work by Miller and Friedman (1999) provides a caveat for this conclusion in that they have demonstrated the existence of both Mesozoic and Tertiary extensional mylonites in the Black Mountains of Death Valley.

The main extensional features within the tectonic setting of Yucca Mountain were established by ca. 15 Ma, namely a basin-and-range structural pattern defined chiefly by north-south oriented basins or troughs. Fault zones associated with the Walker Lane belt, including the Rock Valley fault zone, also were developed at this time.

The late Oligocene was punctuated by deposition of ash-fall tuffs from eruptions east and north of Yucca Mountain (Axen et al., 1993, p. 62). The advent of siliceous volcanism marks an important tectonic development in the early phase of extension: it signals a culmination of regional crustal heating, the so-called "ignimbrite flare-up," during which large volumes of siliceous magma were emplaced in the middle to upper crust (Seedorff, 1991, p. 133).

Like the progress of early extension, magmatism proceeded from north to south through the Great Basin; in the south it generally seems to have lagged behind the extension. Thus, the southwestern Nevada volcanic field may have been generated in an area of crust weakened by deep extensional basins and therefore conducive to volcanic venting (Axen et al., 1993, p. 68, 73), but an alternative interpretation proposed by Sawyer et al. (1994, p. 1314, 1316) was that the Oasis Valley–Timber Mountain caldera complex formed in an area of minor crustal extension and that most of the extension proximal to Yucca Mountain occurred after formation of the caldera complex. A basin analysis by Blakely et al. (1999) indicated that the southwestern Nevada volcanic field (including Yucca Mountain) formed within an assemblage of deep extensional basins, which suggests that the present basin configuration was well established prior to the formation of Yucca Mountain. A clastic sedimentary deposit, the rocks of Pavits Spring (Hinrichs, 1968), and the comparable Esmeralda Formation (Fig. 8; Stewart and Diamond, 1990), also imply that deepening and integration of basins in the Yucca Mountain region occurred prior to formation of the southwestern Nevada volcanic field.

The rocks of Pavits Spring record basin integration and increased structural and topographic relief by way of thick boulder gravels and volcanic arkoses deposited by torrential streams. Increasingly proximal volcanic activity is indicated by increasing contributions of tuffs upsection, including, ultimately, the

major components of the southwestern Nevada volcanic field. The course and extent of basin evolution in the Yucca Mountain region are only generally perceived, but it seems likely that considerable extension and basin deepening preceded the volcanic activity that created Yucca Mountain.

The culminating tectonic event in the geologic evolution of the region and, coincidentally, the initiating event for the structural formation of Yucca Mountain, was the creation of the southwestern Nevada volcanic field. Post-eruptive deflation may have created at least some of the present structural framework of Yucca Mountain; Carr (1990, p. 300), for example, postulated that some post–Paintbrush Group subsidence of Crater Flat basin occurred because of withdrawal from the underlying magma chamber. However, if such a structure is present, it was not detected in seismic-refraction studies (Brocher et al., 1998). Local domainal extension, involving some strike-slip displacements, clockwise rotation of crustal blocks, basin subsidence, and range uplift, continued in the Walker Lane belt during the phase of siliceous volcanism (Sawyer et al., 1994, p. 1314). Yucca Mountain was affected by this activity in the 12.7–9 Ma interval (Scott, 1990; Potter et al., 2004), and subsidence due to extension, continued across the Crater Flat basin and Jackass Flats area and volcanic terrane farther east.

Analysis of faults near Yucca Flat and in the Basin and Range province to the east indicate that the present stress regime originated around 9 Ma; before then, the least compressive stress was oriented in a more westerly or southwesterly direction (Zoback et al., 1981, p. 212; Minor, 1995, p. 10,524). Minor (1995, p. 10,525) concluded that the stress field in the Yucca Mountain region rotated clockwise as much as 65° during the 11–8.5 Ma interval. The clockwise stress rotation is recognized elsewhere in the region (Carr, 1984, p. 84; Zoback et al., 1981, p. 207 and 209; Michel-Noel et al., 1990, p. 155 and 169), but estimates of its timing vary (Wernicke, et al., 1988b, p. 1756). Hardyman and Oldow (1991, p. 295) envision a clockwise stress rotation of as much as 90° in the northern Walker Lane belt that began in the late Oligocene and attained its present state in the late Miocene.

From ca. 11 to 7 Ma, the style of tectonic deformation in the Yucca Mountain region became more clearly one of narrow basin subsidence, possibly accompanied by adjacent range uplift. This style of tectonism continues at present, focused most conspicuously at Frenchman Flat and Yucca Flat east of Yucca Mountain and in Death Valley to the west. Some basins are quiescent or have not been active since the middle Pleistocene, including Mid Valley, Jackass Flats, and Amargosa Desert. Nevertheless, historic seismicity and occasional large earthquakes accompanied by subsidence, such as the Cedar Mountain–Fairview Peak–Dixie Valley earthquakes (Fig. 5), indicate that basin subsidence is sporadic. Presently, strike-slip faulting is active in Rock Valley (Coe et al., 2004) and in the Inyo-Mono terrane to the west.

Contemporary Deformation

Large earthquakes on range-front faults during the past 100 years indicate that Basin and Range extension is still under way.

Epicenter distribution patterns and geodetic strain data indicate that strain presently is concentrated primarily north of Yucca Mountain, in a zone along latitude 37°N (the intermountain seismic belt), in the eastern California shear zone, and in the central Nevada seismic zone (Fig. 5) (Bennett et al., 1999, p. 373, Fig. 1 therein). High geodetic extension rates characterize these active areas (Bennett et al., 1998, p. 566; Savage et al., 1995, p. 20, 266). Dixon et al. (1995, p. 762) noted that northwest motion of the Sierra Nevada block is accomplished by a combination of east-west extension on north-striking normal faults, and by dextral motion on northwest-striking strike-slip faults of the Walker Lane belt and eastern California shear zone (Fig. 5). Geologic evidence suggests that the eastern California shear zone has been a zone of high strain since late Miocene time (10–6 Ma) (Dixon et al., 1995, p. 760). Dixon et al. (1995, p. 761) report 8.8 mm/yr at N9° ± 5° W. The integrated displacement rate across the eastern California shear zone is 12.1 ± 1.2 mm/yr at a vector of N38° ± 5°W (Dixon et al., 1995, p. 767).

The kinematic boundary condition for Basin and Range deformation (the relative motions of the Pacific and North American plates) has been nearly constant for at least the past 3.4 m.y. (Harbert and Cox, 1989, p. 3061), which is within the time span for tectonic activity of the Inyo-Mono domain (Hodges et al., 1989, p. 462). During this time, tectonic activity gradually has shifted westward, from the Death Valley–Furnace Creek fault to the Owens Valley fault (Dixon et al., 1995, p. 765). Dixon et al. (1995, p. 765) suggested that the Walker Lane belt accommodates significant dextral shear. The central Nevada seismic zone trends obliquely across Walker Lane belt, which is an older feature (Savage et al., 1995, p. 20,267). Therefore, it would seem that the westward migration of tectonism in the Inyo-Mono domain and the historical surface-rupturing earthquake activity along the central Nevada seismic zone represent a concentration of crustal strain of regional extent and significant longevity. Active deformation appears to be shifting westward and perhaps northward (Dixon et al., 1995, p. 769), away from any involvement with Yucca Mountain.

The driving mechanism for ongoing extension may be a mantle plume associated with generation of the Yellowstone hot spot (Saltus and Thompson, 1995, p. 1235) or assimilation of previously subducted oceanic lithosphere (Severinghaus and Atwater, 1990, p. 17; Bohannon and Parsons, 1995, p. 957). A mantle plume also may be holding the Great Basin at relatively high elevations north of latitude 37°N (Parsons et al., 1994, p. 85, Fig. 1). However, arguments have been presented against the hot spot/mantle plume interpretation (Hamilton, 1989, p. 758).

The extensional tectonic evolution of the Yucca Mountain region produced significant structures that bear on interpretations of the history of deformation and on the development of tectonic models that include Yucca Mountain. The following sections identify and discuss these regional structures: the Boundary Canyon detachment; the Bullfrog Hills detachment; the Las Vegas Valley shear zone; the Death Valley–Furnace Creek–Fish Lake Valley fault; and northeast-trending strike-slip fault zones located east of Yucca Mountain.

Boundary Canyon Detachment

A major detachment fault (Fig. 13) has denuded the core of the Funeral Mountains, revealing the broad, smooth lower plate surface. It seems clear that the lower plate (i.e., the subjacent crust) rose during or shortly following detachment to give the range its present crest and perhaps much of its overall relief (hence the expression "turtleback" [Wright et al., 1974, p. 53]). Uplift occurred late during the phase of regional Miocene extension. Fission track dates of apatite, sphene, and zircon from the lower plate rock indicate that cooling through the temperature interval 285° to 120° (equivalent to ~10–5 km burial depth) took place between 10 and 9 Ma (Holm and Dokka, 1991, p. 1777), with surface exposure having occurred sometime after 6 Ma (Hoisch and Simpson, 1993, p. 6822).

The elongate domiform or arch-like Funeral Mountains detachment (Fig. 13) and its lower plate of highly metamorphosed Late Proterozoic rocks plunge gently northwestward beneath the almost unmetamorphosed upper plate of Late Proterozoic to Miocene rocks of the Grapevine Mountains, which in most of the range dip gently. Restoration of southern Grapevine rocks atop those of Funeral Mountain indicates the former to have been transported from 10 to 20 km in depth to the west-northwestward along the detachment surface that may be more than 30 km in length (Hamilton, 1988, p. 61). The Boundary Canyon detachment fault, or perhaps more correctly the scarp face of the upper plate, more or less rims the Funeral Mountains and is most accessible at Boundary Canyon (Fig. 13), for which it is named.

Rocks composing the upper plate of the Funeral Mountains detachment are well exposed along the eastern flank of the Funeral Mountains in the vicinity of the Bird Track Hills (Fig. 13). The lower part of this rock sequence consists of the chlorite-grade Stirling Quartzite and the Wood Canyon Formation (Fig. 6), which are complexly and irregularly faulted. This Precambrian section is overlain unconformably by the middle Oligocene Titus Canyon Formation and tilted panels of the Miocene Paintbrush Group (Fig. 8).

The contact between the upper plate and the lower plate along the east side of the Funeral Mountains shows evidence of pronounced shearing, but the amount of slip is unknown. The Titus Canyon Formation and a thick Lower Miocene lava flow and associated tuff are much faulted, but can be seen on remote sensor imagery and on geologic maps to be generally continuous along the Grapevine Mountains for at least 22 km, thus precluding major deformation before eruption of the middle Miocene ash flows. Most of the Cenozoic extension postdates 9 Ma, but may predate 7.5 Ma. This accords with the late Miocene cooling ages, determined by fission-track studies by Hoisch and Simpson (1993, p. 6805) and Holm and Dokka (1991, p. 1775) that record the tectonic denudation of the northwest end of the lower plate of the Funeral Mountains. Tectonic denudation of these midcrustal rocks and the rotation and detachment faulting of the Miocene supracrustal rocks thus were of about the same age and must have been linked kinematically.

Bullfrog Hills Detachment

The Bullfrog Hills (Fig. 13) are an assemblage of highly disrupted and structurally discordant, variably tilted blocks of tuff of the southwestern Nevada volcanic field that are distributed across the Amargosa Desert from a source located between the northern flank of Bare Mountain and the western side of Oasis Valley. The assemblage is separated from Bare Mountain by the shallow, north-dipping, generally east-striking Fluorspar Canyon fault (Fig. 13). This fault represents the near-headwall of a detachment, as well as the accommodation plane for westward translation. The headwall (or breakaway) fault of the Bullfrog Hills detachment system is exposed along a north-trending line north of Bare Mountain that defines at least 1 km of stratigraphic offset that occurred between 12.7 and 11.6 Ma (Fridrich, 1999, p. 184, Fig. 6). This line or zone connects with the Fluorspar Canyon fault. The more evident high-angle faults that segment the Bullfrog Hills farther west terminate against the trace of the low-angle Fluorspar Canyon fault (Fig. 13). After 12.7 Ma, the breakaway zone occupied at least three successively more westward positions (Fridrich, 1999, p. 189).

Extension of the Bullfrog Hills began with northwest-side down faulting during the 12.7–11.6 Ma interval (Hoisch et al., 1997, p. 2818). The faulting produced translation and tilting that ranges from 45° at the head to at least 70° in the hills just east of Beatty (Fridrich, 1999, p. 184). The translated and rotated blocks are separated by small wedge-shaped troughs filled with rock-slide breccia and coarse alluvium (Fridrich, 1999, p. 186). This entire assemblage then was largely blanketed by the Timber Mountain Group tuff and a rhyolite of local extent, which subsequently was faulted; Ammonia Tanks Tuff is tilted 20° to 55° eastward. A cap of 10.7 Ma basalt also is faulted, but is much less tilted (Hoisch et al., 1997, p. 2818). Severe brecciation and sliding occurred in the 11.4 Ma rhyolite and sediments in the northern Bullfrog Hills (Minor et al., 1997). The faulting appears to have become inactive and the Bullfrog Hills stabilized between ca. 9.8 Ma (Weiss et al., 1991, p. A246) and 6.3 Ma (Weiss et al., 1988, p. A399), following the opening of the western Amargosa Desert and Sarcobatus Flat basins (Fig. 3A) after 10 Ma (Weiss et al., 1993; Hoisch et al., 1997, p. 2819).

West of Beatty, the Bullfrog Hills rest on pre-Tertiary rocks along the subhorizontal Bullfrog detachment fault, which apparently is a distal continuation of the Fluorspar Canyon fault (Fig. 13). The Bullfrog detachment fault separates Precambrian schist containing veins of foliated granite from overlying tilted blocks of Miocene tuff. Heating of the Precambrian section during the Miocene apparently was strong enough to reset the K-Ar radiometric systems so that the rocks now yield Miocene ages (McKee, 1983, p. 17). In places, a selvage of highly fragmented Paleozoic section lies above the Bullfrog detachment fault and below the Miocene tuffs (Hamilton, 1988, p. 57). This geometry prompted Maldonado and Hausback (1990) to infer two stacked detachment faults west of Beatty. The lower one, the Bullfrog fault detachment, is clearly the more consequential fault, being an inferred link between the Boundary Canyon fault of the Funeral Mountains detachment and the Fluorspar Canyon fault (Fig. 13; Hoisch et al., 1997, p. 2816). If this inferred fault continuity is correct, there are significant implications for the history of Bare Mountain.

A detachment at Bare Mountain (Fig. 13) is indicated by the Gold Ace fault (Fridrich, 1999, p. 180), a north-striking, east-dipping fault that separates high-grade metamorphic rocks to the west (lower plate) from low-grade to nonmetamorphosed rocks to the east (upper plate). The Gold Ace fault projects to intersect the Fluorspar Canyon fault at a high angle (Fridrich, 1999, p. 180, Fig. 5). Near the northern limit of outcrop, the Gold Ace fault intersects a west-striking fault (Monsen et al. 1992) that also juxtaposes high- and medium-grade metamorphic rocks, the Conejo Canyon fault (Fridrich, 1999, p. 180). Hoisch et al. (1997, p. 2819) and Hoisch (2000) inferred that the Conejo Canyon fault is actually a west-striking segment of the Gold Ace fault, and that this combined fault merges with the Fluorspar Canyon fault (Hoisch, 2000). Because the Gold Ace fault separates rocks of contrasting metamorphic grade, as does the Boundary Canyon fault of the Funeral Mountains, Hoisch (2000) inferred that the Boundary Canyon fault is also a continuation of the Fluorspar Canyon fault. On this basis, Hoisch (2000) concluded that the Boundary Canyon fault extends into Bare Mountain via the Bullfrog-Fluorspar Canyon faults, which thereby define a single regional detachment.

Hoisch (2000) inferred that the present east dip of a north-trending grade discordance fault (Gold Ace) may be explained by horizontal axis rotation from an initial northwest dip, or (less likely) the north-trending, east-dipping grade discordance fault may be a remnant of a system of large mullions within a regional Funeral Mountains–Bullfrog Hills–Bare Mountain detachment (Fig. 13). The mullion interpretation requires that Bare Mountain be rotated 30° counterclockwise to bring a mullion structure into proper northwest alignment with the Bullfrog detachment. Furthermore, the alignment would be enhanced by locating Bare Mountain 5–10 km to the west or southwest in late Miocene time while maintaining the basement exposures in the southern Bullfrog Hills at their present locations. Hoisch (2000) further speculated that translation and rotation were integral components of crustal extension in this region, perhaps leading to opening of the Amargosa Desert basin as well. Notions of wholesale block rotation and translation to accommodate structural alignments and juxtapositions in this region also are argued by Snow and Prave (1994, p. 720); their arguments hinge on pre-Tertiary features and regional strike-slip fault mechanisms. However, work by Stamatakos et al. (1998, p. 1544) demonstrates insignificant, if any, Tertiary vertical axis rotation of Bare Mountain. These mechanisms are discussed in the evaluation of tectonic models (O'Leary, this volume).

Mechanisms of extension west of Bare Mountain require far-traveled translation via detachment, as well as significant uplift (on the order of several kilometers). Hamilton (1988, p. 80) reconciled these mechanisms by inferring that regional detachment began as deep-seated normal faulting. The Gold Ace fault was initially a normal fault that dipped steeply west-northwestward, reaching rocks that were then ~15 km deep (they had been ~25 km deep in Cretaceous time) in the vicinity of the eastern Bullfrog Hills. The present length of the fault along the lower plate as defined is no more than 22 km, so in order to descend 15 km and cut the presently exposed metamorphic rocks, its initial dip would have to have been no gentler than 45°. This dip also accounts for the depth of formation of the garnet-staurolite rocks of northwesternmost Bare Mountain. Hamilton (1988, p. 55) inferred that the initial fault gave way at about the 15 km level to ductile flattening, which presumably accords with the detachment geometry and metamorphic petrology of the present Funeral Mountains.

According to the rolling-hinge detachment model, as slip proceeded on the initially steep fault, the footwall rose and flattened, stranding the thin northeast Bare Mountain upper plate on the rising lower plate as a hinge migrated westward in the lower plate (Hamilton, 1988, p. 50 and 81; Hoisch et al., 1997, p. 2830). Faulting started before 12.7 Ma, and by 8 Ma was inactivated as far west as the northwest Bare Mountain. At ca. 10 Ma, the active fault dipped steeply beneath the Bullfrog Hills region, where mid-crust rocks that were subhorizontal when faulting began were rising into the footwall of the active fault (Hoisch et al., 1997, p. 2829). The shallow hinge of flattening and the deep hinge of pickup of mid-crustal rocks both migrated westward for another 2 m.y. or so, progressively stranding backtilted panels of Miocene rocks and bringing deep rocks to or near the surface. The tectonic lenses and breccias of Paleozoic rocks, now present between lower-plate metamorphic rocks and the panels of Miocene supracrustal rocks of the Bullfrog Hills, were scraped from the hanging wall of a retreating Grapevine megablock (Hamilton, 1988, p. 55 and 61). Klippen of these lenses also lie on topographic crests on the metamorphic rocks south of Fluorspar Canyon. Hoisch et al. (1997) concluded that when the system was inactivated at 7–8 Ma, the final master fault dipped steeply beneath the Grapevine Mountains, which before 12 Ma lay close to the unmetamorphosed Paleozoic strata of Bare Mountain. The trace of the steep, active fault in these terms migrated ~35 km in 4 or 5 m.y. at a rate of ~7–9 mm/yr. Hoisch et al. (1997, p. 2830) calculated a migration rate of 12 mm/yr that operated until ca. 10.3 Ma.

The Las Vegas Valley Shear Zone

The Las Vegas Valley shear zone (Figs. 5 and 14) represents the eastern boundary of the Walker Lane belt south of Rock Valley (Stewart, 1988, p. 688 and 695). The Las Vegas Valley shear zone is important to the Yucca Mountain geologic setting because it forms a major domain boundary (Fig. 5) and plays a role in some tectonic models applicable to Yucca Mountain. However, nothing precise is known about the Las Vegas Valley shear zone because it is buried by Pleistocene alluvium, exhibits little or no seismic activity, and cannot be well characterized using available geophysical data. The shear zone is generally thought to be a right-lateral strike-slip fault, chiefly based on the evidence of displaced traces of Mesozoic thrust faults on either side (Longwell, 1974, p. 985; Stewart, 1988, p. 695) and on the clockwise curvature of the major ranges on the east side. The generally accepted displacement of more than 40 km along the central part of the shear zone (Burchfiel, 1965, p. 185) is thought to have occurred between 15 and 10 Ma (Bohannon, 1984, p. 59; Hudson et al., 1994, p. 273).

The northern reach of the Las Vegas Valley shear zone is subject to widely disparate interpretations (Hinrichs, 1968; Fox and Carr, 1989, p. 42; Caskey and Schweickert, 1992, p. 1325, Figure 3; Burchfiel, 1965, p. 186). Burchfiel (1965, p. 186) considered the northwestern projection of the zone to continue into the Specter Range thrust, as shown on Figure 14. Burchfiel's interpretation requires an episode of substantial south-southeast–directed compression during early Tertiary time to effect 1830 m or more of stratigraphic offset along the 50° to 60° northwest-dipping Specter Range thrust, as well as ~35 km of right-lateral offset along the Las Vegas Valley shear zone as projected into Mercury Valley (Fig. 14).

The Las Vegas Valley shear zone also has been interpreted as an accommodation zone (Guth, 1981, p. 769; Carr, 1984, p. 13; Hamilton, 1988, p. 79) or a "transfer fault" (Duebendorfer and Black, 1992, p. 1109) that marks the lateral margin of a large tract of detachment faults thought to include the Spotted Range and ranges farther southeast (Guth, 1981, p. 770). This interpretation avoids structural problems at the northern end of the shear zone by inferring that lateral displacement decreases to zero somewhere northwest of Indian Springs (Fig. 14), a consequence of extension in this region (Guth, 1981, p. 769). The accommodation model of Duebendorfer and Black (1992) requires 10–20 km of slip to be absorbed by oroclinal bending in the Specter Range, but evidence for such compression during the 14–13 Ma interval has not been recognized in or near Rock Valley. Therefore, arcing the Las Vegas Valley shear zone to the west through Mercury Valley into alignment with the left-lateral Rock Valley fault zone is not a viable tectonic interpretation. However, independent calculation by Caskey and Schweickert (1992, p. 1328) implies that the amounts of extension between correlative structures found north and south of the shear zone are not noticeably different, which diminishes the importance of an accommodation or transfer mechanism.

The Las Vegas Valley shear zone thus is plausibly related to one of two opposed tectonic mechanisms: (1) lateral accommodation that attends detachment faulting, or (2) north-south oriented lateral compression that has resulted in oroclinal bending and some right-lateral slip. The issue of oroclinal bending is of considerable tectonic interest because it implies a mechanism of lateral compression (or "constriction") (Wernicke et al., 1988b, p. 1754) in a tectonic regime thought to be dominated by or exclusively in extension.

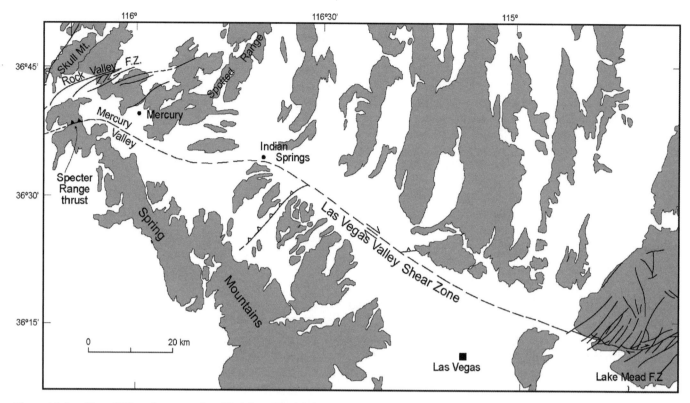

Figure 14. Las Vegas Valley shear zone (modified from Burchfiel, 1965). Mt—mountain, FZ—fault zone.

As much as 55 km of late to middle Miocene north-south crustal shortening is estimated in the northern Black Mountains (Fig. 3A) along the Lake Mead fault zone (Fig. 14; Anderson et al., 1994, p. 1381), which is compatible with both right-lateral slip and domain-boundary compression along the Las Vegas Valley shear zone (Anderson et al., 1994, p. 1403). Paleomagnetic studies indicate that the vertical-axis, clockwise bending in ranges along the north side of the Las Vegas Valley shear zone is not a consequence of simple fault drag (Sonder et al., 1994, p. 786), but represents a broad zone of combined crushing and local rotation of blocks on the order of a few kilometers laterally (Nelson and Jones, 1987, p. 13; Sonder et al., 1994, p. 782).

The sedimentological character of Tertiary strata and structural features near the southern end of the Spotted Range (Fig. 14) suggest that the apparent range-scale drag folding (oroflexing) associated with the Las Vegas Valley shear zone was formed in pre-late Oligocene time (Cole and Cashman, 1999, p. 35). Right-lateral transpression seems to have culminated in a late Miocene event that involved crushing and bending of extended terrane north and east of the shear zone. Extension in the Sheep and Desert Ranges evidently continued late, during deposition of strata tentatively correlated with the Miocene Horse Spring Formation (Guth, 1981, p. 766–767). In that case, right-lateral transpression that possibly had begun as early as 29 Ma must have peaked prior to ca. 14–13 Ma (Hudson et al., 1994, p. 258).

Death Valley–Furnace Creek–Fish Lake Valley Fault

The combined Death Valley–Furnace Creek–Fish Lake Valley fault system may form the only major, throughgoing fault system in the Yucca Mountain region (Fig. 15); it is a major domain boundary that separates a region of high strain rate and seismic activity (the Inyo-Mono domain) from one of relatively low strain rate and highly diverse structure and seismic activity (the Walker Lane belt). The fault system varies in structural style along strike, and links with associated lateral structures are uncertain. Therefore, its role in local fault development is speculative. It may represent the eastern border of a series of transtensional pull-aparts (Burchfiel and Stewart, 1966, p. 439; Blakely et al., 1999, p. 13), or it may represent range front-faults linked by strike-slip segments that are evolving into an increasingly coherent structure propagated northward along a strike distance of ~350 km.

The southern part of the fault system, the Death Valley fault segment, is primarily an oblique right-lateral range-front fault. It follows the salients and reentrants of the Black Mountains front, varying in strike from north-south to N40°W. For the most part, the Death Valley fault dips moderately to steeply west, but toward its southern end, dips range from 35° to 65° east or northeast (Piety, 1996, p. 141 and 318). Fault length is uncertain because of disagreement on definition of its poorly exposed end points. A minimum length of 51 km for the Death Valley fault is based on nearly continuously exposed west-facing scarps (Piety, 1996, p. 142); a minimum length for the Furnace Creek fault is 105 km

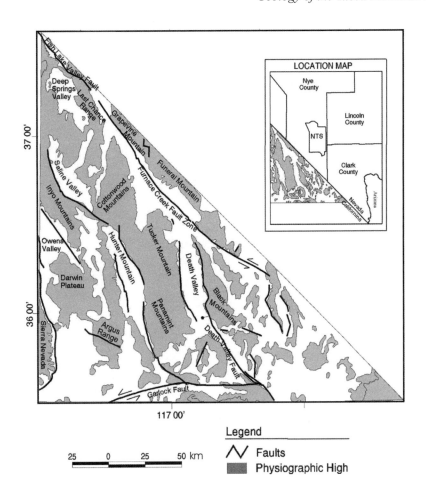

Figure 15. Major faults of the Inyo-Mono domain (modified from Wernicke et al., 1986; and Piety, 1996).

(Piety, 1996, p. 190); and a minimum length for the Fish Lake Valley fault is 80 km (Piety, 1996, p. 181).

The total offset of the Death Valley fault is unknown, but the dip-slip component, estimated from bedrock relief, is ~4570 m (Wills, 1989, p. 197). Hooke (1972, p. 2091) estimated a Holocene (ca. 11–10 ka) dip-slip displacement of ~63 m, based on elevation differences of coeval lakeshore features on the east and west sides of Death Valley. Fleck (1970b, p. 2811) considered that most of the vertical displacement on the Death Valley fault is ancient, probably having its inception before deposition of the Furnace Creek Formation (ca. 6 Ma). Estimates of lateral offset toward the southern end of the fault range from 1.7 to 50 km, depending on the age of offset rock units (Piety, 1996, p. 319). Estimates of late Tertiary and Quaternary offset range from 35 km (Butler et al., 1988, p. 406) to ~20 km (Brady, 1986, p. 2). Estimates of Pleistocene offset toward the southern end of the fault range from ~15–200 m, with estimates of 1.2–3 m per event based on displaced drainages (Piety, 1996, p. 321–322). Toward the southern end of the Black Mountains, the Death Valley fault has mostly strike-slip displacement (Piety, 1996, p. 319). Holocene activity along the Death Valley fault is expressed by a 10.5 m scarp in an alluvial fan near Mormon Point; the average per-event displacement is estimated to be ~2.5 m (Klinger and Piety, 1996, p. 56).

The Furnace Creek fault primarily is a right lateral strike-slip fault that extends through alluvial fans along the central part of Death Valley. The continuous fault trace is well expressed in most remote sensor images, probably because of the well-developed Pleistocene to Holocene scarp that ranges in cumulative relief from 0.3 to 23 m (Piety, 1996, p. 190). Estimates of total lateral offset, based on displaced Precambrian units, are uncertain: they range from 128 km to less than 8 km (Wright and Troxel, 1967, p. 937; Piety, 1996, p. 190). Piety (1996, p. 191) reported estimates of Pleistocene lateral offset of 21 m and 46 m and of single-event Holocene offsets of 1.5–2.7 m or less. Klinger and Piety (1996, p. 56) reported an average lateral displacement per Holocene event of 4.5 m.

A link between the Death Valley fault and the Furnace Creek fault is not well established. They may intersect or merge beneath the alluvial-filled valley between the Funeral and Black Mountains, a 19-km-long gap termed the "transition zone" by Klinger and Piety (1996, p. 9, 44). The structural nature of the inferred linkage is unclear, except that here fault traces and fold forms are relatively short, trend in various directions, and form a relatively wide zone (Klinger and Piety, 1996, p. 44). The main trace of the Furnace Creek fault may veer southeastward along the southern end of the Funeral Mountains and into the Amargosa trough, and even link up with structures along the east side of the Amargosa Desert (Wright and Troxel, 1967, p. 947, Fig. 2 therein).

Toward its northern end, between the Grapevine Mountains (Fig. 15) and the Last Chance Range to the north, the Furnace Creek fault is distributed into a number of fault planes forming a zone that extends into Fish Lake Valley, the northernmost 80 km of which is called the Fish Lake Valley fault. This fault is thought to have propagated northward from the Furnace Creek fault sometime between 12 and 4 Ma (Reheis, 1993, p. 376), and it dies out in a series of folds near the northern end of Fish Lake Valley (Stewart, 1967, p. 133–139). Estimates of maximum lateral displacement range from 25 km (Piety, 1996, p. 182) to 50 km (McKee, 1968, p. 512), and estimates of maximum vertical displacement range to as much as 750 m (Reheis and McKee, 1991, p. 40). The upper Pleistocene dip-slip component on this fault is as great as 64 m (Brogan et al., 1991, p. 1), and a Pleistocene lateral displacement as great as 122 m is recorded (Sawyer, 1991, p. 126). Pleistocene activity along the Fish Lake Valley fault has been high; vertical displacement of as much as 540 m may have accrued within the past 740 ka (Reheis and McKee, 1991, p. 38). However, modeling by Dixon et al. (1995, p. 765), based on space geodesy, implies that activity along the Death Valley–Furnace Creek–Fish Lake Valley fault system has slowed during the past few million years as slip is increasingly taken up to the west, mainly along the Owens Valley fault zone (shown as a straight line on Fig. 15). This transference of right-lateral slip activity to the west is reflected by the historical seismicity along the eastern California shear zone (Fig. 5; Dixon et al., 1995, p. 765) and its convergence northward with the Fish Lake Valley fault.

Northeast-Trending Strike-Slip Fault Zones and the Spotted Range–Mine Mountain Structural Zone

The Spotted Range–Mine Mountain structural zone (Fig. 5; Carr, 1984, p. 30; Stewart, 1988, p. 694, referred to as "section") is distinguished by prominent east-northeast trending, left-lateral, strike-slip faults and fault zones: the Rock Valley fault zone, the Mine Mountain fault, the Wahmonie fault zone, and the Cane Spring fault (Fig. 16). The structural zone forms a discrete section of the Walker Lane domain (Stewart, 1988, p. 694–695); it does not have a counterpart in the adjacent Basin and Range or Inyo-Mono domains.

The largest and most tectonically significant structural component of the Spotted Range-Mine Mountain structural zone is the Rock Valley fault zone (Coe et al., 2004). It is presently seismogenic and is exceeded in size only by the Furnace Creek fault, which occurs at a greater distance from Yucca Mountain. The Rock Valley fault zone coincides with a band of broad aeromagnetic lows bounded by a parallel gradient (−300 to −400 nT) (Glen and Ponce, 1991) along the south side of Little Skull Mountain (Fig. 16) and extending eastward to Frenchman Flat (Fig. 17), a distance of ~40 km. The geophysical data and local stratigraphy and structure indicate that the fault zone is part of a complex structural trough ~5 km wide (Coe et al., 2004). Three major fault sets compose the Rock Valley fault zone:

1. Continuous, dominantly strike-slip faults that strike N65° to 80°E for distances of 15 km or more;

2. Shorter normal, strike-slip, and/or reverse bridging faults that strike N25° to 50°E; and

3. Minor normal and strike-slip faults that strike N10° to 15°W.

The zone is complicated further by N25°E-striking faults that project into Rock Valley from the north. These faults might be related tectonically (but not specifically) to the Cane Spring fault and to the Wahmonie fault zone, which passes through the gap between Skull and Little Skull Mountains (Fig. 16).

Offsets along the fault planes are rarely demonstrable because cross-cutting features are uncommon. Estimates of total lateral offset of no more than 1.5–4 km are based on regional considerations (Barnes et al., 1982) and geophysical data (Kane and Bracken, 1983, p. 9). A few observed lateral offsets are in the range of 30–40 m. However, they appear to be pre-Pleistocene, and a more precise age constraint is unlikely to become available. These large displacements may actually be the cumulative results of several series of smaller events that were spaced closely enough in time to have prevented erosional discrimination of smaller component slips.

Historically, earthquakes have been frequent toward the west end of Rock Valley, in the vicinity of Little Skull Mountain, the Striped Hills, and the Specter Range (Fig. 16). Data summarized by Rogers et al. (1981, p. 9 and 15; 1987, p. 37) indicate that the earthquakes were mostly small magnitude events (M 4.0) that occurred from near surface to ~10 km depth on north- to northeast-striking faults that had left-lateral strike-slip and oblique slip mechanisms (Rogers et al., 1987, p. 31). Most of the strike-slip mechanisms occurred in the 4–9 km depth range. Fault-plane solutions for these pre-1993 earthquakes are in accord with the sense of slip of the mapped faults, but no individual seismogenic faults have been identified (Rogers et al., 1987, p. 37).

The Cane Spring fault is expressed as a conspicuous rectilinear fault-line scarp lineament (Reheis and Noller, 1991, Plate 3 therein) that strikes N54°E along the north flank of Mount Salyer (Fig. 16). The Cane Spring fault itself is mapped for a total length of ~8 km (Frizzell and Shulters, 1990). Slate et al. (1999) project the fault another 19 km to the northwest beneath the alluvial fill in Frenchman Flat). The fault evidently controls the location of Cane Spring, a large perched spring that gives the fault its name. Mapping by Ekren and Sargent (1965) provides little support for a southwest fault projection into Rock Valley, because faults mapped across the eastern flank of Skull Mountain are curvilinear normal faults of varied and minor displacement. These appear to be local faults unrelated to any inferred throughgoing strike-slip zone; in any event, they are old bedrock faults having no morphological expression.

Outcrops show the Cane Spring fault to be a subvertical shear zone ~1.5 m wide. The fault plane is marked by a discontinuous scarp that locally attains a relief of as much as 3 m across the beds of a few downslope gullies that cross a lineament, visible on aerial photographs, west of Cane Spring. Local kinematic

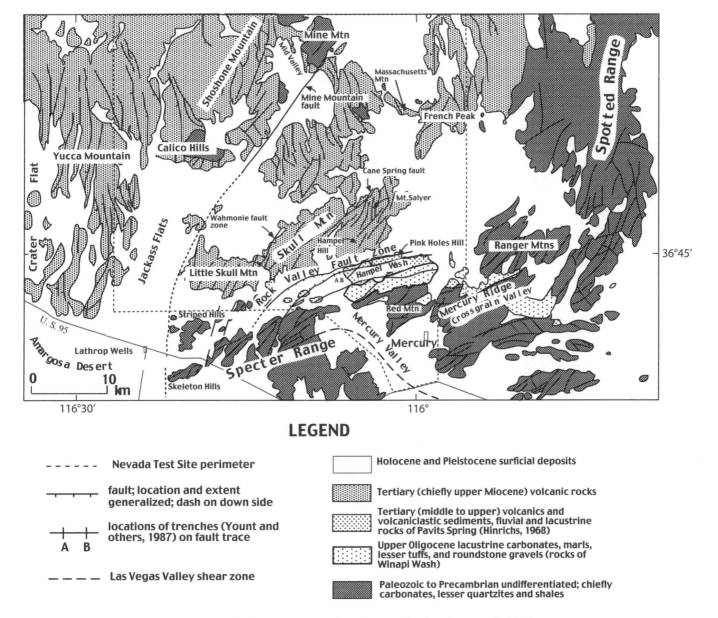

LEGEND

- - - - - - **Nevada Test Site perimeter**

———|——— **fault; location and extent generalized; dash on down side**

——+——+—— **locations of trenches (Yount and others, 1987) on fault trace**
A   B

— — — — **Las Vegas Valley shear zone**

☐ **Holocene and Pleistocene surficial deposits**

▨ **Tertiary (chiefly upper Miocene) volcanic rocks**

▨ **Tertiary (middle to upper) volcanics and volcaniclastic sediments, fluvial and lacustrine rocks of Pavits Spring (Hinrichs, 1968)**

▨ **Upper Oligocene lacustrine carbonates, marls, lesser tuffs, and roundstone gravels (rocks of Winapi Wash)**

▨ **Paleozoic to Precambrian undifferentiated; chiefly carbonates, lesser quartzites and shales**

Figure 16. General geology of the Rock Valley fault zone. Location of trenches A and B from Yount et al. (1987).

features imply left-lateral offset, but gross lithologic contacts indicate a dominantly normal, north-side-down movement. Poole et al. (1965) inferred three generations of alternating dip slip ("yo-yo tectonics") in addition to strike slip, but the basis for this inference is unclear. The contrast in landforms across the fault is pronounced, suggesting that the bulk of the offset has been dip-slip. The southeast side of the fault (upthrown block) shows numerous lineaments diverging south from the fault trace at angles of 30° to 45°. These lineaments probably represent splay faults or fractures indicative of the sinistral mechanism. Total offset along the Cane Spring fault remains unknown. No indications of late Pleistocene activity were observed; aerial photos show that the oldest and deepest stream courses on this slope

cross the fault and are not offset by it. The most recent activity may have been 100 ka or older.

The Mine Mountain fault (Fig. 16; Orkild, 1968) extends along the south flank of Mine Mountain as two N35°E-striking subparallel faults that are separated by as much as 200 m. The faults interconnect and splay and apparently entrain slices tens of meters across. At Mine Mountain, the Tiva Canyon Tuff exhibits left-lateral offset for a distance of 1.2 km. No exposures of the fault have been observed, so the attitude of the fault plane(s) is unknown. Orkild (1968) interpreted the faults as oblique left-lateral, down to the south. The offset Tertiary units dip ~30°W, so given a steeply south-dipping fault (85° or more), purely normal displacement of ~500–600 m could produce the apparent

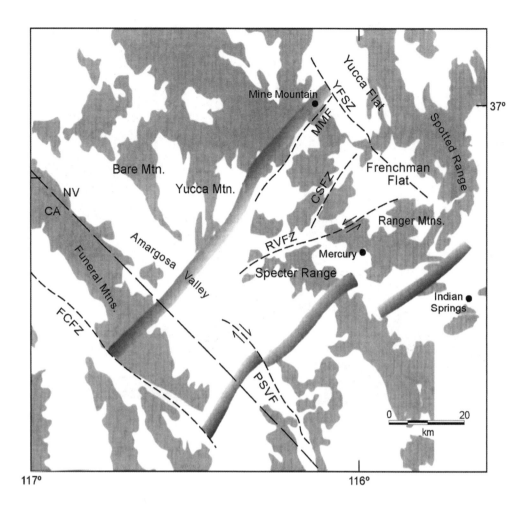

Figure 17. Spotted Range–Mine Mountain structural zone depicted by northeast-trending shaded borders (modified from Carr. 1984). Other faults shown: CSF—Cane Sprong fault zone; FCFZ—Furnace Creek fault zone; PSVF—Pahrump–Stewart Valley fault; RVFZ—Rock Valley fault zone; MMF—Mine Mountain fault; YFSZ—Yucca Flat shear zone.

left-lateral offset shown on a geologic map (Orkild, 1968). Considering slip relations on other faults in the region, an oblique slip seems most likely.

As no detailed Quaternary mapping has been done in the Mine Mountain quadrangle, the relation of faulting to Quaternary stratigraphy is unknown. The surficial Skull Mountain quadrangle map to the south (Swadley and Huckins, 1990) indicates that the fans overlying the projected Mine Mountain fault zone are constructed of late to middle Pleistocene alluvium (Q2b and Q2c). Reconnaissance along and across the southern alluvial flank of Shoshone Mountain (Fig. 2), and examination of aerial photos of this area, revealed evidence of complex faulting, but no evidence of late Quaternary displacements or any scarps in alluvium, or any transcurrent fault trace in alluvium that extends southwest of Mine Mountain (Fig. 16). Weakly etched, short lineaments are visible where the bedrock pediment is thinly covered; these features probably represent erosion focused by shattered bedrock. No throughgoing fault plane was found among the variously tilted and sheared pediment blocks, but a strong northeast-oriented, shear-controlled fabric is evident in numerous bedrock exposures within fan gullies. The breccia typically is sliced by irregular, subplanar fractures having no slip indicators that strike N20° to 45°E, 85°S to 90°.

The total Late Tertiary normal displacement along the Mine Mountain fault is difficult to judge because faulting is distributed across a zone more than 1 km wide and because the volcanic units were deposited on a surface of high relief (as much as 100 m) eroded in faulted Paleozoic blocks and in the overlying Wahmonie Formation. Where evident, the style of displacement is one of obverse dip away from the slope rather than toward it, in contrast to the sense of a rotated slump block. This style, along with the sinistral shear component, indicates that Shoshone Mountain may have pulled away obliquely west-southwest from a subsiding basin and that faulting was preceded by formation of a down-to-basin monocline.

No lineaments or other expressions of Quaternary faulting have been recognized to define a projection of the Mine Mountain fault in the fan deposits graded to Yucca Flat to the east. A smooth 32 mGal gravity gradient that defines the structural west flank of Yucca Flat (Healey et al., 1987) suggests that the fault does not project into Yucca Flat. To the southwest, the situation is more problematic.

The northern strand of the Mine Mountain fault zone was projected by Orkild (1968) southwest across Mid Valley (Fig. 16) along the southeast flank of Shoshone Mountain, where it is depicted as a down-to-the-south range front fault. Seismic profiles illustrated and interpreted by McArthur and Burkhard (1986, p. 61, 63, 67, and 69) cross the projection of the Mine Mountain fault zone in Mid Valley. The profiles indicate disruption of reflections along the projection of the fault zone, but the nature of deformation is ambiguous. Simple large-scale block tilting is not in evidence. The garbled reflections is more consistent with distributed shear rather than a few individual fault planes. Because reflections cannot be traced north across the inferred fault plane profiles, lateral offset rather than normal displacement is indicated.

Maldonado (1985) retained Orkild's range front fault projection, but also projected the more southerly of the two Mine Mountain fault strands southwest across Mid Valley and out across Jackass Flats to a point due west of Little Skull Mountain (Fig. 16). A range front fault certainly exists where Orkild has mapped it, but field work by one of us (DOL) did not reveal any evidence for the left-lateral fault trace projection of Maldonado (1985). Nevertheless, there is good evidence for strike-slip faulting in bedrock exposures along the base of Shoshone Mountain and in a low bluff of Topopah Spring Tuff (evidently an outlier of the Little Skull Mountain) located in Jackass Flats.

The 1:100,000-scale Bouguer gravity map of the Nevada Test Site (Healey et al., 1987) provides little indication of a significant crustal fault along the inferred projection of the Mine Mountain fault zone in northern Jackass Flats. There, the fault projection crosses an area in Jackass Flats of virtually no gradients or conspicuous anomalies. In Mid Valley, however, the projection passes along the northwest flank of a large minimum that represents the main depression of Mid Valley, and the fault thus could be considered a bounding structure to the depression (Fig. 16).

The 1:100,000 aeromagnetic map of the Beatty quadrangle (Glen and Ponce, 1991) shows strongly aligned gradients and separation of distinct anomaly patterns along the projection of the Mine Mountain fault zone into Jackass Flats. The aeromagnetic gradients indicate that the fault zone projection is ~800 m wide along Shoshone Mountain, and that it widens to ~1.5 km as it crosses Jackass Flats south of Calico Hills (Fig. 16). This zone of aligned steep gradients and linear and positive anomalies extends into a crudely annular anomaly pattern of short, steep highs rimmed with negative anomalies, ~8 km in diameter.

The westward extent and the possible interaction of the convergent, westward extensions of the Rock Valley fault zone and the Mine Mountain fault are unknown. Carr (1984, p. 16) projected the Spotted Range–Mine Mountain structural zone of the Walker Lane belt, which is characterized by northeast-striking left-lateral faults, west into California to the Furnace Creek fault zone (Fig. 17). However, no faults resembling the Rock Valley fault zone are known to transect the Funeral Mountains (Fig. 17). The Rock Valley fault zone probably extends no farther west than a line drawn from the west side of Little Skull Mountain south to the west end of the Skeleton Hills (Fig. 16). Laterally sheared Paleozoic rocks and local Miocene volcanic rocks exposed along this line imply the existence of a N5°- to 15°E-striking fault or

shear zone. A fault along this trend also is indicated by gravity and aeromagnetic anomaly gradients, a hydraulic barrier (Winograd and Thordarson, 1975, p. C75 and C84), and seismic reflection data (Brocher et al., 1993, p. 35), and by sparse west-facing scarps in alluvial fans.

Attempts to find a segment of the Rock Valley fault zone west of the line described above (the gravity fault) have been unsuccessful. Lineaments in the Amargosa Desert, however, suggest that a segment of the Rock Valley fault zone exists beneath the Amargosa Desert. On the other hand, the main strands of the Rock Valley fault zone veer to the south into the Specter Range east of the Striped Hills (Fig. 16). Thus, it still is unclear whether the zone extends all the way to the western end of Rock Valley, let alone into Amargosa Desert.

Surface geologic mapping, geophysical evidence, and subsurface investigations by Fridrich (1999, p. 176) and Potter et al. (2004) have led to the inferred presence of a large-offset, east-west–striking concealed fault, referred to, because of its close coincidence with U.S. Route 95, as the Highway 95 fault (Fig. 10). The fault occurs in the subsurface along the northeast margin of the Amargosa Desert, directly south of the southernmost extent of Yucca Mountain and Crater Flat. The Highway 95 structure possesses several unique characteristics. It appears to have a nearly vertical dip and a length of ~15 km, terminating against the Bare Mountain fault on the west and extending to the middle of Fortymile Wash on the east. Potter et al. (2002a) showed the fault just south of the U.S. Highway 95, crossing the highway just southwest of the Lathrop Wells Cone (Fig. 10). Its presence is based on the following observations. A conspicuous alignment of low-lying hills occurs just northeast of U.S. Route 95 and south of Crater Flat. These hills also mark the southwest edge of exposed volcanic rocks. However, the welding characteristics and thicknesses of rocks of the Paintbrush Group, exposed along this margin, do not appear indicative of the extreme distal margin of pyroclastic deposition. Directly south of the low-lying hills that mark the southern extent of Yucca Mountain, moderate to steep aeromagnetic gradients also terminate abruptly. South of the inferred fault location, within northern Amargosa Desert, conspicuous linear magnetic anomalies are not present. South of the inferred fault, a broad gravity high occurs and has been interpreted as a Paleozoic basement high (Ackermann et al., 1988, Figure 3.3, p. 27–30). This interpretation would indicate that a southern block, composed of Paleozoic carbonate rock covered by little or no volcanic rock, is juxtaposed against a northern block, composed of rocks of the Miocene Paintbrush and Crater Flat Groups (Potter et al., 2004).

Geophysical interpretations are, in part, supported by subsurface stratigraphic information. The absence or substantial thinning of magnetized Miocene volcanic rock within the southern block can be confirmed in several deep drill holes. Carr et al. (1995) reported that less than 40 m of tuff, suspected of being part of the Timber Mountain Group, occur above Paleozoic dolomite and limestone in drill hole Felderhoff Federal 25-1, less than 6 km south of the suspected location of the Highway 95 fault (Sweetkind et al., 2001). More recently, two drill holes NC-EWDP-19D1 and NC-EWDP-2DB, which were drilled in close proximity to the Highway 95 fault, indicate an abrupt variation in the thickness and lithologic character of the buried Topopah Spring Tuff. Drill hole NC-EWDP-19D1, located directly south of the inferred trace of the Highway 95 fault and one of the local moderate to steep aeromagnetic gradients, encountered ~130 m of nonwelded tuff that is suspected of being part of the lowermost Topopah Spring Tuff. Although uniformly nonwelded, R.W. Spengler and R.P. Dickerson (U.S. Geological Survey and S.M. Stoller Corp., respectively, written commun., 2002) suggested that much of the localized anomalously thick tuff in NC-EWDP-19D1 may have been preserved on the downthrown side of the Highway 95 fault, thus producing the conspicuous aeromagnetic anomaly. In contrast, drill hole NC-EWDP-2DB, located 2 km to the southwest, within the southern block, encountered only 27 m of the Topopah Spring Tuff, having variations in welding consistent with characteristics of outcrops at the southern extent of Yucca Mountain (R.W. Spengler, written commun., 2001). To best accommodate abrupt differences in the thickness and lithologic character of the Topopah Spring Tuff found between drill holes NC-EWDP-19D and NC-EWDP-2DB, the existence of a splay to the Highway 95 fault, extending to the southeast, also has been suggested (R.W. Spengler and R.P. Dickerson, written commun., 2002). Alternatively, the main trace of the Highway 95 may actually occur farther to the south, between NC-EWDP-19D and NC-EWDP-2DB, instead of the location indicated by Potter et al. (2002a).

Based primarily on the dichotomous relative stratigraphic position of outcrops of Topopah Spring Tuff along different segments of the northern downthrown block, the Highway 95 fault is suspected of having a component of lateral slip. The anomalous stratigraphic setting, wherein welding is present within the Topopah Spring Tuff in drill hole NC-EWDP-2DB, presumably closer to the distal edge of this pyroclastic flow deposit, but is absent in drill hole NC-EWDP-19D that is presumably closer to its source, also suggests lateral slip. However, clear evidence is lacking. Fridrich (1999) noted that B. Slemmons (written commun., 1997) initially proposed the existence of a more extensive structure, called the Carrara fault, which not only coincides with the trace of the Highway 95 fault, but also would extend northward along the southwestern flank of Bare Mountain (dotted line on Fig. 10). Slemmons suggested that the Carrara fault is a right-lateral strike-slip fault. Sweetkind et al. (2001) noted that an outcrop of Miocene Ammonia Tanks Tuff appears displaced to the west on the south side of the inferred trace of the Highway 95 fault relative to where this formation crops out north of the fault (see Swadley and Carr, 1987). In contrast, R.W. Spengler and R.P. Dickerson (written commun., 2002) suggested a component of sinistral lateral movement along the Highway 95 fault, which may explain the development of a deep graben beneath Fortymile Wash (Ponce et al., 2001) as a structurally controlled "pull-apart" basin. Additional deep drilling in southern Fortymile Wash and northern Amargosa Desert may help resolve this uncertainty.

The Quaternary faults discussed here are part of a large set of ~90 faults investigated as part of the Yucca Mountain Project. Several of the more important ones are discussed in the Site Geology chapter (Keefer et al., this volume), and their neotectonic histories are given in detail by Keefer et al. (2004). The full list is given in Appendix 1.

Summary

Yucca Mountain, the site proposed for the nation's first geologic repository for high-level nuclear waste, is located in a part of the Basin and Range province that has a long and complex history and is tectonically active today. The lithologic record in the vicinity of Yucca Mountain extends from late Precambrian through Paleozoic time and again from the late Tertiary to the present. The host rocks for the proposed repository would be Miocene volcanic rocks (mainly quartz latite to rhyolite ash flow tuffs) of the Paintbrush Group.

The tectonic history of the Yucca Mountain region includes a major compressional event during the Mesozoic and a late Tertiary to modern extensional setting. The proposed repository would be constructed in a block ~5 km wide and bounded by two north-trending normal faults. These faults have displacements of hundreds of meters vertically, and although most of that displacement occurred before 7.5 Ma, some activity can be documented for the late Pleistocene.

ACKNOWLEDGMENTS

The authors wish to thank Christopher J. Potter and W. Richard Keefer of the U.S. Geological Survey for help reviews and discussions. Anonymous reviewers with the Department of Energy contributed substantially to an earlier version.

REFERENCES CITED

Ackermann, H.D., Mooney, W.D., Snyder, D.B., and Sutton, V.D., 1988, Preliminary interpretation of seismic-refraction and gravity studies west of Yucca Mountain, Nevada and California, *in* Carr, M.D. and Yount, J.C., eds., Geologic and Hydrologic Investigations of a Potential Nuclear Waste Disposal Site at Yucca Mountain, Southern Nevada: U.S. Geological Survey Bulletin 1790, Chapter 3, p. 23–34.

Anderson, R.E., Barnhard, T.P., and Snee, L.W., 1994, Roles of plutonism, mid-crustal flow, tectonic rafting, and horizontal collapse in shaping the Miocene strain field of the Lake Mead area, Nevada and Arizona: Tectonics, v. 13, p. 1381–1410, doi: 10.1029/94TC01320.

Applegate, J.D.R., Walker, J.D., and Hodges, K.V., 1992, Late Cretaceous extensional unroofing in the Funeral Mountains metamorphic core complex, California: Geology, v. 20, p. 519–522, doi: 10.1130/0091-7613(1992)020<0519:LCEUIT>2.3.CO;2.

Armstrong, R.L., 1968, Sevier Orogenic Belt in Nevada and Utah: Geological Society of America Bulletin, v. 79, p. 429–458.

Asmerom, Y., Snow, J.K., Holm, D.K., Jacobsen, S.B., Wernicke, B.P., and Lux, D.R., 1990, Rapid uplift and crustal growth in extensional environments–an isotopic study from the Death Valley region, California: Geology, v. 18, p. 223–226, doi: 10.1130/0091-7613(1990)018<0223:RUACGI>2.3.CO;2.

Axen, G.J., Taylor, W.J., and Bartley, J.M., 1993, Space-time patterns and tectonic controls of Tertiary extension and magmatism in the Great Basin of the western United States: Geological Society of America Bulletin, v. 105, p. 56–76, doi: 10.1130/0016-7606(1993)105<0056:STPATC>2.3.CO;2.

Barnes, H., and Poole, F.G., 1968, Regional thrust-fault system in Nevada Test Site and vicinity: *in* Eckel, E.B., ed., Nevada Test Site: Geological Society of America Memoir 110, p. 233–238.

Barnes, H., Ekren, E.B., Rodgers, C.L., and Hedlund, D.C., 1982, Geologic and tectonic maps of the Mercury Quadrangle, Nye and Clark Counties, Nevada: U.S. Geological Survey Miscellaneous Investigations Series Map I-1197, scale 1:24,000.

Bennett, R.A., Davis, J.L., and Wernicke, B.P., 1999, Present-day pattern of cordilleran deformation in the western United States: Geology, v. 27, p. 371–374, doi: 10.1130/0091-7613(1999)027<0371:PDPOCD>2.3.CO;2.

Bennett, R.A., Wernicke, B.P., and Davis, J.L., 1998, Continuous GPS measurements of contemporary deformation across the northern Basin and Range Province: Geophysical Research Letters, v. 25, p. 563–566, doi: 10.1029/98GL00128.

Blakely, R.J., Jachens, R.C., Calzia, J.P., and Langenheim, V.E., 1999, Cenozoic basins of the Death Valley extended terrane as reflected in regional-scale gravity anomalies, *in* Wright, L.A., and Troxel, B.W., eds., Cenozoic Basins of the Death Valley Region: Geological Society of America Special Paper 333, p. 1–16.

Bohannon, R.G., 1984, Nonmarine sedimentary rocks of Tertiary age in the Lake Mead region, southeastern Nevada and northwestern Arizona: U.S. Geological Survey Professional Paper 1259, 72 p., 1 plate.

Bohannon, R.G., and Parsons, T., 1995, Tectonic implications of post–30 Ma Pacific and North American relative plate motions: Geological Society of America Bulletin, v. 107, p. 937–959, doi: 10.1130/0016-7606(1995)107<0937:TIOPMP>2.3.CO;2.

Brady, R.H., III, 1986, Stratigraphy and tectonics of the northern Avawatz Mountains at the intersection of the Garlock and Death Valley fault zones, San Bernardino County, California—A field guide, *in* Troxel, B.W., ed., Quaternary Tectonics of Southern Death Valley, California Field Trip Guide: 1986 Annual Meeting and Field Trip of the Friends of the Pleistocene, Pacific Cell, 31 October–2 November 1986, p. 1–12.

Brocher, T.M., Carr, M.D., Fox, K.F., Jr., and Hart, P.E., 1993, Seismic reflection profiling across Tertiary extensional structures in the eastern Amargosa Desert, southern Nevada, Basin and Range Province: Geological Society of America Bulletin, v. 105, p. 30–46, doi: 10.1130/0016-7606(1993)105<0030:SRPATE>2.3.CO;2.

Brocher, T.M., Hunter, W.C., and Langenheim, V.E., 1998, Implications of seismic reflection and potential field geophysical data on the structural framework of the Yucca Mountain–Crater Flat region, Nevada: Geological Society of America Bulletin, v. 110, p. 947–971, doi: 10.1130/0016-7606(1998)110<0947:IOSRAP>2.3.CO;2.

Brogan, G.E., Kellogg, K.S., Slemmons, D.B., and Terhune, C.L., 1991, Late Quaternary faulting along the Death Valley–Furnace Creek fault system, California and Nevada: U.S. Geological Survey Bulletin 1991, 23 p., map scale 1:62,500.

Burchfiel, B.C., 1965, Structural geology of the Specter Range Quadrangle, Nevada, and its regional significance: Geological Society of America Bulletin, v. 76, p. 175–192.

Burchfiel, B.C., and Davis, G.A., 1988, Mesozoic thrust faults and Cenozoic low-angle normal faults, eastern Spring Mountains, Nevada, and Clark Mountains thrust complex, California, *in* Weide, D.L. and Faber, M.L., eds., This Extended Land, Geological Journeys in the Southern Basin and Range: Field Trip Guidebook, Geological Society of America, Cordilleran Section Meeting, p. 87–106.

Burchfiel, B.C., Hamill, G.S., IV, and Wilhelms, D.E., 1983, Structural geology of the Montgomery Mountains and the northern half of the Nopah and Resting Spring Ranges, Nevada and California: Geological Society of America Bulletin, v. 94, p. 1359–1376, doi: 10.1130/0016-7606(1983)94<1359:SGOTMM>2.0.CO;2.

Burchfiel, B.C., Pelton, P., and Sutter, J., 1970, An early Mesozoic deformation belt in south-central Nevada–southeastern California: Geological Society of America Bulletin, v. 81, p. 211–215.

Burchfiel, B.C., and Stewart, J.H., 1966, Pull-apart origin of the central segment of Death Valley, California: Geological Society of America Bulletin, v. 77, p. 439–441.

Burchfiel, B.C., Fleck, R.J., Secor, D.T., Vincelette, R.R., and Davis, G.A., 1974, Geology of the Spring Mountains, Nevada: Geological Society of America Abstracts with Programs, v. 85, p. 1013–1022.

Butler, P.R., Troxel, B.W., and Verosub, K.L., 1988, Late Cenozoic history and styles of deformation along the southern Death Valley Fault zone, California: Geological Society of America Bulletin, v. 100, p. 402–410, doi: 10.1130/0016-7606(1988)100<0402:LCHASO>2.3.CO;2.

Carr, M.D., and Monsen, S.A., 1988, A Field trip guide to the geology of Bare Mountain, *in* Weide, D.L., and Faber, M.L., eds., This Extended Land, Geological Journeys in the Southern Basin and Range: Field Trip Guidebook, Geological Society of America, Cordilleran Section Meeting, Las Vegas, Nevada, Special Publication 2, p. 50–57.

Carr, M.D., Waddell, S.J., Vick, G.S., Stock, J.M., Monsen, S.A., Harris, A.G., Cork, B.W., and Byers, F.M., Jr., 1986, Geology of Drill Hole UE25p#1–A test hole into pre-Tertiary rocks near Yucca Mountain, Southern Nevada: U.S. Geological Survey Open-File Report 86-175, 87 p.

Carr, W.J., 1984, Regional structural setting of Yucca Mountain, southwestern Nevada, and late Cenozoic rates of tectonic activity in part of the southwestern Great Basin, Nevada and California: U.S. Geological Survey Open-File Report 84-854, 109 p.

Carr, W.J., 1990, Styles of extension in the Nevada Test Site region, southern Walker Lane Belt–an integration of volcano-tectonic and detachment fault models, *in* Wernicke, B.P., ed., Basin and Range Extensional Tectonics Near the Latitude of Las Vegas, Nevada: Geological Society of America Memoir 176, p. 283–303.

Carr, W.J., Byers, F.M., Jr., and Orkild, P.P., 1986, Stratigraphic and volcano-tectonic relations of Crater Flat Tuff and some older volcanic units, Nye County, Nevada: U.S. Geological Survey Professional Paper 1323, 28 p.

Carr, W.J., Grow, J.A., and Keller, S.M., 1995, Lithologic and geophysical logs of drill holes Felderhoff Federal 5-1 and 25-1, Amargosa Desert, Nye County, Nevada: U.S. Geological Survey Open-File Report 95-155, 14 p.

Caskey, S.J., and Schweickert, R.A., 1992, Mesozoic deformation in the Nevada Test Site and vicinity: implications for the structural framework of the Cordilleran fold and thrust belt and Tertiary extension north of Las Vegas Valley: Tectonics, v. 11, p. 1314–1331.

Catchings, R.D., 1992, A relation among geology, tectonics, and velocity structure, western to central Nevada Basin and Range: Geological Society of America Bulletin, v. 104, p. 1178–1192, doi: 10.1130/0016-7606(1992)104<1178:ARAGTA>2.3.CO;2.

Chen, J.H., and Moore, J.G., 1979, Late Jurassic independence dike swarm in eastern California: Geology, v. 7, p. 129–133, doi: 10.1130/0091-7613(1979)7<129:LJIDSI>2.0.CO;2.

Chen, J.H., and Moore, J.G., 1982, Uranium-lead isotopic ages from the Sierra Nevada Batholith, California: Journal of Geophysical Research, v. 87, p. 4761–4784.

Coe, J.A., Yount, J.C., O'Leary, D.W., and Taylor, E.M., 2004, Paleoseismic investigations on the Rock Valley fault system, *in* Keefer, W.R., Whitney, J.W. and Taylor, E.M., eds., Quaternary paleoseismology and stratigraphy of the Yucca Mountain area, Nevada: U.S. Geological Survey Professional Paper 1689, p. 175–195.

Cole, J.C., and Cashman, P.H., 1999, Structural relationship of pre-Tertiary Rocks in the Nevada Test Site region, southern Nevada: U.S. Geological Survey Professional Paper 1607, 39 p.

Cole, J.C., Wahl, R.R., and Hudson, M.R., 1989, Structural relations within the Paleozoic basement of the Mine Mountain block–implications for interpretation of gravity data in Yucca Flat, Nevada Test Site, *in* Olsen, C.W. and Carter, J.A., eds., Proceedings of the Fifth Symposium on Containment of Underground Nuclear Explosions: . Mission Research Corporation, CONF-8909163, v. 2, p. 431–455.

Cole, J.C., Trexler, J.H., Jr., Cashman, P.H., and Hudson, M.R., 1994, Structural and stratigraphic relations of Mississippian rocks at the Nevada Test Site, *in* McGill, S.F. and Ross, T.M., eds., Geological Investigations of an Active Margin: Geological Society of America Cordilleran Section Guidebook, 27th Annual Meeting, p. 66–75.

Cole, J.C., Harris, A.G., Lanphere, M.A., Barker, C.E., and Warren, R.G., 1993, The case for pre-middle Cretaceous extensional faulting in northern Yucca Flat, southwestern Nevada: Geological Society of America Abstracts with Programs, v. 25, p. 22.

Corbett, K., Wrucke, C.T., and Nelson, C.A., 1988, Structure and tectonic history of the Last Chance thrust system, Inyo Mountains and Last Chance Range, California, *in* Weide, D.L., and Faber, M.L., eds., This Extended Land, Geological Journeys in the Southern Basin and Range, Field Trip Guidebook, Geological Society of America Special Publication 2: University of Nevada, Las Vegas, Department of Geoscience, p. 269–292.

Crowe, B., Perry, F., Geissman, J., McFadden, L., Wells, S., Murrell, M., Poths, J., Valentine, G.A., Bowker, L., and Finnegan, K., 1995, Status of volcanism studies for the Yucca Mountain site characterization project: LA-12908-MS, Los Alamos, New Mexico, 379 p.

Day, W.C., Potter, C.J., Sweetkind, D.S., Dickerson, R.P., and San Juan, C.A., 1998, Bedrock geologic map of the central block area, Yucca Mountain, Nye County, Nevada: Miscellaneous Investigations Series Map I-2601, U.S. Geological Survey, scale 1:6,000.

Diehl, P., 1976, Stratigraphy and sedimentology of the Wood Canyon Formation, Death Valley Area, California, *in* Troxel, B.W., and Wright, L.A., eds., Geologic Features, Death Valley, California: California Division of Mines and Geology Special Report 106, p. 51–62.

Dilles, J.H., John, D.A., and Hardyman, R.F., 1993, Evolution of Cenozoic magmatism and tectonism along a northeast-southwest transect across the northern Walker Lane, west-central Nevada–Part I, *in* Lahren, M.M., Trexler, J.H., Jr., and Spinosa, C., eds., Crustal Evolution of the Great Basin and the Sierra Nevada: Field Trip Guidebook for the 1993 Joint Meeting of the Cordilleran/Rocky Mountain Sections of the Geological Society of America, p. 409–452.

Dixon, T.H., Robaudo, S., Lee, J., and Reheis, M.C., 1995, Constraints on present-day Basin and Range deformation from Space Geodesy: Tectonics, v. 14, p. 755–772, doi: 10.1029/95TC00931.

Drewes, H., 1963, Geology of the Funeral Peak Quadrangle, California, on the east flank of Death Valley: U.S. Geological Survey Professional Paper 413, 78 p.

Duebendorfer, E.M., and Black, R.A., 1992, Kinematic role of transverse structures in continental extension–an example from the Las Vegas Valley shear zone, Nevada: Geology, v. 20, p. 1107–1110, doi: 10.1130/0091-7613(1992)020<1107:KROTSI>2.3.CO;2.

Dunne, G.C., 1986, Geologic evolution of the southern Inyo Range, Darwin Plateau, and Argus and Slate Ranges, east-central California–an overview: *in* Guidebook and Volume, Field Trip Number 2, Mesozoic Evolution of Southern Inyo, Argus and Slate Ranges, Geologic Evolution of Tucki Mountain, Central Panamint Range, Field Trip Number 14, Stratigraphy and Structure of Metamorphic Framework Rocks, Lake Isabella Area, Southern Sierra Nevada: Cordilleran Section of the Geological Society of America, Pages 3–21.

Dunne, G.C., Gulliver, R.M., and Sylvester, A.G., 1978, Mesozoic evolution of rocks of the White, Inyo, Argus and Slate Ranges, eastern California, *in* Howell, D.G. and McDougall, K., eds., Mesozoic Palcogeography of the Western United States: Pacific Coast Paleogeography Symposium 2, Society of Economic Paleontologists and Mineralogists, p 189–207.

Eaton, G.P., 1982, The Basin and Range Province–origin and tectonic significance: Annual Review of Earth and Planetary Science, v. 10, p. 409–440, doi: 10.1146/annurev.ea.10.050182.002205.

Ekren, E.B., and Byers, F.M., Jr., 1984, The Gabbs Valley range–a well-exposed segment of the Walker Lane in west-central Nevada, *in* Lintz, J., Jr., ed., Western Geological Excursions Volume 4: Geological Society of America, p 203–215.

Ekren, E.B., and Sargent, K.A., 1965, Geologic map of the Skull Mountain Quadrangle, Nye County, Nevada: U.S. Geological Survey Geologic Quadrangle Map GQ-387, scale 1:24,000.

Ekren, E.B., Anderson, R.E., Rogers, C.L., and Noble, D.C., 1971, Geology of the northern Nellis Air Force Base Bombing and Gunnery Range, Nye County, Nevada: U.S. Geological Survey Professional Paper 651, 91 p.

Fleck, R.J., 1970a, Age and tectonic significance of volcanic rocks, Death Valley area, California: Geological Society of America Bulletin, v. 81, p. 2807–2815.

Fleck, R.J., 1970b, Tectonic style, magnitude, and age of deformation in the Sevier orogenic belt in southern Nevada and eastern California: Geological Society of America Bulletin, v. 81, p. 1705–1720.

Forester, R.M., and Smith, A.J., 1994, Late glacial climate estimates for southern Nevada – the ostracode fossil record, *in* Proceedings of the fifth International High-Level Radioactive Waste Management Conference, Las Vegas, Nevada, May 22–26, 1994, American Nuclear Society, LaGrange, Illinois, v. 4, p. 2553–2561.

Fox, K.F., Jr., and Carr, M.D., 1989, Neotectonics and volcanism at Yucca Mountain and vicinity, Nevada: Radioactive Waste Management and the Nuclear Fuel Cycle, v. 13, p. 37–50.

Fridrich, C.J., 1999, Tectonic evolution of the Crater Flat basin, Yucca Mountain region, Nevada: *in* Wright, L.A., and Troxel, B.W., eds., Cenozoic Basins of the Death Valley Region: Geological Society of America Special Paper 333, p. 169–195.

Frizzell, V.A., Jr., and Shulters, J., 1990, Geologic map of the Nevada Test Site,

southern Nevada: U.S. Geological Survey Miscellaneous Investigations Series Map I-2046, scale 1:100,000.

Gilbert, G.K., 1875, Report on the geology of portions of Nevada, Utah, California, and Arizona examined in the years 1871–1872: U.S. Geographical and Geological Surveys West of the 100th Meridian, v. 3, part 1.

Glen, J.M., and Ponce, D.A., 1991, Aeromagnetic map of the Beatty Quadrangle, Nevada–California: U.S. Geological Survey Open-File Report 91-105, scale 1:100,000.

Guth, P.L., 1981, Tertiary extension north of the Las Vegas Valley shear zone, Sheep and Desert Ranges, Clark County, Nevada: Geological Society of America Bulletin, v. 92, p. 763–771, doi: 10.1130/0016-7606(1981)92<763:TENOTL>2.0.CO;2.

Guth, P.L., 1990, Superposed Mesozoic and Cenozoic deformation, Indian Springs Quadrangle, southern Nevada, *in* Wernicke, B.P., ed., Basin and Range Extensional Tectonics Near the Latitude of Las Vegas, Nevada: Geological Society of America Memoir 176, p. 237–249.

Hamilton, W.B., 1987, Crustal extension in the Basin and Range Province, southwestern United States, *in* Coward, M.P., Dewey, J.F., and Hancock, P.L., eds., Continental Extensional Tectonics: Geological Society Special Publication 28, p. 155–176.

Hamilton, W.B., 1988, Detachment faulting in the Death Valley region, California and Nevada, *in* Carr, M.D., and Yount, J.C., eds., Geologic and Hydrologic Investigations of a Potential Nuclear Waste Disposal Site at Yucca Mountain, Southern Nevada: U.S. Geological Survey Bulletin 1790, p. 51–85.

Hamilton, W.B., 1989, Crustal geologic processes of the United States, *in* Pakiser, L.C., and Mooney, W.D., eds. Geophysical Framework of the Continental United States: Geological Society of America Memoir 172, p. 743–781.

Hamilton, W.B., and Myers, W.B., 1966, Cenozoic tectonics of the western United States: Reviews of Geophysics, v. 4, p. 509–549.

Harbert, W., and Cox, A., 1989, Late Neogene motion of the Pacific plate: Journal of Geophysical Research, v. 94, p. 3052–3064.

Hardyman, R.F., and Oldow, J.S., 1991, Tertiary tectonic framework and Cenozoic history of the central Walker Lane, Nevada, *in* Raines, G.L., Lisle, R.E., Schafer, R.W., and Wilkinson, W.H., eds., Geology and Ore Deposits of the Great Basin: Geological Society of Nevada, Symposium Proceedings, v. 1, p. 279–301.

Healey, D.L., Harris, R.N., Ponce, D.A., and Oliver, H.W., 1987, Complete Bouguer gravity map of the Nevada Test Site and vicinity, Nevada: U.S. Geological Survey Open-File Report 87-506, scale 1:100,000.

Heizler, M.T., Perry, F.V., Crowe, B.M., Peters, L., and Appelt, R., 1999, The age of Lathrop Wells volcanic center—An ^{40}Ar/^{39}Ar dating investigation: Journal of Geophysical Research, v. 104, p. 767–804, doi: 10.1029/1998JB900002.

Hillhouse, J.W., Sarna-Wojcicki, A., Reheis, M.C., and Forester, R.M., 2005, Age and paleoenvironments (paleomagnetism, tephra, and ostrocodes) of the Pliocene and Pleistocene Tecopa beds, southeastern, California, *in* Reheis, M.C., ed., Geologic and biotic perspectives on Late Cenozoic drainage histories of the southwestern Great Basin and lower Colorado River regions: U.S. Geological Survey Open-File Report 2005-1204, Conference abstracts, p. 9.

Hinrichs, E.N., 1968, Geologic structure of Yucca Flat area, Nevada, *in* Eckel, E.B., ed., Nevada Test Site: Geological Society of America Memoir 110, p. 239–250.

Hodges, K.V., and Walker, J.D., 1992, Extension in the Cretaceous Sevier orogen, North American Cordillera: Geological Society of America Bulletin, v. 104, p. 560–569, doi: 10.1130/0016-7606(1992)104<0560:EITCSO>2.3.CO;2.

Hodges, K.V., McKenna, L.W., Stock, J., Knapp, J., Page, L., Stemlof, K., Silverberg, D., Wust, G., and Walker, J.D., 1989, Evolution of extensional basins and Basin and Range topography west of Death Valley, California: Tectonics, v. 8, p. 453–467.

Hoisch, T.D., 2000, Conditions of metamorphism in lower-plate rocks at Bare Mountain, Nevada—implications for extensional faulting, *in* Whitney, J.W. and Keefer, W.R., eds., Geology and geophysical characterization studies of Yucca Mountain, Nevada, a potential high-level radioactive-waste repository: U.S. Geological Survey Digital Data Series DDS-0058, 23 p.

Hoisch, T.D., and Simpson, C., 1993, Rise and tilt of metamorphic rocks in the lower plate of a detachment fault in the Funeral Mountains, Death Valley, California: Journal of Geophysical Research, v. 98, p. 6805–6827.

Hoisch, T.D., Heizler, M.T., and Zartman, R.E., 1997, Timing of detachment faulting in the Bullfrog Hills and Bare Mountain area, southwest Nevada—Inferences from ^{40}Ar/^{39}Ar, K-Ar, U-Pb, Fission Track Thermochronology: Journal of Geophysical Research, v. 102, p. 2815–2833, doi: 10.1029/96JB03220.

Holm, D.K., and Dokka, R.K., 1991, Major late Miocene cooling of the middle crust associated with extensional orogenesis in the Funeral Mountains, California: Geophysical Research Letters, v. 18, p. 1775–1778.

Hooke, R.L., 1972, Geomorphic evidence for late-Wisconsin and Holocene tectonic deformation, Death Valley, California: Geological Society of America Bulletin, v. 83, p. 2073–2098.

Houghton, J.G., Sakamoto, C.M., and Gifford, R.O., 1975, Nevada's weather and climate: Nevada Bureau of Mines Special Publication 2, 78 p.

Houser, F.N., and Poole, F.G., 1960, Preliminary geologic map of the Climax Stock and vicinity, Nye County, Nevada: U.S. Geological Survey Miscellaneous Geologic Investigations Map I-328, scale 1:48,000.

Huber, N.K., 1988, Late Cenozoic evolution of the upper Amargosa River drainage system, southwestern Great Basin, Nevada and California: U.S. Geological Survey Open-File Report 87-617, 26 p.

Hudson, M.R., Sawyer, D.A., and Warren, R.G., 1994, Paleomagnetism and rotation constraints for the middle Miocene Southwestern Nevada Volcanic Field: Tectonics, v. 13, p. 258–277, doi: 10.1029/93TC03189.

Jennings, C.W., 1977, Geologic map of California: California Division of Mines and Geology, Geologic Data Map Series, Map No. 2, scale 1:750,000.

Kane, M.F., and Bracken, R.E., 1983, Aeromagnetic map of Yucca Mountain and surrounding regions, southwest Nevada: U.S. Geological Survey Open-File Report 83-616, scale 1:48,000, 19 p.

Keefer, W.R., Whitney, J.W., and Taylor, E.M., eds., 2004, Quaternary paleoseismology and stratigraphy of the Yucca Mountain area, Nevada: U.S. Geological Survey Professional Paper 1689, 206 p.

Keefer, W.R., Whitney, J.W, and Buesch, D.C., 2007, this volume, Geology of the Yucca Mountain site area, in Stuckless, J.S., and Levich, R.A., eds., The Geology and Climatology of Yucca Mountain and Vicinity, Southern Nevada and California: Geological Society of America Memoir 199, doi: 10.1130/2007.1199(03).

Ketner, K.B., 1998, The nature and timing of tectonism in the western facies terrane of Nevada and California—an outline of evidence and interpretations derived from geologic maps of key areas: U.S. Geological Survey Professional Paper 1592, 12 p.

Klinger, R.E., and Piety, L.A., 1996, Late Quaternary activity on the Furnace Creek fault, northern Death Valley, California: Geological Society of America Abstracts with Programs, v. 28, p. A-193.

Labotka, T.C., Warasila, R.L., and Spangler, R.R., 1985, Polymetamorphism in the Panamint Mountains, California—a ^{39}Ar-^{40}Ar study: Journal of Geophysical Research, v. 90, p. 10,359–10,371.

Lewis, M.C., Whittman, C., and Stevens, C.H., 1983, Lower Triassic marine sedimentary rocks in east-central California, in Marzolf, J.E., and Dunne, G.C., eds., Evolution of early Mesozoic tectonostratigraphic environments—southwestern Colorado Plateau to southern Inyo Mountains: Geological Society of America Rocky Mountain and Cordilleran Sections Annual Meeting Guidebook, part 2, Salt Lake City, p. 50–54.

Lipman, P.W., and McKay, E.J., 1965, Geologic map of the Topopah Spring SW Quadrangle, Nye County, Nevada: U.S. Geological Survey Geologic Quadrangle Map GQ-439, scale 1:24,000.

Longwell, C.R., 1945, Low-angle normal faults in the Basin-and-Range Province: Transactions, American Geophysical Union, v. 26, p. 107–118.

Longwell, C.R., 1974, Measure and date of movement on Las Vegas Valley shear zone, Clark County, Nevada: Geological Society of America Bulletin, v. 85, p. 985–990, doi: 10.1130/0016-7606(1974)85<985:MADOMO>2.0.CO;2.

Longwell, C.R., Pampeyan, E.H., Bowyer, B., and Roberts, R.J., 1965, Geology and mineral deposits of Clark County, Nevada: Nevada Bureau of Mines and Geology Bulletin 62.

Lundstrom, S.C., Paces, J.B., Mahan, S.A., Page, W.R., and Workman, J.B., 1999, Quaternary geologic mapping and geochronology of the Las Vegas 1:100,000 sheet and Yucca Mountain Area—Geomorphic and hydrologic response to climate change ear Death Valley: in Slate, J.L. ed., Proceedings of conference on status of geologic research and mapping, Death Valley National Park, U.S. Geological Survey Open-File Report 99-153, p. 110–111.

Majer, E.L., Feighner, M., Johnson, L., Daley, T., Karageorgi, E., Lee, K.H., Williams, K., and McEvilly, T., 1996, Surface geophysics, volume I of Synthesis of borehole and surface geophysical studies at Yucca Mountain, Nevada and vicinity: Berkeley, California, Lawrence Berkeley Laboratory Milestone OB05M.

Maldonado, F., 1985, Geologic Map of the Jackass Flats area, Nye County, Nevada: U.S. Geological Survey Miscellaneous Investigations Series Map I-1519, scale 1:48,000.

Maldonado, F., and Hausback, B.P., 1990, Geologic map of the northeast quarter of the Bullfrog 15-minute quadrangle, Nye County, Nevada: U.S. Geological Survey Miscellaneous Investigations Series Map I-2049, scale 1:24,000.

Maldonado, F., Muller, D.C., and Morrison, J.N., 1979, Preliminary geologic and geophysical data of the UE25a-3 exploratory drill hole, Nevada Test Site, Nevada: U.S. Geological Survey Report USGS-1543-6, 47 p.

Marzolf, J.E., 1990, Reconstruction of extensionally dismembered early Mesozoic sedimentary basins—southwestern Colorado Plateau to the eastern Mojave Desert, in Wernicke, B.P., ed., Basin and Range Extensional Tectonics Near the Latitude of Las Vegas, Nevada: Geological Society of America Memoir 176, p. 477–500.

McAllister, J.F., 1973, Geologic map and sections of the Amargosa Valley borate area—southeast continuation of the Furnace Creek area-Inyo County, California: U.S. Geological Survey Miscellaneous Geologic Investigations Map I-782, scale 1:24,000.

McArthur, R.D., and Burkhard, N.R., 1986, Geological and geophysical investigations of Mid Valley: Lawrence Livermore National Laboratory Report UCID-20740.

McKee, E.H., 1968, Age and rate of movement of the northern part of the Death Valley–Furnace Creek fault zone, California: Geological Society of America Bulletin, v. 79, p. 509–512.

McKee, E.H., 1983, Reset K-Ar ages—evidence for three metamorphic core complexes, Western Nevada: Isochron/West, v. 38, p. 17–20.

Michel-Noel, G., Anderson, R.E., and Angelier, J., 1990, Fault kinematics and estimates of strain partitioning of a Neogene extensional fault system in southeastern Nevada, in Wernicke, B.P., ed., Basin and Range Extensional Tectonics Near the Latitude of Las Vegas, Nevada: Geological Society of America Memoir 176, p. 155–180.

Miller, C., 1978, An Early Mesozoic alkalic magmatic belt in western North America, in Howell, D., and McDougall, K., eds., Mesozoic paleogeography of the western United States: Society of Economic Paleontologists and Mineralogists Pacific Coast Paleogeography Symposium 2, p. 163–174.

Miller, M.G., and Friedman, R.M., 1999, Early Tertiary magmatism and probable Mesozoic fabrics in the Black Mountains, Death Valley, California: Geology, v. 27, p. 19–22, doi: 10.1130/0091-7613(1999)027<0019:ETMAPM>2.3.CO;2.

Minor, S.A., 1995, Superposed local and regional paleostresses: fault-slip analysis of Neogene extensional faulting near coeval caldera complexes, Yucca Flat, Nevada: Journal of Geophysical Research, v. 100, p. 10,507–10,528, doi: 10.1029/95JB00078.

Minor, S.A., Orkild, P.P., Swadley, W.C., Warren, R.G., and Workman, J.B., 1997, Preliminary Digital Geologic Map of the Springdale Quadrangle, Nye County, Nevada: U.S. Geological Survey Open-File Report 97-93, scale 1:24,000

Monsen, S.A., Carr, M.D., Reheis, M.C., and Orkild, P.P., 1992, Geologic map of Bare Mountain, Nye County, Nevada: U.S. Geological Survey Miscellaneous Investigations Series Map I-2201, scale 1:24,000.

Moore, J., and Hopson, C., 1961, The Independence dike swarm in eastern California: American Journal of Science, v. 259, p. 241–259.

Morrison, R.B., 1999, Lake Tecopa—Quaternary geology of the Tecopa Valley, California—a multi-million-year record and its relevance to the proposed nuclear-waste repository at Yucca Mountain, Nevada, in Write, L., and Troxel, B., eds., Cenozoic Basins of the Death Valley Region: Geologic Society of America Special Paper 333, p. 301–344.

Naeser, C.W., and Maldonado, F., 1981, Fission-track dating of the Climax and Gold Meadows stocks, Nye County, Nevada, in Shorter Contributions to Isotope Research in the Western United States: U.S. Geological Survey Professional Paper 1199-E, p. 44–47.

Nelson, M.R., and Jones, C.H., 1987, Paleomagnetism and crustal rotations along a shear zone, Las Vegas Range, Southern Nevada: Tectonics, v. 6, p. 13–33.

Noble, L.F., 1941, Structural features of the Virgin Spring area, Death Valley, California: Geological Society of America Bulletin, v. 52, p. 941–999.

O'Leary, D.W., 1996, Synthesis of tectonic models for the Yucca Mountain area, in Whitney, J.W., ed., Seismotectonic Framework and Characterization of Faulting at Yucca Mountain, Nevada: U.S. Geological Survey Milestone 3GSH100M.

O'Leary, D.W., 2007, this volume, Tectonic models for Yucca Mountain, Nevada, *in* Stuckless, J.S., and Levich, R.A., eds., The Geology and Climatology of Yucca Mountain and Vicinity, Southern Nevada and California: Geological Society of America Memoir 199, doi: 10.1130/2007.1199(04).

Orkild, P.P., 1968, Geologic map of the Mine Mountain Quadrangle, Nye County, Nevada: U.S. Geological Survey Geologic Quadrangle Map GQ-746, scale 1:24,000.

Paces, J.B., Whelan, J.F., Forester, R.M., Bradbury, J.P., Marshall, B.D., and Mahan, S.A., 1997, Summary of discharge deposits in the Amargosa Valley: U.S. Geological Survey Milestone SPC333M4, 53 p.

Paces, J.B., and Whelan, J.F., 2001, Water-table fluctuations in the Amargosa Desert, Nye County, Nevada, *in* Back to the Future—Managing the back end of the nuclear fuel cycle to create a more secure energy future: Proceedings of the 9th International High-Level Radioactive Waste Management Conference, Las Vegas, Nevada, 29 April–3 May 2001, American Nuclear Society, 4 p.

Parsons, T., Thompson, G.A., and Sleep, N.H., 1994, Mantle plume influence on the Neogene uplift and extension of the U.S. Western Cordillera?: Geology, v. 22, p. 83–86, doi: 10.1130/0091-7613(1994)022<0083: MPIOTN>2.3.CO;2.

Piety, L.A., 1996, Compilation of known or suspected Quaternary faults within 100 km of Yucca Mountain, Nevada and California: U.S. Geological Survey Open-File Report 94-112, 404 p., 2 plates.

Ponce, D.A., Blakely, R.J., Morin, R.L., and Mankinen, E.A., 2001, Isostatic gravity map of the Death Valley groundwater model area, Nevada and California: U.S. Geological Survey Miscellaneous Field Studies Map, MF-2381-C, scale 1:250,000.

Poole, F.G., Elston, D.P., and Carr, W.J., 1965, Geologic map of the Cane Spring Quadrangle, Nye County, Nevada: U.S. Geological Survey Geologic Quadrangle Map GQ-455, scale 1:24,000.

Poole, F.G., Stewart, J.H., Palmer, A.R., Sandberg, C.A., Madrid, R.J., Ross, R.J., Jr., Hintze, L.F., Miller, M.M., and Wrucke, C.T., 1992, Latest Precambrian to latest Devonian time—development of a continental margin, *in* Burchfiel, B.C., Lipman, P.W., and Zoback, M.L., eds., The Cordilleran Orogen—Conterminous U.S.: Geological Society of America, Geology of North America, v. G-3, p. 9–56.

Potter, C.J., Dickerson, R.P., Sweetkind, D.S., and Drake, R.M., II, Taylor, Emily M., Fridrich, C.J., San Juan, C.A., and Day, W.C., 2002a, Geologic map of the Yucca Mountain Region, Nye County, Nevada: U.S. Geological Survey Geologic Investigations Series Map I-2755, scale 1:50,000, 37 p. text.

Potter, C.J., Sweetkind, D.S., Dickerson, R.P., and Killgore, M.L., 2002b, Hydrostructural maps of the Death Valley flow system, Nevada and California: U.S. Geological Survey Miscellaneous Field Studies Map MF-2372, scale 1:350,000.

Potter, C.J., Day, W.C., Sweetkind, D.S., and Dickerson, R.P., 2004, Structural geology of the proposed site for a high-level radioactive waste repository, Yucca Mountain, Nevada: Geological Society of America Bulletin, v. 116, p. 858–879, doi: 10.1130/B25328.1.

Quade, J., Forester, R.M., Pratt, W.L., and Carter, C., 1998, Black mats, spring-fed streams, and late-glacial-age recharge in the southern Great Basin: Quaternary Research, v. 49, p. 129–148, doi: 10.1006/qres.1997.1959.

Quade, J., Forester, R.M., and Whelan, J.F., 2003, Late Quaternary paleohydrology and paleotemperature change in southern Nevada: Geological Society of America Special Paper 368, p. 165–188.

Reheis, M.C., 1993, Neogene tectonism from the Southwestern Nevada Volcanic Field to the White Mountains, California–Part II. Late Cenozoic history of the southern Fish Lake Valley fault zone, Nevada and California, *in* Lahren, M.M., Trexler, J.H., Jr., and Spinosa, C., eds., Crustal Evolution of the Great Basin and the Sierra Nevada: Field Trip Guidebook, 1993 Joint Meeting of the Cordilleran/Rocky Mountain Sections of the Geological Society of America, p. 370–382.

Reheis, M.C., and McKee, E.H., 1991, Late Cenozoic history of slip on the Fish Lake Valley fault zone, Nevada and California, *in* Late Cenozoic Stratigraphy and Tectonics of Fish Lake Valley, Nevada and California—Road Log and Contributions to the Field Trip Guidebook: 1991 Pacific Cell, Friends of the Pleistocene, U.S. Geological Survey Open-File Report 91-290, p. 26–45.

Reheis, M.C., and Noller, J.S., 1991, Aerial photographic interpretation of lineaments and faults in late Cenozoic deposits in the eastern part of the Benton Range 1:100,000 Quadrangle and the Goldfield, Last Chance Range, Beatty, and Death Valley Junction 1:100,000 Quadrangles, Nevada and California: U.S. Geological Survey Open-File Report 90-41, 9 p, 4 plates.

Robinson, G.D., 1985, Structure of pre-Cenozoic rocks in the vicinity of Yucca Mountain, Nye County, Nevada—a potential nuclear-waste disposal site: U.S. Geological Survey Bulletin 1647, 22 p.

Rogers, A.M., Harmsen, S.C., and Carr, W.J., 1981, Southern Great Basin seismological data report for 1980 and preliminary data analysis: U.S. Geological Survey Open-File Report 81-1086, 148 p.

Rogers, A.M., Harmsen, S.C., and Meremonte, M.E., 1987, Evaluation of the seismicity of the southern Great Basin and its relationship to the tectonic framework of the region: U.S. Geological Survey Open-File Report 87-408, 196 p.

Saltus, R.W., and Thompson, G.A., 1995, Why is it downhill from Tonopah to Las Vegas?—A case for mantle plume support of the high northern Basin and Range: Tectonics, v. 14, p. 1235–1244, doi: 10.1029/95TC02288.

Sargent, K.A., and Stewart, J.H., 1971, Geologic map of the Specter Range NW Quadrangle, Nye County, Nevada: U.S. Geological Survey Geologic Quadrangle Map GQ-884, scale 1:24,000.

Savage, J.C., Lisowski, M., Svarc, J.L., and Gross, W.K., 1995, Strain accumulation across the central Nevada seismic zone, 1973–1994: Journal of Geophysical Research, v. 100, p. 20,257–20,269.

Sawyer, D.A., Fleck, R.J., Lanphere, M.A., Warren, R.G., Broxton, D.E., and Hudson, M.R., 1994, Episodic caldera volcanism in the Miocene Southwestern Nevada Volcanic Field–revised stratigraphic framework, $^{40}Ar/^{39}Ar$ geochronology, and implications for magmatism and extension: Geological Society of America Bulletin, v. 106, p. 1304–1318, doi: 10.1130/0016-7606(1994)106<1304:ECVITM>2.3.CO;2.

Sawyer, D.A., Wahl, R.R., Cole, J.C., Minor, S.A., Laczniak, R.J., Warren, R.G., Engle, C.M., and Vega, R.G., 1995, Preliminary digital geological map database of the Nevada Test Site area, Nevada: U.S. Geological Survey Open-File Report 95-0567, 43 p., scale 1:130,000.

Sawyer, T.L., 1991, Quaternary faulting and Holocene paleoseismicity of the northern Fish Lake Valley fault zone, Nevada and California, *in* Guidebook for Field Trip to Fish Lake Valley, California-Nevada: Pacific Cell, Friends of the Pleistocene, 31 May 2 June 1991, p. 114–138.

Scholz, C.H., Barazangi, M., and Sbar, M.L., 1971, Late Cenozoic evolution of the Great Basin, western United States, as an ensialic interarc basin: Geological Society of America Bulletin, v. 82, p. 2979–2990.

Scott, R.B., 1990, Tectonic setting of Yucca Mountain, southwest Nevada, *in* Wernicke, B.P., ed., Basin and Range Extensional Tectonics Near the Latitude of Las Vegas Nevada: Geological Society of America Memoir 176, p. 251–282.

Seedorff, E., 1991, Magmatism, extension, and ore deposits of Eocene to Holocene age in the Great Basin—mutual effects and preliminary proposed genetic relationships, *in* Raines, G.L., Lisle, R.E., Schafer, R.W., and Wilkinson, W.H., eds., Geology and Ore Deposits of the Great Basin: Geological Society of Nevada Symposium Proceedings, v. 1, p. 133–178.

Severinghaus, J., and Atwater, T., 1990, Cenozoic Geometry and thermal state of the subducting slabs beneath western North America, *in* Wernicke, B.P., ed., Basin and Range Extensional Tectonics Near the Latitude of Las Vegas, Nevada: Geological Society of America Memoir 176, p. 1–22.

Sharpe, S.E., 2007, this volume, Using modern through mid-Pleistocene climate to bound future variations in infiltration at Yucca Mountain, Nevada, *in* Stuckless, J.S., and Levich, R.A., eds., The Geology and Climatology of Yucca Mountain and Vicinity, Southern Nevada and California: Geological Society of America Memoir 199, doi: 10.1130/2007.1199(05).

Simonds, F.W., and Scott, R.B., 1996, Geology and Hydrothermal Alteration at Calico Hills, Nye County, Nevada: U.S. Geological Survey Milestone 3GTD018M.

Simonds, F.W., Whitney, J.W., Fox, K.F., Ramelli, A.R., Yount, J.C., Carr, M.D., Menges, C.M., Dickerson, R.P., and Scott, R.B., 1995, Map showing fault activity in the Yucca Mountain area, Nye County, Nevada: U. S. Geological Survey Miscellaneous Investigation Series Map I-2520, scale 1:24,000.

Slate, J.L., and 25 others, 1999, Digital geologic map of the Nevada Test Site and vicinity, Nye, Lincoln, and Clark Counties, Nevada and Inyo County, California: U.S. Geological Survey Open-File Report 99-554-A, plate 1, scale 1:250,000.

Smith, D.L., 1991, Large-magnitude Oligocene extension in central Nevada: Geological Society of America Abstracts with Programs, v. 23, p. A188–A189.

Snow, J.K., 1992, Large-magnitude Permian shortening and continental-margin tectonics in the southern Cordillera: Geological Society of America Bulletin, v. 104, p. 80–105, doi: 10.1130/0016-7606(1992)104<0080: LMPSAC>2.3.CO;2.

Snow, J.K., and Prave, A.R., 1994, Covariance of structural and stratigraphic trends—evidence for anticlockwise rotation within the Walker Lane Belt, Death Valley Region, California and Nevada: Tectonics, v. 13, p. 712–724, doi: 10.1029/93TC02943.

Sonder, L.J., Jones, C.H., Salyards, S.L., and Murphy, K.M., 1994, Vertical axis rotations in the Las Vegas Valley shear zone, Southern Nevada—paleomagnetic constraints on kinematics and dynamics of block rotations: Tectonics, v. 13, p. 769–788, doi: 10.1029/94TC00352.

Spaulding, W.G., 1985, Vegetation and climates of the last 45,000 years in the vicinity of the Nevada Test Site, South-Central Nevada: U.S. Geological Survey Professional Paper 1329, 83 p.

Stamatakos, J.A., Ferrill, D.A., and Spivey, K.H., 1998, Paleomagnetic constraints on the tectonic evolution of Bare Mountain, Nevada: Geological Society of America Bulletin, v. 110, p. 1530–1546, doi: 10.1130/0016-7606(1998)110<1530:PCOTTE>2.3.CO;2.

Stevens, C.H., Stone, P., and Belasky, P., 1991, Paleogeographic and structural significance of an upper Mississippian facies boundary in southern Nevada and east-central California: Geological Society of America Bulletin, v. 103, p. 876–885, doi: 10.1130/0016-7606(1991)103<0876: PASSOA>2.3.CO;2.

Stewart, J.H., 1967, Possible large right-lateral displacement along fault and shear zones in the Death Valley–Las Vegas area, California and Nevada: Geological Society of America Bulletin, v. 78, p. 131–142.

Stewart, J.H., 1970, Upper Precambrian and lower Cambrian strata in the southern Great Basin California and Nevada: U.S. Geological Survey Professional Paper 620, 206 p.

Stewart, J.H., 1978, Basin-Range structure in western North America—a review: Cenozoic Tectonics and Regional Geophysics of the Western Cordillera: Geological Society of America Memoir 152, p. 1–31.

Stewart, J.H., 1980, Geology of Nevada, a discussion to accompany the geologic map of Nevada: Nevada Bureau of Mines and Geology Special Publication 4, 136 p.

Stewart, J.H., 1988, Tectonics of the Walker Lane Belt, western Great Basin: Mesozoic and Cenozoic deformation in a zone of shear, *in* Ernst, W.G., ed., Metamorphism and Crustal Evolution of the Western United States: Prentice-Hall, Rubey Volume 7, p. 683–713.

Stewart, J.H., 1992, Walker Lane Belt, Nevada and California—an overview, *in* Craig, S.D., ed., Structure, Tectonics and Mineralization of the Walker Lane: Geological Society of Nevada, Proceedings Volume, Walker Lane Symposium, 24 April 1992, Reno, Nevada, p. 1–16.

Stewart, J.H., and Carlson, J.E., 1978, Geologic map of Nevada: Denver, Colorado, U.S. Geological Survey, scale 1:500,000.

Stewart, J.H., and Diamond, D.S., 1990, Changing patterns of extensional tectonics—overprinting of the basin of the middle and upper Miocene Esmeralda Formation in western Nevada by younger structural basins, *in* Wernicke, B.P., ed., Basin and Range Extensional Tectonics Near the Latitude of Las Vegas, Nevada: Geological Society of America Memoir 176, p. 447–475.

Stewart, J.H., Moore, W.J., and Zietz, I., 1977, East-west patterns of Cenozoic igneous rocks, aeromagnetic anomalies, and mineral deposits, Nevada and Utah: Geological Society of America Bulletin, v. 88, p. 67–77, doi: 10.1130/0016-7606(1977)88<67:EPOCIR>2.0.CO;2.

Stone, P., and Stevens, C.H., 1986, Triassic marine section at Union Wash, Inyo Mountains, California, *in* Guidebook and Volume, Field Trip Number 2, Mesozoic Evolution of Southern Inyo, Argus and Slate Ranges, Geologic Evolution of Tucki Mountain, Central Panamint Range, Field Trip Number 14, Stratigraphy and Structure of Metamorphic Framework Rocks Lake Isabella Area, Southern Sierra Nevada: Prepared for the 82nd Annual Meeting of the Cordilleran Section of the Geological Society of America, 25–28 March 1986, p. 45–51.

Swadley, W.C., and Carr, W.J., 1987, Geologic map of the Quaternary and Tertiary deposits of the Big Dune Quadrangle, Nye County, Nevada, and Inyo County, California: U.S. Geological Survey Miscellaneous Investigations Series Map I-1767, scale 1:48,000.

Swadley, W.C., and Huckins, H.E., 1990, Geologic map of the surficial deposits of the Skull Mountain Quadrangle, Nye County, Nevada: U.S. Geological Survey Miscellaneous Investigations Series Map I-1972, scale 1:24,000.

Sweetkind, D.S., Dickerson, R.P., Blakely, R.J., and Denning, P.D., 2001, Interpretive geologic cross sections for the Death Valley regional flow system and surrounding areas, Nevada and California: U.S. Geological Survey Miscellaneous Field Studies Map MF-2370, scale 1:250,000.

Taylor, W.J., Bartley, J.M., Fryxell, J.E., Schmitt, J.G., and Vandervoort, D.S., 1993, Tectonic style and regional relations of the central Nevada thrust belt, *in* Lahren, M.M., Trexler, J.H., Jr., and Spinosa, C., eds., Crustal Evolution of the Great Basin and the Sierra Nevada: Field Trip Guidebook for the 1993 Joint Meeting of the Cordilleran/Rocky Mountain Sections of the Geological Society of America, p. 57–96.

Trexler, J.H., Jr., Cole, J.C., and Cashman, P.H., 1996, Middle Devonian–Mississippian stratigraphy on and near the Nevada Test Site—implications for hydrocarbon potential: American Association of Petroleum Geologists Bulletin, v. 80, p. 1736–1762.

Tschanz, C.M., and Pampeyan, E.H., 1970, Geology and mineral deposits of Lincoln County, Nevada: Nevada Bureau of Mines and Geology Bulletin 73, 187 p.

Vaniman, D.T., Crowe, B.M., and Gladney, E.S., 1982, Petrology and geochemistry of hawaiite lavas from Crater Flat, Nevada: Contributions to Mineralogy and Petrology, v. 80, p. 341–357, doi: 10.1007/BF00378007.

Weiss, S.I., Noble, D.C., and McKee, E.H., 1988, Volcanic and tectonic significance of the presence of late Miocene Stonewall Flat Tuff in the vicinity of Beatty, Nevada: Geological Society of America Abstracts with Programs, v. 20, p. A399.

Weiss, S.I., McKee, E.H., Noble, D.C., Connors, K.A., and Jackson, M.R., 1991, Multiple episodes of Au-Ag mineralization in the Bullfrog Hills, SW Nevada, and their relation to coeval extension and volcanism: Geological Society of America Abstracts with Programs, v. 23, p. A246.

Weiss, S.I., Noble, D.C., Worthington, J.E., IV, and McKee, E.H., 1993, Neogene tectonism from the Southwestern Nevada Volcanic Field to the White Mountains, California, Part I. Miocene volcanic stratigraphy, paleotopography, extensional faulting and uplift between northern Death Valley and Pahute Mesa, *in* Lahren, M.M., Trexler, J.H., Jr., and Spinosa, C., eds., Crustal Evolution of the Great Basin and the Sierra Nevada: Field Trip Guidebook for the 1993 Joint Meeting of the Cordilleran/Rocky Mountain Sections of the Geological Society of America, p. 353–369.

Wernicke, B.P., Hodges, K.V., and Walker, J.D., 1986, Geological setting of the Tucki Mountain area, Death Valley National Monument, California: Mesozoic and Cenozoic Structural Evolution of Selected Areas, East-Central California, Geological Society of America Cordilleran Section, 82nd Annual Meeting, Guidebook and Volume, Trips 2 and 14, p. 67–80.

Wernicke, B.P., Christiansen, R.L., England, P.C., and Sonder, L.J., 1987, Tectonomagmatic evolution of Cenozoic extension in the North American Cordillera, *in* Coward, M.P., Dewey, J.F., and Hancock, P.L., eds., Continental Extensional Tectonics: Geological Society of London Special Publication 28, p. 203–221.

Wernicke, B., Snow, J.K., and Walker, J.D., 1988a, Correlation of early Mesozoic thrusts in the southern Great Basin and their possible indication of 250–300 km of Neogene crustal extension, *in* Weide, D.L. and Faber, M.L., eds., This Extended Land—Geological Journeys in the Southern Basin and Range: Geological Society of America, Cordilleran Section Meeting, Field Trip Guidebook [Special Publication No. 2], p. 255–267.

Wernicke, B., Axen, G.J., and Snow, J.K., 1988b, Basin and Range extensional tectonics at the latitude of Las Vegas, Nevada: Geological Society of America Bulletin, v. 100, p. 1738–1757, doi: 10.1130/0016-7606(1988)100<1738:BARETA>2.3.CO;2.

Wernicke, B., Snow, J.K., Hodges, K.V., and Walker, J.D., 1993, Structural constraints on Neogene tectonism in the southern Great Basin, *in* Lahren, M.M., Trexler, J.H., Jr., and Spinosa, C., eds., Crustal Evolution of the Great Basin and the Sierra Nevada: Field Trip Guidebook for the 1993 Joint Meeting of the Cordilleran/Rocky Mountain Sections of the Geological Society of America, p. 453–479.

Wills, C.J., 1989, A neotectonic tour of the Death Valley fault zone, Inyo County: California Geology, v. 42, p. 195–200.

Winograd, I.J., and Thordarson, W., 1975, Hydrogeologic and hydrochemical framework, south-central Great Basin, Nevada-California, with special reference to the Nevada Test Site: U.S. Geological Survey Professional Paper 712-C, 126 p., 3 plates.

Wright, L.A., 1989, Overview of the role of strike-slip and normal faulting in the Neogene history of the region northeast of Death Valley, California-Nevada, *in* Ellis, M.A., ed., Late Cenozoic Evolution of the Southern Great Basin: Selected Papers from the Workshop, Nevada Bureau of Mines and Geology Open-File Report 89-1, p. 1–11.

Wright, L.A., and Troxel, B.W., 1967, Limitations on right-lateral, strike-slip displacement, Death Valley and Furnace Creek fault zones, California: Geological Society of America Bulletin, v. 78, p. 933–950

Wright, L.A., Otten, J.K., and Troxel, B.W., 1974, Turtleback surfaces of Death Valley viewed as phenomena of extensional tectonics: Geology, v. 2, p. 53–54, doi: 10.1130/0091-7613(1974)2<53:TSODVV>2.0.CO;2.

Wright, L.A., Troxel, B.W., Burchfiel, B.C., Chapman, R.H., and Labotka, T.C., 1981, Geologic cross section from the Sierra Nevada to the Las Vegas Valley, eastern California to southern Nevada: Geological Society of America Map and Chart Series MC-28M.

Wright, L.A., Thompson, R.A., Troxel, B.W., Pavlis, T.L., DeWitt, E.H., Otton, J.K., Ellis, M.A., Miller, M.G., and Serpa, L.F., 1991, Cenozoic magmatic and tectonic evolution of the east-central Death Valley Region, California, *in* Walawender, M.J., and Hanan, B.B., eds., Geological Excursions in Southern California and Mexico: Geological Society of America Guidebook, 1991 Annual Meeting, p. 93–127.

Yount, J.C., Shroba, R.R., McMasters, C.R., Huckins, H.E., and Rodriguez, E.A., 1987, Trench logs from a strand of the Rock Valley fault system, Nevada Test Site, Nye County, Nevada: U.S. Geological Survey Miscellaneous Field Studies Map MF-1824, scale 1:450.

Zoback, M.L., Anderson, R.E., and Thompson, G.A., 1981, Cenozoic evolution of the state of stress and style of tectonism of the Basin and Range Province of the western United States: Philosophical Transactions of the Royal Society of London, Series A, (300), p. 407–434.

Manuscript Accepted by the Society 18 October 2006

APPENDIX 1. SUSPECTED QUATERNARY FAULTS WITHIN THE YUCCA MOUNTAIN REGION

Minimum distance to Yucca Mountain Proposed Repository (km)	Fault name	Documented Quaternary displacement	Maximum fault length (km)
0	Ghost Dance	No?	7
0	Sundance	No?	0.75
1	Solitario Canyon	Yes	>21
1.5	Drill Hole Wash	No?	4
2	Dune Wash	No?	3
2.5	Bow Ridge	Yes	11.5
2.5	Pagany Wash	No?	4
2.5	Iron Ridge	Yes	9
2.5	Boomerang Point	No?	5
3	Sever Wash	No?	4
3	Midway Valley	Yes?	13
3.5	Fatigue Wash	Yes	17
4	Paintbrush Canyon	Yes	19
4.5	Windy Wash	Yes	25
6	Crater Flat	Yes	20
8	Stagecoach Road	Yes	7
14	Bare Mountain	Yes	20
8.5	Black Cone	Yes	7
19	Rocket Wash-Beatty Wash	Yes?	17
19	Mine Mountain	Yes?	27
22	Wahmonie	Yes?	15
24	Oasis Valley	Yes?	20
27	Rock Valley	Yes	65
29	Cane Spring	No?	27
33	West Specter Range	Yes	9
34	Ash Meadows	Yes	60
36	Yucca Lake	Yes?	17
37	Eleana Range	Yes	13
38	Amargosa River	Yes	15
38	Bullfrog Hills	Yes?	7
40	Yucca	Yes	32
42	Tolicha Pass	Yes?	22
43	Keane Wonder	Yes	25
43	Carpetbag	Yes	30
44	Area Three	Yes?	12
44	Checkpoint Pass	No?	8
46	Plutonium Valley–Halfpint Ridge	No?	26
48	Crossgrain Valley	Yes?	9
48	Pahute Mesa	Yes?	9
48	Mercury Ridge	No?	10
50	Furnace Creek	Yes	145
49	Ranger Mountain	Yes?	5
50	South Ridge	Yes?	19
52	Sarcobatus Flat	Yes?	51
51	Boundary	Yes	7
53	Buried Hills	Yes?	26
53	West Spring Mountains	Yes	60
53	Cockeyed Ridge-Papoose Lake	Yes?	21
55	Death Valley	Yes	100
55	Belted Range	Yes	54
57	Kawich Range	Yes	84
57	Oak Springs	Yes?	21
58	Grapevine	Yes	20
59	Spotted Range	Yes?	30
59	Cactus Springs	Yes?	14

(continued)

APPENDIX 1. SUSPECTED QUATERNARY FAULTS WITHIN THE YUCCA MOUNTAIN REGION (*continued*)

Minimum distance to Yucca Mountain Proposed Repository (km)	Fault name	Documented Quaternary displacement	Maximum fault length (km)
60	Emigrant Valley North	Yes?	28
60	Gold Flat	Yes?	16
61	Kawich Valley	Yes?	43
66	Emigrant Valley South	Yes?	20
65	Chert Ridge	Yes?	14
67	Indian Springs Valley	Yes?	28
67	Grapevine Mountains	Yes?	31
70	Pahrump	Yes	70
70	Fallout Hills	Yes?	8
74	Bonnie Claire	Yes?	27
74	Stumble	Yes?	33
76	West Pintwater Range	Yes	82
76	Towne Pass	Yes	38
77	Jumbled Hills	Yes?	27
80	Cactus Flat–Mellan	Yes?	35
81	East Pintwater Range	Yes?	58
81	North Desert Range	Yes?	24
82	La Madre	Yes?	33
84	Cactus Flat	Yes?	50
82	Groom Range Central	Yes?	31
84	Three Lakes Valley	No?	27
85	Groom Range East	No?	20
87	Cactus Range–Wellington Hills	No?	29
87	Chalk Mountain	Yes?	20
90	Chicago Valley	Yes	20
90	Tin Mountain	Yes	29
92	Tikaboo	Yes	33
92	Stonewall Mountain	Yes	22
95	Hunter Mountain	Yes	85
95	Panamint Valley	Yes	100
97	Penoyer	Yes	56
97	Racetrack Valley	Yes?	22
106	Pahranagat	Yes	91
126	Owens Valley	Yes	110
135	Fish Lake Valley	Yes	83
150	Garlock	Yes	251

Note: From Potter et al. (2002b), Simonds et al. (1995), Day et al. (1998), Piety (1996), and Keefer et al., (2004). No? is used when no evidence for movement was found, but where early Quaternary material, which might have indicated displacement, was not present. Yes? is used when the evidence is equivocal.

Geological Society of America
Memoir 199
2007

Geology of the Yucca Mountain site area, southwestern Nevada

William R. Keefer
John W. Whitney
U.S. Geological Survey, Box 25046, Denver Federal Center, Denver, Colorado 80225, USA

David C. Buesch
U.S. Geological Survey, 1180 Town Center Drive, Las Vegas, Nevada 89144, USA

ABSTRACT

Yucca Mountain in southwestern Nevada is a prominent, irregularly shaped upland formed by a thick apron of Miocene pyroclastic-flow and fallout tephra deposits, with minor lava flows, that was segmented by through-going, large-displacement normal faults into a series of north-trending, eastwardly tilted structural blocks. The principal volcanic-rock units are the Tiva Canyon and Topopah Spring Tuffs of the Paintbrush Group, which consist of volumetrically large eruptive sequences derived from compositionally distinct magma bodies in the nearby southwestern Nevada volcanic field, and are classic examples of a magmatic zonation characterized by an upper crystal-rich (>10% crystal fragments) member, a more voluminous lower crystal-poor (<5% crystal fragments) member, and an intervening thin transition zone. Rocks within the crystal-poor member of the Topopah Spring Tuff, lying some 280 m below the crest of Yucca Mountain, constitute the proposed host rock to be excavated for the storage of high-level radioactive wastes.

Separation of the tuffaceous rock formations into subunits that allow for detailed mapping and structural interpretations is based on macroscopic features, most importantly the relative abundance of lithophysae and the degree of welding. The latter feature, varying from nonwelded through partly and moderately welded to densely welded, exerts a strong control on matrix porosities and other rock properties that provide essential criteria for distinguishing hydrogeologic and thermal-mechanical units, which are of major interest in evaluating the suitability of Yucca Mountain to host a safe and permanent geologic repository for waste storage.

A thick and varied sequence of surficial deposits mantle large parts of the Yucca Mountain site area. Mapping of these deposits and associated soils in exposures and in the walls of trenches excavated across buried faults provides evidence for multiple surface-rupturing events along all of the major faults during Pleistocene and Holocene times; these paleoseismic studies form the basis for evaluating the potential for future earthquakes and fault displacements. Thermoluminescence and U-series analyses were used to date the surficial materials involved in the Quaternary faulting events.

Keefer, W.R., Whitney, J.W., and Buesch, D.C., 2007, Geology of the Yucca Mountain site area, southwestern Nevada, *in* Stuckless, J.S., and Levich, R.A., eds., The Geology and Climatology of Yucca Mountain and Vicinity, Southern Nevada and California: Geological Society of America Memoir 199, p. 53–103, doi: 10.1130/2007.1199(03). For permission to copy, contact editing@geosociety.org. ©2007 Geological Society of America. All rights reserved.

The rate of erosional downcutting of bedrock on the ridge crests and hillslopes of Yucca Mountain, being of particular concern with respect to the potential for breaching of the proposed underground storage facility, was studied by using rock varnish cation-ratio and ^{10}Be and ^{36}Cl cosmogenic dating methods to determine the length of time bedrock outcrops and hillslope boulder deposits were exposed to cosmic rays, which then served as a basis for calculating long-term erosion rates. The results indicate rates ranging from 0.04 to 0.27 cm/k.y., which represent the maximum downcutting along the summit of Yucca Mountain under all climatic conditions that existed there during most of Quaternary time. Associated studies include the stratigraphy of surficial deposits in Fortymile Wash, the major drainage course in the area, which record a complex history of four to five cut-and-fill cycles within the channel during middle to late Quaternary time. The last 2–4 m of incision probably occurred during the last pluvial climatic period, 22–18 ka, followed by aggradation to the present time.

Major faults at Yucca Mountain—from east to west, the Paintbrush Canyon, Bow Ridge, Stagecoach Road, Solitario Canyon, Fatigue Wash, Windy Wash, and Northern and Southern Crater Flat Faults—trend predominantly north, are spaced 1–5 km apart, have bedrock displacements ranging from 125 m to as much as 500 m, and exhibit Quaternary movements of several centimeters to a few meters. Displacements are predominantly down to the west, and bedrock/alluvium contacts commonly are marked by fault-line scarps. The predominant northerly fault trend changes to a more northeasterly trend in adjacent areas south of the site area owing to clockwise vertical-axis rotation. Structural blocks between the block-bounding faults are internally deformed by numerous minor faults, some oriented northwest and exhibiting strike-slip movements.

Investigations to determine the natural resource potential of the Yucca Mountain area—metallic minerals, industrial rocks and minerals, hydrocarbon and other energy resources, and geothermal resources—resulted in findings indicating that a given commodity either (1) is not known to exist in the area, or (2) is present in such low concentrations as to be noneconomic.

Keywords: Yucca Mountain, geologic repository, high-level radioactive waste, southwestern Nevada volcanic field, volcanic stratigraphy, Quaternary geology, structural blocks, faults.

INTRODUCTION

Geologic and related investigations at Yucca Mountain in southwestern Nevada focus on a rectangular area of some 165 km^2 (65 mi^2) that covers the central part of the mountain (Fig. 1) and is informally referred to as the "site area" with respect to the proposed geologic repository for high-level radioactive wastes. Geologic mapping at various scales and detailed stratigraphic and structural studies have been conducted there, and in adjacent areas such as contiguous parts of the Nevada Test Site to the east, since the 1960s, and then were pursued with increased effort since the late 1980s as an integral part of a broad, interdisciplinary characterization program designed to comprehensively evaluate the suitability of the site to host a safe and permanent high-level radioactive waste-storage facility (U.S. Department of Energy, 1988). A synthesis of the principal results of these and associated studies, many of which have been published, is presented in this report.

PHYSIOGRAPHY AND GEOMORPHOLOGY

Physiographic Setting of Yucca Mountain and Vicinity

Yucca Mountain lies in the south-central part of the Great Basin that forms the northern subprovince of the Basin and Range physiographic province (Stuckless and O'Leary, this volume, Fig. 1 therein). More specifically, Yucca Mountain occupies part of the Walker Lane belt, a major structural lineament considered to be a zone of transition between (1) the central and southeastern parts of the Great Basin, characterized by dip-slip normal faulting and typical basin and range topography; and (2) the southwestern Great Basin, typified by dip-slip and strike-slip faulting and irregular topography (Carr, 1984; see O'Leary, this volume). Yucca Mountain itself is situated on the south flank of the southwestern Nevada volcanic field (Fig. 2; also, see Stuckless and O'Leary, this volume, Fig. 9 therein), which consists of a series of volcanic centers from which large

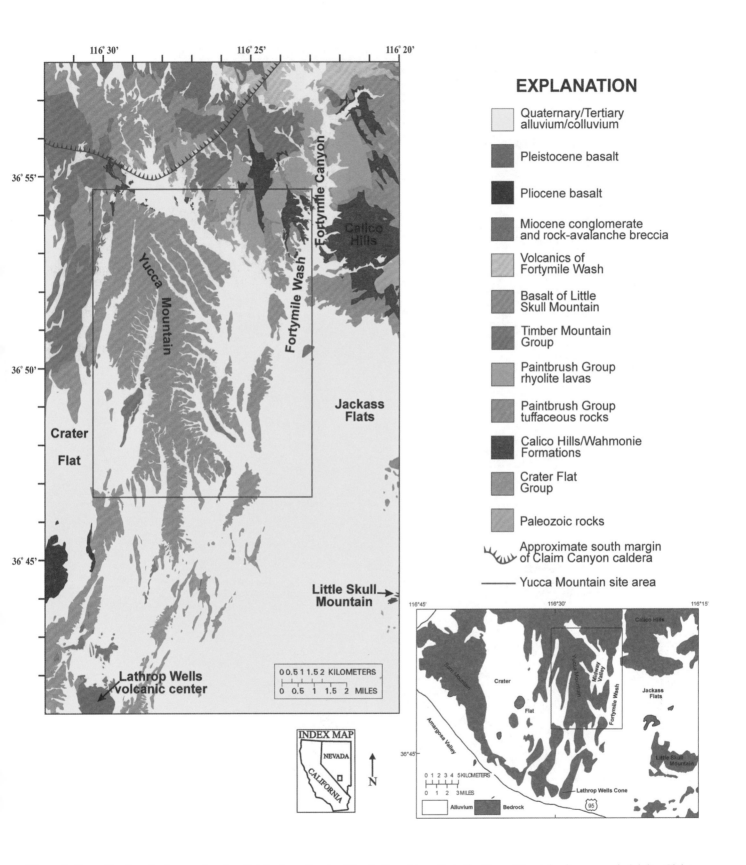

Figure 1. Generalized geologic map showing distribution of major lithostratigraphic units in the Yucca Mountain site area and vicinity. Claim Canyon caldera is in southern part of the southwestern Nevada volcanic field. Modified from Potter et al. (2002a).

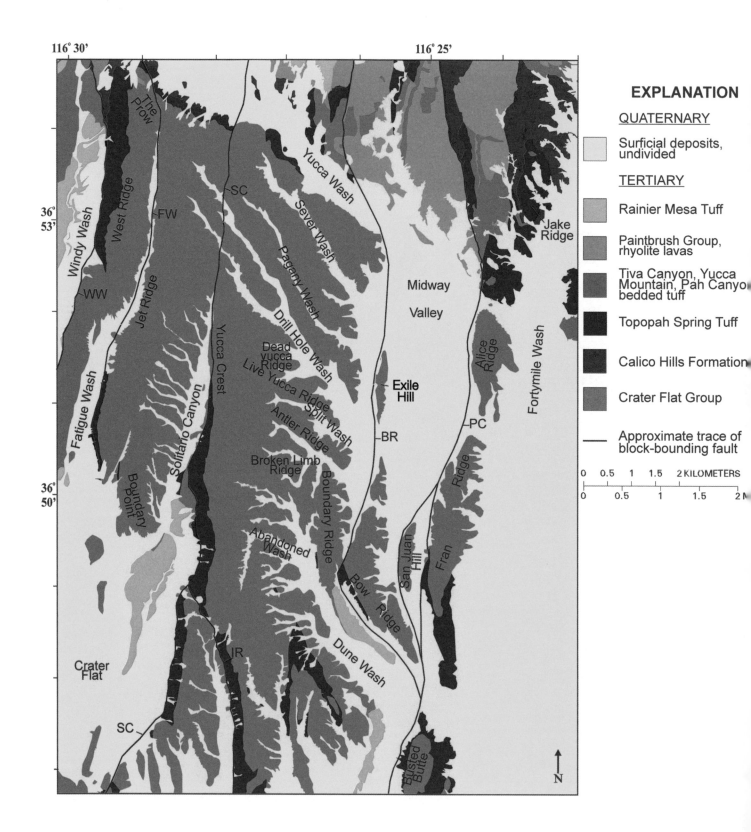

Figure 2. Map of Yucca Mountain site area showing distribution of principal stratigraphic units, major faults, and locations of geographic features named in text. Faults shown with solid lines, although some segments are concealed or inferred beneath Quaternary deposits. Labeled faults: BR—Bow Ridge; FW—Fatigue Wash; IR—Iron Ridge; PC—Paintbrush Canyon; SC—Solitario Canyon; WW—Windy Wash. Generalized from Day et al. (1998a).

volumes of pyroclastic flow and fallout tephra deposits were erupted from ca. 14.0–11.4 Ma (Byers et al., 1976; Sawyer et al., 1994). Accordingly, the mountain and many of the adjacent landforms carry the imprint of the area's extensive volcanic history and its deformational history.

The area surrounding Yucca Mountain can be divided into several clearly defined physiographic elements that combine to produce a variable and diverse terrain typical of the Walker Lane belt (Stewart, 1988; also, see Stuckless and O'Leary, this volume, Fig. 2 therein). Three of these—Yucca Mountain and the flanking landforms to the east and west, Fortymile Wash and Crater Flat, respectively (Fig. 1)—are described below.

Yucca Mountain

Yucca Mountain is a prominent, irregularly shaped upland, 3–8 km wide and ~35 km long, that stretches from near Beatty Wash at the northwest end to near the north edge of the Amargosa Desert at the south end (Stuckless and O'Leary, this volume, Fig. 2 therein). The crest of the mountain reaches elevations of 1500–1930 m, ~125–275 m higher than the floors of adjacent washes and lowlands. The dominantly north-trending pattern of structural blocks characterizing this prominent upland area is controlled by high-angle block-bounding faults (Scott and Bonk, 1984; Day et al., 1998a; Potter et al., 2004) with vertical displacements of several hundred meters in places. The fault blocks, which consist of volcanic rocks of Miocene age, are tilted eastward, so that the fault-bounded, west-facing slopes are generally high and steep in contrast to the more gentle and commonly deeply dissected east-facing slopes (Fig. 3). The valleys generally are narrow and V-shaped along their upper and middle reaches, but locally contain flat, alluviated floors in their lower reaches. Drainage from the west flank of the mountain flows southward down narrow, fault-controlled canyons and out into Crater Flat; drainage from the east flank flows southeastward down Yucca, Drill Hole, and Dune Washes into Fortymile Wash (Fig. 2).

Crater Flat

Crater Flat, flanked by Bare Mountain on the west and Yucca Mountain on the east, is a structural basin ~24 km long and 6–11 km wide (Stuckless and O'Leary, this volume, Fig. 2 therein). The basin has the overall form of a graben (or, more appropriately, a half-graben), its west side having been downdropped several kilometers along the east-dipping Bare Mountain fault and its east side downdropped a few hundred meters along a series of west-dipping normal faults that form the west slope of Yucca Mountain (Carr, 1984; Simonds et al., 1995; Fridrich, 1999). The axial part of the basin floor, covered by alluvial deposits that overlie a thick (as much as 3 km) sequence of Late Cenozoic volcanic rocks, rises gradually from altitudes of ~840 m at the south end to as much as 1280 m at the foot of Yucca Mountain to the north. Four basaltic vents and their associated lava flows form prominent cones that attain heights ranging from 27 to 140 m above the alluviated surface of the central basin area.

Fortymile Wash

Fortymile Wash drains the area east and northeast of Yucca Mountain. From its northern headwaters, it flows southward through the 300 m deep Fortymile Canyon that enters the northeast corner of the site area, continues down the south-sloping piedmont that forms the west end of Jackass Flats, and cuts a nearly linear trench, 150–600 m wide and as much as 25 m deep, into the Quaternary alluvial deposits of the piedmont (Fig. 1). This entrenchment gradually decreases downslope until the wash merges with the general level of the piedmont near the northeast margin of the Amargosa Desert basin.

Other Topographic Features

Three buttes or ridges (Busted Butte and Fran and Alice Ridges) and an alluvial flat (Midway Valley) form prominent topographic features on the east side of Yucca Mountain, and two narrow linear drainage courses (Solitario Canyon and Fatigue Wash) lie to the west. Busted Butte, Fran Ridge, and Alice Ridge (Fig. 2) are faulted bedrock areas rising 110–200 m above the surrounding terrain. Midway Valley, lying between these features and the east slope of Yucca Mountain to the west, is an alluviated lowland that slopes gently eastward from an elevation of ~1220 m in its northwestern part to 1070 m at a low point between Alice and Fran Ridges. Tributaries to Fortymile Wash head in northwest-trending washes along the east slope of Yucca Mountain, the most prominent of which is Yucca Wash (Fig. 2), and flow eastward across Midway Valley. A number of other washes are incised features toward the south end of Yucca Mountain, the largest being Dune Wash.

Drainages in Solitario Canyon and Fatigue Wash rise in upland areas in the northern part of Yucca Mountain at elevations of ~1425 m and 1675 m, respectively, and flow southward into northeastern Crater Flat, where elevations are ~1200 m. The two valleys have been incised some 175–275 m into bedrock, and are fault-controlled (Day et al., 1998a). The north end of a third fault-controlled valley, Windy Wash, also extends into the northwestern part of the site area (Fig. 2). The associated faults (with the same names as the valleys) are discussed in the section "Structural Geology."

Geomorphology

Influence of Tectonism and Quaternary Faulting

As indicated earlier, Yucca Mountain is characterized by a series of fault blocks bounded by subparallel north-striking, primarily dip-slip faults that transect a broad apron of Miocene volcanic rocks and give rise to linear valleys and ridges such as the crest of Yucca Mountain and the adjoining Solitario Canyon (Fig. 2). Fault scarps, commonly visible along these faults, generally are located between the bedrock footwall and Quaternary colluvium on the hanging wall. Because the exposed volcanic rocks weather slowly, many scarps appear sharp, with fault dips of 55° to 75° (Fig. 4). A pattern of enhanced erosion at the base of some scarps near channels and rills indicates that they have

Figure 3. Low-oblique aerial photograph looking southeast across Yucca Mountain, with floor of Solitario Canyon in foreground. Note scarp-like nature of west slope of Yucca Mountain and the dissected terrain across the gently sloping east side. Light-colored band toward top of west slope is the Paintbrush Tuff nonwelded hydrogeologic unit (PTn), which here is ~30 m (100 ft) thick, and underlying ledge is top of densely welded subzone of the vitric zone of the crystal-rich member of the Topopah Spring Tuff. Crest of Yucca Mountain is ~215 m (700 ft) above floor of Solitario Canyon. Photo courtesy of D.W. Wehner, Bechtel-SAIC Corp. Ltd.

been noticeably enhanced by hillslope erosion and, in essence, are fault-line scarps.

Several of the block-bounding faults show evidence of Quaternary displacements, which (1) influenced depositional patterns of surficial materials on hillslopes and on adjacent valley or basin floors, and (2) in places produced visible scarps in bedrock outcrops and surficial deposits along some fault traces. However, low rates of offset and long recurrence intervals between successive faulting events on faults in the site area during Quaternary time (slip rates: 0.002 to 0.02 mm/yr; recurrence intervals: 20 to >100 k.y.; see Keefer et al., 2004) have resulted in subtle landforms and contributed to the preservation of early and middle Pleistocene deposits on Yucca Mountain hillslopes (Whitney and Harrington, 1993).

A striking feature of Yucca Mountain hillslopes is the lack of well-defined, rounded alluvial fans at the base of the slopes. On the west side of Yucca Mountain, hillslopes are of nearly uniform gradients, decreasing gradually from 32° near ridge tops to ~15° near the base, because of the homogeneous nature of the underlying volcanic tuff at the ridge crest, and because the low rates of uplift have not caused oversteepened slopes or high relief. As a result, the lower slopes of Yucca Mountain appear more like pediments than alluvial fans, which is most evident where lower and middle Pleistocene deposits are truncated and overlain by a veneer (<1 m thick) of upper Pleistocene-Holocene alluvium and eolian deposits.

Influence of Volcanism

Bedrock in the Yucca Mountain site area is composed entirely of volcanic outflow sheets whose caldera sources lay north of the site area. Much of the original morphology of this giant sheet of pyroclastic flows and fallout tephra that covered the area of Yucca Mountain and vicinity is no longer preserved, having been broken and segmented by subsequent faulting. A general south-

Figure 4. View looking south along west-facing scarp of the Windy Wash fault. Photograph courtesy of C.J. Potter, U.S. Geological Survey.

ward decrease in elevation may reflect, in part, the regional depositional gradient away from the nearby volcanic centers to the north (Fig. 1). With respect to the volcanic rock sequences now exposed in the site area, differing characteristics between units, particularly the degree of welding, impart varying resistances to erosion, locally creating subdued bench-like topography (Fig. 3). However, the nonwelded, less resistant units commonly are thin compared to the welded, more resistant units, so the effect of differential erosion is of relatively minor geomorphic importance.

Influence of Climate

The effects of climate on the evolution of landforms and on patterns of deposition and erosion at Yucca Mountain are discussed in the section on "Quaternary Geology." Although the present-day climate is dominated by warm, dry conditions, there is evidence that wetter, cooler conditions existed at times in the past (see Sharpe, this volume). Such climate changes could take place at some future time.

STRATIGRAPHY OF THE VOLCANIC ROCKS

Introduction

Mid-Tertiary volcanic rocks, consisting mostly of pyroclastic-flow and fallout tephra deposits with minor lava flows,

dominate the exposed bedrock formations in the Yucca Mountain site area (Fig. 2). Several published descriptive and interpretive reports (for example, Sawyer et al., 1994; Buesch et al., 1996) defined what is now generally recognized as the standard hierarchical sequence of named units and subunits composing the principal volcanic rock groups and formations. The detailed order (and descriptions) of both major and minor subdivisions is given in CRWMS M&O (2000, Tables 4.5-1 and 4.5-2 therein); a summary table listing the succession, general lithologies, and thicknesses of major units is presented in Table 1.

General Features

Division of formations into lithostratigraphic units was initially proposed for the thick tuff sequences in the Yucca Mountain area by Warren et al. (1989). Buesch et al. (1996) applied this terminology in greater detail after close examination and analysis of many samples collected from outcrops and from borehole cores within the site area. In general, the individual formations represent either volumentrically large eruptive units or a series of products interpreted to have formed from compositionally distinct magma bodies in the southwestern Nevada volcanic field. The Tiva Canyon and Topopah Spring Tuffs of the Paintbrush Group (Table 1), which are the most widespread bedrock units at Yucca Mountain, are classic examples of a

Group	Formation/Unit		Thickness in site area[1] (m)	General lithology	Correlative Units	
					Hydrogeologic[2]	Thermal-Mechanical[3]
Timber Mountain	Ammonia Tanks Tuff		Not present in site area	Welded to nonwelded rhyolite tuff	Unconsolidated surficial material	Undifferentiated overburden
	Rainier Mesa Tuff		Generally <30	High-silica rhyolite and quartz latite tuffs		
	Pre–Rainier Mesa Tuff bedded tuff		17[4]	Nonlithified pyroclastic-flow deposits		
Paintbrush	Rhyolite of Comb Peak		≤130	Rhyolite lava flows and related tephra; pyroclastic-flow deposits		
	Tuff Unit "X"		6–23[5]			
	Rhyolite of Vent Pass		0–150			
	Post–Tiva Canyon Tuff bedded tuff		<2–4.5	Pyroclastic-flow and fallout tephra deposits		
	Tiva Canyon Tuff	Crystal-rich member	<50–175	Compositionally zoned (rhyolite to quartz latite) tuff sequence; each member divided into several zones and subzones[6]	_____ a _____ Tiva Canyon welded _____ b _____	_____ a _____ Tiva Canyon welded _____ b _____
		Crystal-poor member				
	Pre–Tiva Canyon Tuff bedded tuff		<1–3[7]	Pyroclastic fallout tephra deposits with thin weathered zones	Paintbrush Tuff nonwelded (PTn)	Paintbrush Tuff nonwelded (PTn)
	Yucca Mountain Tuff		0–55	Nonwelded to densely welded pyroclastic-flow deposit		
	Rhyolite of Black Glass Canyon		2–14	Rhyolite lava flows and related tephra		
	Rhyolite of Delirium Canyon		≤250 (lava) ≤100 (ash flows)			
	Rhyolite of Zig Zag Hill		≤10			
	Pre–Yucca Mountain Tuff bedded tuff		<1–46[7]	Nonwelded pyroclastic-flow deposits		
	Pah Canyon Tuff		0–79	Pyroclastic-flow deposits; abundant large pumice clasts		
	Pre–Pah Canyon Tuff bedded tuff		3–10[7]	Vitric to devitrified and altered fallout tephra and ash-flow tuff		
	Topopah Spring Tuff	Crystal-rich member	0–381	Compositionally zoned (rhyolite to quartz latite) tuff sequence; each member divided into several zones and subzones[6]. Potential repository host rock is within crystal-poor member[8]	_____ c _____ Topopah Spring welded _____ d _____	_____ c _____ Topopah Spring welded[9] _____ d _____
		Crystal-poor member				
	Pre–Topopah Spring Tuff bedded tuff		0–17[7]	Bedded tuffaceous deposits		
	Calico Hills Formation		15–457	Rhyolite tuffs and lavas; contains five pyroclastic units	Calico Hills nonwelded	Calico Hills and lower Paintbrush nonwelded
	Pre–Calico Hills Formation bedded tuff		9–39[7]	Pyroclastic-flow and coarse-grained fallout deposits		

(continued)

Group	Formation/Unit	Thickness in Site Area[1] (m)	General Lithology	Correlative Units	
				Hydrogeologic[2]	Thermal-Mechanical[3]
Crater Flat	Prow Pass Tuff	15–194	Includes four variably welded pyroclastic-flow deposits	Calico Hills nonwelded or Crater Flat unit	———— e ———— Prow Pass welded[10]
	Pre–Prow Pass Tuff bedded tuff	<1–3.5[7]	Pumiceous tuffs and pyroclastic-flow deposits		Upper Crater Flat nonwelded[11]
	Bullfrog Tuff	15–366	Includes two pyroclastic-flow deposits separated by a pumiceous fallout unit		Bullfrog welded[12]
	Pre–Bullfrog Tuff bedded tuff	6–11[7]	Pyroclastic-flow deposits with thin zones of fallout tephra		Middle Crater Flat nonwelded[13]
	Tram Tuff	0–370	Pyroclastic-flow deposits and bedded tuffs		Tram welded[14]
	Pre–Tram Tuff bedded tuff	0–21[7]	Pyroclastic-flow and fallout deposits	Units not defined	Units not defined
	Dacitic lava and flow breccia	111–249[15]	Dacitic lavas and flow breccia; bedded tuff at base		
	Lithic Ridge Tuff	185–304[16]	Pyroclastic-flow deposit		
	Pre–Lithic Ridge Tuff volcanic rocks	45–350+[17]	Pyroclastic-flow deposits and bedded tuffs		

Notes:

[1] Thickness based on identification of formation tops in some 50 boreholes by R.W. Spengler and D.C. Buesch (unpublished data, U.S. Geological Survey), unless otherwise indicated.

[2] Arnold et al. (1995); Flint (1998).

[3] Ortiz et al. 1985.

[4] Thickness in boreholes UE-25 NRG-#2C and UE-25 NRG-42D.

[5] Thicknesses in boreholes near Exile Hill.

[6] Member subdivisions described in Table 4.5.2 of CRWMS M&O 2000, based principally on Buesch et al. (1996).

[7] Thicknesses in the seven boreholes shown in Figures 10 and 11.

[8] Potential repository host rock includes upper lithophysal (lower part), middle nonlithophysal, lower lithophysal, and lower nonlithophysal zones of crystal-poor member of the Topopah Spring Tuff.

[9] Thermal-mechanical Topopah Spring welded unit is divided into lithophysae-rich (upper), lithophysae-poor (middle) and vitrophyre (base) units.

[10] Thermal-mechanical Prow Pass welded unit includes upper part of welded pyroclastic-flow deposit of the Prow Pass Tuff.

[11] Thermal-mechanical Upper Crater Flat nonwelded unit includes the lower part of the welded pyroclastic-flow deposit and underlying units of the Prow Pass Tuff, the pre-Prow Pass bedded tuff, and the upper pyroclastic-flow deposit of the Bullfrog Tuff.

[12] Thermal-mechanical Bullfrog welded unit includes pumiceous fallout unit and upper part of lower pyroclastic-flow deposit of the Bullfrog Tuff.

[13] Thermal-mechanical Middle Crater Flat nonwelded unit includes the lower part of the lower pyroclastic-flow deposit of the Bullfrog Tuff, the pre-Bullfrog Tuff bedded tuff, and the upper part of the lithic-poor unit of the Tram Tuff.

[14] Thermal-mechanical Tram welded unit includes lower part of the lithic-poor unit and underlying units of the Tram Tuff.

[15] Thickness in borehole USW H-6.

[16] Thickness in borehole USW G-3.

[17] Thickness in borehole USW G-2.

Labeled Stratigraphic Horizons:

[a] Contact between moderately welded (above) and densely welded (below) subzones of the vitric zone of the crystal-rich member of the Tiva Canyon Tuff.

[b] Contact between lower nonlithophysal (above) and vitric (below) zones of the crystal-poor member of the Tiva Canyon Tuff.

[c] Contact between moderately welded (above) and densely welded (below) subzones of the vitric zone of the crystal-rich member of the Topopah Spring Tuff.

[d] Contact between densely welded (above) and moderately welded (below) subzones of the vitric zone of the crystal-poor member of the Topopah Spring Tuff; coincides closely with "vitric-zeolitic" boundary mentioned in text.

[e] Contact between pyroxene-rich (above) and welded pyroclastic-flow deposits (below) in upper part of Prow Pass Tuff.

compositional zonation characterized by an upper crystal-rich (>10% crystal fragments) member and a more voluminous, lower crystal-poor (<5% crystal fragments) member (Lipman et al., 1966). A transition zone in crystal abundance, typically 5–10 m thick, is included as a basal unit of the crystal-rich member (Buesch et al., 1996). Lipman et al. (1966) attributed the zoning to fractional crystallization such that the upper part of the magma chamber had evolved to a rhyolitic composition that was the first magma erupted and thus formed the crystal-poor basal part of each ash-flow sheet. Eruption from successively deeper parts of the chambers then produced less siliceous ejecta with a higher proportion of crystals, which formed the crystal-rich upper part of an ash-flow sheet with a quartz-latite composition. Many of the interstratified bedded tuffs and local lava flows that are distinct from overlying and underlying formations (Table 1) probably represent small-volume eruptions.

Criteria for Differentiating Volcanic Rock Units at Yucca Mountain

In the Yucca Mountain area, separation of formations into subunits is based on macroscopic features (for example, degree of welding) of the rocks as they appear in outcrops and borehole cores (Buesch et al., 1996). Their identification is augmented by quantitative mineralogy (Bish and Chipera, 1986; Chipera et al., 1995), borehole geophysics (Muller and Kibler, 1984; Nelson et al., 1991; Nelson, 1996; CRWMS M&O, 1996), rock properties such as density and porosity (Martin et al., 1994, 1995; Moyer et al., 1996; Flint, 1998), and geochemical composition (Spengler and Peterman, 1991; Peterman and Futa, 1996).

Much of the following discussion focuses on the Tiva Canyon and Topopah Spring Tuffs, because each contains rock sequences that exhibit a range of properties that readily provides a basis for detailed stratigraphic subdivision.

Lithologic and Rock-Property Criteria

Important lithologic and rock-property criteria for differentiating the volcanic-rock units include (1) variations in grain size and sorting, (2) relative abundance of volcanic glass (vitric compared to devitrified), (3) degree of welding, (4) types and degree of crystallization, (5) relative abundance of lithophysae, (6) amount and types of glass alteration, and (7) fracture characteristics. Many of these rock properties are graphically portrayed in Figure 5 with respect to different zones within the Tiva Canyon and Topopah Spring Tuffs.

The lithologic and rock property criteria listed above, as well as their respective applications toward subdividing formations and members of formations at Yucca Mountain, were discussed in detail by Buesch et al. (1996). Of these, two are especially important for distinguishing zones and subzones within the volcanic sequences: (1) the presence or absence of lithophysae, which are features used to define some of the principal zones, particularly within the Tiva Canyon and Topopah Spring Tuffs (Fig. 5), and are closely associated with variously welded units; and (2) the degree of welding (Fig. 6), a property that distinguishes many subzones and also provides a principal means of separating hydrogeologic and thermal-mechanical units based on whether they are nonwelded, partially welded, moderately welded, or densely welded zones (Table 1). Such zones are vertically distributed in a single cooling unit of ash-flow tuff, with nonwelded rocks at the top and bottom of the deposit and increasingly welded rocks toward the center (Smith, 1960a, 1960b; see Fig. 5). Relatively thick deposits, such as the Tiva Canyon and Topopah Spring Tuffs, may have the complete welding range, both laterally and vertically (see below), but thin deposits may lack the more highly welded parts. In general, the degree of welding controls porosity, which ranges from 45 to 65% for nonwelded rocks, 25–45% for partially welded rocks, 10–25% for moderately welded rocks, and <10% for densely welded rocks (Buesch, 2000). The degree of welding is therefore of considerable importance to studies of the hydrogeologic and thermal-mechanical properties of the volcanic rock units in the site area (see Flint, 1998; Ciancia and Heiken, 2006).

Mineralogic Criteria

Mineralogy also is important in defining lithostratigraphic units in the site area. As shown in Figure 5, Buesch et al. (1996) observed several crystallization and alteration zones within the Tiva Canyon and Topopah Spring Tuffs. (Note: use of term "zone" in this context is not to be construed as having the same connotation as its use in defining principal formational subdivisions.) The temporal progression of crystallization and alteration in tuffs is well illustrated by the Topopah Spring Tuff. Following eruption and emplacement, the upper and lower parts of the ash flow cooled rapidly, preserving thin nonwelded vitric margins. Glassy parts between these vitric margins and the central devitrified mass retained enough heat to compact and weld, but not crystallize, and became densely welded vitrophyres within the upper and lower vitric zones. The interior of the cooling mass, some 90% of the total volume, retained sufficient heat to promote crystallization of all the glass, thus forming the devitrified, welded core of the formation. The release of water vapor during the crystallization process led to the crystallization of vapor-phase minerals along early-formed fractures and within pockets formed by gas expansion (lithophysal cavities). Vapor-phase minerals are dominantly feldspars and silica minerals, especially tridymite, some of which was subsequently pseudomorphed by quartz.

Phenocryst content in Yucca Mountain tuffs ranges from less than 1 vol% to as much as ~25% (the highest percentages are in the bedded tuff at the base of the Calico Hills Formation and the upper part of the Bullfrog Tuff); lithic fragments average a few vol% (Byers et al., 1976; Broxton et al., 1993). Quartz-latitic units have consistently high phenocryst abundances, but rhyolitic units have variable abundances. Principal phenocrysts are sanidine, plagioclase, quartz, and biotite, and minor varieties include amphibole, clinopyroxene, and orthopyroxene.

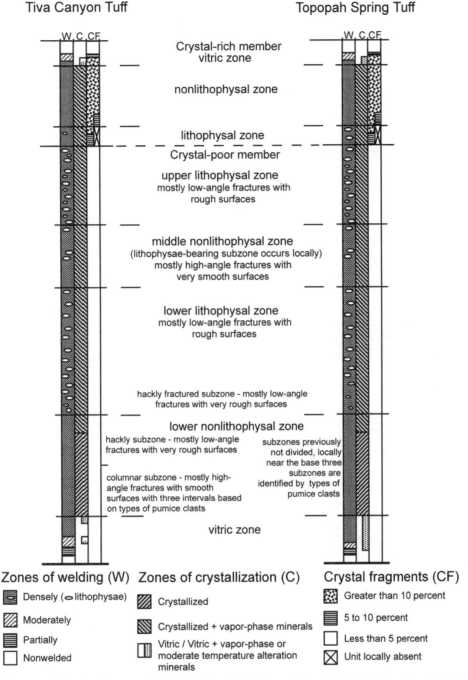

Figure 5. Lithostratigraphic zones in the Tiva Canyon and Topopah Spring Tuffs at Yucca Mountain. Adapted from Buesch et al. (1996). Not to scale.

Geochemical Criteria

Volcanic rocks at Yucca Mountain show systematic variations in their chemical (Lipman et al., 1966) and isotopic compositions (Noble and Hedge, 1969). The most abundant chemical constituents of vitric and devitrified tuffs are SiO_2 and Al_2O_3. On the basis of the abundances of these two constituents, CRWMS M&O (2000, Fig. 4.5-12 therein) showed that (1) the Calico Hills Formation, Yucca Mountain Tuff, and crystal-poor members of the Tiva Canyon and Topopah Spring Tuffs are predominantly high-silica rhyolites; (2) tuffs in the Crater Flat Group exhibit a compositional range that is between high- and low-silica rhyolites; (3) the Lithic Ridge and Pah Canyon Tuffs consist of low-silica rhyolites; and (4) the crystal-rich members of the Tiva Canyon and Topopah Spring Tuffs are largely quartz latites. (Sequence of formations is shown in Table 1.)

Analyses of rock samples collected from several different outcrop localities and boreholes show that trace-element concentrations vary systematically with stratigraphic position. Peterman

A

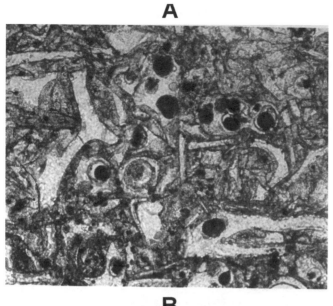

B

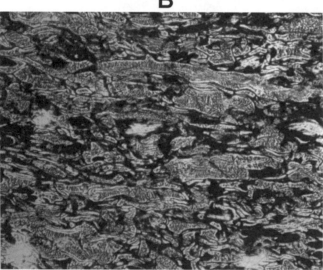

Figure 6. Photomicrograph of vitric (A) and densely welded (B) rocks in the crystal-poor member of the Tiva Canyon Tuff. Figure 6A is ~6 × 8 mm and shows vitric, nonwelded colorless bubblewall shards in a matrix of glass dust; matrix porosity is ~25–35 vol%. B is ~12 × 12 mm, and shows vitric, densely welded tuff with no microscopic porosity; interstitial dust is fused. Photomicrograph courtesy of F.R. Singer, Epsilon Systems Solutions, Inc.

et al. (1993), for example, prepared a graph (Fig. 7) showing concentrations of titanium and zirconium in the sequence of formations cored in borehole UE-25 a#1 (borehole locations shown in Fig. 8). In this borehole, the break between the crystal-rich and crystal-poor members of the Topopah Spring Tuff is clearly evident at a depth of ~160 m (Fig. 7). Similar variations in trace-element concentrations from one borehole to another, as well as to outcrop sections, indicates a general lateral continuity of the volcanic rock units.

Superimposed on the initial composition of the volcanic rocks—that is, glass fragments, lithic inclusions, and phenocrysts—were the variations in mineralogy and chemistry introduced by alteration. Depending on the proportion of secondary minerals precipitated, alteration caused small to large chemical changes in the original rock mass. The initial distribution of vitric and devitrified tuffs (pyroclastic deposits in which high-temperature crystallization changed volcanic glass to a mostly anhydrous mineral assemblage) largely determined the locations of zeolitic and nonzeolitic rocks, respectively, in those parts of Yucca Mountain where the rocks were subjected to zeolitization (CRWMS M&O, 2004, sec. 3.3.5). Both syngenetic and diagenetic alteration were widespread (CRWMS M&O, 2004, sec. 3.3.5). Most syngenetic alteration occurred in and near devitrified-vitric transition zones, and represents a transition from devitrification to glass dissolution and secondary-mineral precipitation of mostly zeolites, clay, and silica phases. The alteration was caused by a combination of water entrained in an ash flow and infiltrating meteoric water that interacted with the rock and occurred during the very late stages of cooling of the erupted material (Levy and O'Neil, 1989). The volume of rock affected by syngenetic alteration was highly variable, especially because much of the alteration was concentrated along and adjacent to fractures. Alteration in the Topopah Spring Tuff, in the interval from the lower non-lithophysal zone to the top of the nonwelded base of the formation (Fig. 5), is the most widespread and volumetrically abundant example of syngenetic alteration in the unsaturated zone in the site area (CRWMS M&O, 2004, sec. 3.3.5). Common mineral constituents in the altered tuffs include alkali feldspar, smectite, heulandite, and silica minerals. Minor constituents include mordenite, calcite, iron and manganese oxides, and erionite.

The most extensive post-cooling mineralogic and geochemical change affecting the rocks at Yucca Mountain has been the diagenetic zeolitization of nonwelded glassy tuffs. This process involved dissolution of glass shards by groundwater at ambient temperatures (e.g., 50 °C or lower) and precipitation of clinoptolite with or without lesser amounts of mordenite, smectite, silica, iron-oxide magnetites and hydroxides, and other minor constituents (CRWMS M&O, 2004, sec. 3.3.5).

Borehole Geophysical-Log Criteria

Suites of geophysical logs, commonly including caliper, gamma-ray, density, induction, resistivity, and neutron logs, were obtained from several tens of boreholes across the Yucca Mountain site area (Nelson, 1993, 1994, 1996). Because these logs reflect changes in rock properties, they can be used to correlate lithostratigraphic features—for example, (1) increased welding causes matrix density to increase and porosity to decrease; (2) mineral alteration (from clays and zeolites) causes a decrease in resistivity and an increase in neutron absorption, resulting in a high apparent neutron porosity; (3) differences in magnetic susceptibility and remanence depend on the chemistry of the rock and Earth's magnetic field at the time of eruption and deposition; and (4) devitrification forms highly magnetic minerals that typi-

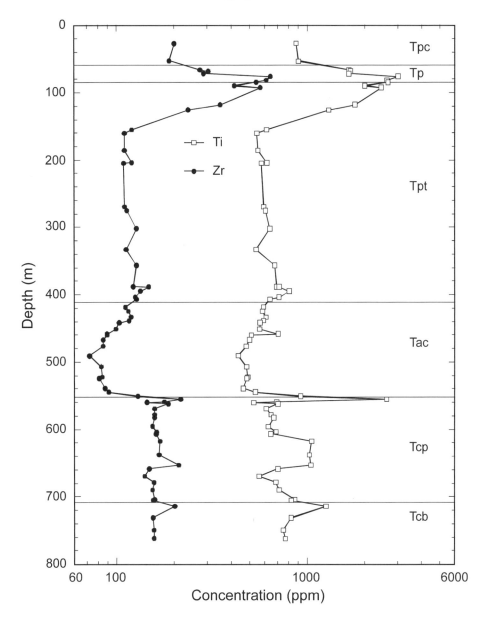

Figure 7. Graph showing concentrations, with depth, of titanium (Ti) and zirconium (Zr) for core samples from borehole UE-25a#1. Location of borehole shown in Figure 8. Stratigraphic units: Tpc—Tiva Canyon Tuff; Tp—Yucca Mountain and Pah Canyon Tuffs; Tpt—Topopah Spring Tuff; Tac—Calico Hills Formation; Tcp—Prow Pass Tuff; Tcb—Bullfrog Tuff. From Peterman et al. (1993).

cally increase the magnetic field of the rocks, whereas alteration typically reduces the intensity of many magnetic properties. Figure 9, showing combined geophysical log and core data obtained in borehole UE-25 UZ#16, illustrates correlations that can be made between log responses and various lithologic and mineralogical features within some of the major stratigraphic units.

Descriptions of Rock Units

Formations and intervening bedded tuff units that compose the Tertiary volcanic rock sequence at Yucca Mountain are shown in Table 1, together with thicknesses and brief generalized lithologic descriptions. Also included are columns showing hydrogeologic and thermal-mechanical units that correlate directly with specific stratigraphic units. Subdivisions of each of the formations and their detailed lithologic descriptions are given

in CRWMS M&O (2000, Tables 4.5-1 and 4.5-2). Two stratigraphic cross sections, Figures 10 and 11, drawn with the top of the Topopah Spring Tuff as a datum, show the distribution of formations across parts of the Yucca Mountain site area. Bedded tuff units, commonly too thin to plot separately at small scales, are included in the basal parts of the overlying formational units. Descriptions of the bedded tuff units also are included with the overlying formations in the following discussions. Unless otherwise indicated, stated thicknesses are based on (1) a tabulation of formation tops as identified in some 50 boreholes by R.W. Spengler and D.C. Buesch (U.S. Geological Survey, unpublished data), and (2) a series of isochore maps presented by Bechtel SAIC Company (2002), based largely on the borehole data in item (1). (Note: Borehole depths and measurements typically are recorded in feet, but in the following descriptions they are converted to meters with feet given in parentheses.)

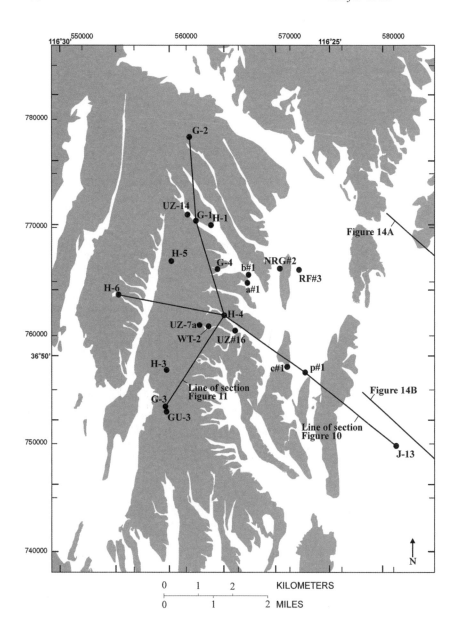

Figure 8. Map of Yucca Mountain site area showing locations of stratigraphic cross sections (Figs. 10 and 11), boreholes mentioned in text, and cross sections across Fortymile Wash (Fig. 14). (Note: borehole numbers not shown with prefixes UE-25 or USW.) Bedrock areas shown in gray, Quaternary deposits are white. Coordinates in UTM, Zone 11.

Pre-Cenozoic Rocks

Pre-Cenozoic rocks, believed to consist primarily of Upper Precambrian and Paleozoic sedimentary strata, underlie the Tertiary volcanic rocks at Yucca Mountain, but little detailed information is available on their thickness and overall lithology. The only direct evidence of their presence within the site area is in borehole UE-25 p#1, which penetrated Paleozoic carbonate rocks in the depth interval 1244–1805 m (4081–5922 ft) (Fig. 10). These rocks, almost entirely dolomites, have been correlated with the Lone Mountain Dolomite and Roberts Mountains Formation on the basis of exposures at Bare Mountain to the west (Monsen et al., 1992), and on the presence of Silurian-age conodonts (M.D. Carr et al., 1986). Summary descriptions of pre-Cenozoic rocks in the Yucca Mountain region are given by Stuckless and O'Leary (this volume).

Pre–Lithic Ridge Volcanic Rocks

The oldest known volcanic rocks in the Yucca Mountain area (>14 Ma; Sawyer et al., 1994) underlie the Lithic Ridge Tuff. Because they are not exposed at Yucca Mountain, little is known about their extent and stratigraphic relations except locally, where they have been penetrated in boreholes. In boreholes USW G-1, USW G-2, and USW G-3 (Fig. 11), the sequence consists of bedded tuffaceous deposits, pyroclastic flow deposits, and quartz-latitic to rhyolitic lavas and flow breccia (Broxton et al., 1989). Crystal fragments are largely plagioclase, with lesser amounts of sanadine and quartz. Penetrated thicknesses vary from ~45 m (148 ft) in USW G-3 to ~350 m (1148 ft) in USW G-2. In borehole UE-25 p#1 (Fig. 10), 180 m (590 ft) of altered tuff lies between the Lithic Ridge Tuff and Paleozoic strata (Muller and Kibler, 1984). Initial compositions of these pre–Lithic Ridge tuffs

EXPLANATION

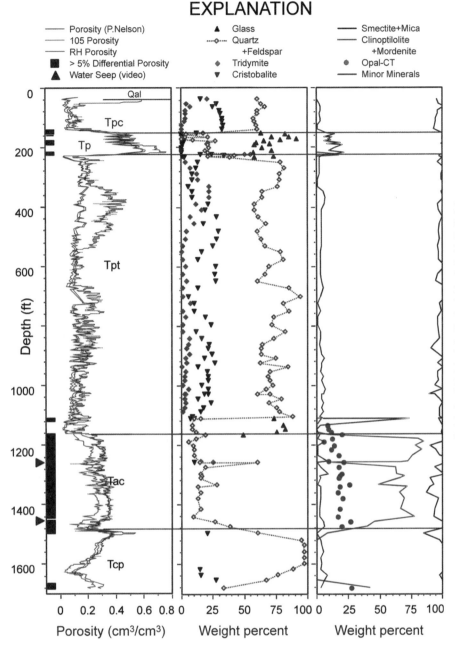

Figure 9. Lithostratigraphy and porosity from cores and geophysical logs and quantitative mineralogy from X-ray diffraction on rock samples from borehole UE-25 UZ#16. For minor minerals in the right-hand column, the scale is reversed, beginning with zero at the far right and increasing in 5% increments to the left. Location of borehole shown in Figure 8. Stratigraphic units: Qal—Quaternary alluvium; Tpc—Tiva Canyon Tuff; Tp—bedded tuffs and upper part of the crystal-rich member of Topopah Spring Tuff; Tpt—Topopah Spring Tuff; Tac—Calico Hills Formation, lowermost part of Topopah Spring Tuff, and bedded tuff; Tcp—Prow Pass Tuff. Abbreviations: ft—feet; cm³—cubic centimeter; 105—sample oven-dried at 105 °C; RH—relative humidity. Data based on Chipera et al. (1995).

are poorly known because they are altered to clays, calcite, and chlorite (Spengler et al., 1981; Bish and Vaniman, 1985). These data have been used to determine their alteration history (Bish and Aronson, 1993).

Lithic Ridge Tuff

The Lithic Ridge Tuff, dated at 14 Ma (Sawyer et al., 1994), is a massive pyroclastic flow deposit (W.J. Carr et al., 1986) ranging in thickness from 185 m (607 ft) at borehole USW G-2 to 304 m (997 ft) in borehole USW G-3 (Fig. 11). The formation is nonwelded to moderately welded, and extensively altered to clay and zeolite minerals. Crystal fragments (quartz, sanadine, plagioclase) average ~10% of the rock, and lithic fragments constitute

5–15%. Many slight variations in the degree of welding, crystal-fragment ratios, and lithic-fragment content indicate that several eruptive surges are represented.

Dacitic Lava and Flow Breccia

Dacitic lava and flow breccia overlie the Lithic Ridge Tuff in deep drill holes in the northern and western parts of the Yucca Mountain site area (Figs. 10 and 11) but are absent elsewhere. The thickness of the unit is 111 m (365 ft) in borehole USW H-1 (Fig. 8; Rush et al., 1984) and 249 m (817 ft) in borehole H-6 (Fig. 10; Craig et al., 1983). In borehole USW G-1, most of the unit is flow breccia made up of angular to subangular dacite fragments, commonly from 2 to 10 cm long, which are intercalated with lava

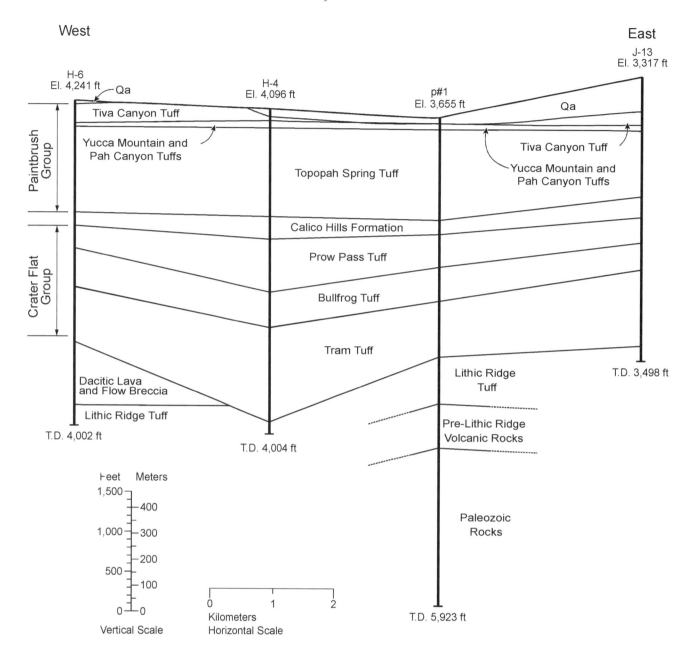

Figure 10. East-west stratigraphic cross section. Datum is top of Topopah Spring Tuff; structure not shown. Abbreviations: Qa—Quaternary alluvium; El.—ground elevation; T.D.—total depth. Based on formation tops identified in the plotted boreholes by R.W. Spengler and D.C. Buesch (U.S. Geological Survey, unpublished data). Bedded tuff units are included at the base of overlying formation. Location of section shown in Figure 8.

blocks ranging from 1 m to more than 17 m thick (Spengler et al., 1981). The breccia is autoclastic, indicating that its formation is primarily due to fragmentation of semisolid and solid lava during relatively slow flow. About 8 m of reworked pyroclastic fallout and bedded tuff deposits underlie the flow breccia in borehole USW G-1 (Spengler et al., 1981).

Crater Flat Group

The Crater Flat Group, dated between 13.5 and 13.0 Ma, consists of three formations of moderate- to large-volume pyro-

clastic flow deposits—Tram, Bullfrog, and Prow Pass Tuffs (Table 1)—and interstratified bedded tuffs (Sawyer et al., 1994). The group ranges in composition from the high-silica rhyolites characterizing most of the younger Paintbrush Group to the distinctive lower silica rhyolites of the Pah Canyon Tuff of the Paintbrush Group (Bish et al., 2002). The Crater Flat Group is distinguished from other pyroclastic units in the vicinity of Yucca Mountain by the relative abundance of quartz and biotite crystal fragments. In addition, the Prow Pass Tuff and, to a lesser degree, some parts of the Bullfrog Tuff contain distinctive lithic clasts of

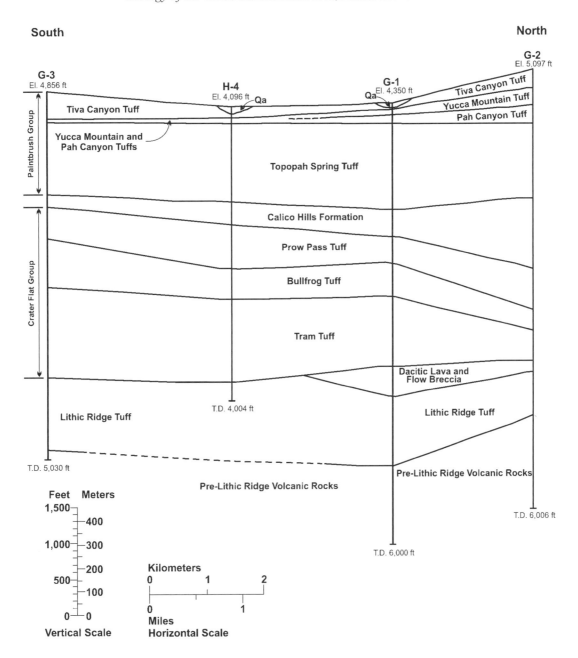

Figure 11. North-south stratigraphic cross section. Datum is top of Topopah Spring Tuff; structure not shown. Abbreviations: Qa—Quaternary alluvium; El.—ground elevation; T.D.—total depth. Based on formation tops identified in plotted boreholes by R.W. Spengler and D.C. Buesch (U.S. Geological Survey, unpublished data). Bedded tuff units are included at base of overlying formation. Location of section shown in Figure 8.

reddish-brown mudstone. The Tram Tuff overlies dacitic lavas and flow breccias in the northern part of Yucca Mountain, and the Lithic Ridge Tuff in the southern part (Figs. 10 and 11; Broxton et al., 1989).

Tram Tuff of the Crater Flat Group

Several depositional units have been distinguished within the Tram Tuff on the basis of the abundance and types of pumice and lithic clasts in pyroclastic-flow deposits and rare bedded tuff interbeds. The most easily recognized stratigraphic divisions are

the lower lithic-rich unit, which can be locally divided into a lower lithic-poor and an upper lithic-rich set of subunits, and an upper lithic-poor unit. Both lithic-rich and lithic-poor units have been identified and described in several boreholes, including UE-25 p#1, USW G-1, UE-25 b#1, USW G-3, and USW H-1 (Spengler et al., 1981; Maldonado and Koether, 1983). In borehole USW G-2, the upper lithic-poor unit is absent and the lithic-rich unit is well developed (Maldonado and Koether, 1983). Welding is variable, and locally the large concentration of lithic clasts (such as in borehole USW G-2) apparently reduced the degree of welding. In general, the lithic-poor unit is more densely welded than the underlying lithic-rich unit. Crystal fragments include quartz, feldspar, abundant biotite (30–50% of phenocrysts in upper part), and very rare hornblende (?).

Argillic and zeolitic alteration is present in both units of the Tram Tuff. In the lithic-poor unit, the alteration appears to be in two zones separated by the zone of maximum welding. The upper and lower parts of the formation are altered to clinoptilolite ± mordenite. In the vicinity of borehole USW G-1, however, analcime appears in the lower part, and in borehole USW G-2 analcime is the dominant zeolite in both the upper and lower parts.

Tram Tuff thicknesses in boreholes range from 104 m to as much as 370 m (340–1213 ft). A regional isopach map by W.J. Carr et al. (1986) shows the thickness to exceed 400 m (1310 ft) in the northern part of Crater Flat to the west.

The lower lithic-rich unit overlies a complex sequence of altered and weathered pyroclastic fallout deposits and minor pyroclastic-flow deposits (e.g., see Diehl and Chornack, 1990). With respect to the seven boreholes plotted in Figures 10 and 11, these pre–Tram Tuff bedded tuffs (included in the Tram Tuff interval) range in thickness from 0 in borehole UE-25 p#1 to 21 m (68 ft) in borehole USW G-2.

Bullfrog Tuff of the Crater Flat Group

Descriptions of the Bullfrog Tuff, which is exposed only in limited outcrops in the northwest corner of the site area, are based primarily on studies of core from boreholes USW G-1 and USW G-4 (Spengler et al., 1981; Spengler and Chornack, 1984). The formation is composed of two pyroclastic-flow deposits, both of which are simple cooling units; they are separated by an interval of pumiceous fallout. Borehole thicknesses range from 67 to 188 m (221–618 ft). Regionally, W.J. Carr et al. (1986) show the formation to be as much as 400 m (1310 ft) thick in an area of maximum deposition in the southern part of Crater Flat.

The upper pyroclastic-flow unit is variably welded and altered to zeolites and/or clay. The lower unit is moderately welded in its central part, and the intervening pumiceous deposit is partly to moderately welded. Pumice clasts constitute as much as 20–25% of the rock; crystal fragments include quartz, feldspar, biotite, and minor pyroxene.

The pre–Bullfrog Tuff bedded tuff unit (included in the Bullfrog Tuff interval) consists primarily of weathered pyroclastic-flow deposits interbedded with thin zones of fallout tephra. Diehl and Chornack (1990) correlated five marker horizons through the sequence between boreholes USW G-1, USW G-2, and USW G-3. Thicknesses of the unit in the seven boreholes in Figures 10 and 11 range from 6 to 11 m (20–37 ft). In addition to an intervening bedded tuff, the Bullfrog Tuff can be differentiated from the overlying Prow Pass Tuff on the basis of crystal assemblages and bulk chemistry (Moyer and Geslin, 1995). The Bullfrog, for example, contains abundant biotite and rare pyroxene, whereas the Prow Pass contains altered orthopyroxene and biotite in about equal amounts.

Prow Pass Tuff of the Crater Flat Group

The Prow Pass Tuff consists of four variably welded pyroclastic-flow deposits formed by eruptions from an unidentified source between 13.0 and 13.25 Ma (Sawyer et al., 1994). Descriptions and unit thicknesses (except for the pre–Prow Pass Tuff bedded tuff) given below are summarized from Moyer and Geslin (1995), based in large part on studies of core samples from boreholes USW G-1, USW G-2, USW GU-3, USW G-4, USW UZ-14, UE-25 a#1, UE-25 c#1 (and nearby c#2 and c#3), and UE-25 UZ#16, and from observations of exposures at the Prow (Fig. 2).

The basal bedded tuff unit (pre–Prow Pass Tuff bedded tuff), <1 m to ~3.5 m (3–11 ft) thick in the boreholes shown in Figures 10 and 11 (included in the Prow Pass Tuff interval), consists of welded and zeolitically altered tuffaceous deposits.

The lowermost pyroclastic-flow deposit of the Prow Pass Tuff (designated unit 1 by Moyer and Geslin, 1995), with an aggregate thickness of 25–70 m (82–230 ft), consists of three subunits separated on the basis of their lithic clast content. The subunits generally are similar, with zeolitically altered matrices. The next overlying unit (unit 2) is a sequence of pyroclastic-flow deposits that have not been subdivided because they lack distinguishing characteristics. Locally preserved ash horizons and abrupt changes in the amounts and sizes of pumice and lithic clasts, however, indicate at least three flow deposits in most boreholes studied. The aggregate thickness ranges from ~3–34 m (10–112 ft). Six subunits defined by changes in the degree of welding or the intensity of vapor-phase alteration characterize the third flow deposit (unit 3). Its thickness ranges from 40 m (131 ft) to nearly 80 m (262 ft). The top unit of the Prow Pass Tuff (unit 4), which ranges from 4 m (13 ft) to as much as 20.5 m (67 ft) thick in cored boreholes, can be divided into three irregularly distributed subunits differentiated by changes in the average diameter and percentage of pumice clasts that decrease stratigraphically upward.

Among its characteristics, the Prow Pass Tuff is distinguished by the presence of altered orthopyroxene in addition to biotite as crystal fragments and by distinctive, fine-grained, oxidized lithic inclusions of red mudstone. In contrast, the overlying Calico Hills Formation contains different amounts of crystal fragments and proportions of quartz in the crystal assemblage. The basal bedded tuff and sandstone units of the Calico Hills serve as consistent stratigraphic markers in several boreholes (Diehl and Chornack, 1990).

Calico Hills Formation

The Calico Hills Formation and the underlying bedded tuffs form one of the most potentially important barriers to the migration of exchangeable cations at Yucca Mountain. Despite its great heterogeneity, the formation has a consistently high matrix porosity (average 28–35%; see Moyer and Geslin, 1995), which indicates an important role for matrix flow of groundwater. Other properties, particularly permeability, are extremely variable and strongly dependent on mineralogy;

permeability decreases by about two orders of magnitude, and sorption by cation exchange increases as much as five orders of magnitude, in the transition from vitric to zeolitic rocks within the formation.

The Calico Hills Formation is a complex series of rhyolite tuffs and lavas that resulted from an episode of volcanism ca. 12.9 Ma (Sawyer et al., 1994). Five pyroclastic units, overlying a bedded tuff unit and, locally, a basal sandstone unit, were distinguished in the Yucca Mountain site area by Moyer and Geslin (1995). The formation is 250 m (820 ft) thick in borehole G-2 toward the northern part of the site area (Figs. 8 and 11) and thins southward to 11 m (37 ft) in borehole H-3 (Fig. 8). The following descriptions are summarized from Moyer and Geslin (1995), whose studies were based on examinations of cores and observations of outcrops in the same boreholes and surface locality as those listed above for the Prow Pass Tuff.

The basal volcaniclastic sandstone unit of the Calico Hills Formation is interbedded with rare reworked pyroclastic-flow deposits; thicknesses of the unit range from 0 to 5.5 m (0–18 ft). The overlying bedded tuff (labeled pre–Calico Hills Formation bedded tuff in Table 1), 9–39 m (30–128 ft) thick, is composed primarily of pyroclastic-fallout deposits. Each of the five pyroclastic units forming the bulk of the formation consists of one or more pyroclastic-flow deposits separated by locally preserved fallout horizons. Ash-fall and ash-flow deposits beneath the repository block give way to lava flows to the north and east.

X-ray diffraction of drill-core samples by Caporuscio et al. (1982), Bish and Vaniman (1985), and Bish and Chipera (1986) and of outcrop samples by Broxton et al. (1993) showed an abundance of authigenic zeolites in all units of the Calico Hills Formation. The pyroclastic units have extremely high clinoptilolite and mordenite contents (40–80%; Caporuscio et al., 1982; Vaniman et al., 1984; Bish and Vaniman, 1985; Bish and Chipera, 1986) that contrast with the somewhat lower zeolite content of the bedded tuffs and basal sandstone (Moyer and Geslin, 1995). Mapping of the distribution of zeolites shows that (1) they are more widely present in the bedded tuffs than in the pyroclastic units, and (2) zeolite mineralization is pervasive in the northern part of Yucca Mountain but absent in some southern locations. In the vicinities of boreholes USW GU-3 and USW H-4, for example, the entire formation is vitric (Moyer and Geslin, 1995). The presence of zeolitized zones within the Calico Hills, and within other formations such as the Prow Pass Tuff, has important implications with respect to paleohydrologic interpretations and the potential development of natural barriers to contaminant movement by groundwater (e.g., see CRWMS M&O, 1998).

The complex series of rhyolite tuffs and lavas in the Calico Hills Formation grades laterally from completely zeolitized to unaltered vitric rock from east to west across the site area. Crystal fragments, which compose as much as 7–12% of some units, predominantly are quartz, feldspar, and biotite, with trace magnetite and accessory clinopyroxene, ilmenite, allanite, and zircon. Lithic clasts make up as much as 40% of the rocks, but the proportion is more commonly in the 15–20% range. The formation is distinguished from the Topopah Spring Tuff by differences in mineralogy and chemical composition; lithostratigraphic units of the former have crystal assemblages with a higher proportion of quartz and higher concentrations of Ca and Ba than units of the latter.

Paintbrush Group

The Paintbrush Group consists of four formations, each primarily composed of pyroclastic-flow deposits interstratified with small-volume pyroclastic-flow and fallout-tephra deposits, and, locally, lava flows and secondary volcaniclastic deposits from eolian and fluvial processes (Buesch et al., 1996). In ascending order, the formations include the Topopah Spring, Pah Canyon, Yucca Mountain, and Tiva Canyon Tuffs (Table 1); they are dated at 12.8–12.7 Ma (Sawyer et al., 1994). This group is one of the most widespread and voluminous caldera-related assemblages in the southwestern Nevada volcanic field (Sawyer et al., 1994). The Topopah Spring Tuff forms the host rock for the proposed repository; therefore, it is one of the most intensely studied formations at Yucca Mountain. Locations of eruptive centers for the Topopah Spring and Pah Canyon Tuffs are uncertain, but the Claim Canyon caldera (Fig. 1) is the identified source of the Tiva Canyon Tuff and possibly the Yucca Mountain Tuff (Byers et al., 1976; Sawyer et al., 1994).

The Paintbrush Group is dominated volumetrically by the Topopah Spring and Tiva Canyon Tuffs. The Yucca Mountain and Pah Canyon Tuffs are minor units but are of potential hydrologic importance because of their high matrix porosity compared to the Tiva Canyon and Topopah Spring, which are largely densely welded with low matrix porosity. The welded tuffs also have higher fracture abundance and connectivity, providing stratified contrasts in unsaturated hydrologic properties in the Paintbrush Group rocks above the proposed repository block.

Descriptions of the formations within the Paintbrush Group are generalized from detailed studies of outcrops and borehole cores by Buesch et al. (1996), supplemented by core descriptions obtained from Geslin et al. (1995); Geslin and Moyer (1995); and Moyer et al. (1995). Divisions of the Tiva Canyon and Topopah Spring Tuffs into members, zones, subzones, and intervals (Buesch et al., 1996) indicates that both formations are simple cooling units within the site area (Lipman et al., 1966). The interaction among depositional, welding, crystallization, and fracturing processes produces unit contacts that range from sharp to gradational. Depositional contacts, such as the bases of pyroclastic-flow and fallout-tephra deposits and redeposited material, are examples of sharp contacts. The tops of these deposits typically are sharp, but may be gradational where there is evidence of reworking or pedogenesis. The transition from nonwelded to densely welded tuff typically is gradational, such as near the base of the Topopah Spring Tuff in boreholes USW GU-3 and USW WT-2. Contacts of several lithostratigraphic units correspond with hydrogeologic and thermal-mechanical unit boundaries throughout Yucca Mountain (Table 1).

Topopah Spring Tuff of the Paintbrush Group

The Topopah Spring Tuff includes the host rock units for the proposed radioactive waste repository. As such, its characteristics are of direct importance to repository design, unsaturated-zone hydrologic flow and radionuclide transport, and total-system performance assessment. A complete description of the Topopah Spring Tuff is presented in Buesch et al. (1996).

The Topopah Spring Tuff is 149–369 m (488–1209 ft) thick as identified in boreholes in the Yucca Mountain site area. The formation is divided into a lower crystal-poor member and an upper crystal-rich member. Vitric rocks form zones at the top and bottom of the formation, and alternating lithophysal and nonlithophysal zones characterize the remaining parts of the two members (Fig. 5). Further subdivision primarily is based on the degree of welding, crystal content and assemblage, and size and abundance of pumice and lithic clasts.

The Topopah Spring Tuff is compositionally zoned with an upward chemical change from high-silica rhyolite in the crystal-poor member to quartz latite (also referred to as quartz trachyte) in the crystal-rich member (Lipman et al., 1966; Sawyer et al., 1994). The lower part of the formation is one of the most chemically homogeneous rock types in the site area (Bish et al., 2002). The homogeneity of the major-element chemistry also extends to trace elements. Somewhat greater chemical variability is seen in the quartz latites of the crystal-rich member.

The crystal-poor member, characterized by 3% (or less) felsic crystal fragments composed mainly of sanadine and plagioclase with traces of quartz and mafic minerals, is divided into vitric rocks of the vitric zone near the base and (in ascending order) devitrified rocks of the lower nonlithophysal, lower lithophysal, middle nonlithophysal, and upper lithophysal zones (Fig. 5; Buesch et al., 1996). The latter four zones form the host rock for the proposed repository. The vitric zone is divided primarily on the basis of degrees of welding, which range upward from a nonwelded to partially welded subzone at the base, through a moderately welded subzone, to a densely welded subzone at the top. The vitric, densely welded subzone, commonly referred to as the vitrophyre, is identified as an important subunit within the Topopah Spring welded thermal-mechanical unit (Table 1).

Within the devitrified, rhyolitic part of the Topopah Spring Tuff, crystal fragments are minor constituents (<5%) of the rock and the remainder consists of fine-grained devitrification minerals. These devitrification products are principally feldspars plus a variable combination of the silica polymorphs tridymite, cristobalite, and quartz. Abundance of quartz is a useful stratigraphic marker within the devitrified, rhyolitic Topopah Spring Tuff, but quartz crystal fragments nevertheless are much less abundant (<0.5%) than groundmass quartz (~20%) throughout this interval. The silica polymorph distributions are particularly important because of their thermal stability, dissolution properties, and other properties that can create inhalation hazards.

A transitional zone, commonly referred to as the vitric-zeolitic transition that is composed of partly devitrified vitrophyre, extends downward from the base of the lower nonlithophysal zone into the crystal-poor vitric zone through a stratigraphic interval ranging from ~3–30 m (10–100 ft) in thickness. In many parts of Yucca Mountain, the moderately welded and nonwelded subzones at the base of the crystal-poor vitric zone are overprinted by zeolite alteration zones (Buesch et al., 1996). Accordingly, a vitric-zeolitic boundary can be drawn that varies within a narrow range of stratigraphic positions, but generally coincides closely with the contact between the moderately welded subzone and the overlying densely welded subzone (Buesch and Spengler, 1999). This boundary is further defined as the contact between the Topopah Spring welded hydrogeologic unit and the underlying Calico Hills nonwelded hydrogeologic unit (Table 1).

The crystal-rich member of the Topopah Spring Tuff is characterized by 10–15% crystal fragments (sanadine and plagioclase, traces of quartz, biotite, pyroxene, and hornblende), with a crystal-transition subzone at the base where crystal abundance increases upward from 3% to 10%. The member is divided into lithophysal, nonlithophysal, and vitric zones (Fig. 5). Rocks in the lower two zones are devitrified, and the division is based on the presence or absence of lithophysae. The vitric zone at the top of the member is distinguished by preservation of the volcanic glass to form rocks with a vitreous luster that typically grade upward from densely welded to nonwelded. This zone is relatively impermeable, which impedes the downward flow of groundwater in the unsaturated zone.

The tuffaceous rock unit (pre–Topopah Spring Tuff bedded tuff) that lies between the Topopah Spring Tuff and the Calico Hills Formation is 0–17 m (0–55 ft) thick in the boreholes plotted in Figures 10 and 11; it is included in the Topopah Spring interval.

Pah Canyon Tuff of the Paintbrush Group

The Pah Canyon Tuff is a simple cooling unit (Christiansen, 1979) consisting of multiple flow units that are composed of low-silica rhyolites (Bish et al., 2002, v. 1, sec. 1, p. 5). The formation reaches a thickness of 72 m (237 ft) in borehole G-2 and thins southward to zero in the vicinity of borehole USW UZ#16 (Fig. 8; Moyer et al., 1996). The formation varies from nonwelded to moderately welded, and, throughout much of the site area, vitric pumice clasts are preserved in a nondeformed matrix that was either sintered or was lithified by vapor-phase mineralization. Crystal fragments in the matrix and in large pumice clasts constitute 5–10% of the rock, with a greater proportion of feldspars relative to mafic minerals (biotite and clinopyroxene). Lithic clasts of devitrified rhyolite (as much as 5% of the rock) are common, and clasts of porphyritic obsidian are in some horizons. Shards are either poorly preserved clear glass or form devitrified material. The high water saturation of porous nonwelded units in the Pah Canyon, as well as in the overlying Yucca Mountain Tuff, leads to a relatively high degree of alteration where there is an underlying barrier to transmission. Because of the relatively impermeable upper vitrophyre of the underlying Topopah Spring Tuff, the alteration of the Pah Canyon Tuff (typically to smectite) generally is more extensive than that of the overlying Yucca Mountain Tuff. Therefore, despite its minor volume, the Pah Canyon Tuff has an important effect on reactions between unsaturated-zone water and the host tuffs.

The pre–Pah Canyon Tuff bedded tuff, 3–10 m thick (10–32 ft) in the boreholes plotted in Figures 10 and 11 (included in the Pah Canyon Tuff interval), consists of moderately well sorted pumiceous tephra with thin layers of lithic-rich fallout and very fine-grained ash at the base.

Rhyolites of Black Glass Canyon, Delirium Canyon, and Zig Zag Hill

Relatively minor amounts of rhyolite lava flows and related tephra deposits crop out locally in the northern part of the Yucca Mountain site area (Day et al., 1998a). The rhyolite of Zig Zag Hill is exposed in one small outcrop in the vicinity of the Prow in the northwest corner of the area (Fig. 2), where it forms a thin unit (thickness 10 m or less) between the Pah Canyon Tuff and the pre–Yucca Mountain Tuff bedded tuff (Table 1). The Delirium Canyon and Black Glass Canyon units are in limited outcrops in the northeast and north-central parts of the site area. Lava flows in the Delirium Canyon are as much as 250 m (820 ft) thick, and ash-flow tuffs are as much as 100 m (328 ft) thick (Table 1); the combined unit is considered to be equivalent to parts of the Rhyolite of Zig Zag Hill and the pre–Yucca Mountain Tuff bedded tuff (Table 1; Day et al., 1998a). The Rhyolite of Black Glass Canyon, 2–14 m (6.5–46 ft) thick, lies stratigraphically between the Yucca Mountain Tuff and the pre–Yucca Mountain Tuff bedded tuff (Table 1; Day et al., 1998a). Crystal fragments in the lavas and tephra consist of 5–10% sanadine and plagioclase and <1% hornblende, biotite, and sphene.

Yucca Mountain Tuff of the Paintbrush Group

The Yucca Mountain Tuff is a simple cooling unit that is nonwelded throughout much of the Yucca Mountain area, but is partially to densely welded where it thickens in the northern and western parts. Although typically vitric in most locations in the central part, the tuff is increasingly devitrified where thickest. The formation is as much as 55 m (180 ft) thick in parts of Yucca Mountain, but thins to zero southward. It is nonlithophysal throughout Yucca Mountain, but contains lithophysae where densely welded in northern Crater Flat. Although chemically similar to the high-silica rhyolites of the Tiva Canyon and Topopah Spring Tuffs, it contains plagioclase and sanidine crystal fragments, which is characteristic of the rhyolitic parts of the Topopah Spring but not those of the Tiva Canyon that contain only sanidine phenocrysts.

The pre–Yucca Mountain Tuff bedded tuff consists of pumiceous, vitric, nonwelded pyroclastic-flow deposits. In the boreholes shown in Figures 10 and 11, the unit, which is included in the Yucca Mountain Tuff interval, ranges from <1 m to as much as 46 m (<3–150 ft) in thickness (Table 1).

Tiva Canyon Tuff of the Paintbrush Group

The Tiva Canyon Tuff is a large-volume, regionally extensive, compositionally zoned (from rhyolite to quartz latite) tuff sequence (Table 1) that forms most of the rocks exposed at the surface in the Yucca Mountain site area (Day et al., 1998a). Thicknesses of those parts of the formation penetrated in boreholes or observed in outcrops range from <50 m to as much as 175 m (165–575 ft). Separation of the formation into a lower crystal-poor member and an upper crystal-rich member, and into zones within each of these members, is based on criteria similar to those discussed above for the Topopah Spring Tuff.

The rhyolitic crystal-poor member is divided into five zones: in ascending order, these are the vitric, lower nonlithophysal, lower lithophysal, middle nonlithophysal, and upper lithophysal zones (Fig. 5; Buesch et al., 1996). Further division into subzones is based on vitric versus devitrified rocks, degree of welding (Fig. 6), differences in pumice clasts, presence or absence of lithophysae, and fracture morphology. The lowest part of the member consists of densely welded to nonwelded high-silica rhyolitic glass. Only ~5% of the rock is composed of crystal fragments (sanadine with traces of hornblende, biotite, and sphene). The crystal-poor member and overlying crystal-rich member are separated by a thin transitional subzone in which there is an upward increase in crystal content and an increase in the proportion of mafic relative to felsic crystal fragments.

The quartz-latitic crystal-rich member, which consists primarily of devitrified nonlithophysal material, locally contains lithophysae near the base; it is capped by a thin (<1 m thick) vitric zone that is preserved only locally and has been eroded from most of Yucca Mountain. Crystal fragments, predominantly sanidine and plagioclase with trace amounts of quartz, biotite, pyroxene, hornblende, and sphene, constitute 10–15% of the rock. The crystal-rich nonlithophysal zone is divided into four subzones based upon such depositional features as abundance of crystal fragments and pumice. Much of this zone has undergone corrosion and alteration, which has substantially increased its porosity compared to the overlying and underlying rocks.

The pre–Tiva Canyon bedded tuff is characterized by thin beds of fallout tephra deposits interbedded with thin oxidized, weathered zones (Diehl and Chornack, 1990). Thicknesses of the unit penetrated in the seven boreholes plotted in Figures 10 and 11 (shown as part of the Tiva Canyon Tuff interval) range from <1 m to 3 m (<3–10 ft).

Post–Tiva Canyon and Pre–Rainier Mesa Tuffs and Lava Flows

Several rhyolite lava flows and fallout tephra deposits are in the upper part of the Paintbrush Group in the vicinity of Yucca Mountain (Buesch et al., 1996; see Fig. 2). These units, lying between the top of the Tiva Canyon Tuff and the base of the pre–Rainier Mesa bedded tuff, include (in ascending order) the post–Tiva Canyon Tuff bedded tuff, rhyolite of Vent Pass, tuff unit "X", and rhyolite of Comb Peak (Table 1). The rhyolitic lavas and ash-flow tuffs of the Vent Pass unit are exposed in the north-central part of the site area where thicknesses are as much as 150 m (490 ft) (Day et al., 1998a). Lavas and tuffs of the Rhyolite of Comb Peak form extensive outcrops in the large area of bedrock in the northeast part of the site area, north of Midway Valley and Yucca Wash (Fig. 2). These rocks aggregate maximum thicknesses of nearly 130 m (426 ft) (Table 1; Day et al., 1998a).

A 6–23-m-thick (20–75 ft) lithic-rich pyroclastic-flow deposit (Table 1), which was penetrated in several boreholes on the west side of Midway Valley near Exile Hill (such as borehole UE-25 RF#3, Fig. 8) and is exposed in the excavation for the north portal of the Exploratory Studies Facility (ESF) (Swan et al., 2001; see Fig. 16), was referred to informally as tuff unit "X" by Carr (1992). The unit is a pumiceous, nonwelded, in part zeolitic ash flow that was tentatively correlated with the Rhyolite of Comb Peak (Table 1) by Buesch et al. (1996). Additional descriptions based on core studies from boreholes on the west side of Exile Hill were given by Geslin et al. (1995).

The post–Tiva Canyon Tuff bedded tuff is a tuffaceous rock unit commonly consisting of numerous depositional sequences separated by possible paleosols (Buesch et al., 1996). Thicknesses in several boreholes near Exile Hill range from <2 to 4.5 m (<7–15 ft) (Table 1; Carr, 1992; Geslin et al., 1995).

Timber Mountain Group

The Timber Mountain Group includes all quartz-bearing pyroclastic-flow and fallout-tephra deposits erupted ca. 11.5 Ma from the Timber Mountain caldera complex, the south edge of which lies just north of the area shown in Figure 1 (Byers et al., 1976; Sawyer et al., 1994). The complex consists of two overlapping, resurgent calderas: an older caldera formed by the eruption of the Rainier Mesa Tuff, and a younger, nested caldera formed by the eruption of the Ammonia Tanks Tuff (Table 1; Minor et al., 1993; Sawyer et al., 1994).

Rainier Mesa Tuff of the Timber Mountain Group

The Rainier Mesa Tuff is a compositionally zoned compound cooling unit consisting of high-silica rhyolite tuff overlain by a considerably thinner quartz latite tuff (Table 1) that is restricted to the vicinity of the Timber Mountain caldera (Byers et al., 1976). The formation is not present across much of Yucca Mountain, but is locally exposed on the downthrown blocks of large faults in valleys toward the south end of the mountain (Day et al., 1998a; see Fig. 2). It is also exposed in the extreme northwest corner of the site area and was penetrated in a few boreholes on the east side. Based on examination of cores from boreholes UE-25 NRG#2, #2B, #2C, and #2D (UE-25 NRG#2 is shown in Figure 8; the other boreholes are nearby), the Rainier Mesa Tuff consists of a nonlithified to lithified and partially welded pyroclastic-flow deposit generally <30 m (98 ft) thick (Geslin and Moyer, 1995; Geslin et al., 1995). A maximum thickness of 240 m (787 ft) was observed in the southwestern part of Crater Flat (Fridrich, 1999). Pumice clasts compose 10–25% of the rocks, crystal fragments 10–20% (quartz, plagioclase, sanadine, biotite), and lithic clasts 1–5%.

The pre–Rainier Mesa Tuff bedded tuff consists of nonlithified fallout-tephra and pyroclastic-flow deposits (Table 1; Geslin and Moyer, 1995; Geslin et al., 1995). The sequence occupies intervals of ~17 m (55 ft) in boreholes UE-25 NRG#2C and UE-25 NRG#2D, and is characterized by moderately well-sorted white pumice lapilli and volcanic lithic clasts.

Ammonia Tanks Tuff of the Timber Mountain Group

The Ammonia Tanks Tuff (Table 1) is not present across Yucca Mountain, but is exposed in the southern part of Crater Flat and was penetrated by one borehole in the Crater Flat area (Fridrich, 1999). There, the formation consists of welded to nonwelded rhyolite tuff, with highly variable thicknesses (maximum as much as 215 m [705 ft]).

Younger Basalt

The youngest volcanic rocks in the Yucca Mountain site area (not included in Table 1) are represented by thin basalt dikes that were intruded along some minor faults near the head of Solitario Canyon (Day et al., 1998a). The dikes consist of fine-grained olivine-bearing basalt, locally with scoria and altered glass, which were dated at 10 Ma (Crowe et al., 1995). Basalt also forms scoria cones, thin lava flows, and flow breccias in Crater Flat to the west (Fig. 1), where they have been studied by Crowe et al. (1995) and Heizler et al. (1999).

Correlation of Lithostratigraphic, Hydrogeologic, and Thermal-Mechanical Units

Three primary stratigraphic systems have been developed to investigate the distribution of lithostratigraphic, hydrogeologic, and thermal-mechanical units at Yucca Mountain. Common to all these systems are the properties of bulk-rock density, grain density, and porosity. Changes in these rock properties result in commensurate changes in many of the associated hydrogeologic and thermal-mechanical properties that define units whose boundaries coincide with a specific stratigraphic contact. (See Ciancia and Heiken [2006] for discussion of geotechnical properties of tuffs at Yucca Mountain.)

As shown in Table 1, lithostratigraphic units within the Tertiary volcanic rock sequence are grouped into five major hydrogeologic units—in descending order, unconsolidated surficial materials, Tiva Canyon welded unit, Paintbrush Tuff nonwelded unit, Topopah Spring welded unit, and Calico Hills nonwelded unit—that were defined principally on the basis of major variations in the degree of welding (Montazer and Wilson, 1984). Hydrogeologic properties of these units were presented by Flint (1998) and will not be discussed here, except to make specific mention of the Paintbrush Tuff nonwelded hydrogeologic unit (PTn; see Fig. 3), which is of special interest to stratigraphic and hydrologic studies in the site area. The distribution and characteristics of this unit are discussed in detail by Moyer et al. (1996) and Buesch and Spengler (1999).

The PTn occupies the stratigraphic interval between the top of the vitric zone in the upper part of the crystal-rich member of the Topopah Spring Tuff upward to the base of the densely welded rocks of the vitric zone in the lower part of the crystal-poor member of the Tiva Canyon Tuff (Table 1; see Buesch et al., 1996). Because of its high porosity (average ~47%; CRWMS M&O, 2000, Table 5-4 therein), the PTn is considered to form a potential permeability boundary affecting the flow of groundwater above the repository block (Flint, 1998).

Stratigraphic units with distinct thermal and mechanical properties within the volcanic rock sequence at Yucca Mountain were identified by Ortiz et al. (1985). As with the hydrogeologic units, the boundaries of thermal-mechanical units (Table 1) are based on changes in macroscopic features that define strati-graphic units and permit the preliminary correlation of labora-tory measurements with specific lithostratigraphic units (Buesch et al., 1996). Analytical data indicate that most thermal-mechani-cal unit boundaries roughly correspond to (1) lithostratigraphic contacts that mark the transition from vitric, moderately welded rocks to densely welded subzones; or (2) the contact between the vitric, moderately welded rocks and devitrified rocks. Additional criteria are based on the percentage of lithophysae.

QUATERNARY GEOLOGY

Introduction

Surficial geologic mapping and chronostratigraphic studies of surface and near-surface deposits, soils, and geomorphic surfaces in the Yucca Mountain site area have resulted in the recognition and differentiation of several principal surficial units, which are com-posed mostly of alluvium and colluvium with minor amounts of eolian and debris-flow sediments that mantle hillslopes and cover the floors of valleys and washes. Figure 12 shows the general distribution of Quaternary deposits in the site area, based on the 1:50,000-scale regional compilation by Potter et al. (2002a). The small scale of the map (Fig. 12) necessitated the combining of vari-ous units and also did not permit the plotting of units that had only limited extent in some areas.

Early studies of Quaternary stratigraphy in the vicinity of Yucca Mountain, particularly those in the area of the Nevada Test Site to the east, by Hoover and Morrison (1980), Hoover et al. (1981), Swadley et al. (1984), and Hoover (1989), resulted in the general recognition of three major units ranging in age from Pliocene (?) and early Pleistocene to late Pleistocene and Holocene. Swadley et al. (1984) mapped these units in Midway Valley (Fig. 2), but no detailed mapping that further subdivided the surficial sequence in that area was published until Taylor (1986) distinguished six differ-ent units in the fluvial-terrace and alluvial-fan deposits along Yucca and Fortymile Washes, as well as in a small area in the northern-most part of Midway Valley, with a strong emphasis on variations in surface characteristics and soil development.

In more recent studies, the Quaternary stratigraphic sequence in the Yucca Mountain site area has been separated into eight indi-vidual units (designated, in ascending order, as QT0, Qa1–Qa7; Table 2), based principally on the mapping of alluvial deposits and overlying geomorphic surfaces and on the logging of some 30 soil pits by Wesling et al. (1992) and Swan et al. (2001) in Midway Val-ley. The principal criteria used for subdivision include (1) relative stratigraphic and geomorphic position, (2) lithologic characteristics, (3) soil-profile development, (4) degree of desert pavement devel-opment, (5) amount and degree of desert varnish accumulation, and (6) degree of preservation of original bar-and-swale topography.

Sedimentologic properties of the various alluvial units are similar. In general, fluvial deposits are predominantly sandy gravel with interbedded gravelly sand and sand; facies include relatively coarse-grained channel bars and intervening finer grained swales. Gravel size ranges from pebble to boulder, and clasts generally are subangular to subrounded. In addition to the predominantly volca-nic-rock detritus forming the deposits, there are varying amounts of pedogenic calcite and opal. A summary of diagnostic surface and soil characteristics for the various surficial units is presented in Table 2.

The relative ages of the deposits, soils, and geomorphic sur-faces around Yucca Mountain are well established. Numerical age control, however, is limited, but the dating of several samples col-lected from mapped units Qa2 through Qa5 at various localities in Midway Valley and Fortymile Wash supports their assigned rela-tive stratigraphic positions. A statistical analysis by S.K. Pezzopane (U.S. Geological Survey, written commun., 2001) of the results obtained from (1) U-series disequilibrium dating of silica- and carbonate-rich materials in soils, and (2) thermoluminescence dat-ing of the silt-size fractions in fluvial and eolian deposits, indicate the following ages: unit Qa2, middle Pleistocene; Qa3, middle (?) to late Pleistocene; Qa4, late Pleistocene; and Qa5, latest Pleisto-cene to early Holocene (see Whitney et al., 2004c). Age ranges are graphically portrayed in Figure 13. The shaded areas are interpreted to represent the main periods of deposition and soil development, or both; for unit Qa3, there appears to have been two distinct depo-sitional cycles. Dates extending beyond the shaded areas could be caused by miscorrelation of the sampled deposits, or they could, in fact, represent valid extensions of the age boundaries, thus indicat-ing that it may not be possible to establish absolute temporal bound-aries between successive units.

With regard to unit Qa1, there is evidence from eolian depos-its at Busted Butte (Figs. 2 and 12; see Menges et al., 2004) that it is associated with a period of deposition as old as the Bishop Ash (Izett et al., 1988), which is dated at 760 ka (Sarna-Wojcicki et al., 1993) and therefore considered to be of early to middle Pleistocene age. Accordingly, the age of unit QT0 is assumed to be greater than 760 ka, possibly as old as Pliocene. Unit Qa6, assumed to be younger than unit Qa5, is assigned a middle to late Holocene age, and unit Qa7 is the deposit presently accumulating along the modern stream courses.

General Distribution and Characteristics of Surficial Deposits

Unit QT0 consists of a single terrace remnant at the north end of Alice Ridge (Fig. 2), forming a prominent bench 46 m above

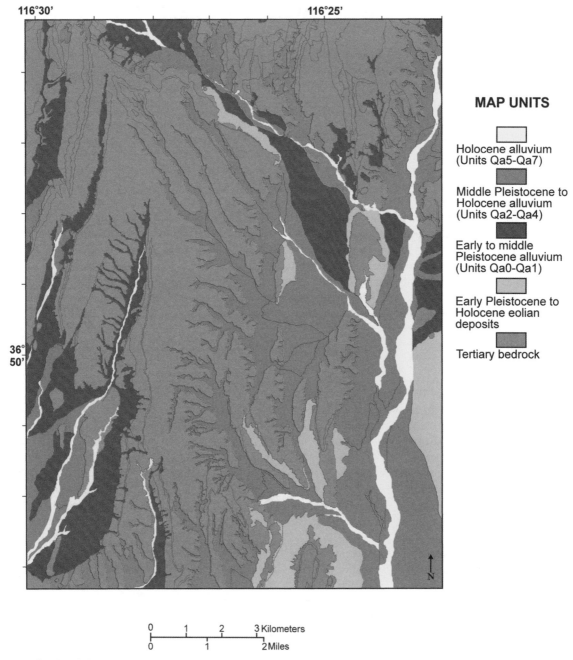

Figure 12. Generalized surficial geologic map of the Yucca Mountain site area. Modified from Potter et al. (2002a).

the modern channel of Yucca Wash. Thickness of the unit appears to be only a few meters, and an early Quaternary to possibly Pliocene age is evident from its highly dissected and eroded nature and its rounded landform morphology. No soil data were collected from the QT0 surface.

Unit Qa1 is preserved at the surface on the Yucca Wash alluvial fan; the fan surface has been dissected by younger drainages and is preserved as slightly rounded interfluves. The unit also is present on the west flank of Yucca Mountain and in northeastern Crater Flat. Locally, the desert pavement associated with the Qa1

surface is well developed, but in most areas it has been extensively degraded. No original bar-and-swale morphology is preserved on the surface. Strongly developed soils are 1.5–2.0 m (5–6.6 ft) thick.

Unit Qa2 is recognized primarily as thin elongated patches of alluvium in northern Midway Valley, where it is inset in unit Qa1 (Wesling et al., 1992). The unit has a well-developed desert pavement that contains darkly varnished clasts (Table 2). The original bar-and-swale morphology has been reduced to the height of the larger clasts on the surface. Where exposed in soil

TABLE 2. SUMMARY OF DIAGNOSTIC SURFACE AND SOIL CHARACTERISTICS OF QUATERNARY MAP UNITS AT YUCCA MOUNTAIN

Map Unit	Surface Characteristics[1]				Soil Characteristics				
	Desert Pavement[2]	Desert Varnish[3]	Rubification[4]	Depositional-bar Relief[5]	Horizon Sequence[6]	Structure[7]	Clay Films[8]	Maximum Reddening[9]	Maximum CaCO₃ Stage Morphology[10]
Qa7	None	1 ± 2 / 12	4	High, unaltered	Cu	sg	n.p.	10YR	n.p.
Qa6	None	0 ± 0 / 0	0	do	A-Ck	sg	n.p.	10YR	n.p.
Qa5	Weak to moderate	1 ± 1 / 28	33	Moderately high, slightly altered.	A-Bwk/Btjk-Bk-Ck	1 vf-f sbk	n.p.-1 n co	10YR	I
Qa4	Moderate to strong	62 ± 27 / 97	87	Low	Av-Btkq-Bkq-Ck	2-3 f-m sbk	3 n-mk pf	7.5YR	I–II
Qa3	Strong	43 ± 28 / 94	54	do	Av-BA-Btkq-Kq/Bkq-Ck	3 m sbk	3 n-mk pf	7.5YR	II–III
Qa2	Strong	80 (est.) / 100 (est.)	100 est.	do	Av-Btq-Btkq-Kq-Bkq-Ck	3 m sbk	3 mk pf	7.5-5YR	IV
Qa1	Locally strong	20 ± 21 / 84	80	None	Av-BA-Btkq-Kqm-Bkq-Ck	m-3 m pl	2 n pf	10-7.5YR	IV
QT0	Degraded						Eroded		

Notes: Source: Whitney et al. (2004b).

[1] See Wesling et al. (1992) for detailed definitions of surface parameters.

[2] Describes the relative degree of interlocking of surface clasts; based on qualitative estimate.

[3] First number is the average varnish cover (percent ± 1σ); second number refers to the percent of varnished clasts; from Wesling et al. (1992).

[4] Percent rubified clasts; from Wesling et al. (1992).

[5] The relative height of depositional bars from the top of the bar to the trough of the adjacent swale.

[6] Refers to the sequence of soil horizons that is representative of each map unit. Abbreviations for master horizons: A—surface horizon characterized by accumulation of organic matter and typically as a zone of illuviation of clay, sesquioxides, silica, gypsum, carbonate, and/or salts; B—subsurface horizon characterized by a redder color, stronger structure development, and/or accumulation of secondary illusial materials (clay, sesquioxide, silica, gypsum, and salts); C—subsurface horizon that may appear similar to dissimilar to the parent material and includes unaltered material and material in various stages of weathering; K—subsurface horizon engulfed with carbonate to the extent that its morphology is determined by the carbonate. Abbreviations for master horizon modifiers; j—used in conjunction with other modifiers to denote incipient development of that particular feature or property; k—accumulation of carbonates; m—strong cementation; q—accumulation of silica; t—accumulation of clay; u—soil properties undifferentiated; v—vesicular structure; w—color of structural B horizon.

[7] Abbreviations: sg—single grained; m—massive; 1—weak; 2—moderate; 3—strong; vf—very fine; f—fine; m—medium; pl—platy; sbk—subangular blocky.

[8] Abbreviations: n.p.—not present; 1—few; 2—common; 3—many; n—thin; mk—moderately thick; pf—ped face; co—colloidal stains.

[9] Hue determined with Munsell Soil Color Chart, Munsell Color Co., Inc. (1988).

[10] Terminology of Gile et al. (1966) and Birkeland (1984).

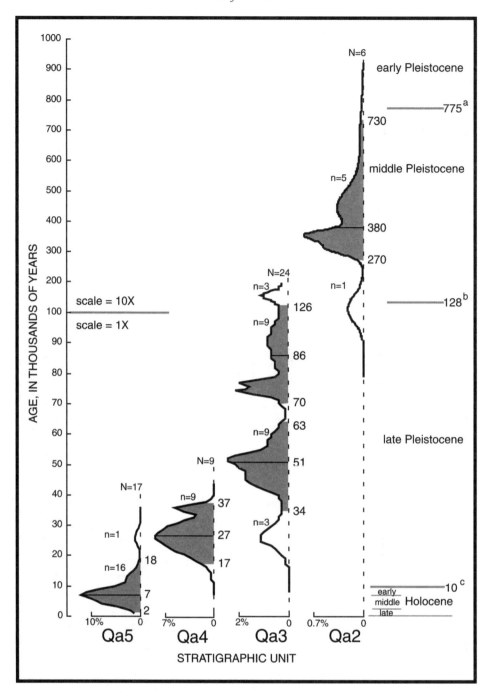

Figure 13. Plot showing age distribution of mapped Quaternary units Qa2-Qa5 in Midway Valley and Fortymile Wash. Shaded areas represent the main periods of deposition and/or soil development. Each of the horizontal axes is a relative scale for each probability density function expressed in percent probability per thousand years. Footnotes: a—Matuyama-Brunhes chronozone boundary (Morrison, 1991); b—astronomical age of marine oxygen-isotope substage 5e boundary (Imbrie et al., 1984); c—arbitrary age suggested for Pleistocene-Holocene boundary (Hopkins, 1975). Ages given in thousands of years; note scale change at 100,000 yr. From Whitney et al. (2004c; unit ages determined by J.D. Paces and S.A. Mahan, U.S. Geological Survey).

pits, thicknesses range from 2.5 (8 ft) to >3.5 m (11.5 ft). Soils are strongly developed, with Av and Bkq horizons formed in eolian sediments capping the deposit.

Unit Qa3 is present as large remnant alluvial-fan surfaces and as fluvial terraces. It is one of the dominant Quaternary map units in the Yucca Mountain site area, and underlies the main Fortymile Wash terrace (Fig. 14). A well-developed desert pavement containing darkly varnished clasts characterizes the Qa3 surface (Table 2). The original bar-and-swale morphology has been reduced to the height of individual clasts (some exceeding

(a)

Calico Fan Site

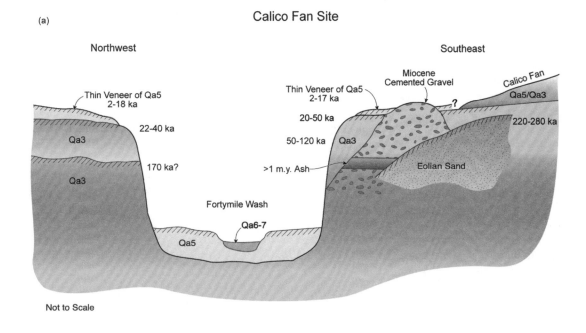

(b)

Yucca Mountain Road Crossing

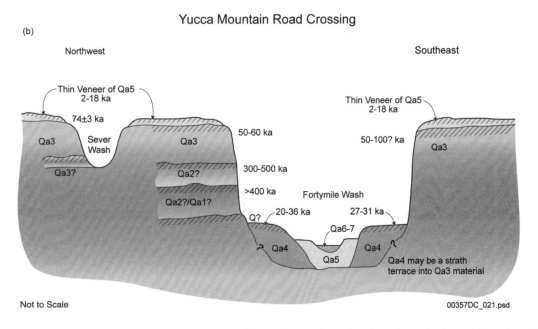

Figure 14. Generalized cross sections showing evolution of Fortymile Wash. Locations of sections shown in Figure 8. Based on CRWMS M&O (2000, Fig. 7.4-4 therein).

30 cm diameter) above the surface. Thickness of the unit averages ~2–2.5 m (6.5–8.2 ft) and locally exceeds 3.3 m (10.8 ft) in soil pits and along the Fortymile Wash terraces. Clay films and a strong blocky structure are characteristic of the argillic soil horizons that also commonly have accumulations of secondary silica and carbonate.

Unit Qa4 consists of small, inset fluvial terrace and alluvial fan remnants on the east side of Yucca Mountain. The desert pavement on the surface ranges from loosely to tightly interlocking and is noticeably less well developed than pavements formed on the older fluvial surfaces. Bar-and-swale relief mostly has been reduced to clast height above the surface. Thickness of the unit averages ~1 m (3.3 ft) and does not exceed 2 m (6.5 ft) where observed in soil pits. The strongly developed Qa4 soil is characterized by a reddened argillic horizon and accumulations of carbonate and silica.

Unit Qa5 covers parts of alluvial fans and forms inset terraces along drainages. The desert pavement is loosely packed and poorly formed, and surface clasts have minor accumulations of rock varnish. Qa5 surfaces display well-developed bar-and-swale morphology, the amount of relief being related to landscape position and sediment sources; coarsest grained bars are in the proximal fan regions. Smaller, lower, partly buried bars lie on distal fans, where the intervening swales are partly filled by fine-grained eolian silts and sands. In soil-pit and trench exposures, the average thickness of Qa5 is ~1 m (3.3 ft), and the maximum observed thickness is ~2.5 m (8.2 ft). Soils are weakly developed, being strongest in swales and weakest on bars.

Unit Qa6 is present along the active washes as low floodplains less than 1 m (3.3 ft) above the active channels and as vegetated bars. No desert pavement has developed, and surface clasts are unvarnished and unweathered. Relief on the Qa6 surface is primarily the result of preservation of original bar-and-swale morphology. Natural outcrops and manmade exposures indicate that the total thickness of the unit does not exceed 2 m (6.5 ft). Soil development is limited to minimal oxidation of the deposit and sparse accumulation of carbonate, which is more concentrated toward the upper 10 cm (4 in) of the deposit, although the matrix typically contains widely disseminated carbonate.

Unit Qa7 consists of deposits along active channels and adjacent floodplains. No desert pavement has formed on the surface, and no desert varnish occurs on clasts except that which may be on clasts reworked from older surfaces. Clasts are unweathered, and the original depositional bar-and-swale relief is unaltered. The total exposed thickness of Qa7 does not exceed 2 m (6.5 ft). No in situ pedogenic alterations were observed, but the matrix contains reworked, disseminated carbonate.

Colluvial and debris-flow deposits are undifferentiated as surficial map units because of their limited areal extent and the limited exposure of all but the youngest deposits. Such deposits generally consist of gravelly silty sands and silty fine- to medium-gravel with pebble to small cobble clasts. They are poorly sorted and nonbedded to crudely bedded. Thicknesses are generally less than 2–3 m (6.5–10 ft) as observed in trench and soil-pit exposures. Most of the colluvial deposits on hillslopes exhibit surface characteristics of units Qa5 and Qa6 (latest Pleistocene to late Holocene), but the deposits having surface characteristics similar to unit Qa4 surfaces (late Pleistocene) commonly are near the toe of the hillslope.

Two types of eolian sediment were observed in the Yucca Mountain site area: (1) reworked eolian deposits within sand ramps surrounding Busted Butte and along the southeastern margin of Midway Valley (Figs. 2 and 12), and (2) thin accumulations of silt and fine sand in the A and B horizons of most surface soils and relict accumulations within some buried soils. Sand ramps at Busted Butte and in southeastern Midway Valley are composed of a stacked sequence of eolian-colluvial units that have textures of pebbly, silty, fine- to medium-grained sand interbedded with sandy pebble to cobble gravel. Gravel clasts are angular to subangular and commonly less than 5 cm (2 in) in diameter, but some clasts are as large as 50 cm (20 in) in diameter. Maximum thickness of the sand-ramp deposits exceeds 15 m (49 ft). A weakly to moderately interlocking desert pavement covers most of the surfaces. Typically, one or more buried soils are within the deposits.

The presence of Bishop Ash (Izett et al., 1988) in lower sand-ramp deposits at Busted Butte (Whitney et al., 1985; Menges et al., 1994, 2004) and at other localities near Yucca Mountain (Hoover, 1989) indicates that those landforms began forming within the region prior to ca. 760 ka (age of Bishop Ash). At Busted Butte, some of the buried soils have been dated as middle to late Pleistocene (Menges et al., 1994, 2004). Multiple buried soils above the Bishop tephra indicate that accumulation of the sand ramps is episodic and punctuated by periods of surface stabilization and soil formation. Numerical ages of 73 ± 9 ka and 38 ± 6 ka from two successive units in the upper 3 m of the deposits in a trench in southern Midway Valley possibly indicate the ages of two of the more recent depositional episodes, and another date of 6 ± 1 ka from a sample of the A soil horizon is indicative of continuing accumulation of eolian sediments during the Holocene (Menges et al., 2004).

A few to several tens of centimeters of eolian silt and fine sand have accumulated on most alluvial geomorphic surfaces in the Yucca Mountain site area and have been incorporated into soil profiles formed on those surfaces. These eolian accumulations are not mapped separately because of their relatively thin nature. Models of desert pavement and soil formation show the importance of eolian accumulations as a source for the fine earth fraction, carbonate, and soluble salts that occur in otherwise clean sandy gravel deposits in arid regions (Birkeland, 1984; McFadden et al., 1987; McFadden and Weldon, 1987; McDonald and McFadden, 1994).

Pedogenic carbonate with subordinate opaline silica (calcrete) is present as slope-parallel deposits and as remobilized fracture fillings. The deposits generally are poorly indurated and fine grained. Ooids and pellets are locally abundant, and preserved fossils are of roots (Stuckless et al., 1998) rather than aquatic animals.

Trenching Activities

Information on the stratigraphic relations among surficial deposits was augmented considerably by the large-scale mapping and detailed descriptions of vertical sequences that were freshly exposed in trenches excavated across those faults suspected of being active during Quaternary time. Within the site area, some 50 trenches were emplaced across such faults (Whitney et al., 2004b) primarily for the purpose of determining the extent of Quaternary tectonic activity with respect to (1) the number, amount of displacement, and age of individual surface-rupturing events causing earthquakes; (2) fault slip rates; and (3) recurrence intervals between successive events on a given fault. Results of the detailed Quaternary fault studies are given in Keefer et al. (2004) and brief summaries are presented in the "Structural Geology" section.

Erosion, Deposition, and Flooding

Studies of past and modern geomorphic processes at Yucca Mountain primarily were designed to estimate the long-term average rates of erosion on the ridge crests and hillslopes of the mountain, thereby to determine the potential for erosional breaching of the proposed underground facility for the storage of high-level radioactive wastes. Flow characteristics within Fortymile Wash are of particular importance because of the concern over whether potential dissolution products from the stored wastes could be entrained by flow within the lower reaches of this drainage system and subsequently become incorporated within the flow of the Amargosa River southwest of Yucca Mountain (Fig. 1).

Landscape Response to Modern Climatic Conditions

In the dry, semiarid climatic regime of the Yucca Mountain area, precipitation and runoff that produces streamflow in Fortymile Wash generally occurs only during infrequent but intense local thunderstorms that produce flash floods and cause extensive hillslope erosion and rapid deposition of coarse debris on alluvial fans and in stream channels. One such event occurred on 21–22 July 1984, when rainfall of ~85 mm (3.35 in) caused a series of debris flows on the south slope of Jake Ridge (Fig. 15), in the northeastern part of the site area (Fig. 2). Coe et al. (1997) reported that (1) 7040 m^3 of debris were stripped from the hillslope and redistributed over an area of 49, 132 m^2, which included a tributary of Fortymile Wash and a part of the wash itself; and

Figure 15. View looking north toward south slope of Jake Ridge (location shown in Fig. 2), showing debris flows and flow tracks (light-colored strips) resulting from intense storm activity on 21–22 July 1984. Photograph courtesy of J.A. Coe, U.S. Geological Survey.

(2) maximum depth of hillslope erosion was 1.8 m. The runoff in Fortymile Wash infiltrates the stream channel at high rates downstream past Yucca Mountain to distal reaches of its alluvial fan (Osterkamp et al., 1994). As a consequence of progressive downstream channel losses and flow attenuation within the wash, channel capacity decreases along the ~24-km-stretch that extends south and southwest from its northern reaches to the northeast edge of Amargosa Valley (Fig. 1). Along this section of Fortymile Wash, large-scale sediment deposition has transformed the entrenched channel into a broadly braided alluvial fan.

Eolian processes of sand movement and dust deposition are presently active around Yucca Mountain. Modern dust deposition in southern Nevada ranges from 4.3 to 5.7 g/m²/year (Reheis and Kihl, 1995). Annual dust flux increases with mean annual temperature but appears to more closely reflect changes in annual precipitation (relative drought conditions) rather than temperature. Playa and alluvial sources produce about the same amount of dust per unit area; however, the total volume of dust produced is much larger from alluvial sources. The mineralogic and major oxide composition of dust samples indicates that sand and some silt is locally derived and deposited, whereas clay and some silt can be derived from distant sources. Modern and Holocene dust has been accumulating below desert pavements and on hillslopes in the site area.

Landscape Response to Climate Change

In contrast to the present warm and dry semiarid conditions, cooler and wetter conditions existed at times in the Yucca Mountain region during the Quaternary (Forester et al., 1999; Sharpe, this volume). The climatic changes followed a cycle consisting of four general phases—interpluvial (present conditions), interpluvial to pluvial transition, pluvial, and pluvial to interpluvial transition. Primary characteristics for each of these phases are briefly summarized below to indicate changes in geomorphic processes that may occur in response to changing climatic conditions in future years at Yucca Mountain.

1. Interpluvial phase. Under warm and dry conditions, there is low vegetation density and little or no grassland. Infrequent hillslope stripping results in local aggradation and alluvial-fan building. Main valleys aggrade slowly or remain essentially stable. Fine-grained eolian material accumulates on geomorphic surfaces and hillslopes. Sporadic large sediment yield from hillslopes continues until most colluvium is removed, and hillslopes begin to stabilize.

2. Interpluvial to pluvial transition phase. As temperature cools and precipitation increases during each season, there is greater vegetation density, hillslopes stabilize, and hillslope-sediment yield decreases. Hillslope deposition is renewed as the removal of colluvium is retarded by vegetation, and there is increased trapping of eolian and other sediments on the hillslopes. The increased retention of surficial materials on hillslopes, combined with greater precipitation, causes a change from aggra-

dation to incision in sections of trunk streams that are above stable base levels.

3. Pluvial phase. Under wetter and cooler conditions, landscape stability is reached through physical weathering of the bedrock, a covering of bouldery colluvium forms on the hillslopes, and there is denser vegetation growth that inhibits erosion.

4. Pluvial to interpluvial transition phase. During the transition to warmer, drier conditions, vegetation becomes less dense, hillslopes destabilize, and sediment yield increases primarily through debris-flow transport of the previously weathered material to the valley floors. Debris-flow stripping occurs during infrequent high-intensity storms, resulting in alluvial-fan building and valley aggradation. Eolian activity may increase.

Flooding History

Glancy (1994) discussed geologic evidence for prehistoric flooding in Coyote Wash, a branch of Drill Hole Wash located between Dead Yucca Ridge and Live Yucca Ridge on the east side of Yucca Mountain (Fig. 2). Trenches excavated across and along the modern-day wash channel, which splits headward into two forks, exposed sediments indicative of multiple flood events, including debris flows. Glancy (1994) concluded that moderately indurated sediments overlying the bedrock and underlying the stream terraces adjacent to the channel probably were deposited during the late Pleistocene or early Holocene (older than 10 ka), and that nonindurated sediments overlying the older sediments were probably of Holocene age (younger than 10 ka). Using surficial boulders near the trenches, Glancy (1994) estimated the magnitude of the flood that deposited them during the Holocene. Assuming the flood was water-dominated (Newtonian fluid) and that all of the boulders were emplaced by the same flood, a peak discharge of 2400 ft³/s was estimated to have occurred in the north fork of Coyote Wash. The combined flows of the north and south forks could result in a peak flow as large as 5000 ft³/s. (Note: Stream-flow and flow-velocity measurements typically are recorded in English units rather than metric units.)

A flood that occurred on 24 February 1969 is believed to have been, overall, the most severe flood in the Amargosa River drainage basin during recent times. The peak flow on that date in Fortymile Wash, at a point just downstream from the Yucca Mountain road crossing (located 3.4 km north and 1.3 km west of the southeast corner of the site area), was estimated by Squires and Young (1984) at ~20,000 ft³/s on the basis of channel geometry and residual evidence discovered during a flood-prediction study. This estimate was independently supported by a witness who described the flow as "wall-to-wall" water, ~4 ft deep, across the 800–900-ft-wide flood plain at the bottom of the incised channel. At an average depth of 4 ft, the cross-sectional flow area would be on the order of 3200–3600 ft². Assuming a peak flow of 20,000 ft³/s, the resultant average velocity would have been ~5.5–6.25 ft/s, depending on cross-sectional area. For comparison, average runoff velocities recorded at a gaging station located near borehole UE-25 J-13 (Fig. 8), 0.8 km south of the Yucca Mountain road crossing, during March 1995 (peak flow of 3,000 ft³/s; see CRWMS M&O, 2000, Table 7.1-1 therein) and February 1998 (peak flow of 200 ft³/s) were 7–8 ft/s and 3 ft/s, respectively.

Fortymile Wash flowed on 3 March 1983, as a result of a regional rainstorm that may have melted some snowpack at the higher basin altitudes (Pabst et al., 1993); the flow peaked at 570 ft³/s, as recorded by the gaging station near borehole UE-25 J-13 (Fig. 8). Fortymile Wash also flowed three times in the summer of 1984 in response to convective rainstorms during a prolonged and uncommonly intensive monsoon-storm season. Magnitudes of the three flows (21–22 July, 22 July, and 19 August 1984) at the recording station near borehole UE-25 J-13 were 1860, ~150, and ~850 ft³/s, respectively (Pabst et al., 1993).

Fortymile Wash did not flow again within the site area for almost 11 years following the 1984 summer storms. It next flowed for 10–12 h on 11 March 1995, in upper-basin reaches as the result of a regional rainstorm and probably was amplified by rainfall-induced snowmelt from highlands north of Yucca Mountain (Beck and Glancy, 1995); peak flow of 3000 ft³/s was recorded at the gaging station near borehole UE-25 J-13. Stretches of the Amargosa River also flowed for 10–12 h on the same day, marking this runoff event as the first documented storm wherein Fortymile Wash and the Amargosa River flowed simultaneously throughout their main-stem-channel reaches into Death Valley. A similarly caused runoff with a peak flow of 200 ft³/s in Fortymile Wash occurred on 22–23 February 1998 (Tanko and Glancy, 2001), at which time there was also flow in the Amargosa River into Death Valley. In summary, Fortymile Wash flowed six times during the 15 years from March 1983 through February 1998, and streamflow data indicated that most of the flows probably continued downstream to Death Valley.

Bedrock Erosion Rates during the Quaternary

A cosmogenic dating technique, primarily involving measurement of the concentrations on bedrock surfaces of ¹⁰Be, was used to calculate the maximum erosion rate of exposures on ridge crests in the Yucca Mountain site area (see Faure, 1986). The dating method assumes that erosion had proceeded at a gradual and constant rate.

Quartz separates from seven samples of tuffaceous rocks of the Tiva Canyon Tuff exposed on Antler Ridge and an adjacent ridge to the south (Fig. 2) were analyzed for ¹⁰Be (Table 3), resulting in a calculated maximum possible erosion rate for these bedrock outcrops of 0.04–0.27 cm/k.y. This rate (1) integrates all erosion occurring on the summit of Yucca Mountain under all climatic conditions that have existed in the area during most (if not all) of the Quaternary; (2) indicates a remarkable erosional stability for this landscape; and (3) compares well with the long-term average erosion rate in hillslope colluvium on the middle to lower hillslopes at Yucca Mountain (U.S. Department of Energy, 1993). The average erosion rate for the seven bedrock analyses on Yucca Mountain is equal to 1.38 m/m.y., which is almost as low as rock erosion rates of <1 m/m.y. measured in Australia (Bierman and Caffee, 2002) and is at the low end of erosion rates of 1.4–20 m/m.y. measured on granite landforms in the Alabama Hills in California (Nichols et al., 2006).

Hillslope Erosion Rates from Dated Colluvial Boulder Deposits

The surface-exposure ages of relict boulder deposits on Yucca Mountain and nearby hillslopes were dated (see below) to calculate the long-term rate of removal of unconsolidated material on the middle and lower hillslopes of Yucca Mountain. In addition, the depth of erosion in 50-m-wide zones on both sides of a deposit, including channel incision, was measured (Whitney and Harrington, 1993). The paleotopographic hillslope surface at each locality was assumed to be represented by the top of the boulder deposit on that hillslope. Because (1) the present relief across the middle hillslopes is low (maximum 2 m), and (2) stripping of hillslopes by debris flows is the dominant process presently moving material down these hillslopes, the modern relief on these hillslopes probably represents a maximum for much of the late Quaternary.

Boulder deposits, with boulders 0.3–2 m in diameter, range from wide continuous mantles to isolated narrow bands bounded

TABLE 3. MAXIMUM BEDROCK EROSION RATES ON YUCCA MOUNTAIN

Sample Number	¹⁰Be Concentration (atoms/g)	Max Erosion Rate	
		cm/k.y.	Uncertainty (cm/k.y.)
CDH-AR-1*	4.71	0.041	(0.028–0.064)
CDH-AR-5	2.33	0.11	(0.083–0.16)
CDH-AR-6	1.95	0.14	(0.10–0.19)
CDH-WR-1*	3.23	0.071	(0.052–0.10)
CDH-WR-2	1.08	0.27	(0.21–0.37)
CDH-WR-5	1.16	0.25	(0.20–0.35)
CDH-WR-6	2.80	0.090	(0.067–0.13)

Note: Samples partially processed by the University of Arizona, Tucson, Arizona, and analyzed at the University of Pennsylvania, Philadelphia, Pennsylvania. Abbreviations: g—gram; cm/k.y.—centimeter/thousand years. Source:CRWMS M&O (1998, Table 3.4-6).

*Samples partially processed by the University of Arizona, and analyzed at PRIME Lab, Purdue University, Lafayette, Indiana.

by gullies. Eleven such deposits were sampled (Whitney and Harrington, 1993) for cation-ratio dating (Table 4)—six on the flanks of Yucca Mountain, three on the southwest hillslope of Skull Mountain (20 km to the east), one on the northeast slope of Little Skull Mountain (10 km to the southeast, Fig. 3), and one on the east slope of Buckboard Mesa (25 km north-northeast of Yucca Wash). The erosion rate was calculated based on the amount of erosion on the hillslope since the boulder deposit formed, divided by the surface-exposure age of the deposit. Both the rock-varnish cation ratio and the in situ ^{36}Cl cosmogenic-nuclide dating methods (Harrington and Whitney, 1987; Whitney and Harrington, 1993; Gosse et al., 1996) were applied (see CRWMS M&O, 2000, section 7.4.2.2, for a detailed discussion on rock-varnish and cosmogenic dating of these deposits). The estimated varnish cation-ratio ages of the analyzed samples range from 100 ka (80–140 ka) to 1020 ka (730–1430 ka), as shown in Table 4, and ages of several of the sampled deposits by cosmogenic dating are given in Table 5. The long-term erosion rates of stripping of unconsolidated material from Yucca Mountain hillslopes were calculated to be <0.5 cm/k.y. (average ~0.2 cm/k.y., based on a range of 0.02–0.6 cm/k.y.; Whitney and Harrington, 1993).

Hillslope Erosion during the Latest Pleistocene-Holocene Interval

The climatic cycles recorded within the valley alluvium in Fortymile Wash and Midway Valley indicate a general landscape stability, punctuated by short pulses of either hillslope stripping or valley incision. The presence of relict boulder deposits that cover parts of most hillsides provides evidence that hillslope stripping was incomplete even through several climate cycles.

The time interval during which alluvial unit Qa5 (latest Pleistocene-Holocene, ca. 18–2 ka; see Fig. 13) was deposited in Mid-

TABLE 5. AGES OF FOUR BOULDER DEPOSITS AROUND YUCCA MOUNTAIN

Boulder deposit location	Calculated cation-ratio age (k.y.)	Calculated cosmogenic-nuclide age (k.y.)
Buckboard Mesa	730–1430	460–765
Skull Mountain Pass	500–930	620–1030
East Side Yucca	320–590	480–805
West Side Yucca	360–660	660–1100

Note: Uncertainties in the cation ratio ages are the 95% confidence limits of the curve regression line. Cosmogenic age 1σ uncertainties are 25% of the mean age. Source: CRWMS M&O (2000, Table 7.4-2 therein).

way Valley and Fortymile Wash can be used to derive semiquantitative boundary values for the amount of erosion then occurring on Yucca Mountain hillslopes. This 16 k.y. period encompasses the last pluvial to interpluvial transition, a time of climatic transition to semiarid conditions favorable for erosional stripping of hillslope sediment. The estimated mean depth of unconsolidated material removed from these hillslopes to form alluvial unit Qa5 in Midway Valley (Forester et al., 1999) is 27 cm. If this mean depth is assumed to have been eroded during these 16 k.y., a rate of 1.7 cm/k.y. for erosion of unconsolidated hillslope material is indicated, although it should be noted that this rate does not incorporate either the eolian-sediment addition to the hillslopes or the sediment that moved through Midway Valley and into Fortymile Wash. Based on an analysis of alluvial deposits in Fortymile Wash, Forester et al. (1999) estimated the depth of erosion of bedrock during the last 15 k.y. to be ~18 cm, which indicates a rate of 1.2 cm/k.y. These relatively short-term erosional rates are larger than the long-term (middle and late Quaternary) rates calculated for Yucca Mountain hillslopes (0.2 cm/k.y.) and bedrock ridges (0.04–0.27 cm/k.y.) (see above).

In the 10 k.y. prior to the deposition of unit Qa5, the climate was wetter, hillslopes were more densely vegetated, and little material was being removed from the surrounding hillslopes. The erosion rate for the complete climatic cycle from 28 to 2 ka for the Yucca Mountain hillslopes therefore was 1.04 cm/k.y. for unconsolidated material and 0.7 cm/k.y. for hillslope bedrock.

Erosional History of Fortymile Wash

Fortymile Wash, the principal tributary of the Amargosa River lying within the site area (Fig. 2), flows through the 25-km-long Fortymile Canyon (Fig.1), and continues southward for about another 20 km along the east side of Yucca Mountain before entering the eastern part of the Amargosa Valley (inset map, Fig. 1). Between the mouth of the canyon and the Amargosa Desert, the stream channel is entrenched as much as 25 m in alluvial fill. The depth of incision decreases over a 6 km stretch, where the channel becomes the head of a long fan that crosses the Amargosa Valley. Analysis of the Fortymile Canyon sedimentary provenance and altitude distribution of volcanic rocks (Lundstrom and Warren, 1994) indicates that the canyon was formed during the late Miocene or Pliocene, sometime before 3 Ma. A

TABLE 4. VARNISH CATION RATIO AGE ESTIMATES FROM BOULDER DEPOSITS AROUND YUCCA MOUNTAIN

Sample	Age (k.y.)
YME-1	440 (*320–590*)
YME-2	100 (*80–140*)
YMW-1	310 (*230–420*)
YMW-2	440 (*330–600*)
YMW-3	480 (*360–660*)
YMN-1	530 (*390–720*)
LSM-1	680 (*500–930*)
SKM-1	550 (*400–750*)
SKM-2	580 (*430–800*)
SKM-3	850 (*600–1180*)
SKM-3A	700 (*510–960*)
BM-1	1020 (*730–1430*)

Note: Error ± 1σ. Source: Modified from CRWMS M&O (1998, Table 3.4-7 therein).

relict gravel deposit exposed in Fortymile Wash contains a different lithology than the Quaternary gravel fills, probably indicating that the present drainage captured a formerly northward-flowing drainage along the moat of the Timber Mountain caldera, north of the site area, sometime between 9 and 3 Ma.

Surficial deposits within and flanking Fortymile Wash record a complex history of aggradation and channel incision, as shown diagrammatically in two cross sections: (1) the northern one (Fig. 14A) located at a point between Alice Ridge west of the wash (Fig. 2) and the western toe of what is termed the Calico Fan across the wash to the east at the east edge of the site area; and (2) the southern one (Fig. 14B) located near the Yucca Mountain road crossing, which is 4 km north and 1.3 km west of the southeast corner of the site area (locations of sections shown in Fig. 8). Multiple episodes of downcutting are evident from a comparison of the different stratigraphic sequences on the east and west walls of the wash, as shown on the two cross sections. At the Yucca Mountain road crossing (Fig. 14B), there are four gravelly alluvial units on the west wall, each capped by a soil representative of pluvial conditions when vegetation was dense and the stream channel was not being aggraded. The buried soils on the west wall are missing from the east wall, indicating that the alluvial fill on the east side of the wash wall is older than the 50–100 ka soils at the top of the fill, but younger than the 300–500 ka buried soil exposed in the west wall. Farther north, at the Calico fan site, the 170 ka buried soil on the west side is missing on the east wall (Fig. 14; note: these older ages are based on U-series analyses). Exposed in gullies in the east wall are upper Tertiary gravels and middle Pleistocene eolian deposits that are overlain by unit Qa3 alluvium, providing evidence of at least two episodes of downcutting that predate unit Qa3. If the 170 ka age on the buried soil in the west wall is valid, then a major incision and erosion of the older alluvium took place during the climatic time of oxygen isotope stage (OIS) 6 of the global climate record (derived from marine cores; see Imbrie et al., 1984), the wettest climatic episode at the end of the middle Pleistocene.

The alluvium of unit Qa3 (Fig. 14) that underlies the main Fortymile Wash stream terrace was subsequently deposited during the interglacial OIS 5e-5a, and it has developed a soil that is primarily of OIS 4 age.

The most recent incision of Fortymile Wash (Lundstrom et al., 1996) probably took place during the latter part of the pluvial episode, OIS 4 (ca. 116–60 ka; Winograd et al., 1988), from ca. 116–60 ka, and the early part of OIS 3 (ca. 55–40 ka). Within 2 m of the present channel of Fortymile Wash are remnants of a strath terrace with a thin alluvial deposit mapped as unit Qa4 at the Yucca Mountain road crossing (Fig. 14B). This terrace likely represents a pause in the downcutting of Fortymile Wash during the relatively short interglacial climate represented by OIS 3. The last 2–4 m of incision probably occurred during the last pluvial climate at Yucca Mountain, 22–18 ka. Aggradation has taken place in the channel and on the lower Fortymile Wash alluvial fan, represented by unit Qa5 deposits, during the Pleistocene-Holocene transition and continuing through the Holocene to the present.

Based solely on thermoluminescence-dating of silt in sand-dominated horizons in soils capping the alluvial units in the west wall of Fortymile Wash and the belief that the oldest dated deposit is younger than 150 ka, Lundstrom et al. (1998) advanced the interpretation that 13 m of aggradation occurred in the wash from 140 to 50 ka, followed by ~20 m of incision between 36 and 24 ka. This interpretation, however, does not account for the presence of buried soils in the west wall that are not present on the east wall (Fig. 14B), which is an important stratigraphic relation that indicates a much longer period (perhaps as much as 500 k.y.) of sediment accumulation along the wash.

In summary, a comprehensive interpretation of Fortymile Wash using all buried soils and the U-series dates obtained from the central wash reveals a complex history of four to five cut-and-fill cycles spanning the middle to late Quaternary. The incision in the wash occurred over a limited vertical range in elevation of not more than several tens of meters. Furthermore, the wash did not cut and fill the same channel each time, but instead migrated laterally across the Fortymile Wash fan. Thus, the channel during the middle and late Quaternary was incised during pluvial periods; then, during the transition to interpluvial climates, when hillslopes were most actively stripped, the wash aggraded and migrated laterally prior to the next cutting cycle.

Potential for Future Erosion and Deposition

Most streams draining the east slope of Yucca Mountain cross Midway Valley and flow into Fortymile Wash (Fig. 3). Although the true base level for these tributary valleys is Fortymile Wash, the effective base level is the floor of Midway Valley that is presently undergoing aggradation because of the existing interpluvial, warm and dry climate. Since at least the beginning of the Holocene, local storms have activated debris-flow stripping of the hillslopes around Midway Valley (e.g., see Fig. 15) resulting in a rising base level as sediments accumulated on the valley floor. If a period of incision were to ensue as a result of a change in climate to one of greater effective moisture, the main drainage courses in Midway Valley would ultimately start to incise the valley floor, then erode headward causing downcutting in the tributary valleys and removal of channel-fill deposits. If wetter climatic conditions continued for a long enough period of time, all of the alluvium in these valleys would be moved to the floor of the valley.

An exposure of the fill in Coyote Wash demonstrates that such a complete emptying of the alluvium in the tributary valleys did not occur during the last glacial cycle (Glancy, 1994). Relict Pleistocene fill documents the incomplete stripping of the valley alluvium during the last two climatic cycles. The climate change to a regime favoring sediment removal that began ca. 28 ka did not last long enough to allow complete sediment removal from these tributary valleys. Since ca. 15–18 ka, when the climate began to become drier, these valleys have been aggraded. The incomplete removal of hillslope and valley alluvium in the tributary valleys during the 10,000–13,000 "wet" years of the last climate cycle indicates that more than 10 k.y. is needed to remove alluvium from these valleys, assuming that the climate for that time interval was favorable for erosion. Based on Coyote Wash data, it would require substantially more than 10 k.y. to effectively remove the alluvium and to begin actively eroding the bedrock floors of the washes. Because evidence shows that aggradation and degradation cycles respond to regional climatic changes, there is no indication, based on an analysis of future climates in the Yucca Mountain region (see Sharpe, this volume), that another period of downcutting of more than a few meters will occur in Fortymile Wash and its tributaries within the next 10 k.y.

Another important factor to consider, relative to future incision of Fortymile Wash and its tributaries, is that the effective base level for Fortymile Wash is the broad expanse of the surface of Amargosa Valley alluvium. No substantial incision within the present valley of Fortymile Wash is possible unless a major incision, or deep headcut, occurs far downstream in the present Amargosa Valley, migrates some 95 km (60 mi) or more upstream through the present fill of Amargosa Valley, and continues headward through the present alluvial fan of Fortymile Wash. Headcutting across the Amargosa Valley over the next 10 k.y. is unlikely, not only because of the long distance involved, but also because no evidence of earlier Quaternary valley incision has been observed along the Amargosa River.

STRUCTURAL GEOLOGY

Introduction

The structural geology of Yucca Mountain and vicinity is dominated by a series of north-striking normal faults along which Tertiary volcanic rocks were tilted eastward and displaced hundreds of meters (predominantly down-to-the-west), primarily during a period of extensional deformation in middle to late Miocene time. These through-going faults divided the site area into several structural blocks, each of which is further deformed by minor intrablock faults (Figs. 16 and 17). The complex pattern of faulting is shown in detail on two bedrock geologic maps based on extensive field investigations conducted largely in 1996 and 1997 as an integral part of the Yucca Mountain site characterization program (U.S. Department of Energy, 1988). The two maps are: (1) a 1:24,000-scale map by Day et al. (1998a) covering the 165 km^2 (65 mi^2) of the site area (Figs. 1 and 2), and (2) a 1:6000-scale map by Day et al. (1998b) covering 41 km^2 (15.7 mi^2) of the central part of the site area that includes the proposed repository block itself. At these scales, it was possible to map individually many of the stratigraphic subdivisions (zones, some subzones, and bedded tuff units) within various volcanic formations and to record faults generally with displacements as little as 5 m at the 1:24,000 scale and as little as 1.5 m at the 1:6000 scale. The site-area map by Day et al. (1998a) incorporated the work of Dickerson and Drake (1998; map scale 1:6000) in the northeastern part of the site area. Detailed results of the 1996–1997 geologic mapping program are discussed by Potter et al. (2004).

The studies by Day et al. (1998a, 1998b) benefited substantially from earlier mapping and structural interpretations of areas within and around the site area by Christiansen and Lipman (1965), Lipman and McKay (1965), and Scott and Bonk (1984). The latter map, at a scale of 1:12,000 and considered to be largely reconnaissance in nature, was particularly useful in that numerous zones within the Tiva Canyon and Topopah Spring Tuffs were defined and mapped, resulting in the delineation of minor faults not previously recognized. Regional map compilations by Frizzell and Shulters (1990) and Potter et al. (2002a) place the geology of Yucca Mountain in a regional setting.

In addition to the maps mentioned above, Simonds et al. (1995) compiled a 1:24,000-scale fault map that incorporated all of the then known information on Quaternary to recent fault activity in the Yucca Mountain site area, which served as a guide for the subsequent trenching and detailed studies of newly exposed surficial-deposit sequences to determine the extent, magnitude, and ages of Quaternary deformational events. Studies of the structural and stratigraphic relations exposed in the trench excavations are described in a series of published reports (Keefer et al., 2004).

Detailed maps and descriptions of faults and fracture systems encountered in the ESF and Cross Drift (CD, Fig. 16) have been presented in several reports, including Beason et al. (1996), Albin et al. (1997), and Mongano et al. (1999). Summary data from these reports are incorporated in discussions of the subsurface characteristics of selected features exposed in the ESF and Cross Drift.

Block-Bounding Faults

Block-bounding faults are spaced 1–5 km apart and include, from east to west within the site area, the Paintbrush Canyon, Bow Ridge, Solitario Canyon, Fatigue Wash, and Windy Wash faults (Fig. 16). The Crater Flat faults lying west of the site area are also included in this discussion of block-bounding faults because they form the west boundary of the structural block that occupies the northwesternmost corner of the site area. Fault descriptions are summarized primarily from (1) bedrock geologic maps of Day et al. (1998a, 1998b) and Dickerson and Drake (1998); (2) a compilation of fault data by Simonds et al. (1995); (3) a regional geologic map compiled by Potter et al. (2002a); (4) detailed descriptions of structural features by Potter et al. (2004); and (5) a series of reports describing results of the mapping of trenches to determine the history of Quaternary deformation along the major faults in and adjacent to the site area (Keefer et al., 2004).

Displacements along block-bounding faults are mainly dip-slip (down-to-the-west), with subordinate strike-slip or oblique-slip components of movement exhibited by some faults. Seismic reflection data have been interpreted to indicate that the faults penetrate and offset the Tertiary-Paleozoic contact beneath Yucca Mountain (Brocher et al., 1998). Strain is transferred between block-bounding faults along relay faults that intersect the block-bounding faults at oblique angles and provide an intrablock

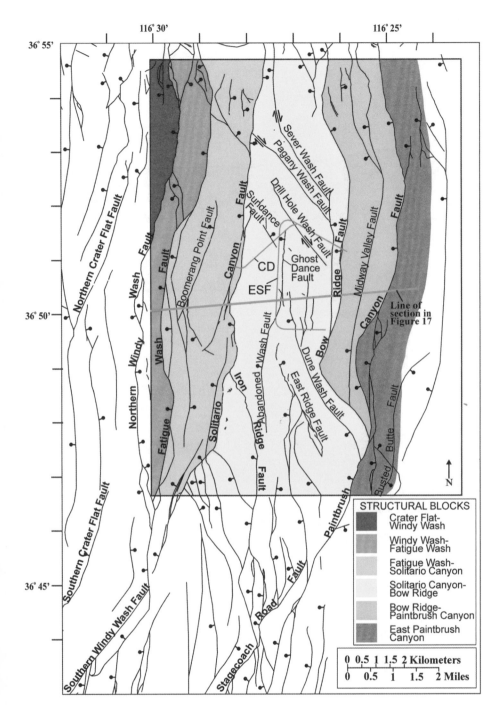

Figure 16. Map showing distribution of faults in Yucca Mountain site area and adjacent areas to south and west. Fault names in bold print indicate faults with demonstrable Quaternary movement; all faults are shown with solid lines although many segments are concealed or inferred. Symbols and abbreviations: bar and bell—downthrown side of fault; arrows—relative direction of strike-slip movement; ESF—Exploratory Studies Facility; CD—Cross Drift. Rectangle defines site area. Based on Potter et al. (2002a).

kinematic link between some of the bounding structures (Day et al., 1998a; Potter et al., 2004). Fault scarps visible along many fault traces dip from 50° to 80° to the west (Fig. 4).

Paintbrush Canyon Fault

The Paintbrush Canyon fault is the major block-bounding fault between Midway Valley to the west and a line of small ridges (Busted Butte, Fran and Alice Ridges) to the east (Figs. 2, 16, and 17). The fault is exposed for a distance of ~5 km in

bedrock forming highlands north of Yucca Wash (Fig. 2), where it is shown by Dickerson and Drake (1998) as a west-dipping (56°–76°) normal fault. In that area, Paintbrush Group rhyolite lava flows are downdropped against rocks of the Topopah Spring and Pah Canyon Tuffs and the Calico Hills Formation, and the fault trace is marked by a discontinuous, west-dipping fault scarp 0.3–4.0 m in height.

The Paintbrush Canyon fault extends to the south beneath the alluvium of Midway Valley for some 5 km before strands are

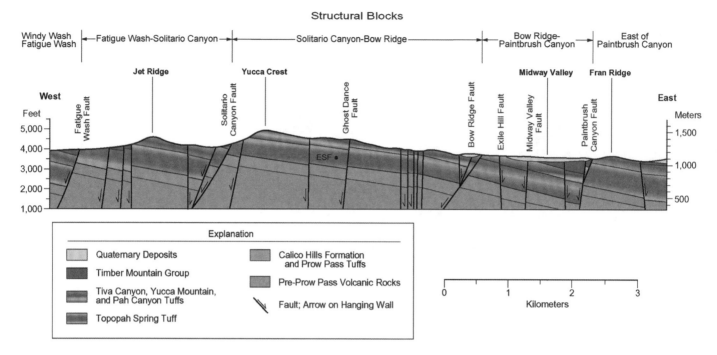

Figure 17. East-west structure section across Yucca Mountain site area. Line of section shown in Figure 16. Not all faults shown are plotted in Figure 16. Datum is mean sea level. ESF—position of Exploratory Studies Facility at intersection with line of section. Simplified from Day et al. (1998a, cross section B–B′).

exposed for ~1 km in bedrock along the west side of Fran Ridge. A major splay trends southwest from a point toward the north end of Fran Ridge, circles around the west side of San Juan Hill and joins the main trace toward the south end of Fran Ridge (Fig. 2). From there northward the fault length is 11 km. However, it may continue southward for another 8 km to a possible intersection with the Stagecoach Road fault beyond the south edge of the site area (Fig. 16), in which case the total fault length may be as much as 19 km (Potter et al., 2002a). The Stagecoach Road fault forms that part of the east boundary of the Solitario Canyon-Bow Ridge structural block that lies south of the site area (Fig. 16).

Estimates of the amount of bedrock displacement on the Paintbrush Canyon fault range from 210 m in the northern segment (Dickerson and Drake, 1998) to as much as 500 m along other segments (Scott and Bonk, 1984; Potter et al., 2004). The fault also shows evidence of multiple surface-rupturing events during the Quaternary, causing offsets of 5.5–8.0 m in surficial deposits as measured in trenches and at natural exposures located near Alice Ridge, Busted Butte, and in the southern part of Midway Valley (Menges et al., 2004). At the Busted Butte locality a series of sand-ramp and colluvial deposits resting on Bishop Ash (dated at 760 ka) are offset (Fig. 18), providing a continuous record of fault movement since early middle Pleistocene time.

Bow Ridge Fault

The Bow Ridge fault is well exposed along a 200-m-long segment on the west side of Exile Hill (Fig. 2), where the Rainier Mesa Tuff is faulted down against the crystal-rich and crystal-poor members of the Tiva Canyon Tuff along a low fault-line bedrock escarpment (Day et al., 1998a). From there north, it extends beneath surficial deposits to the north side of Yucca Wash, a distance of ~4 km, and continues for another 1.5 km to the north edge of the site area, cutting bedrock composed mostly of rhyolite lavas and the Pah Canyon Tuff of the Paintbrush Group (Potter et al., 2002a). South of Exile Hill, the Bow Ridge fault is shown by Day et al. (1998a) to extend southward beneath surficial deposits for ~3.25 km to a point where it is exposed in bedrock (Tiva Canyon Tuff is displaced) for a short distance along the west side of Bow Ridge (Fig. 2). From there, the fault trace is projected to the southeast beneath alluvium for another 2.5 km to a possible intersection with the Paintbrush Canyon fault (Fig. 16), making a total length of ~11.5 km.

Bedrock is displaced ~125 m down to the west along the Bow Ridge fault at the west side of Exile Hill (Scott and Bonk, 1984). The fault dips 75° to 80° W. (Simonds et al., 1995) and net displacement is left-oblique. It was intersected 200 m inside the North Ramp of the ESF, where it was observed to strike north-south and dip 75° W., and to downdrop the pre–Rainier Mesa Tuff bedded tuff against units of the Tiva Canyon Tuff; down-to-the-west dip-slip stratigraphic separation is ~128 m along a 2.7-m-wide brecciated fault zone (Beason et al., 1996). A north-trending fault with down-to-the-east dip-slip offset of 7 m in a 5-m-wide fractured and brecciated zone was intersected some 235 m farther west in the ESF. This feature is believed to be antithetic to, and to terminate against, the Bow Ridge fault at depth and appears to correlate with a strand mapped at the surface in

Figure 18. Exposure of Paintbrush Canyon fault displacing surficial deposits (west side down) on west side of Busted Butte. View is south-southwest, with the Lathrop Wells volcanic center on skyline to right (location shown in Fig. 1). Photograph courtesy of J.A. Coe, U.S. Geological Survey.

the hanging wall block (Figs. 16 and 17; see Day et al., 1998a). Exposures in trenches that were excavated across projections of the Bow Ridge fault beneath surficial deposits at the Exile Hill locality, notably trench 14D described by Menges et al. (1997), reveal small-displacement Pleistocene faulting events with a total offset of 0.5–1.22 m (Menges et al., 2004).

Solitario Canyon and Iron Ridge Faults

The longest continuously exposed fault trace in the site area is associated with the Solitario Canyon fault, which forms the west boundary of the central part of Yucca Mountain that contains the proposed repository block. The segment within the site area is 15 km long (Fig. 2), and to the south it continues for at least another 3 km to where it is shown to have a possible connection with the Southern Windy Wash fault system (Fig. 16; Potter et al., 2002a). There are numerous associated fault splays, particularly toward the south end (Day et al., 1998a; Scott and Bonk, 1984).

The Solitario Canyon fault is well expressed along the east side of Solitario Canyon where, for much of its length, it forms a prominent fault-line scarp as much as 5 m in height along the bedrock-alluvium contact at the base of a large topographic bedrock escarpment (Fig. 2). Bedrock faults split off the main fault trace near the

mouth of Solitario Canyon, and one connects to the southeast with a prominent, west-facing, fault-line scarp as much as 15 m high at the base of a prominent bedrock escarpment. This splay, referred to as the Iron Ridge fault by Scott (1992), extends southeast and south for 8 km and appears to intersect the Stagecoach Road fault south of the site area (Fig. 16; Potter et al., 2002a).

Along the central segment of the Solitario Canyon fault, where two main strands were mapped by Day et al. (1998a; see Fig. 16), units of the Tiva Canyon Tuff in the hanging wall of the eastern strand were downfaulted against rocks of the Topopah Spring Tuff that form all but the upper slopes of the steep west flank of Yucca Mountain (Fig. 2). The down-to-the-west displacement is shown to be 450 m along a fault zone dipping ~65° W. by Day et al. (1998a, cross section B–B'); some left-oblique slip also is indicated by slickensides displayed locally on fault scarps. The western fault strand is covered by surficial deposits for most of its extent. Farther south the faulting involves units of the Topopah Spring, and the down-to-the-west displacement is less owing to the transfer of strain to fault splays. Along the northernmost 3 km segment within the site area, the movement is reversed, with an east-side-down displacement of bedrock of only ~50 m; hence, the Solitario Canyon fault demonstrates a scissors geometry.

A cross drift extending southwestward from near the west end of the northern section of the ESF intersects the central section of the Solitario Canyon fault (see Fig. 16). Only the eastern strand was reached in the boring, at which point the fault plane is defined by an 8–12-cm-thick zone of fault gouge separating rocks in the upper part of the crystal-poor member of the Topopah Spring Tuff in the hanging wall (west side) from rocks in the lower part of that member in the footwall; the down-to-the-west displacement is ~260 m (Mongano et al., 1999). The fault plane strikes N.18°W., and dips 62°W.; slickenside rakes average 40°. Wide zones (30–40 m) of brecciation and fracturing are in both the hanging wall and footwall blocks, being most intense in the latter.

The Iron Ridge fault is a major splay trending south-southeast off the main trace of the Solitario Canyon fault (Figs. 2 and 16). It has an average dip of 68° W. where observed at the surface, with down-to-the-west offset. Along the northern trace of the Iron Ridge fault, rocks in the uppermost Tiva Canyon Tuff are downdropped against the middle part of the Topopah Spring Tuff, a down-to-the-west displacement of ~100 m. Farther south, the amount of displacement increases to ~300 m (Day et al., 1998b).

The Solitario Canyon fault was trenched at 11 locations along the fault trace, with most trenches being sited where the fault extends beneath surficial deposits. Mapping of several of the excavations recorded evidence of multiple middle to late Quaternary surface-rupturing events (Ramelli et al., 2004), with the total amount of displacement ranging from 1.7 to 2.5 m at various sites. One trench was excavated across the Iron Ridge fault, and at least one Quaternary faulting event occurred there with a possible displacement of ~2 m.

Fatigue Wash Fault

The Fatigue Wash fault (Fig. 2) is mapped as a nearly continuous 9-km-long, south-southwest–trending fault along Fatigue Wash (Day et al., 1998a). Except locally, where it forms a fault-line scarp at the base of bedrock escarpments (mainly Yucca Mountain and Pah Canyon Tuffs, and basal units of the Tiva Canyon Tuff) on the east side of the wash, the fault is buried by surficial deposits (Fig. 2). From the mouth of Fatigue Wash, the fault is shown by Potter et al. (2002a) to continue south for a distance of another 8 km to a possible intersection with splays off the Southern Windy Wash fault (Fig. 16) south of the site area (also, see Simonds et al., 1995).

The amount of down-to-the-west displacement of bedrock toward the north end of the Fatigue Wash fault zone is ~100 m, but where it emerges from Fatigue Wash to the south, displacement is ~400 m (Day et al., 1998a, cross section B–B′; see Fig. 17). Average dip of the fault plane is 70° W. (Simonds et al., 1995), and slickenside lineations indicate a moderate amount of left-slip movement.

Studies of surficial deposits exposed in trench excavations across the south-central segment of the Fatigue Wash fault, and measurements of scarp profiles near the trenches, provide evidence that five or more paleoearthquakes occurred on the fault since middle Pleistocene time (Coe et al., 2004). The amount of displacement of the Quaternary units ranges from 1 to 3 m.

Windy Wash Fault

The Windy Wash fault is expressed as a prominent fault-line scarp on the east side of Windy Wash (Fig. 4). It is traceable nearly continuously from the south rim of the Claim Canyon caldera (Fig. 1), one of the eruptive centers in the southwestern Nevada volcanic field (Christiansen and Lipman, 1965), to the southeast edge of Crater Flat, a distance of ~25 km. It is a complex fault system consisting of two main sections, referred to as the Northern Windy Wash and Southern Windy Wash faults (Fig. 16), with down-to-the-west displacements; the two faults are separated by a 4–5-km-long discontinuous zone of east-facing scarps (Simonds et al., 1995). Only about a 5.5-km-long segment of the Northern Windy Wash fault is in the northwest corner of the site area, where it is marked by a west-dipping fault-line scarp at the base of a bedrock escarpment formed largely by units of the Topopah Spring Tuff on the footwall and Yucca Mountain and Tiva Canyon Tuffs on the hanging wall (Fig. 2; Day et al., 1998a). The amount of down-to-the-west displacement of bedrock along this well-exposed segment, on a fault plane with an average west dip of ~65°, is more than 500 m.

Trenches were excavated only across the north end of the Southern Windy Wash fault, the mapping of which provided evidence of as many as eight surface-rupturing events during middle to late Quaternary time that resulted in a total net displacement of 3.7 m in the surficial deposits (Whitney et al., 2004a). With regard to the 5.5-km-long segment of the Northern Windy Wash fault in the northwest corner of the site area, Simonds et al. (1995) showed a nearly continuous scarp along the bedrock-alluvium contact that is interpreted to be indicative of probable Quaternary movement.

Northern and Southern Crater Flat Faults

The Northern and Southern Crater Flat faults lie entirely west of the site area (Fig. 16), but are included here because they form the west boundary of the Windy Wash-Crater Flat structural block to be discussed later. These two faults compose a complex fault system that can be traced discontinuously for a total length of as much as 20 km (Menges and Whitney, 2004) along the east side of Crater Flat, although the relations between the main north and south sections are obscured by surficial deposits in intervening areas. Individual exposures of the fault traces generally are <1 km long, with some being as much as 2 km in length. The fault traces are marked in places by small discontinuous bedrock scarps, subtle scarps and lineaments in alluvium, and short bedrock-alluvium contacts. A 3.5-km-long segment of the southern fault is marked by a linear contact between Pliocene basalt on the east and Quaternary alluvium on the west that locally produces a west-facing scarp (Simonds et al., 1995). Trenches were excavated across both sections of the fault system, showing evidence of at least three Quaternary faulting events that displaced surficial deposits ~0.75 m on the Southern Crater Flat fault (Taylor,

2004) and four to five Quaternary events that displaced surficial deposits 1.2 m on the Northern Crater Flat fault (Coe, 2004). The amount of bedrock displacement could not be determined.

Structural Blocks and Intrablock Faults

The six structural blocks delineated by the block-bounding faults within the Yucca Mountain site area range in width from 1 to 5 km (Fig. 16). Average dip of the tilted volcanic rock units within individual blocks is ~10° E. (Fig. 17), with increasing dips (to as much as 30°) near the east sides of the hanging wall blocks. Each of the blocks is segmented by numerous faults with mostly north to northwest trends. Like the block-bounding faults, displacements are mainly dip-slip, down-to-the-west, but there are some with down-to-the-east offsets that define shallow intervening graben structures (Potter et al., 2004). Notable exceptions are the northwest-trending, largely strike-slip (right lateral) faults in Drill Hole, Pagany, and Sever Washes in the north-central part of the site area (Fig. 16). Principal intrablock features within individual structural blocks are discussed briefly in the following sections.

Structural Block East of the Paintbrush Canyon Fault

Geologic relations across much of the eastern part of the site area, east of the Paintbrush Canyon fault, are poorly known because of the thick blanket of alluvium in Fortymile Wash and over the western part of Jackass Flats (Potter et al., 2002a; see Figs. 1 and 12). However, bedrock exposures on Busted Butte and Fran and Alice Ridges, as well as in the highlands north of Yucca Wash and on both sides of Fortymile Canyon, indicate that a discrete structural block occupies this part of the site area. As yet there is insufficient evidence for defining an eastern block boundary. The easternmost down-to-the-west normal fault mapped in the northeastern part of the site area is inferred by Potter et al. (2002a) to extend south following Fortymile Wash to a point near the north end of Busted Butte, based in part on differences in the attitude of rock units on opposite sides of Fortymile Canyon and in part on the projection of stratal dips in the Topopah Spring Tuff on Fran Ridge with respect to the top of that formation in borehole UE-25 J-13 just east of the wash (see Figs. 8 and 10). Such a fault is shown in Figure 16, but its existence has not been confirmed nor can it be labeled a block-bounding fault on the basis of the available evidence.

Areas of exposed bedrock within the structural block are cut by minor faults. Those faults in the highlands in the northern part are down-to-the-west normal faults involving various units of the Paintbrush Group and the Calico Hills Formation. On Busted Butte and Fran Ridge (Fig. 2), they are mostly splays off the Paintbrush Canyon fault, producing displacements in rocks of the Paintbrush Group and locally forming north-trending zones 0.5–1 km wide. One such fault with down-to-the-west displacement trends north-south through the center of Busted Butte and another, termed the Busted Butte fault (Fig. 16), cuts across the east side with down-to-the-east displacement (Day et al., 1998a).

Bow Ridge–Paintbrush Canyon Block

The Bow Ridge–Paintbrush Canyon structural block is characterized by bedrock areas in both the northern and southern parts separated by a large expanse of surficial deposits in Midway Valley. Several north- to northwest-trending normal faults, most with down-to-the-west displacements, were mapped in rhyolite lavas of the Paintbrush Group in the area that lies between the Bow Ridge and Paintbrush Canyon faults north of Yucca Wash (Dickerson and Drake, 1998). At the south end of the block, south of Midway Valley, a few minor faults outlining some small graben structures were mapped in rocks of the Tiva Canyon Tuff exposed on Bow Ridge. One of these is the Midway Valley fault (Fig. 16), which was shown by Day et al. (1998a) to extend north from the Bow Ridge exposures as a concealed fault beneath alluvium for 8 km before reaching the faulted outcrops north of Midway Valley. Bedrock displacements (normal, down to the west) are shown by Scott and Bonk (1984) and Day et al. (1998a) to be 100 m and 30 m, respectively. Results of geophysical surveys further support the presence of the Midway Valley fault, as well as other north-trending faults beneath the alluvium of the valley floor (Ponce, 1993; Ponce and Langenheim, 1994; Swan et al., 2001).

The Exile Hill fault (Fig. 17) is a minor down-to-the-east, north-trending normal fault along the east side of Exile Hill (Swan et al., 2001); it is shown by Day et al. (1998a) to merge southward with the Midway Valley fault and northward with the eastern strand of the Bow Ridge fault. An exposure in the excavation at the east end of the north portal of the ESF (Fig. 16) shows the bedrock unit referred to as Tuff unit "X" (see Table 1) to be downfaulted against the crystal-rich member of the Tiva Canyon Tuff; estimated displacement is 15–30 m (Swan et al., 2001). Two other minor faults cut bedrock on Exile Hill; these trend northwest with dip-slip to oblique-slip displacements of 10 m or less, and are classed as relay structures by Day et al. (1998a), linking the Bow Ridge and Exile Hill faults. The southeast-trending part of the Bow Ridge fault also is considered to be a relay structure between the main north-trending section of that fault with the Paintbrush Canyon fault to the southeast.

None of the intrablock faults in the Bow Ridge-Paintbrush Canyon structural block shows evidence of Quaternary activity in trenches excavated in surficial deposits across inferred fault trends (Swan et al., 2001).

Solitario Canyon–Bow Ridge Block

The structural block bounded on the west by the Solitario Canyon fault and on the east by the Bow Ridge fault (and in part by the Paintbrush Canyon fault) is areally the largest block in the Yucca Mountain site area, ranging from ~2 to 5 km in width (Fig. 16). Because it also hosts the proposed waste repository, structural features within the block are of special interest and importance to site characterization. Numerous faults with varying orientations and displacement directions were mapped by Day et al. (1998a) and described by Potter et al. (2004). Among the more prominent of these is the Iron Ridge fault (Fig. 16), which is a major splay of the Solitario Canyon fault that was described earlier. In essence, the Iron Ridge fault, with displacements of 180–245 m, bounds the east side of a sub-block within the major block.

The Ghost Dance fault, which trends north-south 150–200 m east of the north-south–oriented main drift of the ESF (Fig. 16), was mapped in considerable detail by Day et al. (1998b). The fault extends south from ~0.25 km south of Drill Hole Wash to Broken Limb Ridge, a distance of 2.5 km (Fig. 2). Farther south, the fault bifurcates, striking to the southwest into the Abandoned Wash fault (Scott and Bonk, 1984) and to the southeast toward (but not into) the Dune Wash fault (Fig. 16). Down-to-the-west displacements along the Ghost Dance fault in surface exposures range from a maximum of 27 m in the central part between Split Wash and Broken Limb Ridge (Fig. 2), where the brecciated zone between splays is as much as 150 m wide, to a minimum of 3 m along segments to the south (Day et al., 1998b).

The Ghost Dance fault does not extend far enough north to be encountered in the northern section of the ESF (Day et al., 1998a). However, a shear with a thin (1–10-cm-thick) gouge zone and less than 0.1 m offset was mapped along the projected north strike of the fault by Mongano et al. (1999). The fault was intersected toward the south end of the north-south–oriented main drift of the ESF (Fig. 16), where the fault was observed to strike N.25°E. with a vertical dip and to have only 1.2 m of down-to-the-west offset in rocks of the crystal-poor member of the Topopah Spring Tuff (Albin et al., 1997). The fault was also exposed in alcoves excavated off the main drift of the ESF, where it displays displacements ranging from 6 m to ~25 m along fault-damage zones 0.6–1.0 m wide (Taylor et al., 1998). The Ghost Dance fault was trenched at several locations, but studies of the excavations recorded no evidence of Quaternary movements (Taylor et al., 2004).

The Sundance fault (Fig. 16) is mapped as a 750-m-long, 70-m-wide brecciated zone of small discontinuous faults trending northwest from Live Yucca Ridge to Dead Yucca Ridge (Fig. 2; Potter et al., 1999). The fault, with down-to-the-east bedrock displacement ranging from 6 to 11 m, terminates west of the trace of the Ghost Dance fault (Day et al., 1998b). It was intersected in both the main drift of the ESF and in the CD (Fig. 16). In the main drift, the fault appears to have several meters of down-to-the-west offset within a 20-cm-thick gouge zone (Mongano et al., 1999); this observed offset is opposite to that observed at the surface. In the CD, the Sundance fault likewise appears to have down-to-the-west displacement of a few meters (Mongano et al., 1999). Like the Ghost Dance fault, there is no evidence to indicate that Quaternary activity took place along the Sundance fault.

From where it branches off the Ghost Dance fault, the Abandoned Wash fault continues southwest and south for ~5 km (Fig. 16). It is exposed in bedrock (Tiva Canyon Tuff) along its northern trace but is buried by alluvium to the south. The fault displays as much as 24 m of down-to-the-west displacement marked by a fault scarp dipping 81° W. (Dickerson and Drake, 2004). In contrast, the southeast-trending Dune Wash fault (Fig. 16) is concealed beneath surficial deposits of Dune Wash for most of its

indicated length of 5 km, being exposed only at the north end where bedrock (Tiva Canyon Tuff) is displaced ~50 m down to the west. To the west, the East Ridge fault (Fig. 16), with as much as 145 m of down-to-the-east displacement, defines the west side of a feature referred to as the Dune Wash graben (Day et al., 1998a). This prominent downfaulted feature may terminate south against the southern extension of the Paintbrush Canyon fault, but the relations are obscured by surficial deposits.

Sever, Pagany, and Drill Hole Washes are prominent northwest-trending drainages in the northern part of the Solitario Canyon–Bow Ridge structural block that appear to be controlled by northwest-striking faults (Fig. 16). The faults were identified on the basis of geophysical investigations, bedrock mapping, and examination of drill cores from Drill Hole Wash (Scott et al., 1984). A similar fault also was inferred to project beneath the Quaternary alluvial deposits of Yucca Wash (Fig. 2) by Scott (1992), but more extensive geologic and geophysical investigations have not confirmed its existence (Langenheim and Ponce, 1994: Dickerson and Drake, 1998; Day et al., 1998a). The Sever Wash and Pagany Wash faults (Fig. 16) are exposed in bedrock and locally have produced small bedrock scarps. The Drill Hole Wash fault (Fig. 16) is concealed by Quaternary alluvium, but two faults encountered in the northern section of the ESF were correlated with the Drill Hole Wash fault zone (Beason et al., 1996). Approximately 4 m of vertical separation was observed on these features, and horizontal slickensides also indicate strike-slip movement, but the total amount of displacement could not be determined. Quaternary alluvial terraces on the floors of the washes do not appear to be displaced by the northwest-trending faults; a trench excavated across the Pagany Wash fault exposed faulted bedrock on the trench floor, but the overlying bedrock regolith and colluvial units are not displaced (Taylor et al., 2004).

The northwest-trending faults are steeply dipping and thought to be strike-slip faults because fault-plane surfaces locally contain slickenside lineations that are nearly horizontal, and vertical displacements generally are less than 5–10 m (Scott et al., 1984). The Sever Wash and Pagany Wash faults show slickenside orientations and Riedel shears that indicate right-lateral slip; the amount of displacement was estimated to be ~40 m on each fault by Scott et al. (1984). These two faults are each ~4 km long; both appear to terminate against the Solitario Canyon fault to the west and, although concealed, are postulated to terminate against a down-to-the-east north-trending fault lying a short distance west of the Bow Ridge fault (Fig. 16; Day et al., 1998b). The Drill Hole Wash fault also is ~4 km long and may terminate against the same north-trending fault.

A closely spaced series of normal faults form an asymmetric graben-like feature that trends north from Boundary Ridge across the toes of Antler and Live Yucca Ridges (Fig. 2); some are shown between the Ghost Dance and Bow Ridge faults on the cross section in Figure 17. Cumulative offset ranges to as much as 30 m. Such fault clusters were referred to as "imbricate fault zones" by Scott (1990), and were considered by him to be characteristic of the more intense deformation that took place along the east side of some structural blocks where dips of compaction foliations become steeper. However, the term "imbricate fault zone" was not used for descriptive purposes by Day et al. (1998a, 1998b), who interpreted the steep foliation dips to be caused by rotation of blocks in a tectonic breccia zone rather than by fault displacements.

Fatigue Wash–Solitario Canyon Block

The prominent feature in the Fatigue Wash–Solitario Canyon structural block is the east-dipping sequence of volcanic rocks that make up Jet Ridge (Fig. 2). Several normal faults, mostly with small offsets in the Tiva Canyon, Yucca Mountain, and Pah Canyon Tuffs, are in the northern part of the block (Fig. 16). The most extensive is a northwest-trending feature ~2.5 km long with down-to-the-east displacement exhibited mainly in rocks of the Yucca Mountain Tuff. A number of faults also cut bedrock (Tiva Canyon Tuff) farther south along the east slope of Jet Ridge, including the 4.5-km-long, north-northeast–trending intrablock Boomerang Point normal fault (Fig. 16). North- to northwest-trending, down-to-the-west normal faults at the south ends of both Jet Ridge and Boomerang Point were considered by Day et al. (1998a) to be relay faults linking the Fatigue Wash and Boomerang Point faults and the Boomerang Point and Solitario Canyon faults, respectively (Fig. 16). Structural relations farther south in this structural block are obscured by surficial deposits.

Windy Wash–Fatigue Wash Block

West Ridge and Fatigue Wash (to the east) occupy that part of the Windy Wash–Fatigue Wash structural block lying within the western part of the Yucca Mountain site area (Figs. 2 and 16). Intrablock structures are mainly small displacement normal faults in the northern and central parts of West Ridge. A cluster of closely spaced, northwest-trending relay faults terminate against the Northern Windy Wash fault to the west and the Fatigue Wash fault to the east (Fig. 16; Day et al., 1998a). Displacements are both down to the southwest and down to the northeast, with a cumulative offset of ~60 m down to the southwest. The structural block terminates just south of the southwest corner of the site area, at the apparent junction between the two bounding faults (Fig. 16).

Crater Flat–Windy Wash Block

Only the northeastern part of the Crater Flat–Windy Wash structural block lies within the site area (Fig. 16). A few north-trending normal faults in bedrock are present in that area, with one fault showing Yucca Mountain Tuff in the hanging wall downdropped (west side down) against ash-flow tuffs of the Calico Hills Formation in the footwall (Day et al., 1998a). Much of the block elsewhere along the east margin of Crater Flat is covered by surficial deposits, so little of the structure can be directly observed. Locations of faults shown on the 1:50,000-scale map compilation by Potter et al. (2002a) are based primarily on interpretation of geophysical surveys within Crater Flat proper.

Vertical Axis Rotation

An important characteristic of the existing fault patterns at and near Yucca Mountain is a noticeable change from the predominant northerly fault trends within the site area proper to more northeasterly trends in adjacent areas toward the south end of the mountain (Fridrich et al., 1999; Rosenbaum et al., 1991; see Fig. 16). This relation is attributed to a progressive north to south increase in post–12.7 Ma vertical-axis rotation clockwise from 0° in the area near the Prow (Fig. 2) to ~30° in an area ~10 km south of the site area. It is interpreted to be the result of (1) right-lateral deformation within the Walker Lane structural belt (see O'Leary, this volume, for location) by Fridrich et al. (1999) and Rosenbaum et al. (1991), or (2) differential displacement on normal faults that shallow with depth (i.e., listric faults) by Stamatakos and Ferrill (1998). Within the site area itself, vertical rotation ranges from 0° at the Prow to 5° at the latitude of Busted Butte (Fig. 2). Commensurate with the north-to-south increase in the clockwise vertical-axis rotation is a general southward increase in displacements along block-bounding faults. This increase in displacement is supported by Potter et al. (2004), who reported that the magnitude of east-west extension was 8% across north-central Yucca Mountain, 10.5% across the southern part of the site area, and 12% in the area still farther south. In intrablock areas, the transition from a less-extended terrane in the northern part of Yucca Mountain to a more-extended terrane farther south generally is expressed by the appearances of numerous closely spaced minor normal faults that coalesce and gain displacement to the south and of wider, fault-bounded half grabens.

Deformation within Fault Zones

Because faults represent zones of poor rock quality resulting in potential hydrologic pathways, or as impediments to flow in some cases, deformation along the faults bordering the proposed repository area has been studied extensively. Map patterns demonstrate that tectonic mixing of various Paintbrush Group lithologies has occurred within the most intensely deformed parts of block-bounding fault systems. This is most apparent in the Solitario Canyon fault system (Scott and Bonk, 1984; Day et al., 1998b). In this wide (as much as 400 m) system, lenses from stratigraphically diverse parts of the Tiva Canyon Tuff are juxtaposed. Slices of Topopah Spring Tuff are also mixed, and in some areas lenses from more than one Paintbrush Group formation are tectonically juxtaposed (Day et al., 1998b). Tectonic mixing is also apparent along the Northern Windy Wash fault system west of the Prow, along the Bow Ridge fault system in the saddle between Bow Ridge and Boundary Ridge, and in the Paintbrush Canyon fault system along the west flank of Fran Ridge (see Figs. 2 and 16; Potter et al., 2004). Individual fault strands within these tectonically mixed zones are brecciated; in some cases the fault-bounded lenses are internally brecciated.

In addition to tectonic mixing, there are areas where coherent blocks of Tiva Canyon Tuff, as much as 250 m wide, dip to the west, opposite to the prevailing easterly dips of the major structural blocks (Day et al., 1998b). Locally, anticlines with axes subparallel to the fault zone are present within individual fault slices and in the immediate footwall of the Solitario Canyon fault. These folds are likely produced by local transpression that folded and rotated volcanic strata. Mapped fold hinges may actually be small-displacement, brittle fault zones lying at shallow structural levels. Small thrust faults are mapped within the Solitario Canyon fault system and in the hanging wall of the Bow Ridge fault near the south portal of the ESF (Day et al., 1998b). The anastomosing pattern of faults that characterizes these fault systems also produced individual fault splays that cut into both the hanging wall and footwall.

As indicated earlier, the eastern (main) strand of the Solitario Canyon fault was encountered in the west end of the CD (Fig. 16), where ~260 m of down-to-the-west offset placed the lower nonlithophysal zone of the Topopah Spring Tuff in the footwall against the upper lithophysal zone of the Topopah Spring Tuff in the hanging wall. However, the tectonic mixing described above also is observed within the fault zone at depth in the CD, where there is a breccia composed of clasts of the overlying lower nonlithophysal zone of the Tiva Canyon Tuff. Footwall deformation (mostly brecciation) is fairly extensive in the area of the drift, extending ~50 m east of the main fault.

Geophysical Surveys

Several geophysical methods, including seismic reflection, gravity, and magnetic surveys, were used in attempts to characterize the subsurface geologic structure within the Yucca Mountain site area (Fig. 19). Such surveys, however, have met with varying degrees of success. Seismic reflection profiling, for example, which was conducted along most of the lines shown in Figure 19, is difficult because the propagation of seismic energy is greatly inhibited by the fracturing and lithologic heterogeneities that characterize much of the thick sequences of volcanic rocks. Gravity data also were obtained along most of the survey lines and were used primarily to interpret regional structure and to assist in locating faults and determining their general displacements in local areas. Ground magnetic surveys and aeromagnetic data were mainly used to infer fault locations and offsets, especially where the relatively magnetic Topopah Spring Tuff was involved in the faulting. Attempts were made to detect and characterize buried faults and geologic heterogeneities by using the magnetotelluric method, but this method was limited unless supplemented by other geophysical techniques.

The results of geophysical surveys in the site area are reported in numerous publications, including Fitterman (1982), Senterfit et al. (1982), Smith and Ross (1982), Pankratz (1982), McGovern (1983), U.S. Geological Survey (1984), Frischknecht and Raab (1984), Reynolds et al. (1985), Ponce (1993), Ponce and Langenheim (1994), Feighner et al. (1996), Majer et al. (1996), Brocher et al. (1998), CRWMS M&O (1998; 2000), and Swan et

al. (2001). Some of the reported findings from these sources are summarized below.

Data from the generally east-trending, 32-km-long seismic reflection survey across Crater Flat, Yucca Mountain, Midway Valley, and Fortymile Wash (lines REG-2 and REG-3, Fig. 19) were interpreted to reflect a series of west-dipping normal faults that project through the volcanic rocks and displace the Tertiary volcanic-rock/pre-Tertiary sedimentary-rock contact at depth (Brocher et al., 1998). Suggestions that this contact is formed by an active detachment fault beneath Yucca Mountain (for example, Scott, 1990; Hamilton, 1988) are therefore inconsistent with the seismic reflection data.

Ponce (1993) and Ponce and Langenheim (1994) conducted gravity and magnetic surveys (Fig. 19) in Midway Valley, from which anomalies were identified that were interpreted to be faults concealed by the thick alluvial deposits covering the central part of the valley. One of the anomalies was presumed to be associated with the Midway Valley fault, with the data indicating a vertical displacement of several tens of meters in the underlying bedrock. Ponce and Langenheim (1994) also interpreted data from ground magnetic surveys to indicate that north-trending faults could be traced continuously across Yucca Wash, thus casting doubt on the existence of a northwest-trending fault along the floor of the wash that had been postulated by earlier investigators (for example, Scott and Bonk, 1984).

Because a primary question to be addressed in the site area is the amount, style, depth, and continuity of faulting in the repository block itself, various geophysical methods were compared to evaluate their effectiveness in imaging both a block-bounding fault (Bow Ridge fault) and a prominent intrablock fault (Ghost Dance fault). In the case of the Bow Ridge fault, only the ground-based gravity and aeromagnetic surveys yielded reliable results. The gravity data show a distinct gravity low on the hanging wall of this block-bounding fault where bedrock is buried by less dense surficial deposits. The aeromagnetic data show a high on the footwall side and a low on the hanging wall side, a relation that is interpreted as a signature of displacement of the relatively magnetic Topopah Spring Tuff. Seismic reflection surveys produced unreliable results.

Ground-based magnetic and magnetotelluric profiling worked well for detecting the Ghost Dance fault, whereas ground-based gravity and standard high-resolution seismic reflection surveys (those with 6–12 m station spacings) did not record significant anomalies. The ground-based magnetic data indicate a characteristic magnetic low, typically ~100 m wide, on the footwall of the fault, and the magnetotelluric data show a clear change in resistivity for the fault. On very high resolution seismic reflection lines (station spacing 1–2 m), displacement of reflections was apparent across the Ghost Dance fault, thus enabling individual splays to be mapped in places.

The general conclusion was that standard geophysical techniques used at Yucca Mountain are best suited for detection of faults with at least tens of meters of offset (CRWMS M&O, 2000, p. 4.6-32).

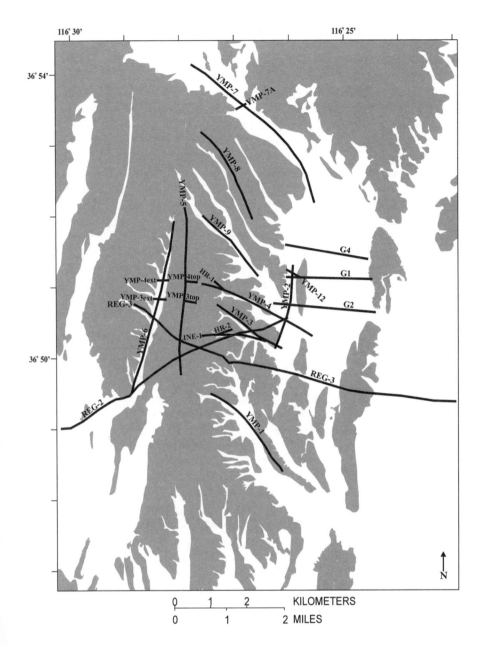

Figure 19. Map showing location of geophysical surveys in the Yucca Mountain site area. Shaded areas are exposed volcanic bedrock. Seismic reflection data were collected along all lines labeled "REG" and "YMP". REG-2 and REG-3 are regional reflection lines (Brocher et al., 1998) and HR-I and HR-2 are very high-resolution seismic reflection lines (station spacings 1–2 m); all others are standard high-resolution seismic reflection lines (station spacing 6–12 m; Feighner et al., 1996). Ground-based gravity data were collected along all lines, except YMP-3 top, YMP-4 top, YMP-7, HR-I, HR-2, and Line-l. Ground magnetic data were collected along all lines except YMP-3 top, YMP-3 ext, YMP-4 top, YMP-4 ext, HR-2, and Line-1. Magnetelluric data were collected only along YMP-3. Lines GI, G2, and G4 are gravity and magnetic surveys of Ponce and Langenheim (1994). Adapted from Swan et al. (2001).

Fractures

Combined three-dimensional studies of fractures in natural and cleared exposures, boreholes, and underground excavations (ESF and CD) led to important conclusions regarding their distribution and characteristics in the Yucca Mountain site area. Attributes of fracture systems within the principal formations that are most closely associated with the proposed repository—Tiva Canyon and Topopah Spring Tuffs, Calico Hills Formation, and Prow Pass Tuff, as well as some of the major units within the PTn hydrogeologic unit—and the study methods used, are described in considerable detail in CRWMS M&O (1998). The data presented in that report were used to characterize fracture systems in support of (1) surface infiltration model development (Flint and Flint, 1994); (2) numerical simulations of discrete fracture networks (Anna and Wallman, 1997); (3) calculations of bulk-rock permeability for use in equivalent continuum models of the unsaturated zone (Schenker et al., 1995; Arnold et al., 1995); (4) studies bearing on the mechanical stability of the proposed repository; and (5) investigations to determine the paleostress history of Yucca Mountain. Some of the general relations that were observed between fracture patterns and lithology and of fracturing in fault zones are summarized briefly below, based on CRWMS M&O (1998).

Fracture characteristics in the pyroclastic flows in the Yucca Mountain site area are controlled primarily by variations in the degree of welding and secondarily by lithophysal development, alteration, and pumice content. Such controls affected fracture spacing, fracture type, number of fracture sets, continuity of individual fractures within each lithostratigraphic unit, and the connectivity of fractures within the network as a whole. Fracture networks commonly act as preexisting lines of weakness in the rock mass, having originated as cooling joints that formed as tensional openings in response to contraction during cooling of the volcanic rock mass; subsequent extensional strain could then be accommodated through distributed slip along the preexisting joint sets. The presence of thin breccia zones along such joints, and observable slip lineations along their surfaces, are indicative of joint reactivation. Tectonic fractures are also common in the volcanic rocks, having been developed independently of the cooling joint sets in response to regional or local stresses, and are recognized as discontinuities across which simple openings (face separations) of <10 cm of displacement have occurred in contrast to reactivated joints.

Because fracturing in zones adjacent to fault planes exerts an important influence on hydrologic flow pathways, many fracture studies focused on the frequency and characteristics of fractures near some of the faults close to the repository block, particularly of fracture sets exposed in the ESF and CD (e.g., see Mongano et al., 1999). Although the amount of fracturing associated with faults depends, in part, on the lithologic units involved, the width of a fracture zone in the immediate vicinity of a fault generally correlates with the amount of fault offset. Intrablock faults with small amounts of displacement (1–5 m) have fracture zones 1–2 m wide, whereas block-bounding faults with tens of meters of offset have zones ranging in widths as much as 6–10 m.

Studies of the Ghost Dance fault, which transects the proposed repository area (Fig. 16), have concentrated on fracture patterns exposed in an excavation for the USW UZ-7a drillpad (location in Fig. 8) and on a cleared pavement on the south flank of Antler Ridge (Fig. 2). One generalization is that the total amount of rock damage and fracturing is greater in the hanging wall than in the footwall. At the USW UZ-7a locality, for example, the intervening rock between the west-dipping main fault and a secondary east-dipping fault 42 m to the west, in the hanging wall, is intensely broken and consists of a complex network of short-length fractures, whereas rocks (lower part of lower lithophysal zone of the Tiva Canyon Tuff) in the footwall east of the main fault trace are noticeably less fractured. At the Antler Ridge locality, there are 13–20 m of cumulative down-to-the-west displacement across several splays of the Ghost Dance fault distributed over a map width of 100–150 m (Day et al., 1998a). The fracture network in various units of the Tiva Canyon Tuff within or proximal to the fault zone is dominated by closely spaced, steeply dipping fractures, many of which show minor offsets, that may be the result of their proximity to the fault, although, alternatively, they may be more closely related to the cluster of closely spaced faults mapped farther east toward the toe of Antler Ridge (Day et al., 1998b). In the case of the Sundance fault, it occupies a well-defined single strand in places where cooling joints are poorly developed in the crystal-rich member of the Tiva Canyon, but where there is a greater abundance of cooling joints the displacement is distributed across a broader zone (Potter et al., 1999).

Stratigraphic Relations across Faults and Timing of Deformation

Stratigraphic relations and geologic map patterns across block-bounding and intrablock faults in the Yucca Mountain site area show evidence of episodic movement during the depositional period (12.8–12.7 Ma) of the Paintbrush Group (Potter et al., 2004). Several examples of such evidence are discussed in detail in CRWMS M&O (2000, p. 4.6-12–4.6-15), a few of which are summarized below:

1. Near the mouth of Solitario Canyon, the stratigraphic interval of the pre–Pah Canyon bedded tuffs and the Pah Canyon Tuff thins across a prominent splay of the Solitario Canyon fault, from a thickness of 7 m on the hanging wall to 2 m on the footwall; as observed by Day et al. (1998a), the top of the Topopah Spring Tuff is offset 13 m whereas the bases of the Yucca Mountain and Tiva Canyon Tuffs are offset only 3 m.

2. At a locality near the Prow (Fig. 2), pre–Yucca Mountain Tuff bedded tuffs thicken abruptly across the north end of the Fatigue Wash fault. Along a parallel fault 150 m to the west, a 45-m-thick rhyolite flow between the Pah Canyon Tuff and the pre–Yucca Mountain Tuff bedded tuffs in the hanging wall is absent in the footwall, indicating that at least 45 m of displacement occurred after deposition of the Pah Canyon.

3. Growth faulting along the Ghost Dance fault during deposition of the crystal-rich member of the Topopah Spring Tuff and overlying bedded tuffs at the base of the Tiva Canyon Tuff is indicated by a 30 m decrease in the thickness of the upper lithophysal zone of the Topopah Spring observed on a lithologic log of borehole USW UZ-7a, which penetrates the fault. Combined with a 15 m offset of the Tiva Canyon Tuff observed during surface mapping, the relations are interpreted by Day et al. (1998b) to indicate that (1) ~15 m of post–Topopah Spring, pre–Tiva Canyon displacement occurred followed by an additional offset of 15 m after deposition of the Tiva Canyon; and (2) a small amount of fault-related topography existed prior to Tiva Canyon time.

4. Numerous minor faults (splays of the Busted Butte fault, Fig. 16) on the west side of Fran Ridge (Fig. 2) and the north end of Busted Butte displace the top of the Topopah Spring Tuff and the pre–Pah Canyon bedded tuffs 1–10 m, but the pre–Tiva Canyon Tuff bedded tuff unit and the base of the Tiva Canyon are unfaulted.

In addition to episodic deformation during the deposition of various units within the Paintbrush Group, there was an episode of faulting and tilting of strata between deposition of the Tiva Canyon Tuff and that of the Timber Mountain Group rocks. Near the mouth of Solitario Canyon, for example, a complex of small faults splaying off the main trace of the Solitario Canyon fault and displacing Paintbrush Group tuffs is overlapped by unfaulted Rainier Mesa Tuff (Fig. 2; Day et al., 1998a). Fridrich et al. (1999) interpreted stratal dips in the site area to indicate that (1) the Tiva Canyon Tuff was tilted 10° to 20° to the east and southeast prior to the deposition of the Rainier Mesa (11.6 Ma); (2) less than 5° of eastward tilting occurred 11.6–10.5 Ma; and (3) less than 5° of eastward tilting occurred after 10.5 Ma. Scott (1990), using compaction foliations, suggested that there is more than 10° of discordance between the Rainier Mesa and Tiva Canyon Tuffs west and northwest of Busted Butte. In much of the site area, however, mapping by Day et al. (1998a) indicated that the Rainier Mesa Tuff was displaced by faulting and tilted nearly the same amount as the Tiva Canyon Tuff.

As indicated in descriptions of the block-bounding faults, deformation also continued through Quaternary time (Keefer et al., 2004).

Geologic Structure of the Pre-Cenozoic Rocks

Little can be said about the structural geology of the Paleozoic and Precambrian rocks that lie beneath Yucca Mountain. They are not exposed in the site area and have been penetrated in only one borehole (borehole UE-25 p#1; see Fig. 10). Based on exposures in other areas, such as Bare Mountain 12 km to the west of Yucca Mountain (Monsen et al., 1992) and Calico Hills 3 km to the east (Potter et al. 2002a), the pre-Cenozoic rocks of the region were highly deformed at some time prior to the deposition of the Tertiary volcanic rocks. Robinson (1985) presented a geologic map of the Proterozoic and Paleozoic rocks of the Yucca Mountain region on which he showed an inferred distribution of Paleozoic strata (Silurian to Mississippian) as directly underlying the volcanic rocks and, for the most part, occupying a broad syncline. Compilations by Sweetkind et al. (2001) and Potter et al. (2002b) show the deep subsurface structure of an extensive region in southwestern Nevada and adjacent parts of California, based largely on the projection of features from structures mapped in exposed areas and on interpretations of available geophysical and borehole information. One of the structures inferred to have involved the Paleozoic rocks beneath Yucca Mountain is an east-west–trending, south-vergent thrust fault block (labeled CP thrust fault by Cole, 1997) that was projected to extend from the CP Hills, some 25 km east of Yucca Mountain, westward to connect with a similarly oriented thrust fault mapped in Lower Paleozoic rocks at Bare Mountain (labeled Panama thrust fault by Potter et al., 2002b). Its actual existence can neither be proved nor disproved, but if present it does not appear to have affected the structural patterns observed in the Tertiary volcanic rocks, or to have given rise to any known seismic activity.

Tectonic Models for Yucca Mountain

Various tectonic models that have been proposed for Yucca Mountain are the subject of a chapter in this volume by D.W. O'Leary. Accordingly, the subject will not be discussed further here, except to note that, in terms of structural style and deformational history, Yucca Mountain is closely linked to Crater Flat

basin to the west (Fig. 1). In view of that relation, Fridrich (1999) proposed that these two features form a single and distinct graben-like structural domain—the Crater Flat domain.

NATURAL RESOURCES

Introduction

Identification and evaluation of the natural resources in the Yucca Mountain area have been the subject of several reports prepared as part of the site characterization program. A detailed discussion of resources potential is given in CRWMS M&O (2001); other reports include (1) Castor et al. (1999) for metallic minerals; (2) Castor and Lock (1995) for industrial rocks and minerals; (3) Barker (1994), Grow et al. (1994), Cashman and Trexler (1995), Trexler et al. (1996), Castor et al. (1999), and French (2000) for hydrocarbon and other energy resources; and (4) Flynn et al. (1996) for geothermal resources. Summary discussions on the various resources, given below, are based largely on one or another of these reports.

Metallic Mineral Resources

Nevada is well known for production of several metallic resources, including gold, silver, copper, mercury, and uranium (Nevada Bureau of Mines and Geology, 1997). Similarly, the region surrounding Yucca Mountain contains deposits or potentially economic resources of these metallic minerals (Castor et al., 1999). Geologic conditions within the site area generally are similar to those in nearby mineralized areas. However, although episodes of alteration and mineralization followed the deposition of the Paintbrush Group tuffaceous rocks in areas a few kilometers away, it appears that the hydrothermal activity resulting in mineral deposits elsewhere did not extend into the Yucca Mountain area. This conclusion is based on studies of the mineralogy, petrography, and alteration of numerous rock samples, geophysical data, remote sensing imagery, and results of chemical analyses, which, combined, show no direct evidence for economic mineralization. Detailed descriptions and interpretations of the studies and tests that were conducted in the site area are presented by Castor et al. (1999), who concluded that the small, largely trace amounts of the minerals that were detected (for example, tin, gold, and uranium) were far below the concentrations or the volumes required for any economic consideration.

Industrial Rocks and Minerals

The Yucca Mountain region contains many deposits of industrial rocks and minerals (Castor and Lock, 1995). Borite, clay minerals, fluorite, and zeolite have been identified in samples from Yucca Mountain; building stone, construction aggregate, limestone, pumice, silica, and vitrophyre/perlite also are present. Based on such factors as quality and quantity of the resource, accessibility, and competition from alternate, more readily available sources of supply elsewhere in the region, none of these commodities are considered to be of economic importance (CRWMS M&O, 2001).

Hydrocarbon and Other Energy Resources

There are few data for determining the extent to which the essential elements for the generation and accumulation of oil and gas—source rocks, favorable maturation history, reservoir rocks, and sealing and trapping conditions—are developed in the Yucca Mountain area. Only one borehole (UE-25 p#1, Figs. 8 and 10) was drilled deep enough to penetrate rocks below the Tertiary volcanic sequence; these pre-Tertiary rocks were identified as strata representing the Lone Mountain Dolomite and Roberts Mountains Formation of Silurian age. No oil shows or residue were reported from an examination of the borehole cores (Carr et al., 1986). To date (2006), no significant volumes of oil or gas have been found in southern Nevada or adjacent California and Arizona.

French (2000), in an assessment of the hydrocarbon potential of the Yucca Mountain area, concluded that, although the basic elements of a viable petroleum system are present, comparisons with known producing fields in the region indicate that (1) the volume of potential source rock is limited, and (2) one of the important seals of the region (an unconformity at the base of valley-fill sediments in some producing areas) is not well developed. Based on these and other factors, French (2000) and Grow et al. (1994) interpreted the geologic conditions at Yucca Mountain to indicate a low potential for the generation and accumulation of oil and gas.

Other energy resources—tar sands, oil shale, and coal—are not known to exist in the rocks underlying Yucca Mountain, not having been detected in any of the boreholes drilled in the area or recognized in outcrops in nearby areas (see Castor et al., 1999).

Geothermal Resources

Flynn et al. (1996), citing geological, geophysical, and geochemical findings, chemical geothermometry, and the very low measured thermal gradient, concluded that there is no potential for geothermal development in the area. This is supported by temperatures measured in springs south of latitude 38°30′ in Nevada, which are uniformly less than 41 °C (Garside and Schilling, 1979).

ACKNOWLEDGMENTS

The synthesis of geologic information presented here is based on a large volume of basic data that was collected and analyzed by scores of investigators involved in the Yucca Mountain Site Characterization program. Although individual contributions forming the basis for much of the descriptive, interpretive, and illustrative content of this report are appropriately cited, we wish to acknowledge certain individual scientists who played key roles in the conduct of field and laboratory studies that were fundamental to developing the structural and stratigraphic framework of the Yucca Mountain site area. Unless otherwise indicated, named individuals are U.S. Geological Survey personnel.

W.C. Day led a team, including R.P. Dickerson (Pacific Western Technology, Inc.), R.M. Drake, III, C.J. Potter, and D.S. Sweetkind, that produced bedrock geologic maps showing in considerable detail major and minor faults and other structural features, many of which had not been recognized previously. As indicated in our report, virtually all of the discussions of bedrock structure and the distribution and displacements of bedrock stratigraphic units are based on the maps, cross sections, and descriptions published by these investigators. A review of a preliminary draft of our report by W.C. Day is also gratefully acknowledged.

R.W. Spengler was a leading member of the group, including J.K. Geslin and T.C. Moyer (Science Applications International Corp.), that was instrumental in defining and describing lithostratigraphic units within the thick volcanic-rock sequences that form Yucca Mountain. Their studies were fundamental to the characterization and distribution of the physical and chemical properties of the rocks that compose and surround the proposed repository block.

Personnel of the Los Alamos National Laboratory, including D.L. Bish, D.E. Broxton, B.A. Carlos, S.J. Chipera, S.S. Levy, and D.T. Vaniman, also contributed basic mineralogical and geochemical data. R.W. Spengler was involved in a major effort to accurately identify lithostratigraphic contacts in boreholes that provided much of the data on rock thicknesses and essential information for the 3-D modeling of the site area.

J.A. Coe, S.C. Lundstrom, C.M. Menges, A.R. Ramelli (Nevada Bureau of Mines and Geology), E.M. Taylor, J.R. Wesling (Geomatrix Consultants, Inc.), and J.C. Yount were principal investigators in the detailed study of Quaternary surficial deposits and the mapping of trench excavations across buried faults that provided evidence of the magnitude and ages of Quaternary faulting events. Ages of sediments and soils were determined principally by J.B. Paces (U-series analyses) and S.A. Mahan (thermoluminescence analyses).

REFERENCES CITED

Albin, A.L., Singleton, W.L., Moyer, T.C., Lee, A.C., Lung, R.C., Eatmon, G.L.W., and Barr, D.L., 1997, Geology of the Main Drift—Station 28+00 to 55+00, Exploratory Studies Facility, Yucca Mountain Project, Yucca Mountain, Nevada: Summary Report by the U.S. Bureau of Reclamation to the U.S. Department of Energy, Yucca Mountain Project Data Tracking Number GS970208314224.005, 312 p., 6 plates.

Anna, L.O., and Wallman, P., 1997, Characterizing the fracture network at Yucca Mountain, Nevada, Part 2, Numerical simulation of flow in a three-dimensional discrete fracture network, *in* Hoak, T.E., Klatwitter, A.L., and Blomquist, P.K., eds., Fractured reservoirs: Characterization and modeling: Rocky Mountain Association of Geologists, Characterization and Modeling Guidebook.

Arnold, B.W., Altman, S.J., Robey, T.H., Barnard, R.W., and Brown, T.J., 1995, Unsaturated-zone fast-path flow calculations for Yucca Mountain groundwater travel time analysis: Sandia National Laboratories SAND 95-0857.

Barker, C.E., 1994, Thermal and petroleum generation history of the Mississippian Eleana Formation and Tertiary source rocks, Yucca Mountain area, southern Nye County, Nevada: U.S. Geological Survey Open-File Report 94-161, 26 p.

Beason, S.C., Turlington, G.A., Lung, R.C., Eatman, G.L.W., Ryter, D., and Barr, D.L., 1996, Geology of the North Ramp—Station 0+60 to 4+00, Exploratory Studies Facility, Yucca Mountain Project, Yucca Mountain, Nevada: Summary Report by the U.S. Bureau of Reclamation to the U.S. Department of Energy, Yucca Mountain Project Data Tracking Number GS960908314224.019, 174 p., 15 plates.

Bechtel SAIC Company, 2002, Geologic framework model: Bechtel SAIC Company MDL-NBS-GS-000002, Rev. 01.

Beck, D.A., and Glancy, P.A., 1995, Overview of runoff of March 11, 1995, in Fortymile Wash and Amargosa River, southern Nevada: U.S. Geological Survey Fact Sheet FS-210-95.

Bierman, P.C., and Caffee, M.C., 2002, Cosmogenic exposure and erosion history of ancient Australian bedrock landforms: Geological Society of America Bulletin, v. 114, p. 787–803, doi: 10.1130/0016-7606(2002)114<0787:CEAEHO>2.0.CO;2.

Birkeland, P.W., 1984, Soils and geomorphology: Oxford University Press, New York, New York, 372 p.

Bish, D.L., and Aronson, J.L., 1993, Paleogeothermal and paleohydrologic conditions in silica tuff from Yucca Mountain, Nevada: Clays and Clay Minerals, v. 41, p. 148–161, doi: 10.1346/CCMN.1993.0410204.

Bish, D.L., Carey, J.W., Carlos, S.J., Chipera, S.J., Guthrie, G.D., Jr., Levy, S.S., Vaniman, D.T., and WoldeGabriel, G., 2002, Summary and synthesis report on mineralogy and petrology Studies for the Yucca Mountain Site Characterization Project: Los Alamos National Laboratory Report LA-UR-02-7840, 1,300 p.

Bish, D.L., and Chipera, S.J., 1986, Mineralogy of drill holes J-13, UE-25A#1, and USW G-1 at Yucca Mountain, Nevada: Los Alamos National Laboratory LA-10764-MS.

Bish, D.L., and Vaniman, D.T., 1985, Mineralogic summary of Yucca Mountain, Nevada: Los Alamos National Laboratory LA-10543-MS.

Brocher, T.M., Hunter, W.C., and Langenheim, V.E., 1998, Implications of seismic reflection and potential field geophysical data on the structural framework of the Yucca Mountain–Crater Flat region, Nevada: Geological Society of America Bulletin, v. 110, p. 947–971, doi: 10.1130/0016-7606(1998)110<0947:IOSRAP>2.3.CO;2.

Broxton, D.E., Byers, F.M., Jr., and Warren, R.G., 1989, Petrography and phenocryst chemistry of volcanic units at Yucca Mountain, Nevada: Los Alamos National Laboratories LA-11503-MS.

Broxton, D.E., Chipera, S.J., Byers, F.M., Jr., and Rautman, C.A., 1993, Geologic evaluation of six nonwelded tuff sites in the vicinity of Yucca Mountain, Nevada for a surface-based test facility for the Yucca Mountain project: Los Alamos National Laboratory LA-12542-MS.

Buesch, D.C., 2000, Application of theoretical relations of density, porosity, and composition in volcanic rocks from Yucca Mountain, Nevada: Geological Society of America Abstracts with Programs, v. 32, no. 7, p. A-89.

Buesch, D.C., and Spengler, R.W., 1999, Stratigraphic framework of the North Ramp area of the Exploratory Studies Facility, Yucca Mountain, in Rousseau, J.P., Kwicklis, E.M., and Gillies, D.C., eds., Hydrology of the unsaturated zone, North Ramp area of the Exploratory Studies Facility, Yucca Mountain, Nevada: U.S. Geological Survey Water-Resources Investigations Report 98-4050, p. 17–44.

Buesch, D.C., Spengler, R.W., Moyer, T.C., and Geslin, J.K., 1996, Proposed stratigraphic nomenclature and macroscopic identification of lithostratigraphic units of the Paintbrush Group exposed at Yucca Mountain, Nevada: U.S. Geological Survey Open-File Report 94-469.

Byers, F.M., Jr., Carr, W.J., Orkild, P.P., Quinlivan, W.D., and Sargent, K.A., 1976, Volcanic suites and related cauldrons of Timber Mountain–Oasis Valley caldera complex, southern Nevada: U.S. Geological Survey Professional Paper 919.

Caporuscio, F., Vaniman, D., Bish, D., Broxton, D., Arney, B., Heiken, G., Byers, F., Gooley, R., and Semarge, E., 1982, Petrologic studies of drill cores USW-G2 and UE25b-1H, Yucca Mountain, Nevada: Los Alamos National Laboratory LA-9255-MS.

Carr, M.D., Waddell, S.J., Vick, G.S., Stock, J.M., Monsen, S.A., Harris, A.G., Cork, B.W., and Byers, F.M., Jr., 1986, Geology of drill core UE25p#1: A test hole into pre-Tertiary rocks near Yucca Mountain, southern Nevada: U.S. Geological Survey Open-File Report 86-175.

Carr, W.J., 1984, Regional structural setting of Yucca Mountain, southwestern Nevada, and Late Cenozoic rates of tectonic activity in part of southwestern Great Basin, Nevada and California: U.S. Geological Survey Open-File Report 84-854.

Carr, W.J., 1992, Structural model for western Midway Valley based on RF drillhole data and bedrock outcrops, in Gibson, J., Swan, F., Wesling, J., Bullard, T., Perman, R., Angell, M., and DiSilvestro, L., Summary and evaluation of existing geological and geophysical data near prospective surface facilities in Midway Valley, Yucca Mountain project, Nye County, Nevada: Sandia National Laboratories SAND90-2491, Appendix A.

Carr, W.J., Byers, F.M., Jr., and Orkild, P.P., 1986, Stratigraphic and volcano-tectonic relations of Crater Flat Tuff and some older volcanic units, Nye County, Nevada: U.S. Geological Survey Professional Paper 1323.

Cashman, P.H., and Trexler, J.H., Jr., 1995, Task 8: Evaluation of hydrocarbon potential, in Evaluation of the geologic relations and seismotectonic stability of the Yucca Mountain area, Nevada nuclear waste site investigation: Mackay School of Mines Progress Report 30, University of Nevada, Reno, Nevada.

Castor, S.B., Garside, L.J., Tingley, J.V., LaPointe, D.D., Desilets, M.O., Hsu, L.-C., Goldstrand, P.M., Lugaski, T.P., and Ross, H.P., 1999, Assessment of metallic and mined energy resources in the Yucca Mountain Conceptual Controlled Area, Nye County, Nevada: Nevada Bureau of Mines and Geology Open-File Report 99-13, Reno, Nevada.

Castor, S.B., and Lock, D.E., 1995, Assessment of industrial minerals and rocks in the controlled area: Nevada Bureau of Mines and Geology, Reno, Nevada, Yucca Mountain Project Data Tracking Number MO 950000000006.002.

Chipera, S.J., Vaniman, D.T., Carlos, B.A., and Bish, D.L., 1995, Mineralogic variation in drill core UE-25 UZ#16, Yucca Mountain, Nevada: Los Alamos National Laboratory LA-12810-MS.

Christiansen, R.L., 1979, Cooling units and composite sheets in relation to caldera structure: Geological Society of America Special Paper 180, p. 29–42.

Christiansen, R.L., and Lipman, P.W., 1965, Geologic map of the Topopah Spring NW quadrangle, Nye County, Nevada: U.S. Geological Survey Geologic Quadrangle Map GQ 444, scale 1:24,000.

Ciancia, M., and Heiken, G., 2006, Geotechnical properties of tuffs at Yucca Mountain, Nevada, in Heiken, G., ed., Tuffs—Their properties, uses, hydrology, and resources: Geological Society of America Special Paper 408, p. 33–89, doi: 10.1130/2007.2408(03).

Coe, J.A., 2004, Quaternary faulting on the Northern Crater Flat fault, in Keefer, W.R., Whitney, J.W., and Taylor, G.M., eds., Quaternary paleoseismology and stratigraphy of the Yucca Mountain area, Nevada: U.S. Geological Survey Professional Paper 1689, p. 145–154.

Coe, J.A., Glancy, P.A., and Whitney, J.W., 1997, Volumetric analysis and hydrologic characterization of a modern debris flow near Yucca Mountain, Nevada: Geomorphology, v. 20, p. 11–28, doi: 10.1016/S0169-555X(97)00008-1.

Coe, J.A., Oswald, J., Vadurro, G., and Lundstrom, S.C., 2004, Quaternary faulting on the Fatigue Wash fault, in Keefer, W.R., Whitney, J.W., and Taylor, E.M., eds., Quaternary paleoseismology and stratigraphy of the Yucca Mountain area, Nevada: U.S. Geological Survey Professional Paper 1689, p. 111–124.

Cole, J.C., 1997, Major structural controls on the distribution of pre-Tertiary rocks, Nevada Test Site vicinity, southern Nevada: U.S. Geological Survey Open-File Report 97-533.

Craig, R.W., Reed, R.L., and Spengler, R.W., 1983, Geohydrologic data for test well USW H-6, Yucca Mountain area, Nye County, Nevada: U.S. Geological Survey Open-File Report 83-856.

Crowe, B., Perry, F., Geissman, J., McFadden, L., Wells, S., Murrell, M., Poths, J., Valentine, G., Bowker, L., and Finnegan, K., 1995, Status of volcanism studies for the Yucca Mountain site characterization project: Los Alamos National Laboratory LA-12908-MS.

CRWMS M&O (Civilian Radioactive Waste Management System Management and Operation Contractor), 1996, Borehole geophysics, in Synthesis of borehole and surface geophysical studies at Yucca Mountain, Nevada and vicinity: CRWMS & M&O, Las Vegas, Nevada, Report BAAA00000-01717-0200-00015, Rev 00, Volume II.

CRWMS M&O, 1998, Yucca Mountain site description: CRWMS M&O, Las Vegas, Nevada, Report B00000000-01717-5700-00019, Rev 01.

CRWMS M&O, 2000, Yucca Mountain site description: CRWMS M&O, Las Vegas, Nevada, Report TDR-CRW-GS-000001, Rev 01.

CRWMS M&O, 2001, Natural resources assessment: CRWMS M&O, Las Vegas, Nevada, Report ANL-NBS-GS-000001, Rev 00.

CRWMS M&O, 2004, Yucca Mountain Site Description: CRWMS M&O, Las Vegas, Nevada, Report TOR-CRW-GS-000001, Rev 02, ICN 001.

Day, W.C., Dickerson, R.P., Potter, C.J., Sweetkind, D.S., San Juan, C.A.,

Drake, R.M., II, and Fridrich, C.J., 1998a, Bedrock geologic map of the Yucca Mountain area, Nye County, Nevada: U.S. Geological Survey Geologic Investigations Series Map I-2627, scale 1:24,000.

Day, W.C., Potter, C.J., Sweetkind, D.C., Dickerson, R.P., and San Juan, C.A., 1998b, Bedrock geologic map of the central block area, Yucca Mountain area, Nye County, Nevada; U.S. Geological Survey Geologic Investigations Series I-2601, scale 1:6000.

Dickerson, R.P., and Drake, R.M., II, 1998, Geologic map of the Paintbrush Canyon area, Yucca Mountain, Nevada: U.S. Geological Survey Open-File Report 97-783, scale 1:6000.

Dickerson, R.P., and Drake, R.M., II, 2004, Geologic map of south-central Yucca Mountain, Nye County, Nevada: U.S. Geological Survey Miscellaneous Field Studies Map MF-2422, scale 1:6000. Map can be printed/downloaded at: http://pubs.usgs.gov/mf2004/mf-2422/.

Diehl, S.F., and Chornack, M.P., 1990, Stratigraphic correlation and petrography of the bedded tuffs, Yucca Mountain, Nye County, Nevada: U.S. Geological Survey Open-File Report 89-3.

Faure, G., 1986, Principles of isotope geology: John Wiley and Sons, New York, New York, 2nd edition.

Feighner, M., Johnson, L., Lee, K., Daley, T., Karageorgi, E., Parker, P., Smith, T., Williams, K., Romero, A., and McEvilly, T., 1996, Results and interpretation of multiple geophysical surveys at Yucca Mountain, Nevada: Lawrence Berkeley National Laboratory LBL-38200, 139 p.

Fitterman, D.V., 1982, Magnetometric resistivity survey near Fortymile Wash, Nevada Test Site, Nevada: U.S. Geological Survey Open-File Report 82-401.

Flint, A.L., and Flint, L.E., 1994, Spatial distribution of potential near surface moisture flux at Yucca Mountain, *in* High Level Radioactive Waste Management: Proceedings of the Fifth Annual International Conference, Las Vegas, Nevada, 22–26 May 1994, American Nuclear Society, La Grange, Illinois, v. 4, p. 2352–2358.

Flint, L.E., 1998, Characterization of hydrogeologic units using matrix properties, Yucca Mountain, Nevada: U.S. Geological Survey Water-Resources Investigations Report 97-4243.

Flynn, T., Buchanan, P., Trexler, D., Shevenell, L., and Garside, L., 1996, Geothermal resource assessment of the Yucca Mountain area, Nye County, Nevada: University and Community College System of Nevada, DI # BA0000000-03255-5705-00002.

Forester, R.M., Bradbury, J.P., Carter, C., Elvidge-Tuma, A.B., Hemphill, M.L., Lundstrom, S.C., Mahan, S.A., Marshall, B.D., Neymark, L.S., Paces, J.B., Sharpe, S.E., Whelan, J.F., and Wigand, P.E., 1999, The climate and hydrologic history of southern Nevada during the Late Quaternary: U.S. Geological Survey Open-File Report 98-635.

French, D.E., 2000, Hydrocarbon assessment of the Yucca Mountain vicinity, Nye County, Nevada: Nevada Bureau of Mines and Geology Open-File Report 2000-2.

Fridrich, C.J., 1999, Tectonic evolution of the Crater Flat Basin, Yucca Mountain region, Nevada, *in* Wright, L.A., and Troxel, B.W., eds., Cenozoic basins of the Death Valley region: Geological Society of America Special Paper 333, p. 169–195.

Fridrich, C.J., Whitney, J.W., Hudson, M.R., and Crowe, B.M., 1999, Space-time patterns of late Cenozoic extension, vertical axis rotation, and volcanism in Crater Flat basin, southwest Nevada, *in* Wright, L.A., and Troxel, B.W., eds., Cenozoic basins of the Death Valley region: Geological Society of America Special Paper 333, p. 197–212.

Frischknecht, F.C., and Raab, P.V., 1984, Time-domain electromagnetic sounds at the Nevada Test Site, Nevada: Geophysics, v. 49, p. 981–992, doi: 10.1190/1.1441742.

Frizzell, V.A., Jr., and Shulters, J., 1990, Geologic map of the Nevada Test Site, southern Nevada: U.S. Geological Survey Miscellaneous Investigations Series Map I-2046, scale 1:100,000.

Garside, L.J., and Schilling, J.H., 1979, Thermal waters of Nevada: Nevada Bureau of Mines and Geology Bulletin, v. 91, p. 163.

Geslin, J.K., and Moyer, T.C., 1995, Summary of lithologic logging of new and existing boreholes at Yucca Mountain, Nevada, March 1994 to June 1994: U.S. Geological Survey Open-File Report 94-451.

Geslin, J.K., Moyer, T.C., and Buesch, D.C., 1995, Summary of lithologic logging of new and existing boreholes at Yucca Mountain, Nevada, August 1993 to February 1994: U.S. Geological Survey Open-File Report 94-342.

Gile, L.H., Peterson, F.F., and Grossman, R.B., 1966, Morphological and genetic sequences of carbonate accumulation in desert soils: Soil Science, v. 101, p. 347–360, doi: 10.1097/00010694-196605000-00001.

Glancy, P.A., 1994, Evidence of prehistoric flooding and the potential for future extreme flooding at Coyote Wash, Yucca Mountain, Nye County, Nevada: U.S. Geological Survey Open-File Report 92-458.

Gosse, J.C., Harrington, C.D., and Whitney, J.W., 1996, Application of in situ cosmogenic nuclides in the site characterization of Yucca Mountain, Nevada: Material Research Society Symposium Proceedings, v. 412, p. 799–806.

Grow, J.A., Barker, C.E., and Harris, A.G., 1994, Oil and gas exploration near Yucca Mountain, Nevada, *in* High Level Radioactive Waste Management: Proceedings of the Fifth Annual International Conference, Las Vegas, Nevada, 22–26 May 1994, American Nuclear Society, LaGrange, Illinois, v. 3, p. 1298–1315.

Hamilton, W.B., 1988, Detachment faulting in the Death Valley region, California and Nevada, *in* Carr, M.D., and Yount, J.C., eds., Geologic and hydrologic investigations of a potential nuclear waste disposal site at Yucca Mountain, southern Nevada: U.S. Geological Survey Bulletin 1790, p. 51–85.

Harrington, C.D., and Whitney, J.W., 1987, Scanning electron microscope method for rock-varnish dating: Geology, v. 15, p. 967–970, doi: 10.1130/0091-7613(1987)15<967:SEMMFR>2.0.CO;2.

Heizler, M.T., Perry, F.V., Crowe, B.M., Peters, Lisa, and Appelt, R., 1999, The age of the Lathrop Wells volcanic center; an ^{40}Ar/^{39}Ar dating investigation: Journal of Geophysical Research, v. 104, no. B1, p. 767–804.

Hoover, D.L., 1989, Preliminary description of Quaternary and late Pliocene surficial deposits at Yucca Mountain and vicinity, Nye County, Nevada: U.S. Geological Survey Open-File Report 89-359.

Hoover, D.L., and Morrison, J.N., 1980, Geology of the Syncline Ridge area related to nuclear waste disposal, Nevada Test Site, Nye County, Nevada: U.S. Geological Survey Open-File Report 80-942.

Hoover, D.L., Swadley, WC, and Gordon, A.J., 1981, Correlation characteristics of surficial deposits with a description of surficial stratigraphy in the Nevada Test Site region: U.S. Geological Survey Open-File Report 81-512.

Hopkins, D.M., 1975, Time-stratigraphic nomenclature for the Holocene epoch: Geoderma, v. 14, p. 2.

Imbrie, J., Hays, J.D., Martinson, D.G., McIntyre, A., Mix, A.C., Morley, J.J., Pisias, N.G., Prell, W.L., and Shackleton, N.J., 1984, The orbital theory of Pleistocene climate: Support from a revised chronology of the marine δ^{18}O record, *in* Berger, A., Imbrie, J., Hays, J., Kukla, G., and Saltzman, B., eds., Milankovitch and Climate, Part I: Reidel Publishing Company, Netherlands, p. 269–305.

Izett, G.A., Obradovich, J.D., and Mehnert, H.H., 1988, The Bishop Ash Bed (middle Pleistocene) and some older (Pliocene and Pleistocene) chemically and mineralogically similar ash beds in California, Nevada, and Utah: U.S. Geological Survey Bulletin 1675, 37 p.

Keefer, W.R., Whitney, J.W., and Taylor, E.M., eds., 2004, Quaternary paleoseismology and stratigraphy of the Yucca Mountain area, Nevada: U.S. Geological Survey Professional Paper 1689.

Langenheim, V.E., and Ponce, D.A., 1994, Gravity and magnetic investigations of Yucca Wash, southwest Nevada, *in* High Level Radioactive Waste Management: American Nuclear Society Annual International Conference, 5th, Las Vegas, Nev., 1994 Proceedings, v. 4, p. 2272–2278.

Levy, S.S., and O'Neil, J.R., 1989, Moderate-temperature zeolitic alteration in a cooling pyroclastic deposit: Chemical Geology, v. 76, p. 321–326.

Lipman, P.W., Christiansen, R.L., and O'Connor, J.T., 1966, A compositionally zoned ash-flow sheet in southern Nevada: U.S. Geological Survey Professional Paper 524-F.

Lipman, P.W., and McKay, E.J., 1965, Geologic map of the Topopah Spring SW quadrangle, Nye County, Nevada: U.S. Geological Survey Geologic Quadrangle Map GQ-439, scale 1:24,000.

Lundstrom, S.C., Paces, J.B., and Mahan, S.A., 1996, Late Quaternary history of Fortymile Wash, southern Nevada: a record of geomorphic response to climate change in the Yucca Mountain region: Geological Society of America Abstracts with Programs, v. 28, no. 7, p. A-552.

Lundstrom, S.C., Paces, J.B., and Mahan, S.A., 1998, Late Quaternary History of Fortymile Wash in the area near the H-Road crossing, *in* Taylor, E.M., ed., Quaternary geology of the Yucca Mountain area, southern Nevada: Field Trip Guide, Annual Meeting of the Friends of the Pleistocene, Pacific Cell, 9–11 October 1998, p. 63–76.

Lundstrom, S.C., and Warren, R.G., 1994, Late Cenozoic evolution of Fortymile Wash: Major change in drainage pattern in the Yucca Mountain, Nevada region during late Miocene volcanism, *in* High Level Radioactive Waste Management: Proceedings of the Fifth Annual International Conference, Las Vegas, Nevada, 22–26 May 1994, American Nuclear Society, La Grange, Illinois, v. 4, p. 2121–2130.

Majer, E.L., Feighner, M., Johnson, L., Daley, T., Karageorgi, E., Lee, K., Williams, K., and McEvilly, T., 1996, Surface geophysics: Volume I of synthesis of borehole and surface geophysical studies at Yucca Mountain, Nevada and vicinity: Lawrence Berkeley National Laboratory, Berkeley, California, Report UCID-39319.

Maldonado, F., and Koether, S.L., 1983, Stratigraphy, structure, and some petrographic features of volcanic rocks at the USW G-2 drill hole, Yucca Mountain, Nye County, Nevada: U.S. Geological Survey Open-File Report 83-732.

Martin, R.J., Price, R.H., Boyd, P.J., and Noel, J.S., 1994, Bulk and mechanical properties of the Paintbrush Tuff recovered from borehole USW NRG-6: Data report: Sandia National Laboratories SAND93-4020.

Martin, R.J., Price, R.H., Boyd, P.J., and Noel, J.S., 1995, Bulk and mechanical properties of the Paintbrush Tuff recovered from borehole USW NRG 7/7A: Data report: Sandia National Laboratories SAND94-1996.

McDonald, E., and McFadden, L.D., 1994, Quaternary stratigraphy of the Providence Mountains piedmont and preliminary age estimates and regional stratigraphic correlations of Quaternary deposits in the eastern Mojave Desert, California, *in* McGill, S.F., and Ross, T.M., eds., Geological investigations of an active margin: Geological Society of America, Cordilleran Section, Fieldtrip Guidebook 8, p. 205–213.

McFadden, L.D., and Weldon, R.J., III, 1987, Rates and processes of soil development on Quaternary terraces in Cajon Pass, California: Geological Society of America Bulletin, v. 98, p. 280–293, doi: 10.1130/0016-7606(1987)98<280:RAPOSD>2.0.CO;2.

McFadden, L.D., Wells, S.G., and Jercinovich, M.J., 1987, Influences of eolian and pedogenic processes on the origin and evolution of desert pavements: Geology, v. 15, p. 504–508, doi: 10.1130/0091-7613(1987)15<504:IOEAPP>2.0.CO;2.

McGovern, T.F., 1983, An evaluation of seismic reflection studies in the Yucca Mountain area, Nevada Test Site: U.S. Geological Survey Open-File Report 83-912.

Menges, C.M., Taylor, E.M., Vadurro, G., Oswald, J.A., Cress, R., Murray, M., Lundstrom, S.C., Paces, J.B., and Mahan, S.A., 1997, Logs and paleoseismic interpretations from trenches 14C and 14D on the Bow Ridge fault, northeastern Yucca Mountain, Nye County, Nevada: U.S. Geological Survey Miscellaneous Field Studies Map 2311.

Menges, C.M., Taylor, E.M., Wesling, J.R., Swan, F.H., Coe, J.A., Ponti, D.J., and Whitney, J.W., 2004, Summary of Quaternary faulting on the Paintbrush Canyon, Stagecoach Road, and Bow Ridge faults, *in* Keefer, W.R., Whitney, J.W., and Taylor, E.M., eds., Quaternary paleoseismology and stratigraphy of the Yucca Mountain area, Nevada: U.S. Geological Survey Professional Paper 1689, p. 41–69.

Menges, C.M., Wesling, J.R., Whitney, J.W., Swan, F.H., Coe, J.A., Thomas, A.P., and Oswald, J.A., 1994, Preliminary results of paleoseismic investigations of Quaternary faults on eastern Yucca Mountain, Nye County, Nevada, *in* High Level Radioactive Waste Management: Proceedings of the Fifth Annual International Conference, Las Vegas, Nevada, 22–26 May 1994, American Nuclear Society, La Grange, Illinois, v. 4, p. 2373–2390.

Menges, C.M., and Whitney, J.W., 2004, Distribution of Quaternary faults at Yucca Mountain, *in* Keefer, W.R., Whitney, J.W., and Taylor, E.M., eds., Quaternary paleoseismology and stratigraphy of the Yucca Mountain area, Nevada: U.S. Geological Survey Professional Paper 1689, p. 23–31.

Minor, S.A., Sawyer, D.A., Wahl, R.R., Frizzell, V.A., Jr., Schilling, S.P., Warren, R.G., Orkild, P.P., Coe, J.A., Hudson, M.R., Fleck, R.J., Lanphere, M.A., Swadley, W.C., and Cole, J.C., 1993, Preliminary geologic map of the Pahute Mesa 30′ × 60′ quadrangle: U.S. Geological Survey Open-File Report 93-299.

Mongano, G.S., Singleton, W.L., Moyer, T.C., Beason, S.C., Eatman, G.L.W., Albin, A.L., and Lang, R.C., 1999, Geology of the ECRB Cross Drift—Exploratory Studies Facility, Yucca Mountain Project, Yucca Mountain, Nevada: Summary Report by the U.S. Bureau of Reclamation to the U.S. Department of Energy, Yucca Mountain Project Data Tracking Number GS990908314224.010, 46 p., 4 plates.

Monsen, S.A., Carr, M.D., Reheis, M.C., and Orkild, P.P., 1992, Geologic map of Bare Mountain, Nye County, Nevada: U.S. Geological Survey Miscellaneous Investigations Map I-2201, scale 1:24,000.

Montazer, P., and Wilson, W.E., 1984, Conceptual hydrologic model of flow in the unsaturated zone, Yucca Mountain, Nevada: U.S. Geological Survey Water-Resources Investigations Report 84-4345.

Morrison, R.B., 1991, Introduction, *in* Morrison, R.B., ed., Quaternary nongla-

cial geology—Conterminous U.S.: Geological Society of America, The Geology of North America, v. K-2, p. 1–12.

Moyer, T.C., and Geslin, J.K., 1995, Lithostratigraphy of the Calico Hills Formation and Prow Pass Tuff (Crater Flat Group) at Yucca Mountain, Nevada: U.S. Geological Survey Open-File Report 94-460.

Moyer, T.C., Geslin, J.K., and Buesch, D.C., 1995, Summary of lithologic logging of new and existing boreholes at Yucca Mountain, Nevada, July 1994 to November, 1994: U.S. Geological Survey Open-File Report 95-102.

Moyer, T.C., Geslin, J.K., and Flint, L.E., 1996, Stratigraphic relations and hydrologic properties of the Paintbrush Tuff nonwelded (PTn) hydrologic unit, Yucca Mountain, Nevada: U.S. Geological Survey Open-File Report 95-397.

Muller, D.C., and Kibler, J.E., 1984, Preliminary analysis of geophysical logs from drill hole UE-25p#1, Yucca Mountain, Nye County, Nevada: U.S. Geological Survey Open-File Report 84-649, 14 p.

Munsell Color Company, Inc., 1988, Munsell soil color charts: Baltimore, Maryland.

Nelson, P.H., 1993, Estimation of water-filled and air-filled porosity in the unsaturated zone, Yucca Mountain, Nevada, *in* High Level Radioactive Waste Management: Proceedings of the Fourth Annual International Conference, Las Vegas, Nevada, 26–30 April 1993, American Nuclear Society, La Grange, Illinois, v. 1, p. 949–954.

Nelson, P.H., 1994, Saturation levels and trends in the unsaturated zone, Yucca Mountain, Nevada, *in* High Level Radioactive Waste Management: Proceedings of the Fifth Annual International Conference, Las Vegas, Nevada, 22–26 May 1994, American Nuclear Society, La Grange, Illinois, v. 4, p. 2774–2781.

Nelson, P.H., 1996, Computation of porosity and water content from geophysical logs, Yucca Mountain, Nevada: U.S. Geological Survey Open-File Report 96-078.

Nelson, P.H., Muller, D.C., Schimschal, U., and Kibler, J.E., 1991, Geophysical logs and core measurements from forty boreholes at Yucca Mountain, Nevada: U.S. Geological Survey Geophysical Investigations Map GP-1001.

Nevada Bureau of Mines and Geology, 1997, The Nevada mineral industry 1996: Nevada Bureau of Mines and Geology Special Publication MI-1996.

Nichols, K.K., Bierman, P.R., Foniri, W.R., Gillespie, A.R., Caffee, M., and Finkel, R., 2006, Dates and rates of arid region geomorphic processes: GSA Today, v. 16, p. 4–10, doi: 10.1130/GSAT01608.1.

Noble, D.C., and Hedge, C.E., 1969, Sr87/Sr86 variations within individual ash-flow sheets: U.S. Geological Survey Professional Paper 650-C, p. C133–C139.

O'Leary, D.W., 2007, this volume, Tectonic models for Yucca Mountain, Nevada, *in* Stuckless, J.S., and Levich, R.A., eds., The Geology and Climatology of Yucca Mountain and Vicinity, Southern Nevada and California: Geological Society of America Memoir 199, doi: 10.1130/2007.1199(04).

Ortiz, T.S., Williams, R.L., Nimick, F.B., Whittet, B.C., and South, D.L., 1985, A three-dimensional model of reference thermal/mechanical and hydrological stratigraphy at Yucca Mountain, southern Nevada: Sandia National Laboratories SAND84-1076.

Osterkamp, W.R., Lane, L.J., and Savard, C.S., 1994, Recharge estimates using a geomorphic/distributed-parameter simulation approach, Amargosa River Basin: Water Resources Association Water Resources Bulletin, v. 30, p. 493–506.

Pabst, M.E., Beck, D.A., Glancy, P.A., and Johnson, J.A., 1993, Streamflow and selected precipitation data for Yucca Mountain and vicinity, Nye County, Nevada, water years 1983–1985: U.S. Geological Survey Open-File Report 93-438.

Pankratz, L.W., 1982, Reconnaissance seismic refraction studies at Calico Hills, Wahmonie, and Yucca Mountain, southwest Nevada Test Site, Nye County, Nevada: U.S. Geological Survey Open-File Report 82-478.

Peterman, Z.E., and Futa, K., 1996, Geochemistry of core samples of the Tiva Canyon Tuff from drill hole UE-25 NRG#3, Yucca Mountain, Nevada: U.S. Geological Survey Open-File Report 95-325.

Peterman, Z.E., Spengler, R.W., Singer, F.R., and Dickerson, R.P., 1993, Isotopic and trace element variability in altered and unaltered tuffs at Yucca Mountain, Nevada, *in* High Level Radioactive Waste Management: Proceedings of the Fourth Annual International Conference, Las Vegas, Nevada, 26–30 April 1993, American Nuclear Society, La Grange, Illinois, v. 2, p. 1940–1947.

Ponce, D.A., 1993, Geophysical investigations of concealed faults near Yucca Mountain, southwest Nevada, *in* High Level Radioactive Waste Management:

Proceedings of the Fourth Annual International Conference, Las Vegas, Nevada, 26–30 April 1993, American Nuclear Society, La Grange, Illinois, v. 1, p. 168–174.

Ponce, D.A., and Langenheim, V.E., 1994, Preliminary gravity and magnetic models across Midway Valley and Yucca Wash, Yucca Mountain, Nevada: U.S. Geological Survey Open-File Report 94-572.

Potter, C.J., Day, W.C., Sweetkind, D.S., and Dickerson, R.P., 2004, Structural geology of the proposed site area for a high-level radioactive waste repository, Yucca Mountain, Nevada: Geological Society of America Bulletin, v. 116, no. 7/8, p. 858–879, doi: 10.1130/B25328.1.

Potter, C.J., Dickerson, R.P., and Day, W.C., 1999, Nature and continuity of the Sundance fault, Yucca Mountain, Nevada: U.S. Geological Survey Open-File Report 98-266.

Potter, C.J., Dickerson, R.P., Sweetkind, D.S., Drake, R.M., II, Taylor, E.M., Fridrich, C.J., San Juan, C.A., and Day, W.C., 2002a, Geologic map of the Yucca Mountain region, Nye County, Nevada: U.S. Geological Survey Geologic Investigations Series I-2755, scale 1:50,000.

Potter, C.J., Sweetkind, D.S., Dickerson, R.P., and Kilgore, M.L., 2002b, Hydrostructural maps of the Death Valley regional flow system, Nevada and California: U.S. Geological Survey Miscellaneous Field Studies Map MF-2372, scale 1:350,000.

Ramelli, A.R., Oswald, J.A., Vadurro, G., Menges, C.M., and Paces, J.B., 2004, Quaternary faulting on the Solitario Canyon fault, *in* Keefer, W.R., Whitney, J.W., and Taylor, E.M., eds., Quaternary paleoseismology and stratigraphy of the Yucca Mountain area: U.S. Geological Survey Professional Paper 1689, p. 89–109.

Reheis, M.C., and Kihl, R., 1995, Dust deposition in southern Nevada and California, 1984–1989: Relations to climate, source area, and source lithology: American Geophysical Union Journal of Geophysical Research, v. 100, p. 8893–8918.

Reynolds, C.B., et al., 1985, Final report, 1985 repository surface facility seismic survey, Yucca Mountain area, NTS, Nye County, Nevada: Charles B. Reynolds and Associates, Albuquerque, New Mexico, Report # MOL.19970415.0158.

Robinson, G.D., 1985, Structure of pre-Cenozoic rocks in the vicinity of Yucca Mountain, Nye County, Nevada—a potential nuclear-waste disposal site: U.S. Geological Survey Bulletin 1647.

Rosenbaum, J.G., Hudson, M.R., and Scott, R.B., 1991, Paleomagnetic constraints on the geometry and timing of deformation at Yucca Mountain, Nevada: American Geophysical Union Journal of Geophysical Research, v. 96, p. 1963–1979.

Rush, F.E., Thordarson, W., and Pyles, D.G., 1984, Geohydrology of test well USW H-1, Yucca Mountain, Nye County, Nevada: U.S. Geological Survey Water-Resources Investigations Report 84-4032.

Sarna-Wojcicki, A.M., Meyer, C.E., Wau, E., and Soles, S., 1993, Age and correlation of tephra layers in Owens Lake drill core OL-92-1 and -2: U.S. Geological Survey Open-File Report 93-683.

Sawyer, D.A., Fleck, R.J., Lanphere, M.A., Warren, R.G., Broxton, D.E., and Hudson, M.R., 1994, Episodic caldera volcanism in the Miocene southwestern Nevada volcanic field: revised stratigraphic framework, $^{40}Ar/^{39}Ar$ geochronology, and implications for magmatism and extension: Geological Society of America Bulletin, v. 106, p. 1304–1318, doi: 10.1130/0016-7606(1994)106<1304:ECVITM>2.3.CO;2.

Schenker, A.R., Guerin, D.C., Robey, T.H., Rautman, C.A., and Barnard, R.W., 1995, Stochastic hydrogeologic units and hydrogeologic properties development for total-system performance assessments: Sandia National Laboratories SAND94-0244.

Scott, R.B., 1990, Tectonic setting of Yucca Mountain, southwest Nevada, *in* Wernicke, B.P., ed., Basin and Range extensional tectonics near the latitude of Las Vegas, Nevada: Geological Society of America Memoir 176, p. 251–282.

Scott, R.B., 1992, Preliminary geologic map of southern Yucca Mountain, Nye County, Nevada: U.S. Geological Survey Open-File Report 92-266, scale 1:12,000.

Scott, R.B., Bath, G.D., Flanigan, V.J., Hoover, D.B., Rosenbaum, J.G., and Spengler, R.W., 1984, Geological and geophysical evidence of structures in northwest-trending washes, Yucca Mountain, southern Nevada, and their possible significance to a nuclear waste repository in the unsaturated zone: U.S. Geological Survey Open-File Report 84-567.

Scott, R.B., and Bonk, J., 1984, Preliminary geologic map of Yucca Mountain, Nye County, Nevada, with geologic sections: U.S. Geological Survey Open-File Report 84-494, scale 1:12,000.

Senterfit, R.M., Hoover, D.B., and Chornack, M.P., 1982, Resistivity sounding investigation by the Schlumberger method in the Yucca Mountain and Jackass Flats area, Nevada Test Site, Nevada: U.S. Geological Survey Open-File Report 82-1043.

Simonds, F.W., Whitney, J.W., Fox, K.F., Ramelli, A.R., Yount, J.C., Carr, M.D., Menges, C.M., Dickerson, R.P., and Scott, R.B., 1995, Map showing fault activity in the Yucca Mountain area, Nye County, Nevada: U.S. Geological Survey Miscellaneous Investigations Map I-2520, 1:24,000 scale.

Sharpe, S.E., 2007, this volume, Using modern through mid-Pleistocene climate proxy data to bound future variations in infiltration at Yucca Mountain, Nevada, *in* Stuckless, J.S., and Levich, R.A., eds., The Geology and Climatology of Yucca Mountain and Vicinity, Southern Nevada and California: Geological Society of America Memoir 199, doi: 10.1130/2007.1199(05).

Smith, C., and Ross, H.P., 1982, Interpretation of resistivity and induced polarization profiles with severe topographic effects, Yucca Mountain area, Nevada Test Site, Nevada: U.S. Geological Survey Open-File Report 82-182, 82 p.

Smith, R.L., 1960a, Ash flows: Geological Society of America Bulletin, v. 71, p. 795–842.

Smith, R.L., 1960b, Zones and zonal variations in welded ash flows: U.S. Geological Survey Professional Paper 354-F, p. 149–159.

Spengler, R.W., Byers, F.M., Jr., and Warner, J.B., 1981, Stratigraphy and structure in volcanic rocks in drill hole USW-G1, Yucca Mountain, Nye County, Nevada: U.S. Geological Survey Open-File Report 81-1349.

Spengler, R.W., and Chornack, M.P., 1984, Stratigraphic and structural characteristics of volcanic rocks in corehole USW-G4, Yucca Mountain, Nevada, with a section on geophysical logs by D.C. Muller and J.E. Kibler: U.S. Geological Survey Open-File Report 84-789.

Spengler, R.W., and Peterman, Z.E., 1991, Distribution of rubidium, strontium, and zirconium in tuff from two deep coreholes at Yucca Mountain, Nevada, *in* High Level Radioactive Waste Management: Proceedings of the Second Annual International Conference, Las Vegas, Nevada, 28 April–3 May 1991, American Nuclear Society, La Grange, Illinois, v. 2, p. 1416–1422.

Squires, R.R., and Young, R.L., 1984, Flood potential of Fortymile Wash and its principal southwestern tributaries, Nevada Test Site, southern Nevada: U.S. Geological Survey Water-Resources Investigations Report 83-4001.

Stamatakos, J.A., and Ferrill, D.A., 1998, Strike-slip fault system in Amargosa Valley and Yucca Mountain, Nevada—comment: Tectonophysics, v. 294, p. 151–160, doi: 10.1016/S0040-1951(98)00082-1.

Stewart, J.H., 1988, Tectonics of the Walker Lane belt, western Great Basin: Mesozoic and Cenozoic deformation in a zone of shear, *in* Ernst, W.G., ed., Metamorphism and crustal evolution of the Western United States: Prentice-Hall, Englewood Cliffs, New Jersey, Rubey Volume 7, p. 683–713.

Stuckless, J.S., and O'Leary, D.W., 2007, this volume, Geology of the Yucca Mountain region, *in* Stuckless, J.S., and Levich, R.A., eds., The Geology and Climatology of Yucca Mountain and Vicinity, Southern Nevada and California: Geological Society of America Memoir 199, doi: 10.1130/2007.1199(02).

Stuckless, J.S., Marshall, B.D., Vaniman, D.T., Dudley, W.W., Peterman, Z.E., Paces, J.B., Whelan, J.F., Taylor, E.M., Forester, R.M., and O'Leary, D.W., 1998, Comments on "Overview of calcite/opal deposits at or near the proposed high-level nuclear waste site, Yucca Mountain, Nevada, USA: pedogenic, hypogene, or both," by C.A. Hill, Y.V. Dublyansky, R.S. Harmon, and C.M. Schluter: Environmental Geology, v. 34, no. 1, p. 70–78, doi: 10.1007/s002540050257.

Swadley, WC, Hoover, D.L., and Rosholt, J.N., 1984, Preliminary report on late Cenozoic faulting and stratigraphy in the vicinity of Yucca Mountain, Nye County, Nevada: U.S. Geological Survey Open-File Report 84-788.

Swan, F.W., Wesling, J.R., Angell, M.M., Thomas, A.P., Whitney, J.W., and Gibson, J.D., 2001, Evaluation of the location and recency of faulting near prospective surface facilities in Midway Valley, Nye County, Nevada: U.S. Geological Survey Open-File Report 01-55.

Sweetkind, D.S., Dickerson, R.P., Blakely, R.J., and Denning, P.D., 2001, Interpretive geologic cross section for the Death Valley regional flow system and surrounding areas, Nevada and California: U.S. Geological Survey Miscellaneous Field Studies Map MF-2370.

Tanko, D.J., and Glancy, P.A., 2001, Flooding in the Amargosa River drainage basin, February 23–24, 1998, southern Nevada and eastern California, including the Nevada Test Site: U.S. Geological Survey Fact Sheet 036-01.

Taylor, E.M., 1986, Impact of time and climate on Quaternary soils in the Yucca

Mountain area of the Nevada Test Site [M.S. thesis]: Boulder, Colorado, University of Colorado.

Taylor, E.M., 2004, Quaternary faulting on the Southern Crater Flat fault, *in* Keefer, W.R., Whitney, J.W., and Taylor, G.M., eds., Quaternary paleoseismology and stratigraphy of the Yucca Mountain area, Nevada: U.S. Geological Survey Professional Paper 1689, p. 135–144.

Taylor, E.M., Menges, C.M., and Beason, S.C., 1998, Characteristics of the Ghost Dance fault at Yucca Mountain, Nevada, *in* High Level Radioactive Waste Management: Proceedings of the Eighth Annual International Conference, Las Vegas, Nevada, 11–14 May 1998, American Nuclear Society, La Grange, Illinois, p. 279–282.

Taylor, E.M., Menges, C.M., and Buesch, D.C., 2004, Results of paleoseismic investigations on the Ghost Dance fault, *in* Keefer, W.R., Whitney, J.W., and Taylor, E.M., eds., Quaternary paleoseismology and stratigraphy of the Yucca Mountain area, Nevada: U.S. Geological Survey Professional Paper 1689, p. 71–88.

Trexler, J.H., Jr., Cole, J.C., and Cashman, P.H., 1996, Middle Devonian-Mississippian stratigraphy on and near the Nevada Test Site: Implications for hydrocarbon potential: American Association of Petroleum Geologists Bulletin, v. 80, p. 1736–1762.

U.S. Department of Energy, 1988, Site Characterization Plan—Yucca Mountain Site, Nevada Research and Development Area, Nevada: U.S. Department of Energy, Office of Civilian Radioactive Waste Management, DOE/RW-0199, 353 p. Accessed online January 9, 2007, at http://www.lsnnet.gov/. Search on Participant number HQO.19881201.0002.

U.S. Department of Energy, 1993, Evaluation of the potential adverse condition "Evidence of extreme erosion during the Quaternary Period" at Yucca Mountain, Nevada: U.S. Department of Energy Topical Report YMP/92-41-TPR, 71 p.

U.S. Geological Survey, 1984, A Summary of geologic studies through January 1, 1983, of a potential high-level radioactive waste repository site at Yucca Mountain, southern Nye County, Nevada: U.S. Geological Survey Open-File Report 44-792.

Vaniman, D., Bish, D., Broxton, D., Byers, F., Heiken, G., Carlos, B., Semarge, E., Caporuscio, F., and Gooley, R., 1984, Variations in authigenic mineralogy and sorptive zeolite abundance at Yucca Mountain, Nevada, based on studies of drill cores USW GU-3 and G-3: Los Alamos National Laboratory LA-9707-MS.

Warren, R.G., Sawyer, D.A., and Covington, H.R., 1989, Revised volcanic stratigraphy of the southwestern Nevada volcanic field, *in* Olsen, C.W., and Carter, J.A., eds., Proceedings of the fifth symposium on containment of underground nuclear explosions, Santa Barbara, California, 19–21 September 1989: Mission Research Corporation CONF-8909163, v. 2, p. 387.

Wesling, J.R., Bullard, T.F., Swan, F.H., Perman, R.C., Angell, M.M., and Gibson, J.D., 1992, Preliminary mapping of surficial geology of Midway Valley, Yucca Mountain, Nye County, Nevada: Sandia National Laboratories Report SAND91-0607, 55 p., scale 1:6000.

Whitney, J.W., and Harrington, C.D., 1993, Relict colluvial boulder deposits as paleoclimate indicators in the Yucca Mountain region, southern Nevada: Geological Society of America Bulletin, v. 105, p. 1008–1018, doi: 10.1130/0016-7606(1993)105<1008:RCBDAP>2.3.CO;2.

Whitney, J.W., Swadley, WC, and Shroba, R.R., 1985, Middle Quaternary sand ramps in the southern Great Basin, California and Nevada: Geological Society of America Abstracts with Programs, v. 17, p. 750.

Whitney, J.W., Simonds, F.W., Shroba, R.R., and Murray, M., 2004a, Quaternary faulting on the Windy Wash fault, *in* Keefer, W.R., Whitney, J.W., and Taylor, E.M., eds., Quaternary paleoseismology and stratigraphy of the Yucca Mountain area, Nevada: U.S. Geological Survey Professional Paper 1689, p. 125–134.

Whitney, J.W., Taylor, E.M., and Menges, C.M., 2004b, Introduction to Quaternary paleoseismology and stratigraphy of the Yucca Mountain area, Nevada, *in* Keefer, W.R., Whitney, J.W., and Taylor, E.M., eds., Quaternary seismology and stratigraphy of the Yucca Mountain area, Nevada: U.S. Geological Survey Professional Paper 1689, p. 1–10.

Whitney, J.S., Taylor, E.M., and Wesling, J.R., 2004c, Quaternary mapping and stratigraphy, *in* Keefer, W.R., Whitney, J.R., and Taylor, E.M., Quaternary paleoseismology and stratigraphy of the Yucca Mountain area, Nevada: U.S. Geological Survey Professional Paper 1689, p. 11–21.

Winograd, I.J., Szabo, B.J., Coplen, T.B., and Riggs, A.C., 1988, A 250,000-year climate record from Great Basin vein calcite: Implications for Milankovitch theory: American Association for the Advancement of Science, Science, v. 242, p. 1275–1280.

Manuscript Accepted by the Society 18 October 2006

.

Geological Society of America
Memoir 199
2007

Tectonic models for Yucca Mountain, Nevada

Dennis W. O'Leary
U.S. Geological Survey, MS 421, Box 25046, Denver Federal Center, Denver, Colorado 80225, USA

ABSTRACT

Performance of a high-level nuclear waste repository at Yucca Mountain hinges partly on long-term structural stability of the mountain, its susceptibility to tectonic disruption that includes fault displacement, seismic ground motion, and igneous intrusion. Because of the uncertainty involved with long-term (10,000 yr minimum) prediction of tectonic events (e.g., earthquakes) and the incomplete understanding of the history of strain and its mechanisms in the Yucca Mountain region, a tectonic model is needed. A tectonic model should represent the structural assemblage of the mountain in its tectonic setting and account for that assemblage through a history of deformation in which all of the observed deformation features are linked in time and space. Four major types of tectonic models have been proposed for Yucca Mountain: a caldera model; simple shear (detachment fault) models; pure shear (planar fault) models; and lateral shear models. Most of the models seek to explain local features in the context of well-accepted regional deformation mechanisms. Evaluation of the models in light of site characterization shows that none of them completely accounts for all the known tectonic features of Yucca Mountain or is fully compatible with the deformation history. The Yucca Mountain project does not endorse a preferred tectonic model. However, most experts involved in the probabilistic volcanic hazards analysis and the probabilistic seismic hazards analysis preferred a planar fault type model.

Keywords: Nevada, tectonic, model, faulting, deformation.

INTRODUCTION

Geologic characterization of Yucca Mountain and its surroundings (Fig. 1) has taken more than 2 decades of investigations carried out by the U.S. Geological Survey, the national laboratories, and numerous academic and consulting groups. The object of this work—to quantify the environmental hazards that might attend a proposed high-level nuclear waste repository at Yucca Mountain—has produced a body of earth science and related data unprecedented in scope, volume, and detail for a single mountain and its setting. Because choice of the site was predicated on the

concept of geologic containment, studies of structural geology and tectonic stability were a large part of the site characterization. These studies were required to evaluate hazards involving seismic ground motion, basaltic volcanism and intrusion, fault slip, and other long-term strain effects, including uplift and subsidence that could result in changes in the structure or physical properties of rock within and surrounding the proposed repository site. Investigations for these purposes are called for by 10CFR960 (U.S. Department of Energy, 1984) as part of the site license application procedure. An additional requirement was that the deformation history be extrapolated into the future for a period of

O'Leary, D.W., 2007, Tectonic models for Yucca Mountain, Nevada, *in* Stuckless, J.S., and Levich, R.A., eds., The Geology and Climatology of Yucca Mountain and Vicinity, Southern Nevada and California: Geological Society of America Memoir 199, p. 105–153, doi: 10.1130/2007.1199(04). For permission to copy, contact editing@geosociety.org. ©2007 Geological Society of America. All rights reserved.

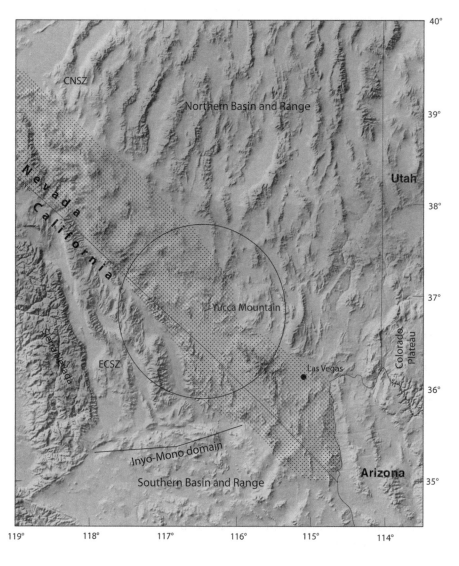

Figure 1. Tectonic setting of Yucca Mountain. Circle shows the 100-km-radius study area. Pale blue—Central Basin and Range; pale green—intermountain seismic belt; pale yellow—eastern California shear zone (ECSZ) and central Nevada seismic zone (CNSZ); stipple pattern—Walker Lane belt.

100 k.y. Therefore, assessment of tectonic activities that could be hazardous for a waste repository has a probabilistic component. This aspect of the investigation was addressed by two panels of experts external to the project. The panels produced a Probabilistic Volcanic Hazard Analysis (PVHA) (CRWMS M&O, 1996) and a Probabilistic Seismic Hazard Analysis (PSHA) (Stepp et al., 2001; Youngs et al., 2003).

Important problems of cause and effect or dynamic interaction still must be addressed. Among these problems is the possible coupling of faulting and igneous activity, including possible structural control of igneous events, the subsurface geometry and possible connectedness of faults that show no connections at the surface, and the spatial distribution of seismogenic strain. The ambiguous and fragmentary nature of geological data, the incomplete history of deformation, and the poorly understood regional tectonic setting highlight the need for a better understanding of the structural framework of Yucca Mountain. A solution to the problems listed above is to rely on a tectonic model that represents the structural framework of Yucca Mountain and explains the origin and the dynamics of deformation that have brought the mountain to its present state. A tectonic model would also relate the sequence and effects of that deformation to the geologic history of surrounding terranes and would provide some capability to predict future deformation. With respect to Yucca Mountain, two specific objectives of a model are to aid in predicting future trends of deformation and likely sources of hazard and to provide a means to assess worst-case scenarios. Two kinds of tectonic processes that might affect repository performance are: earthquake activity (teleseismic shock and local fault displacement) and volcanic eruption and/or intrusion. A tectonic model aids in evaluating these hazards by providing a concept of how faulting and volcanism are generated and controlled by Great Basin tectonism, how faulting and volcanism take place near Yucca Mountain, and how they may be genetically related.

Several tectonic models have been adduced for Yucca Mountain; they range from simplistic cross sections to carefully constrained simulations. Each model was developed to explain a specific problem or structural aspect. Each model favors either the vertical or the horizontal dimension and relies on structural components that are not exposed and are largely invariant through time. Basaltic volcanism is considered in only one of the published models. In this report, the tectonic models that have been proposed for Yucca Mountain are conveniently categorized according to bulk strain geometry: simple shear models, pure shear models, and lateral shear models. In addition, a unique caldera model (Carr, 1982, 1988; W.J. Carr et al., 1986) is excluded from these categories.

This report presents an evaluation of each of the published models for Yucca Mountain. Each model is evaluated in terms of strengths and weaknesses with respect to completeness, internal consistency, and confirmation by all available data. Some of the models are considered "viable models" (U.S. Nuclear Regulatory Commission, 1999, p. C1-C4). However, Yucca Mountain site characterization has been completed, and there is little likelihood of obtaining new data to further discriminate the viable models. Furthermore, none of the viable models is a preferred model, and no attempt has been made to formulate a model under project auspices. The Yucca Mountain site characterization process required that all models be given equal consideration in the interests of objectivity, much in the style of multiple working hypotheses. Nevertheless, some preference is implied by the model rankings given by the PSHA (Wong and Stepp, 1998). Because the models are local, no reference to regional plate tectonics history or speculation is presented as a context for the models; instead, a brief review of the general tectonic framework and evolution of the Great Basin as it pertains to Yucca Mountain is given in following sections. A discussion of the tectonic setting is given to summarize the essential geologic knowledge pertaining to the structure, origin, and boundaries of deformation at Yucca Mountain. An excellent synthesis of the deformation history of Yucca Mountain is provided by Fridrich et al. (1999). A companion paper (Fridrich, 1999) based on the site characterization data discussed herein summarizes critical tectonic elements for Yucca Mountain and its setting and provides a valuable discussion of tectonic models. The geologic setting is described in companion papers in this volume (Stuckless and O'Leary for regional geology and Keefer et al. for site geology).

TECTONIC SETTING OF YUCCA MOUNTAIN

For the Yucca Mountain site characterization project, tectonic setting referred to all of the geologic elements (structural, stratigraphic, volcanic, geomorphic) that characterize, influence, or contribute to the makeup and evolution of Yucca Mountain. Such a setting therefore includes all of the neighboring ranges and bounding basins, the proximal fault zones that distinguish the structural pattern of Yucca Mountain and surrounding areas, and all of the adjacent volcanic fields. Although specific boundaries

cannot be drawn, most of these features, or significant portions of them, occur within 100 km of Yucca Mountain (Fig. 1). Moreover, because seismicity within this radius is relevant to future deformation and ground shaking at the proposed repository site, the 100 km radius is considered to encompass the tectonic setting. Most of the geologic elements discussed here are observed in the Beatty, NV 1° × 2° quadrangle. An excellent summary of the tectonic setting of Yucca Mountain, based on literature published prior to 1989, is presented in Department of Energy Site Characterization Plan Vol. 1, Part A, Chapter 1 (U.S. Department of Energy, 1988).

The tectonic setting of Yucca Mountain is one of poorly understood transitions in strain and crustal properties. At the broadest relevant scale, the setting lies within a transition zone between the Northern Basin and Range and the Southern Basin and Range, more or less between latitudes 36° and 37°N., and between the Colorado Plateau and the southern Sierra Nevada (Fig. 1). This transitional zone is designated the Central Basin and Range (Jones et al., 1992; Wernicke, 1992). The zone is characterized, from north to south, by a decrease in regional elevation of ~1.5 km (Jones et al., 1992) corresponding to a broad increase in Bouguer gravity of ~80 mGals (Saltus and Thompson, 1995). The transition zone includes a broadly defined "amagmatic terrane," typified by lack of igneous activity, and a decrease in heat flow values to the south from 2.25 to 1.5 hfu (heat flow units). A broad belt of seismic activity (the intermountain seismic belt of Smith and Sbar (1974) and Smith (1978)) marks the northern margin of the Central Basin and Range along 37°N. (Fig. 1), and geodetic extension rates across this belt are greater in the Northern Basin and Range than they are to the south.

Yucca Mountain is located within the Walker Lane belt (Fig. 1; Wernicke et al., 2004). The mountain therefore reflects a fault evolution characteristic of basin and range extension, but one complicated by the pronounced dextral shear characteristic of the Walker Lane belt. Yucca Mountain also is an integral part of the southwestern Nevada volcanic field (Stuckless and O'Leary, this volume, Fig. 9 therein), which is centered on one of the largest caldera complexes in the Great Basin (Fig. 2), located at the northern edge of the amagmatic zone (cf. Best et al., 1989, p. 103). Yucca Mountain therefore owes its origin to deformation that attended evolution of the caldera complex and its border areas and also to local extensional faulting of the Central Basin and Range.

Extension and Volcanism in the Central Basin and Range

Extension in the Yucca Mountain region—the Central Basin and Range—appears to have begun in Eocene time following elevation of the crust by overthrust stacking created by Late Cretaceous to early Eocene Cordilleran compression. Late Paleogene extension is recorded in the region by intermontane basin fills of Eocene to late Oligocene age that include the Sheep Pass Formation and the Titus Canyon Formation. These Paleogene units are unconformably overlain by a middle to late Neogene

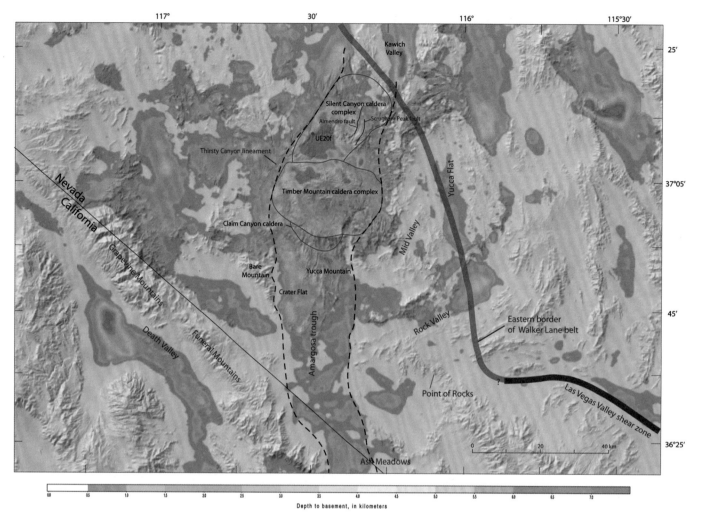

Figure 2. Major tectonic features of the Yucca Mountain region. Dashed lines represent border of the Amargosa trough (Kawich-Greenwater rift; Carr, 1990). Depth to basement from Blakely and Ponce (2001). UE20f—drill hole.

lithosome (having local formation names) that includes chiefly coarse fluvial clastic units and a wide variety of distal and proximal volcanogenic strata dominated by rhyolitic tuffs. Deformation of the Neogene strata records the most recent phase of basin and range extension, between ca. 14 Ma and 9 Ma, that resulted in the creation of Yucca Mountain and development of its major structural features.

Clockwise vertical axis rotation affected Yucca Mountain and adjacent Crater Flat basin between 12 and 11 Ma during the period of peak extension. The rotation may be a localized manifestation of a regional clockwise stress reconfiguration from E-W extension in Paleogene time to NW-SE oblique extension in late Neogene to present (Zoback et al., 1981). Alternatively, the rotation could represent domain-related upper crustal adjustments to bulk right-lateral shear across the Walker Lane belt and the generally increasing influence of dextral shear along the western side of the Basin and Range province within the past 12 Ma (Hudson and Rosenbaum, 1994). Extension of the Central Basin

and Range has "migrated" westward with time and is presently most active in the Death Valley–Owens Valley region (the eastern California shear zone) and northward into the central Nevada seismic zone (Fig. 1).

Volcanism is a significant component of Great Basin tectonism. A broad, north-to-south sweep of explosive felsic volcanism—the "ignimbrite flareup" (Noble, 1972; Best et al., 1989, p. 103; Axen et al., 1993)—in the period from 30 to 7 Ma is thought to reflect the breaking up or steepening of the subducted Farallon plate, allowing volatile-charged asthenospheric basaltic magma to invade the extending lithosphere. In the Yucca Mountain region this phase of volcanism was expressed by creation of the southwestern Nevada volcanic field, beginning around 15.5 Ma (McKee et al., 1999). A series of Plinian or Rotoruan eruptions over a span of nearly 7 m.y. formed the volcanic rocks which compose Yucca Mountain. The chief eruptive sources of the tuff units are the Claim Canyon caldera (Fig. 2) which erupted the 12.8–12.7 Ma Paintbrush Group, and the Timber Mountain caldera complex (Fig. 2), which produced the 11.7–11.45 Ma Timber Mountain Group (Sawyer et al., 1994). It is not clear to what extent felsic volcanism was associated with extension. In the Yucca Mountain region, significant extension occurred late in the evolution of the caldera volcanism (Minor et al., 1993), but the Claim Canyon–Timber Mountain caldera complex itself is only slightly extended. Felsic volcanism transitioned briefly to bimodal (basaltic) activity around 11 Ma then ended abruptly around 7 Ma. The only calderas that show signs of potential resurgence are at Long Valley and Mono Craters, at the western side of the Great Basin.

From ca. 11 Ma into the Pleistocene epoch, alkalic basaltic volcanism sporadically occurred, concentrated chiefly around the margins of the Great Basin in poorly defined fields, zones, or belts. Chemical compositions of the basalts and the general decrease in erupted volumes through time indicate a lithospheric source, at least in the western Great Basin. A case is made for an asthenospheric melt source in the central part of the Great Basin (Fitton et al., 1991; Yogodzinski et al., 1996; Wang et al., 2002), but unless a broad mantle plume is invoked, it is difficult to link asthenospheric magma generation to Pleistocene extension rates and decompression (Bradshaw et al., 1993). Overall, volcanism seems to be waning in an environment of a cooling, strengthening crust. However, the 77 ka date for Lathrop Wells Cone (Fig. 3) at Yucca Mountain (Heizler et al., 1999) indicates that a potential for volcanism near Yucca Mountain still exists.

REGIONAL DEFORMATION

Structural Features and Interpretations of Great Basin Extension

Attempts to establish a unified regional model of Great Basin extension are militated against by the obscure structural relations among the various basins and ranges of the Great Basin. Field observations support the earliest of these models—that the Great Basin formed as a system of horsts and graben (Stewart, 1971; Gilbert, 1928). There is considerable merit to this model, as revealed in the COCORP seismic profile study (Catchings and Mooney, 1991) and in regional Bouguer gravity data. However, this model does not explain the anomalously high elevation of the extended terrane, and the horsts and graben are not involved in extension below the brittle-ductile transition at ~10–15 km depths. The local gravitational collapse along and within the ranges and thick basin alluvium mask a tectonic pattern that must bridge brittle crustal extension phenomena—the basins and ranges—with ductile deformation that must involve much of the rest of the lithosphere (Wernicke, 1981; Hamilton, 1982; Hamilton, 1987; Smith and Bruhn, 1984; Kligfield et al., 1984). Thus, horsts and graben are only part of the tectonic story (Allmendinger et al., 1987).

A synthesis of geological and geophysical data (Eaton et al., 1978) revealed a meridional symmetry across an axis that Eaton (1984) suggested was a back-arc spreading axis, an interpretation suggested earlier by Scholz et al. (1971). The back-arc spreading model looks past the vast tectonic wreckage of the upper few kilometers of the crust and emphasizes the long-wavelength features that indicate the mantle-driven engine of extension, accounting for regional heat-flow anomalies and the anomalous elevation of the Great Basin.

Evidence of large transport distances by extension (e.g., 250 km, Jones et al., 1992, p. 66) and metamorphic core complexes of late Miocene age required an explanation that could not be provided by lateral extension alone (horst and graben formation, or back-arc spreading). Regional detachment combined with lower crustal uplift or thickening provided a tectonic model that is applicable to almost every structural problem in the Great Basin. However, unlike thrust faulting, low-angle (≤30°) detachment fault planes are difficult to explain dynamically. During the 1980s and 1990s two more or less competing detachment models sought to explain the same tectonic features: shallow detachment (Wernicke, 1981; Wernicke et al., 1985; Davis and Lister, 1988), and initially steeply dipping normal faults rotated to shallow dips by a "rolling-hinge" mechanism (Wernicke, 1992; Hamilton, 1988a; Spencer, 1984; Wernicke and Axen, 1988). A significant problem with the detachment model is its role in localized uplift of the metamorphosed middle crust to form the lower plates of detachment faults, especially in the form of core complexes such as the Funeral Mountains and (presumably) Bare Mountain (Fig. 2) (e.g., Jones et al., 1992, p. 77). In keeping with a generally flat MOHO and relatively high density of the mid-crustal rocks, appeal was made to magmatic underplating (Gans, 1987; Thompson and McCarthy, 1990) or to wholesale lateral flow of the middle crust toward areas of increasing detachment (Wernicke, 1992; Jones et al., 1992, p. 67), facilitating the "rolling-hinge" mechanism. A regional driving mechanism for detachment faulting and metamorphic core complex uplift was found in gravitational collapse of the crust thickened by Mesozoic compression (Humphreys, 2000; Burchfiel et al., 1992; Liu, 2001).

Contemporary Seismicity and Strain Data

During the 1990s, GPS (Global Positioning System) and InSAR (Interferometric Synthetic Aperture Radar) made regional patterns of active deformation detectable at a scale of millimeters. On the basis of these data, it became apparent that the northern Basin and Range is moving WNW at a rate of 4.9 ± 1.3 mm/yr (0.19 ± 0.05 in/yr) with respect to the continental interior and the southern Great Basin (Savage et al., 1995, p. 20265). Recent work reported by Bennett et al. (2003, p. 3–18) indicated that the geodetic velocity varies from ~2.8 mm/yr at azimuth N.84° ± 5°W. in the central part of the northern Great Basin to 9.3 ± 0.2 mm/yr at azimuth N.37° ± 2°W. in the western part of the northern Great Basin. Seismic data indicated that the relatively high and varied extension rate and changes in azimuth of the northern Basin and Range are at least partly accommodated by the central Nevada seismic zone and by the intermountain seismic belt (Fig. 1; Savage et al., 1995; Bennett et al., 2003).

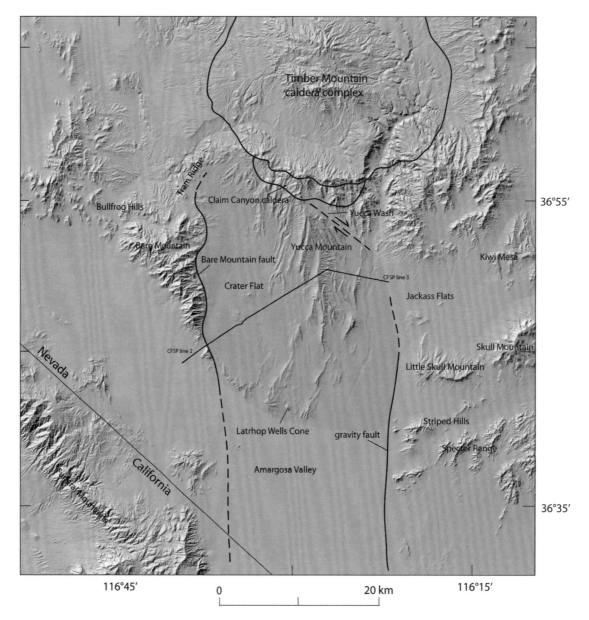

Figure 3. Shaded relief map and physiographic and tectonic features of the Crater Flat domain (pink color indicates extent). CFSP line 2 and 3—Crater Flat seismic profile (Brocher et al., 1998).

The intermountain seismic belt at ~37°N. latitude (Fig. 1; Harmsen and Rogers, 1986, p. 1561; Smith and Arabasz, 1991, p. 192) accommodates the differential extension between the northern and southern Basin and Range provinces; the slip rate in this belt is estimated at ~3.2 mm/yr (Savage et al., 1995, p. 20,267). The southern Basin and Range has an extension rate of 3 mm/yr (0.12 in/yr) or less (Sauber, 1989, p. 123).However, Bennett et al. (2003) did not recognize latitudinal changes in strain; their definition of "central Great Basin" extends from the northern Basin and Range southward into the Yucca Mountain region (Fig. 1) without a break, and their 2.8 mm/yr rate is thus comparable with the ~3 mm/yr rates reported by Savage et al. (1995) and Sauber (1989) for the southern Basin and Range. Ben-

nett et al. (2003, p. 3-1) also noted that the Walker Lane belt takes up ~8.6 ± 0.5 nanostrain/yr along a NW-oriented shear path, thus strongly influencing the strain configuration in the vicinity of Yucca Mountain. The variation in geodetic strain rates and velocity azimuths across the western Great Basin are generally related to present-day transform boundary motion along the San Andreas fault (Liu, 2001; Humphreys, 2000; Bennett et al., 1999; Flesch et al., 2000).

The importance of tangential strain and strike-slip faulting also received attention (Jones et al., 1992, p. 66; Anderson, 1973). Rogers et al. (1991) offered a simple but significant tangential hypothesis for Great Basin extension based entirely on seismic data. The tangential models emphasize north-south shortening, which is estimated to be as much as 20% (40–45 km) for the south-central Great Basin area (Wernicke et al., 1988). Most geologists refer to this strain as "contractional" or "contractile," attributing elastic behavior to the lithosphere analogous to muscle tissue, and inevitably linking it to an orthogonal extension (Bennett et al. 2003, p. 3-25). This notion discounts the role of asthenospheric flow, which must resolve itself as compressional stress in the crust rather than contraction or shortening by tectonic shrinkage. Contraction operates at a scale of meters, creating tensional strain that results in such features as columnar basalt joints or mudcracks. Present geodetic strain data indicate no substantial north-south shortening in the Central Great Basin (Bennett et al., 2003); thus, these data imply uniaxial deformation, hence crustal thinning.

The regional extension models and contemporary strain data are relevant to the origin of Yucca Mountain. Important implications include (1) a seismogenic crust of considerable shear strength that is largely decoupled from viscous deformation of the middle to lower crust; (2) the faulted crust forms large and poorly defined slabs (domains), the margins of which show strike-slip movement (however, randomness at every scale, from outcrop to tens of kilometers, is paradoxically an inherent component of the regional pattern); and (3) time dependence is important—the present style of regional deformation was conditioned by a thick, hot Miocene crust that is cooling and strengthening as it thins; hence, the overall character of deformation is changing and perhaps becoming more localized.

Tectonic Boundaries and Domains

The geologic record and geodetic strain data indicate that Great Basin deformation is compartmentalized in discrete crustal areas or domains of deformation (Wernicke, 1992, p. 555; Bennett et al., 2003, p. 3-17–3-18). Study of satellite radar (SAR) interferometry along the central Nevada seismic zone supports the observation that the Basin and Range east of the central Nevada seismic zone behaves as a rigid block bounded by zones of recurrent deformation (Gourmelen and Amelung, 2005, p. 1476). The Walker Lane belt constitutes a large regional domain within the Central Great Basin. Stewart (1988) recognized within the Walker Lane belt a number of subdomains he called "sections." Within one of these sections (the Goldfield section) is a smaller domain—the Crater Flat domain (Fig. 3)—that is the structurally defined volume of crust within which Yucca Mountain has evolved and presently experiences tectonic deformation (Fridrich et al., 1999, p. 170). In gross structure and deformation history, these domains are analogous to contiguous ice floes that have undergone marginal deformation during motion (i.e., oblique extension) (e.g., Lamb, 1994, p. 4458). Consequently, bounding structures that set boundary conditions for tectonic models commonly are difficult to determine because they tend to be obscured by tracts of damaged rock and peripheral deformation. The pattern of gravity and magnetic anomalies affords perhaps the clearest indication of domain boundaries. Bourne et al. (1998, p. 656)

point out that short-term geodetic measurements of crustal block (domainal) motions should yield the long-term average velocity of deeper, more uniform lithospheric extension.

CRATER FLAT DOMAIN

The chief tectonic feature of the Crater Flat domain is Crater Flat basin, the alluvial surface of which is called Crater Flat (Fig. 3). Latitudinally, Crater Flat basin has the form of a half-graben, deepening slightly toward the west (Fig. 4). Isostatic gravity maps and seismic profiles (McCafferty and Grauch, 1997; Healey et al., 1987; Snyder and Carr, 1982) show that adjacent to Bare Mountain the thickness of Cenozoic basin fill is ~4 km (2.5 mi) (Blakely et al., 1999, p. 12; Snyder and Carr, 1984, Plate 1 therein; Majer et al., 1996, p. 45, 46; Brocher et al., 1996, p. 31; Brocher et al., 1998, p. 960). Yucca Mountain spans the eastern flank of the basin. Gravity data combined with modeling by Snyder and Carr (1982) show that the eastern part of Yucca Mountain rests on the bedrock platform that underlies Jackass Flats (Figs. 3, 4, 5) and is partly buried by alluvium of Jackass Flats. The western and central part of the mountain has subsided and extended into Crater Flat basin where the Ammonia Tanks Tuff, the uppermost member of the Timber Mountain Group, is nearly 400 m deep (Carr and Parrish, 1985).

The gravity data also show that Crater Flat basin is a tongue-shaped depression (Fig. 6) that shallows and narrows to the south but deepens and widens to the north (Fig. 5). Crater Flat basin, as expressed by the isostatic gravity data, is essentially an elongate depression along the western side of a broader trough like feature, herein called the Amargosa trough (Figs. 2, 6; cf. Kawich-Greenwater rift of Carr, 1990). Given this setting, the northern and southern boundaries of the Crater Flat domain are not clearly defined by tectonic elements. The situation is typical of Great Basin structure and partly explains why tectonic descriptions of the Great Basin commonly are illustrated by east-west (perpendicular to strike) cross sections.

Western Domain Boundary

The western boundary of Crater Flat basin, and of the Crater Flat domain, is represented prominently by the Bare Mountain fault (Figs. 3, 7), which has been interpreted as both a single large displacement fault of varied dip and as a series of stepped faults. The gravity gradient along most of the east side of Bare Mountain (Fig. 5) indicates that either the main fault lies outboard of the mountain, buried by alluvium, or that there is a band of synthetic faults as much as 2 km wide, east of the Bare Mountain scarp line (Fridrich, 1999, p. 176; Langenheim, 2000, p. 4). This interpretation may be complicated by a buried wedge of dense landslide debris (Thompson, 2000, p. 2); however, magnetic data indicate that stepped synthetic faults alone probably account for the gravity gradient (Langenheim, 2000, p. 8).

Oblique dextral displacement is indicated near the southern end of Bare Mountain where the Bare Mountain fault curves

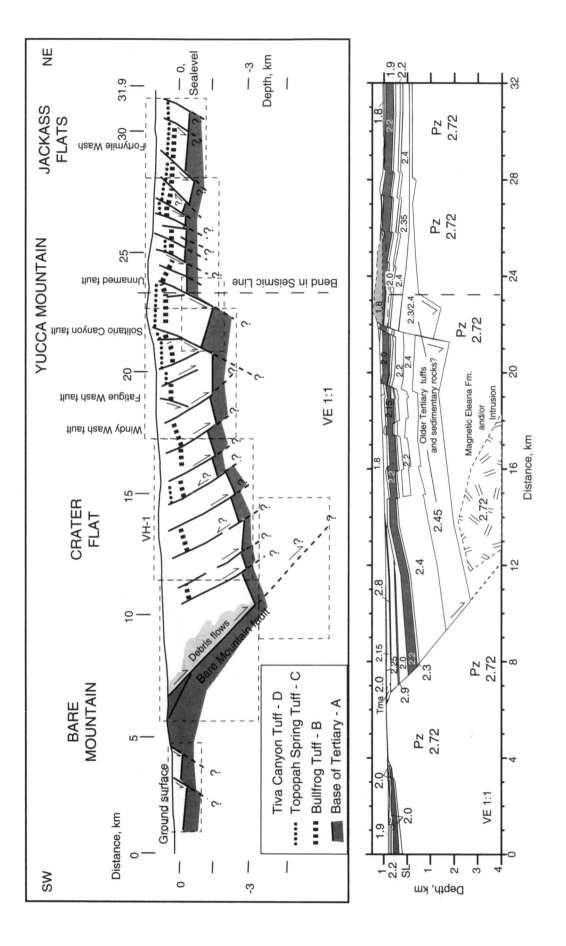

Figure 4. Interpretation of seismic reflection profiles (CFSP lines 2 and 3; Fig. 3) from Bare Mountain east to Jackass Flats, showing inferred east- and west-dipping normal faults across Crater Flat and Yucca Mountain. Densities in lower interpretive cross section are in grams per cubic centimeters. Pz—Paleozoic rocks; Tma—Ammonia Tanks Tuff; VH-1—USGS drill hole. From Brocher et al. (1998, p. 955).

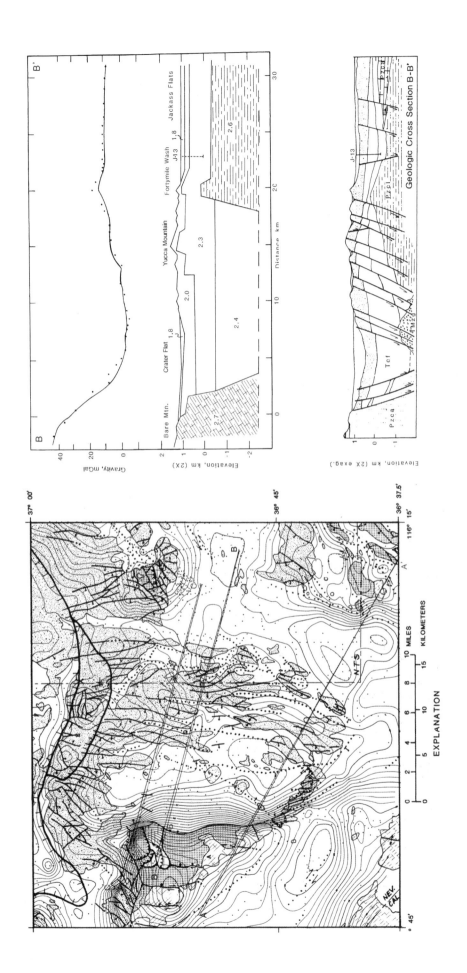

Figure 5. Residual gravity anomalies (contour interval 2 mGal) with superimposed geologic features of Crater Flat domain and location of interpretive cross section B–B' (from Snyder and Carr, 1982, their Figures 7, 9, 12). Stratigraphic units shown on cross section (lower right) are: lower and middle Paleozoic rocks—Pzca; upper Paleozoic clastic rock—Pzcl; Mesozoic granite—Tmzg; Miocene Crater Flat Group—Tcf. Gravity modeling profile (upper right) shows both calculated gravity values (curve at top) and observed values (dots along curve). Densities in grams per cubic centimeter used for the modeling profile are given in the section below the curve. J13—USGS drill hole.

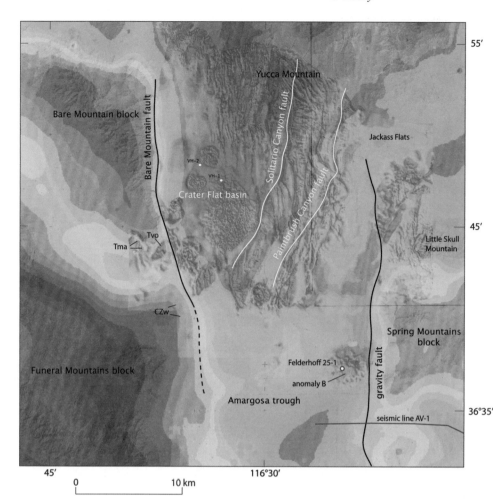

Figure 6. Aeromagnetic map screened on isostatic gravity map and remote sensor image. Blue color represents low isostatic gravity anomaly that defines the Crater Flat basin and western and northern Yucca Mountain. Green to yellow to red colors represent relatively dense crustal rocks of the Funeral Mountains block, Bare Mountain block, and Spring Mountains block. Major faults that conform to gravity gradients are labeled. Purple color corresponds to positive magnetic features of the Crater Flat and Yucca Mountain area (cf. Fig. 9). Tvo, Tma, CZw are outcrops of Miocene dacite lava, Ammonia Tanks Tuff, and Wood Canyon Formation, respectively. Seismic profile line AV-1 from Brocher et al. (1993). VH-1, VH-2, Felderhoff 25-1 are drill holes described in text.

(Fig. 5) to a northwest strike (Fridrich 1999, p. 177). A deep seismic reflection profile (Crater Flat seismic profile CFSP, line 2, Fig. 3; Brocher et al., 1998, p. 956) indicates that the southern end of the Bare Mountain fault dips ~65° east to a depth of ~3.5–6 km (2–3.7 mi, Fig. 4). Below the 6 km depth, the fault was not imaged (Brocher et al., 1998, p. 959).

Eastern Domain Boundary

The eastern domain boundary is most clearly established by a feature identified by gravity surveys and referred to as the gravity fault (Figs. 3, 8; Winograd and Thordarson, 1975, p. C-75). It is inferred to be a north-striking normal fault having down-to-the-west displacements ranging from 150 to ~1000 m (500 to ~3000 ft) beneath surficial deposits of Jackass Flats (Fig. 8). The footwall includes the east-striking Striped Hills and north-dipping Little Skull Mountain (Figs. 3, 8).

North of Little Skull Mountain the gravity fault is not expressed in gravity or aeromagnetic data; therefore, the northeastern boundary of the Crater Flat domain is uncertain. New aeromagnetic data indicate that west of Little Skull Mountain, the trace of the gravity fault veers to the west ~20° (Fig. 9). The fault

trace is lost in generally low magnetic amplitude background in central Jackass Flats (Fig. 9). There, the fault could splay out into several small offset faults, may be buried, or may lose magnetic contrast because of the large volume of volcanic rocks of the Calico Hills (Fig. 9). Fridrich (1999) linked the eastern border of the Crater Flat domain (the gravity fault) to an inferred dextral fault, the Yucca Wash fault, that follows the axis of Yucca Wash (Figs. 3, 8, 9; Fridrich, 1999, p. 173).

Northern Domain Boundary and Pahute Mesa

The inferred Yucca Wash fault separates northern Yucca Mountain from a terrane of greater extension and fault tilting to the north (Fridrich, 1999, p. 174) and on that basis is considered part of the northern border of the Crater Flat domain (Fig. 3). West of the inferred Yucca Wash fault, the northern boundary of the Crater Flat domain is diffuse; it is marked by a transition from systematic down-to-the-west normal faults of Yucca Mountain to the short, local quasi-random radial faults associated with the structure of the southern margin of the Claim Canyon caldera (Figs. 3, 8; Minor et al., 1997, p. 7). The Timber Mountain–Claim Canyon caldera complex appears to be the expression of a large

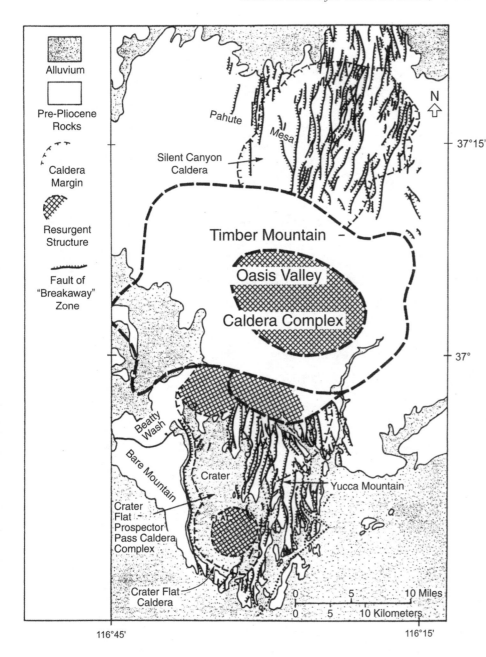

Figure 7. Coaxial fault sets of Yucca Mountain and Pahute Mesa separated by caldera complexes. The Crater Flat–Prospector Pass caldera complex is an essential feature of the caldera model of Carr (1990). From W.J. Carr (1990, p. 293).

intrusive-extrusive igneous mass emplaced within a basement trough several kilometers deep (Blakely et al., 1999, p. 11) (a mile or two, Fig. 2). As such, it is a distinct, discrete tectonic element that bounds the fault system of Yucca Mountain, although its border with Yucca Mountain cannot be identified with any single structural feature comparable to the Bare Mountain fault.

The pattern and style of normal faults expressed in Pahute Mesa north of the Timber Mountain–Claim Canyon caldera complex are aligned with and similar to the fault pattern of the Crater Flat domain, indicating a possible tectonic link between the two areas (Fig. 7; Carr, 1990, p. 291, 293, his Fig. 6). The foundation of Pahute Mesa is the steep-sided, northeast-elongated Silent Canyon caldera, which is filled with ~6 km (19,800 ft) of felsic volcanic rock, producing one of the largest negative

gravity anomalies in the western United States (McKee et al., 1999; Simpson et al., 1986; Healey, 1968). The caldera and its fill are blanketed by ashflows of the Timber Mountain caldera, a major unit of which is a nearly 300-m-thick layer of Rainier Mesa Tuff (Ferguson et al., 1994, p. 4335). The faults of Pahute Mesa form a half-graben at least 2 km deep above the Silent Canyon caldera (Fig. 2; Ferguson et al., 1994). Volcanic strata beneath the Timber Mountain Group are tilted northeastward 2° to 4° (Warren et al., 1985, p. 6), and the Rainier Mesa Tuff (11.6 Ma) is considerably thicker across down-to-the-west faults on the western side of Pahute Mesa than it is on the eastern side, indicating greater extension toward the west in the 12.7–11.6 Ma interval (Fridrich, 1998, p. 15). Fault offsets in the Rainier Mesa Tuff also increase from east to west across Pahute Mesa,

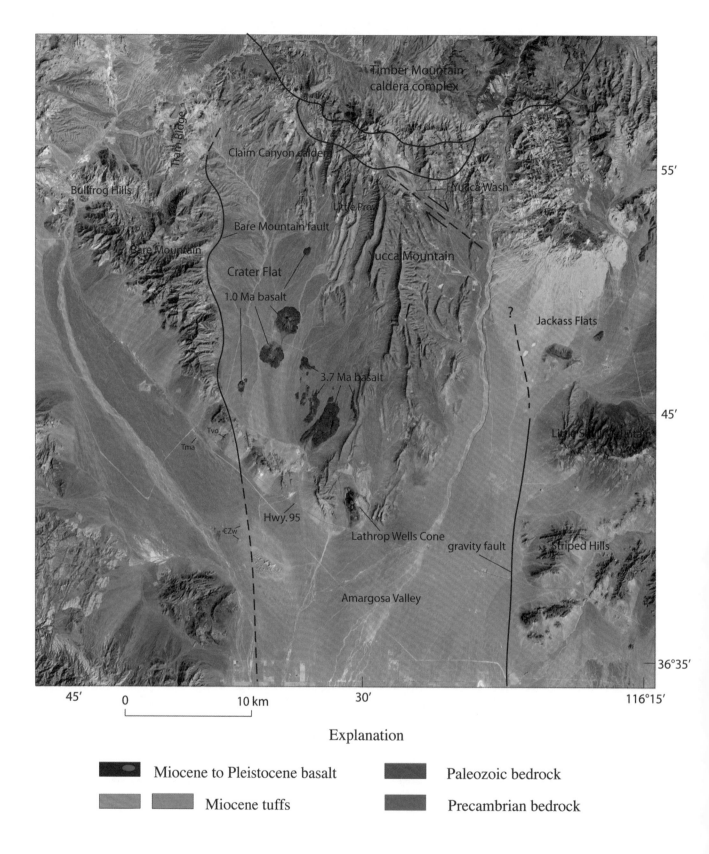

Figure 8. Enhanced remote sensor image shows selected geologic features of Yucca Mountain and surrounding area. (Image processing by J. Dohrenwend.) Tvo—Miocene dacite lava; Tma—Ammonia Tanks Tuff; €Zw—Wood Canyon Formation.

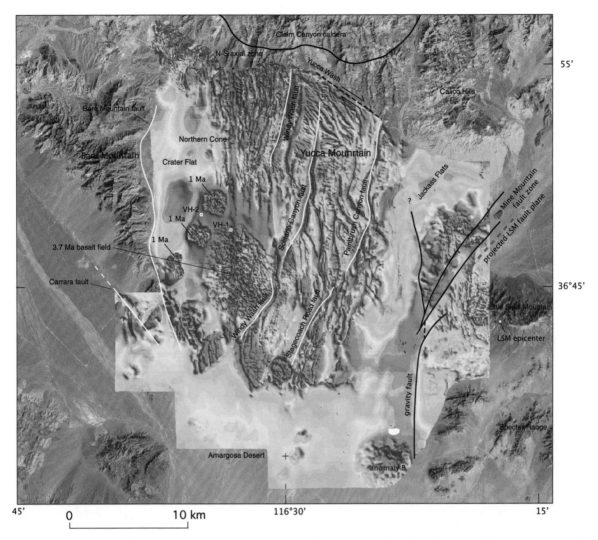

Figure 9. Aeromagnetic map superimposed on remote sensor image mosaic of Yucca Mountain and surrounding area (image enhancement by J. Dohrenwend). Geographic, structural, and magnetic features located and labeled as cited in text. Blue—strong negative magnetization; magenta—strong positive magnetization. Dashed line is trace of the inferred Yucca Wash fault. VH-1 and VH-2 are USGS drill hole locations. LSM—1992 Little Skull Mountain earthquake.

similar to the pattern of increase from east to west seen in the Crater Flat domain (Fridrich, 1998, p. 15). Most of the faults in Pahute Mesa are down to the west, having offsets of ~200 m or less that increase with depth (McKee et al., 1999). The moderate, north-striking, west-directed extension centered in the graben structure has apparently not affected adjacent terrane to the east or west. Fault activity at Pahute Mesa declined after the 11.6 Ma volcanic pulse, as happened in Crater Flat basin (Fridrich, 1998, p. 16).

The fault system in Pahute Mesa implies that the Crater Flat domain may be continued as a tectonic entity north to the edge of the Walker Lane belt, in which case the Timber Mountain–Claim Canyon caldera complex is merely a large plug within this larger domain. The similarities of style, attitude, and timing of faulting in Crater Flat basin and Pahute Mesa indicate a possible genetic relation that has been attributed to extension localized within the Amargosa trough (the Kawich-Greenwater rift of Carr, 1990; p. 284, 286). Crater Flat basin could then be interpreted as the southern extension of a deeply faulted, rift-like component of the Amargosa trough that was tectonically active before and after formation of the caldera complex. Faulting and extension in this extended domain may have been so profound as to have formed the locus of the southwestern Nevada volcanic field (Ferguson et al., 1994, p. 4336). On the other hand, the roots of the caldera complex extend at least 200 km into the lithosphere and upper asthenosphere (Biasi, 2000); therefore, intrusion seems unlikely to have been guided by crustal rifting alone, instead being the precursor to, and facilitator of, rifting (Gans et al., 1989). Alternatively, then, the rift-like character of Crater Flat basin and Pahute Mesa may be a shared feature caused by formation of the caldera complex and only modestly affected by post–12 Ma regional extension.

Southern Domain Boundary

The southern boundary of the Crater Flat domain is arbitrarily defined by the southern margin of Crater Flat basin. The boundary is expressed morphologically by a north-dipping, fault-dissected cuesta that conforms to the isostatic gravity gradient (Figs. 10, 11). The cuesta extends from the southern end of Yucca Mountain west of Lathrop Wells Cone, west to nearly the southern end of Bare Mountain at Steves Pass (Fig. 11). Likewise, the west-dipping normal fault system of Yucca Mountain is terminated along a group of scarps east of the Windy Wash fault (Fig. 11). The southern ends of Yucca Mountain and Crater Flat are each distinct structurally and stratigraphically. The Crater Flat component, which consists of the north-dipping cuesta formed by Timber Mountain Group tuffs and younger deposits, unconformably onlaps the Yucca Mountain component, which consists of two major structural blocks bounded by the west-dipping Stagecoach Road and Windy Wash faults (Fig. 11; Potter et al., 2002). Both of these tectonic components share a common structural feature: en echelon, northwest-striking, down-to-the-southwest faults that segment a south-facing escarpment that extends along the north side of Highway 95 (Fig. 11).

The structural (tectonic) nature of the southern boundary of the domain is unknown. The aeromagnetic map (Fig. 12) shows that the faulted tuff section of Yucca Mountain extends, buried by alluvium, into Amargosa Valley south of the line of scarps facing Highway 95. The magnetic anomalies show that the alluvium-buried tuff masses have sharp, polygonal boundaries and linear internal divisions (Fig. 12). Apart from the 77 ka Lathrop Wells Cone anomaly (LW, Fig. 12), the abrupt, steep gradients imply faulted borders and/or abrupt erosional scarps. The most conspicuous bounding gradients trend N.38°–48°W. and possibly represent a set of fault strikes controlling the tuff salients.

A significant problem with a fault interpretation for the southern margin of Crater Flat is that a general down-to-the-south displacement, indicated by the magnetic anomalies, seems prohibited by the relatively elevated floor of Amargosa Valley; a normal fault geometry is more reasonably down to the north in conformance with the structural declivity of Crater Flat basin. Whatever fault configuration may define the buried, polygonal tuff salients, faulting must have been accompanied by, or followed by, erosion, as several hundred meters of Paintbrush Group tuff, far from a distal pinch-out, are missing from northern Amargosa Valley. A buttress unconformity (Fig. 11; Swadley and Carr,

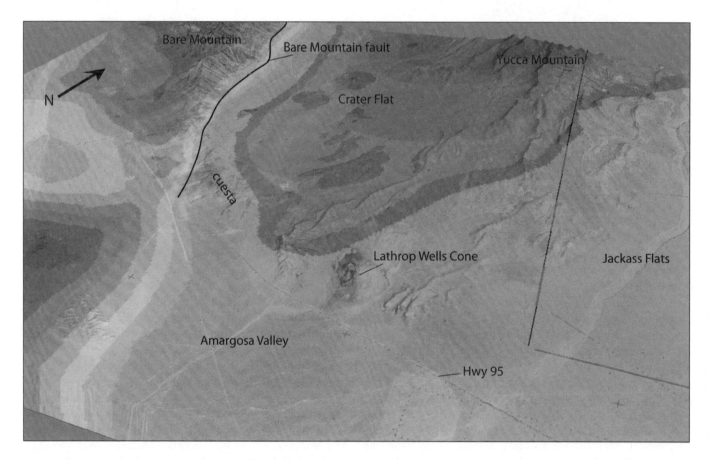

Figure 10. Three-dimensional model shows isostatic gravity map screened on remote sensor image (cf. Fig. 8). Blue to purple tint (less than –20 mGals) indicates shape and extent of Crater Flat basin defined by isostatic gravity anomaly.

Figure 11. Three-dimensional rendition of enhanced remote sensor image (cf. Fig. 8) shows details of the escarpment and cuesta bounding the southern end of Yucca Mountain and Crater Flat. Faults (shown in yellow) from Potter et al. (2002), Swadley and Carr (1987), and McKay and Sargent (1970).

1987; Carr, 1990, p. 292) has almost 100 m of erosional relief, suggesting that the Paintbrush Group had undergone substantial erosion in this area before deposition of the Rainier Mesa Tuff.

The Amargosa Trough

Apart from the structurally distinct but enigmatic line of scarps along Highway 95, the Crater Flat domain seems to be structurally continuous with the Amargosa trough to the south. The low-amplitude, low-gradient, generally moderate to negative magnetic anomalies of northern Amargosa Valley (Figs. 9, 13) indicate essentially flat-lying strata having no faults of large displacement. The Carrara fault seems well defined south of a prominent negative anomaly (Figs. 9, 13); otherwise there are no clear fault trends in Amargosa Valley indicated by geophysical data, particularly large displacement, north-northwest–striking strike-slip faults. Possible sources for the overall negative magnetic field include reversely magnetized basalt flows, Tiva Canyon Tuff, and Rainier Mesa Tuff (Langenheim and Ponce, 1995, p. 14). A relatively thick section (100–200 m) of upper Miocene strata equivalent to the rocks of Pavits Spring (Hinrichs, 1968), and possibly the Oligocene Titus Canyon Formation, could

account for the low magnetization. The magnetic field becomes increasingly negative northward, forming negative embayments against the abruptly contrasting, high-amplitude positive anomalies (Fig. 9) that represent the Paintbrush Group strata. The magnetically negative embayments could indicate Tram Tuff of the Crater Flat Group.

Both the Bare Mountain fault and the gravity fault extend some unknown distance to the south, more or less along the gravity gradients that define the margins of the Amargosa trough. The Bare Mountain fault abruptly loses displacement as well as any evidence of Pleistocene slip south of the cuesta. The southern extension of the Bare Mountain fault lacks sufficient offset and magnetic contrast to appear as a magnetic trace in the Amargosa Valley. The gravity map isograds give some hint as to the general strike of the subdued fault in that area (Figs. 6, 10). The greatly flattened gravity gradient along the Amargosa trough indicates that a single fault trace may not exist, but rather there is a series of faults stepped down into the trough. Bedrock is exposed in Amargosa Valley in the projected footwall of the Bare Mountain fault (Figs. 6, 8; Potter et al., 2002). Outcrop of Ammonia Tanks Tuff south of Highway 95 (Tma, Figs. 6, 8; Swadley and Carr, 1987) and quartz latite north of the highway (Tvo, Figs. 6, 8; Potter et

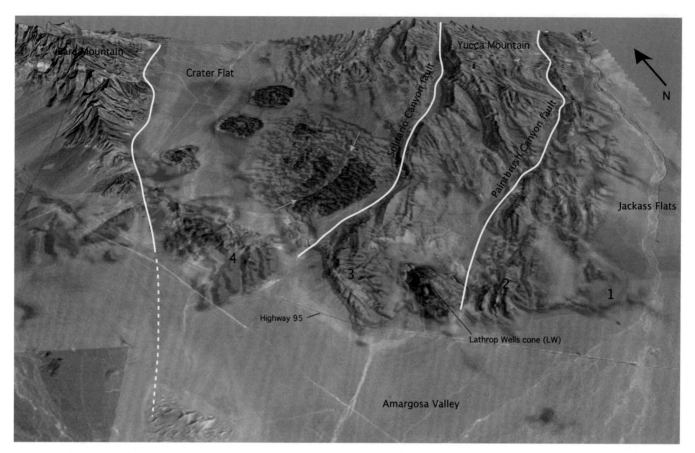

Figure 12. Three-dimensional model with aeromagnetic map screened on enhanced remote sensor image shows magnetic anomalies associated with the escarpment and cuesta that extends along Highway 95 (cf. Fig. 11). Anomalies form four (numbered) polygonal salients extending toward Amargosa Valley. Major faults shown in white; minor fault breaking 3.7 Ma lava field indicated by yellow arrows.

al., 2002) indicate that the irregular and strong positive magnetic anomalies in the area are caused by these shallow buried units. Scattered small outcrops of Devonian to Proterozoic rocks (e.g., €Zw, Figs. 6, 8; Potter et al., 2002) account for small negative magnetic anomalies farther south and east.

Seismic reflection data (line AV-1, Fig. 6; Brocher et al., 1993) indicate that south of Highway 95 the gravity fault constitutes a zone ~2 km wide and that the hanging wall contains Tertiary basin fill between 1.2 and 1.6 km thick. Brocher et al. (1993) inferred the fill to be lakebeds (i.e., playa deposits) abutting spring mounds and fanglomerates along the gravity fault scarp zone. The Felderhoff 25-1 well (Fig. 6; Carr et al., 1995) passed through the 4.0 Ma basalt of anomaly B and penetrated probable Miocene sediments (marl and lacustrine limestone) at a depth of 820 ft. Typical local upper Miocene sedimentary lithologies are recorded to a depth of 1840 ft; Paleozoic bedrock was penetrated at 2000 ft.

The relatively large, flat gravity anomaly combined with the relatively low amplitude magnetic signal implies that the part of Jackass Flats south of Little Skull Mountain (Fig. 6) is a structural bench or platform that is more or less continuous with the floor of the Amargosa trough, and rises slightly westward toward the margin

of Crater Flat basin (Fig. 5; Snyder and Carr, 1982). This bench is not simply the discrete hanging wall of the gravity fault. Carr (1984, p. 76) characterized the structural foundation of Jackass Flats as the "Lathrop Wells rift": a buried, but geophysically prominent, structural trough extending from the northwest end of Ash Meadows (Fig. 2) to southern Jackass Flats (Fig. 3) for a distance of ~30 km. Thus, there appears to be no southern tectonic boundary to the Crater Flat domain in the vicinity of Lathrop Wells; southern Jackass Flats and northern Amargosa Valley are not tectonically separated by a recognizable bounding feature.

Strain in the Crater Flat Domain—Historical and Modern

The least principal stress vector (sigma3) in the Yucca Mountain area trends N.50° to 70°W. and is essentially horizontal (Carr, 1974, p. 1; U.S. Geological Survey [USGS], 1984, p. 4; Zoback and Zoback, 1980; Minster and Jordan, 1987; Wernicke et al., 1988, p. 1752; Zoback, 1989, p. 7105). Prior to around 9–10 Ma sigma3 was oriented in a more westerly or southwesterly direction (Zoback et al., 1981; Minor, 1995). The stress field in the Yucca Mountain region is thought to have rotated clockwise as much as 65° in the 11–8.5 Ma interval (Minor, 1995, p. 10527;

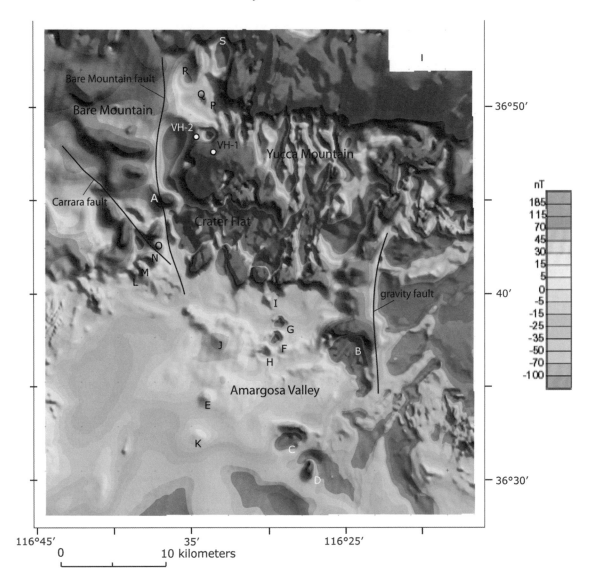

Figure 13. Magnetic anomalies of the Crater Flat domain and adjacent areas, showing relationship to major structural and geographic features. Colors represent magnetic field intensities scaled to the International Geomagnetic Field: blue, negative magnetization; purple, positive magnetization. Color bar indicates intensity intervals in nanoteslas (nT). Letters identify anomalies discussed by O'Leary et al. (2002). VH-1 and VH-2 are U.S. Geological Survey drill holes. Map created by R.J. Blakely, U.S. Geological Survey; modified from version presented by O'Leary et al. (2002, their Fig. 3).

Thompson, 2000, p. 5). The relative magnitudes of sigma1 and sigma2 attained their present values during Plio-Pleistocene time (Bellier and Zoback, 1995, p. 588).

Measured sigma3 values from boreholes at Yucca Mountain are low, near the margin of stability for normal faults that strike N.25° to 30°E. and that have a coefficient of static friction that is equal to or greater than 0.6 (USGS, 1984, p. 21; Stock and Healy, 1988, p. 87). These local stress measurements, obtained within 2000 m (6562 ft) of the surface, may not reflect conditions at seismogenic depths where strike-slip and oblique-slip focal mechanisms are common (Rogers et al., 1991). Because strike-slip and dip-slip mechanisms occur throughout the uppermost 15

km (9.3 mi) of the crust, the relative magnitudes of sigma1 and sigma2 at depth must be nearly equal, a relation described as axially symmetric (Rogers et al., 1991).

Contemporary strain in the Crater Flat domain is difficult to interpret in terms of local structure, paleoslip data, and relation to the Great Basin. A 50-km (31-mi)-aperture trilateration network centered on Yucca Mountain and operated from 1983 to 1993 showed an extensional strain rate of 8 ± 20 nanostrain/yr oriented N.65°W. (Savage et al., 1994, p. 18106). A resurvey in 1998 obtained a strain rate of –2 ± 12 nanostrain/yr at N.65°W., with a monument velocity of ~5 mm/yr N.60°W. with respect to the stable interior of North America (Savage et al., 1999, p. 17631). The low strain rate (Savage et al., 1995, p. 20263) and low seismicity levels (Rogers et al., 1991) in the Crater Flat domain suggest that Yucca Mountain is in a tectonic domain that may be isolated from zones of high strain rate to the west (the central Nevada seismic zone and the eastern California shear zone) and north (the intermountain seismic belt). However, high strain accumulation in the Crater Flat domain was reported by Wernicke et al. (1998) based on GPS surveys conducted from 1991 to 1997. The data indicated uniform north-northwest crustal extension across the Crater Flat domain at a rate of 1.7 ± 0.3 mm/yr over 34 km, or 50 ± 9 nanostrain/yr. This strain rate was considered anomalous on the basis of comparatively low slip rates for the Bare Mountain fault and for faults at Yucca Mountain (Wernicke et al., 1998, p. 2099). Wernicke et al. (1998) asserted that the Little Skull Mountain earthquake had a northwest-dipping nodal plane, thus minimizing the effect of coseismic deformation. Wernicke et al. (1998) also discounted strain effects of the Death Valley–Furnace Creek fault, located ~50 km from Yucca Mountain (Stuckless and O'Leary, this volume, Fig. 3A therein). The anomalous strain was considered to reflect an anomalously high extension rate entirely within the Crater Flat domain.

The strain rate data of Wernicke et al. (1998) were questioned on the basis of possible monument instability and misinterpretation of the Little Skull Mountain fault plane dip (Savage, 1998). A radar interferometry study (Pezzopane et al., 1999) confirmed the southeast dip of the Little Skull Mountain nodal plane and demonstrated as much as 25 ± 5 mm subsidence in an associated area of subsidence of ~8 by 10 km, centered on Little Skull Mountain.

A subsequent strain analysis incorporating geodetic data from 1993 and 1998 was presented by Savage et al. (2001). After removing coseismic effects of the 1992 Little Skull Mountain earthquake, they observed the average extensional strain rate across the monitored area to be 22.8 ± 8.8 nanostrain/yr at N.77.6°W. Hence, extensional strain accumulation within the Crater Flat domain is insignificant.

Strain measurements in the Crater Flat domain from 1999 to 2001 (Wernicke and Davis, 2001) and from 1999 to 2003 (Wernicke et al., 2004) indicate an increasing northward component of velocity with distance toward the west. Wernicke and Davis (2001) concluded that the strain velocity field in the Crater Flat domain is dominated by dextral shear averaging 20–26 nanostrain/yr rather than north-northwest extension at 50 ± 9 nanostrain/yr previously reported by Wernicke et al. (1998). The anomalously high strain rate reported by Wernicke et al. (1998) is now interpreted as a postseismic transient motion caused by the 1992 Little Skull Mountain earthquake (Wernicke and Davis, 2001).

Wernicke et al. (2004) noted that the Yucca Mountain area is influenced by dextral shear associated with Walker Lane belt deformation that increases by ~1.2 mm/yr from the Striped Hills westward to the west side of Bare Mountain, a distance of 60 km. The velocity field is characterized by nearly homogeneous N.20°W. dextral shear of 20 ± 2 nanostrain/yr. This rate is comparable to the dextral shear rate of 23 ± 10 nanostrain/yr reported by Savage et al. (2001) for the 1983–1998 period. Almost half of this shear strain could be contributed by strain along the Death Valley–Furnace Creek fault (Savage et al. 1999). Wernicke et al. (2004) inferred that this strain rate and its variation in space can be explained as viscoelastic strain generated by postseismic relaxation of the Death Valley–Furnace Creek fault, assuming a dislocation strain velocity of 5.78 mm/yr and a locking depth of 30 km for the Death Valley–Furnace Creek fault. Wernicke et al. (2004) speculated that the dextral strain could be caused by a hidden dextral shear zone (an extension of the Pahrump-Stateline fault zone) passing though the Yucca Mountain domain, or from a wide zone of homogeneous simple shear in the upper mantle (i.e., drag imposed by a viscous upper mantle: Bourne et al., 1998; Gan et al., 2000). Gan et al. (2000, p. 16,230) record an average velocity of ~3.0 mm/yr at N36°W for the Yucca Mountain area, which they consider negligible. In contrast to Wernicke et al. (2004), Gan et al. (2000, p. 16,233) consider the Yucca Mountain area to be a rigid block bounding the actively deforming eastern California shear zone to the west. Savage et al. (2001) emphasized the great variability in the measurements of very low strain over very short time periods in the Yucca Mountain area. Decadal variations in strain and order of magnitude imprecision are poorly understood. However, low rates of diffuse dextral shear confined to Crater Flat basin are compatible with some tectonic models.

Structure and Tectonic Framework of Yucca Mountain

The style of faulting at Yucca Mountain is simple: the mountain is formed by generally north-striking normal faults, down-to-the-west (Keefer et al., this volume), that have extended the original stratigraphic pile by 10–40% of its depositional width (Fridrich, 1999). Extension began prior to deposition of the Tiva Canyon Tuff (Fridrich, 1999, p. 189; Scott, 1990, p. 268), but most faulting and tilting occurred between the eruptions of the Tiva Canyon Tuff (12.7 Ma) and the Rainier Mesa Tuff (11.6 Ma) (Day et al., 1998, p. 17–18). It would seem that the main period of extension of the Crater Flat domain is genetically related to, or is at least generally coeval with, the major Miocene caldera activity.

At least three northwest-striking oblique dextral faults are present at the northern end of the mountain (Keefer et al., this volume); their kinematic relation to the north-south–striking, block-bounding faults is not clear, but they probably postdate the normal faulting and reflect internal block strain, possibly related to vertical axis rotation. It is possible that a dextral fault of this group controls the axis of Yucca Wash and marks a tectonic zone of separation from the caldera rim zone to the north (Fridrich, 1999). The existence of a fault in Yucca Wash is controversial (Langenheim et al., 1993, p. 2); some maps show it (Scott and Castellanos, 1984; Maldonado, 1985; Simonds et al., 1995; Scott and Bonk, 1984; Scott, 1990; Frizzell and Shulters, 1990; Fridrich, 1999), others do not (Christiansen and Lipman, 1965; Byers et al., 1976; Day et al., 1998; Potter et al., 2002). Dextral slip is well exposed in bedrock at the northern end of Alice Ridge (Keefer et al., this volume, Fig. 2 therein) on strike with the inferred Yucca Wash fault, and aeromagnetic data indicate at least 70 m of vertical offset is possible there (Bath and Jahren, 1984; Langenheim et al., 1993). Mankinen et al. (2003, p. 30) show a major structural boundary on the southwest side of Yucca Wash, directly beneath the northern edge of Yucca Mountain, expressed as a 10 mGal gravity gradient.

The simple fault system described above is complicated by a large population of splay and relay faults (Keefer et al., this volume, Fig. 16 therein) and by variable displacements of the major faults along strike. Additionally, the footwalls are broken by numerous complex Toreva blocks and graben. Extensive core samples from deep boreholes across the mountain show that the section is extensively brecciated, cemented with gouge, and laced with small-displacement faults and fractures. The enigmatic Ghost Dance fault (Keefer et al., this volume, Fig. 16 therein) has small displacement but at the surface is marked by wide lateral brecciation. This style of deformation—pervasive brecciation—implies that the fault blocks have undergone much internal strain in addition to the large displacement block faulting and block tilting.

An important challenge to a tectonic model is determining which of the block-bounding faults are deep-seated tectonic bounding faults among the faults in the volcanic carapace of Yucca Mountain. The terms "deep-seated" and "volcanic carapace" should be understood in stratigraphic context. The volcanic carapace of Yucca Mountain is the section of faulted tuffs and minor volcaniclastic sediment that rests unconformably on Paleozoic bedrock. A total thickness of 1244 m (4080 ft) of tuff and associated sediment resting on Silurian dolomite was recorded from drill hole UE25p#1 (M.D. Carr et al., 1986; Keefer et al., this volume). The volcanic carapace is estimated to range in thickness from ~1830 m (6000 ft) at the northern end of the mountain to ~610 m (2000 ft) near the southern end (Potter et al., 2002). The basal Tertiary unconformity is a surface of unknown relief across Yucca Mountain. Faults that penetrate the carapace and continue into the Paleozoic section and have offsets of at least 200–300 m are considered "deep seated."

Aeromagnetic data show the most pronounced linear magnetic anomalies associated with faults of Yucca Mountain are those of the Solitario Canyon fault, the Windy Wash fault, the Stagecoach Road fault, and the southern part of the Paintbrush Canyon fault (Fig. 9), as mapped by Potter et al. (2002). Following the magnetic gradients, these faults can be resolved into two major, subparallel faults that extend the length of the mountain: the Solitario Canyon fault (combined Solitario Canyon and Windy Wash faults) and the Paintbrush Canyon fault (combined Paintbrush Canyon and Stagecoach Road faults; Figs. 6, 12; also see Keefer et al., this volume). The near-surface structural continuity of each combined fault is problematic. The variability of displacement and style of the Solitario Canyon and the Paintbrush Canyon faults along strike implies that they may actually be the result of individual structures having become integrated by continuing extension and subsidence of Crater Flat basin.

Comparison of the aeromagnetic map with the isostatic gravity map shows that both the Solitario Canyon and Paintbrush Canyon faults are subparallel to the isostatic gravity gradient that defines the eastern margin of Crater Flat basin (Fig. 6). The conformity implies a close structural association with the basin and suggests that subsidence of the basin is a major cause of Yucca Mountain faulting. The Solitario Canyon and Paintbrush Canyon faults penetrate deeply into the basin, evidence for which includes relatively high groundwater temperatures measured in wells close to these faults, suggesting upward leakage of warm groundwater from a deep carbonate aquifer (Sass et al., 1995, p. 165). Another indication of deep penetration of the Solitario Canyon fault is the presence of a basalt dike ca. 10 Ma (Carr and Parrish, 1985, p. 30) located along part of the fault plane exposed in the Ammo Ridge trench (Simonds et al., 1995) near Little Prow near the northern end of the mountain (Fig. 8; Day et al., 1998).

Changes in strike, dip, and displacement of faults at Yucca Mountain indicate that crustal extension increased toward the south (Fridrich et al., 1999, p. 208). Paleomagnetic data (Rosenbaum et al., 1991, p. 1964; Hudson et al., 1994, p. 270) indicate that vertical-axis clockwise rotation was imposed on the normal-faulted blocks both during and shortly following the peak normal faulting events beginning around 11.6 Ma (Minor et al., 1997, p. 20). As a result, the normal faults have a left-oblique slip component that increases to the south as the angle of rotation increases from north to south from 0° to ~30° (Fig. 14). Virtually no rotation has occurred at the northern end of Yucca Mountain.

The cause of late Miocene vertical-axis rotation is uncertain. It has been ascribed to dextral shear at or near the southern end of Yucca Mountain (Sonder et al., 1994, p. 769; Burchfiel, 1965, p. 186) or, in general, the influence of a strain gradient resulting from differential extension above a detachment fault (Wernicke and Axen, 1988, p. 850; Hagstrom and Gans, 1989, p. 1840; Scott, 1990, p. 275, 279). Rotation also has been attributed to extension of Crater Flat as a pull-apart basin (Fridrich, 1999, p. 210), an increase in listric faulting toward the south, and development of relay ramp slices between fault segments (Stamatakos and Ferrill, 1998, p. 158). Rosenbaum et al. (1991, p. 1977) commented that the regular change in the amount of rotation across the whole mountain is similar to that predicted by models of continuous deformation in a transcurrent shear zone; they offered the strain along the Las Vegas Valley shear zone (Fig. 2) as an example. Minor et al. (1997, p. 33) considered that broadly distributed dextral shear across the southern Walker Lane belt could have caused the distributed, rotated faulting at Yucca Mountain without a discrete, throughgoing strike-slip fault. This interpretation is supported by a zonal distribution of rotation values obliquely across Crater Flat, increasing toward the west and south; vertical axis rotation is not simply concentrated at the southern end of Yucca Mountain. To account for the distribution of rotation azimuths in the Crater Flat tectonic domain, dextral shear would have to have been parallel to the isolines of rotation given by Minor et al. (1997, p. 18). However, this seems to be at too high an angle to account for the fault configuration at the northern end of Amargosa Desert (Fig. 9). Another option is limited shear due to basin

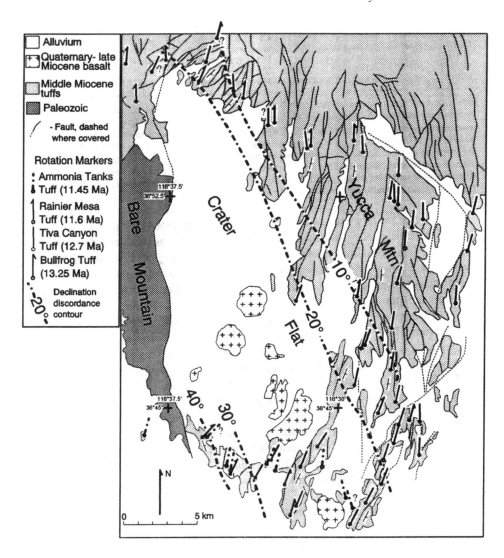

Figure 14. Map of Yucca Mountain and Crater Flat showing extent of vertical axis rotation, locations of paleomagnetic sites (+) and declination discordances (queried if >10°), and contours of equal clockwise declination discordance (dotted lines). From Minor et al. (1997, p. 18).

widening upon uplift and translation of Bare Mountain toward the northwest in the post–12 Ma period, following the suggestion that western Crater Flat basin is a rhombochasm (Fridrich, 1999). The magnetic map data offer no indication of a discrete structure that might have controlled the vertical-axis rotation.

Crater Flat Basin

The distinctive fault-controlled linear magnetic anomaly pattern of Yucca Mountain extends west of the Windy Wash fault, buried by alluvium, for only ~2.5 km to the vicinity of Northern Cone in Crater Flat (Fig. 9). The aeromagnetic map of western Crater Flat indicates a lack of faults expressed by magnetic gradients, and a distinct preponderance of broad, negative anomalies (Fig. 9; Langenheim and Ponce, 1995, p. 9, 10). The geologic map by Potter et al. (2002) shows that the area west of the Windy Wash fault has extensive outcrops of Rainier Mesa Tuff on Tiva Canyon Tuff. Either the Rainier Mesa Tuff masks a closely faulted substrate, or variations in its thickness produce or

enhance the distinctive anomaly pattern. Carr (1982, 1990) concluded from study of core from well VH-2 (Fig. 9) that very few faults are present in the section, including the Timber Mountain Group units, in the western part of the basin. If relatively large displacement faults do exist in this part of the basin, they may be obscured by deep burial or by flows of 10 Ma basalt (e.g., Langenheim, 2000).

A north-south–oriented axial zone ~700 m wide, comprising narrow, closely spaced, north-south-aligned magnetic anomalies, passes through the site of Northern Cone (Fig. 9). Connor et al. (2000) interpreted these anomalies to represent normal faults, based on a ground magnetic survey. Farther south, the north-south axial zone coincides with the north-south–oriented dike-connected vents that form the extrusive axis of the 3.7 Ma basalt field. Carr (1982, p. 4 and 17) inferred that "an important fault or fault zone may lie nearly along the north-south axis of the basin, just west of drill hole VH-1" (Fig. 9). Fridrich (1999, p. 188) inferred an approximately correlative axial feature as a west-side-down fault or faults active between 11.6 and 10 Ma that defined a "structurally distinct subdomain within the Crater Flat basin...."

An important feature of Yucca Mountain tectonic evolution, then, is a two-stage development, a concept discussed by Minor et al. (1997) and Fridrich (1999). In the first stage, extensional faulting of the tuff pile occurred shortly after deposition of the Topopah Spring Tuff at 12.7 Ma, in response to west-directed extension and subsidence of Crater Flat basin. Beginning ca. 11.7 Ma, Bare Mountain underwent relatively rapid uplift and translation to the northwest. This accompanied vertical-axis rotation and formation of northwest-striking dextral faults, graben, and north-northwest relay and splay faults, linking and producing continuity along the Solitario Canyon and Paintbrush Canyon faults, and subsidence of western Crater Flat basin with accompanying rock slides off Bare Mountain. The second stage resulted in trap-door subsidence of western Crater Flat basin to the north after ca. 10–9 Ma (Fridrich, 1999), giving western Crater Flat and Crater Flat basin their present form and structure.

Basaltic Volcanism

Basaltic volcanism is a distinctive feature of late Miocene to late Pleistocene tectonism in Crater Flat and in the Amargosa trough near Yucca Mountain (Fig. 2). The oldest basalts shortly postdate deposition of the Ammonia Tanks Tuff and range in age between 11.3 and 10.5 Ma (Crowe, 1990); they are considered basalts of the silicic cycle, as silicic caldera eruptions occurred in the area until ca. 7 Ma. The next period of basalt eruption occurred between 4.4 and 3.7 Ma. Lavas of this series are partly exposed in Crater Flat (Fig. 8) but are buried in the Amargosa Valley to the south (e.g., anomaly B, Figures 6, 13; O'Leary et al., 2002). The next younger basalts are the ca. 1.0 Ma volcanoes located in Crater Flat (Fig. 8). The youngest basalt eruption is the 77 ka Lathrop Wells Cone (Figs. 8 and 11) at the southern end of Yucca Mountain.

All of the basalts of the Crater Flat domain are moderately evolved, moderately potassic trachybasalts; some are almost sodic enough to be termed hawaiites (LeBas et al., 1986). In bulk chemistry and trace-element content, they are typical basalts of the western Great Basin (Rogers et al., 1995; Farmer et al., 1989; Fleck et al., 1996). The basalts of Pleistocene age are conspicuously enriched in LIL (large ion lithophile) trace elements. In general, eruptive volumes have decreased with time, and the individual Pleistocene eruptive centers appear to have formed from small, isolated, and chemically distinct source volumes. The characteristics of all these basalts indicate they were formed by partial melting of an enriched (metasomatized) ancient lithospheric mantle at a depth range between 45 and 65 km. The Plio-Pleistocene basalts show no evidence of crustal contamination or substantial reservoir fractionation; they apparently traversed the entire crust to points of eruption in a matter of hours or, at most, days. This situation speaks for local and direct through-the-crust conduits active at ca. 4 Ma, 1.0 Ma, and 77 ka, with the loci of activity drawing into Crater Flat basin and, finally, to the south-

ern basin margin at 77 ka. A tectonic model for Yucca Mountain should consider the presence of a strong, relatively cool and intact lithospheric mantle (Jones et al., 1992, p. 76), hosting scattered enclaves of residual melt and a lithosphere subject to transient brittle fracture.

A tectonic link between the mantle sources and the eruptive centers is unknown. Only one intrusive source for the late Miocene basalt series is known—the dike present in the Solitario Canyon fault at Little Prow, toward the northern end of Yucca Mountain (Fig. 8; Day et al., 1998). The exposed lavas that cap Little Skull Mountain, Skull Mountain, and Kiwi Mesa (Figs. 3, 8) have no known eruptive source. However, high-resolution aeromagnetic data and recent drilling results imply intrusive loci in western Crater Flat basin and in eastern Jackass Flats. The late Miocene basalts have all been severely dismembered by post–10 Ma faulting and subsequent erosion. It is likely that a magmatic source for such basalt magma and a tectonic mechanism for eruption are no longer operable in the Crater Flat domain.

It is generally thought that the eruptive centers are localized along dikes. A series of dikes and eruptive centers essentially coincide with the north-south magnetic axial zone in Crater Flat basin (Fig. 8) and form a central axis for the 3.7 Ma basalt field in Crater Flat. This suggests a rift-centered eruption scenario in which lava flowed from a central fracture-controlled eruptive axis in Crater Flat, forming a nearly symmetrical flow distribution. The prominent northeast-oriented arcuate lineament seen in the 3.7 Ma basalt anomaly (Fig. 12) reflects a normal fault (Potter et al., 2002) subparallel to the Windy Wash fault (Fig. 9). There, Yucca Mountain faulting was superimposed on any north-striking faults that controlled intrusion. It seems unlikely that Pleistocene fault slip or weak fault planes at Yucca Mountain facilitated intrusion of the Plio-Pleistocene magmas (cf. Connor et al., 2000, p. 426).

The tectonic significance of the small-volume Plio-Pleistocene alkali-olivine basaltic volcanic eruptions is presumably linked to their distribution and recurrence. Two distributions, or spatial clusters, have been recognized (Fig. 15): the north-northwest–elongated Crater Flat volcanic zone (CFVZ; Crowe and Perry, 1989) and the broad, northeast-oriented Death Valley–Pancake Range belt (Vaniman et al., 1982, p. 341; Crowe et al., 1983, p. 4; Carr, 1984, p. 30), also designated the Crater Flat–Lunar Crater zone (Smith et al., 2002). Neither of the distributions correlates with regional patterns of deformation or shows a consistent pattern in recurrence. Individual volcanic centers show no consistent relation to a particular tectonic setting within each distribution. Nevertheless, the locations of the volcanic centers reflect a scheme of deformation that involves the upper mantle, and the recurrence reflects local failure mechanisms that resulted in immediate intrusion of small, chemically isolated melt volumes from depths of 45–60 km. Three tentative conclusions are offered: (1) The clustering in the CFVZ or DVPR is a subjective aggregation and has no tectonic meaning; (2) a yet unrecognized pattern of intrusion is controlled

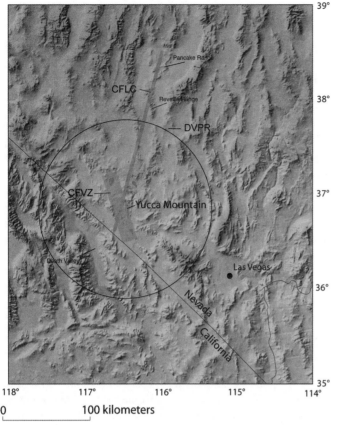

Figure 15. Inferred zonations of Plio-Pleistocene basaltic volcanism in the Yucca Mountain region: CFVZ—Crater Flat volcanic zone; DVPR—Death Valley–Pancake Range belt; CFLC—Crater Flat–Lunar Crater zone. Circle shows the 100-km-radius study area.

by regional strain that is integrated at a subcrustal depth and hence has no relevance to the observable residue of late Miocene crustal deformation; and (3) the post-Miocene basaltic volcanism represents a phase of tectonic activity too feeble, deep seated, and sparsely manifested to unequivocally support any tectonic model discussed here.

EVALUATION OF TECTONIC MODELS

The Crater Flat–Prospector Pass Caldera Model

The Crater Flat-Prospector Pass caldera model (Fig. 16) was formulated by Carr (1982, 1984, 1988, 1990) to account for two major tectonic problems: the then unknown source for the Crater Flat Group, and the form and structure of Crater Flat basin. Briefly, the model postulates that Crater Flat basin reflects the structure of a subsided (now buried) caldera (the "Crater Flat caldera") thought to be the source of the Crater Flat Group.

Evidence for the Caldera Model

The caldera model is based on the following relations and assumptions:

1. A thick sequence of welded Bullfrog Tuff was penetrated in USGS drillhole VH-1 within the area of a broad, positive magnetic anomaly (Fig. 13) thought to indicate the presence of a thick, circular body of volcanic rock in Crater Flat that represented a resurgent structure (Fig. 7).
2. The negative gravity anomaly of Crater Flat is indicative of an underlying graben-like structure (Fig. 5); the outline of the basin appears to conform to the shape of a caldera.
3. The location of several structural and volcanic features (including the Bare Mountain fault and some Yucca Mountain faults and the Lathrop Wells basalt Cone) could be controlled by an inferred caldera rim.

Two buried calderas were inferred to lie north of the inferred Crater Flat caldera: the Tram caldera (later named the Prospector Pass segment of the Crater Flat caldera (W.J. Carr et al., 1986, p. 21) and an "older tuffs" caldera beneath Yucca Mountain (Fig. 16; Carr, 1982, p. 11). The Tram caldera was inferred based on:

1. Arcuate dikes in Bare Mountain that seem to correspond in age and composition to lava beneath the Tram Tuff; the lavas were thought possibly to represent early eruptions from the Tram caldera.
2. Thick Tram Tuff (457 m) in Beatty Wash (near the northern margin of Fig. 16).
3. Truncation of the Tram Tuff in northern Crater Flat by a fault that "may be a caldera wall" (Carr, 1982, p. 10).

The fact that the Tram and Lithic Ridge Tuffs are underlain by and contain dacites made it seem likely that the lavas formed an extensive pile beneath Crater Flat prior to eruption of the Crater Flat Group (cf. Brocher et al., 1998, p. 969) and therefore was adduced as evidence for the caldera. Carr (1984, p. 71) inferred that the Paintbrush Canyon fault may mark the eastern edge of such a caldera, or at least of a "large tectonic sag." Carr (1984, p. 72) further stated that there is "a good relationship between the location of fault segments active in the Quaternary and the proposed location of the caldera margins or ring fracture zones." But on p. 60 of the same publication Carr (1984, p. 60) noted that a conspicuous exception to this relationship is shown by the northeast curvilinear alignment of 1.0 Ma basalt cones (Fig. 8) that transect the site of the inferred caldera in Crater Flat. Carr (1982, p. 11; 1984, p. 77) and Snyder and Carr (1982) identified the volcano alignment with a possible post caldera "rift" zone (Fig. 16).

Following publication of evidence that supported a detachment model for Yucca Mountain (Scott and Hofland, 1987; Myers, 1987; Scott and Whitney, 1987; Hamilton, 1988b), Carr (1990, p. 299) integrated the caldera model with a detachment model and abandoned the notion that a caldera rim structure had a tectonic influence on fault patterns in Yucca Mountain. Instead, he (1) emphasized the graben-like structure of Crater Flat and the "trapdoor" character of the inferred Crater Flat caldera complex (Carr, 1990, p. 290); (2) related the faults of Yucca Mountain with a coaxial zone of like faults in Pahute Mesa (Fig. 7; Carr, 1990, p. 290); and (3) proposed that they all originated by "gravitational sliding toward the volcano-tectonic depression" (Carr 1990, p. 289), which he named the Kawich-Greenwater rift (Fig. 2). In this revision, the Bare

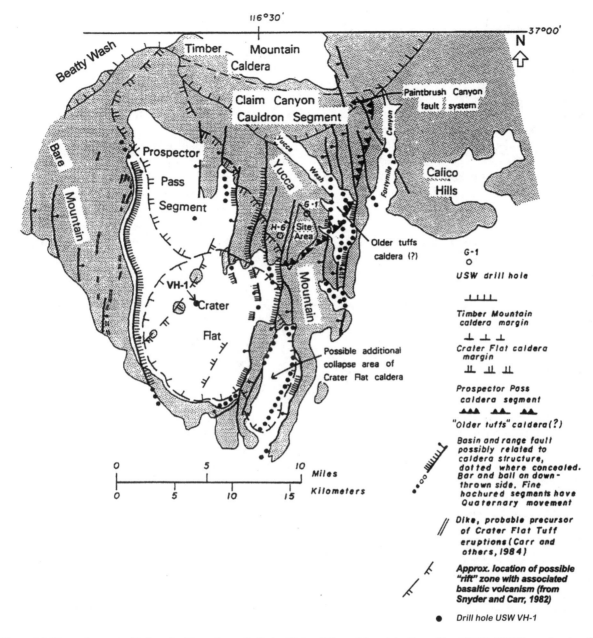

Figure 16. Size and extent of inferred calderas beneath Crater Flat and Yucca Mountain. From Carr (1984). "Rift" zone borders from Snyder and Carr (1982, Fig. 4 therein). Stippled area is bedrock.

Mountain fault controlled subsidence of the caldera complex rather than being a local peripheral feature of the complex. Carr (1990, p. 290) reported that the faults at Yucca Mountain accord with a northwest-oriented regional extensional stress. The faults were no longer seen to be reactivated caldera rim features, except where they correlated with "properly oriented" segments of the inferred buried caldera (Carr, 1990, p. 300).

Evidence against the Caldera Model

The lack of demonstrable associations between a supposedly buried caldera and more recently acquired data militates against the Crater Flat caldera model:

1. Paleomagnetic studies (Rosenbaum et al., 1991; Hudson et al., 1994) explain the curvature of faults at Yucca Mountain as having been a result of vertical axis rotation that occurred ca. 12.7 Ma and later, well after eruption of the 13.45–13.1 Ma Crater Flat Group.

2. Analysis of aeromagnetic data indicated that the prominent positive anomaly in Crater Flat originated within the Precambrian or Paleozoic section rather than from structures within the Tertiary section (Brocher et al., 1996, p. 32; Langenheim and Ponce, 1995, p. 15).

3. A seismic reflection profile across Crater Flat (Brocher et al., 1998) gave no evidence for deformation in Crater Flat

apart from block faulting of broadly warped, essentially homoclinal Tertiary strata.

The caldera model places peak tectonic activity in Crater Flat at ca. 13.45 Ma and requires that all subsequent deformation be guided by relict caldera rim structures. This hypothesis does not address the origins and mechanism of late Neogene and Quaternary strain effects, such as (1) distributed and recurrent faulting at Yucca Mountain; (2) origins and impetus for basaltic volcanism in Crater Flat; (3) mechanisms for vertical-axis rotation at the southern half of Yucca Mountain and the strike-slip component of faulting; (4) post–9 Ma uplift of Bare Mountain (Hoisch et al., 1997); (5) evidence for Quaternary faulting at Busted Butte (Keefer et al., this volume, Fig. 2 therein); and (6) the fact that styles of faulting similar to those at Yucca Mountain in Mid Valley, Yucca Flat, and on Pahute Mesa (Fig. 2) originated independent of any relict guiding caldera structures.

Crater Flat basin apparently took its present form beginning around 13 Ma (Fridrich, 1999, p. 182), when older, tuff-filled graben became part of a larger, extended graben along the Bare Mountain fault. Nevertheless, the possibility remains that the deeper reaches of Crater Flat basin may be the site of one or more calderas or at least cauldron subsidence during an early stage of development of the southwestern Nevada volcanic field (Mankinen et al., 2003). Mankinen et al. (2003, p. 33) noted the striking geophysical similarity of subbasins within the Crater Flat basin to those in deep basins elsewhere in the region; such subbasins could reflect early, deeper calderas, but these must predate eruption of the Crater Flat Group (ca. 13 Ma) because sources for the Crater Flat Group are in the Silent Canyon caldera complex (Sawyer et al., 1994; McKee et al., 1999). If Crater Flat basin is the southern part of a deeper rift that includes the Silent Canyon caldera and that predates the Timber Mountain–Claim Canyon caldera complex (Fig. 7), then further study could be guided by speculation by Mankinen et al. (2003) that the deep foundations of Crater Flat basin could include one or more pre–14 Ma calderas completely obscured by post–13 Ma deposition and extension. Early "Crater Flat" volcanism could account for the pre–13 Ma tuffs found low in the section of the rocks of Pavits Spring in Rock Valley to the east (Fig. 2; Hinrichs, 1968) and for thick pre-Bullfrog tuffs inferred to be present in Crater Flat basin (Brocher et. al., 1998, p. 969). A caldera model may account for some of the tectonic history of Crater Flat, but it does not account for Plio-Pleistocene deformation and post–12.7 Ma extension.

Simple Shear (Detachment Fault) Models

The hallmark of detachment faulting is creation of a succession of rotated fault blocks that rest cleanly on a low-angle shear plane (the "detachment fault") below which are older, lower-plate rocks that have extended by viscous or ductile behavior. Extension is thus accomplished in the brittle upper crust by multiple listric faults that jointly separate and rotate blocks of the upper plate in a common direction. Hence, because one geometric axis of the deforming body rotates out of its original position, it is convenient to group all detachment fault models under the genetic classification of simple shear.

Evidence for Detachment Fault Models

Detachment models have been applied to Yucca Mountain and its tectonic setting on the strength of four main arguments:

1. Proximity—Late Miocene detachment faulting occurred west of Yucca Mountain at Bare Mountain, the Bullfrog Hills, and the Funeral Mountains (Fig. 3; Hoisch and Simpson, 1993; Hoisch et al., 1997; Fridrich, 1999, p. 180).
2. Geometry—Resemblance of Yucca Mountain faults to tilted dominos with rollover (local increase of hanging wall dip toward the footwalls) suggests that they are listric faults that accompany detachment faulting (Scott, 1990, p. 251).
3. Field observation—Detachments were reported at the Tertiary-Paleozoic contact in places east and south of Yucca Mountain. An interpreted detachment fault at the Tertiary-Paleozoic contact in the Calico Hills (Fox and Carr, 1989), Rock Valley (Myers, 1987), and Point of Rocks (Fig. 2) led to the conclusion that a detachment fault forms the Tertiary-Paleozoic contact beneath Yucca Mountain at a depth of 1.5–2.5 km (0.9–1.6 mi) (Scott, 1990, p. 258).
4. Regional tectonic interpretation—A major deep detachment is thought to extend from near the Sheep Range in Nevada (Stuckless and O'Leary, this volume, Fig. 12 therein) west to Death Valley in California (Death Valley system breakaway fault zone, Wernicke et al., 1988, p. 1746, 1747; Sheep Range extensional terrane, Guth, 1981, p. 764).

Hamilton (1988a, p. 62) proposed a detachment at Yucca Mountain as part of a regional "rolling-hinge" model (Fig. 17). In this model, Bare Mountain was seen as the uplifted lower part of the footwall (lower plate), and the east-sloping profile of Bare Mountain was interpreted to be the exhumed detachment plane (Fig. 17) projected east under Crater Flat to become the surface of detachment under Yucca Mountain. The evolution of the rolling hinge and the chronology of uplift at Bare Mountain meant that detachment faulting at Yucca Mountain ceased at ca. 12 Ma (Hoisch et al., 1997, p. 2829; Fridrich, 1999, p. 192) as the rolling hinge rolled westward to create the Funeral Mountains detachment (Hamilton, 1988a). If faulting at Yucca Mountain represented headwall detachment, as proposed by Scott and Whitney (1987, p. 332), it was a relatively minor and short-lived event in a scheme of regional deformation that manifested itself most powerfully in the Funeral Mountains and the east flank of Death Valley.

Scott (1990, p. 269) noted the resemblance of the faults at Yucca Mountain to tilted dominos (Wernicke and Burchfiel, 1982, p. 109). This resemblance, along with a perceived detachment at the Tertiary-Paleozoic contact exposed in the Calico Hills, Rock Valley, and Point of Rocks, led Scott (1990) to conclude that a detachment fault also forms the Tertiary-Paleozoic contact beneath Yucca Mountain at a depth of 1.5–2.5 km (Fig. 18).

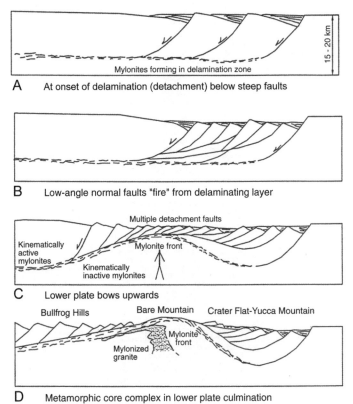

Figure 17. Rolling hinge model with reference to Bare Mountain and Crater Flat (modified by W.B. Hamilton from Lister and Davis, 1989).

Scott (1990) inferred the presence of two, possibly three detachment faults under Yucca Mountain, the deeper ones being more in accord with the regional concept of Wernicke et al. (1988, p. 1750) than with the local Yucca Mountain upper plate assemblage. Using a conceptual cross section for illustration (Fig. 19), Scott (1990, p. 276) projected the Fluorspar Canyon fault over Bare Mountain and east, under Crater Flat, to meet the shallow Yucca Mountain detachment, and projected the Bullfrog Hills detachment fault east under Bare Mountain as the deeper one. He included all of the deformation in Bare Mountain within this detachment envelope ("middle plate") eastward to the breakaway fault zone near the Sheep Range (Guth, 1981). Although Scott (1990, p. 276) showed the Bare Mountain fault cutting the Yucca Mountain-Fluorspar Canyon detachment fault (Fig. 19), he noted that extension (presumably related to detachment) continued at Yucca Mountain into the Pleistocene.

A corollary of Scott's (1990, p. 272) treatment of the detachment model is his assumption that vertical-axis rotation at Yucca Mountain is an expression of an underlying dextral bend or shear zone. The inferred detachment represents a zone of partial decoupling across which narrowly confined shear is distributed into the tuff blocks according to the model of Hardyman (1978) and Hardyman and Oldow (1991, p. 291).

Fox and Carr (1989, p. 44, 47) inferred detachment at Yucca Mountain based on the interpretations of Scott (1986, p. 411), but they emphasized the significance of Crater Flat as a pull-apart feature that controlled fault activity at Yucca Mountain (Fig. 20). Fox and Carr (1989) also inferred that the postulated low-angle "extensional fault" at the base of the Tertiary section is a small fragment of a subregional Miocene detachment, a fragment locally reactivated in the Quaternary by sliding toward the extensional axis of Crater Flat. In this sense, their view of Yucca Mountain deformation is more akin to mass movement than to a tectonic detachment mechanism. They also emphasized that extension in Crater Flat, hence, Quaternary movement of Yucca Mountain faults, is related to the northwest-directed translation of the Inyo-Mono domain to the west (Fig. 1).

Fox and Carr (1989, p. 46) inferred that local extension at Yucca Mountain was reactivated around 3.7 Ma in conjunction with basaltic volcanism in Crater Flat. They noted the presence of basaltic ash in Quaternary fault fissures at Yucca Mountain and suggested that the coincidence was related to a stress-strain cycle: minimum principal stress was signaled by faulting, fissuring, and volcanism; subsequent calcrete precipitation within the fault crevices and fissures exerted a compressive stress that increased the least principal stress, but eventually this relatively mild strengthening effect was overcome by the regional extensile strain and the cycle began anew. Fox and Carr (1989, p. 47) cited a periodicity of ca. 75 ka based on a composite average recurrence rate on the Windy Wash fault during the past 300 k.y.

Carr (1990, p. 290) attempted to associate Yucca Mountain and the Kawich-Greenwater rift (Fig. 2) with a detachment structure following the concepts of Wernicke (1981), Wernicke and Burchfiel (1982), Howard and John (1987), and Spencer (1984). According to Carr (1990), the east side of the rift (i.e., Yucca Mountain itself) constitutes the headwall for detachments farther to the west. The result is an array of faults (Fig. 21) explained in the context of structure of the Bullfrog Hills and Death Valley. However, in projecting the faults of Yucca Mountain to an undetermined depth into the Paleozoic section, Carr (1990, p. 300) indicated no detachment at all. In doing this, Carr (1990, p. 299, 300) gave the term "headwall" a special meaning and stated that the faults of Yucca Mountain-Crater Flat are essentially planar and "need not be underlain by a regional detachment." Nevertheless, these faults were considered to be largely gravitational features of a "breakaway zone" of a detachment within the Kawich-Greenwater rift.

Ferrill et al. (1996, p. 6-4) proposed two variants of a detachment beneath Yucca Mountain: Model A (Fig. 22A) assumes that the faults of Yucca Mountain developed as the headwall of the "Bullfrog Hills detachment system," (cf. Fig. 19; Bullfrog Hill detachment fault) which is thought to accommodate as much as 275% extension. Yucca Mountain faults were isolated from the Bullfrog Hills detachment system by displacement of the Bare Mountain fault (Figs. 19, 22A). Continued motion of the Bare Mountain fault led to formation of a deeper, east-directed detachment plane. According to this model, the older, shallower, west-

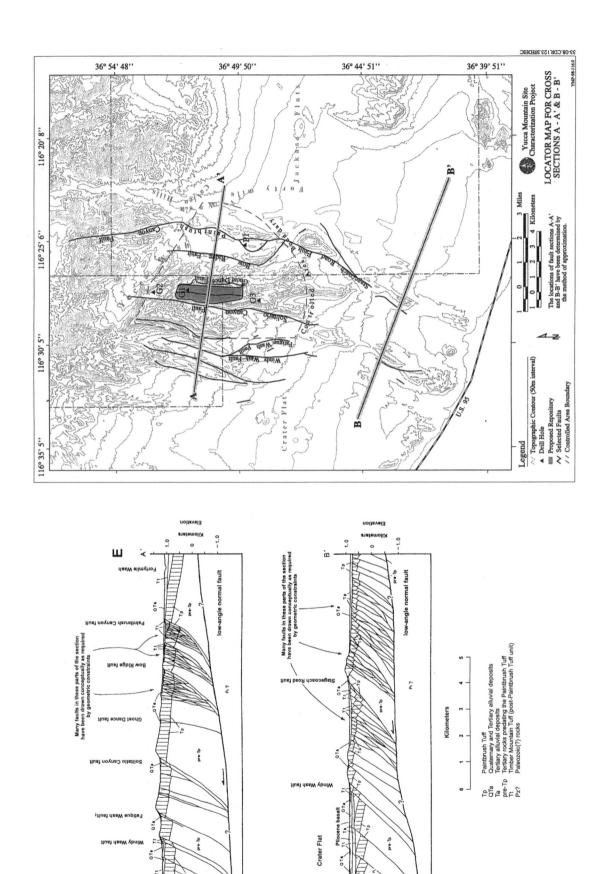

Figure 18. Cross sections of Yucca Mountain showing inferred shallow detachment fault. From Scott (1990, Figs. 3, 4 therein).

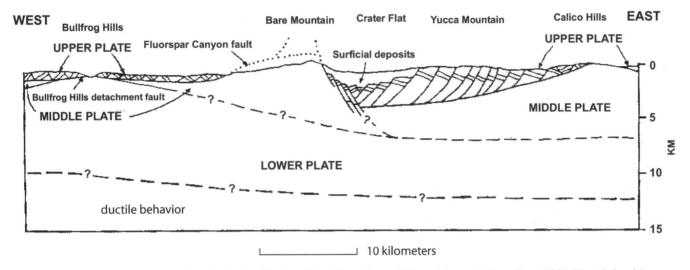

Figure 19. Conceptual cross section showing inferred levels of detachment beneath Yucca Mountain. From Scott (1990, Fig. 15 therein).

directed detachment accounts for the imbricate faulting at Yucca Mountain, whereas the younger, deeper, east-directed detachment accounts for hanging-wall collapse into rollover and formation of Crater Flat basin.

Model variant B (Fig. 22B) holds that the Bare Mountain fault is the driving listric (detachment) fault at a depth of ~6 km, and that Yucca Mountain faults are antithetic to this deep, east-directed Bare Mountain detachment. In this version of the model, faults antithetic to the Bare Mountain listric fault are also listric faults synthetic to a breakaway fault located somewhere to the east in Jackass Flats. The result is a curious "bathtub" profile having listric faults at each end that merge at a common plane of detachment. It is not clear how slip is partitioned between the two apparently competing listric faults and along the common detachment surface.

According to model variant A, extension at Yucca Mountain is genetically linked to the Bullfrog Hills detachment system but not to subsidence of Crater Flat, which requires a separate tectonic mechanism (east-directed extension). Uplift of Bare Mountain is not an integral part of either deformation process but merely serves to separate two distinct extension events. The model does not explain the reversal of slip direction after ca. 11 Ma. If east-directed extension presently drives fault slip at Yucca Mountain, then displacement must occur below the upper (older) detachment. In effect, this makes model variant A the kinematic equivalent of model variant B. Both these models help explain the westward subsidence of Crater Flat with time, and they are compatible with a succession of relatively young, eastward-dipping faults in Crater Flat (Brocher et al., 1998, p. 955), even though the model profiles do not show such faults.

Support for detachment models of Yucca Mountain also is based on geophysical data and on simulated mechanical behavior. Oliver and Fox (1993) used gravity data that Snyder and Carr (1982) had used to demonstrate a structural trough beneath Crater Flat (Fig. 23). Oliver and Fox (1993, p. 1812) matched the gravity profile by juxtaposing crustal slices of differing density

and polygony. When the slices were arranged to give the Bare Mountain fault a 27° dip and the Yucca Mountain "detachment" a dip of 12°, the simulated gravity profile fit the Snyder and Carr (1982) data (Fig. 5).

Young et al. (1993) used a computer simulation technique to evaluate detachment hanging-wall deformation mechanisms (flexural slip, slip line, domino, vertical shear) and found that the assumptions required to model detachment-style rollover at Yucca Mountain did not comply well with field data. Vertical shear provided the most acceptable mechanism for creating appropriate rollover. However, much of the vertical shear discussed and depicted by Scott (1990, p. 259, 270) to explain hanging-wall rollover at Yucca Mountain is conceptual (Fig. 19). Such faults are "required by geometric constraints" (Scott, 1990, p. 260).

Finite-element modeling was applied by Ofoegbu and Ferrill (1998) to the problem of detachment-related fault slip (Fig. 22A). A five-layer linear elastic model was used, and the initial stress state included previous fault slip on simulated Yucca Mountain fault planes. In order for the model to work, it was necessary to treat each fault as a weakly cohesive or cohesionless layer of at least 150 m thickness and decoupled from confining rock. Slip was produced on a selected fault by reducing its coefficient of static friction. Under reasonable confining stress, a friction angle of 0.93° is required. The model implies also that a relatively large proportion of fault displacement is taken up by deformation of the hanging wall and footwall. Ofoegbu and Ferrill (1998, p. 72) observed that slip rates in the detachment fault and in the steep, off-branching perturbed fault differed by up to six orders of magnitude. They concluded that a detachment fault is likely to slip aseismically in response to slip events that may occur at seismic rates on the off-branching steep faults. In reaching this conclusion, however, it seems that the modeled mechanism violates the concept of detachment faulting, as steep fault perturbation is not supposed to generate strain in the detachment fault. Rather, the detachment is the master slip

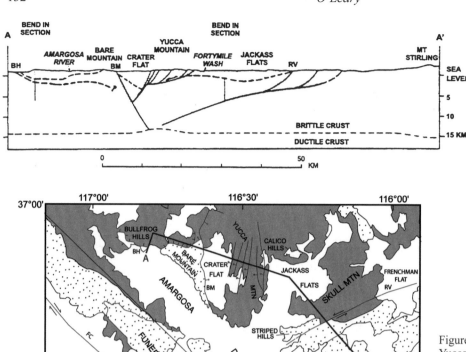

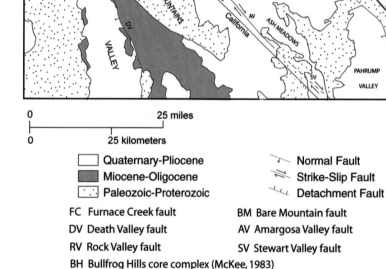

Figure 20. Detachment structures inferred near Yucca Mountain. Modified from Fox and Carr (1989, Fig. 2 therein).

plane, and motion along it is supposed to generate slip along the faults of the upper plate and distribute strain among them by virtue of independent motion. The model implies that detachment can only work along a weak layer that has an uncommonly low angle of friction or that presents significant rheological contrast with the suprajacent layer.

Implications of Detachment Fault Models

Detachment models adequately explain the distributed normal fault system at Yucca Mountain and the hanging-wall roll-over exhibited by each fault block. The mechanism of listric faulting linked to a detachment at depth is well established by exposures of similar fault systems elsewhere in the region. These models also adequately explain vertical-axis rotation at Yucca Mountain as a consequence of differential slip rate rather than profound crustal shear mechanisms linked to deformation of the Walker Lane belt. Because all rotated normal faults of the upper plate are rooted in a common slip plane (the detachment), all faulting is necessarily distributed, and (if the detachment level is deep enough) all rooted normal faults are equally seismogenic and could produce simultaneous earthquakes of equivalent and relatively small magnitudes. Because the hidden structures are

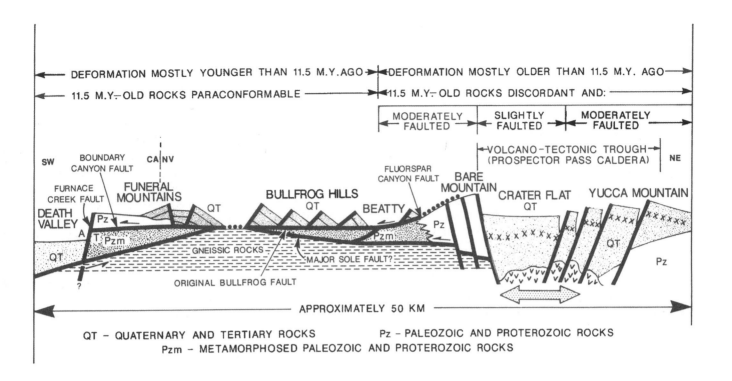

Figure 21. Model of crustal extension from Death Valley to Yucca Mountain. Arrow under Crater Flat indicates "pull-apart." From Carr (1990, Fig. 11 therein).

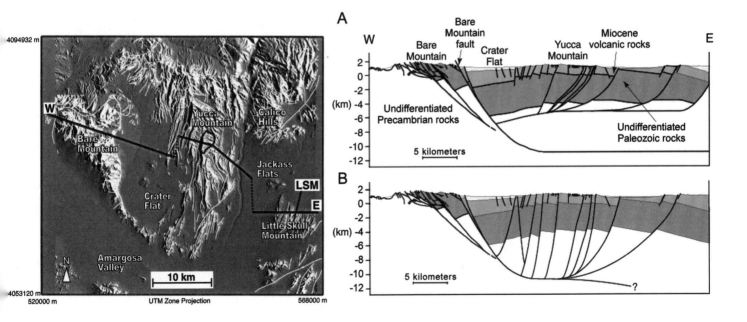

Figure 22. Diagrammatic cross sections show two different versions of a detachment fault model for Yucca Mountain. A—Shallow detachment fault system. B—Deep detachment fault system. Map is a digital elevation model of the Crater Flat domain. From McKague et al. (1996, p. 3–11).

subhorizontal slip planes within the brittle crust, they effectively isolate any lower-plate deformation from structure expressed within the upper plate or at the surface, and in fact, they imply a substantial contrast in structural style across the detachment. Consequently, these models require consideration of two super-imposed seismic source zones (an upper plate and a lower plate seismic source zone), and they provide no explanation for passage of basaltic magma through the lower crust. Listric fault mechanisms require a fixed (or rigid) headwall that does not participate in deformation related to extension; the rigid headwall does not undergo uplift in response to unloading of the lower plate. Listric fault models that make the Bare Mountain fault a headwall fault do not account for the 2–3 km of uplift of Bare Mountain since 13 Ma (Fridrich, 1999, p. 182), whereas the rolling-hinge model requires substantial uplift of Bare Mountain in response to upper plate unloading of only 4 km or less overburden.

Evidence against Detachment Fault Models

Shallow detachment at the Tertiary-Paleozoic contact (Scott, 1990, p. 273) can be eliminated as a credible model for Yucca Mountain. Scott (1990, p. 259) interpreted the Yucca Mountain faults to be listric on the basis of rollover or a local increase of hanging-wall dip toward the footwalls. Although he drew a comparison to the listric faults exhibited in seismic reflection profiles from the Gulf of Mexico, his interpretive profiles of Yucca Mountain showed domino structures that required huge amounts of basal shearing (Fig. 18) and implausibly tight curvatures to

be truly listric with the Paleozoic contact at ~2 km depth. The amount of structural deformation required to accommodate listric faulting low in the Miocene volcanic tuff section should be evident in core records, but the rocks show no evidence of such damage. The only major deformation found at depth at Yucca Mountain is the breccia in the Paleozoic limestone recovered from well UE-25 p#1 (M.D. Carr et al., 1986, p. 21, 74). Scott (1990, p. 273) referred this to a fault of "unknown attitude" although M.D. Carr et al. (1986, p. 25, 74) made a good case for deformation related to a steeply dipping fault a short distance to the east. The important point, however, is that the breccia is in the presumed lower plate, not in the upper plate where it should be, and it shows no shear fabric and no alignment parallel to the inferred detachment.

All the Tertiary-Paleozoic contacts exposed east and south of Yucca Mountain are erosional and/or depositional contacts, not slip surfaces (USGS, 1995), and interpretation of the deep seismic reflection profile across Yucca Mountain shows that high-angle faults offset the Tertiary-Paleozoic contact, thus precluding a shallow detachment beneath the mountain (Brocher and Hunter, 1996). However, Brocher et al. (1998, p. 967) noted that the seismic reflection data do not preclude a detachment deep in the Paleozoic section.

Detachment models that incorporate Bare Mountain or that involve a deformation scheme within and west of Bare Mountain (Hamilton, 1988a, p. 55; Hamilton, 1988b, p. 184; Scott, 1990, p. 276, his Fig. 15; McKague et al., 1996, p. 3–11, their Fig. 3-6)

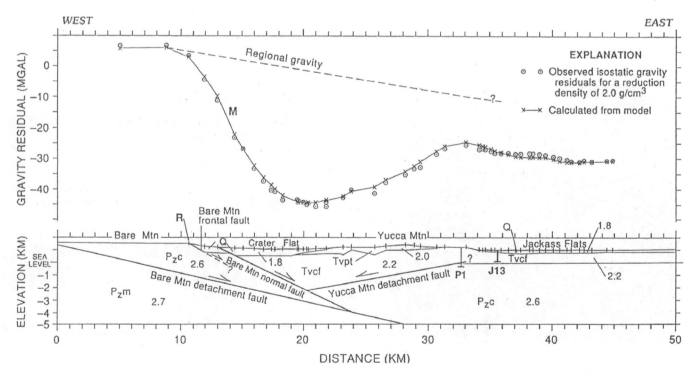

Figure 23. Interpreted detachment faults under Yucca Mountain as modeled using gravity data. Numbers with units are densities in grams per cubic centimeter assumed in the model. No vertical exaggeration. Q—Quaternary alluvium; Tvpt—Paintbrush and Timber Mountain Group tuff; Tvcf—Crater Flat Group and older volcanic rocks; Pzc—Paleozoic carbonates; Pzm—lower Paleozoic schist and gneiss; R—Bare Mountain range front; M—maximum gravity gradient. From Oliver and Fox (1993).

are limited by timing and geometry. Peak extension of Yucca Mountain occurred within the 1.1 m.y. period from 12.7 to 11.6 Ma; by 11.7 Ma, Bare Mountain was already an elevated range. Displacement on the Bare Mountain fault would have severed detachments at crustal depths above ~6 km (3.7 mi) shortly after 12.7 Ma, well before 11.7 Ma. Furthermore, any regional deep crustal detachment slip at or above the brittle-ductile transition was terminated by ca. 12 Ma. Hence, the rolling-hinge detachment model offers no explanation for deformation in the Crater Flat domain younger than 12 Ma. For example, the low cuesta along the southern flank of the basin formed after ca. 10 Ma and involves stratal tilting of as much as 10° north into the basin, a style of deformation that is not a continuation of earlier structural patterns (Fridrich, 1999, p. 190).

A further problem is that none of the detachment fault models address lateral boundary conditions to extension in Crater Flat. Each of the models depends on structures that extend beyond the east or west tectonic borders of the Crater Flat domain and are not resolved with respect to known or postulated boundary structures. Directly north of Yucca Mountain a large volume of magma resided in the crust (Broxton et al., 1989, p. 5983) throughout the period of inferred maximum detachment activity, precluding detachment north of some undefined model boundary. Likewise, the origin of the cuesta at the south end of the basin is not considered in any of the models. None of the detachment models provides a structural solution for the eastern border of the Crater Flat domain, as no fixed headwall is identified. The model cross sections shown in Figure 22 place the headwall east of Little Skull Mountain, but by incorporating Little Skull Mountain into the listric upper plate, a tectonic problem is created: Little Skull Mountain is a north-dipping cuesta cut by down-to-the-west oblique faults; the northward tilt requires a post-9-Ma tectonic event not provided by the listric fault model that attempts to link the post–9 Ma down-to-the-west faults at Little Skull Mountain with the pre–11.6 Ma faults at Yucca Mountain and the Bullfrog Hills.

Deep detachment faults (or systems) projected west of the Sheep Range by Guth (1981) and Wernicke et al. (1988, p. 1746) are incompatible with the long-lived strike-slip faulting within the Spotted Range-Mine Mountain structural zone (Carr, 1984, 1990) and the east-directed extension east of the CP Hills (Stuckless and O'Leary, this volume, Fig. 12 therein). Models of east-vergent detachment do not accommodate the tectonic style and deformation history of Little Skull Mountain and strike-slip dominated faulting farther east.

The history of localized late Neogene basin deformation with varied and opposed senses of flank collapse, indicates that a systematic west-directed sense of detachment faulting has not been a part of crustal evolution in Neogene time within the Walker Lane belt east of Bare Mountain. The structure of the Specter Range (Figs. 3 and 9) suggests that regional detachment operated east of Bare Mountain, but this is pre-late Oligocene deformation, possibly coeval with detachment-level shearing in the Funeral and Grapevine Mountains (Fig. 2) (Applegate et al., 1992, p. 521;

Hoisch and Simpson, 1993, p. 6823; Hamilton, 1988b, p. 59). Brocher et al. (1993, p. 44) pointed out that the apparent continuity of seismic reflections in basinal units south of the Specter Range suggests little or no faulting within the last 8.5–11 Ma; thus, detachment was not active there in late Miocene time.

A common point of objection regarding contemporary detachment faulting is lack of seismic activity as well as conflicts with the earthquake record (Arabasz and Julander, 1986, p. 63, 69; Jackson and White, 1989, p. 17, 24). Ofoegbu and Ferrill (1998, p. 67) proposed that a breakaway fault for detachment under Yucca Mountain surfaces east of Little Skull Mountain (Fig. 22A). The Little Skull Mountain earthquake occurred in 1992 at ~11 km depth on a N.60°E.-striking, 65°–70°SE–dipping fault (Smith et al., 2000), which projects to surface more or less along the southwest projection of the Mine Mountain fault (Fig. 9). Aftershock foci climbed this fault plane to within 5 km of ground surface, with some energy release even shallower. Aftershocks also occurred on a variety of other local faults, some strike-slip, but none having a shallow "detachment" aspect. The inferred detachment fault was not susceptible to slip under conditions that generated slip on a steeply dipping fault that transects the inferred detachment as well as slip on ancillary faults of differing attitudes.

The sparse record of small (ML, local magnitude; ≤2.0) earthquakes at or near Yucca Mountain give focal depths as great as 11 km; fault-plane solutions indicate oblique left-lateral slip with a substantial dip-slip component on faults dipping from 55° to 65° (Harmsen and Bufe, 1992, p. 33, 34). The largest recorded Yucca Mountain earthquake (ML = 2.1), at 11 km focal depth, had an inferred nodal fault plane dip of 74° for the primary focal mechanism (Harmsen and Bufe, 1992). These data imply that fault slip beneath Yucca Mountain occurs on steeply dipping faults of moderate frictional strength at depths where detachment faults are inferred to exist. Either detachment faulting does not operate at present under Yucca Mountain, or it does so by aseismic creep, or there are no detachment faults.

Slip along low-angle listric faults and detachment faults requires special conditions. Detachment can only work along a weak layer that has an unusually low angle of friction and little or no cohesive strength, as is common with undrained slumping in saturated sediments and in the marine environment (Bradshaw and Zoback, 1988). Exposed detachments typically show evidence of ductile deformation in the lower plate, which implies presence of a weak layer. Brun et al. (1994, p. 320) were able to develop a rolling-hinge-type structure in sandbox experiments only by placing a discrete low-viscosity material where they wished footwall uplift to occur. Otherwise, their models resulted in an entirely different structure. Likewise, McClay and Ellis (1987, p. 342) were able to create a tilted domino fault succession, but only on a tilted table; the faults were initiated at the proper tilted attitudes but did not rotate into those attitudes from a previously steeper attitude.

Detachment faults behave somewhat like compound slump sheets, except that detachments are rooted in the crust. A "deep detachment" model, with slip surfaces located at depths from 6 to 15 km could bring ductile deformation, and subhorizontal slip, into play, but the model requires the block-bounding faults to behave like dominos. However, domino rotation presumes tensile behavior at the base and uniform frictional slip across the entire width of the slip plane, which is unrealistic when applied to depths of 6 km at Yucca Mountain, even in the presence of extreme pore pressure. Normal faulting in the brittle crust typically begins at high angles (~55° to 70°) and may extend with little or no curvature down to the depths of ductile deformation. Consequently, the rotation of upper crustal fault planes to angles shallower than 30° requires either substantial shear along the basal contact (Gross and Hillemeyer, 1982, p. 263; the rotated domino or "bookshelf" deformation mechanism) or plastic deformation and uplift of the footwall (the rolling-hinge mechanism). Although there is no doubt that detachment on this scale has occurred in areas of the Mojave Desert and in southern Arizona (i.e., south of latitude 37°N) (Davis and Lister, 1988; Dokka, 1989), it is questionable whether appropriate conditions exist today in the crust of the Central Basin and Range to facilitate such extension mechanisms.

Pure Shear (Planar Fault) Models

Pure shear models assume a viscous middle crust overlain by a quasi-elastic or brittle upper crust. The dominant mode of deformation approximates pure shear whereby the orientations of geometric axes of the deforming volume remain unchanged during deformation. The result is a variety of riftlike or grabenlike elongate basins in the upper crust having their long axes normal to the direction of extension. These models are also called planar fault models because faults do not change dip (become listric) with depth. The viscous middle crust distributes strain by viscous (or ductile) deformation; hence, these models incorporate buoyancy, which affects local subsidence and uplift of the suprajacent fault blocks.

Evidence for Pure Shear Models

Present-day extension is manifested throughout most of the Great Basin by normal fault displacement earthquakes that exhibit focal mechanisms on steeply dipping faults at depths approaching 19 km (Doser and Smith, 1989, p. 1385). Deformation that approximates or incorporates pure shear extension seems to operate in the Basin and Range at present, and there is evidence that pure shear mechanisms have operated throughout the Great Basin in the past.

Two general kinds of pure shear model have been applied to Yucca Mountain: a half-graben model and a pull-apart or rift model. In the half-graben model, Crater Flat basin is the hanging wall of the Bare Mountain fault, and it behaves somewhat like a falling trapdoor; slip on the Bare Mountain fault controls basin subsidence, and the block-bounding faults of Yucca Mountain are antithetic to the Bare Mountain fault. In the pull-apart or rift model, a master fault is not required; rather, behavior of

internal fault sets determines the structural configuration. This model has Crater Flat controlled by an axial fracture zone; the structural configuration of the basin is simply a lateral propagation of the deep axial fracture zone by a variety of flanking faults and fractures.

The simplest of the pure shear models is the volcano-tectonic rift model advanced by Carr (1990, p. 300). Crater Flat basin is a conspicuous depression within the Kawich-Greenwater rift (i.e., the Amargosa trough: Figs. 2, 6), the axis of which is defined by aligned gravity anomalies that indicate other, shallower basement depressions (Carr, 1990, p. 287). Crater Flat basin is attributed to several episodes of magmatic inflation, doming, and caldera and sector collapse (Carr, 1990, p. 290) within a steep-sided basement trough. Thus, the faults at Yucca Mountain are essentially planar subsidence structures created by opening of the rift (Carr, 1990, p. 300). Figure 21 shows that opening of the rift was bidirectional, centered on an axis (obscured by intrusion), even though the abrupt western side (i.e., Bare Mountain fault) results in an asymmetric graben (Carr, 1990, p. 286). The form of Crater Flat basin and its association with the caldera complex led Carr (1990, p. 300) to interpret it as a sector graben, an area of subsidence caused by evacuation of a body of magma from the base of the crust during or shortly following eruption of the Topopah Spring Tuff. This interpretation, and similar speculations by Fridrich (1999, p. 184), accords with the timing and magnitude of initial faulting of Yucca Mountain and with the shape and position of the basin. Brun et al. (1994, p. 321) effectively simulated this kind of structure, in cross section, with a sandbox model that portrayed a low-density viscous mass at the base of the crust.

Apart from an appeal to magmatic activity and sector collapse, Carr (1990) did not develop a regional mechanism for rift genesis that would link Crater Flat basin to the entire extent of the Kawich-Greenwater rift. The main conclusion was that the rift formed the headwall for detachments west of Crater Flat (Carr, 1990, p. 299). However, the rift model provides a tectonic link between the fault systems in Crater Flat–Yucca Mountain and those at Pahute Mesa to the north. Accordingly, Crater Flat basin can be understood as the southern end of a rift-controlled basin that projects south from the Basin and Range province deep into the Walker Lane belt (Fig. 2). This riftlike aspect of the model downplays the notion of the Bare Mountain fault as a conventional range-front fault. It implies that Pleistocene extensional faulting at Yucca Mountain is not a function of antithetic slip controlled by the Bare Mountain fault but is instead controlled by axial fractures within the deepest part of the Amargosa trough (i.e., Crater Flat basin).

A rift model for Yucca Mountain, as part of the "Amargosa Desert rift zone" (i.e., the Amargosa trough or the Kawich-Greenwater rift; Fig. 2), was further elaborated by Brocher et al. (1998). Brocher et al. (1998, p. 968) presented a "simplified model" (i.e., one designed only to facilitate interpretation of the seismic profile [CFSP lines 2, 3, Fig. 3], specifically to account for a large population of inferred, east-dipping, normal faults beneath Crater Flat). Although Brocher et al. (1998, p. 947) referred to the Amargosa Desert rift zone as an asymmetric half-graben, a typical graben-forming mechanism was not presented, nor was a rift model comparable to that of Carr (1990, p. 300) offered; rather, a kind of evolved, pull-apart model that depends on changing behavior of the brittle crust in response to its changing thickness through time was presented. Brocher et al. (1998, p. 950) divided the rift zone into two subdomains on the basis of fault block tilt: a "west-tilted Crater Flat domain" and an "east-tilted Yucca Mountain domain" (Figs. 4, 24). The presence of east-side-down faults in Crater Flat was interpreted entirely on the basis of the seismic reflection profile and aeromagnetic anomalies (Brocher et al., 1998, p. 961). Brocher et al. 1998, p. 956, 962) inferred the east-dipping faults to be present as far east as the Solitario Canyon fault on the basis of the westward tilt of reflections within the Bullfrog Tuff in the upper 700 m of the profile (Fig. 4, Bullfrog Tuff-B). The longitudinal extent of the east-dipping faults is restricted. They noted, "Because these east-facing scarps reverse polarity to west-facing scarps just a few kilometers north and south of the seismic line, we infer that these east-dipping and west-dipping faults operated simultaneously, and that their interaction in the subsurface has been complex" (Brocher et al., 1998, p. 966–967).

Deformation of a relatively thin (~11 km) upper crust began in middle Miocene time. A series of east-dipping faults formed in a more or less symmetrical, rift-like basin bounded by the Bare Mountain fault and by the Solitario Canyon fault to the east against which most of the Crater Flat faults terminate (Fig. 24B). As the crust cooled and the brittle upper crust thickened to 15 km, west-dipping faults originated under Yucca Mountain and increased in number to the east; the enclave of east-dipping faults in Crater Flat became immobilized and stranded high in the thickening brittle crust, trapped between the Bare Mountain fault and the Solitaro Canyon fault (Fig. 24A).

The graben-like aspect of Crater Flat basin was emphasized by Fridrich (1999, p. 170) in his characterization of the Crater Flat domain. Fridrich (1999, p. 193) considered planimetric aspects, including northwest-directed dextral shear (a feature of the Walker Lane belt), vertical-axis rotation, and doming of the caldera complex. Consequently, Fridrich (1999, p. 193) considered the Crater Flat domain to be a "hybrid basin of complex origin." He offered two alternative interpretations: Crater Flat basin is a rhombochasm, a pull-apart modified by imposed distributed dextral shear, or it is a sphenochasm, a pull-apart anchored at its northeastern corner and subject to increasing extension toward the south such that the basin has opened radially, like a fan. These general alternative characterizations are compatible with most known tectonic features of the Crater Flat domain, but no specific tectonic mechanism is proposed. It is not clear how formation of the faulted cuesta at the southern end of Crater Flat basin relates to a sphenochasm mechanism.

Treatment of the Crater Flat domain as a complex graben or half-graben was undertaken by application of a boundary-element model (Janssen and King, 2000). The primary objective was to create a structural cross section that simulates the Crater Flat domain based on observed structure and on known or

assumed crustal properties and boundary conditions. The model is a two-layer model that includes a brittle, seismogenic upper crust 12–15 km thick and cut by planar faults that dip 75°, underlain by a viscous lower crust of higher density subject to pure

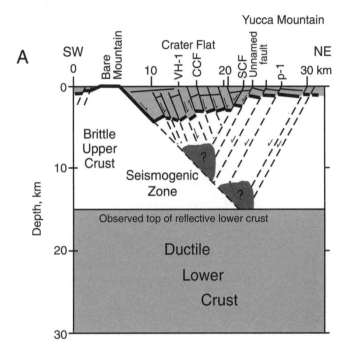

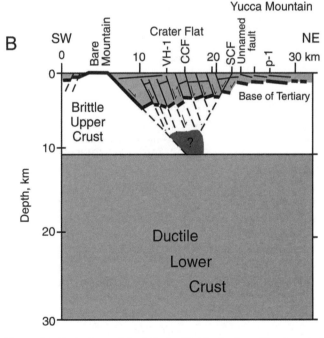

Figure 24. Tectonic model of Crater Flat basin from Brocher et al. (1998, p. 968). A—present fault configuration; B—middle Miocene fault configuration. VH-1 and p-1—USGS boreholes. CCF—central Crater Flat fault; SCF—Solitario Canyon fault. (Queried areas in brittle crust are inferred intrusions that resolve space problems created by faulting (Brocher et al., 1998, p. 969).

shear deformation (Fig. 25). In reality, the upper, brittle crust and the lower, viscous crust are transitional (Lamb, 1994, p. 4464), but the nature of the transition is difficult to model because the distribution of traction or basal shear stress is poorly known and rheological properties are poorly constrained. In the model, both layers of the crust behave as an elastic body during fault slip (at the time of an earthquake). After the earthquake, the lower crust accommodates the stress perturbation by creep, but the upper crust does not completely relax or recover its preseismic strength; its long-term elastic modulus is decreased. Over many earthquake cycles, the upper crust becomes considerably less elastic than its 15 km thickness would indicate; its reduced elastic modulus defines the effective elastic thickness of the crust. The effective elastic thickness of upper crust in the southern Great Basin is ~2 km (Stein et al., 1988, p. 13,326), a fact that at least partly accounts for relatively high structural relief across short distances in the Basin and Range.

Six major faults were assumed to control the overall structure of Yucca Mountain and Crater Flat basin (Fig. 26). The amount of slip on each fault was fixed on the basis of data from Scott (1990) in order to replicate the structural relief. It was found that intersection of faults or variations of dip of as much as 30° did not appreciably influence the profile; total fault slip and effective elastic thickness had much greater effects on structural relief. However, neither Bare Mountain nor Yucca Mountain could be sufficiently elevated under the initial slip conditions on the known faults (Fig. 25C). In order to achieve credible elevations and eliminate a necking effect because of too few faults, additional faults had to be added to the model in plausible locations west of Bare Mountain, in Jackass Flats, and within Crater Flat (the "Crater Flat fault"; Figs. 25, 26). Boundary condition fault 1 (Fig. 25B) is inferred to be one or more faults in Amargosa Valley subparallel to Bare Mountain. The Carrara fault (Fig. 9) could represent one such fault, despite its relatively small inferred normal displacement. Boundary condition fault 2 (Fig. 25B) is inferred to be a northern projection of the gravity fault of Winograd and Thordarson (1975) or a set of faults related to down-to-the-west faults exposed on the west flank of the Calico Hills (Frizzell and Shulters, 1990).

The "Crater Flat" fault (Fig. 25B) could be represented by one or several faults of large cumulative displacement buried in Crater Flat, such as indicated by the seismic reflection profile (Brocher et al., 1998, p. 967) or the magnetic anomaly data (Fig. 9). The relevance of a major fault or fault zone in Crater Flat was emphasized by Fridrich (1999, p. 188), who noted the concentrated tectonic activity in the western one-third of Crater Flat basin between 11.6 and 10 Ma, between the Bare Mountain fault and two major (possibly connected) down-to-the-west faults at the northern and southern ends of the basin (Fridrich, 1999, p. 188). The concentration of extension in this part of the basin appears to have created a distinct subbasin (cf. Fig. 25E), possibly formed as a transtensional pull-apart along the southern part of the Bare Mountain range front (Fridrich, 1999, p. 189). However, it is important to realize that total slip could be achieved by

numerous small faults as well as by single faults of great displacement (which were chosen for modeling convenience).

Assigning a total slip of ~1 km to the hidden Crater Flat fault improved the elevation of Yucca Mountain in the model profile. Elevation could be gained also by assuming the mountain is a site of maximum depositional thickness, thus adding elevation without the need for faulting in Crater Flat basin, or a combination of depositional thickness and faulting could equally well improve the profile. An amount of postslip erosion and deposition of ~30% of maximum relief was added to the profile to produce a cross section that approximates the profile of the Crater Flat domain (Fig. 27). Results of the boundary-element model show:

1. A two-layer crustal model that incorporates buoyancy, elasticity, and viscosity can explain fault-block dips at Yucca Mountain as a result of slip on planar faults and consequent block adjustment.

2. Block dips are relatively insensitive to fault-plane dip and subsurface fault intersections but are relatively sensitive to displacement and effective elastic thickness.

3. The anomalous elevation of Yucca Mountain within Crater Flat basin can be accounted for by original deposition or preexisting topography or by slip on presently hidden faults within Crater Flat. Subsidence in Jackass Flats and in the valley west of Bare Mountain also requires slip on buried faults.

Implications of Pure Shear Models

Because pure shear models explicitly involve deformation of the lower crust, they offer a mechanism for basaltic volcanism coupled to basin faulting. In the rift model, intersection of convergent faults with axial fractures at the base of the seismogenic crust could focus dilational strain, even at depths of 15–20 km, and thereby facilitate the ascent of basaltic magma to higher crustal levels (Fig. 28). The Bare Mountain fault and the Paintbrush Canyon–Stagecoach Road fault likely would be the primary intersecting faults at the deepest crustal level; interaction of these faults at a sufficient strain threshold could be accompanied by basaltic intrusion. If decompression melting of basalt can occur in the Central Basin and Range, the pure shear models provide the crustal conditions for localized melting in the upper mantle in the neighborhood of deep, basin-controlling faults, as well as the locus of magma ascent. These models imply that faulting and volcanism are coupled processes and that future volcanism will either penetrate the Bare Mountain fault or focus on deep fault intersections at the southern end of the basin, and that faulting in Crater Flat will precede and accompany volcanism.

A pure shear mechanism explains the fundamental graben-like structure of Crater Flat basin, and because a pure shear mechanism can be tied directly to lower crustal ductile deformation, it can adequately account for extension throughout Quaternary time. Pure shear models adequately explain the most recent tectonic developments in and near the Crater Flat domain: namely, earthquakes having steep focal plane mechanisms that occur at

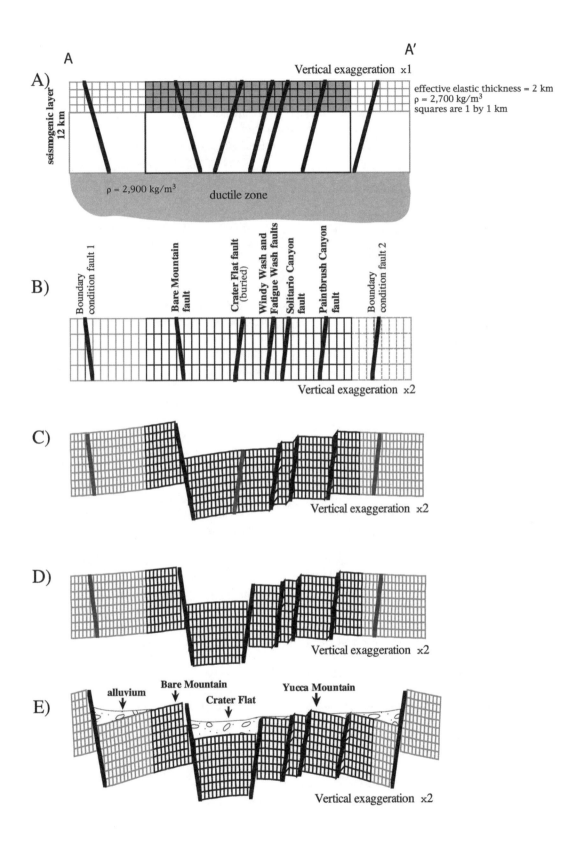

Figure 25. Simplified east-west cross section of the Crater Flat domain depicted as a complex half-graben (see Fig. 26 for A–A' profile location on map plan). Panels B to E show brittle crust only; E shows that slip on boundary condition faults provides for appropriate relief for Yucca Mountain. Boundary condition fault 1—inferred fault in Amargosa Valley; boundary condition fault 2—gravity fault. From Janssen and King (2000).

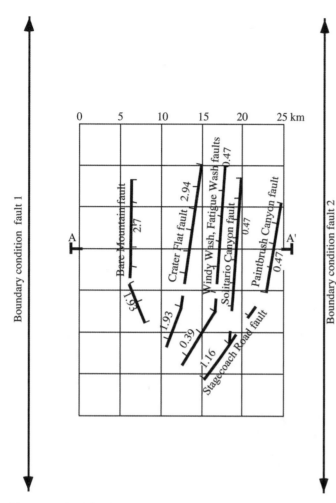

Figure 26. Simplified fault distribution of the Crater Flat domain used for the planar fault model of Janssen and King (2000). A–A' shows location of model cross section shown in Figure 25. Numbers are displacements (km) from Scott (1990). Hachures on downthrown side. Model area indicated by arbitrary grid in km.

happens in the basin east of the rift axis is largely independent of what happens west of the rift axis. The model implies that Crater Flat basin is propagating to the south, which perhaps could explain the progression of extension and subsidence toward the southwestern corner of the basin.

Evidence against Pure Shear Models

The half-graben model works well only near the central latitudinal axis of Crater Flat basin. The model fails to account for the decreased throw and splitting of the Bare Mountain fault in the vicinity of the caldera complex, and it does not account for the structural style at the southern end of Crater Flat. However, imposition of dextral shear across the model solves some of these problems, most notably by treating the caldera complex as a fixed plug that concentrates strain along its southern margin. The model leaves open the possibility that the half-graben formed prior to the caldera complex and that post-middle-Miocene faulting and vertical axis rotation are unique to Crater Flat basin, which is isolated from deformation north of the caldera complex. The half-graben model implies that basaltic intrusion in Crater Flat could be guided by faults, but to infer that the block-bounding faults of Yucca Mountain would guide intrusion toward Yucca Mountain, or that the east-dipping faults of Crater Flat would guide magma away from Yucca Mountain, depends on which variant of the model is preferred.

The rift model does not explain the origin of the cuesta that bounds the southern rim of the basin and that shows no evidence of axial symmetry. The model does not account for hanging-wall rollover if each block-bounding fault at Yucca Mountain extends as an independent plane through the brittle crust. Fault blocks that have the aspect ratio of slabs ~2 by 15 km would not be subject to rollover. However, if the faults merge at depth (cf. Ferrill et al., 1999) to create thicker, weaker slabs, rollover could occur. The model does not account for the asymmetry of Crater Flat basin, for uplift of Bare Mountain relative to Jackass Flats, or for vertical axis rotation in Crater Flat.

The rift model of Brocher et al. (1998) does not explain why (1) Crater Flat formed prior to Yucca Mountain; or (2) the early, east-dipping faults deepened the basin, but the west-dipping faults left Yucca Mountain at an anomalously high elevation. The model also contradicts the geologic evidence that subsidence and extension in the Crater Flat domain progressed toward the west, resulting in an asymmetric basin (Fridrich, 1999, p. 189) and does not explain conditions that result in a normal-fault system of opposing dips. Presumably, the latter is related to a critical thickness of the upper crust, inasmuch as the model geometry indicates that as the brittle crust thickens and the basin widens, the east-dipping faults synthetic to the Bare Mountain fault should slip, and those antithetic to the Solitario Canyon fault and unable to slip should be cut by new west-dipping faults. Although Brocher et al. (1998, p. 966) acknowledged the presence of west-dipping faults in Crater Flat basin north and south of the seismic profile, these are not factored into the model. The model is too specifically tied to the seismic profile to be applied to the whole Crater Flat basin.

various depths in the seismogenic brittle crust, and locations and genesis of basaltic intrusion in Crater Flat basin and elsewhere in the Amargosa trough. The pure shear mechanism accounts for both uplift and subsidence (including hanging-wall rollover) of block-faulted crust. These models can easily be modified to include vertical-axis rotation, which is not easily accounted for in simple shear models.

The rift model implies that Crater Flat basin is a segment of a much larger, longer tectonic feature in which faults at Pahute Mesa and at Yucca Mountain are genetically linked and that the caldera complex is a local aberration much like a knot in the middle of a splitting wood plank. Because rift-controlled extension is more or less symmetrical, the model accounts for the unbalanced slip budget between the Bare Mountain fault and the Yucca Mountain fault system. If the Bare Mountain fault and one or more crustal faults at Yucca Mountain are driven by a deep master fracture zone in the axis of Crater Flat basin, the faults may be largely independent of each other in terms of slip budget; what

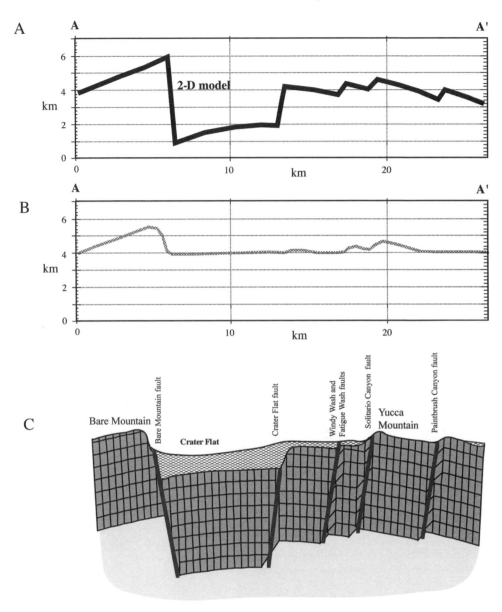

Figure 27. (A) Profile of two-dimensional boundary element model of section A–A′ (cf. Fig. 25E). (B) Generalized topography of Yucca Mountain, Crater Flat, Bare Mountain at latitude of Kiwi Mesa (cf. Fig. 3). (C) Combined profiles A and B with differences adjusted by simulated erosion and deposition to match profile B. From Janssen and King (2000, Fig. 12).

Lateral Shear Models

Lateral shear models are based on application of horizontal shear stress to create translation (lateral offset) as well as extension (pull-apart). The result is an alignment of strike-slip fault segments that link pull-apart basins dominated by oblique faulting (Sims et al., 1999; Burchfiel and Stewart, 1966; Blakely et al., 1999). This style of deformation is well documented in the Inyo-Mono domain west of the Death Valley–Furnace Creek fault (Stuckless and O'Leary, this volume, Fig. 5 therein). Death Valley has been modeled as a series of obliquely extending rhombochasms (Wright and Troxel, 1973) connected by northwest-striking dextral faults (Wright, 1989; Blakely et al., 1999, p. 13). The intervening ranges are more or less structurally isolated, passive blocks that can undergo deformation apart from the widening pull-apart basins.

Evidence for Lateral Shear Models

Evidence of right-lateral shear is widespread in the Walker Lane belt, but evidence for transtensional basins linked by strike-slip faults is sparse (Blakely et al., 1999, p. 13). A model proposed by Hardyman (1978) for the central Walker Lane belt and presented by Hardyman and Oldow (1991, p. 291) implies that a strike-slip fault may be present but hidden beneath a shallow detachment. The model describes a "transtensional nappe" which actually requires that the detachment (listric fault tract) be bounded by a pair of strike-slip faults and that the detachment faults have a fixed geometry with respect to the strike-slip faults, visible or not. Hardyman and Oldow (1991, p. 295) cited as the best examples of this style of faulting the faults in the Gabbs Valley where subdomains of listric normal faults of similar polarity exhibit dips of 60° to 20° and have displacements of several centimeters to several tens of meters or more. How-

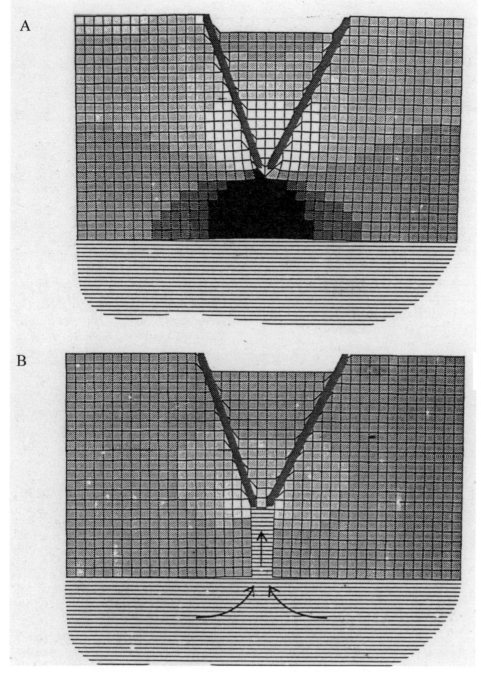

Figure 28. Two layer crust model: brittle layer (grid pattern) on viscous layer (horizontal line pattern). (A) Normal faults converge near base of the brittle crust layer resulting in local strain field: dark shading represents dilational strain, light shading represents compressional strain. (B) Dilational strain beneath convergent fault tips optimizes extensional fracturing creating a path for dike intrusion. From G. King and B. Janssen (unpub. data, 1996).

ever, the listric fault pattern of the Gabbs Valley is distinctly different from that of Yucca Mountain and, in fact, none of the criteria or geometry required for Hardyman's model exists at Yucca Mountain. Hardyman and Oldow (1991, p. 295) do cite high-angle normal faults in the central Walker Lane belt that cut Tertiary strata, have dip-slip and oblique-slip offsets, display straight-line map traces, and have variable strike orientations. They note that some of these faults presumably penetrate the crust, having guided the emplacement of Tertiary dikes. These faults, not subsumed by Hardyman's (1978) model, more closely resemble those that cut Yucca Mountain than do those of the Gillis and Gabbs Valley Ranges.

A model consisting of a north-northwest–striking dextral strike-slip fault zone passing beneath Yucca Mountain (Fig. 29) is presented by Caskey and Schweickert (1992) and Schweickert and Lahren, 1994, 1997). The inferred fault zone was defined as the Amargosa Desert fault system by Schweickert and Lahren (1994, p. A-250; 1997, p. 25), a system that comprises the Stewart Valley, Pahrump-Stateline, and (not shown) Ivanpah faults for a total length of ~250 km. Projection of the Pahrump-State-

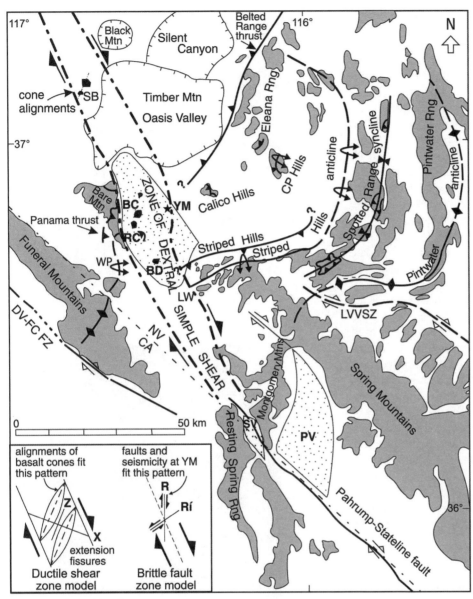

LVVSZ   Las Vegas Valley shear zone
DV-FC FZ   Death Valley - Furnace Creek fault zone
SV   Stewart Valley fault
PV   Pahrump Valley
SB   Sleeping Butte
BC   Black Cone
RC   Red Cone
BD   Big Dune Cone (Lathrop Wells Cone)
YM   Yucca Mountain
WP   Winters Peak anticline

■ Pleistocene volcanic rocks
▨ Paleozoic rocks exposed in highlands
▨ Basins

Figure 29. Amargosa Desert fault system. Dot-dash lines indicate approximate boundaries of the dextral shear zone. From Schweickert and Lahren (1997, their Fig. 1).

line fault zone toward Crater Flat follows a N.45°W. trend, as indicated by various negative Bouguer gravity anomalies that probably reflect pull-aparts along the fault zone (Wright, 1989; Donovan, 1991, p. 77, 80, 81).

Evidence for the Amargosa Desert fault system includes gravity, seismic, structural, stratigraphic, and paleomagnetic data, the distribution of springs and basaltic volcanic centers,

and patterns of late Quaternary surface faulting (Schweickert and Lahren, 1997, p. 25). Right-lateral offset of 30 km or more is based on separation of Bare Mountain and the Striped Hills (Caskey and Schweickert, 1992, p. 1324; Schweickert and Lahren, 1994, p. A-250; 1997, p. 25). Fault offset is inferred on the premise that Bare Mountain and the Striped Hills had formed a continuous Mesozoic fold structure. However, no throughgoing surface traces of the fault zone exist in the tuffs of the southwestern Nevada volcanic field. To explain the absence of such traces, Schweickert and Lahren (1997, p. 35) appealed to the model of shallow detachment described by Hardyman and Oldow (1991, p. 291). They attributed the vertical-axis rotations at Yucca Mountain to ~25 km of dextral displacement that may have occurred since ca. 11.5 Ma, consistent with dextral shear features near Yucca Mountain. However, they also pointed out that study of the exposed rotational normal faults of Yucca Mountain and Crater Flat will provide little information on the character of the strike-slip faults at depth. This statement concerning Yucca Mountain does not hold for the fault system farther south, however, where the Pahrump-Stateline fault zone consists of two prominent subparallel strands ~5 km apart that exhibit normal, west-side-down and dextral oblique offset (Hoffard, 1991, p. 49, 82). The faulting there was active from late Tertiary to late Quaternary time.

A planimetric version of the half-graben model was essayed by Janssen and King (2000) in order to account for dextral shear in the Crater Flat domain. The fault blocks at Yucca Mountain were simulated by an array of parallel beams (Fig. 30A); the beams were fixed by "pivots" at their southern ends (but were allowed some adjustment along small local faults) along a line parallel to the regional shear vector, and Bare Mountain was fixed. Right lateral shear was imposed from the northwest along the northern end of the beam array (i.e., along the caldera rim and Yucca Wash), and a series of north-south–striking faults was placed in Jackass Flats between Fortymile Wash and Little Skull Mountain to accommodate left-lateral distortion of Crater Flat basin. The model results generally resemble the Yucca Mountain fault system and deformation across Crater Flat basin as it might have appeared prior to 11.6 Ma (Fig. 30B). A combination of the profile model (Figs. 25, 27) and the planimetric model (Fig. 30) resulted in a three-dimensional model (Fig. 31).

Implications of Lateral Shear Models

A discrete shear zone that passes through Crater Flat could account for vertical-axis rotation and for the centers of Quaternary and Neogene basaltic volcanism inside and outside Crater Flat. This model implies that future volcanism in Crater Flat will be narrowly confined. The model is not only compatible with detachment faulting; it requires detachment in order to hide the inferred transcurrent shear zone in the lower crust. The model implies that slip on the buried strike-slip fault would activate listric faulting across Yucca Mountain. However, in explaining Quaternary faulting at Yucca Mountain, the model should point to evidence of northwest-striking Quaternary slip outside the basin, as such slip is required by the model mechanism to drive deformation at Yucca Mountain. To the contrary, the model does not explain structure at the caldera rim or structure along the cuesta at the southern end of the basin where the entire history of late Miocene deformation is exposed.

A prime question directing formulation and application of lateral shear models for Yucca Mountain is whether oblique dex-

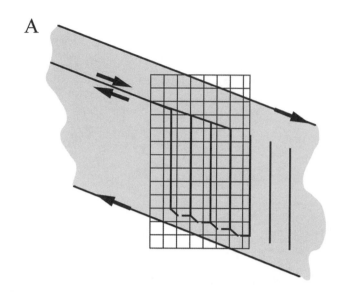

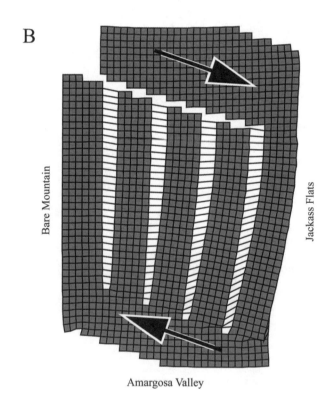

Figure 30. (A) Application of dextral shear to the model grid; right-lateral fault represents inferred Yucca Wash fault; small, complex faults at south end of the blocks facilitate clockwise rotation; two N-S faults at right side of grid (i.e., in Jackass Flats) are added to prevent undesired strain effects in the grid area. (B) Slip model shows normal displacement decreases toward the south, whereas sinistral slip increases; however, net displacement decreases toward the south and apparent eastward "thrusting" occurs north of the inferred Yucca Wash fault. From Janssen and King (2000, their Fig. 9).

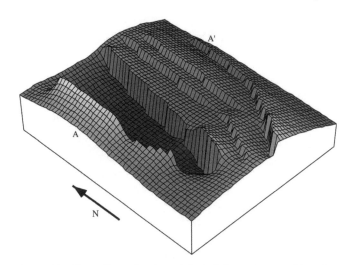

Figure 31. Three-dimensional model of deformation resulting from slip on faults shown in Figure 26. Vertical exaggeration, 3.5×. A–A′ indicates location of profile shown in Figure 25. From Janssen and King (2000, their Fig. 11).

tral shear is confined to Crater Flat basin (i.e., the basin itself is becoming distorted because of distributed [diffuse], regional shear) (Minor et al., 1997, p. 33), or whether shear is imposed by a regional right-lateral fault or narrowly confined shear zone that passes through or into Crater Flat basin (Wernicke et al., 2004): Is lateral shear imposed by deep ductile deformation over a broad zone and expressed within individual overlying basins, or is it propagated through the brittle crust by long strike-slip faults (Lamb, 1994; Bourne et al., 1998; King et al., 1994)?

Paleomagnetic studies (Hudson et al., 1994, p. 274) suggest that dextral shear that affected the region of the southwestern Nevada volcanic field occurred in discrete zones that were discontinuous in length and diachronous in age. Nonsystematic distributions of vertical-axis rotations in time and space within the southwestern Nevada volcanic field, as reported by Hudson et al. (1994), imply that individual basins have responded uniquely to distributed northwest-oriented dextral shear driven by post–12.7 Ma extension south of Yucca Mountain and west of the Spring Mountains (cf. Brocher et al., 1993, p. 45). However, a buried zone of dextral shear could have a wider extent—the projected contours of rotation across Crater Flat imply presence of a zone of diffuse dextral shear that is aligned with, and possibly part of, a larger belt of clockwise rotation and dextral shear that extends at least 60 km farther to the northwest (Hudson et al., 1996, p. A-451; Minor et al., 1997, p. 20). The data imply that middle Miocene normal extension was essentially confined to the Crater Flat domain and may have been associated with caldera magmatism (Minor et al., 1997, p. 28), whereas later vertical-axis rotation was imposed from outside the domain via dextral shear associated with evolution of the Walker Lane belt (Minor et al., 1997, p. 33).

It seems clear that lateral shear deformation that created pull-apart basins in conjunction with right-lateral slip has operated, and continues to operate, in the Inyo-Mono domain west of the

Funeral Mountains, but this style of deformation is not evident at Yucca Mountain. Models that call on diffuse shear, such that individual basins deform in individual ways at different times, are not well formulated. They are referred to as sphenochasm or rhombochasm structures and thus call on elements of pure shear deformation. Diffuse shear limited to Crater Flat basin can explain localizations of basaltic volcanism and late concentration of extension toward the southwestern corner of Crater Flat. Crater Flat basin appears to have formed by orthogonal extension; lateral shear was imposed on the basin during a subsequent episode of deformation. Whether the lateral shear was diffuse or more narrowly confined is uncertain and therefore the object of alternative tectonic models.

In emphasizing the varieties and relations of planimetric features, including vertical-axis rotation, lateral shear models deal with a dimension not well treated by the other kinds of models. Lateral shear models for Yucca Mountain, however, are difficult to support in general because of the lack of evident shear structures required to drive local deformation; appeal to hidden, buried, or intermittently active crustal features amounts to special pleading for mechanisms that cannot be verified or that are unique in the overall tectonic environment.

Evidence against Lateral Shear Models

Some observations appear to be inconsistent with the existence of a large, throughgoing dextral fault zone or shear zone beneath Crater Flat:

1. The inferred fault zone exhibits no throughgoing surface displacement in the northern Amargosa trough and in the vicinity of Crater Flat. Basin analysis finds no clear expression of the Amargosa Desert fault system north of Amargosa Valley; it shows, rather, that the Stateline fault zone may merge with the northeastern margin of the Funeral Mountains (Blakely et al., 1999, p. 10).
2. Inferred movement along the zone appears to have been intermittent with long periods of inactivity. The fault system seems to have been active into late Oligocene time (ca. 25 Ma), then inactive until ca. 12.7 Ma, when it experienced activity during volcanism centered on this time; then another period of quiescence was followed by activity ca. 3.7 Ma. A 17 m.y. hiatus in extension-related movement along a 250-km-long fault system in the Walker Lane belt is an unusual lapse of activity.
3. An alternative interpretation of the geology (Snow, 1992, p. 94, 96; Snow and Prave, 1994, p. 713) projects the Striped Hills structure west to an anticlinal axis in the southern Funeral Mountains (Fig. 29), and shows no offset in folds and south-vergent structures spanning the inferred trace of the Amargosa Desert fault system. Exhumation ages and original burial depths, and the structural plunges of the Striped Hills and Bare Mountain, are too different to comply with an originally continuous Mesozoic structure (Stamatakos and Ferrill, 1998, p. 152).

4. Observations of vertical-axis rotation indicate it cannot always be interpreted as diagnostic of a discrete fault zone. For example, in the Tolicha Peak area near Black Mountain (Fig. 29), 13.7 Ma Grouse Canyon Tuff is rotated 10° to 30° clockwise, whereas the unconformably overlying Rainier Mesa Tuff is unrotated; 10 km southwest, Rainier Mesa Tuff is rotated 30° clockwise, whereas Ammonia Tanks Tuff and 9.4 Ma Thirsty Canyon Tuff are unrotated (Hudson et al., 1996). This temporal and spatial variability is incompatible with a fixed throughgoing fault. Furthermore, the vertical-axis rotation within the Crater Flat basin does not accommodate 25 km of dextral offset, nor do any of the post-Miocene features between Black Mountain and Stewart Valley account for any large dextral offset. A best-fit profile across the inferred shear zone in Crater Flat suggests that only 10 km of lateral offset could be accounted for by vertical-axis rotation (Stamatakos and Ferrill, 1998, p. 154). Evidence of possible Quaternary faulting in Amargosa Valley closest to Yucca Mountain is provided by a group of N.70°E.-trending lineaments and subdued scarps that are inferred to represent the extension of the left-lateral Rock Valley fault zone (Donovan, 1991).

5. Apparent north-striking right-lateral faults in northwestern Bare Mountain are actually pre-Miocene down-to-the-southeast normal faults that have been rotated out of their original attitudes and are located several kilometers west of the inferred Amargosa Desert fault system (Stamatakos and Ferrill, 1998, p. 152).

Other interpretations of Quaternary and late Tertiary strain phenomena suggest that Quaternary transcurrent features are more likely oriented oblique to the Walker Lane belt than along it. For example, Carr (1984, p. 30) related all of the basaltic extrusion later cited by Schweickert and Lahren (1997, p. 30) to the north-northeast-trending Death Valley-Pancake Range belt (Fig. 15), a zone of concentrated Quaternary faulting (Carr, 1984, p. 33), seismicity (Rogers et al., 1983, p. 4, 12), and basaltic volcanism that evolved largely in the past 6 m.y. (Crowe et al., 1995). Savage et al. (1995) documented the central Nevada seismic zone that cuts across the Walker Lane belt from the northern end of the eastern California shear zone (Fig. 1). Moderate to large earthquakes that have occurred within the zone (e.g., Pleasant Valley, Dixie Valley, Fairview Peak, and Cedar Mountain earthquakes) appear to be responses of individual faults to stress within a broad N.15°W.-trending shear zone rather than successive ruptures along a throughgoing fault. Savage et al. (1995, p. 20267) documented significant extensional strain across the central Nevada seismic zone (Fig. 1) but virtually no strain in the immediate vicinity of Yucca Mountain (Savage et al. 1995, p. 20266). These observations imply that long-term extensional strain leading to faulting is currently being concentrated along the eastern California shear zone and the central Nevada seismic zone rather than along a 250-km-long fault system within and subparallel to the Walker Lane belt.

SYNTHESIS AND CONCLUSIONS

The tectonic models that have been applied to Yucca Mountain, with exception of the caldera model of Carr (1984) and the planar fault model of Janssen and King (2000), are big-concept models that have been brought to bear on a locally complex and particular situation. These models have been widely applied to resolve tectonic problems at regional scales throughout the Great Basin. The extent to which these models work for Yucca Mountain reflects the extent that Yucca Mountain has been influenced by regional deformation; the extent to which these models fail reflects the fact that they were not designed to account for the peculiarities of the Crater Flat domain. In a sense, the problems cited herein highlight the shortcomings of any regional-scale conceptual model applied to a particular real-world case.

The Yucca Mountain project did not seek to formulate a unique model or to identify a "preferred" model for Yucca Mountain. The course of geology, however, inevitably tends toward formulating and refining a useful explanation that rationalizes all the facts and guides fruitful research. For example, no one maintains the fiction that the geosyncline model and the plate tectonics model are equally valid models for mountain building. It seems desirable—and perhaps inevitable—that a fully valid model for Yucca Mountain will be constructed from all the data at hand.

How might this be accomplished? Because Yucca Mountain site-characterization studies are substantially completed, no data surprises are likely to alter the known structural framework and geological history of the Crater Flat domain. Possibly the way to attain the "good model" is to consider what a group of geologists, selected on the basis of their knowledge of and expertise in the subject at hand, thought about the models described here when asked to evaluate them with respect to Probabilistic Volcanic Hazards Analysis (PVHA: CRWMS M&O, 1996) and Probabilistic Seismic Hazards Analysis (PSHA: Wong and Stepp, 1998). In PVHA the experts (Table 1) were asked individually to express an opinion on the relevance of tectonics to recurrence and spatial distribution of volcanic events with respect to their overall conceptual model(s) for the occurrence of volcanism in the Yucca Mountain region (including volcanic history, tectonic regime, magma dynamics, and sources).

TABLE 1. PROBABILISITIC VOLCANIC HAZARD ANALYSIS PANEL MEMBERS

Expert	Affiliation
Richard W. Carlson	Carnegie Institution of Washington
Bruce M. Crowe	Los Alamos National laboratory
Wendell A. Duffield	U.S. Geological Survey
Richard V. Fisher	University of California at Santa Barbara (emeritus)
William R. Hackett	WRH Associates
Mel A. Kuntz	U.S. Geological Survey
Alexander R. McBirney	University of Oregon (emeritus)
Michael F. Sheridan	State University of New York, Buffalo
George A. Thompson	Stanford University
George P.L. Walker	University of Hawaii

Not all the experts considered tectonism to be significant for basaltic volcanism. The PVHA experts (Table 1) who considered geological control of magma ascent formed two general camps of opinion: (1) location and timing of intrusion is a function of mantle petrogenesis (Carlson, Walker), and (2) location and timing of intrusion is controlled by crustal tectonics (Hackett, Kuntz, McBirney, Sheridan, Thompson). Most of the experts acknowledged that magma ascent is related to extension (Crowe, Fisher, Hackett, McBirney, Sheridan, Thompson), but only McBirney, Sheridan, and Thompson offered explicit statements on what might be called tectonic models. The model of choice among those who offered even general opinion clearly is that of a pull-apart basin controlled by local but deep-seated normal faults. Strike-slip faulting related to Walker Lane belt deformation was acknowledged as a possible factor (Crowe, McBirney), but strike-slip faulting alone was not acceded to be a control on magma ascent. No expert cited detachment faulting.

Evaluation of tectonic models in PSHA (Wong and Stepp, 1998) was more rigorous. The instructions required explicit consideration of tectonic models "Based on…data, a relative preference for…alternatives can be expressed by weights in the logic tree. A very strong preference for one alternative over the other (i.e., the data strongly support one interpretation over the other) usually is represented by weights such as 0.9 and 0.1. If there is no preference for either hypothesis (i.e., the data equally support either alternative), they are assigned equal weights (0.5 and 0.5 for two hypotheses)" (Wong and Stepp, 1998, p. 4–3). The teams (Table 2) were offered the models discussed in this report and a summary of the evaluations presented here and were required to rank models according to the likelihood that these models accounted for faulting at Yucca Mountain. The experts were allowed to modify or to combine the models in any way that addressed the issue of fault geometry and fault plane interrelations. The teams each identified a "preferred model" and one or more contingent models that might modify the action of the preferred model. The range of models is given in Table 2, with each team's assessment and ranking by weight.

The caldera model was not credible to any of the teams. Most teams considered the "lateral shear" model as two variants: (1) a transcurrent strike-slip fault along which Crater Flat basin is a right step, or (2) a more "diffuse Walker Lane" dextral shear that has exerted an asymmetric clockwise torque on Crater Flat basin. Most teams gave very low weight to the first variant (the Amargosa Desert fault system), and two teams gave it no credibility. The model was weighted by three teams in the interests of objectivity and completeness and because the model is based on "hidden" structures that could not be assessed. Thus, in the absence of falsification, there remains a remote possibility that the hidden structure exists in combination with detachment. It is this latter consideration that led team ASM (Table 2) to accord a weighting of 0.25 for the strike-slip model as a hidden component of a detachment model itself given a weighting of 0.15. Only two of the six teams entertained some component of dextral shear as part of their preferred model.

Detachment models were ranked slightly higher than lateral shear models. Team DFS considered detachment only as an adjunct to the lateral shear model: consideration of one required consideration of the other. Teams RYA and SBK (Table 2) emphasized that any possible detachment is aseismic and therefore relevant only to constraining widths of block-bounding faults.

The preferred or most credible model was the pure shear (planar fault) model (weighted 0.6–1.0). Only two of six teams emphasized some component of oblique dextral shear, and team RYA (Table 2) proposed a "coalescent fault" model that sees the planar fault model as an "end member" of that model. A planar fault model has numerous advantages: It does not need to import structure from outside the domainal boundaries; the boundaries are the model constraints. It accords with the fact that different shifts in tectonism have affected the Crater Flat domain with time. It also is compatible with the notion that the entire lithosphere has participated in extension, the different levels of strain and deformation style related to a layered lithosphere. It implicitly acknowledges that a large degree of randomness characterizes the Great Basin.

If Yucca Mountain is considered to be an evolving crustal entity, a simple way to describe it is that it is a slab of rock that is slowly and intermittently sliding into a deepening hole. Crater Flat basin therefore is interpreted to be the key to tectonic evolution of Yucca Mountain; as the basin widens and deepens sporadically, the Miocene volcanic section of Yucca Mountain subsides and extends basinward, incorporating a combination of down-to-basin faulting and mass movement. Yucca Mountain itself looks like an incipient slab slide, the toe controlled by the Bare Mountain fault and the surface faults possibly extending no more than a kilometer into the Paleozoic substrate. Yucca Mountain is a carapace, a cap of young (Miocene) strata on a much older, much more deformed basement. The basement has a stress history (including late Miocene hydration and/or heating) going back to continental margin deformation, which guides and conditions deformation of the overlying carapace. Therefore, the mapped faults are a subset of a larger, buried fault population relevant to seismicity, volcanism, and hydrology. Likewise, Crater Flat basin is not a simple hole: from east to west it resembles a trapdoor hinged along the Paintbrush Canyon fault; from north to south it resembles an asymmetric sag that deepens to the north. The strain pattern indicates that the basin is torqued clockwise by a northwest-directed shear couple broadly imposed by distributed shear within the Walker Lane belt. The Bare Mountain fault is essentially a local tear fault along the west side of the basin, one deep enough to affect the upper mantle. This simple tectonic summary has aspects that could support a fully developed tectonic model for Yucca Mountain:

- It explains the structural isolation of Yucca Mountain.
- It explains the character and progress of faulting across the mountain.
- It accounts for the local deformation, such as vertical axis rotation and Quaternary volcanism, within the broader context of extension within the Walker Lane belt.

TABLE 2. TECTONIC MODELS EVALUATED BY THE PROBABILISTIC SEISMIC HAZARD ANALYSIS EXPERT TEAMS

Teams	Caldera Model	Detachment model	Planar fault model	Lateral shear model
ASM	0.0	Ranked second (0.15); favored version has detachment at 6+ km depth.	"Greatest credibility" (0.6); foundation for preferred model variants of which are: 1. diffuse dextral shear, 2. rhombochasm.	Ranked third; relevant only in combination with detachment in which context it has a probability of 0.25.
AAR	0.0	Not credible alone, but in association with preferred model, it has a probability of 0.2.	Pull-apart with dextral shear couple (0.6).	0.05; for regional strike-slip fault included in detachment model.
DFS	0.0	Relevant only to the strike-slip fault model in which association has probability of 0.2.	"Domino model" preferred (0.8) modified by "diffuse" shear.	0.05
RYA	0.0	An "end member" of preferred "coalescent fault" model, but no seismic detachment.	An "end member" of preferred "coalescent fault" model.	0.0 ("unlikely fault geometry").
SBK	0.0	(0.01); no seismic detachment.	Oblique rift is preferred model (0.99) with "Walker Lane" lateral shear.	Transcurrent strike-slip has "extremely low weight" (0.001); regional dextral shear (0.01).
SDO	0.0	0.0	Preferred model (1.0) modified by distributed shear; basin cross fault has probability of 0.5.	0.0

Note: Each three-member team is identified by the first letter of each member's last name. Numbers in parentheses are weights assigned in logic trees to models (Youngs et al., 2003). 0.0 means no weight or probability was assigned.

- It provides insight into mechanisms and controls for local faulting and basaltic intrusion considered as potential hazards for a proposed nuclear waste repository at Yucca Mountain.

ACKNOWLEDGMENTS

C. J. Fridrich (USGS) was my able colleague through much of the site characterization work on the Yucca Mountain Project. Our many discussions of the tectonic development of Yucca Mountain helped form my critical approach to tectonic models, and his review of this paper greatly aided its presentation and corrected many errors. I thank R. Keefer (USGS) for his review and edit, for providing clarity and professional example. This report also benefited from discussions and field work over the years with Warren Hamilton (USGS), Silvio Pezzopane (USGS), F. William Simonds (USGS), Will Carr (USGS), John Stamatakos (Center for Nuclear Waste Regulatory Analyses), and Geoffrey King (Institut de Physique du Globe), all of whom helped my understanding of Great Basin tectonics.

REFERENCES CITED

Allmendinger, R.W., Hauge, T.A., Hauser, E.C., Potter, C.J., Klemperer, S.L., Nelson, K.D., Knuepfer, P.L.K., and Oliver, J., 1987, Overview of the COCORP 40°N transect, western United States—The fabric of an orogenic belt: Geological Society of America Bulletin, v. 98, no. 3, p. 308–319, doi: 10.1130/0016-7606(1987)98<308:OOTCNT>2.0.CO;2.

Anderson, R.E., 1973, Large-magnitude late Tertiary strike-slip faulting north of Lake Mead, Nevada: U.S. Geological Survey Professional Paper 794, 18 p.

Applegate, J.D.R., Walker, J.D., and Hodges, K.V., 1992, Late Cretaceous extensional unroofing in the Funeral Mountains metamorphic core complex, California: Geology, v. 20, p. 519–522, doi: 10.1130/0091-7613(1992)020<0519:LCEUIT>2.3.CO;2.

Arabasz, W.J., and Julander, D.R., 1986, Geometry of seismically active faults and crustal deformation within the Basin and Range Province, northeastern Nevada, *in* Mayer, L., ed., Extensional tectonics of the western United States—A perspective on processes and kinematics: Boulder, Colorado, Geological Society of America Special Paper 208, p. 43–74.

Axen, G.J., Taylor, W.J., and Bartley, J.M., 1993, Space-time patterns and tectonic controls of Tertiary extension and magmatism in the Great Basin of the western United States: Geological Society of America Bulletin, v. 105, p. 56–76, doi: 10.1130/0016-7606(1993)105<0056:STPATC>2.3.CO;2.

Bath, G.D., and Jahren, C.E., 1984, Interpretations of magnetic anomalies at a potential repository site located in the Yucca Mountain area, Nevada Test Site: U.S. Geological Survey Open-File Report 84-120, 40 p.

Bellier, O., and Zoback, M.L., 1995, Recent state of stress change in the Walker Lane zone, western Basin and Range province, United States: Tectonics, v. 14, no. 3, p. 564–593, doi: 10.1029/94TC00596.

Bennett, R.A., Davis, J.L., and Wernicke, B.P., 1999, Present-day pattern of Cordilleran deformation in the western United States: Geology, v. 27, no. 4, p. 371–374, doi: 10.1130/0091-7613(1999)027<0371:PDPOCD>2.3.CO;2.

Bennett, R.A., Wernicke, B.P., Niemi, N.A., and Friedrich, A.M., 2003, Contemporary strain rates in the northern Basin and Range province from GPS data: Tectonics, v. 22, no. 2, p. 3–1 – 3–31.

Best, M.G., Christiansen, E.H., Denio, A.L., Gromme, C.S., McKee, E.H., and Noble, D.C., 1989, Eocene through Miocene volcanism in the Great Basin of the western United States: New Mexico Bureau of Mines and Mineral Resources Memoir, v. 47, p. 91–133.

Biasi, G.P., 2000, Constraints on Basin and Range extensional timing and style from tomographic imaging in southern Nevada: Seismological Research Letters, v. 71, no. 1, p. 214.

Blakely, R.J., and Ponce, D.A., 2001, Map showing depth to Pre-Cenozoic basement in the Death Valley ground-water model area, Nevada and California: U.S. Geological Survey Miscellaneous Field Studies Map MF-2381-E, scale 1:250,000.

Blakely, R.J., Jachens, R.C., Calzia, J.P., and Langenheim, V.E., 1999, Cenozoic basins of the Death Valley region as reflected in regional-scale gravity anomalies, *in* Wright, L.A., and Troxel, B.W., eds., Cenozoic basins of the Death Valley region: Boulder, Colorado, Geological society of America Special Paper 333, p. 1–16.

Bourne, S.J., England, P.C., and Parsons, B., 1998, The motion of crustal blocks driven by flow of the lower lithosphere and implications for slip rates of continental strike-slip faults: Nature, v. 391, p. 655–659, doi: 10.1038/35556.

Bradshaw, G.A., and Zoback, M.D., 1988, Listric normal faulting, stress refraction, and the state of stress in the Gulf Coast basin: Geology, v. 16, p. 271–274, doi: 10.1130/0091-7613(1988)016<0271:LNFSRA>2.3.CO;2.

Bradshaw, T.K., Hawkesworth, C.J., and Gallagher, K., 1993, Basaltic volcanism in the southern Basin and Range—No role for a mantle plume: Earth and Planetary Science Letters, v. 116, p. 45–62, doi: 10.1016/0012-821X(93)90044-A.

Brocher, T.M., and Hunter, W.C., 1996, Seismic reflection evidence against a shallow detachment beneath Yucca Mountain, Nevada, *in* High-Level Radioactive Waste Management Proceedings of the Seventh International Conference, Las Vegas, Nevada, p. 148–150.

Brocher, T.M., Carr, M.D., Fox, K.F., Jr., and Hart, P.E., 1993, Seismic reflection profiling across Tertiary extensional structures in the eastern Amargosa Desert, southern Nevada, Basin and Range province: Geological Society of America Bulletin, v. 105, p. 30–46, doi: 10.1130/0016-7606(1993)105<0030:SRPATE>2.3.CO;2.

Brocher, T.M., Hart, P.E., Hunter, W.C., and Langenheim, V.E., 1996, Hybrid-source seismic reflection profiling across Yucca Mountain, Nevada—Regional lines 2 and 3: U.S. Geological Survey Open-File Report 96-28, 110 p.

Brocher, T.M., Hunter, W.C., and Langenheim, V.E., 1998, Implications of seismic reflection and potential field geophysical data on the structural framework of the Yucca Mountain–Crater Flat region, Nevada: Geological Society of America Bulletin, v. 110, no. 8, p. 947–971, doi: 10.1130/0016-7606(1998)110<0947:IOSRAP>2.3.CO;2.

Broxton, D.E., Warren, R.G., and Byers, F.M., 1989, Chemical and mineralogic trends within the Timber Mountain–Oasis Valley caldera complex, Nevada—Evidence for multiple cycles of chemical evolution in a long-lived silicic magma system: Journal of Geophysical Research, v. 94, no. B5, p. 5961–5985.

Brun, J.-P., Sokoutis, D., and Van Den Driessche, J., 1994, Analogue modeling of detachment fault systems and core complexes: Geology, v. 22, p. 319–322, doi: 10.1130/0091-7613(1994)022<0319:AMODFS>2.3.CO;2.

Burchfiel, B.C., 1965, Structural geology of the Specter Range quadrangle, Nevada, and its regional significance: Geological Society of America Bulletin, v. 76, p. 175–192.

Burchfiel, B.C., and Stewart, J.H., 1966, Pull-apart origin of the central segment of Death Valley, California: Geological Society of America Bulletin, v. 77, p. 439–442.

Burchfiel, B.C., Cowan, D.S., and Davis, G.A., 1992, Tectonic overview of the Cordilleran Orogen in the western United States, *in* Burchfiel, B.C., Lipman, P.W., and Zoback, M.L., eds., The Cordilleran Orogen: Conterminous U.S.: Boulder, Colorado, Geological Society of America, The Geology of North America, v. G-3, p. 407–480.

Byers, F.M., Jr., Carr, W.J., Christiansen, R.L., Lipman, P.W., Orkild, P.P., and Quinlivan, W.D., 1976, Geologic map of the Timber Mountain caldera area, Nye County, Nevada: U.S. Geological Survey Miscellaneous Investigations Series Map I-891, scale 1:48,000.

Carr, M.D., Waddell, S.J., Vick, G.S., Stock, J.M., Monsen, S.A., Harris, A.G., Cork, B.W., and Byers, F.M.J., 1986, Geology of drill hole UE25 p#1—A test hole into pre-Tertiary rocks near Yucca Mountain, southern Nevada: U.S. Geological Survey Open-File Report 86-175, 87 p.

Carr, W.J., 1974, Summary of tectonic and structural evidence for stress orientation at the Nevada Test Site: U.S. Geological Survey Open-File Report 74-176, 53 p.

Carr, W.J., 1982, Volcano-tectonic history of Crater Flat, southwestern Nevada, as suggested by new evidence from drill hole USW-VH-1: U.S. Geological Survey Open-File Report 82-457, 23 p.

Carr, W.J., 1984, Regional structural setting of Yucca Mountain, southwestern Nevada, and late Cenozoic rates of tectonic activity in part of the South-

western Great Basin, Nevada and California: U.S. Geological Survey Open-File Report 84-854, 109 p.

Carr, W.J., 1988, Volcano-tectonic setting of Yucca Mountain and Crater Flat, southwestern Nevada: U.S. Geological Survey Bulletin 1790, p. 35–85.

Carr, W.J., 1990, Styles of extension in the Nevada Test Site region, southern Walker Lane Belt—An integration of volcano-tectonic and detachment fault models, *in* Wernicke, B.P., ed., Basin and Range extensional tectonics near the latitude of Las Vegas, Nevada: Boulder, Colorado, Geological Society of America Memoir 176, p. 283–303.

Carr, W.J., and Parrish, L.D., 1985, Geology of drill hole USW-VH-2, and structure of Crater Flat, southwestern Nevada: U.S. Geological Survey Open-File Report 85-475, 41 p.

Carr, W.J., Byers, F.M.J., and Orkild, P.P., 1984, Stratigraphic and volcano-tectonic relations of Crater Flat Tuff and some older volcanic units, Nye County, Nevada: U.S. Geological Survey Open-File Report 84-114, 42 p.

Carr, W.J., Byers, F.M.J., and Orkild, P.P., 1986, Stratigraphic and volcano-tectonic relations of Crater Flat Tuff and some older volcanic units, Nye County, Nevada: U.S. Geological Survey Professional Paper 1323, 28 p.

Carr, W.J., Grow, J.A., and Keller, S.M., 1995, Lithologic and geophysical logs of drill holes Felderhoff Federal 5-1 and 25-1, Amargosa Desert, Nye County, Nevada, U.S. Geological Survey Open-File Report 95-155, 14 p.

Caskey, S.J., and Schweickert, R.A., 1992, Mesozoic deformation in the Nevada Test Site and vicinity—Implications for the structural framework of the Cordilleran fold and thrust belt and Tertiary extension north of Las Vegas Valley: Tectonics, v. 11, no. 6, p. 1314–1331.

Catchings, R.D., and Mooney, W.D., 1991, Basin and range crustal and upper mantle structure, northwest to central Nevada: Journal of Geophysical Research, v. 96, p. 6247–6267.

Christiansen, R.L., and Lipman, P.W., 1965, Geologic map of the Topopah Spring NW quadrangle, Nye County, Nevada: U.S. Geological Survey Quadrangle Map GQ-444, scale 1:24,000.

Connor, C.B., Stamatakos, J.A., Ferrill, D.A., Hill, B.E., Ofoegbu, G.I., Conway, F.M., Sagar, B., and Trapp, J., 2000, Geologic factors controlling patterns of small-volume basaltic volcanism: application to a volcanic hazards assessment at Yucca Mountain, Nevada: Journal of Geophysical Research, v. 105, no. 1, p. 417–432, doi: 10.1029/1999JB900353.

Crowe, B.M., 1990, Basaltic volcanic episodes of the Yucca Mountain region—High level radioactive waste management, Volume 1: American Nuclear Society, p. 65–73.

Crowe, B.M., and Perry, F.V., 1989, Volcanic probability calculations for the Yucca Mountain site—Estimation of volcanic rates: Proceedings, Nuclear Waste Isolation in the Unsaturated Zone, Focus '89, American Nuclear Society, p. 326–334.

Crowe, B.M., Vaniman, D.T., and Carr, W.J., 1983, Status of volcanic hazard studies for the Nevada nuclear waste storage investigations: Los Alamos National Laboratory, LA-9325-MS, 47 p.

Crowe, B., Perry, F., Geissman, J., McFadden, L., Wells, S., Murrell, M., Poths, J., Valentine, G.A., Bowker, L., and Finnegan, K., 1995, Status of volcanism studies for the Yucca Mountain Site Characterization Project: Los Alamos National Laboratory, LA-12908-MS, UC-802.

Civilian Radioactive Waste Management System Management & Operating Contractor, 1996, Probabilistic volcanic hazard analysis for Yucca Mountain, Nevada: BA0000000 -01717-2200-00082 REV 0. Las Vegas, Nevada. Prepared for U.S. Department of Energy, Yucca Mountain Site Characterization Project. Accessed online January 9, 2007, at http://www.lsnnet.gov/. Search on Participant number MOL.19971201.0221.

Davis, G.A., and Lister, G.S., 1988, Detachment faulting in continental extension; perspectives from the southwestern U.S. Cordillera, *in* Clark, S.P.J., et al., ed., Processes in continental lithospheric deformation, Boulder, Colorado: Geological Society of America Special Paper 218, p. 133–159.

Day, W.D., Dickerson, R.P., Potter, C.J., Sweetkind, D.S., San Juan, C.A., Drake, R.M., II, and Fridrich, C.J., 1998, Bedrock geologic map of the Yucca Mountain area, Nye County, Nevada: U.S. Geological Survey Geologic Investigations Series I-2627, 21 p., scale 24,000.

Dokka, R.K., 1989, The Mojave extensional belt of southern California: Tectonics, v. 8, no. 2, p. 363–390.

Donovan, D.E., 1991, Neotectonics of the southern Amargosa Desert, Nye County, Nevada and Inyo County, California [Master's thesis]: Reno, University of Nevada, 151 p.

Doser, D.I., and Smith, R.B., 1989, An assessment of source parameters of earthquakes in the Cordillera of the western United States: Seismological Society of America Bulletin, v. 79, p. 1383–1409.

Eaton, G.P., 1984, The Miocene Great Basin of western North America as an extending back-arc region: Tectonophysics, v. 102, p. 275–295, doi: 10.1016/0040-1951(84)90017-9.

Eaton, G.P., Wahl, R.R., Prostka, H.J., Mabey, D.R., and Klienkopf, M.D., 1978, Regional gravity and tectonic patterns—Their relation to late Cenozoic epeirogeny and lateral spreading in the western Cordillera, in Smith, R.B., and Eaton, G.P., eds., Cenozoic tectonics and regional geophysics of the western Cordillera: Geological Society of America Memoir 152, p. 51–91.

Farmer, G.L., Perry, F.V., Semken, S., Crowe, B., Cirtos, D., and DePaolo, D.J., 1989, Isotopic evidence of the structure and origin of subcontinental lithospheric mantle in southern Nevada: Journal of Geophysical Research, v. 94, p. 7885–7898.

Ferguson, J.F., Cogbill, A.H., and Warren, R.G., 1994, A geophysical-geological transect of the Silent Canyon caldera complex, Pahute Mesa, Nevada: Journal of Geophysical Research, v. 99, no. B3, p. 4323–4339, doi: 10.1029/93JB02447.

Ferrill, D.A., Stamatakos, J.A., and Simms, D., 1999, Normal fault corrugation—Implications for growth and seismicity of active normal faults: Journal of Structural Geology, v. 21, p. 1027–1038, doi: 10.1016/S0191-8141(99)00017-6.

Ferrill, D.A., Stirewalt, G.L., Henderson, D.B., Stamatakos, J.A., Morris, A.P., Spivey, K.H., and Wernicke, B.P., 1996, Faulting in the Yucca Mountain region: Critical review and analyses of tectonic data from the central Basin and Range: Washington D.C., U.S. Nuclear Regulatory Commission, NUREG/CR-6401.

Fitton, J.G., James, D., and Leeman, W.P., 1991, Basic magmatism associated with late Cenozoic extension in the western United States—Composition variations in space and time: Journal of Geophysical Research, v. 96, no. B8, p. 13693–13711.

Fleck, R.J., Turrin, B.D., Sawyer, D.A., Warren, R.G., Champion, D.E., Hudson, M.R., and Minor, S.A., 1996, Age and character of basaltic rocks of the Yucca Mountain region, southern Nevada: Journal of Geophysical Research, v. 101, no. B4, p. 8205–8227, doi: 10.1029/95JB03123.

Flesch, L.M., Holt, W.E., Haines, A.J., and Shen-Tu, B., 2000, Dynamics of the Pacific-North American plate boundary in the western United States: Science, v. 287, p. 834–836, doi: 10.1126/science.287.5454.834.

Fox, K.F., Jr., and Carr, M.D., 1989, Neotectonics and volcanism at Yucca Mountain and vicinity, Nevada: Radioactive Waste Management and the Nuclear Fuel Cycle, v. 13, no. 1–4, p. 37–50.

Fridrich, C.J., 1998, Tectonic evolution of the Crater Flat basin, Yucca Mountain region, Nevada: U.S. Geological Survey Open-File Report 98-33, 43 p.

Fridrich, C.J., 1999, Tectonic evolution of the Crater Flat basin, Yucca Mountain region, Nevada, in Wright, L.A., and Troxel, B.W., eds., Cenozoic Basins of the Death Valley region: Boulder, Colorado, Geological Society of America Special Paper 333, p. 169–195.

Fridrich, C.J., Whitney, J.W., Hudson, M.R., and Crowe, B.M., 1999, Space-time patterns of late Cenozoic extension, vertical axis rotation, and volcanism in the Crater Flat basin, southwest Nevada, in Wright, L.A., and Troxel, B.W., eds., Cenozoic Basins of the Death Valley Region: Boulder, Colorado, Geological Society of America 333, p. 197–212.

Frizzell, V.A., Jr., and Shulters, J., 1990, Geologic map of the Nevada Test Site, southern Nevada: U.S. Geological Survey Miscellaneous Investigations Series Map I-2046, scale 1:100,000.

Gan, W., Svarc, J.L., Savage, J.C., and Prescott, W.H., 2000, Strain accumulation across the eastern California shear zone at latitude 36°30□N: Journal of Geophysical Research, v. 105, no. B7, p. 16229–16236, doi: 10.1029/2000JB900105.

Gans, P.B., 1987, An open-system, two-layer crustal stretching model for the eastern Great Basin: Tectonics, v. 6, p. 1–12.

Gans, P.B., Mahood, G.A., and Schermer, E., 1989, Synextensional magmatism in the Basin and Range province—A case study from the eastern Great Basin: Boulder, Colorado, Geological Society of America Special Paper 233, 53 p.

Gilbert, G.K., 1928, Studies of basin-range structure: U.S. Geological Survey Professional Paper 153, 92 p.

Gourmelen, N., and Amelung, F., 2005, Postseismic mantle relaxation in the central Nevada seismic belt: Science, v. 310, p. 1473–1476, doi: 10.1126/science.1119798.

Gross, W.W., and Hillemeyer, F.L., 1982, Geometric analysis of upper-plate fault patterns in the Whipple-Buckskin detachment terrane, California and Arizona, in Frost, E.G., and Martin, D.L., eds., Mesozoic-Cenozoic tectonic evolution of the Colorado River region, California, Arizona, and Nevada: San Diego, California, Cordilleran Publishers, p. 257–265.

Guth, P.L., 1981, Tertiary extension north of the Las Vegas Valley shear zone, Sheep and Desert Ranges, Clark County, Nevada: Geological Society of America Bulletin, v. 92, no. 10, p. 763–771.

Hagstrom, J.T., and Gans, P.B., 1989, Paleomagnetism of the Oligocene Kalamazoo Tuff: Implications for middle Tertiary extension in east central Nevada: Journal of Geophysical Research, v. 94, p. 1827–1842.

Hamilton, W.B., 1982, Structural evolution of the Big Maria Mountains, northeastern Riverside County, southeastern California, in Frost, E.G., and Marin, D.L., eds., Mesozoic-Cenozoic tectonic evolution of the Colorado River region, California, Arizona, and Nevada: San Diego, California, Cordilleran Publishers, p. 1–27.

Hamilton, W., 1987, Crustal extension in the Basin and Range Province, southwestern United States, in Coward, M.P., Dewey, J.F., and Hancock, P.L., eds., Continental extensional tectonics: Geological Society [London] Special Publication 28, p. 155–176.

Hamilton, W.B., 1988a, Detachment faulting in the Death Valley region, California and Nevada: U.S. Geological Survey Bulletin 1790, p. 51–85.

Hamilton, W.B., 1988b, Death Valley tectonics—Hingeline between active and inactivated parts of a rising and flattening master normal fault, in Gregory, J.L., and Baldwin, E.J., eds., Geology of the Death Valley region: Santa Ana, California, South Coast Geological Society, p. 179–205.

Hardyman, R.F., 1978, Volcanic stratigraphy and structural geology of the Gillis Canyon quadrangle, northern Gillis Range, Mineral County, Nevada [Ph.D. dissertation thesis]: Reno, University of Nevada, 248 p.

Hardyman, R.F., and Oldow, J.S., 1991, Tertiary tectonic framework and Cenozoic history of the central Walker Lane, Nevada, in Raines, G.L., Lisle, R.E., Schafer, R.W., and Wilkinson, W.H., eds., Geology and ore deposits of the Great Basin: Geological Society of Nevada Symposium Proceedings, Reno, Nevada, 1–5 April 1990, v. 1, p. 279–301.

Harmsen, S.C., and Bufe, C.G., 1992, Seismicity and focal mechanisms for the southern Great Basin of Nevada and California: 1987 through 1989: U.S. Geological Survey Open-File Report 91-572, p. 208.

Harmsen, S.C., and Rogers, A.M., 1986, Inferences about the local stress field from focal mechanisms: applications to earthquakes in the southern Great Basin of Nevada: Bulletin of the Seismological Society of America, v. 76, p. 1560–1572.

Healey, D.L., 1968, Application of gravity data to geologic problems at Nevada Test Site, in Eckel, E.B., ed., Nevada Test Site: Boulder, Colorado, Geological Society of America Memoir 110, p. 65–74.

Healey, D.L., Harris, R.N., Ponce, D.A., and Oliver, H.W., 1987, Complete bouguer gravity map of the Nevada Test Site and vicinity, Nevada: U.S. Geological Survey Open-File Report 87-506, scale 1: 100,000.

Heizler, M.T., Perry, F.V., Crowe, B.M., Peters, L., and Appelt, R., 1999, The Age of Lathrop Wells volcanic center—An ^{40}Ar/^{39}Ar dating investigation: Journal of Geophysical Research, v. 104, no. B1, p. 767–804, doi: 10.1029/1998JB900002.

Hinrichs, E.N., 1968, Geologic map of the Camp Desert Rock quadrangle, Nye County, Nevada: U.S. Geological Survey Geologic Quadrangle Map GQ-726, scale 1:24,000.

Hoffard, J.L., 1991, Quaternary tectonics and basin history of Pahrump and Stewart Valleys, Nevada and California [Master's thesis]: Reno, University of Nevada, 138 p.

Hoisch, T.D., and Simpson, C., 1993, Rise and tilt of metamorphic rocks in the lower plate of a detachment fault in the Funeral Mountains, Death Valley, California: Journal of Geophysical Research, v. 98, no. B4, p. 6805–6827.

Hoisch, T.D., Heizler, M.T., and Zartman, R.E., 1997, Timing of detachment faulting in the Bullfrog Hills and Bare Mountain area, southwest Nevada: inferences from ^{40}Ar/^{39}Ar, K-Ar, U-Pb and fission-track thermochronology: Journal of Geophysical Research, v. 102, no. B2, p. 2815–2833, doi: 10.1029/96JB03220.

Howard, K.A., and John, B.E., 1987, Crustal extension along a rooted system of low-angle normal faults—Colorado River extensional corridor, California and Arizona, in Coward, M.P., Dewey, J.F., and Hancock, P.L., eds., Continental extensional tectonics: Geological Society of London Special Paper 28, p. 299–312.

Hudson, M.R., and Rosenbaum, J.G., 1994, Broad transfer zones—Examples of vertical-axis rotation and discontinuous faulting in the Great Basin: GSA Abstracts with Programs, v. 26, no. 2, p. 61.

Hudson, M.R., Sawyer, D.A., and Warren, R.G., 1994, Paleomagnetism and rotation constraints for the middle Miocene southwestern Nevada volcanic field: Tectonics, v. 13, no. 2, p. 258–277, doi: 10.1029/93TC03189.

Hudson, M.R., Minor, S.A., and Fridrich, C.J., 1996, The distribution, timing, and character of steep-axis rotations in a broad zone of dextral shear in southwestern Nevada: Geological Society of America Abstracts with Programs, v. 28, no. 7, p. A-451.

Humphreys, E.D., 2000, Two fundamental causes of Great Basin deformation: Geological Society of America Abstracts with Programs, v. 32, no. 7, p. A-461.

Jackson, J.A., and White, N.J., 1989, Normal faulting in the upper continental crust—Observations from regions of active extension: Journal of Structural Geology, v. 11, p. 15–36, doi: 10.1016/0191-8141(89)90033-3.

Janssen, B., and King, G., 2000, Tectonic modeling of Yucca Mountain, Chapter N, *in* Whitney, J.W., and Keefer, W.R., eds., Geologic and geophysical characterization studies of Yucca Mountain, Nevada, a potential high-level radioactive-waste repository: U.S. Geological Survey Digital Data Series DDS-058, p. 1–18.

Jones, C.H., Wernicke, B.P., Farmer, G.L., Walker, J.D., Coleman, D.S., McKenna, L.W., and Perry, F.V., 1992, Variations across and along a major continental rift—An interdisciplinary study of the Basin and Range Province, western USA: Tectonophysics, v. 213, p. 57–96, doi: 10.1016/0040-1951(92)90252-2.

Keefer, W.R., Whitney, J.W., and Buesch, D.C., 2007, this volume, Geology of the Yucca Mountain site area, southwestern Nevada, *in* Stuckless, J.S., and Levich, R.A., eds., The Geology and Climatology of Yucca Mountain and Vicinity, Southern Nevada and California: Geological Society of America Memoir 199, doi: 10.1130/2007.1199(03).

King, G., Oppenheimer, D., and Amelung, F., 1994, Block versus continuum deformation in the western United States: Earth and Planetary Science Letters, v. 128, p. 55–64, doi: 10.1016/0012-821X(94)90134-1.

Kligfield, R., Crespi, J., Naruk, S., and Davis, G.H., 1984, Displacement and strain patterns of extensional orogens: Tectonics, v. 3, p. 577–609.

Lamb, S.H., 1994, Behavior of the brittle crust in wide plate boundary zones: Journal of Geophysical Research, v. 99, no. B3, p. 4457–4483, doi: 10.1029/93JB02574.

Langenheim, V.E., 2000, Constraints on the structure of Crater Flat, southwest Nevada, derived from gravity and magnetic data, Chapter C, *in* Whitney, J.W., and Keefer, W.R., Geologic and geophysical characterization studies of Yucca Mountain, Nevada, a potential high-level radioactive-waste repository: U.S. Geological Survey Digital Data Series DDS-058, 11 p.

Langenheim, V.E., and Ponce, D.A., 1995, Ground magnetic studies along a regional seismic-reflection profile across Bare Mountain, Crater Flat and Yucca Mountain, Nevada: U.S. Geological Survey Open-File Report 95-834, 36 p.

Langenheim, V.E., Ponce, D.A., Oliver, H.W., and Sikora, R.F., 1993, Gravity and magnetic study of Yucca Wash, southwest Nevada: U.S. Geological Survey Open-File Report 93-586-A, 14 p.

LeBas, M.J., LeMaitre, R.W., Streckeisen, A., and Zanettin, B., 1986, A chemical classification of volcanic rocks based on the total alkali-silica diagram: Journal of Petrology, v. 27, no. 3, p. 745–750.

Lister, G.S., and Davis, G.A., 1989, The origin of metamorphic core complexes and detachment faults formed during Tertiary continental extension in the northern Colorado River region, U.S.A: Journal of Structural Geology, v. 11, p. 65–94, doi: 10.1016/0191-8141(89)90036-9.

Liu, M., 2001, Cenozoic extension and magmatism in the North American Cordillera—The role of gravitational collapse: Tectonophysics, v. 342, p. 407–433, doi: 10.1016/S0040-1951(01)00173-1.

Majer, E., Feighner, M., Johnson, L., Daley, T., Karageorgi, E., Lee, K.H., Kaelin, B., Williams, K., and McEvilly, T., 1996, Synthesis of borehole and surface geophysical studies at Yucca Mountain, Nevada and vicinity, Volume I: Surface geophysics: Berkeley, California, Lawrence Berkeley National Laboratory Report UCID-39319.

Maldonado, F., 1985, Geologic map of the Jackass Flats area, Nye County, Nevada: U.U. Geological Survey Miscellaneous Investigations Series Map I-1519, scale 1:48,000.

Mankinen, E.A., Hildenbrand, T.G., Fridrich, C.J., McKee, E.H., and Schenkel, C.J., 2003, Geophysical setting of the Pahute Mesa-Oasis Valley region, southern Nevada: Nevada Bureau of Mines and Geology Report 50, Mackay School of Mines, University of Nevada Reno, Nevada, 45 p.

McCafferty, A.E., and Grauch, V.J.S., 1997, Aeromagnetic and gravity anomaly maps of the southwestern Nevada volcanic field, Nevada and California: U.S. Geological Survey Geophysical Investigations Map GP-1015, scale 1:250,000.

McClay, K.R., and Ellis, P.G., 1987, Geometries of extensional fault systems developed in model experiments: Geology, v. 15, p. 341–344, doi:

10.1130/0091-7613(1987)15<341:GOEFSD>2.0.CO;2.

McKague, H.L., Stamatakos, J.A., and Ferrill, D.A., 1996, Type I faults in the Yucca Mountain region: San Antonio, Texas, Center for Nuclear Waste Regulatory Analyses CNWRA 96-007, Rev. 1.

McKay, E.J., and Sargent, K.A., 1970, Geologic map of the Lathrop Wells quadrangle, Nye County, Nevada: U.S. Geological Survey Geologic Quadrangle Map GQ-883, scale 1:24,000.

McKee, E.H., 1983, Reset K-Ar ages: Evidence for three metamorphic core complexes, western Nevada: Isochron/West, v. 38, p. 17–20.

McKee, E.H., Hildenbrand, T.G., Anderson, M.L., Rowley, P.D., and Sawyer, D.A., 1999, The Silent Canyon caldera complex—A three-dimensional model based on drill-hole stratigraphy and gravity inversion: U.S. Geological Survey Open-File Report 99-555, 79 p.

Minor, S.A., 1995, Superposed local and regional paleostresses—Fault-slip analysis of Neogene extensional faulting near coeval caldera complexes, Yucca Flat, Nevada: Journal of Geophysical Research, v. 100, no. B6, p. 10507–10528, doi: 10.1029/95JB00078.

Minor, S.A., Hudson, M.R., and Fridrich, C.J., 1997, Fault-slip data, paleomagnetic data, and paleostress analyses bearing on the Neogene tectonic evolution of northern Crater Flat basin, Nevada: U.S. Geological Survey Open-File Report 97-285, 41 p.

Minor, S.A., and 12 others, 1993, Preliminary geologic map of the Pahute Mesa 30'x60' quadrangle, Nevada: U.S. Geological Survey Open-File Report 93-299, 39 p., scale 1:250,000.

Minster, J.B., and Jordan, T.H., 1987, Vector constraints on western U.S. deformation from space geodesy, neotectonics, and plate motion: Journal of Geophysical Research, v. 92, p. 4798–4804.

Myers, W.B., 1987, Detachment of Tertiary strata from their Paleozoic floor near Mercury, Nevada: Geological Society of America Abstracts with Programs, v. 19, p. 783.

Noble, D.C., 1972, Some observations on the Cenozoic volcano-tectonic evolution of the Great Basin, Western United States: Earth and Planetary Science Letters, v. 17, p. 142–150, doi: 10.1016/0012-821X(72)90269-5.

O'Leary, D.W., Mankinen, E.A., Blakely, R.J., Langenheim, V.E., and Ponce, D.A., 2002, Aeromagnetic expression of buried basaltic volcanoes near Yucca Mountain, Nevada: U.S. Geological Survey Open-File Report 02-020, 52 p.

Ofoegbu, G.I., and Ferrill, D.A., 1998, Mechanical analyses of listric normal faulting with emphasis on seismicity assessment: Tectonophysics, v. 284, p. 65–77, doi: 10.1016/S0040-1951(97)00168-6.

Oliver, H.W., and Fox, K.F., 1993, Structure of Crater Flat and Yucca Mountain, southeastern Nevada, as interpreted from gravity data, *in* High level radioactive waste management: Proceedings of the Fourth Annual International Conference, Las Vegas, Nevada, 26–30 April 1993, American Nuclear Society, Inc., La Grange Park, Illinois, v. 2, p. 1812–1817.

Pezzopane, S.K., Carande, R.E., and Smith, K.D., 1999, Preliminary surface displacement of the 1992 Little Skull Mountain earthquake measured by satellite radar interferometry for the Yucca Mountain region, Nevada: Eos (Transactions, American Geophysical Union), Spring Meeting 80, v. 80, no. 17, p. S1.

Potter, C.J., Dickerson, R.P., Sweetkind, D.S., Drake, R.M.I., Taylor, E.M., Fridrich, C.J., San Juan, C.A., and Day, W.C., 2002, Geologic map of the Yucca Mountain region, Nye County, Nevada: U.S. Geological Survey Geologic Investigations Series I-2755, scale 1:50,000.

Rogers, A.M., Harmsen, S.C., Carr, W.J., and Spence, W., 1983, Southern Great Basin seismological data report for 1981 and preliminary data analysis: U.S. Geological Survey Open-File Report 83-669, p. 240, one plate.

Rogers, A.M., Harmsen, S.C., Corbett, E.J., Priestley, K., and dePolo, D., 1991, The seismicity of Nevada and some adjacent parts of the Great Basin, *in* Slemmons, D.B., Engdahl, E.R., Zoback, M.D., and Blackwell, D.D., eds., Neotectonics of North America: Boulder, Geological Society of America, Continent-Scale Maps of North America, Decade Map Volume, p. 153–184.

Rogers, N.W., Hawkesworth, C.J., and Ormerod, D.S., 1995, Late Cenozoic basaltic magmatism in the western Great Basin, California and Nevada: Journal of Geophysical Research, v. 100, no. B7, p. 10287–10301, doi: 10.1029/94JB02738.

Rosenbaum, J.G., Hudson, M.R., and Scott, R.B., 1991, Paleomagnetic constraints on the geometry and timing of deformation at Yucca Mountain, Nevada: Journal of Geophysical Research, v. 96, no. B2, p. 1963–1979.

Saltus, R.W., and Thompson, G.A., 1995, Why is it downhill from Tonopah to Las Vegas?—A case for mantle plume support of the high northern Basin and Range: Tectonics, v. 14, no. 6, p. 1235–1244, doi: 10.1029/95TC02288.

Sass, J.H., Dudley, W.W., Jr., and Lachenbruch, A.H., 1995, Chapter 8—Regional thermal setting, *in* Oliver, H.W., Ponce, D.A., and Hunter, W.C., eds., Major results of regional geophysical investigations of Yucca Mountain and vicinity, Nevada: U.S. Geological Survey Open-File Report 95-74, p. 199–218.

Sauber, J., 1989, Geodetic measurement of deformation in California: Washington D.C., NASA Technical Memoir 100732, 211 p.

Savage, J.C., 1998, Detecting strain in the Yucca Mountain area, Nevada: Science, v. 282, p. 1007, doi: 10.1126/science.282.5391.1007b.

Savage, J.C., Lisowski, M., Gross, W.K., King, N.E., and Svarc, J.L., 1994, Strain accumulation near Yucca Mountain, Nevada, 1983–1993: Journal of Geophysical Research, v. 99, no. B9, p. 18103–18107, doi: 10.1029/94JB01551.

Savage, J.C., Lisowski, M., Svarc, J.L., and Gross, W.K., 1995, Strain accumulation across the central Nevada seismic zone, 1973–1994: Journal of Geophysical Research, v. 100, no. B10, p. 20257–20269, doi: 10.1029/95JB01872.

Savage, J.C., Svarc, J.L., and Prescott, W.H., 1999, Strain accumulation at Yucca Mountain, Nevada: Journal of Geophysical Research, v. 104, no. B8, p. 17625–17631.

Savage, J.C., Svarc, J.L., and Prescott, W.H., 2001, Strain accumulation near Yucca Mountain, Nevada, 1993–1998: Journal of Geological Research, v. 106, no. B8, p. 16483–16488.

Sawyer, D.A., Fleck, R.J., Lanphere, M.A., Warren, R.G., Broxton, D.E., and Hudson, M.R., 1994, Episodic caldera volcanism in the Miocene southwestern Nevada volcanic field—Revised stratigraphic framework, $^{40}Ar/^{39}Ar$ geochronology, and implications for magmatism and extension: Geological Society of America Bulletin, v. 106, p. 1304–1318, doi: 10.1130/0016-7606(1994)106<1304:ECVITM>2.3.CO;2.

Scholz, C.H., Barazangi, M., and Sbar, M.L., 1971, Late Cenozoic evolution of the Great Basin, Western United States, as an ensialic interarc basin: Geological Society of America Bulletin, v. 82, p. 2979–2990.

Schweickert, R.A., and Lahren, M.M., 1994, Amargosa fault system near Yucca Mountain, Nevada: Geological Society of America Abstracts with Programs, v. 26, no. 7, p. A250.

Schweickert, R.A., and Lahren, M.M., 1997, Strike-slip fault system in Amargosa Valley and Yucca Mountain, Nevada: Tectonophysics, v. 272, no. 1, p. 25–42, doi: 10.1016/S0040-1951(96)00274-0.

Scott, R.B., 1986, Extensional tectonics at Yucca Mountain, southern Nevada: Geological Society of America Abstracts with Programs, Rocky Mountain Section, v. 18, no. 5, p. 411.

Scott, R.B., 1990, Tectonic setting of Yucca Mountain, southwest Nevada, *in* Wernicke, B.P., ed., Basin and Range extensional tectonics near the latitude of Las Vegas, Nevada: Boulder, Colorado, Geological Society of America Memoir 176, p. 251–282.

Scott, R.B., and Bonk, J., 1984, Preliminary geologic map of Yucca Mountain, Nye County, Nevada with geologic sections: U.S. Geological Survey Open-File Report 84-494, 9 p., scale 1:12,000.

Scott, R.B., and Castellanos, M., 1984, Stratigraphic and structural relations of volcanic rocks in drill holes USW GU-3 and USW G-3, Yucca Mountain, Nye County, Nevada, U.S. Geological Survey Open-File Report 84-491, 94 p.

Scott, R.B., and Hofland, G.S., 1987, Fault-slip paleostress analysis of Yucca Mountain, Nevada: EOS, Transactions, American Geophysical Union, v. 68, no. 44, p. 1461.

Scott, R.B., and Whitney, J.W., 1987, The upper crustal detachment system at Yucca Mountain, SW Nevada: Geological Society of America Abstracts with Programs, v. 19, p. 332–333.

Simonds, F.W., Whitney, J.W., Fox, K.F., Ramelli, A.R., Yount, J.C., Carr, M.D., Menges, C.M., Dickerson, R.P., and Scott, R.B., 1995, Map showing fault activity in the Yucca Mountain area, Nye County, Nevada: U.S. Geological Survey Map I-2520, scale 1:24,000.

Simpson, R.W., Jachens, R.C., and Blakely, R.J., 1986, A new isostatic residual gravity map of the conterminous United States with a discussion on the significance of isostatic residual anomalies: Journal of Geophysical Research, v. 91, no. B8, p. 8348–8372.

Sims, D., Ferrill, D.A., and Stamatakos, J.A., 1999, Role of ductile décollement in the development of pull-apart basins—Experimental results and natural examples: Journal of Structural Geology, v. 21, no. 5, p. 533–554, doi: 10.1016/S0191-8141(99)00010-3.

Smith, R.B., 1978, Seismicity, crustal structure, and intraplate tectonics of the interior of the western Cordillera, *in* Smith, R.B., and Eaton, G.P., eds., Cenozoic tectonics and regional geophysics of the western Cordillera: Boulder, Colorado, Geological Society of America Memoir 152, p. 111–144.

Smith, R.B., and Arabasz, W.J., 1991, Seismicity of the intermountain seismic

belt, *in* Slemmons, D.B., Engdahl, E.R., Zoback, M.D., and Blackwell, D., eds., Neotectonics of North America: Boulder, Colorado, Geological Society of America, Continent-Scale Maps of North America, Decade Map Volume, p. 185–228.

Smith, R.B., and Bruhn, R.L., 1984, Intraplate extensional tectonics of the eastern Basin-Range—Inferences on structural style from seismic reflection data, regional tectonics, and thermal-mechanical models of brittle-ductile deformation: Journal of Geophysical Research, v. 89, no. B7, p. 5733–5762.

Smith, R.B., and Sbar, M.L., 1974, Contemporary tectonics and seismicity of the western United States with emphasis on the Intermountain Seismic Belt: Geological Society of America Bulletin, v. 85, p. 1205–1218, doi: 10.1130/0016-7606(1974)85<1205:CTASOT>2.0.CO;2.

Smith, K.D., Brune, J.N., dePolo, D., Savage, M.K., Anooshehpoor, R., and Sheehan, A.F., 2000, The 1992 Little Skull Mountain earthquake sequence, southern Nevada Test Site, Chapter K, *in* Whitney, J.W., and Keefer, W.R., eds., Geologic and geophysical characterization studies of Yucca Mountain, Nevada, a potential high-level radioactive-waste repository: U.S. Geological Survey Digital Data Series DDS-058, 16 p.

Smith, E.I., Keenan, D.L., and Plank, T., 2002, Episodic volcanism and hot mantle—Implications for volcanic hazard studies at the proposed nuclear waste repository at Yucca Mountain, Nevada: GSA Today, v. 12, no. 4, p. 4–10, doi: 10.1130/1052-5173(2002)012<0004:EVAHMI>2.0.CO;2.

Snow, J.K., 1992, Large-magnitude Permian shortening and continental-margin tectonics in the southern Cordillera: Geological Society of America Bulletin, v. 104, p. 80–105, doi: 10.1130/0016-7606(1992)104<0080:LMPSAC>2.3.CO;2.

Snow, J.K., and Prave, A.R., 1994, Covariance of structural and stratigraphic trends—Evidence for anticlockwise rotation within the Walker Lane belt, Death Valley region, California and Nevada: Tectonics, v. 13, p. 712–724, doi: 10.1029/93TC02943.

Snyder, D.B., and Carr, W.J., 1982, Preliminary results of gravity investigations at Yucca Mountain and vicinity, southern Nye County, Nevada: U.S. Geological Survey Open-File Report 82-701, 36 p.

Snyder, D.B., and Carr, W.J., 1984, Interpretation of gravity data in a complex volcano-tectonic setting, southwestern Nevada: Journal of Geophysical Research, v. 89, no. B12, p. 10193–10206.

Sonder, L.J., Jones, C.H., Salyards, S.L., and Murphy, K.M., 1994, Vertical axis rotations in the Las Vegas Valley shear zone, southern Nevada: Paleomagnetic constraints on kinematics and dynamics of block rotations: Tectonics, v. 13, no. 4, p. 769–788, doi: 10.1029/94TC00352.

Spencer, J.E., 1984, Role of tectonic denudation in warping and uplift of low-angle normal faults: Geology, v. 12, p. 95–98, doi: 10.1130/0091-7613(1984)12<95:ROTDIW>2.0.CO;2.

Stamatakos, J.A., and Ferrill, D.A., 1998, Strike-slip fault system in Amargosa Valley and Yucca Mountain, Nevada—Comment: Tectonophysics, v. 294, p. 151–160, doi: 10.1016/S0040-1951(98)00082-1.

Stein, R.S., King, G.C.P., and Rundle, J.B., 1988, The growth of geological structures by repeated earthquakes, 2. Field examples of continental dip-slip faults: Journal of Geophysical Research, v. 93, p. 13319–13331.

Stepp, J.C., Wong, I., Whitney, J., Quittmeyer, R., Abrahamson, N., Toro, G., Youngs, R., Coppersmith, K., Savy, J., Sullivan, T., and Yucca Mountain PSHA Members, 2001, Probabilisitic seismic hazard analyses for ground motions and fault displacement at Yucca Mountain, Nevada: Earthquake Spectra, v. 17, no. 1, p. 113–151.

Stewart, J.H., 1971, Basin and range structure—A system of horsts and grabens produced by deep-seated extension: Geological Society of America Bulletin, v. 82, p. 1019–1044.

Stewart, J.H., 1988, Tectonics of the Walker Lane belt, western Great Basin—Mesozoic and Cenozoic deformation in a zone of shear, *in* Ernst, W.G., ed., Metamorphism and crustal evolution of the western United States, Vol. VII: Englewood Cliffs, New Jersey, Prentice-Hall, Inc., p. 684–713.

Stock, J.M., Healy, J.H., Hickman, S.H., and Zoback, M.D., 1985, Hydraulic fracturing stress measurements at Yucca Mountain, Nevada, and relationship to the regional stress field: Journal of Geophysical Research, v. 90, no. B10, p. 8691–8706.

Stock, J.M., and Healy, J.H., 1988, Stress field at Yucca Mountain, Nevada, *in* Carr, M.D., and Yount, J.C., eds., Geologic and hydrologic investigations of a potential nuclear waste disposal site at Yucca Mountain, southern Nevada: U.S. Geological Survey Bulletin 1790, p. 87–93.

Stuckless, J.S., and O'Leary, D.W., 2007, this volume, Geology of the Yucca Mountain region, *in* Stuckless, J.S., and Levich, R.A., eds., The Geology and Climatology of Yucca Mountain and Vicinity, Southern Nevada and California: Geological Society of America Memoir 199, doi: 10.1130/2007.1199(02).

Swadley, W.C., and Carr, W.J., 1987, Geologic map of the Quaternary and Tertiary deposits of the Big Dune quadrangle, Nye County, Nevada, and Inyo County, California: U.S. Geological Survey Miscellaneous Investigations Series Map I-1767, scale 1:48,000.

Thompson, G.A., 2000, Perspectives on Basin and Range structure and basaltic volcanism—Bare Mountain-Crater Flat area, Nye County, Nevada, Chapter E, *in* Whitney, J.W., and Keefer, W.R., eds., Geologic and geophysical characterization studies of Yucca Mountain, Nevada, a potential high-level radioactive-waste repository: U.S. Geological Survey Digital Data Series DDS-058, 7 p.

Thompson, G.A., and McCarthy, J., 1990, A gravity constraint on the origin of highly extended terranes: Tectonophysics, v. 174, p. 197–206, doi: 10.1016/0040-1951(90)90392-L.

U.S. Department of Energy, 1984, General guidelines for the recommendation of sites for the nuclear waste repositories: Federal Register, v. 49, no. 236.

U.S. Department of Energy, 1988, Site Characterization Plan—Yucca Mountain Site, Nevada Research and Development Area, Nevada: U.S. Department of Energy, Office of Civilian Radioactive Waste Management, DOE/RW-0199, 353 p. Accessed online January 9, 2007, at http://www.lsnnet.gov/. Search on Participant number HQO.19881201.0002.

U.S. Geological Survey, 1984, A summary of geologic studies through January 1, 1983, of a potential high-level radioactive waste repository site at Yucca Mountain, southern Nye County, Nevada: U.S. Geological Survey Open-File Report 84-792, p. 103.

U.S. Geological Survey, 1995, Characterization of detachment faults in the Yucca Mountain region—Summary report for Site Characterization Plan, Study 8.3.1.17.4.5: U.S. Geological Survey Administrative Report, Milestone Number 3GTD500M. Accessed online January 9, 2007, at http://www.lsnnet.gov/. Search on Participant number MOL.20000425.0570.

U.S. Nuclear Regulatory Commission, 1999, Issue resolution status report key technical issue—Structural deformation and seismicity, Rev. 2: Washington D.C., U.S. Nuclear Regulatory Commission. (Can only find JOL.19991214.0623 in LSN, which contains the color figures for rev 2 of this report).

Vaniman, D.T., Crowe, B.M., and Gladney, E.S., 1982, Petrology and geochemistry of hawaiite lavas from Crater Flat, Nevada: Contributions to Mineralogy and Petrology, v. 80, p. 341–357, doi: 10.1007/BF00378007.

Wang, K., Plank, T., Walker, J.D., and Smith, E.I., 2002, A mantle melting profile across the Basin and Range, southwestern USA: Journal of Geophysical Research, v. 107, no. B1, p. 5-1–5-21.

Warren, R.G., Byers, F.M., Jr., and Orkild, P.P., 1985, Post-Silent Canyon caldera structural setting for Pahute Mesa, *in* Olsen, C.W., and Donahue, M.L., eds., Proceedings, Third Symposium on the Containment of Underground Nuclear Explosions, CONF-850953, Lawrence Livermore National Laboratory, Livermore, California, v. 2, p. 3–30.

Wernicke, B., 1981, Low-angle normal faults in the Basin and Range Province—Nappe tectonics in an extending orogen: Nature, v. 291, p. 645–648, doi: 10.1038/291645a0.

Wernicke, B.P., 1992, Cenozoic extensional tectonics of the U.S. Cordillera, *in* Burchfiel, B.C., Lipman, P.W., and Zoback, M.L., eds., The Cordilleran orogen—Conterminous U.S., The geology of North America: Geological Society of America v. G-3, p. 553–581.

Wernicke, B., and Axen, G.J., 1988, On the role of isostasy in the evolution of normal fault systems: Geology, v. 16, p. 848–851, doi: 10.1130/0091-7613(1988)016<0848:OTROII>2.3.CO;2.

Wernicke, B., and Burchfiel, B.C., 1982, Modes of extensional tectonics: Journal of Structural Geology, v. 4, no. 2, p. 105–115, doi: 10.1016/0191-8141(82)90021-9.

Wernicke, B.P., and Davis, J.L., 2001, Second report of results from geodetic monitoring of the Yucca Mountain area using continuous GPS—DOE Grant DE-FC08-98NV12081: Prepared for U.S. Department of Energy. Accessed online January 9, 2007, at http://www.lsnnet.gov/. Search on Participant number ALE.20040511.7206.

Wernicke, B., Walker, J.D., and Beaufait, M.S., 1985, Structural discordance between Neogene detachments and frontal Sevier thrusts, central Mormon Mountains, southern Nevada: Tectonics, v. 4, p. 213–246.

Wernicke, B.P., Axen, G.J., and Snow, J.K., 1988, Basin and Range extensional tectonics at the latitude of Las Vegas, Nevada: Geological Society of America Bulletin, v. 100, p. 1738–1757, doi: 10.1130/0016-7606(1988)100<1738:BARETA>2.3.CO;2.

Wernicke, B.P., Davis, J.L., Bennett, R.A., Elosegui, P., Abolins, M., Brady, R.J., House, M.A., Niemi, N.A., and Snow, J.K., 1998, Anomalous strain accumulation in the Yucca Mountain area, Nevada: Science, v. 279, p. 2096–2100, doi: 10.1126/science.279.5359.2096.

Wernicke, B., Davis, J.L., Bennett, R.A., Normandeau, J.E., Friedrich, A.M., and Niemi, N.A., 2004, Tectonic implications of a dense continuous GPS velocity field at Yucca Mountain, Nevada: Journal of Geophysical Research, v. 109, no. B12404, p. 1–13, doi: 10.1029/2003JB002832.

Winograd, I.J., and Thordarson, W., 1975, Hydrogeologic and hydrochemical framework, south-central Great Basin, Nevada-California, with special reference to the Nevada Test Site: U.S. Geological Survey Professional Paper 712-C, 126 p.

Wong, I.G., and Stepp, J.C., 1998, Probabilistic seismic hazard analyses for fault displacement and vibratory ground motion at Yucca Mountain, Nevada; Prepared for the U.S. Geological Survey by the Civilian Radioactive Waste Management System Management and Operating Contractor: Oakland, California, Office of Civilian Radioactive Waste Management, U.S. Department of Energy Milestone Report SP32IM3. Accessed online January 9, 2007, at http://www.lsnnet.gov/. Search on Participant number MOL.19981207.0393.

Wright, L.A., 1989, Overview of the role of strike-slip and normal faulting in the Neogene history of the region northeast of Death Valley, California-Nevada, *in* Ellis, M.A., ed., Late Cenozoic evolution of the southern Great Basin: Nevada Bureau of Mines and Geology Open File Report 89-1, p. 1–11.

Wright, L.A., and Troxel, B.W., 1973, Shallow-fault interpretation of Basin and Range structure, southwestern Great Basin, *in* de Jong, D.A., and Scholten, R., eds., Gravity and tectonics: New York, John Wiley and Sons, p. 397–407.

Yogodzinski, G.M., Naumann, T.R., Smith, E.I., Bradshaw, T.K., and Walker, J.D., 1996, Evolution of a mafic volcanic field in the central Great Basin, south central Nevada: Journal of Geophysical Research, v. 101, no. B8, p. 17425–17445, doi: 10.1029/96JB00816.

Young, S.R., Morris, A.P., and Stirewalt, G., 1993, Geometric analysis of alternative models of faulting at Yucca Mountain, Nevada, *in* High level radioactive waste management: Proceedings of the Fourth Annual International Conference, Las Vegas, Nevada, 26–30 April 1993, p. 1818–1825.

Youngs, R.R., Arabasz, W.J., Anderson, R.E., Ramelli, A.R., Ake, J.P., Slemmons, D.B., McCalpin, J.P., Doser, D.I., Fridrich, C.J., Swan, F.H., III, Rogers, A.M., Yount, J.C., Anderson, L.W., Smith, K.D., Bruhn, R.L., Knuepfer, P.L.K., Smith, R.B., dePolo, C.M., O'Leary, D.W., Coppersmith, K.J., Pezzopane, S.K., Schwartz, D.P., Whitney, J.W., Olig, S.S., and Toro, G.R., 2003, A methodology for probabilisitc fault displacement hazard analysis (PFDHA): Earthquake Spectra, v. 19, no. 1, p. 191–219, doi: 10.1193/1.1542891.

Zoback, M.L., 1989, State of stress and modern deformation of the Basin and Range Province: Journal of Geophysical Research, v. 94, p. 7105–7128.

Zoback, M.L., and Zoback, M.D., 1980, State of stress in the conterminous United States: Journal of Geophysical Research, v. 85, no. B11, p. 6113–6156.

Zoback, M.L., Anderson, R.E., and Thompson, G.A., 1981, Cainozoic evolution of the state of stress and style of tectonism of the Basin and Range Province of the western United States: Royal Society of London Philosophical Transactions, v. A300, p. 407–434.

MANUSCRIPT ACCEPTED BY THE SOCIETY 18 OCTOBER 2006

Geological Society of America
Memoir 199
2007

Using modern through mid-Pleistocene climate proxy data to bound future variations in infiltration at Yucca Mountain, Nevada

Saxon E. Sharpe
Desert Research Institute, 2215 Raggio Parkway, Reno, Nevada 89512-1095, USA

ABSTRACT

Planetary and synoptic-scale atmospheric features are important because they set the stage for differing climate regimes in the Yucca Mountain area—whether in past, present, or future time. Climate proxy records in the region show that numerous climate regimes occurred during the past 800 k.y. ranging from warm interglacial periods (similar to modern climate) to cool or cold and wet glacial periods. The current climate at Yucca Mountain is arid, with an annual average precipitation of ~17.7 cm/yr. Most of the annual precipitation occurs during winter or during July and August monsoons. Annual average temperatures generally range from 15° to 18 °C but can exceed 40 °C during summer. Continuously deposited calcite at Devils Hole, Nevada, provides a precise chronology that can be used to calibrate other climate proxy data that provide estimates of the nature and magnitude of past climate events. During past glacial periods, mean annual temperature may have been as much as 10° to 15 °C cooler than present temperatures, with mean annual precipitation as much as 1.4–3 times present precipitation. These records of past climate are used to bound estimates of future climate to assess future potential infiltration. Five maximum infiltration scenarios are estimated to occur within the next 500 k.y. providing that anthropogenic disturbance does not modify or alter long-term climate change.

Keywords: Yucca Mountain, climate change, paleoclimate, infiltration, future climate, orbital parameters.

INTRODUCTION

Estimates of future variation in infiltration are necessary to assess the long-term hydrologic integrity of a high-level radioactive waste repository. Infiltration is defined as the flow of surface water downward across the atmosphere-soil or the atmosphere-bedrock interface (CRWMS M&O, 2004). Climate is a primary control on infiltration because factors such as diurnal and seasonal temperature cycles, precipitation in the form of rain or snow, relative humidity, and solar radiation flux affect infiltration processes.

Evaluating future infiltration scenarios is challenging, because it involves estimating future climates. Because future climates are not known, the method used herein relies on paleoclimatic reconstructions from lake and other records in the Yucca Mountain area (Fig. 1) to provide patterns in the timing and nature of past climates to bound estimates of future climate and maximal infiltration scenarios. Without bounding criteria—which

Sharpe, S.E., 2007, Using modern through mid-Pleistocene climate proxy data to bound future variations in infiltration at Yucca Mountain, Nevada, *in* Stuckless, J.S., and Levich, R.A., eds., The Geology and Climatology of Yucca Mountain and Vicinity, Southern Nevada and California: Geological Society of America Memoir 199, p. 155–205, doi: 10.1130/2007.1199(05).

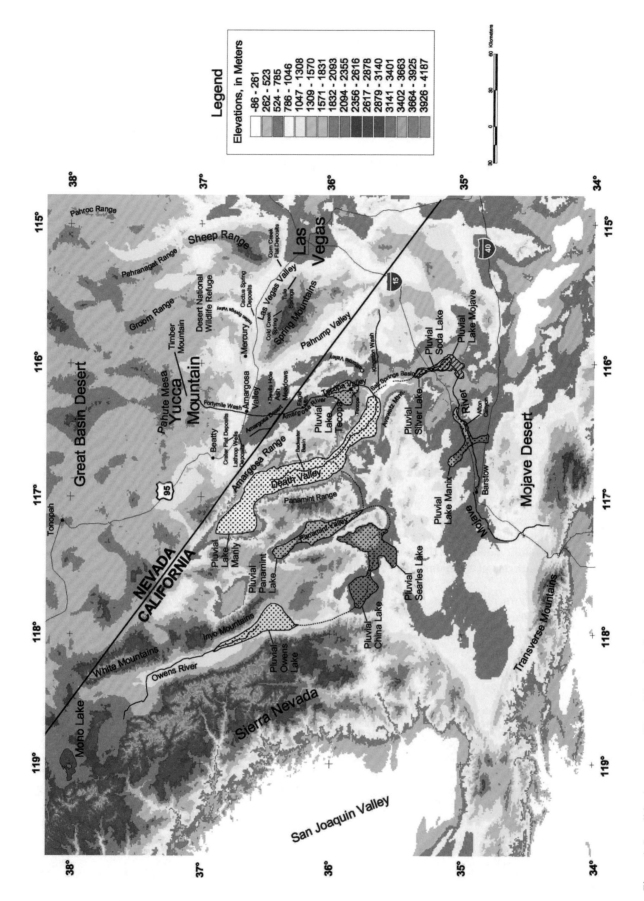

Figure 1. Localities important to Yucca Mountain climate records. Pluvial lake highstand areas are modified from Enzel et al. (2003); Smith and Bischoff (1997).

include the frequency, nature, and duration of maximal and high infiltration events—the program would need to generate for safety reasons a continuous, maximum infiltration event to evaluate repository performance throughout the next tens of thousands of years.

This chapter is divided into three sections: modern climate, paleoclimate, and bounding future variations in infiltration. The modern climate section first discusses forcing mechanisms that have operated in the same way for many hundred thousands of years with different magnitudes and on varying time scales. This section then describes site climatology. The paleoclimate section provides an overview of past environments in the Yucca Mountain region utilizing different climate proxy records. It documents the timing, duration, magnitude, and character of past climates in the Yucca Mountain area and establishes the rationale for bounding future variations in infiltration. The future infiltration section integrates material from previous sections and establishes timing relations between calculated Earth orbital parameters and past climate cycles to forecast the potential timing and magnitude of future climate for input to infiltration models.

Approach and Assumptions

Climate in the Yucca Mountain area is influenced by many factors from local topography that can produce microclimates to El Niño–Southern Oscillation events that can affect climate on multiyear time frames and to millennial-scale climate states that are correlated with change in astronomical parameters. Evaluation of modern climate is necessary to relate climatic events to near-surface processes such as infiltration, runoff, and evapotranspiration. Modern climate information also aids in environmental analyses of repository design facilities and atmospheric dispersion models. Evaluation of past climate regimes, particularly temperature and precipitation, is needed to assess the relation of past climate to past hydrologic conditions. Estimates of potential future climate and hydrology are needed to evaluate repository performance.

Anthropogenic Influence on Climate at Yucca Mountain

The Intergovernmental Panel on Climate Change (IPCC), established in 1988 by the World Meteorological Organization and the United Nations Environment Programme, concludes that "the Earth's climate system has demonstrably changed on both global and regional scales after the preindustrial era, with some of these changes attributable to human activities" (Watson et al., 2001). Regardless of what percentage of the changes are human-induced, the implication for the Yucca Mountain area is that observed historical climate patterns from recent decades are not representative of century- or millennial-scale past climate and may not be representative of future climate.

How long-term responses to anthropogenic disturbance will be manifested in infiltration in the Yucca Mountain region is uncertain. The IPCC has produced a series of reports and papers

assessing available information on the science, impacts, and economics of climate change. The panel reported results from different future climate models based on conditions of CO_2 increasing 1% per year (mean for 2071–2100 A.D.) with and without sulfate forcing. Model results were averaged to a single case, and *agreement* was defined as at least four of the five CO_2-only and three of the four increased CO_2-with-sulfate-aerosol cases agreeing (Giorgi et al., 2001, Figs. 10.3 and 10.4 therein).

For western North America, these model simulations show increased summer and winter temperatures, a small increase in winter precipitation, and disagreement regarding summer precipitation (Giorgi et al., 2001, Figs. 10.4 and 10.6 therein). Alternatively, Thompson et al. (1998, Fig. 3 therein) estimate climate change for the western United States resulting from a doubling of greenhouse gases from the preindustrial level. In this analysis, January temperatures are estimated to increase by 2–3 °C; July temperatures are estimated to increase 3–4 °C; and January and July precipitation amounts are expected to decrease 10–30 mm in the Yucca Mountain area. Regarding inconsistency in climate change forecasts, the general consensus is that temperature effects are more likely to be correctly forecast than precipitation effects (Giorgi et al., 2001, Figs. 10.4 and 10.6 therein). Because future climate models include large geographic areas and many types of terrain, it is unrealistic to extract specific values for the Yucca Mountain area for the purpose of estimating infiltration.

It is estimated that temperature and CO_2 emissions will stabilize in a few centuries (Watson et al., 2001, Figs. 5-1 and 5-2 therein). Even if greenhouse gas emissions peak and decrease within the next 100 yr; however, the climate system will not respond immediately (Wigley, 2005). The climate system, particularly the oceans and cryosphere (the component of the climate system consisting of all snow, ice, and permafrost on and beneath the surface of the Earth and ocean) has a long response time; therefore, thousands to tens of thousands of years could pass before sea level and ice caps reach equilibrium (Watson et al., 2001, Figs. 5-1 and 5-2 therein).

Some scientists suggest that the next glacial period could be postponed as a result of greenhouse emissions. For example, Berger and Loutre (2002) hypothesize that an irreversible greenhouse effect could become the climate of the future if CO_2 concentrations increase to 750 ppmv (parts per million by volume) during the next 200 yr and return to natural levels (~225 ppmv) by 1000 yr from now. This interglacial period would last to 50,000 yr into the future, significantly affect the northern hemisphere ice sheet for approximately the next 50,000 yr (Loutre and Berger, 2000), and postpone the next glacial maximum for 100,000 yr (Berger and Loutre, 2002). Archer and Ganopolski (2005) predict that a carbon release from fossil fuels or methane hydrate deposits could prevent glaciation for the next 500,000 yr. Ruddiman et al. (2005) suggest that if anthropogenic contributions to greenhouse gases were absent, the Earth's climate would no longer be in an interglacial state but would be moving toward temperatures typical of glacial periods. If anthropogenic disturbance delays the astronomically predicted onset of the next glacial period and the

Earth has either an exceptionally long interglacial or tropical climate regime like those in past high-CO_2 climates, then using the timing and magnitude of past climates to forecast future climates would not be applicable.

Because much greater-than-modern infiltration scenarios are of concern here, currently estimated global-warming scenarios are considered to be insignificant in terms of future high-infiltration events at Yucca Mountain. Some increases in precipitation may occur, but all models predict higher temperatures that may more than offset precipitation increases because of increased evaporation. Winograd et al. (1998) report that high-intensity, short-duration summer convective storms provide approximately one-third of annual precipitation and only a small fraction (possibly 10%) of recharge to the Spring Mountains today. This indicates that infiltration in the Yucca Mountain area is a winter-precipitation–dominated phenomenon. Therefore, increased warm-season precipitation projected by some of the global-warming models for the Yucca Mountain area is not likely to result in a maximum infiltration scenario.

Given the uncertainty of future climate estimates with respect to global-warming scenarios and that estimated future warmer and slightly wetter climates may occur which are thought not to result in greatly increased infiltration, this analysis does not include effects attributable to human activities. If global-warming estimates are refined in the future to show that anthropogenically driven climate change will substantially increase precipitation in southern Nevada, however, then a global-warming scenario likely would be significant in terms of infiltration.

Key Assumptions for Bounding Estimates of Future Variations in Infiltration

The approach used herein is a five-step process. First, compare the general characteristics of past climate with Earth orbital parameters to establish a relation between eccentricity, precession, and obliquity and interglacial and glacial periods. Second, compare the timing of the Devils Hole (Fig. 1) isotope record (ca. 568 to ca. 4.5 ka) to the calculated timing of change in Earth orbital parameters to identify the pattern and timing of past periods of infiltration greater than today. Third, identify the nature and timing of general past climate states (glacial, interglacial, monsoon, or intermediate) suggested by the Owens Lake, California, paleoenvironmental record and other climate proxy records from the region. Fourth, select present-day meteorological stations to represent these past climate states so that the record of daily temperature and precipitation from these stations can represent these past periods. Finally, bound future infiltration scenarios using the timing of calculated orbital parameters, the nature of past climate states, as well as temperature and precipitation records from modern stations.

This forecast method was devised and developed by R.M. Forester, U.S. Geological Survey (retired), who suggested a specific link between the Devils Hole chronology, a pattern of climate change, and the relation of eccentricity and precession (U.S. Geological Survey, 2001). This method assumes that the general nature and sequencing of climate state characteristics are similar and repeated through time and includes the following key assumptions (U.S. Geological Survey, 2001).

1. Climate was sequential within the past two 400 k.y. eccentricity cycles; the Earth is currently at the beginning of the next 400 k.y. eccentricity cycle. Known past climate sequences can be important for estimating future infiltration because they imply that some past climate or aspects of past climate will recur in the future. The past is the key to the future.

2. Past climate change and infiltration scenarios can be timed with an Earth orbital clock of precession and eccentricity. The orbital clock of precession and eccentricity can be calculated into the future allowing for an assessment of potential infiltration scenarios based on past scenarios. These infiltration scenarios may be used as input by total system performance-assessment and infiltration models.

3. Characteristics of late Quaternary glacial and interglacial climates differ from each other in a systematic way. The nature of these particular past climates and their analogous infiltration scenarios correspond to the pattern of past eccentricity and precession values. Future infiltration scenarios may be estimated by calculating future eccentricity and precession values. Thus, analysis of future infiltration inputs can focus on one particular infiltration sequence rather than the most conservative approach of using one maximum value throughout the future.

4. Long-term, Earth-based, climate-forcing functions, such as tectonic change, have remained relatively constant during the past 500 k.y. and will remain relatively constant for approximately the next 500 k.y. Long-term, Earth-based, climate-forcing functions operating on the hundreds of thousands to millions of years time scales almost certainly will alter future climates from those known from the past 400 k.y. time series.

Assumption 4 is important because climate beyond the next 500 k.y. may change in non-sequential ways as it has in the past because of forcing functions. What is termed the mid-Pleistocene climate transition marks a period of change in the dominant response of the Earth's climate from 41 k.y. obliquity cycles to 100 k.y. periodicities. This has been documented in basins in the Atlantic Ocean or Pacific Ocean or both between 1.5 Ma and 600 ka (Rutherford and D'Hondt, 2000); between 1.2 and 1 Ma (Berger et al., 1994); between 900 and 600 ka (Williams et al., 1988); ca. 640 ka ago (Mudelsee and Schulz, 1997); and between 870 and 450 ka (Hall et al., 2001). These data sets show that the response of the Earth to orbital forcing has varied considerably during the last million years and support the assumption that long-term, Earth-based, climate-forcing functions have remained relatively constant only during the past 500 k.y.

Uncertainties using This Approach

Uncertainties using this approach to estimate future infiltration include the possibility that change in orbital parameters may be correlated with some other factors that independently cause climate change. These factors could include solar variability (Gauthier, 1999; Sharma, 2002; Jouzel, 2001; Shackleton, 2000; Bond et al., 2001; Rind, 2002), celestial phenomena such as galactic cosmic ray flux (Shaviv and Veizer, 2003), the content of atmospheric carbon dioxide (Ruddiman, 2003a, 2003b; Cuffey and Vimeux, 2001), the effects of wind and tidal forcing on the ocean's mass flux (Wunsch, 2002), ice-sheet volume and behavior combined with CO_2 levels (Loutre and Berger, 2000), sea-surface temperatures and ice cover (Knorr and Lohmann, 2003; Helmke et al., 2002), and a threshold such as radiation windows (Shaffer et al., 1996). It also is possible that future climates may not have late Pleistocene analogs because of anthropogenic influences (Hay et al., 1997), as discussed above. None, some, or all of these factors may be involved.

Additionally, for any assessment of future infiltration it is important to remember that the Earth itself is a dynamic system that responds to changes in insolation with complex terrestrial interrelations that profoundly affect climate. Feedback processes leading to local-to-global effects also occur. Sometimes the effects may be small or self-cancelling. Effects can be additive, however, producing significant changes in precipitation and temperature. Some examples of feedback processes:

- Radiative forcing, the measure of the influence a factor has in altering the balance of incoming and outgoing energy in the Earth-atmosphere system expressed in watts per square meter (Wm^{-2}), arises from changes in atmospheric composition, alteration of surface reflectance, and variation in the output of the sun. Radiative forcing can result in either warming or cooling, depending on the factor. Some factors include aerosols (black carbon and mineral dust), contrails, ozone, sulfate, and organic carbon (Albritton et al., 2001).
- Snow and ice cover (e.g., growth and shrinkage of glaciers) and land use affect reflective characteristics (albedo) of the Earth's surface and energy transfer to the atmosphere.
- Oceanic processes (changes in sea level, temperature, ocean basin shape, salinity, abyssal circulation, and El Niño–Southern Oscillation events) can generate gain or loss of energy between the oceans and atmosphere.
- Changes in the hydrologic cycle can change the net transfer of water between hemispheres and alter thermohaline circulation; a seasonal or geographic redistribution of precipitation can change plant composition and density as well as affect erosion.
- Tectonic change, such as mountain building, can alter regional climate and vegetation by producing a rain shadow on the lee side of a mountain range and increasing precipitation on the windward side.

The method used herein assumes that the nature and sequencing of past climate characteristics are similar and repeated through time and that the correspondence will continue in the future. Other infiltration forecast methodologies might develop a different rationale, resulting in different future infiltration scenarios.

MODERN CLIMATE

As the Earth's energy budget changes, so does climate (Barry and Chorley, 1992; Imbrie et al., 1992). Greatly simplified, global climate may be considered as processes operating within the atmosphere and hydrosphere to minimize temperature differences arising from the unequal reception of energy in different locations and seasons. Insolation is the amount of incoming solar radiation that is received over a unit area of Earth's surface. As a consequence of insolation imbalance, energy is transported toward the poles from the equator by air and ocean circulation. Changes in Earth's insolation during millennia result in changes in the energy budget between equatorial regions and poles. Thus, solar radiation is a forcing mechanism and a key factor in climate change.

Solar Insolation

Incoming solar insolation at the top of Earth's atmosphere can cause change in two basic ways: (1) changes in total solar irradiance that influence the total energy received annually by Earth, and (2) changes in latitudinal and seasonal distribution of solar insolation arising from variations in Earth's orbital parameters. Total solar irradiance changes a fraction of a percent in relation to solar magnetic activity (Barry and Chorley, 1992). Total solar irradiance and other factors may affect climate globally (Eddy, 1976; Willson, 1997) through cosmic radiation and cloud formation combined with enhancement of precipitation (Muller and MacDonald, 2002). Changes in the distribution of solar insolation arise from variations in Earth's orbital parameters (eccentricity, precession, and obliquity). These parameters are a function of change in the Earth-Sun distance, the orientation of Earth's axis of rotation relative to its orbit, and(or) the position of Earth's orbit relative to the center of mass of the solar system or some other non-Earth reference. Eccentricity (variation in the shape of Earth's elliptical orbit) changes annual total radiation received at the top of Earth's atmosphere via variations in the Earth-Sun distance. Precession (the slow migration of Earth's axis that traces out a cone combined with the rotation of the axis of Earth's orbit) and obliquity (the angle of tilt of Earth's axis of rotation) change the seasonal and latitudinal distribution of insolation at the top of Earth's atmosphere, but not total insolation.

Orbital parameters vary on a cyclical basis. Berger and Loutre (1991) and Muller and MacDonald (2002) describe the behavior and timing of Earth orbital parameters and the criteria to calculate these parameters, past and future. Calculating past timing of these parameters enables their comparison with climate proxy records, such as the Devils Hole isotope record (Winograd et al., 1992) discussed later in this chapter. Calculating future timing of these parameters enables estimates of future variation in infiltration. Because eccentricity, precession, and obliquity vary with different frequencies, they sometimes will act collectively to reinforce or dampen insolation departures from average. For example, high eccentricity amplifies the seasonal effects of precession (Crowley and North, 1991).

Planetary- and Synoptic-Scale Features

Planetary- and synoptic-scale atmospheric features are important because they set the stage for differing climate regimes in the Yucca Mountain area—whether in past, present, or future time. Planetary-scale features occupy areas with horizontal dimensions of several thousand kilometers and have durations of approximately one week. Synoptic-scale atmospheric features are smaller than planetary-scale features: several hundred to a few thousand kilometers, with durations from a few days to a few weeks (Ahrens, 1994).

Planetary-Scale Features

Principal factors that govern planetary-scale features include the spherical shape of Earth, the fact that it spins, tilt of Earth's rotational axis with respect to the plane of its orbit, distribution of the oceans and continents, effects of constituents in the atmosphere on the flow of energy in the form of radiation (all wavelengths) through the system, and absorption and emission of this energy at interfaces such as those separating the atmosphere from the hydrosphere and lithosphere.

Effects stemming from Earth's rotation, atmospheric heat and moisture, and surface friction include winds (the polar easterlies, westerlies, and trade winds), cells of rising and subsiding air, and high and low pressure systems. These large-scale influences set the stage for more regional processes, such as suppressed precipitation from 30° to 35° in the north and south latitudes. These processes, in turn, produce their own effects in a cascading manner down to very small scales. This connectivity ensures that climates of individual locations, such as Yucca Mountain, are affected by influences around the entire Earth including the world's oceans, its vegetation and biology, and cryosphere. Correspondingly, large-scale influences are usually the integrated effects of numerous, small-scale processes and, therefore, one scale is not more important than another.

El Niño-Southern Oscillation. The El Niño–Southern Oscillation also influences Yucca Mountain climate. Warm-ocean, El Niño, and cool-ocean, La Niña, conditions with respect to long-term average temperatures alternate in intervals typically of two to seven years. During the northern hemisphere cool season, approximately October through March, La Niña in southern Nevada is associated with drier than usual conditions, and El Niño is associated with wetter than usual conditions. These surface effects are expressions of major shifts in the storm tracks to other latitudes as the jet stream responds to changes in atmo-spheric temperature and ocean heat content produced by El Niño and La Niña.

El Niño is closely associated with flood frequency and heavy precipitation in the southwest (Redmond et al., 2002) and, therefore, variations in the rate and intensity of recurrence of El Niño are of great importance and relevance to Yucca Mountain. Anderson (1992) statistically examined historical El Niño–Southern Oscillation records to show that the frequency of the warm-ocean El Niño phase varied on preferred time scales of 90, 50, and 22 yr, since A.D. 622 and that during the Medieval Warm Period (ca. 600–1000 A.D.), El Niño events were less common. Farther back in time, paleoenvironmental records from Australia and South America indicate that El Niño–Southern Oscillation events in early Holocene time (10–7.5 ka) were much reduced in amplitude or were expressed differently because of altered climatic and oceanic boundary conditions (McGlone et al., 1992).

Proxy records from tree rings and other sources show that there have been significant variations in precipitation in the southwestern United States during the past 1500 yr with the recent century among the wettest within that time period (Redmond et al., 2002, Fig. 9 therein). Abundant winter precipitation in the local Yucca Mountain area in response to the 1969 and 1993 El Niño–Southern Oscillation events caused sufficient flow in the Amargosa River to form shallow lakes in Death Valley (Grasso, 1996). During the 1983 El Niño–Southern Oscillation, winter and summer precipitation events were so large that the Amargosa flow gauge at Tecopa, California (35°53′N, 116°14′W) (Fig. 1), 100 km south of Yucca Mountain, was destroyed by flooding (Grasso, 1996).

Pacific Decadal Oscillation. On longer time scales, periods of warmer or wetter climate lasting decades and longer have been documented. Such periods include a large-scale, slowly varying pattern of ocean temperatures in the central and northern Pacific called the Pacific Decadal Oscillation. The Pacific Decadal Oscillation appears to modulate the effect of El Niño on the southwestern United States (Mantua et al., 1997). The cause or causes of the Pacific Decadal Oscillation are not well understood, although the oscillation appears to be related to El Niño and La Niña.

The southwestern region recently has experienced a period with above-normal precipitation, the wettest in the past century, from the late-1970s through the mid-1990s. The Pacific Decadal Oscillation was consistently in the positive, or warm, phase during this time. The Southwest has subsequently experienced significant drought for much of the last decade, the first widescale drought in the West and Southwest in 30 yr. From the late-1940s to 1977 also was very dry and encompassed the severe drought of the 1950s. During both of these dry periods, the Pacific Decadal Oscillation was consistently negative or in the cool phase. McCabe et al. (2004) suggest that the interplay of positive and negative phases of the Pacific Decadal Oscillation and the Atlantic Multidecadal Oscillation influence drought frequency in the United States. These patterns indicate that during the twentieth century, variations in the north Pacific have affected winter precipitation in the Southwest, including the Yucca Mountain area, and that recent short-term precipitation records should be interpreted with reference to these possible external influences. At the same time, temperatures have been rising in southern Nevada for the past 30–40 yr for unknown reasons. Other research has shown through a variety of indicators (direct thermometer measurements, plant blooming dates, spring runoff dates) that winter and spring appear to be warming much more than summer or fall (Cayan et al., 2001) in the western United States.

Tree ring data from southern and Baja California indicate that shifts in the Pacific Decadal Oscillation from positive to negative have occurred throughout the past 400 yr (Biondi et al., 2001). The known major Pacific Decadal Oscillation reversals of 1947 and 1977 are matched by reversals in tree growth time series from these sites. These records also indicate that more pronounced climate transitions occur when shifts from El Niño to La Niña coincide with Pacific Decadal Oscillation reversals (Biondi et al., 2001). Longer-term data sets have caused us to question how representative the relatively short-term instrumental records may be. This also brings into question how long those records must be to establish representativeness. Thus, the foundation of our understanding of *modern* climate may need to be reconsidered.

Synoptic-Scale Features

Present-day synoptic weather patterns affect the Southwest and control certain semi-permanent atmospheric pressure features over and near the United States. These weather patterns depend primarily on modern temperature and humidity properties of the land or ocean underlying the system air mass. These are the Pacific High (eastern north Pacific), Aleutian Low (Gulf of Alaska, winter), Bermuda High (western north Atlantic), and summertime thermal low (Southwestern United States) (Ahrens, 1994, Fig. 11.3 therein). Seasonal changes in position and strength of these centers of action influence winds and storm movement. Many Pacific cyclones affecting Yucca Mountain form in the vicinity of the Aleutian Low and arrive from the west or northwest, often on a trajectory that curves around or over the southern part of the Sierra Nevada.

The Yucca Mountain area is on the climate gradient associated with the rise from the low-elevation Mojave Desert to the higher elevation Great Basin (Fig. 1). Because of its latitude, the Yucca Mountain area is affected by two main influences during the annual cycle. During the cool parts of the year, the area is affected by mid-latitude westerly winds and associated storm systems. During summer, this band of upper air (i.e., tropospheric) winds weakens and retreats toward the United States–Canada border, leaving the Yucca Mountain area under the influence of the southwest monsoon.

Precipitation. Precipitation in southern Nevada arises primarily from three airflow trajectories and moisture origins in the Pacific, Gulf of Mexico, and continental regions. The most important to the Yucca Mountain area is the Pacific trajectory, followed to a lesser extent by the continental and Gulf trajectories (Benson and Klieforth, 1989). The polar front, usually oriented east-west, lies approximately beneath the jet stream and is the zone that usually separates cool northern air from warm southern air. During the winter, the polar front moves as far south as 30°N and retreats poleward in summer to near 50°N (Lutgens and Tarbuck, 1998). Yucca Mountain is at ~37°N (Fig. 1). Thus, the Yucca Mountain area receives more precipitation as the polar front expands southward in winter and less precipitation as the front contracts northward in summer. The position of the jet stream and storm track depends on the season as well as geographic and topographic influences (e.g., ocean and land, mountains and valleys). The average position of the storm track can change slowly at decadal to millennial scales, remain more or less stationary for months, or change abruptly in a few hours to days or weeks.

Winter disturbances typically are frontal storms that have large-scale, synoptic organization and structure, on the order of hundreds to more than a thousand kilometers in horizontal dimensions. Cool-season storms help to equalize horizontal temperature differences between the tropics and polar latitudes, which radiative processes continually recreate. The storms usually have a warm sector, with southerly or southwesterly winds in advance (east) of the core of the storm, and a trailing (west) cool sector, with northerly to northwesterly winds. The transition between sectors manifests itself as a wind shift as the storm passes. Storms occurring in summer are smaller, the size of individual thunderstorms, with horizontal dimensions (e.g., mesoscale) of just a few kilometers. On occasion, individual storms can merge into larger scale assemblages that last longer and produce heavier rains.

The Sierra Nevada and Transverse Mountains (Fig. 1) either can block or impede atmospheric moisture transport from the Pacific Ocean to Yucca Mountain, especially during winter, producing a rain-shadow effect. Eastward-moving air must ascend the Sierra Nevada, which is high at this latitude (numerous 4270 m peaks), skirt the range to the south, or (only occasionally) follow a more northerly trajectory. In any case, intervening mountain ranges can remove much of the moisture that might have been in the air originally. Nearly all precipitation is from imported moisture because the southern Nevada region is too arid to resupply much moisture back to the overlying atmosphere from vegetation and other local surface sources.

Winter. During winter, the eastward extension of the Pacific High directs most cyclonic storms away from the Southwestern United States by deflecting the jet stream toward more northerly latitudes. Thus, the desert Southwest region has relatively few storm passages and tends to have mild, dry winter weather. On occasion, the Pacific High weakens or moves, and the jet stream shifts to help bring storms, precipitation, and cooler air into the Southwest (Mock, 1996). Although relatively infrequent, these storms are a very important contributor to annual recharge and streamflow in the Southwest.

An example of this wet-weather pattern occurred during the 2004–2005 winter. In early January 2005, lows off the California coast forced the polar jet stream south. A subtropical jet stream (often referred to as the Pineapple Express) brought moisture-laden air from the tropics, over the Hawaiian Islands, and onto the west coast of the United States. El Niño was not thought to be the primary contributing factor for this series of heavy precipitation events (http://www.ncdc.noaa.gov/oa/climate/research/2005/california-storms2005.html). By 18 January 2005, Las Vegas, Nevada, recorded a total of 4.42 inches (112 mm) of rainfall which was 96% of its seasonal rainfall total (WRCC, 2006). This synoptic pattern resembles the pattern for glacial periods discussed later in this chapter because the jet-stream position is thought to have had a prolonged southerly position aimed at the Transverse Mountains of southern California (Fig. 1) during glacial periods.

Summer. As spring transitions into summer, an east-west ridge of higher pressure forms at upper levels, essentially producing a western extension of the subtropical Bermuda High in the Atlantic. Through early summer, this feature migrates slowly north to permit the northward intrusion of very moist tropical air into the southwestern United States by July. Gulf of California sea surface temperatures are thought to be a major factor in determining the timing, rainfall amount, and northwestward extent of the Mexican or North American monsoon (Mitchell et al., 2002). The often abrupt arrival of this southwest monsoon is accompanied by greatly decreased vertical stability and numerous, and often heavy, thunderstorms. Yucca Mountain lies in a transition zone, where the influence of the monsoon is significant; the heaviest showers of the year usually occur during July and August. Less commonly, in September and October, remnant moisture exported northeastward from dying tropical storms off Baja California also can produce very heavy precipitation.

Site Climatology

Site climatology is influenced by local hills and valleys, drainage channels, rock outcrops and cliffs, hill slopes, and similar sized features. It operates at small scales relative to synoptic and regional features. Terrain can channel, accelerate, or block the movement of air and affect the vertical component of air motion and, thus, precipitation mechanisms. Much of the observed fine-scale spatial variation in precipitation in the mountainous western United States (Mock, 1996; Blumen, 1990) arises from the way that terrain influences flow pattern, on large and small scales.

Topography provides a significant influence regionally and locally, at scales down to those recorded by measurement stations. The following sections on temperature, precipitation, humidity, wind, solar radiation, evaporation, atmospheric stability, and air quality rely primarily on data from the U.S. Department of Energy (DOE) meteorological monitoring sites (Fig. 2). These data are summarized by the Western Regional Climate Center at http://www.yuccamountain.dri.edu (WRCC, 2006). Additional data from the Nevada Test Site (http://www.nts.dri.edu) and regional meteorological stations (http://www.wrcc.dri.edu/climsum.html) also are available.

Nine DOE monitoring sites (Fig. 2, sites 1 through 9) were established to provide representative data regarding meteorological conditions in topographically diverse settings at and around Yucca Mountain and to provide data for estimating atmospheric dispersion to evaluate the consequences of potential airborne releases. DOE sites 1–5 were installed in December 1985 as part of an environmental monitoring network. Sites 6–8 were added in July 1992, and site 9 was added in January 1993 primarily to provide localized airflow characteristics related to the Exploratory Studies Facility. Five of the nine sites (3, 5, 6, 7, and 8) were downgraded to precipitation sites in 1999 with accompanying temperature and humidity measurements. Monitoring equipment installed at sites 1–9 varies. Onsite data loggers record meteorological conditions including mean, extreme, standard deviation, and total summaries using a range of time periods. Wind gusts occurring in a three-second period and extreme daily one-minute average wind speed and temperature values are recorded. All sites have two precipitation gages: one gage records by increments of 0.01 inch (0.254 mm); the other is a standard storage gage. Types of monitoring equipment are listed in Table 1. The period of record for meteorological parameters for each site as well as the start and end date used for summary calculations are listed in Table 2.

Seventeen supplementary precipitation sites (401–417) were added to the monitoring network in 1997 to extend precipitation data collection. Sites 405 and 415 have all-season and storage precipitation gages. Site 401 was downgraded to only a storage gage on October 30, 2001. The remaining supplementary precipitation sites have calibrated tipping-bucket rain gages. They currently (2006) are maintained by the Nevada System of Higher Education (http://hrc.nevada.edu/chemistry/hydrologic.htm).

Site 1 has a 60 m tower, instrumented at two levels, with wind and temperature sensors at 10 and 60 m above ground level (m-agl). Horizontal wind speed and direction are measured at both levels, and vertical wind speed is measured at 10 m-agl. Site 1 temperature, relative humidity, and pyranometers (used for measuring solar radiation) are located at 2 m-agl, and barometric pressure is nominally located at the surface. The recording precipitation gage at site 1 is heated to capture snowfall as it occurs. Sites 2, 4, and 9 include towers instrumented at 10 m-agl with wind and temperature sensors virtually the same as the 10 m-agl at site 1. These sites also record temperature, relative humidity, and solar radiation at 2 m-agl. Barometric pressure is recorded at the surface. Sites 3, 5, 6, 7, and 8 have temperature and relative humidity sensors at 2 m-agl. Site 5 includes a barometer at the surface.

The following discussion summarizes results from all nine DOE meteorological monitoring sites. Monthly values for temperature, precipitation, barometric pressure, relative humidity, wind speed and direction, and mean daily total solar radiation are listed for site 1 (WRCC, 2006) in Table 3. Annual values of the parameters listed above and the location of each site are shown in Table 4.

Temperature

Temperatures range from cool in the winter (~6 °C) to hot in summer (~29 °C). At site 1, for example, the mean daily minimum is 2.1 °C in December, and the mean daily maximum is

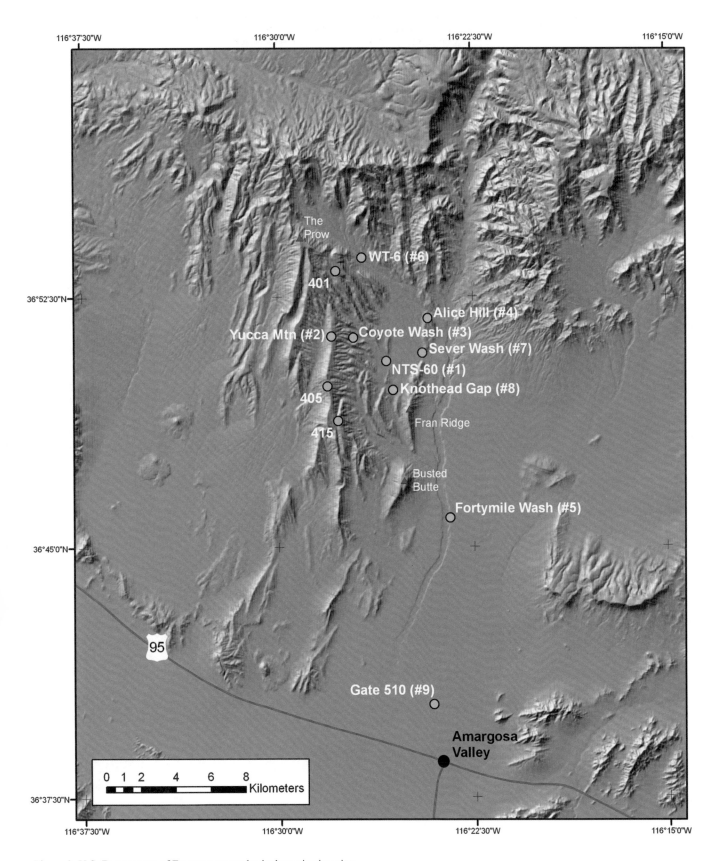

Figure 2. U.S. Department of Energy meteorological monitoring sites.

TABLE 1. TYPES OF MONITORING EQUIPMENT INSTALLED IN THE FIELD TO MEASURE VARIOUS ENVIRONMENTAL PARAMETERS AT U.S. DEPARTMENT OF ENERGY METEOROOLOGICAL MONITORING SITES 1 TO 9, YUCCA MOUNTAIN

Parameter	Equipment
Wind speed	Cup anemometer with photochopper
Wind direction	Vane, with potentiometer at Sites 2 through 9 and resolver at Site 1
Temperature and Delta-temperature	Mechanically aspirated shields with thermistor
Relative humidity	Capacitance sensors at Sites 1 through 9
Barometric pressure	Aneroid wafer
Precipitation	Tipping-bucket, 8-inch orifice (20.32 cm), 0. 01-inch tip (0.254 mm)
Solar radiation	Pyranometer
Vertical wind speed	Propeller anemometer with optical chopper

34.9 °C in July (Table 3). Average monthly and annual temperatures are higher at lower elevations. The modest elevation (838–1478 m) at Yucca Mountain DOE sites is enough to prevent occurrence of the extremely hot temperatures reached in other, lower southwestern deserts. In the dry and cloudless air, surfaces cool efficiently by radiation, and daily ranges can be large.

Low humidity and clear skies allow surface temperatures to decrease significantly with increasing elevation, especially during daylight hours. This is less true at night and depends on local (sometimes very local) exposure and station site geometry. Unless it is cloudy or windy, surface-based temperature inversions form nearly every night, with warmer air aloft overlying cooler air near the surface. Such situations are stable and usually persist until daybreak. These conditions produce surface heating, particularly in the summer with its high Sun, which disrupts this vertical layering and soon produces temperatures that decrease with elevation. For this reason, sites on the sides or tops of even small hills often have warmer minimums than sites in adjoining low spots. For example, the December mean daily minimum at site 4 on Alice Hill is 2.9 °C whereas the mean daily minimum at nearby site 7 in Sever Wash is −1.4 °C (Table 4).

Atmospheric moisture absorbs the infrared radiation emitted by the ground as it cools. In the very dry desert air, water vapor is not available to absorb this upward flux and re-radiate it back down toward the surface, so the surface cools very rapidly. Only in July and August, when the southwest monsoon brings extremely moist air to the Yucca Mountain area on occasion, is it humid enough to significantly decrease the rate at which the atmosphere cools. Well into late spring or early summer, with sufficiently dry air, the Yucca Mountain area can reach temperatures at or below freezing. For example, the lowest recorded daily minimum temperature at site 1 for April is −2.4 °C and May is 0.3 °C (Table 3).

The average annual temperature for the period of record for all stations (Table 2) ranges from 15.1 °C at site 6 to a high of 18.2 °C at site 9 (Table 4). Generally, these two stations also record the lower (site 6) and upper (site 9) average monthly temperatures. The mean daily maximum temperature for all stations is highest in July (ranging from 32.7 to 38.8 °C) and the mean daily minimum temperature is lowest in December

(varying from −1.4 to 3.1 °C). Site 9 and site 2 register the highest and lowest, respectively, daily maximum temperatures, as well as the annual highest and lowest mean daily maximum temperatures (Table 4). These two stations also generally record the highest and lowest daily maximum temperatures, respectively, for each month throughout the year. Site 6 monthly temperature values are similar to site 2 values, however, and site 5 values are similar to site 9 values. Site 7 records the lowest mean daily minimum temperature averaged for each month for the period of record and the lowest daily minimum temperature (−14.8 °C) of all sites. The highest daily maximum temperature, 44.7 °C, was recorded at site 9 on 18 July 1998. Monthly temperature values for site 1 generally occur in the middle of the monthly values for the other stations (Table 3).

Precipitation

Annual precipitation is low in the Yucca Mountain area and occurs in two main seasons, during the winter months and during the southwest monsoon in July and August. On a monthly average for each station's period of record, most precipitation falls in February at all stations. The greatest average monthly total for February is 51.6 mm (site 7), and the least average monthly total for February is 33.2 mm (site 9). Maximum daily precipitation also is high in July, however; occasionally, maximum daily values in July exceed maximum daily values in February (WRCC, 2006). Monthly values for site 1 precipitation are listed in Table 3. As with temperature, these monthly values generally occur in the middle of the monthly values for the other stations except for maximum one-hour totals where site 1 records very high values in February and June compared to the other stations.

Maximum daily values are highly variable among stations, underscoring the effects of topography and highly variable weather patterns in the Yucca Mountain area. Even heavy thunderstorms may deposit little precipitation on low elevation surfaces. In areas with arid climates, relative variability of aggregated precipitation totals is very large on all time scales, from daily to decadal. Relative variability is a measure of statistical dispersion of the frequency distribution (e.g., standard deviation), divided by the mean. Temperature data do not show

TABLE 2. PERIOD OF RECORD FOR U.S. DEPARTMENT OF ENERGY METEOROLOGICAL MONITORING SITES 1 TO 9, YUCCA MOUNTAIN

	Site 1 (NTS-60)	Site 2 (Yucca Mountain)	Site 3 (Coyote Wash)	Site 4 (Alice Hill)	Site 5 (Fortymile Wash)	Site 6 (WT-6)	Site 7 (Sever Wash)	Site 8 (Knothead Gap)	Site 9 (Gate-510)
Start and End Dates for Period of Record									
Precipitation	12/1/85–12/31/05	8/23/89–12/31/05	8/23/89–12/31/05	2/5/90–12/31/05	8/23/89–12/31/05	7/1/92–12/31/05	6/27/92–12/31/05	7/2/92–12/31/05	1/1/93–12/31/05
Temperature	12/1/85–12/31/05	12/1/85–12/31/05	12/2/85–12/31/05	12/1/85–12/31/05	12/1/85–12/31/05	7/1/92–12/31/05	7/1/92–12/31/05	7/2/92–12/31/05	1/1/93–12/31/05
Barometric Pressure	3/1/89–12/31/05	8/1/89–12/31/05	8/1/89–7/15/99	2/5/90–12/31/05	9/19/89–12/31/05	10/1/92–7/15/99	10/1/92–7/14/99	10/2/92–7/15/99	1/1/93–12/31/05
Relative Humidity	1/1/99–12/31/05	12/1/85–12/31/05	12/2/85–12/31/05	12/1/85–12/31/05	12/1/85–12/31/05	7/1/92–12/31/05	7/1/92–12/31/05	7/2/92–12/31/05	1/1/93–12/31/05
Wind Speed	12/1/85–12/31/05	12/1/85–12/31/05	12/6/85–7/15/99	12/1/85–12/31/05	12/1/85–7/13/99	10/1/92–7/15/99	7/2/92–7/14/99	7/2/92–7/15/99	1/1/93–12/31/05
Wind Gust	1/1/96–12/31/05	10/1/93–12/31/05	10/1/93–7/15/99	10/1/93–12/31/05	10/1/93–7/13/99	10/1/93–7/15/99	10/1/93–7/14/99	10/1/93–7/15/99	10/1/93–12/31/05
Solar Radiation	7/13/93–12/31/05	9/1/93–12/31/05	9/1/93–7/15/99	9/1/93–12/31/05	9/1/93–7/13/99	7/1/92–7/15/99	7/1/92–7/14/99	7/1/92–7/15/99	1/1/93–12/31/05
Start and End Dates Used for Summary Calculations									
Precipitation	1/1/86–12/31/05	9/1/89–12/31/05	9/1/89–12/31/05	2/5/90–12/31/05	9/1/89–12/31/05	7/1/92–12/31/05	7/1/92–12/31/05	7/2/92–12/31/05	1/1/93–12/31/05
Temperature	1/1/86–12/31/05	1/1/86–12/31/05	1/1/86–12/31/05	1/1/86–12/31/05	1/1/86–12/31/05	7/1/92–12/31/05	7/1/92–12/31/05	7/2/92–12/31/05	1/1/93–12/31/05
Barometric Pressure	3/1/89–12/31/05	8/1/89–12/31/05	8/1/89–6/30/99	2/5/90–12/31/05	10/1/89–12/31/05	10/1/92–6/30/99	10/1/92–6/30/99	11/2/92–6/30/99	1/1/93–12/31/05
Relative Humidity	1/1/99–12/31/05	1/1/86–12/31/05	1/1/86–12/31/05	1/1/86–12/31/05	1/1/86–12/31/05	7/1/92–12/31/05	7/1/92–12/31/05	7/2/92–12/31/05	1/1/93–12/31/05
Wind Speed	1/1/86–12/31/05	1/1/86–12/31/05	1/1/86–6/30/99	1/1/86–12/31/05	1/1/86–6/30/99	10/1/92–6/30/99	7/1/92–6/30/99	7/2/92–6/30/99	1/1/93–12/31/05
Wind Gust	1/1/96–12/31/05	10/1/93–12/31/05	10/1/93–6/30/99	10/1/93–12/31/05	10/1/93–6/30/99	10/1/93–6/30/99	10/1/93–6/30/99	10/1/93–6/30/99	10/1/93–12/31/05
Solar Radiation	8/1/93–12/31/05	9/1/93–12/31/05	9/1/93–6/30/99	9/1/93–12/31/05	9/1/93–6/30/99	7/1/92–6/30/99	7/1/92–6/30/99	7/1/92–6/30/99	1/1/93–12/31/05

Note: Locations are shown in Figure 2.

TABLE 3. MONTHLY AVERAGES FOR U.S. DEPARTMENT OF ENERGY METEOROLOGICAL MONITORING SITE 1, YUCCA MOUNTAIN*

Parameter	Jan.	Feb.	March	April	May	June	July	August	Sep.	Oct.	Nov.	Dec.
Temperature °C												
Average	6.5	8.0	11.5	15.0	20.0	25.4	28.8	27.9	23.5	17.7	10.1	6.1
Highest Recorded Daily Maximum[†,§]	23.4	26.3	29.3	31.7	39.0	40.6	42.3	41.2	36.9	34.1	26.2	21.5
(day/year)	(31/2003)	(26/1986)	(21/2004)	(7/1989)	(28/2003)	(15/2000)	(9/2002)	(15/2002)	(2&31/1988)	(8/1996)	(4/1988)	(16/1998)
Mean Daily Maximum[†,§]	11.3	12.8	16.9	20.6	26.0	31.5	34.9	34.1	29.5	23.4	15.4	11.1
Lowest Recorded Daily Minimum[†,§]	−7.8	−11.1	−3.9	−2.4	0.3	4.5	10.9	13.7	6.9	0.4	−6.1	−11.7
(day/year)	(14/1997)	(6/1989)	(23/1995;1/1997)	(10/1999)	(2/1991)	(17/1995)	(18/1987)	(7/1999)	(26/1986)	(31/1991)	(27/1994)	(22/1990)
Mean Daily Minimum[†,§]	2.5	3.8	6.2	9.1	13.4	18.2	21.9	21.4	17.5	12.3	5.6	2.1
Monthly Average # Hours ≥ 32 °C[†]	0.0	0.0	0.0	0.0	22.9	119.1	226.2	183.5	47.0	2.2	0.0	0.0
Monthly Average # Hours ≤ 0 °C[†]	80.5	48.8	14.4	3.7	0.2	0.0	0.0	0.0	0.0	0.1	22.3	99.3
Precipitation (tipping-bucket)												
Average Monthly Total mm	21.8	35.7	18.1	10.2	9.2	7.2	11.7	12.4	7.6	8.9	8.3	11.8
Maximum Daily total[§] mm (day/year)	35.3	54.1	26.7	28.7	16.8	25.8	36.6	30.0	29.0	26.2	22.6	25.4
(day/year)	(17/1988)	(23/1998)	(20/1991)	(14/2003)	(26/1999)	(6/1987)	(13/1999)	(4/1987)	(25/1997)	(27/2004)	(21/1996)	(7/1992)
Maximum 1 hr. total mm	4.8	8.4	14.7	5.8	13.7	19.3	19.1	21.1	10.4	6.1	9.9	5.8
# Hours Precipitation ≥ 0.25 mm	22.9	30.6	18.0	10.1	8.1	4.5	4.5	5.7	5.5	8.1	6.9	12.2
# Hours Precipitation ≥ 2.5 mm	1.9	4.0	1.3	1.1	0.9	0.8	1.3	1.2	1.0	1.4	1.1	1.1
Mean Barometric Pressure[†] (mb)	889	887	885	884	883	883	886	886	886	887	888	889
Mean Relative Humidity[†] (%)	44	49	36	33	22	16	20	24	23	30	38	42
Hour 0400 (Pacific Standard Time)	52	57	46	45	33	25	30	34	31	37	47	49
Hour 1000 (Pacific Standard Time)	39	44	31	28	19	14	18	21	19	25	32	36
Hour 1600 (Pacific Standard Time)	33	36	23	20	13	9	13	14	13	21	27	32
Hour 2200 (Pacific Standard Time)	48	53	38	37	24	17	22	25	25	33	42	45
Wind												
Mean Speed 10 m (m/s)[†]	2.9	3.3	4.0	4.3	4.0	4.0	3.9	3.8	3.6	3.4	3.2	2.9
Maximum 3-s Wind Gust 10m (m/s)	20.4	24.8	21.9	27.1	27.6	24.6	22.7	24.1	24.6	27.1	22.0	27.1
(day/year)	(8/2005)	(2/2003)	(8/2002)	(15/2002)	(10/2004)	(16/1998)	(24/2002)	(31/1998)	(11/2004)	(25/1996)	(8/2002)	(14/2003)
Prevailing Direction (deg)*	337	337	337	180	180	180	180	180	180	337	337	337
Mean Speed 60 m (m/s)**	3.0	3.4	3.7	4.3	3.9	3.8	3.5	3.3	3.1	3.2	2.8	2.7
Maximum 3s Gust 60 m (m/s)	23.9	29.3	28.3	30.1	27.0	30.0	23.2	31.3	23.5	30.4	24.5	27.5
Mean Daily Total Solar Radiation (MJ/m²/d)	9.9	12.6	18.9	23.7	27.2	29.9	28.8	26.0	21.6	16.4	11.4	9.4

Note: Location is shown in Figure 2; m—meter, s—second, deg—degrees, MJ—megajoules, d—day).

*WRCC (2006).

[†]Values are taken from 1-s data averaged over 1 hr. (day/year)—day/year value occurred, as applicable.

[§]Calendar day, midnight to midnight.

*Highest frequency of 16-point compass.

**Values are taken from 1-s data averaged over 10 min.

TABLE 4. ANNUAL VALUES FOR U.S. DEPARTMENT OF ENERGY METEOROLOGICAL SITES 1 TO 9*

Parameter	Site 1 (NTS-60)	Site 2 (Yucca Mountain)	Site 3 (Coyote Wash)	Site 4 (Alice Hill)	Site 5 (Fortymile Wash)	Site 6 (WT-6)	Site 7 (Sever Wash)	Site 8 (Knothead Gap)	Site 9 (Gate-510)
Latitude	36°50'34"N	36°51'19"N	36°51'17"N	36°51'51"N	36°45'52"N	36°53'40"N	36°50'49"N	36°49'42"N	36°40'17"N
Longitude	116°25'50"W	116°27'56"W	116°27'06"W	116°24'15"W	116°23'26"W	116°26'45"W	116°24'28"W	116°25'35"W	116°24'17"W
Elevation	1143 m	1478 m	1279 m	1234 m	953 m	1315 m	1081 m	1131 m	838 m
Temperature (°C)									
Average	16.7	15.7	16.5	16.8	17.7	15.1	15.9	16.0	18.2
Highest Recorded Daily Maximum†§	42.3	39.9	41.2	42.3	44.1	40.6	43.2	42.5	44.7
(month/day/year)	(7/9/02)	(7/9/02)	(7/9/02)	(7/9/02)	(7/9/02)	(7/9/02)	(7/18/05)	(7/18/98)	(7/18/98)
Mean Daily Maximum†§ (month)	34.9 (Jul)	32.7 (Jul)	33.5 (Jul)	34.3 (Jul)	36.8 (Jul)	33.8 (Jul)	36.7 (Jul)	35.9 (Jul)	38.8 (Jul)
Lowest Recorded Daily Minimum†§	−11.7	−12.5	−12.2	−12.6	−13.1	−10.4	−14.8	−11.9	−9.5
(month/day/year)	(12/22/90)	(2/6/89)	(12/22/90)	(12/22/90)	(12/22/90)	(12/22/98)	(12/22/98)	(12/22/98)	(12/23/98)
Mean Daily Minimum†§ (month)	2.1 (Dec)	3.1 (Dec)	2.7 (Dec)	2.9 (Dec)	1.9 (Dec)	0.5 (Dec)	−1.4 (Dec)	0.1 (Dec)	1.4 (Dec)
Total # Hours ≥ 32 °C and above	601	292	424	512	858	458	818	755	1093
Total # Hours ≤ 0 °C and below	270	340	257	221	224	466	568	440	248
Precipitation									
Annual Average Tipping-Bucket mm (entire period of record)	162.9	183.1	195.7	192.2	143.5	213.9	202.4	188.7	113.3
Annual Average Tipping-Bucket mm (1996–2005)	196.9	197.3	215.7	205.9	154.5	207.1	205.9	189.4	112.4
Annual Average Storage-Gage mm (1996–2005)	212.6	207.6	231.4	205.1	155.0	227.3	208.5	204.1	121.4
Maximum Daily total§ mm (tipping bucket period of record) (month/day/year)	54.1 (2/23/98)	50.0 (2/23/98)	48.0 (2/23/98)	59.4 (2/23/98)	50.0 (2/23/98)	44.7 (2/21/05)	64.8 (7/13/99)	59.9 (12/7/92)	45.5 (2/12/03)
Maximum 1 hr. total mm (month)	21.1 (Aug)	30.0 (Jul)	22.1 (Jul)	30.7 (Jul)	29.0 (Jul)	16.3 (Jul)	31.2 (Jul)	26.9 (Aug)	13.5 (Jul)
Total # Hours Precipitation ≥ 0.25 mm	137	147	140	143	122	155	148	147	113
Total # Hours Precipitation ≥ 2.5 mm	17	21	21	22	15	26	24	22	12
Annual Average Barometric Pressure† (mb)	886	851	871	876	905	867	892	887	917
Highest Daily Average (month/day/year)	904 (2/10/02)	866 (2/10/02)	886 (12/11;&12/97)	893 (2/10/02)	924 (2/10/02)	882 (12/24/93;12/11&12/97)	908 (12/11&12/97)	903 (11/26/92;12/24/93;12/11/97)	936 (2/10/02)
Lowest Daily Average (month/day/year)	867 (3/1/90&91;2/29/92)	831 (2/27/97)	853 (2/27/97)	858 (2/27/97)	887 (12/19/90)	848 (2/27/97)	874 (2/27/97)	869 (2/27/97)	899 (2/27/97)
Annual Average Relative Humidity† (%)	31	28	29	28	29	33	34	33	30
Hour 0400 (Pacific Standard Time)	41	33	36	34	37	43	48	45	40
Hour 1600 (Pacific Standard Time)	21	22	22	21	19	22	21	20	18
Wind									
Mean Annual Speed 10 m (m/s)†	3.6	4.3	2.6	4.5	4.4	4.0	3.2	3.1	4.4
Maximum 3-s Wind Gust 10 m (m/s)	27.6	38.7	–	37.9	30.4	29.9	–	–	33.1
(month/day/year)	(5/10/04)	(9/26/05)	–	(8/31/98)	(10/25/96)	(6/16/98)	–	–	(7/30/03)
Prevailing direction (deg)#	337	157	–	180	360	315	–	–	22
Average Annual Daily Total Solar Radiation MJ/m²/d	19.7	19.9	19.6	21.1	20.3	19.8	20.1	20.1	21.5

Note: Sites are shown in Figure 2; m—meter, s—second, deg—degrees, MJ—megajoules, d—day.
*WRCC (2006).
†Values are taken from 1-s data averaged over 1 hr. (month/day/year)—month/day/year value occurred, as applicable.
§Calendar day, midnight to midnight.
#Highest frequency of 16-point compass.

such high variability. Thus, longer records are needed for precipitation data than for temperature data to obtain a *representative* mean.

Another feature of arid climates is that much of the annual precipitation falls in just a few concentrated episodes. Typically, in this part of the United States, the wettest day brings about a quarter to a third of the annual mean precipitation (Table 4), and about once in 50–100 yr, the wettest annual day can rival the mean annual total in the driest locations. Previous estimates from Atlas 2 by the National Oceanic and Atmospheric Administration (Miller et al., 1973) have been updated by the National Weather Service Hydrometeorological Design Studies Center and placed online (www.nws.noaa.gov/ohd/hdsc). Because values from 1973 are in such widespread use, old and new estimates (following in brackets) for the Yucca Mountain area (36.904°N, 116.481°W, 1587 m elevation) are given here. They show that in a 6 h period, ~19 mm [20 mm] of precipitation will fall in a randomly placed gage ~50 times in 100 yr and that ~43 mm [63 mm] would fall about once in 100 yr. For a 24 h period, ~28 mm [30 mm] of precipitation is expected about every other year and ~71 mm [96 mm] could be expected during a randomly selected 100 yr period. The newer values are greater than the previous values in part because the region experienced a somewhat wetter precipitation regime from the late-1970s to the mid-1990s.

The average annual tipping-bucket precipitation values show that the highest value, 213.9 mm, occurred at site 6 and the lowest, 113.3 mm, occurred at site 9 (Table 4). The highest maximum daily total of all sites measured 64.8 mm at site 7 on 13 July 1999. The lowest maximum daily total of all sites measured 44.7 mm at site 6 on 21 February 2005. Maximum one-hour totals occur in July and August with a maximum recorded value of 31.2 mm at site 7 (Table 4). The number of hours per month with precipitation greater than or equal to 0.25 mm was highest in February for all sites ranging from 36.8 h at site 7 to 22.7 h at site 5 (WRCC, 2006). The number of hours per year with precipitation greater than or equal to 2.5 mm ranged from 26 (site 6) to 12 h (site 9) (Table 4). Although Yucca Mountain climate is considered to be semiarid or arid, hourly, daily, and monthly maximum values can be considerable.

Tipping-bucket and storage gage precipitation values were collected from all nine stations, although the period of record is longer for tipping-bucket data than for storage gage data. From 1996 to 2005 when both instruments were in use for all nine stations, the annual average storage gage totals were almost always greater than the tipping-bucket totals (Table 4) indicating that the tipping-bucket values often may underestimate annual precipitation. These differences are likely because the storage gage catches everything, although it may lose a little to evaporation. The tipping-bucket gages tend to undermeasure during heavy rainfall rates, or events with high winds, and they typically measure a little bit less than the total because of the water left in the bucket that did not make the last tip.

Humidity

The atmosphere in southern Nevada is characterized by very low relative and absolute humidity, especially in summer. Absolute humidity refers to the number of water molecules as a fraction of total air molecules. Relative humidity refers to what the air could contain. For the same amount of moisture, relative humidity varies inversely with temperature. Thus, for the same amount of moisture, relative humidity is low in mid-afternoon and higher at night and is higher in winter than in summer for the same time of day and on a daily average. Although absolute humidity is usually very low, occasionally—during the monsoon season (mostly July and August)—short episodes of high absolute humidity can occur with dew points reaching 23 °C. In the lower atmosphere, relative humidity increases with elevation, reflecting the decrease in temperature with elevation, whereas absolute humidity typically decreases with elevation.

Mean relative humidity is lowest for all stations in June and July and highest in December through February (WRCC, 2006). Monthly averages for each station are lowest at 1600 h and highest at 0400 h (WRCC, 2006). Monthly values for site 1 are listed in Table 3; annual values for all sites are listed in Table 4.

Wind

Wind is one of the most variable atmospheric elements in time and space. Wind is the dominant meteorological parameter involved in characterizing atmospheric dispersion because airflow controls the transport pathway and dilution of airborne material. Atmospheric dispersion refers to the mixing and transport of momentum, kinetic energy, or a contaminant (heat, particles or gas) by the atmospheric processes of molecular diffusion, turbulent diffusion, and advection. Therefore, wind is an important meteorological parameter at Yucca Mountain.

Winds have local and large-scale origins, ranging from small-scale heating differences on the scale of millimeters to as much as the size of the globe. In a typical desert environment, surface and upper flows are coupled much more strongly during daytime and often completely decoupled at night. Wind speeds usually increase with elevation, but there are many exceptions to this generalization. In the free atmosphere, winds increase with elevation in winter. In the summer, winds decrease away from the surface, in part reflecting low-level northward transport associated with the monsoon. No matter how hard the wind is blowing, wind velocity is always zero at the ground surface. Therefore, a larger variation exists within a few vertical meters for wind than for almost any other atmospheric parameter. Topographic effects—such as channeling, steering, waves, rotors, accelerations, quiet zones, cold air trapping, and other phenomena—are common.

Wind velocity is also a vector quantity, which complicates the task of formulating simple or adequate summaries of wind effects. Scalar properties suffice for some processes. For example, evaporation depends on wind speed and is not affected by wind direction, unless the moving air mass carries a directionally varying property, such as temperature or moisture content.

For other processes, information on wind speed and direction must be summarized with probability distributions. The strongest winds in southern Nevada are likely to be associated with thunderstorms. For example, Table 4 lists maximum gusts at sites 2 (38.7 m/s), 4 (37.9 m/s), and 9 (33.1 m/s). These gusts occurred just before or during precipitation events (WRCC, 2006). Stations 1, 5, and 6, with lower maximum wind speeds (~27–30 m/s), did not have any precipitation associated with these wind gusts (WRCC, 2006). In the dry desert air, very strong downdrafts can develop through evaporative cooling of drops falling in concentrated rain shafts. The strongest thunderstorm winds will preferentially be in the direction of storm movement, which is from southern and western quadrants. Wind is also a major factor in removal of moisture near the surface after recent wetting by a rainstorm. When such moisture is available, evaporative losses are increased considerably by strong winds.

Wind patterns are a result of local topography and synoptic- and regional-scale weather patterns (CRWMS M&O, 1997). The primary influence on local wind is topography because it channels winds along the axes of valleys and generates diurnal winds due to air density differences over varying elevations. Local topography can generate winds because the common diurnal wind cycle of airflow is toward higher terrain in the daytime and away from higher terrain at night. This movement of air is caused by air-pressure differences that arise from air-density differences (caused by temperature differences between the air and Earth's surface at equal elevations over higher and lower terrain). The diurnal cycle occurs most often during clear sky conditions. Downslope winds during nighttime hours frequently are called drainage winds, because they typically follow the directions of hydrologic drainage in complex terrain.

Airflow at Yucca Mountain is channeled north and south by the north-south alignment of Yucca Mountain and Fran Ridge, located to the east of Fortymile Wash (Fig. 2). Wind direction is variable among sites and during different seasons, however (WRCC, 2006). For example, sites 1 and 8 have northwest and southerly winds throughout most of the year, but winds from the south blow a greater percentage of the time relative to northwest winds from March to August. Sites 2 and 4, located on ridgetops, have greater variability in wind direction than sites at lower elevations in the valley and wash areas. Winds blow from all directions at all times of the year at site 2. Although site 4 has winds from all directions at all times of the year, southerly winds during March through August are a dominant component. Sites 3 and 6 are similar in that they have northwesterly flow throughout the year and southeasterly flow March through August. Site 7 has northwest winds and south-southeast winds for most of the year. Winds recorded at site 5, in Fortymile Wash, are channeled north and south for most of the year, although a lesser north-northeast component is evident during the winter months. Site 9 has north-northeast winds throughout the year, but a south-southeasterly component is strongly evident March through August.

Change in diurnal direction also occurs. Airflow is generally from the south during the day. At night, winds flow from the north, northwest, or northeast—depending on local topography. The prevailing direction listed in Table 4 is the greatest number of hours the wind blew from that direction using a 16-point compass. Numerous other ways could be used to determine prevailing direction.

Wind speed increases at almost all sites from March through August relative to the rest of the year (WRCC, 2006). The highest mean monthly wind speed (4.9 through 5.5 m/s) occurs at site 4 from March through June. Site 5 records values almost equal to site 4 in March, June, October, and December, however. Site 3 has the lowest mean monthly wind speed (2.3–3.1 m/s) for all months of the year. Wind speed generally is greater in March for all stations. Wind speed is greater during the day than at night at all sites (WRCC, 2006).

The maximum wind gust recorded at each station and date of occurrence are listed in Table 4. When maximum wind gusts for each month are compared for all stations, hilltop sites 2 and 4 have the strongest gusts. The only exception is the month of July, when site 9 recorded a gust of 33.1 m/s on 30 July 2003 compared to site 2 (28.5 m/s on 29 July 1995) and site 4 28.3 m/s on 11 July 1996 and 19 July 2003). The 33.1 m/s value at site 9 is also the maximum gust recorded at this location (Table 4). Again, as discussed earlier with temperature, site 1 monthly average wind-speed values are approximately mid-range when compared with the other eight stations. Maximum wind gusts at site 1, however are low compared to the other stations—probably because of its sheltered location.

Solar Radiation

Southern Nevada has abundant sunshine, and with relatively few manmade sources to absorb or redirect (scatter) light, the atmosphere is a little more transparent in the Yucca Mountain area than in urbanized regions to the south and west. This radiant energy is absorbed at the air-soil interface and converted primarily to the physical heating of the atmosphere. It also is readily available to evaporate whatever water exists at the surface. Although the DOE meteorological monitoring sites do not monitor cloud-free days, Desert Rock at the Nevada Test Site averages 195 clear days per year (period of record June 1978 to May 1988) (WRCC, 2006).

Mean daily solar radiation is highest for all stations in June and lowest in December and January. Monthly values for site 1 are listed in Table 3. Average annual values for all sites are listed in Table 4.

Evaporation and Transpiration

Evaporation is important to the Yucca Mountain project because it is one factor that affects moisture content of soil and, hence, groundwater recharge. Rates of water loss are strong functions of wind, atmospheric humidity, temperature, and, to a lesser extent, solar radiation. There are few direct local measurements of actual or potential evaporation. The station at Boulder City, Nevada, however, shows a long-term average (1931 through 2002) of 116.02 in/yr (2947 mm/yr) from a standard National

Weather Service evaporation pan, kept full so that water availability is not a limiting factor (http://www.wrcc.dri.edu/htmlfiles/westevap.final.html).

Transpiration from desert plants is relatively low because of limited water available to evaporate and the high efficiency of desert plant life in taking up water. Moisture is lost from the soil directly and by the wicking action of plants. Plants take up water from a deep, long taproot or from extensive, shallow roots. Taproots can be tens of meters long and draw moisture from deep in the soil whereas shallow roots take up water during rare rainy episodes.

Atmospheric Stability

Atmospheric stability is an indicator of the potential strength of horizontal and vertical atmospheric mixing processes. Stability can be considered a measure of the tendency of the air to react to vertical displacement (CRWMS M&O, 1997). Stability data are used to model atmospheric dispersion of airborne material. Regional airflow, topographic channeling, diurnal and seasonal cycles, wind speed, wind direction, and percentage occurrence of wind direction influence atmospheric stability at Yucca Mountain.

Data from DOE sites 1–9 indicate that stability ranges from very stable (category F, restricted mixing conditions occurring during nights with little cloud cover and low wind speed) to extremely unstable (category A, vigorous mixing conditions occurring during days with strong to moderate insolation and low wind speed). The neutral category (Class D) is associated with moderate mixing conditions, occurring during either night or day with moderate to high wind speeds. The stable periods minimize vertical mixing and dilution of airborne pollutants (CRWMS M&O, 1997).

The Yucca Mountain area typically has unstable and neutral atmospheric stability conditions during daytime hours and stable conditions typically during nighttime hours (CRWMS M&O, 1997). Transition periods from northerly nighttime to southerly daytime flow also produce unstable conditions (CRWMS M&O, 1997). Heating of the ground surface through solar radiance during the largely cloudless daytime periods contributes to instability, thus effectively enhancing mixing conditions by creating large negative vertical temperature gradients. Conversely, clear sky during the nighttime hours allows the ground surface to cool leading to positive vertical temperature gradients (temperatures increasing with height) that suppress vertical mixing.

When the extremely unstable Category A condition is met at sites 1, 3, and 8, winds are generally from the southeast or south-southeast (WRCC, 2006). When Category A is met at sites 2, 4, and 9, winds occur from all directions; however, the winds are generally from the south. Wind patterns at each individual site are similar for all seasons of the year for Category A. Sites 2 and 4 are on hills, and site 9 is in Fortymile Wash (Fig. 2).

When the moderately stable Category F air condition is met at site 1, winds are predominately from the northwest (WRCC, 2006). When these stability conditions are met at sites 2 and 9, winds are from all directions. Moderately stable air occurs at these two sites at night, however, with northwest winds. When

the moderately stable Category F air condition is met at site 3, winds are from west-northwest at night and southeast during the day for all seasons of the year. This reflects the location of site 3 in a narrow wash. Site 4 moderately stable category winds blow from all directions; however, they are north-northeasterly a large percentage of the time.

When the neutral Category D condition is met at sites 1 and 8 for each season of the year, winds are generally from either the northwest or a southerly direction (WRCC, 2006). Additionally, site 1 shows predominately southerly winds during the day and northwesterly winds at night year around. When the neutral Category D condition is met at sites 2 and 4, winds are from all directions, reflecting station location on the top of hills. At site 2 in the summer months, most winds are from the east (90°) through the southwest (170°) with few winds from the other quadrants. Site 3 reflects channeling by terrain because it is located in a narrow canyon. Winds are from the west-northwest and south-southeast when conditions are met for Category D at site 3. When the neutral Category D condition is met at site 4, winds are predominately north-northeast and south for all seasons of the year. When Category D conditions are met at site 9, the winds are predominately from either the north-northeast or south-southeast in all seasons of the year. At this site, neutral air occurs with northeast winds during the day and southeast winds at night.

When different stability conditions are met for each site, wind directions are reasonably constant throughout the year at each individual site for each stability category (WRCC, 2006). Topographic constraints near each site produce some differences, however. For example, site 3 winds are the most channeled for all stability categories because the site is located in a narrow wash (Fig. 2). Site 2 winds are the least constrained for all stability categories because it is located on the top of a hill. Site 1 is partially constrained because it is located lower than the surrounding terrain in a relatively open area.

Air Quality

The Yucca Mountain Project ambient air-quality-monitoring program includes total suspended particulate matter and inhalable particulate matter (PM_{10}) sampling. Carbon monoxide, nitrogen dioxide, ozone, sulfur dioxide, nitric oxide, and the oxides of nitrogen were monitored from October 1991 through September 1995. Particulate matter monitoring began at sites 1 and 5 in 1989 and at sites 6 and 9 in 1992 (CRWMS M&O, 1999). The air-quality monitoring program consistently showed levels well below the applicable National Ambient Air Quality Standards. The highest reported PM_{10} concentration for a 24 h period was 67 $\mu g/m^3$, which is 45% of the applicable standard concentration level (CRWMS M&O, 1999). Most values did not exceed 15 $\mu g/m^3$.

Summary of Modern Climate

Planetary- and synoptic-scale features set the stage for differing climate regimes in the Yucca Mountain area. Geography, such as the Sierra Nevada, and local topography, such as hills and valleys, influence regional and local climate. Nine DOE meteorological monitoring stations have recorded temperature, precipitation, barometric pressure, relative humidity, wind speed and direction, and mean daily total solar radiation since as early as December 1985.

PALEOCLIMATE

Paleoclimate proxy records are valuable for this study because they identify sustained periods in the past with anomalously different climate relative to the modern instrumental record. Instrumental records in the western United States typically span decades to, at most, a century; they do not cover the range of climatic variability that Yucca Mountain has had in the past or will likely have during its post-closure period. This section documents the timing, magnitude, and character of past climate change in the Yucca Mountain area.

The Yucca Mountain regional area contains a robust late Quaternary paleoclimatic record from a variety of sources. The primary records of past climate change come from stratigraphic successions of plant and animal fossils as well as stable oxygen ($\delta^{18}O$) and carbon ($\delta^{13}C$) isotopes. Equally important age relations of the climate records are derived from U-series disequilibria ($^{230}Th/U$) and radiocarbon (^{14}C) dating, tephrochronology, paleomagnetic polarity stratigraphy, and stratigraphic position.

Paleoclimate data can be classified into three groups for this project: (1) providing information on site climate change at Yucca Mountain; (2) providing local late Quaternary climate change records; or (3) providing long regional records encompassing mid-Pleistocene to recent climate change. These data categories have different temporal resolutions. Site records can record several hundred thousand years; local records usually are limited to the past ~40 k.y., the limit of radiocarbon dating; and long regional records can encompass hundreds of thousands of years.

Paleoclimate records representing glacial periods are key to this study because precipitation was greater and temperature and evaporation were less during these times relative to the modern, interglacial climate. This suggests that infiltration was greater during glacial periods than during interglacial periods. Many paleoclimate proxy records, such as pluvial lake sediments, support the idea of increased infiltration and groundwater flow during glacial periods. Increased groundwater and river discharge as well as direct precipitation on lake surfaces during glacial periods enlarged and maintained these lakes as a direct result of increased local and regional precipitation and snowfall in the glaciated mountains. Lake records also are important because they establish a 400 k.y. cycle that is used to estimate future climate cycles. Thus, lake records provide an important component to this analysis.

Site Records of Climate Change

Site records are those on and within Yucca Mountain. They include data sets collected from calcite and silica precipitated in fractures within Yucca Mountain and calcite precipitated in the soils on or near Yucca Mountain. Isotopic and chemical data from unsaturated-zone minerals support that their source was from descending meteoric water (Whelan et al., 1994; Vaniman et al., 2001). Based on chloride simulations and data collected by Sonnenthal and Bodvarsson (1998), perched waters appear to contain a substantial component of older waters from a period of higher precipitation, which may date to late Pleistocene or early Holocene time periods.

Data from secondary minerals, mainly low-temperature calcite and opal in fractures and cavities, are used to evaluate hydrological conditions in the unsaturated zone and the response of the hydrogeologic system to climatic change through time (Paces et al., 1998). These secondary mineral data from Yucca Mountain do not provide high-resolution paleoclimatic data; however, at the depth of the proposed repository, uranium concentration and $\delta^{18}O$ values indicate that unsaturated-zone percolation and seepage-water chemistries have responded to changes in climate during the past 300 k.y. Variation in concentrations of uranium and $\delta^{18}O$ values in opal and calcite correspond to the timing of glacial and interglacial events in the Devils Hole record (Whelan et al., 2006, Fig. 4 therein). Large variations in seepage flux at the proposed repository horizon did not occur, however.

Local Records of Past Climate

Local records are within the Yucca Mountain area and include plant macrofossil data collected from packrat middens and sediments as well as biotic remains associated with wetland and spring deposits. Packrat midden records are temporally discontinuous records relative to the time scales considered here, although site-specific records can approach 7 k.y. in length (Spaulding, 1985). Paleo-wetland and spring deposits are also discontinuous records, because most basins within the Yucca Mountain precipitation area are situated well above the regional groundwater table. Therefore, the stratigraphic records of these deposits tend to capture only episodes representing high water tables. Erosion of these deposits may occur during ensuing dry climate episodes, thus yielding an even more discontinuous sedimentary record. These records often identify the timing and magnitude of the last glacial period, however, so that this information may be used to calibrate previous glacial episodes.

Packrat Middens

Packrat middens are accumulations of organic debris typically rich in plant fragments. Middens are common in the deserts of western North America and are an important source of paleoenvironmental information. Packrats, rodents of the genus *Neotoma*, are widespread and share the trait of collecting large amounts of vegetal material and caching it in their dens. When located in a sheltered location such as a cave, middens can be preserved for tens of thousands of years. The vegetal material in the middens represents plants that grew close to the midden site, and because they often are identifiable to the species level, they offer a means of determining what species were present at a given time in the past, determined by radiocarbon dating of the remains.

Because midden data rely on radiocarbon dating, plant assemblages older than ca. 45 ka are generally at or beyond the limit of radiocarbon dating and, therefore, the utility of midden data in understanding past climates is restricted to late Marine Isotope Stage (MIS) 3 (ca. 58 ka to ca. 34 ka) and MIS 2 (ca. 34 ka to ca. 12 ka) times. MIS refers to a period of time associated with a glacial or interglacial climate state. MIS numbers were established from studies using marine carbonate $\delta^{18}O$ records reflecting change in $\delta^{18}O$ values of ocean water as continental ice sheets expanded and contracted (Imbrie et al., 1984; Shackleton and Opdyke, 1973, Fig. 7 therein). Even-numbered MIS represent glacial stages, whereas odd-numbered MIS represent interglacial stages.

The composition of modern plant communities in the Yucca Mountain region changes in response to elevation-dependent variation in temperature and precipitation regimes. Presently, at the lowest elevations below ~1000 m and in most arid habitats, desert scrub vegetation is predominant, typified by such heat-loving plants as creosote bush (*Larrea tridentata*) and white bursage (*Ambrosia dumosa*). These communities give way to mixed desert scrub (hopsage, *Grayia spinosa*; desert thorn, *Lycium andersonii*) above ~1400 m elevation. These communities often transition to scrub vegetation dominated by blackbrush (*Coleogyne ramosissima*) at slightly higher elevations. Pigmy conifer woodland, dominated by Utah juniper (*Juniperus osteosperma*) and piñon (*Pinus monophylla*), occurs above ~1800 m elevation. On higher mountains in the region, montane conifer forest—typified by white fir (*Abies concolor*) and ponderosa pine (*Pinus ponderosa*)—occurs above ~2200 m, whereas subalpine conifer forest characteristically dominated by bristlecone pine (*Pinus longaeva*) occurs above ~2700 m elevation (Beatley, 1976; Spaulding, 1990).

Paleoclimate versus modern climate

To understand how past climates differed from those of the present, a large data set—including the macrofossil assemblages from 200 radiocarbon-dated packrat midden samples—was compiled from studies conducted throughout southern Nevada (Forester et al., 1999; Spaulding 1985, Table 6 therein; Wigand and Rhode, 2002). This packrat midden data set indicates that woodland was common from ca. 35–12 ka in contrast to the desert scrub vegetation currently widespread in the area. The most common tree species in MIS 2 packrat middens from the area were Utah juniper and limber pine (*Pinus flexilis*) (Spaulding, 1985). White fir and bristlecone pine were found in midden samples from a number of higher elevation sites. Bristlecone pine was restricted to calcareous rocks, as it is today (Spaulding, 1990, Fig. 9.15 therein; Thompson, 1990). Limber pine grew at elevations as low as 1600 m, ~1000 m below its modern elevation in the Sheep and Spring Mountains (Fig. 1; Wigand and Rhode, 2002). Piñon, common throughout the woodland of the region

today, is rare in midden samples from the Yucca Mountain area, and during late MIS 3 and most of MIS 2, apparently occurred no farther north than the Amargosa Desert at 36° N latitude (Koehler et al., 2005; Spaulding, 1990). Cold-tolerant shrubs typical of Great Basin desert and woodland, indicating relatively cold and dry conditions, were common in MIS 2 assemblages (Thompson, 1990; Spaulding, 1985).

Distribution of common plant species during MIS 3 and MIS 2, within and outside the Yucca Mountain region, indicates a climate different from that of today. Warm-desert shrubs and succulents, such as creosote bush, were restricted during these stages to more southerly latitudes in the present Sonoran Desert (Spaulding, 1990) located south of Nevada in California, Arizona, and Mexico. At these southerly latitudes, south of 34°N, pigmy conifer woodland supported a wide array of tree and succulent species, whereas the Yucca Mountain area supported fewer such species and a wider array of shrubs, presently growing in semiarid habitats, such as blackbrush and snowberry (*Symphoricarpos longiflorus*) (Spaulding, 1990). Subalpine woodland, which presently exists only on the highest mountains of the region, descended to elevations of ~1800 m (Thompson, 1990) and all the way to the valley floors (on rocky substrates, at least) farther north in the Great Basin (Spaulding, 1985; Spaulding, 1990). Wells and Woodcock (1985) report an elevational displacement of Utah juniper 1200–1500 m below modern elevations from 19 to 13 ka on the mountain flanks of Death Valley.

Relative displacement of plant species downslope and to more southerly latitudes during MIS 3 and MIS 2 indicates colder and wetter conditions relative to modern times, just as those plant species grow in colder and wetter conditions at higher elevations and in more northerly latitudes today. Koehler et al. (2005) report a MIS 2 biogeographic boundary at ~36° N latitude in the central Mojave Desert. During the last glacial period, single needle pinyon and associated mild-mesic vegetation grew south of ~36° N latitude whereas colder, xeric juniper woodland steppe grew to the north. This distribution indicates that the jet stream may have been resident at 36° N latitude, at least seasonally, during this time period. Climate during MIS 2 must have involved cold, perhaps snowy winters and cool, probably dry summers. This interpretation is consistent with interpretations of past climate from the Owens Lake (Fig. 1) core and other climate proxy records.

Quantitative estimates of past temperatures and precipitation indicated by plant species in packrat middens can be made by examining the current range of these species (Thompson et al., 1999). Thompson et al. (1999) note that while their reconstructed last glacial maximum (20.5–18 ka) temperatures and those reconstructed by Spaulding (1985) do not differ greatly (mean annual temperature [MAT] ~8 °C and ~7 °C lower than present, respectively), the difference in reconstructed precipitation is substantial. Thompson et al. (1999) arrive at a full-glacial mean annual precipitation (MAP) of 2.1–2.6 times current MAP, compared to 1.3–1.4 times current MAP reconstructed by Spaulding (1985) for that time. The difference in precipitation estimates lies in the baseline data selected by Spaulding, which reflected much wetter modern climatic conditions than the baseline data used in Thompson et al. (1999). Consequently, the relative change in precipitation reflected in Spaulding's reconstruction was substantially lower. Using the quantitative techniques described by Thompson et al. (1999), these authors estimated that the last glacial maximum was from 4.9 to 5.5 °C colder than present with a mean annual precipitation (MAP) from 1.4 to 1.7 times that of present.

Wetland and Spring Deposits

Wetland and spring discharge is rare in southern Nevada today because the climate is arid and effective moisture—commonly defined as precipitation minus evaporation—is low. Spring discharge at elevations typically above ~2000 m is supported by winter storms and snowpack on the higher mountains (Winograd and Riggs, 1984; Winograd et al., 1998). Spring discharge at low elevations typically comes from water in the regional carbonate or volcanic aquifers (Winograd and Thordarson, 1975) that is recharged at high elevation and over large areas. Sedimentary deposits on the valley floors throughout the southern Nevada region, however, record evidence of increased spring discharge such as wet meadows, seeps, flowing springs, streams, and wetlands during times of greater effective moisture relative to today (Quade et al., 2003; Jayko et al., 2005; Hillhouse et al., 2005; Bright and Anderson, 2005).

Relying on exposed stratigraphy plus U-series, luminescence, and radiocarbon geochronology, Lundstrom et al. (1999) document multiple episodes of groundwater discharge in the northern Las Vegas Valley, Pahrump Valley, and Amargosa Desert (Fig. 1) during the past ~120 k.y. Although dates are discontinuous, fan deposition and aggradation occurred during 120–50 ka, probably in response to high-intensity rainfall, runoff, and erosion of uplands.

During MIS 2, springs and wetlands on the valley floors supported abundant aquatic vegetation (sedge and cattails), fauna (ostracodes, diatoms, and mollusks), and waterfowl (ducks and wading birds) (Mehringer, 1967; Mawby, 1967; Taylor, 1967; Quade et al., 1995). A diverse vertebrate community from large mammals such as mammoths and camels, to small mammals such as pikas, marmots, and ground squirrels, also lived on the valley floors (Grayson, 1993). The existence of fossils of small mammals (which today live at either the upper tree line or in the northern United States) in sediments, packrat middens, and caves in the northern Las Vegas Valley (Fig. 1) and nearby localities supports the temperature reconstructions from the plant macrofossils discussed above (Grayson, 1993).

The existence and annual persistence of groundwater discharge and permanent through-flowing wetlands at low elevation require that past levels of effective moisture were much higher than today (Quade et al., 1995). Inference of past water table rises, however, by as much as 100 m based on an assumed depth to water beneath one spring deposit by Quade et al. (1995, Table 5 therein) is not supported by more recent data collected through the Nye County Early Warning Drilling Program (http://www.nyecounty.com/index.htm). Data from wells located south of Yucca Mountain along potential groundwater flow paths indicate that the maximum Pleistocene groundwater table rise was 17–30 m (Paces and Whelan, 2001). Presently, the regional groundwater table is less than 20 m below the Lathrop Wells Spring discharge sediments (Paces and Whelan, 2001). The estimated water table elevations in the Yucca Mountain area vary with the characteristics of the aquifer involved. For example, systems with greater transmissivity have greater flow-through and, hence, rise less than systems with lower transmissivity, given equal amounts of recharge. Therefore, a small rise in the water table of a transmissive aquifer could reflect a change to a much wetter climate.

Three local discharge records that provide insight into the nature of past climate are discussed below. These include an ostracode record from Corn Creek Flat, a well-dated section in the Las Vegas Valley; an isotope record from Cactus Springs, a well-dated section north of the Las Vegas Valley; and diatomaceous deposits near Lathrop Wells, north of U.S. Highway 95 and south of Crater Flat, down the regional flow gradient from Yucca Mountain (Fig. 1).

Corn Creek Flat. Corn Creek Flat lies near the center of the upper Las Vegas Valley (Fig. 1) at an elevation of 840 m. Two sections of wetland sediments ~200 m apart (OCI-11 and LPM-34) have been analyzed (Quade, 1986; Quade and Pratt, 1989; Quade et al., 2003; Quade et al., 1995). Three informal stratigraphic units—denoted B, D, and E—which were described by Haynes (1967) and Quade (1986) are found in these sections and other localities in southern Nevada. Sediments comprising units B and D occur throughout the Las Vegas Valley, indicating that they were deposited in extensive wetlands and springs discharging at a higher rate than today (Quade, 1986; Quade and Pratt, 1989; Quade et al., 2003).

Quade et al. (2003) tentatively correlate deposits in the Las Vegas Valley dating >41 ^{14}C ka with MIS 6 and a series of discharge-related deposits between <26.3 and 16.4, ~13.9 to 13.5, and 11.6 to ~9.5 ^{14}C ka with MIS 2 and the early Holocene. Units D and E, originally defined by Haynes (1967) at Tule Springs, may be correlative with MIS 2 or MIS 1 or both lake highstands of Lake Manly in Death Valley, Lake Mojave in Silver Lake, and to a certain extent, Searles Lake (Fig. 1).

Based on δ^{18}O of fossil ostracodes, Quade et al. (2003) estimate that the MAT during MIS 6 (unit B_2) was at least 10.8 °C colder than today and at least 5.6 °C colder during the last glacial maximum (unit D). If a vital effect (biologically precipitated calcite not formed in isotopic equilibrium with the water) of 0.8–1.0% on ostracode valves is assumed, however, then valley bottom temperatures were warmer than their unadjusted MIS 2 estimate by ~2–3 °C. Warmer temperatures are not consistent with other data, however.

Cactus Springs. The Cactus Springs isotope record occurs in a well-dated section north of the Las Vegas Valley. Quade et al. (2003) report on ostracode assemblages (site LPM-35) from this locality. These deposits probably represent the upper part of unit D or more likely unit E. Dates on the middle of unit D/E$_1$

range from $13,690 \pm 80$ to $13,350 \pm 60$ [14]C yr B.P. and are thought to span the period of greatest effective moisture in this section. The section represents a wet meadow environment in the basal unit with flowing springs possibly derived from a valley aquifer but without extensive discharge of regional groundwater in the middle, and a transition to a drier environment in unit E_2, which has a date of 10,030 ^{14}C yr B.P.

Oxygen isotopic compositions of fossil bivalves from Cactus Springs were compared to modern bivalve $\delta^{18}O$ values of shell carbonate (Sharpe et al., 1994). Oxygen isotope data from the bivalve *Pisidium* spp., living in Cold Creek Spring in the Spring Mountains (Fig. 1) at 1940 m and found as a fossil in the Cactus Springs (930 m) section (CRWMS M&O, 2000, Fig. 6.3-18 therein), provide a way to compare modern data from high elevations to data from low-elevation fossil localities without concern for different vital effects. The $\delta^{18}O$ values for living *Pisidium* spp. from the Cold Creek Spring locality averaged 18.7‰ (n = 8, range 18.3–19.5‰), and the fossil site sample values averaged 19.6‰ (n = 6, range 19.0–20.1‰). The $\delta^{18}O$ values of water collected from a small pond receiving flow from the Cold Creek Spring averaged ~ −14‰, so the modern bivalve values are ~32.7‰ greater than the water values (Sharpe et al., 1994).

Because the $\delta^{18}O$ value of a bivalve is determined by isotopic composition and the temperature of the water in which the organism lived, fossil data cannot be directly converted into a $\delta^{18}O$ value for the paleowater. The similarity between the modern and fossil bivalve $\delta^{18}O$ values indicates, however, that the paleowater $\delta^{18}O$ and temperature at the fossil site on the valley bottom may have been comparable to those found today at the Cold Creek Spring locality at an elevation of 1940 m. Modern recharge to the Spring Mountains occurs primarily from winter precipitation with values of ~°–14‰ (Winograd and Riggs, 1984). Therefore, the low $\delta^{18}O$ values of paleowater on the valley bottom, as indicated by the fossil bivalves, are consistent with the expansion of the polar cell into this region during glacial times.

Lathrop Wells diatomite. The Lathrop Wells diatomite deposits occur at the southern margin of Crater Flat (Fig. 1), ~18 km southwest of Yucca Mountain at an elevation of 792.5 m. These spring deposits originated from discharge from the regional water table and are comprised of pale-green mudstones, local secondary carbonate, siliceous rhizoliths, and diatomite (Quade et al., 1995). Diatomite is sediment composed primarily of the opaline frustules of diatoms (single-celled algae).

Various studies provide the basis for interpreting the stratigraphy, ostracode paleontology, paleohydrology, and age of these deposits (Paces et al., 1993; Paces et al., 1996, Paces et al., 2001; Quade et al., 1995; Quade et al., 2003, Table 2 therein; Brennan and Quade, 1997, Table 1 therein). Although Swadley and Carr (1987) believed that these deposits are Pliocene to lower Quaternary based on fission-track and K-Ar dating, the bulk of the reported dates and vertebrate fossils recovered primarily from the diatomite in these deposits indicate MIS 6 to MIS 2 ages for the deposits (Paces et al., 1993; Paces et al., 1997, Fig. 18 therein; and Quade et al., 2003, Fig. 6 and Table 1 therein).

Isotopic evidence (Paces et al., 1993) indicates that the Lathrop Wells diatomite deposits were derived from a regional groundwater source and not from surface water or a perched aquifer (Paces and Whelan, 2001). Strontium and uranium isotopic ratios for authigenic materials in these deposits are similar to those from regional groundwater sampled in nearby wells. These data exclude a surface water source, and $^{234}U/^{238}U$, $\delta^{87}Sr$, and $\delta^{13}C$ data from authigenic materials in the deposit are inconsistent with perched water compositions expected from interactions with local rock sources.

Reconstruction of climate from aquatic microfossils and stable isotope data in the Las Vegas and Indian Springs Valley (CRWMS M&O, 2000) at Corn Creek Flat, Cactus Springs, and Lathrop Wells (Fig. 1) is consistent with packrat midden and plant macrofossil climate reconstruction. Because the Las Vegas and Indian Springs Valleys are bounded by some of the highest mountains in the region, however, their hydrological response to Pleistocene climate change may have been accentuated by local upland recharge relative to that in the immediate Yucca Mountain flow system. The Lathrop Wells diatomite, by contrast, represents the response of the Yucca Mountain paleohydrological system to climate change without significant effects of local high-mountain recharge.

Long Regional Records of Quaternary Climate Change

Long regional records of Quaternary climate change are critical for understanding the timing, magnitude, and frequency of past climates in the Yucca Mountain region. Long records provide linkages among orbital parameters, which force, or at least time, climate change and interpretable climate records. Such records, from sources close to Yucca Mountain, have the advantage of identifying global climate cyclicity within a temporal framework and specific patterns of past regional climate changes that are relevant to the repository site. Comparison and integration of these climate proxy data provide a local and regional picture of variation in past temperature, precipitation, and hydrology during glacial and interglacial climate regimes. These past climate proxy records, when linked to global circulation patterns and orbital parameters, illuminate the process, timing, and potential drivers of past climate and provide insight into potential future climates.

Regional records are from outside the Yucca Mountain area, but within ~160 km of Yucca Mountain. Three sites with long-term regional climate records are Devils Hole, Nevada; Owens Lake, California; and Death Valley, California (Fig. 1). Regional records from these sites can identify the rate and timing of climate change, as well as the duration of climate states, but the magnitude of that change may or may not apply precisely to the Yucca Mountain area.

Devils Hole, Nevada, is currently a large, open extensional fracture within the carbonate aquifer, located in the Ash Meadows discharge area ~60 km southeast of Yucca Mountain (Fig. 1). During the past 568 k.y., the fracture generally has maintained the opening, and calcite has slowly precipitated on the fracture walls, leaving a stable isotope record of the composition of the water in the aquifer. Because of its well-constrained chronology (Ludwig et al., 1992, Tables 1 and 2 therein; Landwehr et al., 1997; Winograd et al., 2006), data from Devils Hole provide a precise timing of global climate change applicable to the Yucca Mountain area. The isotope record from Devils Hole, however, does not provide a clear sense of past volumes of precipitation or absolute temperatures.

Owens Lake, California, occupies a structural graben immediately east of the Sierra Nevada ~150 km west of Yucca Mountain (Fig. 1). Its sediments contain an ~800 k.y. proxy record of precipitation and runoff from the Sierra Nevada (Smith and Bischoff, 1997). The Owens Lake sediment core provides a record of past changes in temperature and precipitation, but the timing of those changes is constrained by a relative chronology or potentially correlative chronology (Smith et al., 1997; Litwin et al., 1999).

Death Valley, California (Li et al., 1996), located ~80 km west of Yucca Mountain, is a fault-controlled desert basin. It lies 86 m below sea level. During glacial periods, however, it contained deep freshwater and saline lakes that were supported by flow in the Amargosa River and its tributaries, such as Fortymile Wash adjacent to Yucca Mountain, and occasionally other sources such as overflow from the Owens River and Mojave River paleolake systems (Fig. 1).

Devils Hole, Nevada

The Devils Hole record is significant for studies at Yucca Mountain because it provides a precise chronology for past glacial and interglacial periods recorded in the Yucca Mountain region. The principal research at Devils Hole (Winograd et al., 1992; Winograd et al., 1988; Winograd et al., 2006) has focused on the excellent chronology of recorded isotopic changes. The chronology is now well established—using thermal-ionization mass-spectrometric uranium-series and protactinium-231 analyses (Ludwig et al., 1992; Edwards et al., 1997; Winograd et al., 2006). Errors are reported at 2 σ. Accurately dated calcite layers record isotopic variation in atmospheric precipitation in the recharge area of the regional aquifer (Winograd et al., 1992) from ca. 568 to 4.5 ka.

Because light isotopes of O and H are preferentially enriched in the vapor phase during evaporation or condensation of water, an enrichment that increases as temperature decreases, these isotopes can be used as tracers of precipitation air-mass sources and recharge conditions. Thus, larger $\delta^{18}O$ (and δD) values are indicators of warmer seasons or climates, or tropical air mass sources, and smaller values are indicators of cooler seasons or climates, or higher latitude air mass sources. Hence, $\delta^{18}O$ values are smaller in glacial periods and greater in interglacial periods. Because precipitation pathways reflect relative dominance of polar (glacial) versus tropical (interglacial) circulation, precise dating of the Devils Hole $\delta^{18}O$ record provides a climate change chronology.

The Devils Hole $\delta^{18}O$ isotope curve (Figs. 3A to 3C) shows sequential fluctuations between isotopically lighter and heavier values that, respectively, track a progression of glacial and interglacial climates from ca. 568 to 4.5 ka (Winograd et al., 1988; Winograd et al., 2006). Winograd et al. (2006) show that the Devils Hole record for the period 160 to 4.5 ka is a proxy of Pacific Ocean sea surface temperature off the California coast and possibly the eastern tropical Pacific. They indicate that sea surface temperature and Devils Hole may be responding to the same forcing mechanism through an atmospheric teleconnection.

Significantly for Yucca Mountain studies, the shape of the Devils Hole $\delta^{18}O$ isotopic curve compares well with other paleoclimatic records from Greenland, Antarctica, China, the Indian Ocean, the western equatorial and southwest Pacific, Siberia, South America, and Europe. Comparisons include composite records from the global oceans established by the Spectral Mapping Project (Imbrie et al., 1993; Lea et al., 2003), $\delta^{18}O$ values of ice from cores taken in Antarctica (EPICA, 2004; Landwehr and Winograd, 2001) and Greenland (Grootes et al., 2001, Fig. 4 therein; NGICP, 2004), and other paleoclimatic records reflecting glacial and interglacial climate states (Landwehr et al., 1997; Smith et al., 1997; Jannik et al., 1991; Lowenstein et al., 1999; Ku et al., 1998; Morrison, 1999; Negrini et al., 2000, Fig. 11 therein; Pahnke et al., 2003; Prokopenko et al., 2001; Petit et al., 1999; Rousseau, 2003; Tzedakis et al., 1997; Tzedakis et al. 2004; Wang et al., 2004; Xie et al., 2003; Yuan et al., 2004).

Uncertainty in the Devils Hole record is nominal. A time lag between atmospheric precipitation and deposition of calcite (travel time) for the past 160 k.y. is <2000 yr (Winograd et al., 2006, Appendix A, Supplemental materials therein). Samples were taken every 0.25 mm during this time period, and dating errors within the past 80 k.y. are well within the travel time estimate: several hundred years at 2 σ (Winograd et al., 2006, Tables 1 and 2 therein). Travel times for time periods >160 k.y. are probably also within 2000 yr (Isaac Winograd, U.S. Geological Survey [retired], oral commun., 2006). In the part of the core older than 80 ka, one sample represents an average time interval of ~1800 yr (Winograd et al., 1992), which is still within the estimated travel time period.

Because these uncertainties are small, a description of the generalized conditions that lead to observed isotopic trend patterns within the Devils Hole record can be made. For example, as continental glaciers expand, the polar front and latitudinal position of associated storm tracks move southward (Kutzbach and Webb, 1993). The seasonal or annual southerly position of polar air steepens the thermal gradient between the Devils Hole recharge areas and the largely tropical and subtropical oceanic moisture source areas thousands of kilometers west and south of Yucca Mountain.

The Devils Hole record and climate proxy records from both hemispheres provide critical evidence that orbital parameters, at a minimum, represent a clock that signals the beginning of glacial periods. Although changes in insolation (related to changes in orbital parameters) are commonly cited as a primary cause of climate change, the specific mechanisms of the origins and terminations of glacial periods remain unresolved. These mechanisms probably involve complex interactions among orbital, solar, marine, and terrestrial climate-forcing functions that operate in different ways. The importance, or result, of a particular forcing function will vary according to its distance and relation to the proxy studied. Regardless, the existence of a chronology of past climate change specific to the Yucca Mountain region provides crucial bounding parameters needed for Yucca Mountain site characterization.

Owens Lake, California

The Owens Lake record is important to understanding past climate and hydrology in the Yucca Mountain area because it pro

vides a record of snowpack in the Sierra Nevada above Owens Lake (Smith et al., 1997; Forester et al., 1999) and hence, the nature, rate of change, and duration of past glacial and interglacial periods. Although at a much lower elevation than the upper reaches of the Owens River, the Yucca Mountain area has cool and wet weather when the Sierra Nevada receives abundant snowfall when the polar front moves latitudinally to its southerly position. Because the Owens Lake drainage is in the same latitudinal zone as that of Yucca Mountain, ~150 km to the east, it can be assumed that variations in one can be related to variations in the other.

Owens Lake is a present-day playa (elevation 1081 m) in Inyo County with a sill, or spillway, at 1145 m (Bacon et al., 2006). The playa contains a thick sequence of lacustrine deposits

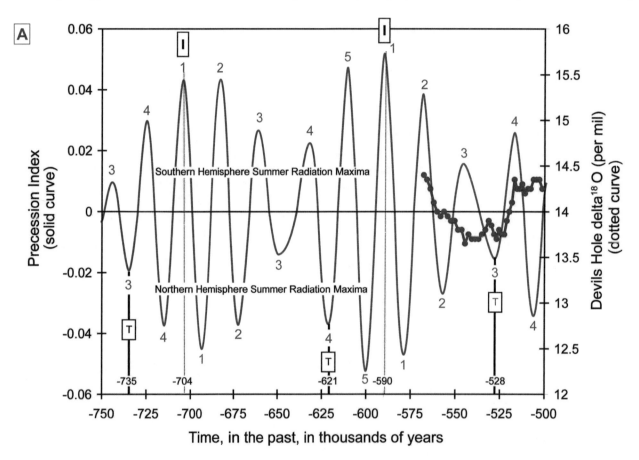

Figure 3. (A) Relation of precession to the Devils Hole stable isotope climate proxy record during the past 568 k.y.: –568 to –500 ka (Landwehr et al., 1997; Berger, 1978). Stable isotope data (closed circles) are reported relative to Vienna standard mean ocean water (VSMOW). The precession index is calculated using axial precession and elliptical precession to quantify the Earth-Sun distance on 21 June, the summer solstice in the northern hemisphere and winter solstice in the southern hemisphere. Colors designate general climate states: red—interglacial; blue—glacial; green—intermediate. I—initiation of transition from interglacial to glacial climate; T—initiation of transition from glacial to interglacial climate. The I to I event equals a precession sequence. Ages for I and T are shown near the x-axis. Numbers 1 through 4 or 5 equal summer solar radiation maxima; numbers at the top of the graph are summer solar radiation maxima in the southern hemisphere; numbers at the bottom of the graph are summer solar radiation maxima in the northern hemisphere. MIS equals Marine Isotope Stage. Continuation of the diagram is given as Figs. 3B and 3C. (B) Relation of precession to the Devils Hole stable isotope climate proxy record during the past 568 k.y.: –500 to –250 ka (Landwehr et al., 1997; Berger, 1978). *—MIS substages as in Winograd et al. (1997, Fig. 7 therein); †—MIS substages as in Prokopenko et al. (2001, Fig. 3 therein). (C) Relation of precession to the Devils Hole stable isotope climate proxy record during the past 568 k.y.: –250 ka to present (Landwehr et al., 1997; Berger, 1978; Winograd et al., 2006). Stars designate the two tie points between calcite samples in cores DH-11, DHC2-3, and DHC2-8 (Winograd et al., 2006).

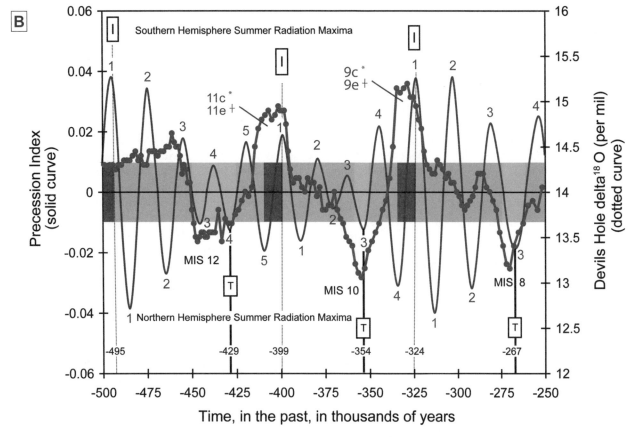

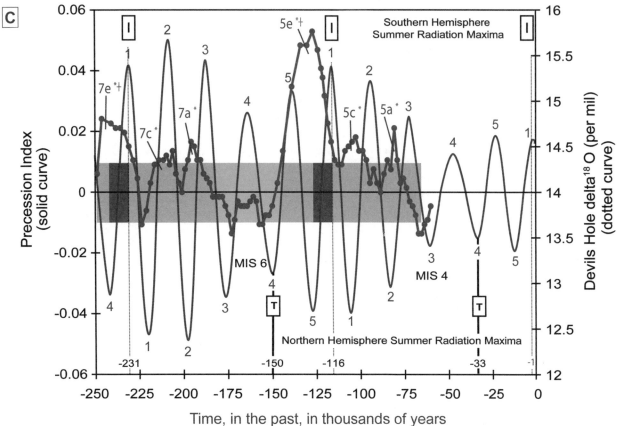

which include diatom, ostracode, pollen, and geochemical proxies for paleohydrology and climate. Three cores were drilled to a total depth of 322.86 m in the south-central part of the playa (Smith and Bischoff, 1997). The composite core represents 80% of the section. Three other cores drilled nearby provide additional sediment for a high-resolution study of the upper part of the Owens Lake section (Benson et al., 1996, 1997).

The cores from Owens Lake span the past 750 k.y. and provide a record of alternating periods of high-volume (glacial periods) and low-volume (interglacial periods) runoff primarily from creeks originating in the high-elevation, east-draining slopes of the Sierra Nevada (Smith and Bischoff, 1997). The original chronology for the Owens Lake record was derived primarily from an age model based on a sediment accumulation rate (Bischoff et al., 1997a), unlike the Devils Hole stable isotope record which has a chronology derived from direct radiometric dating. As with any age model based on sediment-mass accumulation rates, some events will be assigned ages that are too young or too old simply because natural sediment-accumulation rates are not constant.

Litwin et al. (1999) provide a 230 k.y. duration climate proxy record for Owens Lake core OL-92 based on pollen profiles. Warm and cold climate intervals were identified based on pollen assemblages, and these pollen intervals were determined to correspond to particular MIS. This technique better resolves the earlier chronology (Bischoff et al., 1997a) for this period.

Li et al. (2004) use a time-depth model for the 32–83 m interval in the OL-92 core based on a model developed by Bischoff and Cummins (2001). This chronology places the MIS 6/5 boundary at 140 ka, which agrees with the Termination II age reported by Winograd et al. (1992). Li et al. (2004) report warm and dry climate conditions resulting in closed conditions at Owens Lake from 140 to 123, 113 to 91, and 84 to 72.3 ka (identified as MIS substages 5e, 5c, and 5a, respectively). These time frames coincide with increased $\delta^{18}O$ values recorded in the Devils Hole record (Fig. 3C) establishing similar, yet independent chronologies of climate change between Devils Hole and Owens Lake. Therefore, just as the undated Spectral Mapping Project (SPECMAP) marine record (Imbrie et al., 1984) was synchronized to an orbital time scale, the Owens Lake record is synchronized here to the Devils Hole chronology.

All of the Owens Lake climate proxy records indicate some intervals that can be attributed to glacial periods and other intervals that can be attributed to interglacial periods as initially reported by Smith et al. (1997). During the past 400 k.y., microfossils from the Owens Lake core document four major cool or wet periods or both (MIS 10, 8, 6, and 2) (U.S. Geological Survey, 2001, Fig. 11 therein), which also are documented in other climate proxy records (MIS 10, 8, 6, 4, and 2) as discussed below. MIS ages vary with the proxy record and location. Both the Owens Lake microfossil record (U.S. Geological Survey, 2001) and Li et al. (2004) suggest rapid changes between cold/wet and warm/dry climates. These rapid transitions occur within one or two millennia to as little as a few centuries.

The Owens Lake ostracode record provides a good estimate of the nature of different climate states. This is an important component needed to estimate future climate parameters, and it is central to key Assumption 3: the characteristics of late Quaternary glacial and interglacial climates differ from each other in a systematic way. Table 5 lists four generalized climate states based on the Owens Lake ostracode record. The first column refers to MIS 12 through 1, with MIS 12 being the oldest.

The time series in Table 5 is based on the Devils Hole $\delta^{18}O$ chronology beginning in MIS 12 through MIS 2 and into MIS 1 (Winograd et al., 1992, Fig. 3 therein; Winograd et al., 2006, Fig. 2 therein). The timing between MIS listed in Table 5 was determined by locating the inflection points on the Devils Hole isotope record. These points are found between curve high-point and low-point reversals. The ages at which the curves reverse direction denote glacial or interglacial periods (Figs. 3B and 3C). The uppermost peaks in the curve (large $\delta^{18}O$ values) represent interglacial periods, and the troughs represent glacial periods. Glacial periods are noted as even numbered MIS in Figures 3B and 3C.

The estimated length of time that the glacial or interglacial periods lasted was based on change in the slope of the isotope curves near the reversal peaks or troughs. A one-value cutoff point designating all glacial or all interglacial periods could not be chosen because each individual glacial or interglacial event had its own set of values particular to the preceding climate interval and factors associated with climate and groundwater mechanisms. Estimated durations of glacial and interglacial states, based on a change in slope in the Devils Hole isotope curve, however, generally are consistent with the timing of glacial and interglacial onset and duration reported in the literature.

The middle columns of Table 5 show time intervals designated as monsoon and intermediate climate states based on the occurrence of certain ostracodes. The intermediate climate state is a transitional state occurring between glacial and interglacial periods and vice versa. It designates climate periods commonly wetter and cooler than interglacial climates. The monsoon state generally occurs in the Owens Lake record following interglacial climate states. It is characterized by hotter summers with increased summer rainfall relative to today.

Past climates differed from those of today because the predominant circulation pattern of the atmosphere was different from that which typifies the modern world. Such rapid changes from warm and dry (interglacial) to cold and wet (glacial) climates at Owens Lake indicate a southerly shift in the average position and strengthening of the polar front and associated polar jet stream. An alternative viewpoint is presented by Davis (1989) and Zielinski and McCoy (1987), however, who argue that the position of some major atmospheric circulation features did not change during the late Quaternary period.

The present atmospheric circulation pattern and a significant rain-shadow effect are reasons for today's arid to semiarid climate in the Yucca Mountain region. The presence of a glacial and interglacial biostratigraphy within the Owens Lake microfossil record indicates that, like the Devils Hole record, the Owens Lake record is relatively continuous and can be interpreted in terms of global climate changes that are associated with orbital parameters. This linked evidence enables the Owens Lake record to serve as a guide to the magnitude of future infiltration events at nearby Yucca Mountain.

Death Valley, California

Data from Death Valley, California, also record a sequence of climate events similar to the Devils Hole and Owens Lake records, further documenting the regional character of climate change in the Yucca Mountain region. Fresh and saline lake phases in Death Valley and Owens Lake essentially are synchronous during the past 200 k.y., the length of the Death Valley record.

The Death Valley lake record is important to the Yucca Mountain paleohydrology and paleoclimate story because a combination of low temperatures as well as surface and ground-water sources maintained lakes 175–300 m deep during glacial periods (Forester et al., 2005; Ku et al., 1998). Therefore, glacial period effective moisture was very different than modern effective moisture. Death Valley was potentially fed by three major water sources at different times: (1) drainage from the Sierra Nevada via the Owens River and through Owens Lake, China Lake, Searles Lake, Panamint Valley, leading to Death Valley; (2) the Mojave River flowing from the Transverse Mountains into the southern side of Death Valley; and (3) the Amargosa River draining the highlands north of Yucca Mountain via Fortymile Wash and flowing into Death Valley on the southeast margin of the basin (Fig. 1; Forester et al., 2005).

Death Valley paleohydrologic and paleoclimatic data are primarily from a 186 m core (DV93-1) from lake deposits (surface elevation 85 m below sea level) in the Badwater Basin (36°14′N, 116°48′W) (Fig. 1) of Death Valley. Four distinct playa or lake environments occurred in Death Valley during the past 200 k.y.: dry mud flats, playa salt pans, layered halite of permanent saline lakes, and black mud with sedimented halite. The chronology of these depositional environments has been established by U-series dates of bedded salts (Roberts and Spencer, 1995, Fig. 7 therein; Li et al., 1996). As discussed by Forester et al. (2005), however, previously reported ages of 128–120 ka for core depth interval ~128 m to 109 m (Ku et al., 1998, Table 2 therein) probably are older and represent the MIS 6–5e transition. This interpretation is based on the original ^{230}Th/^{234}U ratios (Ku et al., 1998, Table 2 therein) which are low, and ratios such as these are considered to be unreliable (Muhs, 2002); on the ostracode stratigraphy; and on other paleohydrologic records in the vicinity.

Forester et al. (2005) discuss the ostracode record contained in Core DV93-1. The ostracode record shows that the hydrologic setting in Death Valley ranged from deep, relatively freshwater lakes supported by local streams to wetlands supported by spring discharge during the past 200 k.y. MIS 6 was much colder and, at times, relatively wet compared to succeeding periods. Additionally, hydrologic settings during MIS 6 were more varied and

complex, persisting longer than in subsequent periods. Finally, the hydrologic settings occurring during the transition from MIS 6 to MIS 5e oscillated among halite-precipitating brine lakes, saline groundwater and spring-discharge supported wetlands, and slightly saline stream-supported lakes.

Fluid inclusions in halite crystals precipitated from the lake water record surface brine temperatures at the time of halite precipitation. The inclusions were studied (Roberts and Spencer, 1995; Spencer and Roberts, 1998; Lowenstein et al., 1998) using the methods described by Roberts and Spencer (1995) and Lowenstein et al. (1998). The resulting maximum homogenization temperatures of halite fluid inclusions (Th_{MAX}) reflect the maximum water temperature at which the halite precipitated (Roberts and Spencer, 1995; Spencer and Roberts, 1998; Lowenstein et al., 1998). Spencer and Roberts (1998) suggest 10 °C colder-than-modern summer and winter maximum air temperatures in the ephemeral lake-salt pan interval from 192 to 186 ka and 15 °C colder-than-modern summer and winter maximum air temperatures in the perennial lake interval from 128 to 120 ka. This last interval actually may be older, however, and date to MIS 6 time, as discussed above.

Lowenstein et al. (1998) and Lowenstein et al. (1999) determined that fluid-inclusion homogenization temperatures for virtually all of the past 100 k.y. were lower than modern temperatures. Halites dated ca. 100 ka had the largest Th_{MAX} values in the 100 k.y. record: from 23 to 35 °C, with four values 30 °C or above. The higher values are similar to the modern late spring and early summer mean daily maximum air temperatures at Yucca Mountain (Table 3). Halites dated between 60 and 35 ka had brine temperatures between 23 and 28 °C which are 6–11 °C below modern temperatures. Halites dated from the last glacial period (MIS 2), between 35 and 10 ka, had brine temperatures between 19 and 30 °C which are ~4–15 °C below modern temperatures. For MIS 2, the range of brine temperature values is consistent with and supportive of the temperature reconstructions based on packrat midden and ostracode data sets (Lowenstein et al., 1998).

Sedimentary structures of muds and evaporites, evaporite mineralogy, and analysis of fluid inclusions from core DV93-1 and other cores (Li et al., 1996; Roberts and Spencer, 1995; Roberts and Spencer, 1998; Spencer and Roberts, 1998; Lowenstein et al., 1998; Anderson, 1999; D.E. Anderson and Wells, 2003; Lowenstein, 2002; Forester et. al., 2005) provide a paleolimnologic and temperature history for the Death Valley Basin that can be compared to other proxy data from the Owens Lake core, the Devils Hole oxygen isotope record, and other lacustrine records in the Mojave Desert.

Comparison of Regional Records to Distant Records

Other climate proxy data record climate episodes similar in magnitude and timing to the Owens Lake and Death Valley sediment core data. Lake and glacial records from the region show that climate varied synchronously and substantively through time. Figure 4 compares the Devils Hole isotopic record with lake core and sediment records in California; a sediment core in

TABLE 5. CORRELATION BETWEEN CLIMATE STATES, REPRESENTATIVE OSTRACODES, AND MARINE ISOTOPE STAGES FOR THE OWENS LAKE CORE FOR THE PAST 400,000 YEARS*

Climate state and representative ostracode / Marine isotope stage/substage	Interglacial (IG) Limnocythere sappaensis			Monsoon (M) Limnocythere bradburyi			Intermediate (IM) Limnocythere ceriotuberosa			Glacial (G) Cytherissa lacustris Candona caudata		
	Begin (yr B.P.)[§]	End (yr B.P.)	Duration[†] (yr)	Begin (yr B.P.)	End (yr B.P.)	Duration (yr)	Begin (yr B.P.)	End (yr B.P.)	Duration (yr)	Begin (yr B.P.)	End (yr B.P.)	Duration (yr)
12							425,000	410,000	15,000			
11	410,000	405,000	5000									
11				405,000	403,000	2000						
11	403,000	398,000	5000									
11				398,000	397,000	1000						
11	397,000	397,000										
			T[#]: 10,000			T: 3000						
10							397,000	364,000	33,000			
10										364,000	348,000	16,000
10							348,000	336,000	12,000			
									T: 45,000			
9	336,000	323,000	13,000									
9				323,000	323,000							
9							323,000	276,000	47,000			
8										276,000	262,000	14,000
8							262,000	247,000	15,000			
7E				247,000	247,000							
7E	247,000	246,000	1000									
7E				246,000	245,000	1000						
7E	245,000	244,000	1000									
7E				244,000	244,000							
7E	244,000	243,000	1000									
7E				243,000	242,000	1000						
7E	242,000	235,000	7000									
7E				235,000	234,000	1000						
7E	234,000	232,000	2000									
7D							232,000	225,000	7000			
7D										225,000	219,000	6000
7C							219,000	210,000	9000			
7C				210,000	210,000							
7C							210,000	201,000	9000			
7B										201,000	200,000	1000
7A							200,000	184,000	16,000			
			T: 12,000			T: 3000			T: 41,000			T: 7000
6										184,000	147,000	37,000
6							147,000	140,000	7000			
5E				140,000	138,000	2000						
5E	138,000	119,000	19,000									
5D							119,000	109,000	10,000			

(continued)

TABLE 5. CORRELATION BETWEEN CLIMATE STATES, REPRESENTATIVE OSTRACODES, AND MARINE ISOTOPE STAGES FOR THE OWENS LAKE CORE FOR THE LAST 400,000 YEARS (*continued*)

Climate state and representative ostracode	Interglacial (IG) *Limnocythere sappaensis*			Monsoon (M) *Limnocythere bradburyi*			Intermediate (IM) *Limnocythere ceriotuberosa*			Glacial (G) *Cytherissa lacustris Candona caudata*		
	Begin	End	Duration	Begin	End	Duration	Begin	End	Duration	Begin	End	Duration
Marine isotope stage/substage	(yr B.P.)	(yr B.P.)	(yr)	(yr B.P.)	(yr B.P.)	(yr)	(yr B.P.)	(yr B.P.)	(yr)	(yr B.P.)	(yr B.P.)	(yr)
5C	109,000	95,000	14,000									
5B							95,000	81,000	14,000			
5A	81,000	81,000	0									
5A				81,000	80,000	1000						
			T: 33,000			T: 3000			T: 24,000			
4							80,000	70,000	10,000			
4										70,000	60,000	10,000
4							60,000	58,000	2000			
									T: 12,000			
3	58,000	56,000	2000									
3							56,000	34,000	22,000			
2							34,000	24,000	10,000			
2										24,000	24,000	0
2							24,000	23,000	1000			
2										23,000	22,000	1000
2							22,000	21,000	1000			
2										21,000	20,000	1000
2							20,000	19,000	1000			
2										19,000	19,000	0
2							19,000	18,000	1000			
2										18,000	18,000	0
2							18,000	12,000	6000			
									T: 20,000			T: 2000
1	12,000	0	12,000									

*Owens Lake record is synchronized here to the Devils Hole δ^{18}O chronology (Winograd et al., 1992; Winograd et al., 2006). Numbers rounded to nearest 1000 yr.
†Duration of climate state substage.
§Years before present.
#Total years of substages.

Lake Baikal, Siberia, and the Vostok, Antarctica, ice core record. The Devils Hole, Baikal, and Vostok records are plotted so that the glacial periods are peaks and the interglacial periods are troughs. The biogenic silica record from Lake Baikal, Siberia, (Prokopenko et al., 2001, Fig. 3 therein), covering the past 500 k.y. (Fig. 4), records substages e through a for MIS 9, 7, and 5. The authors suggest that these interglacial stages correspond to precessional insolation peaks (Prokopenko et al., 2001, Fig. 2 therein). Additionally, the climate change record based on pollen in sediment cores from Owens Lake and Searles Lake is similar to a number of proxy climate records from France, Greece, western North America, and marine sediment cores off the southern California coast (Litwin et al., 1999).

Regional records compare favorably with other published paleoenvironmental records. Sulfate minerals in the Death Valley core record patterns of oxygen isotopic change that compare well with the SPECMAP record of marine carbonate and global ice volume variation, and the Summit Ice core in Greenland (Yang et al., 1999, Fig. 5 therein). Yang et al. (1999) concluded that the regional records of Death Valley, Owens Lake, and Devils Hole are responding to climate changes, but manifesting them differently. Phillips et al. (1994) discuss a correspondence between Searles Lake and Summit, Greenland. Low water episodes at Searles Lake are synchronous with the interstadial episodes determined by δ^{18}O values at Summit, with both records indicating relatively long stadials punctuated by brief interstadials. Phillips et al. (1994) suggest that both records are responding to climatic forcing. The 400 k.y. δ^{18}O record from Taylor Dome, Antarctica, and δD Vostok record also are similar in timing (Grootes et al., 2001, Fig. 3 therein). Many other climate proxy records from southeastern California and

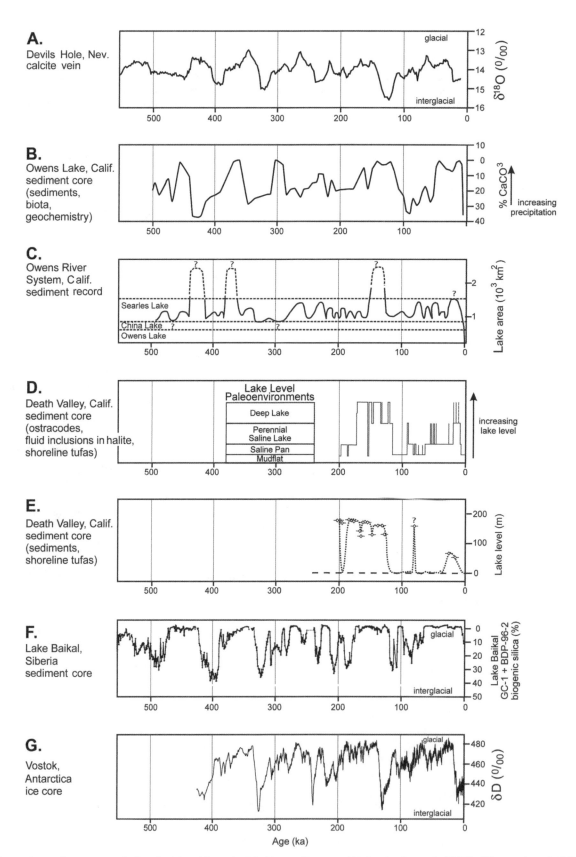

Figure 4. Comparison of proxy records for glacial and interglacial climate. Sources: (A) Landwehr et al. (1997); Winograd et al. (2006); (B) Smith et al. (1997); (C) Jannik et al. (1991); (D) Lowenstein et al. (1999); (E) Ku et al. (1998); (F) Prokopenko et al. (2001); (G) Petit et al. (1999, 2001).

southern Nevada show similar timing and magnitude of recurrent climate events, which indicate a global forcing mechanism to which these different climate proxies are responding.

Comparison among Regional Records

Critical questions—including the timing of lake highstands, discerning lacustrine compared to spring or wetland deposits, and periods of flow-through in the Amargosa and Mojave Rivers and Owens River system—are continuing to be resolved. Increased effective moisture during the pluvial periods led to increased groundwater recharge and ultimately to increased groundwater discharge to springs and lakes (Quade and Pratt, 1989; Forester et. al., 2005). Additionally, increased inflow to lakes by surface water and precipitation on the lake surface also elevated lake levels. An integrated picture of the past hydrology of the southeastern California and southwestern Nevada area is still developing, however.

The Owens River System

Jannik et al. (1991) established the chronology of environmental change in the Owens River system for the past 2 m.y. based on lake sediment dated by ^{36}Cl, U/Th, ^{14}C, and magnetostratigraphy (Fig. 4). Both Jannik et al. (1991) and Smith (1984) report a 400 k.y. periodicity in the Owens River system lake records, which is the same length of time required for orbital cycles. The ^{36}Cl record for the past 700 k.y. in the Owens system supports very high lake phases at times during MIS 16, 12, 10, and 6 (Jannik et al., 1991). Lakes in the entire Owens system (Owens, China, Searles, Panamint) overflowed numerous times during the past, with Searles Lake being the terminal sink in most overflow periods during the past 1 m.y. Apparently, Searles Lake was not the terminal sink during MIS 6 and 2, however. Jayko et al. (2005) report deep lakes in Panamint Valley (Fig. 1) during MIS 6 and 2.

Glacial advances, recorded by high plagioclase feldspar content in the Owens Lake core, overlap with times of glacial advance established in the Sierra Nevada by Phillips et al. (1996, Table 1 therein) based on ^{36}Cl dates on glacial moraines. Chemical analyses of sediment in Owens Lake show a rock-flour record with two major ice advances during MIS 6 and major advances during MIS 4, 3, and 2, which also correspond to ^{36}Cl dates on alpine glacial moraines in the Sierra Nevada (Bischoff et al., 1997b). Shoreline deposits around the northeast margins of Owens Lake indicate that the lake reached a late Pleistocene maximum elevation of 1140 m (59 m lake depth) in MIS 2 at ~20,000 ^{14}C yr B.P. (Orme et al., 2005). A 1160 m highstand is reported by Bacon et al. (2006) at ~27,000 cal ^{14}C yr B.P., however, based on integration of stratigraphic analysis, published surface stratigraphic data, and subsurface core data.

Amargosa River

Menges and Anderson (2005) suggest that the full modern course of the Amargosa River was relatively recently established by a succession of discrete diachronous events such as headward erosion and knickpoint migration from below or spillover from above, or both, that breached topographic paleodivides. These events began near Beatty, Nevada, (Fig. 1) sometime after 7–4 Ma. The Amargosa River probably breached a former paleodivide (Morrison, 1999; Mahan et al., 2005), possibly near Eagle Mountain (Menges and Anderson, 2005), in mid-Pleistocene (possibly MIS 6) time.

It is unclear if the Amargosa River were a source for Lake Manly in Death Valley during MIS 6. Jayko et al. (2005) suggest Panamint Lake overflowed into Death Valley at this time. Forester et al. (2005), however, report the MIS 6 lake in Death Valley was supported by elevated Amargosa streamflow.

Morrison (1999) reports exposed lake sediments (Lake Tecopa) in the Tecopa Valley, California (Fig. 1). According to Morrison, the climatic history of pluvial and interpluvial cycles during the past 1 m.y. in Tecopa Valley records significant increases in effective precipitation, streamflow, flood magnitude, erosion rate, groundwater recharge, water tables and potentiometric surfaces relative to modern values until Lake Tecopa was breached at ca. 186 ka (Morrison, 1999). Hillhouse et al. (2005), however, suggest that the lower Tecopa beds represent lacustrine, playa, stream, and spring deposits rather than the predominately lacustrine sediments interpreted by Morrison (1999). Ostracode assemblages do not add support for a Tecopa Valley deep lake at 200 ka (Hillhouse et al., 2005).

Mojave River

The Mojave River (Fig. 1) flowed beyond the present city of Barstow, California (Fig. 1), beginning ca. 500 ka, episodically filling proximal basins during wet periods (Miller, 2005). Lake Manix (Fig. 1), the upper-most basin, contains deposits spanning ~500,000–19,000 ^{14}C yr B.P. During periodic highstands, Lake Manix overtopped its sill and flowed east-northeast toward the Soda Lake (Fig. 1) basin. Reheis and Redwine (2005) report evidence of a sill, once as high as ~558 m (differentially corrected GPS data) that likely controlled the Lake Manix lake level prior to ca. 30 ka. They report that Lake Manix overflowed toward the Soda Lake basin well before ca. 30–18 ka, prior to initiating the incision of Afton Canyon (Fig. 1) at ca. 19 ka (Miller, 2005).

These overflow events resulted from significantly increased precipitation relative to today. Prolonged lake highstands lasting from 2 to 3 k.y. recorded in the Mojave River basin beginning as early as 22 ka were produced by episodic large-scale floods resulting from increased precipitation (Wells et al., 2003). Values of stream discharge reaching Afton Canyon are estimated to have been two-to-three times larger than modern extremes (Wells et al., 2003).

Mahan et al. (2005) report two clearly identified groundwater discharge events bracketed between ca. 190 and 140 ka and ca. 65 and 20 ka in lower California Valley (Fig. 1). The older event corresponds with pluvial MIS 6, and the younger event may represent MIS 4 or 2. Indications of depositional discontinuities are absent from each of these sections, indicating relatively stable groundwater discharge during each interval.

The Mojave River probably connected with Death Valley sometime after ca. 500 ka and may have been connected during MIS 6 (Miller, 2005). Controversy exists as to the age and extent of a highstand in the Death Valley–Silver–Soda Lake basins (Fig. 1) in MIS 5e/6 (Hooke, 1999; Hooke, 2002; Enzel et al., 2002; Enzel et al., 2003; Hooke, 2005). Hooke argues for a highstand of a single contiguous lake from northern Death Valley to southern Soda Lake from ca. 186 to ca. 128 ka, whereas Enzel et al. (2002) and Wells et al. (2003) counter that the highstand to which Hooke is referring comprises highstands in at least two separate lake basins at distinctly different times between ca. 30 and 9 ka. Data from Mahan et al. (2005) support Wells et al. (2003) Lake Mojave chronology and indicate that no overflow of Lake Mojave occurred after 11 ka.

Differentiation between Lacustrine Deposits and Spring and Wetland Deposits

Bright and Anderson (2005) resampled the ostracode fauna in Core DU-2, Lake Dumont (K.C. Anderson and Wells, 2003) and took new samples from nearby outcrops in the Salt Spring Basin located on the divide between the Mojave and Death Valley watersheds (Fig. 1). They determined that the sediments in the basin are wetland deposits fed by local water sources rather than lacustrine deposits as reported earlier by K.C. Anderson and Wells (2003). Based on a sedimentation rate of ~1000 yr m^{-1} (K.C. Anderson and Wells, 2003), a relatively permanent wetland setting occurred between ca. 27 to ca. 25 ka, and more ephemeral wetlands occurred at ca. 29, 23, and 18 ka. Furthermore, no ostracodes indicative of high spring discharge or stream conditions were found. No indication of a lake supported by the Mojave River is preserved in core DU-2 or in nearby outcrops; therefore, it is improbable that a lake fed by the Mojave River existed in the Salt Spring Basin at this time. Knott (2005) reports that sediment cores taken from Soda Lake playa (Fig. 1) show no lakes during OIS 18, 16, and 6.

Other Records

Reheis (1999, Fig. 1 therein) and Reheis et al. (2002a) report lake highstands 25–70 m above late Pleistocene highstands shortly after 660 ka (MIS 16) in the northwestern Great Basin. Reheis et al. (2003) discovered that soils accumulate silt with the incorporation of eolian dust over time. This accumulation can change the rate of overall soil development resulting in soil development rate increases with age as evidenced in soil-horizon index values. Based on a ^{36}Cl model from Kurth et al. (2002), ages previously reported by Reheis et al. (2002a) at Thorne Bar near Walker Lake, Nevada north of Mono Lake (Fig. 1) indicate revised correlations of shorelines to MIS 6, 8, 10, and possibly 16, further supporting a regional record of greater effective moisture during pluvial periods (Reheis et al., 2003).

At 70 m above the late Pleistocene highstand, submerged basins thought to have been previously isolated were part of an extensive Lake Lahontan. Reheis suggests that to reach the highest levels of Lake Columbus–Rennie (located in present-day Columbus Salt Marsh and Fish Lake Valley, Nevada, 180 km northwest

of Yucca Mountain), a two to three times increase in precipitation and a temperature decrease of 8 °C would have been required (Reheis, 1999). Ancient Lake Russell, where Mono Lake stands today, records a minimum of three large-lake periods in the early-to-middle Pleistocene with levels between 250 and 330 m higher than the present 1950 m elevation of Mono Lake (Reheis et al., 2002b). Estimates using modern groundwater recharge indicate that drainage additions account for only a small part of these high lake levels. The lakes progressively decreased in size, indicating a long-term drying trend from early to late Pleistocene (Reheis et al., 2002a).

Benson (1999, Fig. 8 therein) provides a comparison of lake cycles to glacial-interglacial events in the western Great Basin. He concludes that alpine glacial periods generally were wet and interglacial periods generally were dry, although glacial and interglacial periods included dry and wet intervals. Benson (1999) estimates that late Pleistocene MIS 2 condensation air temperatures were only a few degrees colder than today. An abrupt decrease in δ^{18}O values in Owens Lake sediment, however, at ca. 13 ka indicates a "profound increase in wetness" (Benson et al., 1996).

Glaciated mountain ranges near the Yucca Mountain area include the White Mountains and possibly the Spring Mountains (Fig. 1). The White Mountains supported relatively large glaciers likely dating to MIS 2, whereas the Spring Mountains may or may not have supported glaciers (Osborn and Bevis, 2001). Van Hoesen et al. (2000) argue, however, that cirques and two morainal deposits in the Spring Mountains near Las Vegas, Nevada, are evidence for glaciation, although the age of the deposits is not known. Controversy exists as to whether these are indeed morainal deposits; they may be fluvial (for a discussion of soil properties and previous work in this locality, see Reheis et al., 1992). Regardless of whether these deposits are morainal or fluvial, at an elevation of 2286 m above mean sea level, their presence implies a much colder and wetter climate than exists there today.

Summary of Past Climate Records

Comparison and integration of climate proxy data provide a local and regional picture of variations in past temperature, precipitation, and hydrology in glacial and interglacial climate regimes. These past climate proxy records, when linked to global circulation patterns and orbital parameters, illuminate the sequence, process, timing, magnitude, and potential drivers of past climate.

These climate proxy data indicate the following key points.

1.   Numerous climate states occurred during the past 800 k.y. ranging from warm interglacial periods (similar to modern climate) to cool or cold and wet glacial periods. The past 800 k.y. contained glacial periods of different magnitudes ranging from cold and very wet to cool and wet relative to today. The glacial maximum temperature in MIS 2 is estimated to have been between 5 and 7 °C colder than the present 13 °C average regional temperature with MAP

between 1.4 and 2.6 times that of the present 125 mm yr. This glacial period is considered to have been cool and dry compared to previous glacial periods.

2. MAT was lower and MAP was substantially higher than modern MAT and MAP for sustained periods at numerous times during the last 800 k.y. MAT is estimated to have ranged from 4 °C to as much as 10° or 15 °C below modern temperatures, and precipitation may have been from 1.4 to three times modern precipitation during certain periods.
3. Past climate states contained periods of high variability with warmer periods occurring in glacial stages and cool episodes occurring in warm climate periods.
4. The modern interglacial climate is the least common of climate states.
5. The modern climate is one of less effective moisture compared to other climate states.

BOUNDING FUTURE VARIATIONS IN INFILTRATION

Predicting future climate for hundreds of thousands of years to evaluate repository performance is problematic because of the many uncertainties discussed above. No group of experts would support or come to consensus on any such prediction. A method for estimating generalized future climate states is needed, however, to establish bounding estimates for future infiltration. Paleoenvironmental and paleohydrologic data are used here as the basis for estimating the magnitude, nature, and timing of potential future climate states whose characteristics provide input for infiltration models.

These future climate scenarios do not represent a future climate forecast or prediction, but instead describe a sequential series of climate states each with a different set of temperature and precipitation properties that are derived from generalized reconstructions of past climates. The duration and timing of these generalized future states come from known future characteristics of Earth orbital parameters. Four generalized climate states—interglacial, monsoon, intermediate, and glacial—are based on the Owens Lake ostracode record (Table 5). Numerous other climate states occurred in the past and will occur in the future. Only four states were selected, however, to simplify model simulations of net infiltration.

Infiltration associated with each climate state varies. Climates wetter and cooler than today that persisted for centuries or millennia are of the greatest potential consequence because such climates produce the highest levels of infiltration, percolation, and recharge. This results in higher water tables or increased groundwater transmissivity and discharge volumes or both relative to present hydrologic conditions. The modern interglacial climate and currently predicted future global-warming scenarios are of least consequence, as previously discussed, because they produce less infiltration than the other climate states.

Methodology

The methodology used here is composed of five steps. First is comparing general characteristics of past climates with eccentricity, obliquity, and precession, which comprise the Earth orbital parameters. This establishes the relation between orbital parameters and different past glacial (even numbered MIS) and interglacial (odd numbered MIS) stages during the past 800 k.y. and provides a basis to bound future climates. This comparison is fundamental to understanding how pluvial lake levels and the Devils Hole record present a case for the greatest possible future effective moisture scenarios for Yucca Mountain. Second is comparing the timing of the Devils Hole isotope chronology to calculated chronologies of Earth orbital parameters. The Devils Hole stable isotope record, recovered from the Yucca Mountain area, is the only accurately dated chronology of the timing and duration reflecting major global climate events on Earth (Winograd et al., 1992). Comparing the timing of the Devils Hole record to the timing of orbital parameters provides the basis for estimating the timing and duration of future climate states. Third is identifying the nature and timing of general past climate states indicated by the Owens Lake, California, paleoenvironmental record. The Owens Lake record is the only long paleoenvironmental record in the region and so offers the only data for examining relative climate-driven environmental change that can be expressed in relative effective moisture terms. These relative effective moisture terms form the basis for characterizing generalized future climate states. The fourth step is selecting present-day meteorological stations to represent these past climate states. A record of continuous daily temperature and precipitation from these stations is needed to calculate model-derived future infiltration estimates. Although these meteorologic stations are selected as best-case analogs for past climates, it is important to understand that subsets of the modern climate cannot rigorously define past climates. Finally, the fifth step is estimating the bounds of future infiltration scenarios using the timing of calculated orbital parameters combined with the nature of past climate states as well as temperature and precipitation records from modern stations.

Characteristics of Past Climate and Orbital Parameters

Past and future timing of Earth's orbital parameters (obliquity, eccentricity, and precession) can be constructed accurately from celestial mechanics calculations, assuming there are no perturbations from any large bodies passing through the solar system (Hartmann, 1994). Berger and Loutre (1991) and Muller and MacDonald (2002) describe the behavior and timing of Earth orbital parameters and the criteria used to calculate these parameters, past and future. Comparison of an accurate chronology of Earth-based climate change with the past orbital parameter chronology offers the opportunity to define the timing of Earth-based climate change in orbital chronological terms.

Once the timing of climate change is expressed in orbital chronological terms, that timing can be extended into the future to establish the timing and duration of generalized climate states. It is critical that the reader understand that this step is intended only to identify the most general characteristics of the nature and timing of future climate change. For example, this methodology provides the basis to estimate that glacials are of a given duration and that they might be expected to occur at particular times in the future. Figures 5A to 5D show the magnitude and timing of precession and eccentricity for the past 1 m.y. (Berger, 1978; A. Berger, 2000, personal commun.; Berger and Loutre, 1991).

Eccentricity

Eccentricity (dashed curve in Figs. 5A to 5D) is the degree to which the orbit of the Earth departs from a circle. It plays a key role in the nature of Earth's insolation (Hartmann, 1994). The shape of Earth's orbit ranges from nearly circular (e = 0.004) to more elliptical (e = 0.06) over ~100 k.y. cycles. Four 100 k.y. cycles form a 400 k.y. cycle (Berger and Loutre, 1991, Fig. 4a therein). If Earth's orbit were circular and centered on the Sun, incoming solar radiation over the tropics would be the same in all months because the Earth-Sun distance would be constant. Also, energy input to the northern and southern hemispheres would be symmetrical seasonally [i.e., the northern hemisphere would receive the same amount of energy in summer (June) as the southern hemisphere in its equivalent summer season (Decem-

ber)]. Therefore, when the orbit is more elliptical, energy input to the northern and southern hemispheres is not seasonally equal.

Eccentricity modulates the amplitude of precession cycles; high eccentricity produces a strong precessional cycle. The next 100 k.y. eccentricity cycle will produce a relatively circular, rather than elliptical, orbit (Berger and Loutre, 2002). The last time a relatively circular orbit occurred was 400 ka (Fig. 5C), so it is expected that insolation for the next 100 k.y. will be similar to that from 400 to 300 ka (Droxler et al., 2003).

Precession

Precession (solid curve in Figs. 5A to 5D) affects latitudinal and seasonal redistribution of solar radiation at the top of the atmosphere (Crowley and North, 1991). The climatic effect of precession is to change the distance between the Earth and Sun during any given season. This changes distribution of incoming solar radiation on Earth. Two components make up the precession index, which is basically a measure of the Earth-Sun distance on June 21, the summer solstice in the northern hemisphere and the winter solstice in the southern hemisphere.

Precession is composed of two components. The first component, axial precession, is the wobble of Earth about an axis

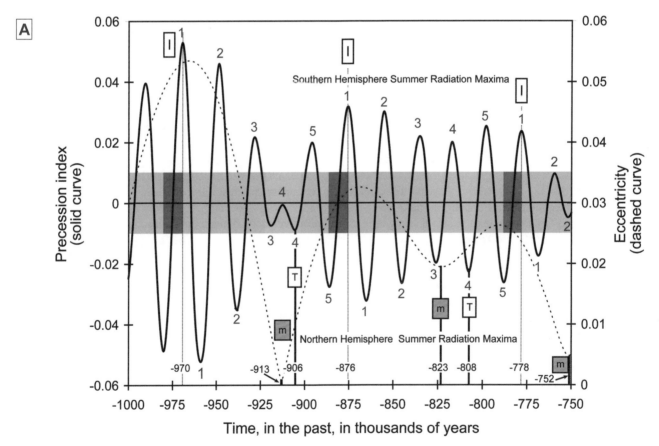

Figure 5. (A) Precession and eccentricity for the past 1 m.y.: −1 m.y. −750 ka (Berger, 1978). As in Figure 3. Continuation of the diagram is given as Figures 5B, 5C, and 5D. (B) Precession and eccentricity for the past 1 m.y.: −750 ka to −500 ka (Berger, 1978). (C) Precession and eccentricity for the past 1 m.y.: −500 ka to −250 ka (Berger, 1978). (D) Precession and eccentricity for the past 1 m.y.: −250 ka to 0 (Berger, 1978).

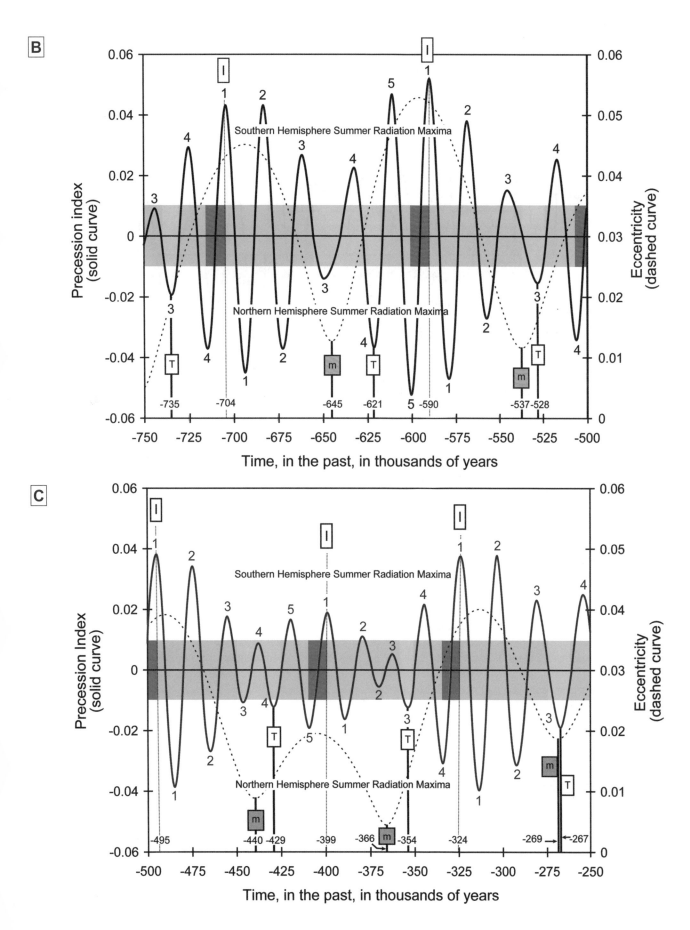

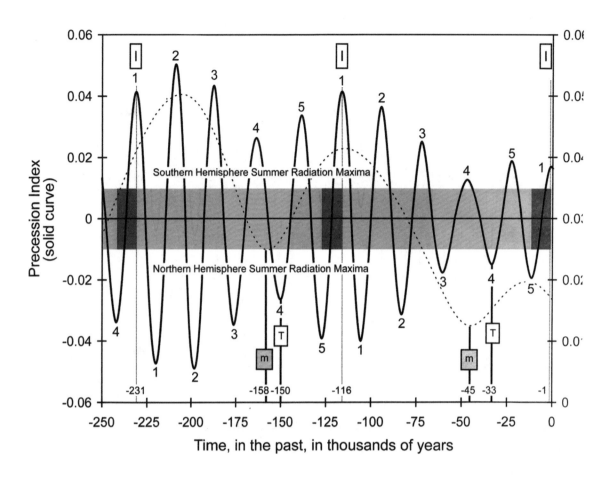

of symmetry resulting in the North Pole describing a circle in space, much like the axis of a spinning top. The second component, elliptical precession, is the axis of the orbital ellipse slowly rotating in the opposite direction of axial precession. These two effects together are called precession of the equinoxes, and these changes occur with 19 and 23 k.y. cycles. A decrease in the Earth-Sun distance at any given season causes an increase in radiation during that season. For example, perihelion occurs presently in northern winter. Consequently, parts of the winter hemisphere receive as much as 10% more solar radiation at present than they will 11 k.y. from now when perihelion will occur in the summer (Crowley and North, 1991).

Obliquity

Obliquity influences the seasonal cycle in high latitudes on time scales of ~40 k.y. (Crowley and North, 1991). Obliquity refers to the tilt of the Earth's axis which varies between ~22 and 25°. An increase in obliquity (tilt) concentrates annual radiation toward the poles and reduces radiation at the equator.

Eccentricity and Precession Cycles

Figures 5A to 5D show eccentricity minima (lowercase m) denoting a more circular orbit. The precession index maxima near the numbers 1 through 4 or 5 at the top of Figures 5A

to 5D indicate summer solar radiation maxima in the southern hemisphere. Conversely, the precession index minima near the numbers 1 through 4 or 5 at the bottom of the graph indicate summer solar radiation maxima in the northern hemisphere. Capital T (T = initiation of transition from glacial to interglacial climate) marks the first northern hemisphere summer solar radiation maximum after the eccentricity minimum. Dates for these events are shown toward the bottom of the graph. The letter I (I = initiation of transition from interglacial to glacial climate) at the top of the graph marks the second southern hemisphere precession peak after the T event. All the I events for the past ~900 k.y. are located two southern hemisphere maxima precession peaks forward in time from each T event (Figs. 5A to 5D). The span from one I event to the next encompasses a precession sequence. The number of precession peaks or cycles in past sequences is randomly either four or five, also noted by Ruddiman (2003a).

The past 800 k.y. include two full eccentricity cycles, each ~400 k.y. long. At present, the Earth is at the end of the 400 k.y. to 0 yr cycle and poised to begin a new 400 k.y. cycle by repeating orbital parameter relations that existed during the past 400 k.y. (Ruddiman, 2005; Droxler et al., 2003; U.S. Geological Survey, 2001; Poore and Dowsett, 2001, Fig. 3 therein; Loutre and Berger, 2000; Hodell et al., 2000; Bauch et al., 2000; Kindler and Hearty, 2000; and Murray et al., 2000). The best-dated Devils Hole chronology spans just the last 400-k.y.-long cycle with age control of isotope records older than ca. 400 ka having large standard deviations, which are related to the limitations of U-series dates. Past climate proxy data may be used, however, to help determine if a systematic relation exists between the characteristics and magnitude of glacial and interglacial climate couplets during the last two eccentricity cycles (supporting key Assumption 3).

Although a strict repetition of climate characteristics is not expected from or implied by the available data, similarities in general characteristics for glacial and interglacial sequences are evident. The lake record in the western Great Basin suggests that MIS in precession sequences with five peaks had larger lakes than MIS in precession sequences with four peaks, with the possible exception of MIS 4. The absolute size of a lake in a particular basin is a function of many climatic and nonclimatic factors; however, lake sizes during MIS 16, 12, 6, and 2 (all precession sequences with five cycles) suggest high effective moisture generated by some combination of increased precipitation or lowered temperature or both relative to lake sizes during MIS 14, 10, and 8 (U.S. Geological Survey, 2001; Knott, 1999; Jannik et al., 1991; Smith et al., 1997; Whitney and Harrington, 1993; Reheis, 1999; Morrison, 1999), all precession sequences with four cycles. MIS 18 is a precession sequence with four cycles, whereas MIS 20 and 22 are in precession sequences with five cycles. Reheis et al. (2002a) present some evidence for large lakes during MIS 18; however, deposits representing these older MIS are not well preserved or well dated.

The marine isotope record during the past 800 k.y., providing a general proxy for ice volume [although ocean temperature appears to play an important role (Shackleton, 2000)], also indicates that MIS in precession sequences with five cycles had larger ice sheets than MIS in precession sequences with four cycles. The largest ice sheets recorded by the marine isotope record during the past 800 k.y. interval occurred during MIS 16, 12, 6, and 2, although these sheets varied in relative size (indicating that these glacial periods were not of the same magnitude) (U.S. Geological Survey, 2001; Crowley and North, 1991, Fig. 6.1 therein; Oviatt et al., 1999, Fig. 2 therein). MIS 18, 14, 10, 8, and 4 ice sheets appeared to cover less area and were not as thick as ice sheets during other glacial MIS. With the exception of MIS 4, these are all found in precession sequences with four cycles.

It is possible that MIS with very large ice sheets could produce climates with greater effective moisture in the vicinity of Yucca Mountain relative to MIS with smaller ice sheets (U.S. Geological Survey, 2001). As mentioned earlier, effective moisture does not necessarily reflect precipitation; cold, dry glacial periods can have greater effective moisture than warm, wet glacial periods. Smaller lakes could have resulted from less effective moisture compared to the periods with large lakes if the overall climate were very wet but the temperature was warm. As continental ice sheets expand in area and thickness (become higher in elevation), they tend to deflect dry and very cold arctic high-pres-

sure air masses southward during the entire year (an annual cold and dry climate state), or just during the winter if high pressure cells retreat northward in summer (Kutzbach et al., 1993, Figs. 4.16 and 4.17 therein).

Uncertainties exist in the 800–400 k.y. time frame, however, because tectonic activity may have affected topography and, hence, the record from which climate was interpreted (Reheis et al., 2002a) (key Assumption 4). It also is possible that a shifting of the center of mass of the continental ice sheets from the west in the older glacials to the east in the younger glacials may have significantly impacted Great Basin climate during this time period.

Relation of the Timing of the Devils Hole Record to Calculated Orbital Parameters

The Devils Hole record (Landwehr et al., 1997) contains the most robust information and most accurate dates about climate change in the Yucca Mountain region, although the U-series method is limited to ~500 k.y. Other long, dated climate records exist, but typically their chronologies are not well dated or rely on extensive interpolation between dates or both. Because of this drawback, the chronology of continental climate records often is inferred from the correlation of glacial and interglacial stages with marine climate records that, in turn, have their chronologies derived from correlation with orbital properties. For these reasons, Devils Hole is used as the continuously dated, climate-linked chronology for this analysis. The greater $\delta^{18}O$ values in the Devils Hole record interglacial climates, the smaller values record glacial climate, and the intermediate values record what is termed herein as intermediate climates (inferred from Winograd et al., 1992; Landwehr and Winograd, 2001).

The Devils Hole chronology is used here to ask if this Earth-based record of climate change fits orbital parameter sequences. Because the Devils Hole record is well dated, it is possible to use it to find related patterns in orbital parameters rather than using orbital parameters to date a climate proxy record, as is often the case with ice or marine records. Comparing the Devils Hole $\delta^{18}O$ record from calcite and U-series ages (Landwehr et al., 1997, Table 1 therein; Winograd et al., 2006) with orbital parameter and age data (Fig. 3; Berger and Loutre, 1991) establishes a pattern linking precession, eccentricity, and terminations in glacial and interglacial cycles during the past 400 k.y. of the Devils Hole record (U.S. Geological Survey, 2001). Neither obliquity (operating on a ~41–44 k.y. cycle) nor orbital inclination (Muller and MacDonald, 2002) were found to have a consistent relation with the Devils Hole record. See Ruddiman (2003a) and Huybers and Wunsch (2005) for discussions on how obliquity helps force deglaciation.

The I events for the ~500 k.y. Devils Hole record correspond to times when greater Devils Hole $\delta^{18}O$ values (interglacials and other warm periods) are changing toward smaller values. These interglacial periods are shown as red bars in Figures 3B and 3C and Figures 5A to 5D. The T events correspond to times when smaller Devils Hole $\delta^{18}O$ values (glacial periods) are changing toward greater values (Figs. 3B and 3C). Terminations of glacial periods (blue bars, Figs. 3B and 3C, Figs. 5A to 5D) follow eccentricity minima.

The timing, pattern, and magnitude of each glacial period correspond with the number of precession peaks in a precession sequence (I to I event). Glacial cycles in precession sequences with five peaks generally occur between northern hemisphere summer radiation maxima 3 and 4. When compared to the Devils Hole record, the precession sequences with five precession peaks have a glacial period (MIS 12, 6, 4, 2) with two episodes (double-trough) of low isotope values (Figs. 3B and 3C). The precession sequences with four precession peaks have a single low isotope value (MIS 10, 8) near the southern hemisphere summer radiation maxima 3. The lightest isotopic values recorded in the Devils Hole record for double-trough glacials are ~13.5‰ and for single-trough glacials are ~13‰.

This pattern shows that each 400 k.y. cycle can be divided into glacial, interglacial, and intermediate (transitions between glacial and interglacial and vice versa) climate states based on precession index values and paced by eccentricity minima. These data sets support the first two key assumptions: (1) climate is sequential; therefore, past timing can be used to forecast the future timing of change; and (2) a relation exists between the timing of glacial and interglacial cycles and the timing of changes in certain Earth orbital parameters. The relation between past climate change and precession can provide the basis to use a precessional clock to time climate change in the future.

Comparison of the Owens Lake and Devils Hole Records with Orbital Parameters

By relating the pattern of variation in orbital parameters in Figures 5A to 5D to the climate records for Owens Lake (Table 5) and Devils Hole (Figs. 3A to 3C), the following observations and definitions are evident.

1. The second northern hemisphere summer solar radiation maximum going forward in time from an eccentricity minima begins the interglacial climate state (red bands on Figs. 3 and 5). This interglacial climate state always begins at the last northern hemisphere summer solar radiation maximum, either #4 or #5 depending on the number of precession peaks in a sequence, just prior to the I event. This interglacial state lasts to the I event (southern hemisphere maximum #1).

2. From the I event to where the precession curve crosses zero between the southern hemisphere summer solar radiation maximum #3 and northern hemisphere summer solar radiation maximum #3, intermediate with short episodes of monsoon climate occurs (green bands following red bands on Figs. 3 and 5).

3. The glacial climate (blue bands on Figs. 3 and 5) is defined as beginning where the intermediate climate ends in #2 above. The end of the glacial climate is defined as the point where the precession curve crosses zero just forward in time following a T event [the northern hemisphere sum-

mer solar radiation maximum precession #3 (if a four-sequence) or #4 (if a five-sequence)].

4. An intermediate climate (green bands following blue bands on Figs. 3 and 5) is defined to exist following the end of the glacial climate until the final northern hemisphere summer radiation maxima in the precession sequence. Intermediate climates always end at the northern hemisphere summer radiation maxima prior to the next I event.

For example, the eccentricity minimum at 269 ka noted as a heavy vertical line segment marked m on Figure 5C is closely followed at 267 ka by a minimal precession value noted as T. This point, T, generally corresponds in time with minimal δ¹⁸O values in the Devils Hole record (Figs. 3B and 3C), signaling a shift from a glacial toward an interglacial climate. This relation, discernible from ~429 to 4.5 ka consistently identifies all of the primary reversals in the Devils Hole record.

The repetitive pattern of the Devils Hole isotope record suggests that MIS 4, 3, and 2 could be combined into a single longer segment for the modeling purposes of this analysis. The Owens Lake and Devils Hole records contain patterns that support combining these three MIS. Each precession sequence (I event to I event) from 425 to 4.5 ka in the Devils Hole chronology begins with an I event in an interglacial period, moves into a glacial period, and then moves toward another interglacial period as it nears the next I event (Figs. 3A to 3C). If glacial MIS 4 and 2 are defined as separate MIS in the last precession sequence, this sequence would be the only sequence containing three interglacial (MIS 5, 3, and 1) and two glacial periods (MIS 4 and 2).

Muller and MacDonald (2002) include a short account of Nicholas Shackleton recounting Cesare Emiliani's designation of MIS 3. Apparently, Emiliani based its designation on the 41 k.y. obliquity cycle (41 k.y. prior to MIS 2), even though MIS 3 warming was not as pronounced as in previous interglacial periods. If MIS 2 is considered to be the second low isotope value in the double trough (MIS 4, MIS 2) glacial, the four precession sequences during the past 400 k.y. would display a similar pattern and timing.

Larger ice sheets and larger lakes occurred in MIS 16, 12, 6, and 2 compared to MIS 18, 14, 10, 8, and 4, as discussed above. If MIS 2 and 4 are considered one glacial event in this precession sequence with five precession cycles, these past magnitude patterns are repeated. For these reasons, MIS 2 and 4 are considered here as one *type* of glacial representing the climatic nature and characteristics of MIS 2. This sequence simplifies specification of estimated future climate states for infiltration modeling and largely preserves the cycle of precession sequences for the past 425 k.y.

It is important to note that reversal points in the Devils Hole δ¹⁸O record are selected in this study to mark the beginnings and ends of glacial and interglacial periods. This is not conventional (Winograd et al., 1997; Kukla et al., 2002a) but better suits the purposes of this study because they mark the beginning of a change. The time periods associated with the δ¹⁸O values from the Devils Hole record that reach a plateau following a glacial period define interglacial periods for this analysis. This is the *warmest* part of the full interglacial rather than a full interglacial as conventionally defined (see Winograd et al., 1997, Table 1 therein). The intermediate climate, as defined here, includes the *less than warmest* interglacial periods, true intermediate climate and near-glacial periods.

Given these parameters, the general nature of glacial and interglacial climate does not change precisely at the primary reversal points. Instead, reversals begin a trend toward a glacial or interglacial climate. A substantial amount of time elapses from these primary reversals before the next climate state is reached, and smaller reversals occur within each general trend. Interglacial climates generally reach those plateaus of $\delta^{18}O$ values ~20–25 k.y. after the glacial reversals (U.S. Geological Survey, 2001). The Devils Hole $\delta^{18}O$ profile shows a relatively smooth curve, indicating a continuous transition toward and into either glacial or interglacial climates, because each Devils Hole data point integrates ~1800 yr (Winograd et al., 1992). Examination of a higher resolution curve, such as the deuterium record of the past 420 k.y. from Antarctica (Petit et al., 1999, Fig. 1 therein), shows a pattern of numerous small-magnitude climate reversals that occur on decade and century time scales not presently visible in the Devils Hole record.

Note the lower variability in the Devils Hole record prior to ca. 470 ka (Figs. 3A and 3B). Although glacial period MIS 14 may be recorded at the T event at ca. 528 ka, the $\delta^{18}O$ curve is relatively flat across the following estimated interglacial climate state. The relative invariability of these $\delta^{18}O$ values could result from a number of factors. First, the site did not record a change in recharge during this time period. Second, the glacial and interglacial pattern established by the Devils Hole record subsequent to 470 ka is coincidental. Third, the dates are not accurate based on the uncertainty this far back in the record. Fourth, the climate signal during this period was lost in the regional aquifer from mixing of waters with different ages and isotopic values or hydrologic head relations between recharge and discharge change. Fifth, climate during this time did not accentuate differences in the isotopic value of snow by increasing and decreasing thermal gradient between source area and recharge area. Sixth, the earliest part of the Devils Hole record was influenced by a shift in climate, Earth processes, or some other factor.

The largest discrepancy between the end of an interglacial period designated by a decrease in the large $\delta^{18}O$ values in the Devils Hole record and a precession (I event) occurs at the end of interglacial Stage 5e. The isotope peak is at 126.7 ka in the Devils Hole record while the I event occurs at 116 ka (Fig. 3C). When sea-level records are considered, however, the timing of the I event is consistent with a change from an interglacial period. Records from sediments and corals from the Bahamas, Barbados, New Guinea, and the eastern Pacific Rise (Henderson Island) indicate a sea-level highstand occurred ca. 135 ka (Henderson and Slowey, 2000; Gallup et al., 2002; Esat et al., 1999; Stein et al., 1993), consistent with the Devils Hole chronology, which indicates that Stage 5e began at about this time. Muhs (2002)

reports that U-series dates on corals from Bermuda, the Bahamas, Hawaii, and Australia indicate that the last interglacial period had a sea level at least as high as present (2002) from ca. 128–116 ka. Therefore, the sea-level highstand data are consistent with the onset of stage 5e in the Devils Hole record and the I event in the precession sequence. A possible explanation is that the large $\delta^{18}O$ values in the Devils Hole record for 5e (relative to the other interglacial $\delta^{18}O$ values in the Devils Hole record) may reflect a change in the vapor path (limited rainout) rather than the timing of the end of the interglacial period (U.S. Geological Survey, 2001). If this timing is used, all of the I events and available Devils Hole interglacial reversal point ages are within 2500 yr or less of each other, a good agreement between data sets (U.S. Geological Survey, 2001).

Correspondence between the timing of I events (following several large $\delta^{18}O$ values representing warmer or drier conditions in the recharge area or both) in the latter part of the Devils Hole record and maximum precession (increased summer solar radiation) in the southern hemisphere summer (Figs. 3A to 3C) indicates that northern hemisphere climate begins a cooling trend when heat is being added to the southern hemisphere. This relation indicates that a link between glacial and interglacial periods and tropical insolation may exist, although it is possible that there is no causal relation.

Mechanisms and linkages for orbital forcing, a tropical moisture source, and short- and long-term climatic events are discussed in Winograd (2001); Landwehr and Winograd (2001); Cane (1998); Kerr (2001); Cane and Evans (2000); Clement et al. (2004); Clement et al. (2001); Clement and Cane (1999); Cane and Clement (1999); Seager et al. (2000); Clement and Seager (1999); Khodri et al. (2001); Kukla and Gavin (2005); Kukla and Gavin (2004); Kukla et al. (2002b); Ortiz et al. (2004); Pierrehumbert (1999); and Vandergoes et al. (2005). Furthermore, Kukla et al. (2002a), in a comprehensive paper on interglacial climates, suggest "the orbital shift to the warming of the tropics and cooling of the high latitudes in autumn is strongly indicated as the primary cause of the interglacial decline."

Describing the Patterns

The timing and pattern of interglacial to glacial periods in the Devils Hole record show a remarkable consistency during the last eccentricity cycle (~400 k.y.). As discussed above, the ends of interglacial episodes correspond with the I events when $\delta^{18}O$ values in Devils Hole calcite decrease moving forward in time. The path taken by Devils Hole $\delta^{18}O$ from an I to a T event is oscillatory in nature reflecting a climate path of cold and warm events. This complex, climate-change path also is known from numerous long records around Earth. Cold episodes during an interglacial are termed substages d and b, and the warmer intervals are termed substages e, c, and a. Substage e is always the oldest and substage a is always the youngest (Fig. 3C).

From 250 to 60 ka, interglacial periods MIS 7 and 5 contained cold and warm episodes. Warm episodes—or substages, 7e, 7c, 7a, 5e, 5c, and 5a—occur as peaks in the Devils Hole record (Fig. 3C; Landwehr and Winograd, 2001, Fig. 1a therein). Cold episodes—or substages 7d, 7b, 5d, and 5b—occur as troughs between the warm episodes in the Devils Hole record at ca. 223, 200, 112, and 88 ka, respectively. Troughs in the Devils Hole isotopic record also occur during MIS 11 (388 and 377 ka) and during MIS 9 [314 and 296 ka (Fig. 3B)].

Prokopenko et al. (2001, Fig. 3 therein) designate the peaks in biogenic silica in the Lake Baikal record (indicating warm climatic periods) at ca. 333 ka and 287 ka (9e and 9a, respectively); whereas Landwehr and Winograd (2001, Fig. 1a therein) label the interglacial in the Devils Hole record at ca. 330 ka as 9c rather than 9e (Fig. 3B). The MIS 11 climatic optimum in the Lake Baikal record is provisionally labeled 11e by Prokopenko et al. (2001). This interglacial period corresponds to 11c at ca. 400 ka in the Devils Hole record (Fig. 3B; Landwehr and Winograd, 2001, Fig. 1a therein). Interglacial substages 11c, centered at ca. 410 ka, and 9c, centered at ca. 330 ka (after Winograd et al., 1997, Fig. 2 therein), correspond to e events, as reported by Prokopenko, and not c events based on precession sequence patterns described herein.

Warm substages generally occur between the southern hemisphere summer radiation maxima 1 and 2 and between 2 and 3. The past 400 k.y. of the Owens Lake ostracode record (Table 5) based on correlation to the Devils Hole chronology also largely supports this pattern. This pattern is not as pronounced in the Devils Hole record prior to ~420 ka, possibly because of the reasons discussed above. Cold and warm episodes associated with the numbered substages also appear in other paleoenvironmental records worldwide (Woillard, 1978; Litwin et al., 1999, Fig. 3a therein; Adam, 1988, Fig. 1 therein; Shackleton and Opdyke, 1973, Figs. 8 and 9 therein).

Identify the Nature and Timing of Climate States using the Owens Lake Record

Four basic climate states (interglacial, monsoon, intermediate, and glacial) occurring during the past 400 k.y. were identified using modern geographic and hydrologic distributions of ostracode (Table 5; Forester, 1983; Forester, 1985; Forester, 1986, Figs. 1, 2, and 3 therein; Forester, 1987) and diatom taxa recovered from the Owens Lake sedimentary record (CRWMS M&O, 2000; U.S. Geological Survey, 2001, Fig. 11 therein; Sharpe, 2003). Numerous other climate states also occurred during this time, but four general states were selected to simplify model simulations of net infiltration. The sequence proceeds from interglacial to glacial climate states and back again. Transitions between these states are termed intermediate climate states. Short bursts of monsoonal climate states occur within the intermediate climate state.

Monsoonal states were identified in the Owens Lake record by the occurrence of the ostracode *Limnocythere bradburyi*. The known modern distribution of this ostracode occupies a relatively narrow latitudinal band east and west of Mexico City, Mexico, and the southwestern corner of New Mexico (Smith and Forester,

1994), which indicates that this species is linked to the summer monsoon season and that it cannot tolerate cold winters (Forester, 1985). Most of the rain in the Mexico City area occurs during the summer and fall and is produced by tropical cyclone systems.

The presence of this ostracode in Owens Lake can be explained best by an expansion and intensification of the summer rain system (monsoons) from moisture sources originating in the Gulf of California or Gulf of Mexico (U.S. Geological Survey, 2001). This distribution also implies a more equitable climate at times in the past than exists presently at Owens Lake and a source of water that was, at times, derived from summer rain rather than snowmelt (U.S. Geological Survey, 2001, Table 2 therein). *L. bradburyi* was recovered in Owens Lake sediments at the end of periods of long, seasonal continental heating in the northern hemisphere. These time periods were during the transition from the end of interglacials (MIS 11, MIS 9, MIS 5) to the beginning of intermediate climate states. It also was recovered during the transition from the end of intermediate to the beginning of interglacial climate (MIS 8-7 and MIS 6-5) (Table 5).

L. bradburyi inhabited Owens Lake for at most ~1000–2000 yr intervals, with a total cumulative duration during each MIS of ~3000 yr. A simplified representation of monsoonal climate was necessary to model infiltration during these warm and wet episodes. Therefore, the ~3000 yr cumulative duration has been divided into two monsoon intervals, each 1500 yr long, evenly distributed within each intermediate climate state moving from interglacial to glacial states. Although this greatly oversimplifies the past climate that the ostracode record indicates, it includes the climatic event represented by monsoon intervals, thus making it possible to model and estimate future infiltration during these episodes.

It is thought that MIS 11 is an analog for our current climate status (Droxler et al., 2003). To model future infiltration, a point in time during MIS 11 must be selected that corresponds to our present climate point in time. Once determined, this point marks the beginning of future climate sequences for the infiltration model. If anthropogenic warming doesn't permanently alter climate, we are likely at or nearing the end of an interglacial period.

The initial step in determining what point in MIS 11 was equivalent to our modern climate was to select a past/present analog point of 403,970 yr B.P. in the MIS 11 sequence at Owens Lake between the occurrence of ostracodes *Limnocythere sappaensis* and *L. bradburyi* (inferred from CRWMS M&O, 2000, Fig. 6.4-10 therein; U.S. Geological Survey, 2001). The large *L. sappaensis* abundance peak in MIS 11 reflects a mid-stage warm and dry climate (similar to present day) and the enhanced monsoon reflecting the *L. bradburyi* abundance peak had (and has) yet to occur. Because the present interglacial is nearing its end, the analog point was placed closer to the monsoon climate indicator than to the interglacial climate indicator at an Owens Lake chronology age of ca. 404 ka (U.S. Geological Survey, 2001).

The timing of the analog point (ca. 404 ka) occurs within the *Limnocythere bradburyi* event (405–403 ka) in Table 5. That is, it appears that *L. bradburyi* arrived sooner at Owens Lake (by ~1000 yr) than it should have. The timing of the analog point, however, was chosen by using the isotope values and timing of the Devils Hole chronology. The analog point had to correspond to a point in the Devils Hole record where the isotopic values were increasing in response to monsoonal flow, after 405.4 ka. Because the sampling interval of the Devils Hole calcite represents an average time interval of ~1800 yr at 2 σ (Winograd et al., 1992), the timing discrepancy occurs within this uncertainty.

Figure 6 shows how the Owens Lake ostracode assemblages represent these different combinations of temperature and precipitation or levels of effective moisture. The interglacial climate (modern) state is comparable to our relatively warm present climate state. It has the least effective moisture compared to the other climate states. The monsoon climate state is characterized by hotter summers with increased summer rainfall relative to today. The intermediate climate state is a transition from glacial state to interglacial state or vice versa and has cooler and wetter summers and winters relative to today. The glacial climate state (climates cooler and wetter than today) has the greatest effective moisture of these four selected climate states. Glacial states are of particular importance to the performance of the proposed underground high-level radioactive nuclear waste repository because periods of substantially cooler and wetter climate relative to today will increase infiltration.

Selecting Present-Day Meteorological Stations as Analogs to Past Climate States

Continuous daily temperature and precipitation values from present-day meteorological stations are required to calculate model-derived future infiltration estimates. Therefore, meteo-

rological stations representing the past four basic climate states (interglacial, glacial, intermediate, and monsoon) were selected, in part, based on geographic factors and the limiting hydrologic and physical factors estimated from modern distributions of fossil ostracode and diatom assemblages recovered from the Owens Lake record (U.S. Geological Survey, 2001; Forester, 1983; Forester, 1985; Forester, 1986) as well as nearby vegetation and pollen records (Thompson et al., 1999; Mensing, 2001).

Stations based on geographic location rather than elevation in the Yucca Mountain area were chosen as analog climate sites because the shifting of atmospheric circulation patterns over time manifests itself more in terms of latitude and longitude than elevation. The present-day late spring through early autumn season in the Yucca Mountain region is characterized by the residence of a tropical high-pressure system whereby sinking air and clear skies help produce the high summer temperatures. Evidence from many sources described above indicates that the subtropical high-pressure system was not resident in the Yucca Mountain area during glacial and intermediate climate states. Therefore, evaporation would have been much lower then than at present, so infiltration probably was much higher during those climate states when the tropical high-pressure system was not resident. For these reasons, present-day meteorological stations positioned with respect to the seasonal location of the polar front and associated low and high pressure zones were selected as analogs for past climate. These stations better represent seasonal distribution of temperature, precipitation, snowfall, and humidity than stations located on an elevational gradient in southern Nevada.

Stations (Fig. 7, Table 6) were chosen to represent upper (wetter) and lower (drier) bounds (U.S. Geological Survey, 2001; Sharpe, 2003). Only meteorological stations with relatively complete and long records were considered as analogs

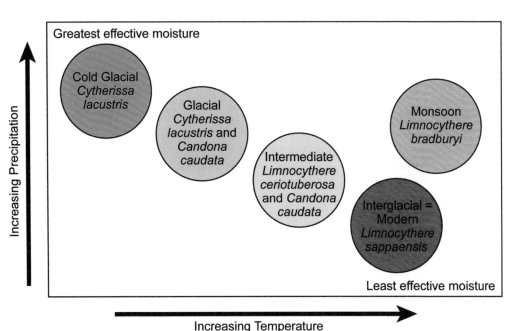

Figure 6. Climate state and relative magnitude of associated parameters based on the Owens Lake ostracode record.

Figure 7. Modern meteorological stations used as future climate analogs.

for past climates. The number of past climate states and representative meteorological stations were limited to facilitate and simplify model simulations of net infiltration.

Present-Day Climate

The present-day climate state is represented by regional meteorological stations in the Yucca Mountain area. Modern climate in the Yucca Mountain region averages 13.4 °C MAT and 125 mm MAP (Thompson et al., 1999, Table 4 therein). These values integrate a number of meteorological stations throughout the Yucca Mountain region (Nevada Divisions 3 and 4) during a 30 yr period. Currently, precipitation minus open-water evaporation is −100 cm/yr (Winter, 1990, Plate 2 therein). When MAT and MAP are averaged for all nine of the YMP stations for their individual periods of record, average annual temperature and average annual total precipitation are 16.5 °C and 177 mm respectively (WRCC, 2006). Although warmer and wetter than the regional record reported by Thompson et al. (1999), the period of record from these stations is at the most 20 yr long and is comprised of only nine local Yucca Mountain sites and not numerous regional stations.

Monsoon Climate

Nogales, Arizona, and Hobbs, New Mexico (Fig. 7), were chosen as the monsoon average upper bound climate analogs based on modern and fossil distribution of the ostracode *Limnocythere bradburyi*. Stations in Arizona and New Mexico were chosen to represent the monsoon climate state because these areas receive monsoonal precipitation and, therefore, represent a summer-fall wet cycle. MAT for the current known distribution of *L. bradburyi* is from 15 to 20 °C, and the summer rain cycle produces from 50 to 100 cm of rain per year, with some areas receiving 200 cm/yr (Forester, 1985).

Station data from Nogales, Arizona, and Hobbs, New Mexico, were combined to represent the monsoon climate state because monsoonal precipitation appears to vary depending on whether the air mass originates in the northern Gulf of California (wet Arizona monsoons) or in the southern Gulf of California or tropical eastern Pacific Ocean (New Mexico monsoons) (Mitchell et al., 2002). These stations also have relatively long period records compared to other stations that also could represent monsoon climate. MAT at Nogales and Hobbs averages ~17 °C, and MAP averages ~415 mm/yr at these stations. Precipitation minus open-water evaporation at these stations is ~ −120 cm/yr (Winter,

TABLE 6. PRESENT-DAY METEOROLOGICAL STATIONS SELECTED AS ANALOGS FOR CLIMATE STATES

Climate State*	Analog Meteorological Stations[†]	Latitude	Longitude	Elevation (m^2)[§]	MAT (°C)[#]	MAP (mm/yr)**
Glacial, MIS 6/16–Average upper bound	Lake Yellowstone, Wyo. (485345) (1948–2005)	44°33'	110°24'	2,368	0. 0	508
Glacial, MIS 6/16–Average lower bound	Browning, Mont. (241202) (1894–1989)	48°34'	113°01'	1,329	4.3	381
	Simpson 6NW, Mont. (247620) (1948–2005)	48°59'	110°19'	835	4.9	254
Glacial, MIS 2/4–Average upper bound	Browning, Mont. (241202) (1894–1989)	48°34'	113°01'	1,329	4. 3	381
	Simpson 6NW, Mont. (247620) (1948–2005)	48°59'	110°19'	835	4.9	254
Glacial, MIS 2/4–Average lower bound	Elko, WB Airport, Nev. (262573) (1888–2005)	40°50'	115°47'	1,539	7.8	238
Glacial, MIS 8/10–Average upper bound	Chewelah, Wash. (451395) (1948–2005)	48°15'	117°43'	509	8.0	533
Glacial, MIS 8/10–Average lower bound	Rosalia, Wash. (457180) (1948–2005)	47°14'	117°22'	732	8.3	451
	St. John, Wash. (457267) (1963–2005)	47°06'	117°35'	594	9.3	430
	Spokane, WSO Airport, Wash. (457938) (1889–2005)	47°38'	117°32'	719	8.9	408
Intermediate–Average upper bound	Rosalia, Wash. (457180) (1948–2005)	47°14'	117°22'	732	8.3	451
	St. John, Wash. (457267) (1963–2005)	47°06'	117°35'	594	9.3	430
	Spokane, WSO Airport, Wash.(457938) (1889–2005)	47°38'	117°32'	719	8.9	408
Intermediate–Average lower bound	Beowawe, Nev. (260795) (1949–2005)	40°36'	116°29'	1,433	8.9	222
	Delta, Utah (422090) (1938–2005)	39°20'	112°35'	1,408	10.1	199
Monsoon–Average upper bound	Nogales, Old Nogales, Ariz. (025922) (1892–1948)	31°20'	110°57'	1,189	17.3	421
	Hobbs, N.Mex. (294026) (1914–2005)	32°42'	103°08'	1,103	16.6	409
Monsoon–Average lower bound	Yucca Mountain regional stations			1,524	13.4[††]	125[††]
Modern or interglacial climate	Yucca Mountain regional stations			1,524	13.4[††]	125[††]

*MIS—marine isotope stage.
[†]Data obtained from WRCC (2006). Station identification numbers in parentheses followed by period of record in parentheses.
[§]Elevations are above mean sea level.
[#]MAT—mean annual temperature. MAT is calculated by converting °F to °C.
**MAP—mean annual precipitation. MAP is calculated by converting inches to millimeters.
[††]Thompson et al. (1999).

1990, Plate 2 therein). The monsoon climate analog average lower bound is represented by the Yucca Mountain regional climate stations because the modern climate represents conservative estimates of the MAT and MAP of *L. bradburyi* occurrence.

Glacial Climate

Three magnitudes of glacial climate are inferred from distinct ostracode assemblages in the Owens Lake stratigraphic record (U.S. Geological Survey, 2001). These differing magnitudes are designated by representative MIS stages: cold-wet (MIS 6/16), cold-dry (MIS 2/4) and warm-wet (MIS 8/10). Upper and lower MAT and MAP values for each glacial MIS at Yucca Mountain were estimated so that modern meteorological stations representing those values could be selected. Upper and lower bounds are represented by stations in Wyoming, Montana, Nevada, and Washington (Fig. 7; Sharpe, 2003). Precipitation minus open-water evaporation ranges from +25 cm/yr (upper bound) to −60 cm/yr (lower bound) (Winter, 1990, Plate 2 therein).

To determine the magnitude of these three glacial climates, MAP and MAT for MIS 2 were estimated based on vegetation recovered from packrat middens (Thompson et al., 1999, Table 4 therein). The MIS 2 values at Yucca Mountain estimated by Thompson et al. (1999) were 266–321 mm MAP and 7.9–8.5 °C MAT. These values agree fairly well with estimates from pollen assemblages in Owens Lake between 16,200 and 15,000 cal yr B.P. (Mensing, 2001). Based on the pattern described previously, MIS 2 and 4 are considered here as one glacial event, MIS 2/4.

Elko, Nevada, was selected as the lower bound for MIS 2/4 with a MAP of ~238 mm and a MAT of ~8 °C. Elko was selected because it can have cold, wet, and snowy winters influenced by either Polar lows or Arctic highs, and cool and dry summers resulting from the presence of cool westerly flows and the absence of subtropical highs in the region.

The upper bound of MIS 2/4 is also the lower bound of MIS 6/16, the Browning and Simpson, Montana, stations (Fig. 7; Table 6). This is an upper bounding estimate because average annual temperatures for these stations are 3–4 °C below the

MIS 2/4 temperature estimates. These Montana stations were selected as the lower bound for MIS 6/16 because MIS 6 had greater effective moisture than MIS 2, 8, or 10, and MIS 16 appears to have had greater effective moisture than MIS 6 (Knott, 1999; Jannik et al., 1991; Whitney and Harrington, 1993; Smith and Bischoff, 1997; Reheis, 1999; Oviatt et al., 1999; Reheis et al., 2002a). Therefore, a MAP of 300 mm or more and a MAT colder than 8 °C were required. These stations average less than 5 °C MAP and 318 mm MAP. Greater effective moisture does not necessarily signify increased precipitation, however. Low temperatures can play a critical role in determining effective moisture; hence, increased effective moisture can occur under conditions of very low temperatures and low precipitation.

The upper bound for MIS 6/16 is Lake Yellowstone, Wyoming, because this region is dominated by polar air masses and the ostracode *Cytherissa lacustris* (found during glacial periods in Owens Lake) currently (2006) is living in Lake Yellowstone, Wyoming, a very fresh and cold lake (Fig. 7). The MAT at this station is very cold (0 °C) because of its high elevation and latitude and, therefore, provides a lower bounding estimate on the coldest temperature. The MAP is 508 mm/yr at this site. The lower bound MIS 6/16 analog stations, Browning and Simpson, Montana, are slightly more in line with estimated MIS 6 temperatures (4.3 and 4.9 °C, respectively) and average slightly above the estimated 300 mm MIS 2 MAP, although *C. lacustris* has not been reported in this locality.

MIS 8 and 10 were wetter and warmer than either MIS 2 or 6. Therefore, MIS 8 and 10 likely had MAP much greater than 300 mm and MAT greater than 8 °C. The area east of the Cascade Range in the State of Washington was chosen as the lower bound full-glacial MIS 8/10 analog and as the average upper bound analog for the intermediate climate state. This includes climate stations Rosalia, Spokane, and St. John, Washington (Fig. 7; Table 6), with an average MAT of ~9 °C and an average MAP of ~430 mm/yr. This choice was made because the region (1) is east of a high mountain range in a rain shadow similar to the Yucca Mountain region; (2) is winter-precipitation dominated; (3) is under the influence of the polar front during the winter; (4) is situated near the average position of the polar front throughout the year; and (5) does not have extended dominance by cold Arctic high-pressure air. Ostracodes recovered from the glacial MIS 8 and 10 in the Owens Lake core also occur at present (2006) in eastern Washington, supporting the link between ostracode distribution and climate. Because the glacial MIS 8/10 upper bound required wetter and slightly cooler climate than MIS 2, Chewelah, Washington (Fig. 7), was selected based on similar geographic criteria and the fact that it has a MAP of ~533 mm and a MAT of ~8 °C.

Intermediate Climate

The Spokane, Rosalia, and St. John climate stations (Fig. 7) also were selected to represent the upper bound intermediate (glacial-transition) climate in U.S. Geological Survey (2001; Table 2 therein). Precipitation minus open-water evaporation is ~0 cm/yr at these stations (Winter, 1990, Plate 2 therein). With intermediate climates drier and warmer than MIS 2, but wetter and cooler than present day, MAP for the intermediate climates may have been more than 125 mm, but less than ~275 mm, and MAT may have been from 8 to 13 °C (U.S. Geological Survey, 2001; Sharpe, 2004). Beowawe, Nevada, and Delta, Utah (Fig. 7), were chosen as the intermediate lower bound climate analogs because they represent cool, winter wet seasons, warm to cool and dry summers, and lie on the east sides of large mountain ranges (U.S. Geological Survey, 2001, Table 2 therein). Their MAT averages above 9 °C, and MAP averages 211 mm/yr (Table 6). Precipitation minus open-water evaporation is −60 cm/yr at these stations (Winter, 1990, Plate 2 therein).

Figure 8 shows temperature and precipitation values for each of the climate state upper and lower bounds. If an upper or lower bound is represented by more than one climate station, the values are averaged to show a general comparison among the climate states. For example, the glacial MIS 6/16 lower bound Browning and Simpson, Montana, values are averaged. All values are cooler and wetter than modern values except for the monsoon temperature upper bound. Infiltration is greater during cooler and wetter climate states.

Estimating the Bounds of Future Infiltration Scenarios

Eccentricity and precession cycles and the timing of the four future climate states—glacial, interglacial, intermediate, and monsoon—for the next 500 k.y. are shown in Figures 9A and 9B. As in the previous figures that show orbital parameters, m, I, and T events are designated, and climate states are represented by colored bars. As discussed previously, the intermediate climate state has begun or will begin soon and will end ~30 k.y. from now based on the analogy with the Owens Lake record and past timing of precession cycles (Sharpe, 2004; U.S. Geological Survey, 2001). Accordingly, the glacial state is estimated to begin between 30 and 38 k.y. after present (A.P.) and continue until ca. 50 k.y. A.P.

Note that a flattening of the eccentricity cycle occurs at 95.5 k.y. A.P., as eccentricity remains almost constant for ~40 k.y. This flattening affects the magnitude of the corresponding precession sequence because eccentricity amplifies or dampens precession. The precession sequence here is the only one containing three precession peaks, rather than four or five, in the entire 1.5 m.y. time span evaluated in this analysis.

Because no previous pattern for a three-precession cycle sequence was available, the intermediate/monsoon climate states were determined to be one precession cycle shorter, lasting through southern hemisphere maximum two rather than three. This adjustment makes durations of the glacial and following intermediate climate states similar to past durations, so that consistency with the methodologies described above was maintained. If the intermediate/monsoon climate state continued to just beyond the southern hemisphere summer radiation maximum #3 as in previous cycles, then the following glacial, intermediate, and interglacial states would be compressed into 17 k.y. in less than one precession cycle.

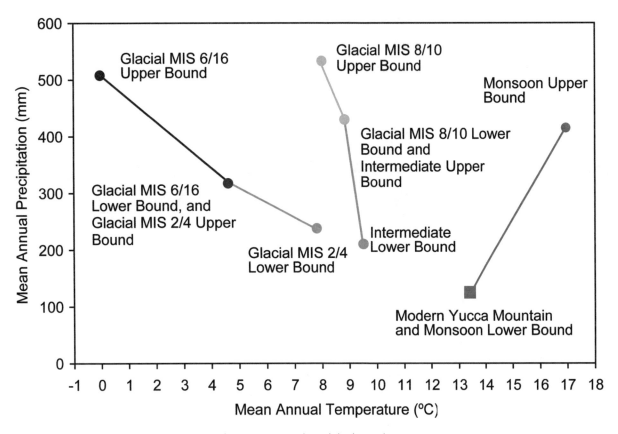

Figure 8. Modern meteorological station mean annual temperature and precipitation estimates.

Future glacial states should have different characteristics, just as past glacial states have differed from one another. Based on the Devils Hole record and other paleoenvironmental data discussed herein, precession sequences with five high-amplitude (several index values which are greater than ~0.04 and less than ~−0.04) precession peaks host relatively colder, greater effective moisture MIS 6/16 equivalent glacials. The Devils Hole data record a double-trough glacial period in MIS 6 (Fig. 3C). Note that during the next 500 k.y., from 241 to 355 k.y. A.P., only one precession sequence containing five precession cycles occurs. It is a low-amplitude precession sequence; therefore, no MIS 6/16 equivalent glacial state is estimated to occur during the next 500 k.y.

Based on the Devils Hole record and other paleoenvironmental data discussed herein, precession sequences with five low-amplitude precession peaks host relatively cooler drier glacials. MIS 12 occurs in a low-amplitude five precession peak cycle (Fig. 3B). MIS 4 and 2 (currently considered two separate glacial periods) occur in the other low-amplitude five precession peak sequence within the past 500 k.y. (Fig. 3C). As discussed earlier, this pattern suggests that MIS 4 and 2 may be a double-troughed glacial similar to MIS 12 with the MIS 3 period as the warm period between the troughs. This pattern of a double-trough glacial period in a five-precession sequence is consistent with the entire past 500 k.y. of the Devils Hole record. Because

MIS 12 paleoclimate data are not well constrained, MIS 2/4 are used here to represent a cool, dry MIS 2/4 glacial period based on the climate characteristics of MIS 2.

Based on the Devils Hole record and other paleoenvironmental data discussed herein, precession sequences with four low-amplitude precession peaks host relatively warmer, wetter glacial periods. These glacial period characteristics are represented by MIS 10 and MIS 8 (Fig. 3B). Note that these glacial periods have a single trough in the Devils Hole record.

Using this pattern, the magnitude of future glacial states for this time period is estimated to be equivalent to MIS 8/10 for the next three glacial periods (centering at ca. 44, ca. 114, and ca. 206 k.y. A.P.) (Fig. 9A). A MIS 2/4 equivalent centers at ca. 309 k.y. A.P. during a five-precession cycle with low amplitude (Fig. 9B). The next two glacial periods are MIS 8/10 equivalents (centering at ca. 405 and ca. 477 k.y. A.P.).

Based on the next ~500 k.y. of precession sequences, future interglacial (modern) climate periods will last between 10 and 12 k.y. and occur ~13% (65 k.y.) of the time. Interglacial climate is the warmest and driest of all climate states. This climate state has been dominant in the Yucca Mountain area for only the past 7–8 k.y. Regional MAT and MAP are estimated to be ~13 °C and 125 mm/yr, respectively.

Intermediate climate states are highly variable in duration. They will last between 13 and 52 k.y. and occur more than 68%

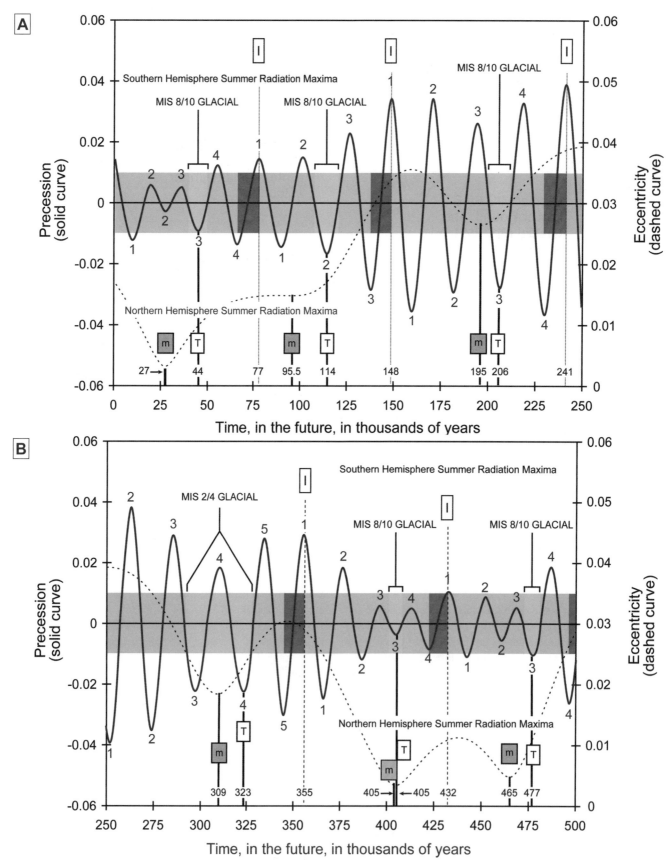

Figure 9. (A) Relation between precession and eccentricity from present to 500 k.y. after present (A.P.): 0 to 250 ka (Berger, 1978). As in Fig. 3. Continuation of the diagram is given as Fig. 9B. (B) Relation between precession and eccentricity from present to 500 k.y. A.P.: 250 to 500 ka (Berger, 1978).

of the time during the next 500 k.y. (>340 k.y.). Monsoon climate states occurred in the past and are estimated to occur 3% of the time within that 68%. Intermediate climate states range from an upper bound of ~8.8 °C and 430 mm/yr to 9.5 °C and 211 mm/yr. Monsoon climate states range from ~13–17 °C MAT and 125–415 mm MAP.

Five glacial climate periods lasting between 8 and 14 k.y. and one glacial climate period lasting ~38 k.y. are estimated (Figs. 9A and 9B). The percentage of time duration for glacial periods during the next 500 k.y. is 19% (95 k.y.). These future glacial episodes will vary from each other in magnitude, ranging from relatively warm and wet to cold and dry (Table 6). Future glacial period upper bound (most conservative, MIS 6/16) estimates for MAT and MAP in the Yucca Mountain area are 0 °C and 508 mm, respectively; however, this magnitude of climate change is not estimated to occur within the next 500 k.y. because a high-amplitude five-precession sequence does not occur during this time.

Published estimates of past temperature and precipitation for the Yucca Mountain area and western Great Basin during glacial periods range from 4 to 15 °C colder than today and precipitation from 1.4 to three times modern. Average MAT and MAP from DOE sites 1–9 are ~17 °C and 177 mm/yr, respectively. If past glacial climate estimates are correct, using these values would place past glacial MAT and MAP at Yucca Mountain between 2 and 13 °C and 248–531 mm/yr, respectively. These values support the estimated future glacial MAT and MAP (Table 6) ranging from 0 to 9 °C and from 238 to 533 mm/yr, respectively.

CONCLUSIONS

Climatology and meteorology studies in the Yucca Mountain area have resulted in the following key observations and conclusions:
- The present-day (2006) arid climate of the Yucca Mountain area can be understood in terms of global-scale atmospheric circulation and regional-to-local physiographic features. In general terms, the area is under the influence of mid-latitude westerly winds and associated storm systems during the cool part of the year, and under the influence of moist air advected from the eastern tropical Pacific Ocean and Gulf of California during the summer.
- Climate change during the past several hundred thousand years can be understood partially in terms of changes in atmospheric circulation patterns, physiographic features, and predictable variations in the Earth's orbital characteristics. Regional and local evidence indicates that the Yucca Mountain site has had, during the past several hundred thousand years, many different climate states ranging from glacial to interglacial periods. Periods of sustained greater effective moisture, commonly defined as precipitation minus evaporation, occurred during glacial and intermediate climate periods. Thus, temperature is as important as precipitation in determining effective moisture. Greater infiltration and recharge occurred during the glacial and intermediate climate periods than during interglacial periods. Although Yucca Mountain had glacial climates, it did not undergo glaciation.
- The Devils Hole record provides the opportunity to compare the timing of millennial scale climate change on Earth to orbital parameters. That comparison suggests that the chronology of climate change may be timed with precession; however, no cause and effect are implied here. The Owens Lake record, which has a chronology independent of the Devils Hole record, provides estimates of magnitude and duration of past climate states, as do other regional paleoclimate records. Accordingly, assuming that the correlation would persist into the future, these relations allow estimates for bounding future infiltration scenarios.

ACKNOWLEDGMENTS

This study was supported by U.S. Department of Energy Cooperative Agreement DE-FC28-04RW12232. I thank Eric Smistad, U.S. Department of Energy, for his support throughout this project. Rick Forester developed the method for estimating future climate scenarios, and without his initial idea and continued thoughtful and extensive contributions, this chapter would not exist. Thanks go to Schon Levy, Marith Reheis, John Barron, and Joe Whelan who provided review comments that greatly improved this chapter. I also appreciate Isaac Winograd, Kelly Redmond, W. Geoff Spaulding, and Laura Edwards who took time to constructively discuss many different aspects of this chapter.

REFERENCES CITED

Adam, D.P., 1988, Correlations of the Clear Lake, California, Core CL-73–4 pollen sequence with other long climate records, *in* Sims, J.D., ed., Late Quaternary Climate, Tectonism, and Sedimentation in Clear Lake, Northern California Coast Ranges: Boulder, Colorado, Geological Society of America Special Paper 214, p. 81–95.

Ahrens, C.D., 1994, Meteorology Today, An Introduction to Weather, Climate, and the Environment: St. Paul, Minnesota, West Publishing, 544 p.

Albritton, D.A., Allen, M.R., Baede, A.P.M., Church, J.A., Cubasch, U., Xiaosu, D., Yihui, D., Ehhalt, D.H., Folland, C.K., Giorgi, F., Gregory, J.M., Griggs, D.J., Haywood, J.M., Hewitson, B., Houghton, J.T., House, J.I., Hulme, M., Isaksen, I., Jaramillo, V.J., Jayaraman, A., Johnson, C.A., Joos, F., Joussaume, S., Karl, T., Karoly, D.J., Kheshgi, H.S., LeQuere, C., Maskell, K., Mata, L.J., McAvaney, B.J., McFarland, M., Mearns, L.O., Meehl, G.A., Meira-Filho, L.G., Meleshko, V.P., Mitchell, J.F.B., Moore, B., Mugara, R.K., Noguer, M., Nyenzi, B.S., Oppenheimer, M., Penner, J.E., Pollonais, S., Prather, M., Prentice, I.C., Ramaswamy, V., Ramirez-Rojas, A., Raper, S.C.B., Salinger, M.J., Scholes, R.J., Solomon, S., Stocker, T.F., Stone, J.M.R., Stouffer, R.J., Trenberth, K.E., Wang, M.-X., Watson, R.T., Yap, K.S., and Zillman, J., 2001, Summary for Policymakers. A report of Working Group I of the Intergovernmental Panel on Climate Change, *in* Houghton, J.T., Ding, Y., Griggs, D.J., Noguer, M., van der Linden, P.J., Dai, X., Maskell, K., and Johnson, C.A., eds., Climate Change 2001: The Scientific Basis. Contribution of Working Group I to the Third Assessment Report of the Intergovernmental Panel on Climate Change: Cambridge, United Kingdom and New York, New York, Cambridge University Press, 881 p.

Anderson, D., 1999, Latest Quaternary (<30 ka) late high-stand fluctuations and evolving paleohydrology of Death Valley, *in* Slate, J.L., ed., Proceedings of Conference on Status of Geologic Research and Mapping in Death

Valley National Park, 9–11 April 1999: Las Vegas, Nevada, U.S. Geological Survey Open-File Report 99-153, Denver, Colorado, p. 124–131.

Anderson, D.E., and Wells, S.G., 2003, Latest Pleistocene lake highstands in Death Valley, California, *in* Enzel, Y., Wells, S.G., and Lancaster, N., eds., Paleoenvironments and Paleohydrology of the Mojave and Southern Great Basin Deserts: Boulder, Colorado, Geological Society of America Special Paper 368, p. 115–128.

Anderson, K.C., and Wells, S.G., 2003, Latest Quaternary paleohydrology of Silurian Lake and Salt Spring Basin, Silurian Valley, California, *in* Enzel, Y., Wells, S.G., and Lancaster, N., eds., Paleoenvironments and Paleohydrology of the Mojave and Southern Great Basin Deserts: Boulder, Colorado, Geological Society of America Special Paper 368, p. 129–141.

Anderson, R.Y., 1992, Long-term changes in the frequency of occurrence of El Nino events, *in* Diaz, H.F., and Markgraf, V., eds., El Nino, Historical and Paleoclimatic Aspects of the Southern Oscillation: New York, New York, Cambridge University Press, p. 419–433.

Archer, D., and Ganopolski, A., 2005, A movable trigger: Fossil fuel CO_2 and the onset of the next glaciation: Geochemistry Geophysics Geosystems, v. 6, no. 5, p. 1–7, doi: 10.1029/2004GC000891.

Bacon, S.N., Burke, R.M., Pezzopane, S.K., and Jayko, A.S., 2006, Last glacial maximum and Holocene lake levels of Owens Lake, eastern California, USA: Quaternary Science Reviews, v. 25, no. 11–12, p. 1264–1282, doi: 10.1016/j.quascirev.2005.10.014.

Barry, R.G., and Chorley, R.J., 1992, Atmosphere, Weather and Climate: New York, New York, Routledge, 392 p.

Bauch, H.A., Erlenkeuser, H., Helmke, J.P., and Struck, U., 2000, A paleoclimatic evaluation of Marine Oxygen Isotope Stage 11 in the High-Northern Atlantic (Nordic Seas): Global and Planetary Change, v. 24, no. 1, p. 27–39, doi: 10.1016/S0921-8181(99)00067-3.

Beatley, J.C., 1976, Vascular Plants of the Nevada Test Site and Central-Southern Nevada: Ecologic and Geographic Distributions: Oak Ridge, Tennessee, Energy Research and Development Administration.

Benson, L., 1999, Records of millennial-scale climate change from the Great Basin of the western United States, *in* Clark, P.U., Webb, R.S., and Keigwin, L.D., eds., Mechanisms of Global Climate Change at Millennial Time Scales, Washington, D.C., American Geophysical Union, Monograph 112, p. 203–225.

Benson, L., and Klieforth, H., 1989, Stable isotopes in precipitation and ground water in the Yucca Mountain region, southern Nevada: Paleoclimatic implications, *in* Peterson, D.H., ed., Aspects of Climate Variability in the Pacific and the Western Americas, Washington, D.C., American Geophysical Union, Geophysical Monograph 55, p. 41–59.

Benson, L.V., Burdett, J.W., Kashgarian, M., Lund, S.P., Phillips, F.M., and Rye, R.O., 1996, Climatic and hydrologic oscillations in the Owens Lake Basin and adjacent Sierra Nevada, California: Science, v. 274, p. 746–749, doi: 10.1126/science.274.5288.746.

Benson, L., Burdett, J., Lund, S., Kashgarian, M., and Mensing, S., 1997, Nearly synchronous climate change in the Northern Hemisphere during the Last Glacial termination: Nature, v. 388, p. 263–265, doi: 10.1038/40838.

Berger, A.L., 1978, Long-term variations of daily insolation and Quaternary climate changes: Journal of Atmospheric Sciences, v. 35, no. 12, p. 2362–2367, doi: 10.1175/1520-0469(1978)035<2362:LTVODI>2.0.CO;2.

Berger, A., and Loutre, M.F., 1991, Insolation values for the climate of the last 10 million years: Quaternary Science Reviews, v. 10, p. 297–317, doi: 10.1016/0277-3791(91)90033-Q.

Berger, A., and Loutre, M.F., 2002, An exceptionally long interglacial ahead?: Science, v. 297, no. 5585, p. 1287–1288, doi: 10.1126/science.1076120.

Berger, W.H., Yasuda, M.K., Bickert, T., Wefer, G., and Takayama, T., 1994, Quaternary Time Scale for the Ontong Java Plateau: Milankovitch Template for Ocean Drilling Program Site 806: Geology, v. 22, no. 5, p. 463–467, doi: 10.1130/0091-7613(1994)022<0463:QTSFTO>2.3.CO;2.

Biondi, F., Gershunov, A., and Cayan, D.R., 2001, North Pacific decadal climate variability since 1661: Journal of Climate, v. 14, no. 1, p. 5–10, doi: 10.1175/1520-0442(2001)014<0005:NPDCVS>2.0.CO;2.

Bischoff, J.L., Stafford, T.W., Jr., and Rubin, M., 1997a, A time-depth scale for Owens Lake sediments of Core OL-92: radiocarbon dates and constant mass-accumulation rate, *in* Smith, G.I., and Bischoff, J.L., eds., An 800,000-Year Paleoclimatic Record from Core OL-92, Owens Lake, Southeast California: Boulder, Colorado, Geological Society of America, Special Paper 317, p. 91–98.

Bischoff, J.L., Menking, K.M., Fitts, J.P., and Fitzpatrick, J.A., 1997b, Climatic oscillations 10,000–155,000 yr B.P. at Owens Lake, California, reflected in glacial rock flour abundance and lake salinity in Core OL-92: Quaternary Research, v. 48, no. 3, p. 313–325, doi: 10.1006/qres.1997.1933.

Bischoff, J.L., and Cummins, K., 2001, Wisconsin glaciation of the Sierra Nevada (79,000–15,000 yr B.P.) as recorded by rock flour in sediments of Owens Lake, California: Quaternary Research, v. 55, p. 14–24, doi: 10.1006/qres.2000.2183.

Blumen, W., 1990, Atmospheric processes over complex terrain: Meteorological Monographs, v. 23, no. 45, 323 p.

Bond, G., Kromer, B., Beer, J., Muscheler, R., Evans, M.N., Showers, W., Hoffmann, S., Lotti-Bond, R., Hajdas, I., and Bonani, G., 2001, Persistent solar influence on North Atlantic climate during the Holocene: Science, v. 294, no. 5549, p. 2130–2136, doi: 10.1126/science.1065680.

Brennan, R., and Quade, J., 1997, Reliable Late-Pleistocene stratigraphic ages and shorter groundwater travel times from ^{14}C in fossil snails from the southern Great Basin: Quaternary Research, v. 47, p. 329–336, doi: 10.1006/qres.1997.1895.

Bright, J., and Anderson, K.C., 2005, Re-interpretation of Pleistocene Lake Dumont, Salt Spring basin, California, based on ostracode faunal analysis, *in* Miller, D.M., Menges, C.M., and McMacklin, M.R., eds., Geomorphology and tectonics at the intersection of Silurian and Death Valleys, 2005 Guidebook Pacific Cell Friends of the Pleistocene, p. B1–B10.

Cane, M.A., 1998, A role for the tropical Pacific: Science, v. 282, no. 5386, p. 59–61, doi: 10.1126/science.282.5386.59.

Cane, M., and Clement, A.C., 1999, A role for the tropical Pacific coupled ocean-atmosphere system on Milankovitch and millennial time scales. Part II: Global impacts, *in* Clark, P.U., Webb, R.S., and Keigwin, L.D., eds., Mechanisms of Global Climate Change at Millennial Time Scales: Washington, D.C., American Geophysical Union, Geophysical Monograph 112, p. 373–383.

Cane, M.A., and Evans, M., 2000, Do the tropics rule?: Science, v. 290, no. 5494, p. 1107–1108, doi: 10.1126/science.290.5494.1107.

Cayan, D.R., Kammerdiener, S.A., Dettinger, M.D., Caprio, J.M., and Peterson, D.H., 2001, Changes in the onset of spring in the western United States: Bulletin of the American Meteorological Society, v. 82, no. 3, p. 399–415, doi: 10.1175/1520-0477(2001)082<0399:CITOOS>2.3.CO;2.

Clement, A.C., and Cane, M., 1999, A role for the Tropical Pacific coupled ocean-atmosphere system on Milankovitch and millennial time scales. Part I: A modeling study of Tropical Pacific variability, *in* Clark, P.U., Webb, R.S., and Keigwin, L.D., eds., Mechanisms of Global Climate Change at Millennial Time Scales: Washington, D.C., American Geophysical Union, Geophysical Monograph 112, p. 363–371.

Clement, A., and Seager, R., 1999, Climate and the tropical oceans: Journal of Climate, v. 12, no. 12, p. 3383–3401, doi: 10.1175/1520-0442(1999)012<3383:CATTO>2.0.CO;2.

Clement, A.C., Cane, M.A., and Seager, R., 2001, An orbitally driven tropical source for abrupt climate change: Journal of Climate, v. 14, no. 11, p. 2369–2375, doi: 10.1175/1520-0442(2001)014<2369:AODTSF>2.0.CO;2.

Clement, A.C., Hall, A., and Broccoli, A.J., 2004, The importance of precessional signals in the tropical climate: Climate Dynamics, v. 22, p. 327–341, doi: 10.1007/s00382-003-0375-8.

Crowley, T.J., and North, G.R., 1991, Paleoclimatology: New York, New York, Oxford University Press, 339 p.

CRWMS M&O, 1997, Regional and local wind patterns near Yucca Mountain: CRWMS M&O, Las Vegas, Nevada, B00000000-01717-5705-00081 REV 00.

CRWMS M&O, 1999, Environmental baseline file for meteorology and air quality: CRWMS M&O, Las Vegas, Nevada, B00000000-01717-5705-00126 REV 00, 23 p.

CRWMS M&O, 2000, Yucca Mountain Site Description: CRWMS M&O, Las Vegas, Nevada, TDR-CRW-GS-000001 REV 01 ICN 01.

CRWMS M&O, 2004, Yucca Mountain Site Description: TDR-CRW-GS-000001 REV 02 ICN 01: Las Vegas, Nevada.

Cuffey, K.M., and Vimeux, F., 2001, Covariation of carbon dioxide and temperature from the Vostok ice core after deuterium-excess correction: Nature, v. 412, no. 6846, p. 523–527, doi: 10.1038/35087544.

Davis, O.K., 1989, The regionalization of climatic change in western North America, *in* Leinen, M., and Sarnthein, M., eds., Paleoclimatology and Paleometeorology: Modern and past patterns of global atmospheric transport: Proceedings of the NATO Advanced Research Workshop, 17–19 November 1987: NATO ASI Series, Series C: Mathematical and Physical Sciences: Oracle, Arizona, Kluwer Academic Publishers, p. 617–636.

Droxler, A.W., Poore, R.Z., and Burckle, L.H., 2003, Earth's climate and orbital eccentricity: The Marine Isotope Stage 11 question: Washington, D.C., American Geophysical Union, Geophysical Monograph 137, 240 p.

Eddy, J.A., 1976, The Maunder Minimum: Science, v. 192, no. 4245, p. 1189–1201, doi: 10.1126/science.192.4245.1189.

Edwards, R.L., Cheng, H., Murrell, M.T., and Goldstein, S.J., 1997, Protactinium-231 dating of carbonates by thermal ionization mass spectrometry: Implications for quaternary climate change: Science, v. 276, no. 5313, p. 782–786, doi: 10.1126/science.276.5313.782.

Enzel, Y., Knott, J.R., Anderson, K., Anderson, D.E., and Wells, S.G., 2002, Is there any evidence of mega-lake Manly in the eastern Mojave desert during Oxygen Isotope Stage 5e/6? A comment on R. LeB. Hooke (1999), Lake Manly(?) Shorelines in the eastern Mojave Desert, California; Quaternary Research v. 52, p. 328–336: Quaternary Research, v. 57, no. 1, p. 173–176, doi: 10.1006/qres.2001.2300.

Enzel, Y., Wells, S.G., and Lancaster, N., 2003, Late Pleistocene lakes along the Mojave River, southeast California, *in* Enzel, Y., Wells, S. G., and Lancaster, N., eds., Paleoenvironments and paleohydrology of the Mojave and southern Great Basin Deserts: Boulder, Colorado, Geological Society of America Special Paper 368, p. 61–77.

EPICA, 2004, Eight glacial cycles from an Antarctic ice core: Nature, v. 429, p. 623–628, doi: 10.1038/nature02599.

Esat, T.M., McCulloch, M.T., Chappell, J., Pillans, B., and Omura, A., 1999, Rapid fluctuations in sea level recorded at Huon Peninsula during the penultimate deglaciation: Science, v. 283, no. 5399, p. 197–201, doi: 10.1126/science.283.5399.197.

Forester, R.M., 1983, Relationship of two lacustrine ostracode species to solute composition and salinity: Implications for paleohydrochemistry: Geology, v. 11, no. 8, p. 435–438, doi: 10.1130/0091-7613(1983)11<435: ROTLOS>2.0.CO;2.

Forester, R.M., 1985, Limnocythere bradburyi N. SP.: A modern ostracode from central Mexico and a possible quaternary paleoclimatic indicator: Journal of Paleontology, v. 59, no. 1, p. 8–20.

Forester, R.M., 1986, Determination of the dissolved anion composition of ancient lakes from fossil ostracodes: Geology, v. 14, p. 796–798, doi: 10.1130/0091-7613(1986)14<796:DOTDAC>2.0.CO;2.

Forester, R.M., 1987, Late Quaternary paleoclimate records from lacustrine ostracodes, *in* Ruddiman, W.F., and Wright, H.E. Jr., eds., North America and Adjacent Oceans during the Last Deglaciation: Boulder, Colorado, Geological Society of America, Geology of North America, v. K-3, p. 261–276.

Forester, R.M., Bradbury, J.P., Carter, C., Elvidge-Tuma, A.B., Hemphill, M.L., Lundstrom, S.C., Mahan, S.A., Marshall, B.D., Neymark, L.A., Paces, J.B., Sharpe, S.E., Wheland, J.F., and Wigand, P.E., 1999, The climatic and hydrologic history of southern Nevada during the late Quaternary: U.S. Geological Survey Open-File Report 98-635, 63 p.

Forester, R.M., Lowenstein, T., and Spencer, R.J., 2005, An ostracode based paleolimnologic and paleohydrologic history of Death Valley: 200 to 0 ka: Geological Society of America Bulletin, v. 117, p. 1379–1386, doi: 10.1130/B25637.1.

Gallup, C.D., Cheng, H., Taylor, F.W., and Edwards, R.L., 2002, Direct determination of the timing of sea level change during Termination II: Science, v. 295, no. 5553, p. 310–313, doi: 10.1126/science.1065494.

Gauthier, J.H., 1999, Unified structure in Quaternary climate: Geophysical Research Letters, v. 26, no. 6, p. 763–766, doi: 10.1029/1999GL900086.

Giorgi, F., Hewitson, B., Christensen, J., Hulme, M., Storch, H.V., Whetton, P., Jones, R., Mearns, L., and Fu, C., 2001, Regional Climate Information—Evaluation and Projections, *in* Watson, R.T., ed., Climate Change 2001: The Scientific Basis, Contribution of Working Group I to the Third Assessment Report of the Intergovernmental Panel on Climate Change: New York, New York, Cambridge University Press, p. 583–638.

Grasso, D.N., 1996, Hydrology of modern and late Holocene lakes, Death Valley, California, U.S. Geological Survey Water-Resources Investigations Report 95-4237, 54 p.

Grayson, D.K., 1993, The Desert's Past: A natural prehistory of the Great Basin: Washington, D.C., Smithsonian Institution Press, 356 p.

Grootes, P.M., Steig, E.J., Stuiver, M., Waddington, E.D., Morse, D.L., and Nadeau, M.-J., 2001, The Taylor Dome Antarctic ^{18}O record and globally synchronous changes in climate: Quaternary Research, v. 56, no. 3, p. 289–298, doi: 10.1006/qres.2001.2276.

Hall, I.R., McCave, I.N., Shackleton, N.J., Weedon, G.P., and Harris, S.E., 2001, Intensified Deep Pacific Inflow and Ventilation in Pleistocene Glacial Times: Nature, v. 412, no. 6849, p. 809–812, doi: 10.1038/35090552.

Hartmann, D.L., 1994, Global Physical Climatology, International Geophysics Series: San Diego, California, Academic Press, v. 56, 411 p.

Hay, W.W., DeConto, R.M., and Wold, C.N., 1997, Climate: is the past the key to the future?: Geologische Rundschau, v. 86, no. 2, p. 471–491, doi: 10.1007/s005310050155.

Haynes, C.V., 1967, Quaternary geology of the Tule Springs Area, Clark County, Nevada, *in* Wormington, H.M., and Ellis, D., eds., Part 1 of Pleistocene Studies in Southern Nevada, Anthropological Papers No. 13: Carson City, Nevada, Nevada State Museum, 411 p.

Helmke, J.P., Schulz, M., and Bauch, H.A., 2002, Sediment-color record from northeast Atlantic reveals patterns of millennial-scale climate variability during the past 500,000 years: Quaternary Research, v. 57, no. 1, p. 49–57, doi: 10.1006/qres.2001.2289.

Henderson, G.M., and Slowey, N.C., 2000, Evidence from U-Th dating against northern hemisphere forcing of the penultimate deglaciation: Nature, v. 404, no. 6773, p. 61–66, doi: 10.1038/35003541.

Hillhouse, J., Sarna-Wojcicki, A., Reheis, M., and Forester, R., 2005, Age and Paleoenvironments (Paleomagnetism, Tephra, and Ostracodes) of the Pliocene and Pleistocene Tecopa Beds, Southeastern California, *in* Reheis, M.C., ed., Geologic and biotic perspectives on Late Cenozoic drainage history of the southwestern Great Basin and lower Colorado River region: conference abstracts, U.S. Geological Survey Open-File Report 2005-1404, 24 p.

Hodell, D.A., Charles, C.D., and Ninnemann, U.S., 2000, Comparison of interglacial stages in the south Atlantic sector of the Southern Ocean for the past 450 kyr: Implications for marine isotope stage (MIS) 11: Global and Planetary Change, v. 24, no. 1, p. 7–26, doi: 10.1016/S0921-8181(99)00069-7.

Hooke, R.L., 1999, Lake Manly(?) shorelines in the eastern Mojave desert, California: Quaternary Research, v. 52, no. 3, p. 328–336, doi: 10.1006/qres.1999.2080.

Hooke, R.L., 2002, Is there any evidence of mega-lake Manly in the eastern Mojave desert during oxygen isotope stage 5e/6?: Quaternary Research, v. 57, no. 1, p. 177–179, doi: 10.1006/qres.2001.2299.

Hooke, R.L., 2005, Where was the southern end of Lake Manley during the Blackwelder stand?, *in* Reheis, M.C., ed., Geologic and biotic perspectives on Late Cenozoic drainage history of the southwestern Great Basin and lower Colorado River region: conference abstracts: U.S. Geological Survey Open-File Report 2005-1404, 24 p.

Huybers, P., and Wunsch, C., 2005, Obliquity pacing of the late Pleistocene glacial terminations: Nature, v. 434, p. 491–491, doi: 10.1038/nature03401.

Imbrie, J., Hays, J.D., Martinson, D.G., McIntyre, A., Mix, A.C., Morley, J.J., Pisias, N.G., Prell, W.L., and Shackleton, N.J., 1984, The orbital theory of Pleistocene climate: Support from a revised chronology of the marine delta ^{18}O record, *in* Berger, A., Imbrie, J., Kukla, J.H.G., and Saltzman, B., eds., Milankovitch and climate, Understanding the Response to Astronomical Forcing: Hingham, Massachusetts, Reidel Publishing Company, p. 269–305.

Imbrie, J., Boyle, E.A., Clemens, S.C., Duffy, A., Howard, W.R., Kukla, G., Kutzbach, J., Martinson, D.G., McIntyre, A., Mix, A.C., Molfino, B., Morley, J.J., Peterson, L.C., Pisias, N.G., Press, W.L., Raymo, M.E., Shackleton, M.J., and Toggweiler, J.R., 1992, On the structure and origin of major glaciation cycles, 1. Linear responses to Milankovitch forcing: Paleoceanography, v. 7, no. 6, p. 701–738.

Imbrie, J., Mix, A.C., and Martinson, D.G., 1993, Milankovitch theory viewed from Devils Hole: Nature, v. 363, no. 6429, p. 531–533, doi: 10.1038/363531a0.

Jannik, N.O., Phillips, F.M., Smith, G.I., and Elmore, D., 1991, A ^{36}Cl chronology of lacustrine sedimentation in the Pleistocene Owens River system: Geological Society of America Bulletin, v. 103, p. 1146–1159, doi: 10.1130/0016-7606(1991)103<1146:ACCOLS>2.3.CO;2.

Jayko, A.S., Forester, R.M., Kaufmann, D., Phillips, F., Mahan, S., and McGeehin, J., 2005, Late Pleistocene Lakes, Panamint Valley, California, *in* Reheis, M.C., ed., Geologic and biotic perspectives on Late Cenozoic drainage history of the southwestern Great Basin and lower Colorado River region: conference abstracts, U.S. Geological Survey Open-File Report 2005-1404, 24 p.

Jouzel, J., 2001, Milankovitch and ice core records: Eos (Transactions, American Geophysical Union) (Supplement), v. 82, no. 47, p. F1.

Kerr, R.A., 2001, The tropics return to the climate system: Science, v. 292, no. 5517, p. 660–661, doi: 10.1126/science.292.5517.660.

Khodri, M., Leclainche, Y., Ramstein, G., Braconnot, P., Marti, O., and Cortijo, E., 2001, Simulating the amplification of orbital forcing by ocean feedbacks in the last glaciation: Nature, v. 410, no. 6828, p. 570–574, doi: 10.1038/35069044.

Kindler, P., and Hearty, P.J., 2000, Elevated marine terraces from Eleuthera (Bahamas) and Bermuda: Sedimentological, petrographic and geochronological evidence for important deglaciation events during the Middle

Pleistocene: Global and Planetary Change, v. 24, no. 1, p. 41–58, doi: 10.1016/S0921-8181(99)00068-5.

Knorr, G., and Lohmann, G., 2003, Southern Ocean origin for the resumption of Atlantic thermohaline circulation during deglaciation: Nature, v. 424, p. 532–536, doi: 10.1038/nature01855.

Knott, J.R., 1999, Quaternary stratigraphy and geomorphology of Death Valley, *in* Slate, J.L., ed., Proceedings of Conference on Status of Geologic Research and Mapping, Death Valley National Park, 9–11 April 1999: Las Vegas, Nevada, U.S. Geological Survey Open-File Report 99-153, p. 90–96.

Knott, J.R., 2005, Lake Manly-A Brief Review, *in* Reheis, M.C., ed., Geologic and biotic perspectives on Late Cenozoic drainage history of the southwestern Great Basin and lower Colorado River region: conference abstracts, U.S. Geological Survey Open-File Report 2005-1404, 24 p.

Koehler, P.A., Anderson, R.S., and Spaulding, W.G., 2005, Development of vegetation in the Central Mojave Desert of California during the Late Quaternary: Paleography: Paleoclimatology, Paleoecology, v. 215, p. 297–311, doi: 10.1016/j.palaeo.2004.09.010.

Ku, T.L., Luo, S., Lowenstein, T.K., Li, J., and Spencer, R.J., 1998, U-series chronology of lacustrine deposits in Death Valley, California: Quaternary Research, v. 50, p. 261–275, doi: 10.1006/qres.1998.1995.

Kukla, G.J., Bender, M.L., de Beaulieu, J.-L., Bond, G., Broecker, W.S., Cleveringa, P., Gavin, J.E., Herbert, T.D., Imbrie, J., Jouzel, J., Keigwin, L.D., Knudsen, K.-L., McManus, J.F., Merkt, J., Muhs, D.R., Müller, H., Poore, R.Z., Porter, S.C., Seret, G., Shackleton, N.J., Turner, C., Tzedakis, P.C., and Winograd, I.J., 2002a, Last interglacial climates: Quaternary Research, v. 58, no. 1, p. 2–13, doi: 10.1006/qres.2001.2316.

Kukla, G.J., Clement, A.C., Cane, M.A., Gavin, J.E., and Zebiak, S.E., 2002b, Last interglacial and early glacial ENSO: Quaternary Research, v. 58, no. 1, p. 27–31, doi: 10.1006/qres.2002.2327.

Kukla, G., and Gavin, J., 2004, Milankovitch climate reinforcements: Global and Planetary Change, v. 40, p. 27–48, doi: 10.1016/S0921-8181(03)00096-1.

Kukla, G., and Gavin, J., 2005, Did glacials start with global warming?: Quaternary Science Reviews, v. 24, p. 1547–1557, doi: 10.1016/j.quascirev.2004.06.020.

Kurth, G.E., Phillips, F.M., and Reheis, M.C., 2002, The relationship between lake-filling cycles in the western Great Basin and Pleistocene Epoch climate changes: Eos (Transactions of American Geophysical Union), Fall Meeting Supplement, Abstract, v. 83, no. 47, p. PP71B–0399.

Kutzbach, J.E., and Webb, T., 1993, Conceptual Basis for Understanding Late-Quaternary Climates, *in* Wright, H.E. Jr., Kutzbach, J., Webb, T., Ruddiman, W., Street-Perrott, F., and Bartlein, P., eds., Global Climates Since the Last Glacial Maximum: Minneapolis, Minnesota, University of Minnesota Press, p. 5–11.

Kutzbach, J.E., Geutter, P.J., Behling, P.J., and Selin, R., 1993, Simulated climatic changes: Results of the COHMAP climate-model experiments, *in* Wright, H.E. Jr., Kutzbach, J., Webb, T., Ruddiman, W., Street-Perrott, F., and Bartlein, P., eds., Global Climates Since the Last Glacial Maximum: Minneapolis, Minnesota, University of Minnesota Press, p. 24–93.

Landwehr, J.M., Coplen, T.B., Ludwig, K.R., Winograd, I.J., and Riggs, A.C., 1997, Data from Devils Hole Core DH-11: U.S. Geological Survey Open-File Report 97-792, 8 p.

Landwehr, J.M., and Winograd, I.J., 2001, Dating the Vostok ice core record by importing the Devils Hole chronology: Journal of Geophysical Research, v. 106, no. D23, p. 31,853–31,861, doi: 10.1029/2001JD900065.

Lea, D.W., Pak, D.K., and Spero, H.J., 2003, Sea surface temperatures in the Western Equatorial Pacific during Marine Isotope Stage 11, *in* Droxler, A.W., Poore, R.Z., and Burckle, L.H., eds., Earth's Climate and Orbital Eccentricity, The Marine Isotope Stage 11 Question: Washington D.C., American Geophysical Union, Geophysical Monograph 137, p. 1–15.

Li, J., Lowenstein, T.K., Brown, C.B., Ku, T.-L., and Luo, S., 1996, A 100 ka record of water tables and paleoclimates from salt cores, Death Valley, California: Paleogeography, Paleoclimatology, Paleoecology, v. 123, no. 1-4, p. 179–203, doi: 10.1016/0031-0182(95)00123-9.

Li, H.C., Bischoff, J.L., Ku, T.L., and Zhu, Z.Y., 2004, Climate and hydrology of the Last Interglaciation (MIS 5) in Owens Basin, California: Isotopic and geochemical evidence from core OL-92: Quaternary Science Reviews, v. 23, p. 49–63, doi: 10.1016/S0277-3791(03)00215-4.

Litwin, R.J., Smoot, J.P., Durika, N.J., and Smith, G.I., 1999, Calibrating Late Quaternary terrestrial climate signals: Radiometrically dated pollen evidence from the southern Sierra Nevada, USA: Quaternary Science Reviews, v. 18, p. 1151–1171, doi: 10.1016/S0277-3791(98)00111-5.

Loutre, M.F., and Berger, A., 2000, Future climatic changes: Are we entering an exceptionally long interglacial?: Climatic Change, v. 46, no. 1-2, p. 61–90, doi: 10.1023/A:1005559827189.

Lowenstein, T.K., 2002, Pleistocene lakes and paleoclimates (0 to 200 ka) in Death Valley, California, *in* Hershler, R., Madsen, D.B., and Currey, D.R., eds., Great Basin Aquatic Systems History: Washington, D.C., Smithsonian Contributions to the Earth Sciences, no. 33, p. 109–120.

Lowenstein, T.K., Li, J., and Brown, C.B., 1998, Paleotemperatures from fluid inclusions in halite: Method verification and a 100,000-year paleotemperature record, Death Valley, California: Chemical Geology, v. 150, no. 3-4, p. 223–245, doi: 10.1016/S0009-2541(98)00061-8.

Lowenstein, T.K., Li, J., Brown, C., Roberts, S.M., Ku, T.-L., Luo, S., and Yang, W., 1999, 200 k.y. paleoclimate record from Death Valley salt core: Geology, v. 27, no. 1, p. 3–6, doi: 10.1130/0091-7613(1999)027<0003:KYPRFD>2.3.CO;2.

Ludwig, K.R., Simmons, K.R., Szabo, B.J., Winograd, I.J., Landwehr, J.M., Riggs, A.C., and Hoffman, R.J., 1992, Mass-spectrometric ^{230}Th ^{234}U-^{238}U dating of the Devils Hole calcite vein: Science, v. 258, p. 284–287, doi: 10.1126/science.258.5080.284.

Lundstrom, S.C., Paces, J.B., Mahan, S.A., Page, W.R., and Workman, J.B., 1999, Quaternary geologic mapping and geochronology of the Las Vegas 1:100,000 sheet and Yucca Mountain area: Geomorphic and hydrologic response to climate change near Death Valley, *in* Slate, J.L., ed., Proceedings of Conference on Status of Geologic Research and Mapping in Death Valley National Park, 9–11 April 1999: Las Vegas, Nevada: U.S. Geological Survey Open-File Report 99-153, p. 110–111.

Lutgens, F.K., and Tarbuck, E.J., 1998, The Atmosphere, An Introduction to Meteorology: Upper Saddle River, New Jersey, Prentice-Hall.

Mahan, S.A., Miller, D.M., Menges, C.M., and Yount, J.C., 2005, Late Quaternary stratigraphy and luminescence geochronology of the northeastern Mojave Desert, with emphasis on the Valjean Valley area, *in* Miller, D.M., Menges, C.M., and McMacklin, M.R., eds., Geomorphology and tectonics at the intersection of Silurian and Death Valleys, 2005 Guidebook Pacific Cell Friends of the Pleistocene, p. D1–D37.

Mantua, N.J., Hare, S.R., Zhang, Y., Wallace, J.M., and Francis, R.C., 1997, A Pacific interdecadal climate oscillation with impacts on salmon production: Bulletin of the American Meteorological Society, v. 78, no. 6, p. 1069–1079, doi: 10.1175/1520-0477(1997)078<1069:APICOW>2.0.CO;2.

Mawby, J.E., 1967, Fossil vertebrates of the Tule Springs Site, Nevada, *in* Wormington, H.M., and Ellis, D., eds., Part 2 of Pleistocene Studies in Southern Nevada, Anthropological Papers No. 13: Carson City, Nevada, Nevada State Museum, p. 105–128.

McCabe, G.J., Palecki, M.A., and Betancourt, J.L., 2004, Pacific and Atlantic ocean influences on the multidecadal drought frequency in the United States: Proceedings of the National Academy of Sciences of the United States of America, v. 101, no. 12, p. 4136–4141, doi: 10.1073/pnas.0306738101 (www.pnas.org/cgi/doi/).

McGlone, M.S., Kershaw, A.P., and Markgraf, V., 1992, El Niño/Southern Oscillation climatic variability in Australasian and South American paleoenvironmental records, *in* Diaz, H.F., and Markgraf, V., eds., El Niño, Historical and Paleoclimatic Aspects of the Southern Oscillation: New York, New York, Cambridge University Press, p. 435–462.

Mehringer, P.J., 1967, Pollen analysis of the Tule Springs Site, Nevada, *in* Wormington, H.M., and Ellis, D., eds., Part 3 of Pleistocene Studies in Southern Nevada, Anthropological Papers No. 13: Carson City, Nevada, Nevada State Museum, p. 129–200.

Menges, C.M., and Anderson, D.E., 2005, Late Cenozoic Drainage History of the Amargosa River, Southwestern Nevada and Eastern California, *in* Reheis, M.C., ed., Geologic and biotic perspectives on Late Cenozoic drainage history of the southwestern Great Basin and lower Colorado River region: conference abstracts, U.S. Geological Survey Open-File Report 2005-1404, 24 p.

Mensing, S.A., 2001, Late-Glacial and Early Holocene vegetation and climate change near Owens Lake, eastern California: Quaternary Research, v. 55, no. 1, p. 57–65, doi: 10.1006/qres.2000.2196.

Miller, D.M., 2005, Summary of the Evolution of the Mojave River, *in* Reheis, M.C., ed., Geologic and biotic perspectives on Late Cenozoic drainage history of the southwestern Great Basin and lower Colorado River region: conference abstracts, U.S. Geological Survey Open-File Report 2005-1404, 24 p.

Miller, J.F., Frederick, R.H., and Tracy, R.J., 1973, Precipitation-Frequency Atlas of the Western United States, NOAA Atlas 2, Volume VII-Nevada: Silver Spring, Maryland, U.S. Department of Commerce, National Oceanic and Atmospheric Administration, 43 p.

Mitchell, D.L., Ivanova, D., Rabin, R., Brown, T.J., and Redmond, K., 2002, Gulf of California sea surface temperatures and the North American Monsoon: Mechanistic implications from observations: Journal of Climate, v. 15, no. 17, p. 2261–2281, doi: 10.1175/1520-0442(2002)015<2261: GOCSST>2.0.CO;2.

Mock, C.J., 1996, Climatic controls and spatial variations of precipitation in the western United States: Journal of Climate, v. 9, p. 1111–1125, doi: 10.1175/1520-0442(1996)009<1111:CCASVO>2.0.CO;2.

Morrison, R.B., 1999, Lake Tecopa: Quaternary geology of Tecopa Valley, California, a multimillion-year record and its relevance to the proposed nuclear-waste repository at Yucca Mountain, Nevada, *in* Wright, L.A., and Troxel, B.W., eds., Cenozoic Basins of the Death Valley Region: Geological Society of America Special Paper 333, p. 301–344.

Mudelsee, M., and Schulz, M., 1997, The Mid-Pleistocene Climate Transition: Onset of 100 ka Cycle Lags Ice Volume Build-Up by 280 ka: Earth and Planetary Science Letters, v. 151, no. 1-2, p. 117–123, doi: 10.1016/S0012-821X(97)00114-3.

Muhs, D.R., 2002, Evidence for the timing and duration of the last interglacial period from high-precision uranium-series ages of corals on tectonically stable coastlines: Quaternary Research, v. 58, no. 1, p. 36–40, doi: 10.1006/qres.2002.2339.

Muller, R.A., and MacDonald, G.J., 2002, Ice Ages and Astronomical Causes, Data, Spectral Analysis and Mechanisms, Springer-Praxis Books in Environmental Sciences: New York, New York, Springer, 318 p.

Murray, R.W., Knowlton, C., Leinen, M., Mix, A.C., and Polsky, C.H., 2000, Export production and terrigenous matter in the central equatorial Pacific Ocean during interglacial Oxygen Isotope Stage 11: Global and Planetary Change, v. 24, no. 1, p. 59–78.

Negrini, R., Erbes, D., Faber, K., Herrera, A., Roberts, A., Cohen, A., Wigand, P., and Franklin Foit, J., 2000, A paleoclimate record for the past 250,000 years from Summer Lake, Oregon, USA: I. Chronology and magnetic proxies for lake level: Journal of Paleolimnology, v. 24, p. 125–149, doi: 10.1023/A:1008144025492.

NGICP, 2004, High-resolution record of Northern Hemisphere climate extending into the last interglacial period: Nature, v. 431, p. 147–151, doi: 10.1038/nature02805.

Orme, A.R., Orme, A.J., and Piscitello, B., 2005, Late Pleistocene Climate and Tectonic Impacts on the Owens River Cascade, *in* Reheis, M.C., ed., Geologic and biotic perspectives on Late Cenozoic drainage history of the southwestern Great Basin and lower Colorado River region: conference abstracts, U.S. Geological Survey Open-File Report 2005-1404, 24 p.

Ortiz, J.D., O'Connell, S.B., Del Viscio, J., Dean, W., Carriquiry, J.D., Marchitto, T., Zheng, Y., and van Geen, A., 2004, Enhanced marine productivity off western North America during warm climate intervals of the past 52 k.y.: Geology, v. 32, no. 6, p. 521–524, doi: 10.1130/G20234.1.

Osborn, G., and Bevis, K., 2001, Glaciation in the Great Basin of the western United States: Quaternary Science Reviews, v. 20, no. 13, p. 1377–1410, doi: 10.1016/S0277-3791(01)00002-6.

Oviatt, C.G., Thompson, R.S., Kaufman, D.S., Bright, J., and Forester, R.M., 1999, Reinterpretation of the Burmester Core, Bonneville Basin, Utah: Quaternary Research, v. 52, no. 2, p. 180–184, doi: 10.1006/qres.1999.2058.

Paces, J.B., and Whelan, J.F., 2001, Water-table fluctuations in the Amargosa Desert, Nye County, Nevada, Back to the Future—Managing the Back End of the Nuclear Fuel Cycle to Create a More Secure Energy Future, *in* Proceedings of the 9th International High-Level Radioactive Waste Management Conference (IHLRWM), Las Vegas, Nevada, 29 April–3 May 2001, American Nuclear Society, LaGrange Park, Illinois (CD-ROM).

Paces, J.B., Taylor, E.M., and Bush, C., 1993, Late Quaternary history and uranium isotopic compositions of ground water discharge deposits, Crater Flat, Nevada, *in* High Level Radioactive Waste Management, Proceedings of the Fourth Annual International Conference, Las Vegas, Nevada, 26–30 April 1993, American Nuclear Society, LaGrange Park, Illinois, p. 2, 1573–1580.

Paces, J.B., Neymark, L.A., Marshall, B.D., Whelan, J.F., and Peterman, Z.E., 1996, Letter report: Ages and origins of subsurface secondary minerals in the Exploratory Studies Facility (ESF). Milestone 3GQH450M, Results of sampling and age determination: U.S. Geological Survey, MOL.19970324.0052, 44 p.

Paces, J.B., Whelan, J.F., Forester, R.M., Bradbury, J.P., Marshall, B.D., and Mahan, S.A., 1997, Summary of discharge deposits in the Amargosa Valley, Milestone SPC333M4 to DOE-YMPSCO: U.S. Geological Survey, MOL.19990105.0321, 23 p.

Paces, J.B., Neymark, L.A., Marshall, B.D., Whelan, J.F., and Peterman, Z.E., 1998, Inferences for Yucca Mountain unsaturated-zone hydrology from secondary minerals, *in* High-Level Radioactive Waste Management, Proceedings of the Eighth International Conference, Las Vegas, Nevada, 11–14 May 1998, American Nuclear Society, LaGrange Park, Illinois, p. 36–39.

Paces, J.B., Neymark, L.A., Marshall, B.D., Whelan, J.F., and Peterman, Z.E., 2001, Ages and origins of calcite and opal in the Exploratory Studies Facility Tunnel, Yucca Mountain, Nevada: Water-Resources Investigations Report 01-4049, U.S. Geological Survey, 95 p.

Pahnke, K., Zahn, R., Elderfield, H., and Schulz, M., 2003, 340,000-year centennial-scale marine record of Southern Hemisphere climatic oscillation: Science, v. 301, p. 948–952, doi: 10.1126/science.1084451.

Petit, J.R., Jouzel, J., Raynaud, D., Barkov, N.I., Barnola, J.-M., Basile, I., Bender, M., Chappellaz, J., Davis, M., Delaygue, G., Delmotte, M., Kotlyakov, V.M., Legrand, M., Lipenov, V.Y., Lorius, C., Pepin, L., Ritz, C., Saltzman, E., and Stievenard, M., 1999, Climate and atmospheric history of the past 420,000 years from the Vostok Ice Core, Antarctica: Nature, v. 399, no. 6735, p. 429–436, doi: 10.1038/20859.

Petit, J.R., Jouzel, J., Raynaud, D., Barkov, N.I., Barnola, J.-M., Basile, I., Bender, M., Chappellaz, J., Davis, M., Delaygue, G., Delmotte, M., Kotlyakov, V.M., Legrand, M., Lipenov, V.Y., Lorius, C., Pepin, L., Ritz, C., Saltzman, E., and Stievenard, M., 2001, Vostok Ice Core Data for 420,000 Years, IGBP PAGES/World Data Center for Paleoclimatology Data Contribution Series #2001–076, http://hurricane.ncdc.noaa.gov/pls/paleo/ftpsearch.icecore, NOAA/NGDC Paleoclimatology Program, Boulder, Colorado.

Phillips, F.M., Campbell, A.R., Smith, G.I., and Bischoff, J.L., 1994, Interstadial climatic cycles: A link between western North America and Greenland?: Geology, v. 22, no. 12, p. 1115–1118, doi: 10.1130/0091-7613(1994)022<1115:ICCALB>2.3.CO;2.

Phillips, F.M., Zreda, M.G., Benson, L.V., Plummer, M.A., Elmore, D., and Sharma, P., 1996, Chronology for fluctuations in Late Pleistocene Sierra Nevada glaciers and lakes: Science, v. 274, no. 5288, p. 749–751, doi: 10.1126/science.274.5288.749.

Pierrehumbert, R.T., 1999, Subtropical water vapor as a mediator of rapid global climate change, *in* Clark, P.U., Webb, R.S., and Keigwin, L.D., eds., Mechanisms of Global Climate Change at Millennial Time Scales: Washington, D.C., American Geophysical Union, Geophysical Monograph 112, p. 339–361.

Poore, R.Z., and Dowsett, H.J., 2001, Pleistocene reduction of polar ice caps: Evidence from Cariaco Basin marine sediments: Geology, v. 29, no. 1, p. 71–74, doi: 10.1130/0091-7613(2001)029<0071:PROPIC>2.0.CO;2.

Prokopenko, A.A., Karabanov, E.B., Williams, D.F., Kuzmin, M.I., Shackleton, N.J., Crowhurst, S.J., Peck, J.A., Gvozdkov, A.N., and King, J.W., 2001, Biogenic silica record of the Lake Baikal response to climatic forcing during the Brunhes: Quaternary Research, v. 55, no. 2, p. 123–132, doi: 10.1006/qres.2000.2212.

Quade, J., 1986, Late Quaternary environmental changes in the upper Las Vegas Valley, Nevada: Quaternary Research, v. 26, no. 3, p. 340–357, doi: 10.1016/0033-5894(86)90094-3.

Quade, J., and Pratt, W.L., 1989, Late Wisconsin groundwater discharge environments of the southwestern Indian Springs Valley, southern Nevada: Quaternary Research, v. 31, no. 3, p. 351–370, doi: 10.1016/0033-5894(89)90042-2.

Quade, J., Mifflin, M.D., Pratt, W.L., McCoy, W., and Burckle, L., 1995, Fossil spring deposits in the southern Great Basin and their implications for changes in water-table levels near Yucca Mountain, Nevada, during Quaternary time: Geological Society of America Bulletin, v. 107, no. 2, p. 213–230, doi: 10.1130/0016-7606(1995)107<0213:FSDITS>2.3.CO;2.

Quade, J., Forester, R.M., and Whelan, J.F., 2003, Late Quaternary paleohydrologic and paleotemperature change in southern Nevada, *in* Enzel, Y., Wells, S.G., and Lancaster, N., eds., Paleoenvironments and Paleohydrology of the Mojave and Southern Great Basin Deserts: Boulder, Colorado, Geological Society of America Special Paper 368, p. 165–188.

Redmond, K.T., Enzel, Y., House, P.K., and Biondi, F., 2002, Climate variability and flood frequency at decadal to millennial time scales, *in* House, P.K., Webb, R.H., Baker, V.R., and Levish, D.R., eds., Ancient Floods, Modern Hazards, Principles and Applications of Paleoflood Hydrology: Washington, D.C., American Geophysical Union, Water Science and Application 5, p. 21–45.

Reheis, M., 1999, Highest pluvial-lake shorelines and Pleistocene climate of the western Great Basin: Quaternary Research, v. 52, no. 2, p. 196–205, doi: 10.1006/qres.1999.2064.

Reheis, M., and Redwine, J., 2005, Old Shorelines of Lake Manix: Implications for Afton Canyon Incision, *in* Reheis, M.C., ed., Geologic and biotic perspectives on Late Cenozoic drainage history of the southwestern Great Basin and lower Colorado River region: conference abstracts, U.S. Geological Survey Open-File Report 2005-1404, 24 p.

Reheis, M.C., Sowers, J.M., Taylor, E.M., McFadden, L.D., and Harden, J.W., 1992, Morphology and genesis of carbonate soils on the Kyle Canyon Fan, Nevada, USA: Geoderma, v. 52, p. 303–342, doi: 10.1016/0016-7061(92)90044-8.

Reheis, M.C., Sarna-Wojcicki, A.M., Reynolds, R.L., Repenning, C.A., and Mifflin, M.D., 2002a, Pliocene to middle Pleistocene lakes in the western Great Basin: Ages and connections, *in* Hershler, R., Madsen, D.B., and Currey, D.R., eds., Great Basin Aquatic Systems History, Smithsonian Contributions to the Earth Sciences, Number 33: Washington, D.C., Smithsonian Institution Press, p. 53–108.

Reheis, M.C., Stine, S., and Sarna-Wojcicki, A.M., 2002b, Drainage reversals in Mono Basin during the late Pliocene and Pleistocene: Geological Society of America Bulletin, v. 114, no. 8, p. 991–1006, doi: 10.1130/0016-7606(2002)114<0991:DRIMBD>2.0.CO;2.

Reheis, M., Redwine, J., Adams, K., Stine, S., Parker, K., Negrini, R., Burke, R., Kurth, G., McGeehin, J., Paces, J., Phillips, F., Sarna-Wojcicki, A., and Smoot, J., 2003, Pliocene to Holocene lakes in the western Great Basin: New perspectives on paleoclimate, landscape dynamics, tectonics, and paleodistribution of aquatic species, *in* Easterbrook, D.J., ed., Quaternary Geology of the United States, INQUA 2003 Field Guide Volume, XVI INQUA Congress: Reno, Nevada, Desert Research Institute, p. 155–194.

Rind, D., 2002, The Sun's role on climate variations: Science, v. 296, no. 5568, p. 673–677, doi: 10.1126/science.1069562.

Roberts, S.M., and Spencer, R.J., 1995, Paleotemperatures preserved in fluid inclusions in halite: Geochimica et Cosmochimica Acta, v. 59, no. 19, p. 3929–3942, doi: 10.1016/0016-7037(95)00253-V.

Roberts, S.M., and Spencer, R.J., 1998, A desert responds to Pleistocene climate change: Saline lacustrine sediments, Death Valley, California, USA, *in* Alsharhan, A.S., Glennie, K.W., Whittle, G.L., and Kendall, C.G.S.C., eds., Quaternary Deserts and Climatic Change, Proceedings of the International Conference on Quaternary Deserts and Climatic Change, Al Ain, United Arab Emirates, 9–11 December 1995: Brookfield, Vermont, A.A. Balkema Company, p. 357 370.

Rousseau, D.-D., 2003, The Continental Record of Stage 11: A Review, *in* Droxler, A.W., Poore, R.Z., and Burckle, L.H., eds., Earth's Climate and Orbital Eccentricity, The Marine Isotope Stage 11 Question: Washington D.C., American Geophysical Union, Geophysical Monograph 137, p. 213–222.

Ruddiman, W.F., 2003a, Orbital insolation, ice volume and greenhouse gases: Quaternary Science Reviews, v. 22, p. 1597–1629, doi: 10.1016/S0277-3791(03)00087-8.

Ruddiman, W.F., 2003b, The anthropogenic greenhouse era began thousands of years ago: Climatic Change, v. 61, p. 261–293, doi: 10.1023/B:CLIM.0000004577.17928.fa.

Ruddiman, W.F., 2005, Cold climate during the closest Stage 11 analog to recent millennia: Quaternary Science Reviews, v. 24, p. 1111–1121, doi: 10.1016/j.quascirev.2004.10.012.

Ruddiman, W.F., Vavrus, S.J., and Kutzbach, J.E., 2005, A test of the overdue-glaciation hypothesis: Quaternary Science Reviews, v. 24, p. 1–10, doi: 10.1016/j.quascirev.2004.07.010.

Rutherford, S., and D'Hondt, S., 2000, Early Onset and Tropical Forcing of 100,000 Year Pleistocene Glacial Cycles: Nature, v. 408, no. 6808, p. 72–75, doi: 10.1038/35040533.

Seager, R., Clement, A.C., and Cane, M.A., 2000, Glacial cooling in the tropics: Exploring the roles of tropospheric water vapor, surface wind speed, and boundary layer processes: Journal of Atmospheric Sciences, v. 57, no. 13, p. 2144–2157, doi: 10.1175/1520-0469(2000)057<2144:GCITTE>2.0.CO;2.

Shackleton, N.J., 2000, The 100,000-year ice-age cycle identified and found to lag temperature, carbon dioxide, and orbital eccentricity: Science, v. 289, no. 5486, p. 1897–1902, doi: 10.1126/science.289.5486.1897.

Shackleton, N.J., and Opdyke, N.D., 1973, Oxygen isotope and palaeomagnetic stratigraphy of equatorial Pacific Core V28-238: Oxygen isotope temperatures and ice volumes on a 10^5 and 10^6 year scale: Quaternary Research, v. 3, p. 39–55, doi: 10.1016/0033-5894(73)90052-5.

Shaffer, J.A., Cerveny, R.S., and Dorn, R.I., 1996, Radiation windows as indicators of an astronomical influence on the Devil's Hole chronology: Geology, v. 24, no. 11, p. 1017–1020, doi: 10.1130/0091-7613(1996)024<1017:RWAIOA>2.3.CO;2.

Sharma, M., 2002, Variations in solar magnetic activity during the last 200,000 years: Is there a sun-climate connection?: Earth and Planetary Science Letters, v. 199, no. 3-4, p. 459–472, doi: 10.1016/S0012-821X(02)00516-2.

Sharpe, S.E., 2003, Future Climate Analysis-10,000 Years to 1,000,000 Years A.P.: Desert Research Institute, Reno, Nevada, MOD-01-001 REV 01, http://hrcweb.nevada.edu/qa/Report/MOD-01-001.pdf

Sharpe, S.E., 2004, Chapter 6, Climate: Past, Present, and Future, *in* Bechtel SAIC Company, ed., Yucca Mountain Site Description: Las Vegas, U.S. Department of Energy, DOC.20040504.0006, TDR-CRW-GS-0000001 Rev 02 ICN 01, p. 6–1 to 6–99.

Sharpe, S.E., Whelan, J.F., Forester, R.M., and McConnaughey, T., 1994, Molluscs as climate indicators: Preliminary stable isotope and community analysis, *in* High Level Radioactive Waste Management, Proceedings of the Fifth Annual International Conference, Las Vegas, Nevada, 22–26 May 1994, American Nuclear Society, LaGrange Park, Illinois, p. 2538–2544.

Shaviv, N.J., and Veizer, J., 2003, Celestial driver of Phanerozoic climate?: GSA Today, v. 13, no. 7, p. 4–10, doi: 10.1130/1052-5173(2003)013<0004:CDOPC>2.0.CO;2.

Smith, A.J., and Forester, R.M., 1994, Estimating Past Precipitation and Temperature from Fossil Ostracodes, *in* High Level Radioactive Waste Management, Proceedings of the Fifth Annual International Conference, Las Vegas, Nevada, 22–26 May 1994, American Nuclear Society, LaGrange Park, Illinois, p. 2545–2552.

Smith, G.I., 1984, Paleohydrologic regimes in the southwestern Great Basin, 0–3.2 m.y. ago, compared with other long records of 'global' climate: Quaternary Research, v. 22, p. 1–17, doi: 10.1016/0033-5894(84)90002-4.

Smith, G.I., and Bischoff, J.L., 1997, Core OL-92 from Owens Lake: Project rationale, geologic setting, drilling procedures, and summary, *in* Smith, G.I., and Bischoff, J.L., eds., An 800,000-Year Paleoclimatic Record from Core OL-92, Owens Lake, Southeast California: Boulder, Colorado, Geological Society of America Special Paper 317, p. 1–8.

Smith, G.I., Bischoff, J.L., and Bradbury, J.P., 1997, Synthesis of the paleoclimate record from Owens Lake Core OL-92, *in* Smith, G.I., and Bischoff, J.L., eds., An 800,000-Year Paleoclimatic Record from Core OL-92, Owens Lake, Southeast California: Boulder, Colorado, Geological Society of America Special Paper 317, 143–160.

Sonnenthal, E.L., and Bodvarsson, G.S., 1998, Percolation flux estimates from geochemical and thermal modeling, *in* High-Level Radioactive Waste Management, Proceedings of the Eighth International Conference, Las Vegas, Nevada, 11–14 May 1998, American Nuclear Society, LaGrange Park, Illinois, p. 130–132.

Spaulding, W.G., 1985, Vegetation and climates of the last 45,000 years in the vicinity of the Nevada Test Site, south-central Nevada: U.S. Geological Survey Professional Paper 1329, 83 p.

Spaulding, W.G., 1990, Vegetational and climatic development of the Mojave Desert: The last glacial maximum to the present, *in* Betancourt, J.L., Van Devender, T.R., and Martin, P.S., eds., Packrat Middens, The Last 40,000 Years of Biotic Change: Tucson, Arizona, University of Arizona Press, p. 166–199.

Spencer, R.J., and Roberts, S.M., 1998, Magnitude of climate change in Death Valley, California, USA between 100 and 200 ka BP: Comparison with modern systems, *in* Alsharhan, A.S., Glennie, K.W., Whittle, G.L., and Kendall, C.G.S.C., eds., Quaternary Deserts and Climatic Change, Proceedings of the International Conference on Quaternary Deserts and Climatic Change, Al Ain, United Arab Emirates, 9–11 December 1995: Brookfield, Vermont, Balkema Publishing Company, p. 371–380.

Stein, M., Wasserburg, G.J., Aharon, P., Chen, J.H., Zhu, Z.R., Bloom, A., and Chappell, J., 1993, TIMS U-Series dating and stable isotopes of the last interglacial event in Papua New Guinea: Geochimica et Cosmochimica Acta, v. 57, no. 11, p. 2541–2554, doi: 10.1016/0016-7037(93)90416-T.

Swadley, W.C., and Carr, W.J., 1987, Geologic Map of the Quaternary and Tertiary Deposits of the Big Dune Quadrangle, Nye County, Nevada, and Inyo County, California: U.S. Geological Survey, Miscellaneous Investigations Series Map I-1767, 1:48,000.

Taylor, D.W., 1967, Late Pleistocene molluscan shells from the Tule Springs area, *in* Wormington, H.M., and Ellis, D., eds., Part 8 of Pleistocene Studies in Southern Nevada, Anthropological Papers No. 13, Carson City, Nevada, Nevada State Museum, p. 396–399.

Thompson, R.S., 1990, Late Quaternary vegetation and climate in the Great Basin, *in* Betancourt, J.L., Van Devender, T.R., and Martin, P.S., eds., Packrat Middens, The Last 40,000 Years of Biotic Change: Tucson, Arizona, University of Arizona Press, p. 200–239.

Thompson, R.S., Hostetler, S.W., Bartlein, P.J., and Anderson, K.H., 1998, A strategy for assessing potential future changes in climate, hydrology, and vegetation in the Western United States: U.S. Geological Survey, Circular 1153, 20 p.

Thompson, R.S., Anderson, K.H., and Bartlein, P.J., 1999, Quantitative paleoclimatic reconstructions from late Pleistocene plant macrofossils of the Yucca Mountain region: U.S. Geological Survey Open-File Report 99-338, 38 p.

Tzedakis, P.C., Andrieu, V., deBeaulieu, J.-L., Crowhurst, S., Follieri, M., Hooghiemstra, H., Magri, D., Reille, M., Sadori, L., Shackleton, N.J., and Wijmstra, T.A., 1997, Comparison of terrestrial and marine records of changing climate of the last 500,000 years: Earth and Planetary Science Letters, v. 150, p. 171–176, doi: 10.1016/S0012-821X(97)00078-2.

Tzedakis, P.C., Roucoux, K.H., de Abreu, L., and Shackleton, N.J., 2004, The duration of forest stages in southern Europe and interglacial climate variability: Science, v. 306, p. 2231–2235, doi: 10.1126/science.1102398.

U.S. Geological Survey, 2001, Future Climate Analysis: U.S. Geological Survey, ANL-NBS-GS-000008 REV 00 ICN 01, March 14, 2000, 83 p.

Vandergoes, M.J., Newnham, R.M., Preusser, F., Hendy, C.H., Lowell, T.V., Fitzsimons, S.J., Hogg, A.G., Kasper, H.U., and Schluchter, C., 2005, Regional insolation forcing of late Quaternary climate change in the southern Hemisphere: Nature, v. 436, p. 242–245, doi: 10.1038/nature03826.

Van Hoesen, J.G., Orndorff, R.L., and Saines, M., 2000, Evidence for Pleistocene glaciation in the Spring Mountains, Nevada, in Abstracts with Programs: Boulder, Colorado: Geological Society of America, v. 32, no. 7, p. A-16.

Vaniman, D.T., Chipera, S.J., Bish, D.L., Carey, J.W., and Levy, S.S., 2001, Quantification of unsaturated-zone alteration and cation exchange in zeolitized tuffs at Yucca Mountain, Nevada, USA: Geochimica et Cosmochimica Acta, v. 65, no. 20, p. 3409–3433, doi: 10.1016/S0016-7037(01)00682-2.

Wang, X., Auler, A.S., Edwards, R.L., Cheng, H., Cristalli, P.S., Smart, P.L., Richards, D.A., and Shen, C.-C., 2004, Wet periods in northeastern Brazil over the past 210 kyr linked to distant climate anomalies: Nature, v. 432, p. 740–743, doi: 10.1038/nature03067.

Watson, R.T., Albritton, D.L., Barker, T., Bashmakov, I.A., Canziani, O., Christ, R., Cubasch, U., Davidson, O., Gitay, H., Griggs, D., Halsnaes, K., Houghton, J., House, J., Kundzewicz, Z., Lal, M., Leary, N., Magadza, C., McCarthy, J.J., Mitchell, J.F.B., Moreira, J.R., Munasinghe, M., Noble, I., Pachauri, R., Pittock, B., Prather, M., Richels, R.G., Robinson, J.B., Sathaye, J., Schneider, S., Scholes, R., Stocker, T., Sundararaman, N., Swart, R., Taniguchi, T., and Zhou, D., 2001, Summary for policymakers, in Watson, R.T., ed., Climate Change 2001: Synthesis Report, An Assessment of the Intergovernmental Panel on Climate Change: New York, New York, Cambridge University Press, 397 p.

Wells, P.V., and Woodcock, D., 1985, Full-glacial vegetation of Death Valley, California: Juniper woodland opening to Yucca semidesert: Madrono, v. 32, no. 1, p. 11–23.

Wells, S.G., Brown, W.J., Enzel, Y., Anderson, R.Y., and McFadden, L.D., 2003, Late Quaternary geology and paleohydrology of pluvial Lake Mojave, Southern California, in Enzel, Y., Wells, S.G., and Lancaster, N., eds., Paleoenvironments and Paleohydrology of the Mojave and Southern Great Basin Deserts: Boulder, Colorado, Geological Society of America Special Paper 368, p. 79–114.

Whelan, J.F., Vaniman, D.T., Stuckless, J.S., and Moscati, R.J., 1994, Paleoclimatic and paleohydrologic records from secondary calcite: Yucca Mountain, Nevada, in High Level Radioactive Waste Management, Proceedings of the Fifth Annual International Conference, Las Vegas, Nevada, 22–26 May 1994: American Nuclear Society, LaGrange Park, Illinois, p. 4, 2738–2745.

Whelan, J.F., Paces, J.B., Neymark, L.A., Schmitt, A.K., and Grove, M., 2006, Impact of Quaternary Climate on Seepage at Yucca Mountain, Nevada, in Proceedings of the International High-Level Radioactive Waste Management Conference (IHLRWM), Las Vegas, Nevada, 30 April–4 May 2006: American Nuclear Society, LaGrange Park, Illinois, p. 199–206.

Whitney, J.W., and Harrington, C.D., 1993, Relict colluvial boulder deposits as paleoclimatic indicators in the Yucca Mountain region, southern Nevada: Geological Society of American Bulletin, v. 105, p. 1008–1018, DOI: 10.1130/0016-7606(1993)105<1008:RCBDAP>2.3.CO;2.

Wigand, P.E., and Rhode, D., 2002, Great Basin vegetation history and aquatic systems: The last 150,000 years, in Hershler, R., Madsen, D.B., and Cur-

rey, D.R., eds., Great Basin Aquatic Systems History: Washington, D.C., Smithsonian Contributions to the Earth Sciences, no. 33, p. 309–367.

Wigley, T.M.L., 2005, The climate change commitment: Science, v. 307, p. 1766–1769, doi: 10.1126/science.1103934.

Williams, D.F., Thunell, R.C., Tappa, E., Rio, D., and Raffi, I., 1988, Chronology of the Pleistocene Oxygen Isotope Record: 0–1.88 m.y. B.P.: Palaeogeography, Palaeoclimatology, Palaeoecology, v. 64, no. 221–240.

Willson, R.C., 1997, Total solar irradiance trend during Solar Cycles 21 and 22: Science, v. 277, p. 1963–1965, doi: 10.1126/science.277.5334.1963.

Winograd, I.J., 2001, The magnitude and proximate cause of ice-sheet growth since 35,000 yr B.P: Quaternary Research, v. 56, no. 3, p. 299–307, doi: 10.1006/qres.2001.2272.

Winograd, I.J., and Thordarson, W., 1975, Hydrogeologic and hydrochemical framework, south-central Great Basin, Nevada-California, with special reference to the Nevada Test Site: U.S. Geological Survey Professional Paper 712-C, 125 p.

Winograd, I.J., and Riggs, A.C., 1984, Recharge to the Spring Mountains, Nevada: Isotopic evidence: Boulder, Colorado, Geological Society of America Abstracts with Programs, abstract, v. 16, p. 698.

Winograd, I.J., Szabo, B.J., Coplen, T.B., and Riggs, A.C., 1988, A 250,000-year climate record from Great Basin vein calcite: Implications for Milankovitch Theory: Science, v. 242, p. 1275–1280, doi: 10.1126/science.242.4883.1275.

Winograd, I.J., Coplen, T.B., Landwehr, J.M., Riggs, A.C., Ludwig, K.R., Szabo, B.J., Kolesar, P.T., and Revesz, K.M., 1992, Continuous 500,000-year climate record from vein calcite in Devils Hole, Nevada: Science, v. 258, p. 255–260, doi: 10.1126/science.258.5080.255.

Winograd, I.J., Landwehr, J.M., Ludwig, K.R., Coplen, T.B., and Riggs, A.C., 1997, Duration and structure of the past four interglaciations: Quaternary Research, v. 48, p. 141–154, doi: 10.1006/qres.1997.1918.

Winograd, I.J., Riggs, A.C., and Coplen, T.B., 1998, The relative contributions of summer and cool-season precipitation to groundwater recharge, Spring Mountains, Nevada, USA: Hydrogeology Journal, v. 6, p. 77–93, doi: 10.1007/s100400050135.

Winograd, I.J., Landwehr, J.M., Coplen, T.B., Sharp, W.D., Riggs, A.C., Ludwig, K.R., and Kolesar, P.T., 2006, Devils Hole, Nevada, $\delta^{18}O$ record extended to the mid-Holocene: Quaternary Research, v. 66, no. 2, p. 202–212, doi: 10.1016/j.yqres.2006.06.003.

Winter, T.C., 1990, Plate 2: Distribution of the difference between precipitation and open-water evaporation in North America, in Wolman, M.G., and Riggs, H.C., eds., Surface Water Hydrology: Boulder, Colorado, Geological Society of America, Geology of North America, v. O-1, 374 p.

Woillard, G.M., 1978, Grande Pile peat bog: A continuous pollen record for the last 140,000 years: Quaternary Research, v. 9, p. 1–21, doi: 10.1016/0033-5894(78)90079-0.

WRCC, 2006, Western Regional Climate Center, Desert Research Institute: http://www.wrcc.dri.edu/.

Wunsch, C., 2002, What is the thermohaline circulation?: Science, v. 298, no. 5596, p. 1179–1181, doi: 10.1126/science.1079329.

Xie, S., Lai, X., Yi, Y., Gu, Y., Liu, Y., Wang, X., Liu, G., and Liang, B., 2003, Molecular fossils in a Pleistocene river terrace in southern China related to paleoclimate variation: Organic Chemistry, v. 34, p. 789–797.

Yang, W., Krouse, H.R., Spencer, R.J., Lowenstein, T.K., Hutcheon, I.E., Ku, T.-L., Li, J., Roberts, S.M., and Brown, C.B., 1999, A 200,000-year record of change in oxygen isotope composition of sulfate in a saline sediment core, Death Valley, California: Quaternary Research, v. 51, no. 2, p. 148–157, doi: 10.1006/qres.1998.2022.

Yuan, D., Cheng, H., Edwards, R.L., Dykoski, C.A., Kelly, M.J., Zhang, M., Qing, J., Lin, Y., Wang, Y., Wu, J., Dorale, J.A., An, Z., and Cai, Y., 2004, Timing, duration, and transitions of the last interglacial Asian monsoon: Science, v. 304, p. 575–578, doi: 10.1126/science.1091220.

Zielinski, G.A., and McCoy, W.D., 1987, Paleoclimatic implications of the relationship between modern snowpack and Late Pleistocene equilibrium-line altitudes in the mountains of the Great Basin, Western USA: Arctic and Alpine Research, v. 19, no. 2, p. 127–134, doi: 10.2307/1551246.

MANUSCRIPT ACCEPTED BY THE SOCIETY 18 OCTOBER 2006

Printed in the USA